SOCIAL STRATIFICATION AND INEQUALITY

CLASS CONFLICT IN HISTORICAL AND COMPARATIVE PERSPECTIVE

SOCIAL STRATIFICATION AND INEQUALITY

CLASS CONFLICT IN HISTORICAL AND COMPARATIVE PERSPECTIVE

SECOND EDITION

Harold R. Kerbo

California Polytechnic State University
San Luis Obispo

McGRAW-HILL, INC.

New York St. Louis San Francisco Auckland Bogotá Caracas
Hamburg Lisbon London Madrid Mexico Milan Montreal New Delhi
Paris San Juan São Paulo Singapore Sydney Tokyo Toronto

This book was set in Times Roman by the College Composition Unit
in cooperation with York Graphic Services, Inc.
The editors were Phillip A. Butcher, Katherine Blake, and Edwin Hanson;
the production supervisor was Leroy A. Young.
The cover was designed by Carla Bauer.
New drawings were done by ECL Art.
R. R. Donnelley & Sons Company was printer and binder.

SOCIAL STRATIFICATION AND INEQUALITY
Class Conflict in Historical and Comparative
Perspective

3 4 5 6 7 8 9 0 DOC DOC 9 0 9 8 7 6 5 4 3 2

ISBN 0-07-034192-3

Library of Congress Cataloging-in-Publication Data

Kerbo, Harold R.
    Social stratification and inequality: class conflict in
  historical and comparative perspective / Harold R. Kerbo.—2nd ed.
        p.   cm.
    Includes bibliographical references (p.   ) and index.
    ISBN 0-07-034192-3
    1. Social classes—United States.   2. Social conflict—United
  States.   3. Equality—United States.   4. Social mobility—United
  States.   I. Title
  HN90.S6K47   1991
  305.5'0973—dc20   90-20513

For Kathy, Nicole, and Emily

CONTENTS

PREFACE

The 1980s were good years for many Americans; they were bad years for many others. Since the early 1980s, when the first edition of this book was published, income inequality has grown considerably. The United States, in fact, moved from only an average level of income inequality compared to other industrial nations to the position of highest income inequality (at least by some measures discussed in Chapter 2). Part of this change has occurred because the middle-income group in the United States has been shrinking. At the same time the upper-income segment has grown, while the lower-income group has grown more than any other segment.

Change in the level of income inequality in the United States is only one of the significant changes in the nature of social stratification in the 1980s. As was noted in the first edition of this book, my primary task has been to provide an up-to-date, comprehensive examination of social stratification in human societies. The added task of this second edition is an attempt to understand the very important changes in social stratification that have occurred in this country as well as in other nations in the world since 1980. In addition to general updating, this edition has become much more comparative, as the new subtitle should suggest.

Before I summarize the general subject matter and chapter content of this book, let me note the most significant changes. First, as indicated above, the second edition has required extensive updating. Chapter 2, on the dimensions of inequality in the United States, has been extensively rewritten to include the changes in inequality during the Reagan years. Significant changes have also been made in the theory chapters. Most important, the old Chapter 4, on paradigms of social stratification, has been dropped to make room for additions elsewhere. The idea of paradigms of social stratification, however, has been retained in reduced form in the chapter on classical theories (the new Chapter 4), in order to provide a means for students to classify and make sense of the differences in stratification theories contained in Chapters 4, 5, and elsewhere.

The chapters on the various classes in the United States, poverty, and social mobility have, of course, required extensive updating because of the new studies on these subjects and the changes of the 1980s. It is especially in Chapter 9, on the working and middle class, that I have included data and research on why these changes have occurred in the United States. To adequately understand the changes in social stratification in the United States, however, it is more necessary than in the past to understand the world stratification system and other countries. In this regard, Chapter 15, on the modern world system, has been extensively changed and updated for an understanding of the position of core nations like the United States, as well as the noncore. The biggest change has occurred with an additional chapter on social stratification in Japan (Chapter 13). As everyone will agree, Japan is a country that Americans must learn more about. But there are other reasons for including a chapter on social stratification in Japan: Japan is the first nation without a western cultural base to achieve advanced industrial status. So far the theories on the nature of social stratification in industrial, capitalist societies have been grounded in the experiences of western societies. Thus, Japan provides us with a most interesting comparison and a test of the western theories of social stratification. Finally, with respect to changes in the second edition, updating Chapter 14, on social stratification in communist societies, has been challenging, to say the least. I have included the basic changes up to the first half of 1990 and have tried to provide a sense of where things seem to be going in the Soviet Union and Eastern Europe. No doubt this task has been speculative, but we can look to some basic principles of social stratification in industrial societies (capitalist or communist) to help us in this task.

Having described the general changes, let me now outline the basic arrangement of the chapters and subject matter.

Within Part One of this text, the first chapter begins with some preliminary questions for the study of social stratification suggested by the life histories of two people found at either extreme of the stratification system of the United States. From these questions, which I hope will raise further questions and interest, the chapter moves to basic definitions and an outline of major types of stratification systems. Chapter 2 is for the most part descriptive: The extent and degree of inequality in the United States are the subjects. Chapter 3 presents an overview of the history of inequality in human societies. But rather than merely provide a description of inequality and social stratification in many types of societies, Chapter 3 is also designed to provide an idea of the progression of inequality in human societies—that is, where we came from and how we arrived at our present state of inequality.

Building upon the descriptive base of Part One, Part Two takes up the difficult task of explaining the nature of social stratification. Chapter 4 describes the classical theories of Marx, Weber, and Durkheim, while Chapter 5 describes the more contemporary theories related to these three. The discussion of stratification theory comes together toward the end of Chapter 5 with a scheme representing the conflict process of social stratification taken from the variety of conflict theories previously examined. In elementary form, this scheme helps set the stage for an examination of the class systems of industrial nations.

The primary focus of Part Three is the class system of the United States. Chapter 6 introduces a number of preliminary issues (for example, a working definition of class in the United States, class distributions, occupational prestige, subjective class identification). But most importantly, Chapter 6 provides continuity by outlining the major structural bases of class inequality in the United States. Following our discussion of the conflict process of social stratification from Chapter 5, Chapter 6 describes the historical development and importance of the occupational structure, bureaucratic authority structures, and capitalist property structure as battlegrounds for class conflict and the process of inequality in the United States.

The next four chapters are devoted to description and analysis of major class segments in the United States. Chapters 7 and 8 are concerned with the upper class and corporate class, respectively. Chapter 7 examines the power and historical position of wealthy capitalist families—the dominant actors according to the traditional ruling-class perspective. Chapter 8 examines the power and historical position of the new corporate elite of advanced bureaucratic capitalism. While by no means accepting a simple managerial elite or managerial revolution thesis, Chapter 8 presents much of the rapidly emerging research on the United States corporate structure (on such aspects as interlocking directorates, corporate ownership and control, and corporate concentration) to show the importance of the United States corporate structure in understanding inequality and social stratification. In short, Chapters 7 and 8 examine the top of the stratification system.

Going below the top, Chapters 9 and 10 consider the middle class, working class, and lower class (or poor). Contained in these chapters are the usual discussions of class lifestyles, class inequalities, and socialization differences—in essence, the major outcomes and consequences of class location. At this point racial and sex inequality are brought in and related to social stratification in general. Equally important, however, and a major focus of Chapters 9 and 10, is the place of the middle class, working class, and poor in the process of class conflict in the United States. Rather than having us view those below the top as powerless, dependent actors (as a mass-society perspective would have it); a *process* of class conflict requires us to consider how inequalities of wealth, power, and income are shaped by the actions and opportunities not only of elites, but also of those below the elite level. For example, Chapter 10 concludes with an examination of the welfare state as a response to class conflict.

Chapters 11 and 12 conclude the examination of the United States class system by considering the processes of social mobility and the legitimation of inequality. Chapter 11 includes recent theory and research on social mobility and the complex subject of status attainment, as well as an extensive critique of this material, using recent cross-national and historical information. The legitimation of class inequality as a process is the subject of Chapter 12, with a focus both on the sociopsychological aspect of this process and on more specific attempts to render elite rule and political-economic policy acceptable to those below the elite level.

Finally, Part Four takes us beyond social stratification within advanced capitalist societies such as the United States. As noted above, Chapter 13 attempts a comprehensive analysis of social stratification in Japan, while Chapter 14 provides information on social stratification in communist societies, with a primary focus on the Soviet Union. The goals of these chapters are to trace the similarities and differences in social stratification between communist and capitalist industrial societies and to show the wider utility of the conflict perspective of social stratification followed in the present text. Then, expanding the unit of analysis beyond individual nations, Chapter 15 presents the recently growing research and theory on the world economic system. Following the world system perspective, the focus is on the place of nations within a system of international class conflict and on how many of the principles of class conflict within nations have wider application.

Before concluding this preface I should note that, as in the first edition, the basic orientation of this book continues to follow a general conflict perspective. This is not to say that other perspectives have been neglected, but it is to say that with the subject of social stratification I continue to believe that a conflict perspective of some variety is most useful in understanding the subject matter. A central, often violent question about social stratification continues to be how valued goods and services are to be distributed in a society. This underlying conflict is sometimes hidden, sometimes tamed, but no less behind all systems of social stratification. When overt conflict over the distribution of valued goods and services is relatively low, it only means that the system of stratification has been somewhat successful in managing such conflict (at least for a time). As I complete work on this edition, I have been learning about Thai society at Chulalongkorn University, walking the streets of Bangkok and observing the extremes of inequality in a developing country experiencing rapid change. Unlike Cambodia, Burma, and Vietnam, for example, and since the bloody massacre of students in 1976, Thailand has recently experienced less overt violence over the question of who gets what and why. But this does not mean that no conflict is behind the distribution of wealth and poverty in Thailand. It only means that the question of who gets what and why has been somehow tamed for the present. How this can be done in a country with extensive poverty is one of the most interesting and important subjects in the study of social stratification.

ACKNOWLEDGMENTS

As every writer of a book of this nature comes to recognize, scientific analysis is clearly a collective enterprise. I am indebted to many social scientists whose works are discussed and cited in the pages of this book. Also, as every writer comes to recognize, there are those in one's more immediate social environment who deserve appreciation. My wife and daughters have been very understanding during the many months of work devoted to this book. Again, I am dedicating the book to them.

Many social scientists and students have provided useful comments and suggestions that have helped me in my work on this edition. For example, the students at Mills College in Professor Constance Jones's seminar on social stratification offered helpful observations. I would like to thank Bill Domhoff, Ken'ichi Tominaga, Hermann Strasser, and Leonard Broom for their encouragement and assistance in locating information. John McKinstry, Keiko Nakao, Mariko Inoe, and Jeffrey Broadbent have been helpful in providing comments and information for the new chapter on Japan, as were Katsuhiro Jinzaki, Nobuo Kawabe, and Naoyuki Kodaira at Hiroshima University. Mikk Titma of the Soviet Sociological Association deserves special thanks for his comments on the Soviet chapter, provided at a time when dramatic events were underway in his Estonian homeland. At McGraw-Hill, I would like to thank my editor, Phillip Butcher, as well as Edwin Hanson, senior editing supervisor, and Katherine Blake, assistant editor, for their professional work and encouragemnt.

McGraw-Hill and I would like to extend our thanks to the following reviewers of the second edition for their valuable critiques and suggestions: Charles Dudley, Virginia Polytechnic Institute and State University; Allan Johnson, Hartford College; John Leggett, Rutgers University; Albert Simkus, Vanderbilt University; and Eve Spangler, Boston College. Finally, we would like once again to acknowledge our indebtedness to the reviewers of the first edition: Karl Alexander, Johns Hopkins University; Daniel Chirot, University of Washington; L. Richard Della Fave, North Carolina State University; Patrick Horan, University of Georgia; Gerhard Lenski, University of North Carolina; Paul Montagna, CUNY–Brooklyn College; Robert Perrucci, Purdue University; and William Sampson, Northwestern University.

Harold R. Kerbo

SOCIAL STRATIFICATION AND INEQUALITY

CLASS CONFLICT IN HISTORICAL AND COMPARATIVE PERSPECTIVE

PART ONE

INTRODUCTION

PERSPECTIVES AND CONCEPTS IN THE STUDY OF SOCIAL STRATIFICATION

In understanding human beings and human societies, no subject is more important than social stratification. A system of social stratification helps shape how people live, their opportunities for a better life, and their mental health and life expectancy. On a more general level, a system of social stratification has an important influence on events such as war and peace, economic expansion or stagnation, unemployment and inflation, and government policies of many kinds.

Most people, of course, are aware of the fact that some people are rich while others are poor. But people in general are usually less aware of the rather systematic social forces that structure such outcomes. They prefer to think that people themselves are responsible for their lot in life. This type of belief is especially strong among the nonpoor and whites in the United States with its values of freedom and individualism. Most people, too, are aware of the fact that some individuals have more influence than others, with the power to shape national issues of war and peace, economic well-being, and general social welfare. But, again, people are usually much less aware of how a system of stratification forms the basis for such influence. They prefer to think that great men and women determine historical events; the possibility that great men and women are themselves a product of a system of social stratification is less obvious to most people.

We can begin our study of social stratification on the level of individual life histories. Individual life histories alone, of course, can tell us very little about an overall *system* of social stratification. It should also be recognized that the subject of sociology, and thus social stratification, is concerned with group

3

properties, social structures, and social forces. In other words, sociology is concerned primarily with groups or aggregates of people, not individual biographies. For example, if sociologists want to understand crime or mental illness they are interested in the social forces that help produce such phenomena. On an individual level many *unique* influences may be shaping human behavior. Thus, to increase the power of our explanations or sociological theories, we concern ourselves with more general social forces that affect many people. As in any science, our intent is to get the most general explanations or understanding out of the least number of variables.

With this in mind, however, we can examine individual biographies as examples, and for the questions they raise. For maximum effect, let us consider a life history on both extremes of the stratification system in the United States.

Michael

Michael was born in August 1965, in the low-income, predominantly black, area of Los Angeles they call Watts. There is some distinction in the place and timing of Michael's birth, not only because he was born six months after his mother began a jail term, but also because his birth occurred a few days after one of the worst race riots in United States history—a race riot that was only one of the first of over 300 that sprang up, one after another, through 1968 (Salert and Sprague 1980). Given these circumstances we have a rather detailed description of Michael's early life provided by Richard Meyers of the *Los Angeles Times*; it is a life history that parallels the troubled history of Watts since Michael was born (see the *Los Angeles Times,* August 10, 1980).

Michael's mother was involved in a daily struggle to find money for food and shelter for herself and a 1-year-old handicapped child when a knife fight led to her arrest and jail term. Despite considerable pressure to the contrary, Michael's mother, Judy, did not give up her baby born while in prison. Michael joined his handicapped brother in a foster home (separately) until Judy could care for her children adequately. During his three years in the foster home, Michael was healthy and developed with the likes and dislikes of any young child—he "hated green peas and haircuts," he loved his toys, dog, and ice cream; and he enjoyed playing with his foster father's tools.

Judy was out of prison after three years, but was also out of work and a place to live. For the next seventeen months she lived in ten different locations—including her mother's apartment, two foster homes, her stepfather's back porch, and a truck. With an unemployment rate of almost 20 percent in the area, jobs were extremely scarce. She reports working for a time with a temporary government work project, and for a time as an aide in a parole office. She also tried her hand at being a pimp for gay men, which brought her considerably more money, but also a life she rejected in order to provide a home for her children. Pregnant again at age 18, she gave up hustling for welfare and her children.

Judy was happy when Michael was returned to her, although she cried for many days when Michael cried for his foster parents. She began receiving a welfare check, like 265,221 other people in the area. But the amount received, despite California's more "generous" assistance level, was inadequate for her needs and the needs of three children. (By 1990 in California, a mother with three children could receive about $800 per month with a basic welfare grant under Aid to Families with Dependent Children.) Judy and her three children were forced to live with relatives in a three-bedroom apartment that was home for 13 people.

To some extent Judy and Michael's prospects improved when Judy married a man who was employed as a janitor. They moved to a rented apartment of their own in a low-income housing project. Like most mothers, Judy loved her children and did her best in providing for them. Michael remembers she always wrote "I love you" on his lunch sack when he began school. She saved to buy Christmas presents for the kids, and did volunteer work at Michael's preschool.

With marriage Judy had her fourth child. But as is too often the case for many poor children, the relatively good times did not last. Judy's marriage began breaking up, and she turned to drugs. The children were chased by rats in the apartment, rats that sometimes woke them up at night in their beds, and Michael was bitten by a tarantula. Again they moved, and again Judy was alone with her children.

Their new apartment was not much better, but the rats were less of a problem. Judy was back on the welfare rolls, and the area they lived in was one of the most crime-prone and violent. Judy first placed Michael in a Catholic school to keep him away from the crime and gangs in the public school, but it did not last. Both Judy and Michael describe being embarrassed when comparing themselves with the parents and children in this new school, with the embarrassment reaching a peak when Judy could not afford 11 cents for required pencil and eraser at the school. Michael was placed in the public school.

Michael saw a man killed for the first time when he was 7 years old. The man was driving an ice cream truck in front of Michael's apartment when several young boys stopped the truck, beat the man, and took $12. Other residents in the area took all the ice cream out of the truck. This was only the first of many people Michael saw killed before he was 15.

Michael's 16-month-old sister was killed when she fell from their apartment stairs. Judy took the death with much grief and alcohol. Shortly afterward, when Michael was in the third grade, he was again placed in a foster home. This time it was because of a child abuse charge against Judy. Michael had broken his arm, but was unable to convince anyone that it had happened in a fall away from home. Again Judy found it difficult to live with her life. Michael remembers crying night after night for his mother. The alleged child abuse, however, did appear unfounded, and Michael was returned to Judy after a judge became convinced of her innocence.

At about this time Michael also found the influence of street gangs difficult to resist. He was arrested for shoplifting in the third grade. By the time he was 10 there were other arrests and gang fights for Michael. By age 15 he had experienced anger over his mother's beating and gang rape by young boys, he had seen more men killed, and he had to bear the fact that his and his mother's possessions were stolen time and time again. He had seen his mother sick because of hunger and he had stolen food. Michael still lived in the area of the 1965 Watts riot, which in 1990 had an even higher rate of crime and unemployment. Also, by the age of 15, Michael was in jail; and nine months after the story on Michael appeared in the *Los Angeles Times* his mother was found shot to death.

The future for Michael, along with millions of children in similar circumstances in this country, does not look good. Judging from the experience of most middle-aged men in the area of Watts, we might expect Michael to be in and out of the unemployment lines throughout his life; and when work is found it will be low paid and low skilled. Of course, there is the strong possibility he will be in and out of prison as well, if not killed like many young people in places like Watts.

We can feel sorry and angry for, and about, Judy and Michael; but sorrow and anger are not the intent of the above description. The description is meant to illustrate not just the misfortunes of one family, but the experience of many families who are poor (of no matter what race) in the United States. Such experiences are no doubt varied for, contrary to popular belief, the poor represent a diverse segment of our population. But the poor do have many common problems that are presented by their common position at the bottom of the stratification system in an affluent society. We will consider the questions this case presents for the study of social stratification after we examine the case of David.

David

David was born at the other end of the stratification system in this country—at the top. His parents were not only rich, they were among the superrich and powerful. David was born in 1915, the youngest of six children. His father had assets of at least $0.5 billion, which he had inherited from his father (Collier and Horowitz 1976:133). David, like Michael, grew up in a number of dwellings though, as might be expected, there were a number of differences. For one, the several dwellings were all owned by the family—all at the same time. As for other differences, the homes were substantially less crowded than Michael's first (three bedrooms for thirteen people), and it is rather doubtful that they had rats, spiders, and cockroaches.

First, there was their New York City townhouse on Fifth Avenue. Then, for the weekends, there was the Pocantico Hills estate in New York. The

3,500-acre Pocantico estate is five times the size of Central Park in New York City, with a 250-acre park of its own. At Pocantico, David and his brothers and sister could "go to the stone stables and have the riding master take them out on the trails; they could check out one of the fleet of electric cars that sailed silently around the grounds . . . " (Collier and Horowitz 1976:182). It took $50,000 a year to maintain the "Big House" on this estate, and a total of $500,000 per year to maintain the whole estate.

During the summers David's family spent most of its time at its estate in Seal Harbor, Maine. Here the children could go sailing in the many boats or go on long walks to the "cabin" deep in the woods on the estate (Collier and Horowitz 1976:181–182). Finally, if they really wanted to get away, there was a home in the Virgin Islands, a Venezuela ranch, and the Grand Teton Mountains ranch (Dye 1979:158).

We would expect that David was much like Michael as a 2-year-old child. He was curious about his environment, he loved to play with his toys, and, though never mentioned in biographies, we might expect that he liked ice cream. But David had a much wider and safer environment to explore, and his toys were more numerous and expensive. After this young age, the differences grew much wider. David did not grow up with street crime and violence, it is doubtful he ever saw a man killed, and his schools were much different. He went to the elite Lincoln School near the Pocantico Hills estate, then attended Harvard and the London School of Economics, and earned a Ph.D. in economics at the University of Chicago (Kutz 1974:71).

As a young child, David appeared serious and "responsible," and he was informally selected from among his brothers to carry on the family business interests (Collier and Horowitz 1976:220; Dye 1979:158). After World War II David began work at his uncle's bank as an assistant manager of the foreign department. He spent three years at that job, and in 1950 he was promoted to a vice-president. By 1952 he was senior vice-president; in 1962, president; and in 1969, chairman of the board and chief executive officer (Kutz 1974:73–99). He retired from these positions in 1981.

Before retirement, David Rockefeller was described as the most powerful private citizen in the United States; "the only man who would have to step down to become president of the United States" (Collier and Horowitz 1976:431; Dye 1979:157–158). As one corporate executive put it to the *Wall Street Journal* (April 3, 1981), Mr. Rockefeller "is the equivalent of a head of state. He is the chairman of the board of the Eastern establishment." All this is an exaggeration—at least to some degree. At Chase Manhattan Bank David Rockefeller chaired a board of directors that included men from top positions at American Express Company, Chrysler, Continental Corporation, Equitable Life Assurance, Exxon, General Electric, General Motors, IBM, Sears Roebuck, Standard Oil of Indiana, Union Carbide, and United States Steel (U.S. Senate Committee on Governmental Affairs 1978b:898). In addition, the bank's trust department controlled significant stock in such companies as Exxon, IT&T, Morgan Bank, Standard Oil of California,

Mobil, and Aetna Life and Casualty (U.S. Senate Committee on Governmental Affairs 1978a).

David Rockefeller has also been chairman of the Museum of Modern Art, on the board of Harvard University, a trustee of the Carnegie Foundation, a trustee of the University of Chicago and the John F. Kennedy Library, and director of the Council on Foreign Relations (Dye 1979:159). He repeatedly turned down cabinet posts offered by Presidents Kennedy, Johnson, and Nixon (Collier and Horowitz 1976:403).

David Rockefeller is noted for his hard work, but he does have the time and means to play. As a wine connoisseur, he is part owner of a French vineyard; and in his Pocantico home, he has "a renowned temperature-controlled [wine] cellar sealed with a bank-vault door." As a yachtsman, he has three 40-foot boats at his Seal Harbor estate in Maine; as an art collector, he has one of the best collections of Impressionist and post-Impressionist paintings (Collier and Horowitz 1976:321). And one must not forget his beetle collection (bugs, not Beatle records); dating back to his childhood days, his collection is reported to be one of the best in the world, with two species named after him (Collier and Horowitz 1976:221).

Added to all this, David's personal real estate holdings include residences in Manhattan and Pocantico, the vacation homes at Seal Harbor and in the Caribbean, a sheep ranch in Australia, and several thousand acres in the Virgin Islands and the Brazilian interior (Collier and Horowitz 1976:423). It is difficult to obtain precise figures on the total wealth of people like David Rockefeller, but one "conservative" estimate of the present Rockefeller family wealth (excluding family holdings in real estate and financial institutions) was $4 billion (Kutz 1974:71).

The two life histories just described illustrate the obvious fact that while some people in this nation are very rich, others are very poor. And it might be well to note that we can find many more people in Michael's position than we can in David Rockefeller's position. But these two life histories have been presented for a more important reason; they suggest several questions that must be considered in any study of social stratification.

1 Most basic, of course, is the question "*Why* is Michael so poor while David Rockefeller is so rich?" A popular explanation (especially in the United States) for wealth and poverty is directed toward individual qualities. The rich, it is often believed, are rich because of their superior talents and motivation. The poor, in turn, are believed to be poor because of their lack of talent and motivation and low moral qualities. It is doubtful that anyone would question the exceptional talent of David Rockefeller. But the key question is how this talent developed or where it came from. Also, we must ask how many among the poor have exceptional talent, or even average talent, that is never given a chance to develop. If a poor child were adopted at birth by a family like the

Rockefellers, how would this child turn out? Similarly, what if David Rocke-feller had been adopted by a poor family? Unless we are willing to say the rich are usually biologically superior in some way (which is absurd), we must look further. In the two cases described above, social background differences are obvious. But this presents further questions.

2 How does class background influence how people turn out or where they end up in the class system? Does class background primarily influence oppor-tunities for more and better education, job opportunities, and opportunities for more income; or does it also shape personal characteristics like intelligence, aspirations, and self-evaluations? Family class background is often used as an explanation for social conditions like poverty and crime, as well as for why some people end up affluent and in respected positions in the society. But this is only a partial explanation. With this explanation we may blame Michael's mother for the way Michael is ending up: Despite her love for Michael, why was she in jail when Michael was born? Why did she have children she could not support? Why did she allow Michael to get involved with gangs? By them-selves, however, such questions provide little help in a *general* understanding of inequality and social stratification. On the one hand, if we blame Judy for Michael's outcome, we may have to blame Judy's parents, and their parents, until we go back to the early slaves. (Do we blame them for being captured and sold as slaves?) On the other hand, we must not forget what Judy had to face in raising Michael. These questions lead us to other questions.

3 Why do social backgrounds differ? In essence, we have returned to our first question without making much progress. At this point we must ask ques-tions about the nature of society rather than of individuals. What are the po-litical, economic, and social forces that help produce inequality and social stratification? In related questions we must ask if inequality is somehow nec-essary and beneficial for the overall society. Or is inequality best understood as a conflict relation, with the greater power of the more affluent producing their greater share of valued goods and services? Even if we find inequality to be beneficial in some way, we must also ask if the *degree* of inequality we find in the United States is beneficial for the overall society. Or does the degree of inequality in this country primarily benefit the more affluent, resulting in the exploitation of others?

4 Putting aside questions concerning the causes of inequality, we have oth-ers pertaining to the maintenance of inequality. For example, why is it that many of the poor either accept or tolerate their low position? A question often posed is "Why do people on the bottom rebel?" Perhaps a more important question (given over 33 million poor in this country) is "Why do the poor so seldom rebel?" Blacks and other minorities did rebel in the 1960s. But most of the poor in this country are white, and the black rebellion has subsided (for now) without significant improvement for most blacks.

5 With respect to the brief biographies of Michael and David Rockefeller, could we find similar biographies in other countries today (both capitalist and communist)? In other words, how similar or different is the level of inequality and system of social stratification in this country compared with others, past and present?

6 Finally, with respect to David Rockefeller's power in this society (and the world), what is the basis of his power, and that of others like him? Is this power more an outcome of his family wealth, or of his institutional position with Chase Manhattan Bank (the second largest bank in the United States)?

As we will see in coming chapters, questions such as these have no simple answers. But these questions are among the most important that a serious examination of social stratification must attempt to answer. There is an even more general question, however, from which the others follow. As Lenski (1966) puts it, the study of social stratification is an attempt to answer the question of *who gets what, and why*. With limited valuable resources, we want to know why some (like the Rockefellers) get a much greater share of these resources. When we ask such a question it becomes necessary to link personal misfortune (such as Michael's) and fortune (such as David Rockefeller's) with more general social arrangements or social structure. It is this task that will guide what follows.

DEFINITIONS AND CONCEPTS

Before proceeding there is the usual matter of basic definitions and concepts. Because a few words or concepts may be used differently by social scientists than by the public, or even than by other social scientists, we must be precise. At the same time, we have to avoid overdoing the definitions and concepts now or we will only compound the confusion. For this reason our discussion at this point will be as brief as possible. We will define only the most important terms and concepts, leaving others for discussion as appropriate. Further, we will define the terms and concepts that follow as simply as possible. Complexity and additional specification may be added in later chapters when such specification becomes necessary and useful.

Social Stratification and Inequality

We must begin with a most basic concept that describes a necessary precondition for social stratification, but that must not be confused with social stratification. This condition is *social differentiation,* which occurs, quite simply, when we find people with distinct individual qualities and social roles. People are differentiated in terms of biological characteristics such as sex, size, strength, and agility and in every society they are differentiated (at least to some degree) by social roles, work tasks, or occupations. Some people do the hunting, others chop wood, and still others care for children or gather plants in the forest. As societies become more complex technologically, the division of labor increases—the number of tasks, occupations, and roles grows also. In short, an increased division of labor means more differentiation.

It is important to recognize that social differentiation does *not* necessarily suggest that differences in personal qualities or work roles are ranked on a hierarchy, or evaluated differently. As Heller (1969:3) notes, "Positions may be differentiated from one another and yet not *ranked* relative to each other. For example, in our society the position of the adolescent is generally not considered superior to that of infant, merely different." Social differentiation, however, sets the stage for inequality and social stratification.

Social inequality is the condition whereby people have unequal access to valued resources, services, and positions in the society. Such inequality can emerge in terms of how individuals and groups are themselves ranked and evaluated by others, but, most importantly, social inequality is related to differing positions in a social structure. Social inequality often emerges from social differentiation for two basic reasons. On the one hand, because of the human capacity to apply meaning to events and things, to develop judgments of what is "good," "bad," or preferable, social evaluation is often applied to differences. Thus, individual characteristics and different positions or roles may be valued unequally or ranked from superior to inferior. In this sense we refer to social inequality in terms of prestige or honor. As we will see in coming chapters, it is only in this limited respect that we can say social inequality has been present in all human societies.

On the other hand, and more importantly, inequality may emerge from social differentiation because some roles or social positions place some people in a position to acquire a greater share of valued goods and services. In this case we refer to inequality in terms of the access to favored positions in the society, although social evaluation or prestige will usually follow as a secondary matter, because people who have positions favored in the society will be evaluated highly.

For example, in societies where physical strength is important in providing the necessities of life, the strong may be able successfully to demand greater rewards and, consequently, greater respect. In more complex societies with an expanded division of labor, those in the position of coordinating and organizing the work of others obtain more authority. Such authority will be used to acquire greater rewards. Also, acquiring a surplus of goods and services in and of itself usually leads to even more rewards. This is because an unequal exchange may develop. When some people control what others want and need, they are able to demand additional goods and services in return for distributing these necessities.

We come finally to the most important concept for our purpose—social stratification. As the root term suggests, *strata* is implied in this concept. By adding the term *social* we are saying that human beings in social positions are stratified from high to low as strata of rock are layered one upon another. But at this point social stratification is not clearly distinguished from social inequality, so we must mean more if separate terms are used. *Social stratification* means that inequality has been hardened or *institutionalized,* and there is a *system of social relationships* that determines who gets what, and why. When we say *institutionalized* we mean that a system of layered hierarchy has been established. People have come to expect that individuals and groups with certain positions will be able to demand more influence and respect and accumulate a greater share of goods and services. Such inequality may or may not be accepted equally by a majority in the society, but it is recognized as the way things are.

By a system of social stratification we also mean that something like rules have been developed "explaining" how rewards are distributed and why they are distributed in such a way. For example, the rules may explain that some receive greater rewards because they are the human representative of some god or because they are believed to contribute more to the well-being of the total society.

Some sociologists prefer the term *structured inequality* in place of the term *social stratification.* As Heller (1969:4) writes, "The term *structured* indicates an arrangement of elements: the inequality is not random but follows a pattern, displays relative constancy and stability, and is backed by ideas that legitimize and justify it."

Other sociologists add a further dimension to the meaning of social stratification. Along with what we have described as institutionalized inequality and a system of rules "explaining" unequal distribution, they add the condition of hereditary inequalities. As Mayer and Buckley (1955:7) put it, "The central focus of stratification study is the fact that, over a number of generations, those individuals who fill positions in any particular level of positional hierarchy tend to be recruited from the corresponding level of the hierarchy of individuals and subgroups." Those advantaged usually find ways to assure that their offspring will be advantaged.

When class or strata placement is primarily hereditary, we refer to such placement as *ascription.* That is, people are placed in positions in a stratification system because of qualities beyond their control (for example, because of race, sex, or class at birth). When class or strata placement is due primarily to qualities that can be controlled by individuals, we refer to such placement as *achievement.* That is, people obtain their place in the stratification system because they have merit, because they live up to certain ideals, or because they follow certain achievement rules. However, because in most societies strata placement is based on a varying mixture of ascription and achievement, we have chosen not to limit our definition of social stratification to cases of ascription.

Class Divisions and Social Mobility

Because much of our concern in coming chapters will be the stratification systems of industrial societies, a brief introductory comment is necessary with respect to class divisions and social mobility. (Again, more detail will be added when needed.) The concept of class, as we will see, has provoked a lot of controversy among sociologists. Generally, we can define *class* as a grouping of individuals with similar positions and similar political and economic interests within the stratification system. The controversy over class involves such questions as (1) the criteria most important in distinguishing classes, (2) the number of class divisions that exist, (3) the extent to which individuals (themselves) must recognize these divisions if they are to be meaningful, and (4) whether or not class divisions (as defined here) even exist in the United States and other industrial societies.

In coming chapters we will present evidence supporting the dominant view that class is a meaningful and very important concept in the context of the United States, and that class divisions are based upon three main criteria: a person's position in the *occupational structure,* a person's position in *authority structures* (how many people a person must take orders from versus how many people a person can give orders to), and a person's ownership of *property* (or, more specifically, the ownership of property that produces profit, such as stock ownership). These three criteria tend to intersect, producing more or less distinct class divisions.

A typical listing of class divisions in the United States is made primarily in terms of occupational and economic divisions. Given that the United States is an industrial capitalist nation, such divisions are of prime importance in the stratification system. These class divisions are often labeled upper class, upper middle class, lower middle class, working class, and lower class. Similar labels, specifying occupation more distinctly, are capitalist class (upper class), higher nonmanual (higher white-collar), lower nonmanual (lower white-collar), skilled manual (skilled blue-collar), unskilled manual (unskilled blue-collar), and the poor (primarily unemployed).

Because of our stress on the three intersecting criteria for class location (occupation, authority, property), a slightly altered class breakdown will be employed. This class breakdown provides more recognition of the fact that the United States is a bureaucratized industrial society as well as a capitalistic industrial society. That is, people are ranked by authority as well as occupational and economic standing.

Upper class will be used to signify those families high in property ownership, with high authority flowing from such ownership. These are the old established families with significant ownership of major corporations, such as the Rockefellers, the Du Ponts, the Mellons, and the Fords.

The *corporate class* will be used to signify people with high authority and power in major corporations (and often government), usually without extensive ownership in these corporations. These people include top corporate executives (presidents, vice-presidents, and so on) and corporate board members. There is some evidence that the upper class is shrinking in importance while this corporate class is growing in importance.

The *middle class* will be used to signify those with relatively little property, but high-to-middle positions in occupation (nonmanual labor) and authority.

Further distinction will be made with respect to the upper middle class (lesser corporate managers, doctors, lawyers, and so forth) and lower middle class (office workers, clerks, salespeople).

The *working class* will be used to signify people with little or no property, middle-to-low positions in occupation (manual labor), and little or no authority. A further distinction will be made with respect to skilled and unskilled manual workers.

Last, the *lower class* will be used to signify those individuals with no property, who are often unemployed and have no authority (that is, the poor). A more detailed discussion of these class divisions in the United States will be presented in Chapter 6.

The rather ambiguous term *status* should be discussed in conjunction with class. This term is ambiguous because sociologists often use it to mean different things. On the one hand, status is often used to indicate positions in a social structure—for example, student, teacher, father, child—with certain rights and duties attached to such positions. On the other hand, status is often used to indicate something like class position within a hierarchy. In this usage, however, the criterion of status consists of occupational prestige, or the popularly ranked esteem and respect associated with high to low occupational attainment. In coming chapters we will use the term *status* in this second sense, although it will be used sparingly and specifically because of our rejection of the primary importance of status or prestige divisions in the stratification system. (The reasons for this require more justification later.)

Any analysis of a class system is incomplete without due consideration of social mobility. As we will see, a class system may in part be distinguished from other types of stratification systems because of the greater possibility of achievement or changes in class placement. In reality, of course, ascription is never eliminated, and what exists is a varied mixture of achievement and ascription. *Social mobility* may be defined as individual or group movement within the class system. We can speak of both vertical and horizontal mobility, or the movement of individuals up and down the class system compared with their movement across positions of roughly equal rank.

Given that class systems are based (at least to some degree) on achievement, we would expect them to display extensive patterns of vertical social mobility. Combining this expectation with the American stress on equality of opportunity, we can understand why the study of social mobility has become almost an obsession among American sociologists. We have numerous studies designed to measure the extent of vertical mobility in the United States, as well as many studies attempting to measure the exact mixture of achievement versus ascriptive factors that determine where people end up in the class system. (This second type of study is called *status attainment research.*)

We may note at this point that research indicates social mobility is extensive in the United States, although most of it is short range. The extent of mobility varies, depending on where we look in the class system (top, middle, or bottom) and race. However, the research also indicates that both ascriptive factors (such as race and family class background) and achievement factors (such as educational attainment) play a part in class placement in the United States, with ascriptive factors playing a larger part than our values proclaim.

VARIETIES OF HUMAN STRATIFICATION SYSTEMS

The final task of this chapter is to give a brief description of varieties of human systems of social stratification. It must be stressed that we will concentrate here on description. In Chapter 3 we will explore these varieties of stratification systems more fully from an historical perspective. Approaching a subject as vast as that of varieties of social stratification systems means we have to generalize and simplify. To do so, however, is of value, for among the varieties we do find most societies tending toward one of a few ideal types of stratification systems. By ideal types of stratification systems we mean general forms, or groupings, of systems that are broadly similar. What such a tendency toward a few ideal types indicates is that human beings have generally found only a few types of stratification systems to be most successful in providing social order in the face of sometimes extremely high levels of inequality.

Social scientists are not in complete agreement on the most useful typology or method of comparing social stratification systems, but five ideal types are most commonly described: *primitive communal, slavery, caste, estate* or *feudal,* and *class systems.* (For a discussion similar to what follows, see Heller 1987.) Each of these five ideal types can be compared on five basic characteristics of stratification systems: normatively closed versus open divisions, the actual method of status or class placement, the major method of legitimation, the predominant form of inequality, and the comparative level of inequality in each type of stratification system. However, it should be noted that, given our definition of social stratification stressing structured inequalities, it is somewhat inaccurate to suggest that all primitive communal societies have a *system* of social stratification. As we will see, the inequalities in many of these societies are relatively minor, unstructured, and informal. But for the sake of comparison, this type of society can be included in the typology as long as the above point is recognized.

With respect to the first main characteristic, these societies vary according to the degree of normative closure or openness between the hierarchical divisions or ranks within the stratification system. We say *normative* because we are referring to norms or values prescribing relatively open versus closed rankings. For example, social norms may stress that individuals are free, following certain rules, to leave their present rank (or rank at birth) by moving into a higher or lower rank. Conversely, in other societies such vertical mobility may be prohibited.

Closely following the first characteristic, we find differing methods by which people are *actually* placed within ranks in the stratification system. These methods range along a continuum from *ascription* to *achievement.* As noted earlier, ascription refers to placement beyond the control of the individual. Placement is determined by such characteristics as the rank of one's parents, sex, or race. Achievement refers to placement based on individual merit or, as the name suggests, achievement. Few societies can be located at either extreme end of the ascription–achievement continuum (the caste system is one exception); most have a varying mixture of ascription and achievement.

All societies must, at least to a degree, employ some method for justifying the existence of inequality among its population. This method typically follows a process referred to as *legitimation*. Such a process is of primary importance in societies maintaining a high degree of inequality among its members (which is to say most societies in the past 10,000 years or so). For example, those at the bottom of the stratification system must in some way be convinced that their low position is "right and proper." Otherwise social order and structured inequalities can be maintained only through use of physical force—a method that can be very costly in lives and resources, and in the long run is often unsuccessful. Most societies, in fact, rely upon a number of methods of legitimation, although one or two tend to predominate.

Tradition or *custom* as a method of legitimation forces attention to the past. People may be taught that this is how things have always been, thus closing their minds to any possible alternatives to a present distribution of valued goods and services. A more systematic *ideological* justification may also be used. Although such an ideological justification may rely in part on tradition, here we are speaking of a more systematic belief system often pointing to the superior qualities of those at the top of the stratification system and/or to their "important" contribution to the overall social well-being as justification for their greater share of valued goods and services.

Often similar to more secular ideological justifications are religious beliefs. Here the "superior qualifications" of those on top of the stratification system are not as important. Rather, the existing system of stratification is deemed legitimate because a deity or supernatural force wills it so. Accompanying a religious justification we typically find promised rewards (usually in the next life or in heaven) for those who obey the rules and obligations of their present class or caste position. Finally, there are varying methods of *legal* justification. These are based either on laws enforcing the rights, privileges, and duties of existing ranks backed up by the authority of the state or on legal procedures that claim to ensure a fair set of rules in assigning ranks and rewards.

Three major dimensions or kinds of inequality can be found in most human societies. These three are (1) inequalities of honor, *status,* or prestige; (2) inequalities of *economic* influence and material rewards; and (3) inequalities based on military, political, or bureaucratic *power.* In most societies all three types of inequalities are present and are usually interrelated. For example, when a person is favored with respect to one type of inequality, he or she is usually well off with respect to others as well. But in different types of stratification systems one of the three tends to be most important. In other words, a high position within one dimension of inequality can be used to obtain a high position in the others. Remembering that all three dimensions of inequality are present in most societies, we will indicate the dimension most important in each type of stratification system.

We can provide a rough estimate of the overall degree of inequality in these differing ideal types of stratification systems. Our estimate is based primarily upon the range of inequality between elites and the common people in each society. This estimate is made with respect to economic and power values which are more easily represented across societies. Considering the five types of stratification systems, overall inequality ranges from a very low level in primitive communal societies to a high level in slave, caste, and estate societies and a medium level in class or industrial societies. The reasons for this range in the level of inequality are of major importance for an overall understanding of social stratification, and because they are so important, we will focus on them later.

Primitive Communal Societies

Societies labeled *primitive communal* represent the earliest forms of social organization. (As noted above, formal systems of stratification are absent.) Their economy is based on simple hunting and gathering methods of killing or trapping animals, with little use of agricultural methods of food production. Because hunting and gathering methods of food production usually result in a depletion of resources in the immediate environment (how rapidly depends on the size of the tribe and climate conditions), these people tend to be nomadic or seminomadic. Also, because of their primitive methods of food production and nomadic lifestyle, an accumulation of material possessions generally is impossible. What goods and food they have is usually divided more or less equally among all members of the tribe.

Primitive communal societies may have chiefs, respected leaders, medicine men, or shamans who have more influence or power within the tribe. However, their influence over others is relatively limited and restricted to their ability to perform valuable functions for the tribe as a whole. Thus, positions such as chief are achieved positions with an open method of placement. The predominant form of inequality—in fact often the only major form of inequality—is status or honor. Because of some important function served by a particular individual, such as in providing food, a higher status position may be obtained, with few if any material rewards above the general level found among other tribal members. No legal, religious, or systematic ideological justifications are offered for the existence of inequalities of status. Most importantly, with the overall level of inequality very low, none is needed. The inequalities of status that are found are simply explained by tradition. That is, the best hunter is customarily awarded greater status/honor.

In concluding this brief initial discussion of primitive communal societies (we will have much more to say in Chapter 3), we should note that this ideal type is very general (as are the others), and includes primitive societies with slightly differing levels and forms of inequality.

One important distinction can be made between what has been called *bands,* which are nonranked and nonstratified; and *tribes,* which are ranked but nonstratified (see Sahlins and Service 1960; Fried 1973). In the band we find unlimited higher status positions based exclusively on individual abilities. Higher status is given to some, such as the best hunter, and if there are ten or fifteen good hunters there are ten or fifteen higher-status positions (that is, higher status is given to all that achieve it).

In the tribe, however, while still nonstratified, the higher status positions are more formalized, with a specific number of higher-status positions. Those with the higher-status positions perform specific tribal functions, such as presiding over rituals or overseeing the distribution of goods and resources. Thus, in contrast to the band, in the tribe higher status is not an unlimited commodity, and elementary rules of succession have developed.

However, a main point must be stressed: In primitive communal societies in general (including the band and the tribe), the only significant form of inequality is status, with no one able to achieve material or power resources significantly above others in the society.

Slavery

One of the most persistent historical forms of inequality has been *slavery.* This form of domination emerged soon after human beings settled down in established agricultural communities, reaching its high point with early agrarian civilizations. It can be found here and there in slightly altered forms, but with a few major characteristics dominating. First of all, it is an economic relationship, the ownership of human beings, and an economic form of inequality dominates. Throughout history the position of slave has been acquired in many ways—through birth, military defeat, falling into debt, or, as with United States slaves, through capture and then commercial trade. Likewise, throughout history the level of hardship and misery for slaves has varied, as has their hope of freedom.

Contrary to the American experience, slavery has not always been an hereditary condition, nor has it always been a normatively closed system. Especially in ancient slave societies, freedom could be purchased or otherwise acquired by the slave. Thus, although slavery was often an ascribed status, achievement out of slave status could be attained. Slavery in the United States was compounded by what will be described below as caste. Only in a few societies like our own did racial caste produce a more closed, hereditary slave status.

The level of inequality between the slave and the owner, as well as between the common people and elites in agrarian slave societies, was great. But, again, the level of inequality varied greatly. In some societies slaves did have legal rights and were treated fairly well, in contrast to the United States experience. In some ancient societies, slaves were sometimes highly rewarded, and even placed in positions of high authority. Elites sometimes felt that slaves could be controlled and trusted with power more than nonslaves, who might aspire to the kingship.

The two primary means of legitimation in slave societies were legal and ideological. Slave status was usually a legal property relation sanctioned by state authority. Ideological justification varied from racist beliefs "explaining" the inferior qualities of slaves (thus making them "fit" for slavery) to nonracial ideologies. The latter type of ideology was more common throughout history because the combination of racial caste and slavery was less common. The more usual type of ideological justification for slavery can be found in ancient Greek civilization, where Aristotle wrote that "it is clear that some men are by nature free, and others slaves, and that for these latter slavery is both expedient and right."

Caste

Nowhere has the *caste* system approximated the ideal type as closely as in India. In fact, some authors maintain (see Dumont 1970) that a caste system in the full sense of the term has existed only in India. Although our focus at this point will be India, we will note caste characteristics found in other localities. With respect to the Indian caste system, there is no clear information on its origins. It seems to have grown from a system of domination by nomadic Aryan invaders about 4,000 years ago (Wells 1971:203; Pfeiffer 1977:213).

In the Indian caste system four main divisions or castes (*varnas*), with priests (Brahmans) and a warrior caste (Kshatriyas) on top of this highly rigid hierarchy, developed. In addition to the four main castes there are *many* subcastes (*jatis*), with much local variation based on occupational specialization. But everyone in the population is not located in a particular caste or subcaste. A large number of people are literally "outcastes," that is, outside of the caste system. These people, commonly referred to as *untouchables,* are considered by others to be so lowly and unclean as to have no place within this system of stratification.

Most important among the distinguishing characteristics of a caste system are its almost complete normative closure and very rigid ranks. Unlike a class system, for example, there are no ambiguous gray areas in which one class or rank shades into another; rather, the divisions are well defined and clear. Along with this, extreme normative closure specifies that no one born into one caste can be socially mobile, either up or down. Although there have been some cases of marriage across caste lines (Dumont 1970), and in special cases a whole subcaste has moved up in rank, this system represents extreme ascription.

Another important aspect of a caste system is the very high degree of institutionalization and acceptance of rigid ranks, as well as the rights and duties of each caste. It is a highly ritualistic system, meaning that strict rules must be observed whenever people from differing castes come into contact. For example, untouchables are considered so unclean as to be required to hide whenever anyone from a higher caste (or, more accurately, anyone with a caste position) is in the area or, if this is not possible, they are required to bow with their faces to the earth.

The acceptance of such ritual and caste inequality in India, especially among the lowest castes and untouchables (until this century), seems quite remarkable. It is this acceptance that has led some, as noted above, to suggest that a caste system has existed in its fullest sense only in India. As evidence of this acceptance, in an "extensive search" through the historical literature, Moore (1978:62) could find no report of revolts by untouchables in India before this century.

An immediate question arises: What accounts for this remarkable acceptance (especially by those toward the bottom of the stratification system)? The best answer, it seems, can be found with the method of justification or legitimation of caste inequalities. In India the Hindu religion has provided such a justification through an elaborate code spelling out the obligations, rights, and overall workings of the caste system. If accepted (which no doubt they generally were), these religious beliefs provided the sanctions necessary for enforcement of caste duties and obligations.

The Hindu religion maintains a belief in reincarnation—that souls are reborn after death. For enforcement of caste duties the key is that individuals are believed to experience reincarnation upward or downward within the caste system, depending on how well they respect their caste duties and obligations. Thus, depending on the acceptance of this religious belief, and the evidence suggests that such acceptance was typical (Dumont 1970), we find an incredibly strong mechanism for maintaining the stratification system. No one wants to be reborn as an untouchable, least of all the untouchables, who best know the miseries of this position. Furthermore, we can understand the contempt received by untouchables; they are those believed to have sinned most in a previous life.

As might be expected with such rigid closure and ascribed rankings, the degree of inequality within the Indian caste system has been high. Incumbents of top caste positions maintain vast amounts of wealth and power, while those below remain very poor. But economic and power differences are not the most prominent forms of inequality. Rather, as the Indian caste system has operated, it is status inequality that dominates. The caste rankings are primarily status ranks, while inequalities of wealth and power flow from, or are traditionally attached to, the inequalities in status.

Before concluding our discussion of the Indian caste system it is important to note that India has been in a period of change in this century, especially since independence from English domination after World War II. A quasi-democratic form of government along British lines has been established, and there have been systematic attempts to reduce the old inequalities of caste. With an ascriptive system so deeply ingrained through the centuries, however, resistance to change is perhaps understandable. It has been primarily since

World War II that we find periodic clashes among caste members and untouchables over inequalities.

As mentioned above, at least some characteristics of caste can be found outside India. One country that has had a stratification system roughly similar to a caste system for at least a relatively brief period of time is Japan (Reischauer and Craig 1978; Hane 1982). From the early 1600s to the middle 1800s, during what is called the Tokugawa Period in Japan, the shogun rulers established a very rigid system of closed caste ranks to maintain strict control as European countries threatened Japan with colonization. At the top of the caste rankings were the shogunate warrior-bureaucrats, their samurai military elite, and the higher aristocracy (called *daimyo*). This top caste was followed by peasants (who were very poor, but given a relatively high status position due to their honorable work in rice production), then artisans, and merchants at the bottom (who were often well off economically, but involved in a traditionally low status and "dirty" occupation). And, as in the Indian caste system, there was even a group of outcastes called *eta* or *hinin* (and today more often called *burakumin*) who were treated much like the Indian outcastes described above. (The term *eta* actually means "heavily polluted," and the term *hinin* means "nonhuman" in Japanese.)

It is common to hear any form of inequality based on ascription referred to as a caste ranking. For example, race and sexual inequalities are often referred to as caste divisions, and so is the ascriptive status maintained by old upper-class families in countries such as the United States. Most of the controversy over the existence of caste outside of India, however, has been focused on black racial inequality in the United States (see Cox 1948; Sio 1969; Dumont 1970).

We do, of course, find racial ascription maintained by a racist ideology. But, it is argued, the most important aspect of a highly institutionalized system of caste inequality is lacking with respect to black–white divisions in the United States. Most significant is that there has never been a high degree of acceptance of racial ascription in the United States, especially among blacks. We can conclude by noting only that there are at least some caste characteristics found with race and sexual ascription in modern societies like the United States.

Estate

There is also a controversy over whether *feudalism,* or the *estate* system, is primarily a relationship based on military power or economic dominance (see Heller 1969:57). Marc Bloch disputes the economic view by describing the origins of feudalism in military power held by some families during Europe's early Middle Ages (Bloch 1961). Marx, of course, stressed the relation of economic dominance whereby one class owned the major means of production (in this case land) while others lived at its mercy. We may enter this debate only by suggesting that in the early European age of feudalism the military power aspect was dominant, while an economic form of control (enforced by the state) increased in importance later. But, to be completely accurate, in the final stage of European feudalism bureaucratic state power also became an important element, as in late eighteenth-century France.

A form of feudalism existed in many, if not most, agrarian societies, but it was in Europe during the Middle Ages that a form of feudalism developed most conforming to the described ideal type. By the twelfth century in Europe the feudal system was firmly established. This system centered around the land holdings of an originally military class termed a nobility. There were ties of obedience, agrarian labor, and protection between the nobility and subjects (mostly peasants or serfs) called a vassalage. Peasants were required to supply labor and military service to their lords (nobility) when needed, in exchange for the necessities of life and protection from external threats.

During the early period of feudalism Europe was a continent of overlapping and fragmented areas of authority. Land was dominated primarily by rather independent noble kinship groups, but with shifting alliances to other noble families in an area. As these ties between noble families became more extensive, more dominant noble families emerged, forming kingdoms. Later, what we know of as modern states further institutionalized the authority of the more dominant nobility.

It was with the consolidation of early feudal states around the twelfth century that the true form of an *estate system* fully emerged. For it was with state sanction that estate ranks, similar to classes, were formalized and given justification or legitimation through law. Three estates were defined by law—the priestly class (the first estate); the nobility (the second estate); and commoners (or everyone else, including artisans, merchants, and peasants), who accounted for the lowest rank (or third estate). Thus, in the early stages of feudalism custom or tradition justified the structured social inequalities. But with the growth of the state, legal sanction became of greater importance.

However, religion always played a justifying role. The church, primarily the Roman Catholic Church, was a hierarchical institution which through its teachings supported the tradition of worldly inequality. And later, with the emergence of the state, the higher church officials were given legal sanction as the first estate. In this later stage of feudalism, the Church usually gave supporting religious sanction to the secular rulers through an ideology of divine right of kings.

With respect to normatively closed versus open ranks or estates, closure represented the primary form. However, the degree of closure varied. Especially in early feudalism, when estates were not yet given formal legal sanction, there was some chance of social mobility. For example, an exceptionally bright peasant could achieve a high religious position, or an exceptionally skilled warrior could achieve a position among nobility. But in the later stages of feudalism the ranks became more rigid. Hereditary placement became more strictly the rule—ascription predominated. Marriage across estate or class lines was forbidden, assuring hereditary closure.

The span of inequality between the elites (in this case the first and second estates) and the masses (or the third estate) was high. In fact, as will be discussed in more detail later, it was in this type of society that relative inequality reached its highest level (see Lenski 1966). With the technological superiority of this type of agrarian society there was a much greater output of material goods and, for the most part, the surplus of material goods went to the elites.

Class

The industrial revolution ultimately shaped a new system of stratification we call a *class system*. Some characteristics of a class system have existed before—during the Roman Empire, for example—but it was not until the emergence of industrial societies that this kind of stratification system could survive and spread around the world. This is not to say that class systems throughout the world are identical. Many differences can be found, although industrial societies tend to have the broadly similar characteristics of stratification outlined below. In other words, although we can identify an ideal type of class system, there is more variation in this type than in some others (such as caste and feudal systems).

One of the most important aspects of class societies is their industrial (in contrast to agrarian) economic base. With the changing economic substructure during the late feudal period in Europe, the old nobility lost its position of economic and political dominance. At the same time, the ascriptive inequalities and rigid estate divisions gave way. The new industrial societies required a different system of stratification if they were to expand and prosper—that is, if the new dominant economic class was to expand and prosper.

A stratification system was required that could respond to the need for an educated, more skilled work force to operate in the more complex industrial economy. And it had to be a stratification system that would, at least to some degree, allow for class placement in terms of ability or merit, rather than in terms of the ascriptive criteria of previous stratification systems. Thus, we find normatively open ranks based to a greater degree on achievement rather than ascription. We say "to a greater degree" based on achievement because, as will be considered more fully in later chapters, ascription is really still a significant method of placement.

With a stress on open ranks and achievement in class societies, however, it does *not* follow that there is also a normative stress on equality. Rather, inequality is accepted, if not highly valued, in class societies. The normative stress (never a complete reality) is on inequality resulting from the existence of equality of opportunity or free competition. The belief is that those with the greatest ability will be rewarded most highly. The actual level of inequality between elites and the general population, however, is reduced in comparison with previous ideal types of stratification systems. Elites in class societies do not have fewer material benefits than their counterparts in feudal, caste, or slave societies, but the general population is better off, at least materially (that is, the separation between elites and the masses has been reduced).

The above comments have hinted at how the important legitimation process operates in class societies. We must now outline this process more specifically. The same problem exists for class societies as for the others; those less advantaged in the society must be convinced, at least to some degree, that their low position is somehow right or fair. In class societies inequalities are justified in large measure by an ideology of equality of opportunity (see Huber and Form 1973; Feagin 1975). Thus, the normative stress on open ranks and achievement itself becomes part of the legitimation process.

To some degree this ideology has been institutionalized through the legal system. Gone are the legal sanctions *overtly* supporting ascriptive inequalities found in feudal or estate societies. In their place are laws intended to promote free competition or equality of opportunity (laws intended to prevent monopolistic business practices, promote equal access to education and job opportunities, and so on). But as will be evident upon a more detailed analysis of the United States class system, these laws are in part an aspect of the legitimation of inequality and are often circumvented in actual application.

In early class systems the most prominent form of inequality was economic. Either the ownership (or control) of the means of production (that is, industrial capital) or occupational skill brought high economic reward that influenced status and political power. However, as will be described in later chapters, today the dominance of economic inequalities is weakened. Some argue that what can be called modern, advanced, or postindustrial societies are replacing early industrial societies. In these societies most aspects of the class system have remained. But the most prominent form or base of inequality is said to differ.

Generally, the view is that economically based inequalities are not as important now as inequalities in bureaucratic power. With the ownership of the means of production (capital or factories) no longer securely in the hands of wealthy families and with the growth of corporate and government bureaucratic institutions, it is said that top positions in these bureaucratic institutions are the most prominent forms of class superiority in advanced industrial societies.

Related to this view we typically find a convergence theory suggesting that all types of advanced industrial societies, whether Asian, capitalist, or communist, are becoming more similar with respect to the basis of social stratification (Galbraith 1971; Kennedy 1987). Events in the Soviet Union and the Eastern European communist countries at the beginning of the 1990s certainly suggest this is possible, but the merits of the postindustrial society and convergence theories will be considered more fully in later chapters.

Finally, Table 1-1 has been included to summarize our discussion of the major types of stratification systems throughout history. Across the top of Table 1-1 you will find the defining characteristics of each type of stratification sys-

TABLE 1-1
CHARACTERISTICS OF STRATIFICATION SYSTEMS

Type of system	Ranks	Placement	Form of legitimation	Primary basis of ranking
Primitive communal	Open	Achievement	Tradition	Status-honor
Slave system	Generally closed	Usually ascription	Legal ideology	Economic
Caste system	Closed	Ascription	Religious ideology	Status-honor
Estate, feudal	Primarily closed	Primarily ascription	Legal ideology	Economic
Class	Primarily open	Mix of ascription, achievement	Legal ideology	Economic, bureaucratic authority

tem, with the five major types of stratification systems listed down the left side of the table.

THE ORGANIZATION OF CHAPTERS

Having outlined some of the major issues in the study of social stratification and defined basic terms, it will be useful to familiarize the reader with the order in which major issues will be approached. In Part One of this book, after the present introductory chapter, we will consider the extent of inequality in the United States. Our concern in Chapter 2 will be the degree to which valued goods and services, health, political influence, and other important aspects of life are unequally distributed. In Chapter 3 the focus will be on the history of inequality in human societies. We will examine how inequality and systems of social stratification evolved from the earliest societies thousands of years ago up to the present.

The chapters in Part Two will present various theories of social stratification and theoretical controversies. Chapter 4 will examine the classical theories of Marx, Weber, and Durkheim, and Chapter 5 will examine current functional and conflict theories.

Part Three is concerned primarily with social stratification in the United States. It will begin with Chapter 6 and an overview of class, class divisions, and the study of social stratification by American sociologists. Chapters 7 through 10 will be devoted to major classes in the United States—the upper class, corporate class, middle and working class, and poor. Two chapters will follow (Chapters 11 and 12) on the subjects of social mobility and the legitimation of inequality (or how inequality is made acceptable or tolerable, especially for those toward the bottom of the stratification system).

Finally, Part Four will present information on social stratification in Japan, communist societies, and among nations. Because Japan is the first industrial society without a Western cultural tradition, an examination of Japan's class system will provide an interesting test of our ideas about social stratification developed in Western societies. Chapter 14 will examine social stratification primarily in the Soviet Union. This chapter will be especially useful, given our extensive examination of stratification in the United States and given that the Soviet Union claims to have drastically altered the nature of class conflict in its society. We will find that the similarities between these two nations are more striking than the differences. And in Chapter 15 we will find that something like a system of stratification is not confined to national boundaries. Nations themselves are divided within an international system of stratification that is in many ways similar to class divisions and class conflicts within nations. Combined with Chapter 3 (on the history of inequality in human societies), Chapters 13, 14, and 15 will demonstrate that whenever groups of people are faced with the question of distributing valued resources, some degree of class inequality and class conflict is found, no matter what type of society (except the most primitive) or size of human group is involved.

DIMENSIONS OF INEQUALITY IN THE UNITED STATES

In our beginning discussion of the life histories of Michael and of David Rockefeller we got a rough idea that inequality certainly exists in the United States. But we must be more specific. How many others are on the top and bottom of the stratification system? How many are in between? What is the general distribution of valued resources and opportunities throughout the stratification system? A key question in the study of social stratification, as noted in the previous chapter, is who gets what, and why. In starting such a study it is helpful, and logical, to address the first part of this question—"Who gets what?" In other words, before examining systems of social stratification, how these systems developed, how they operate, and why they operate in various ways, we want to consider patterns or *dimensions of inequality*. This is the task of our present (and second) introductory chapter.

Before going to the detailed statistics on inequality in the United States, however, it might be useful to present a general summary of the trends in inequality in the United States. With one of the most common measures of income inequality, we will see that the United States now has the highest level of inequality among the major industrial nations. And these are not just abstract figures. After spending some time in the other industrial nations of the world, you can clearly see and feel the differences in inequality. (An American who had lived in Japan once told me "the United States is now like a Third World country" after returning to his homeland for the first time in ten years.) Indeed, in the United States we find a mix of Third World and First World characteristics more than in other industrial nations. Traveling around this country, you find the Third World and First World in separate regions, with people of First World America trying to isolate themselves from what they find in the other.

It is important to recognize that these conditions of inequality in the United States are not simply due to Third World immigrants, nor is the inequality being reduced. In fact, the inequality has been growing considerably since the late 1970s. In part this is because of change in the world economy and the less competitive position of the U.S. economy within this changing world economy. We will see that the middle-paying jobs in the United States are shrinking, while the jobs paying poverty wages are increasing. Some of the reasons for this will be considered in the last chapter on the modern world system and worldwide stratification. But in part the increasing inequality is due to political policies which we will examine in other chapters.

There was economic recovery in the second half of the 1980s, after the worst recession since the 1930s in the first half of the 1980s. We will see, however, that the recovery was different than before: Many people missed the recovery. The unemployment rate was cut in half by the end of the 1980s, but unemployment remains higher compared to other times of economic recovery. And the unemployed who remain have been, on average, unemployed for a longer period of time than in previous periods of recovery.

And there are the homeless. No one knows exactly how many there were by 1990, but it is unlike any other time since the Great Depression. The most cited figure is that there were at least *1 million* homeless people in the United States by the end of the 1980s, a time of scandals in which hundreds of millions of dollars from the Department of Housing and Urban Development that were to help increase low-income housing went to the rich. The characteristics of the homeless also have changed. There are the mentally ill sleeping in the streets, but most homeless people are able and willing to work, and, in fact many do have jobs. These jobs pay only poverty wages, however, and these people are still unable to afford housing. And the most surprising new statistic is that about *one-third* of the homeless are now families with children.

It must be stressed that our intent in this chapter is primarily *descriptive* rather than analytical. We will begin by describing the distribution of income and wealth, then proceed to standards of living and health. In the final section we will describe inequalities in government services and the tax policies that lead to inequalities in who pays for these services. These types of inequalities are among the most important, although by no means the only ones of importance. There are, for example, other nonmaterial inequalities, and inequalities based upon caste like divisions of race and sex. These will be examined in other chapters. But the patterns of inequality examined below will provide us with a base image of inequality in a Western industrial society that will make further study of social stratification more meaningful.

INCOME AND WEALTH INEQUALITY

Two of the most important types of inequality are inequalities of income and wealth. These two are of major importance because it is income and wealth that bring other valued goods and services, not to mention the basic necessities of life. The relationship between income and necessities like food, shelter, and health care will be described after our discussion of income and wealth. Income and wealth, however, are also generalized commodities that, depending upon the quantity and how they are used, bring power and influence. The relationship income and wealth have to power and influence will be the subject of later chapters.

By *income* we mean money, wages, and payments that periodically are received as returns from an occupation or investments. Income is the means by which most Americans obtain the necessities and simple luxuries of life; and a wage or salary (rather than investments) sustains the vast majority of people in this country. *Wealth* is accumulated assets in the form of various types of valued goods, such as real estate, stocks, bonds, or money held in reserve. Wealth is anything of economic value that is bought, sold, stocked for future disposition, or invested to bring an economic return. As might be expected, most Americans have little or no wealth; whatever they have attained in the form of wages and salaries cannot be accumulated because it must be used for immediate necessities. Income is distributed in a highly unequal manner in this country, but wealth is distributed even more unequally.

Income Inequality

A simple method of considering income inequality is by looking at a population distribution within specified income categories. Table 2-1 presents such a distribution for all families (as well as for whites, blacks, and Hispanics) in the United States as of 1987. Of more than 65 million families, for example, 1.8 percent had annual incomes of less than $2,500; 2.6 percent had incomes be-

TABLE 2-1
PERCENTAGE DISTRIBUTION OF FAMILIES (WHITE AND NONWHITE) BY INCOME LEVEL, 1987

Annual income (dollars)	Percentage of all families	Percentage of white families	Percentage of black families	Percentage of Spanish origin families
Under 2,500	1.8	1.3	5.0	3.4
2,500–4,999	2.6	1.9	8.5	5.2
5,000–7,499	3.6	2.9	8.7	7.3
7,500–9,999	3.6	3.2	7.8	7.1
10,000–12,499	4.6	4.2	7.1	7.7
12,500–14,999	4.5	4.4	5.4	7.0
15,000–19,999	9.5	9.3	11.8	11.7
20,000–24,999	9.2	9.1	10.0	10.2
25,000–34,999	17.5	18.1	13.6	15.7
35,000–49,999	20.2	21.2	12.8	14.0
50,000 and over	22.9	24.4	9.5	10.9

Source: U.S. Bureau of the Census. 1989. *Current Population Reports,* "Money Income and Poverty Status of Families and Persons in the United States: 1987," table 10, p. 34.

tween $2,500 and $4,999; and, at the other end of the spectrum, 22.9 percent had incomes of $50,000 or more.

The income distribution presented in Table 2-1 does not give us an accurate picture of the extremes, because many people make substantially more than $50,000 a year. As an example of the extremes, about 36,000 people reported incomes of $1 million or more in 1986, and over 1.5 million people had incomes of more than $100,000 in 1986 (U.S. Bureau of the Census, *Statistical Abstracts of the United States,* 1989:315). At the other extreme, almost 10 million people reported incomes of less than $3,000 in 1986 (though many of these people were, no doubt, in families with other wage earners). If we consider $3,000 and $1 million as the income extremes (which, of course, continues to *underestimate* the extremes), we find an income ratio of 1 to 500, or incomes that are more than 500 times the lowest.

As we will see in later chapters, an important issue in the study of social stratification and inequality, especially in the United States, is inequality by race and ethnic origin. We will see that race, ethnicity, and class are related to each other in complex ways, with racial divisions often having, to some degree, class divisions at their base. But for now we need first to consider the level of income inequality by race and Hispanic origin. In Table 2-1 we find that both blacks and Hispanics made up a much higher percentage of people with incomes of $2,500 or less in 1987, and much fewer with incomes of $50,000 or more compared to whites.

In contrast to considering the distribution of people or families within income categories (as in Table 2-1), we can consider the distribution of total income among select population categories. A standard method of doing so is to divide the population into income fifths and compare population shares with income shares. Table 2-2 presents this information for 1988. In this year the lowest fifth of families in the United States received 4.6 percent, the next low-

TABLE 2-2
PERCENTAGE OF AGGREGATE FAMILY
INCOME RECEIVED BY EACH FIFTH
AND HIGHEST 5 PERCENT, 1988

All families	Percentage of aggregate income
Lowest fifth	4.6
Second fifth	10.7
Middle fifth	16.7
Fourth fifth	24.0
Highest fifth	44.0
Highest 5 percent	17.2

Source: U.S. Bureau of the Census. 1989. *Current Population Reports,* "Money Income and Poverty Status of Families and Persons in the United States: 1988." table 5, p. 31.

est fifth received 10.7 percent, and the highest fifth received 44.0 percent of all income. In other words, the lowest 20 percent of families received only 4.6 percent of the total income, while the highest 20 percent of families received 44.0 percent of the total. Table 2-2 also shows that the highest 5 percent of families received 17.2 percent of aggregate income, or over three times the share they would have received under conditions of income equality.

It is useful to note at this point that the median family income in 1988 was $30,850, while the upper income limit of the lowest 20 percent of families was only $14,450 (meaning those families in the lowest fifth had $14,450 or less in annual income). The upper income limit for the second lowest fifth was $25,100, while it was $36,600 for the third fifth, and $52,910 for the fourth fifth (the upper limit for the top 20 percent and top 5 percent, of course, is held by the richest family).

The vast majority of people in this country must depend upon some type of employment (as opposed to wealth) for their income, and the occupational structure is of primary importance in creating an unequal distribution of income. Table 2-3 presents the median incomes within general occupational categories for 1987. For males, the highest occupational category (executive, administrative, and managerial occupations) shows a median income of $33,094, while the lowest (farm workers) shows a median income of only $6,479. It is also interesting to note that for females the highest figure is substantially lower than that for men ($19,643). Roughly the same income discrepancy is found between males and females with respect to education level in Table 2-3. As we will see in later chapters, part of the male–female inequality is due to sex discrimination, but this discrimination operates within the occupational structure in a number of important ways.

The extent of income inequality by occupation is severely underestimated in Table 2-3 because we are considering only very general occupational categories. Within each occupational category many people are making much less and much more than is indicated by the median. This underestimation is especially evident at the top, where many managers of major corporations have exceptionally high salaries (for example, more than 300 corporate executives had incomes of more than $1 million in 1988; see *Los Angeles Times,* June 4, 1989).

Having considered some aspects of current income inequality, we will go on to two further questions. What was the previous pattern of income inequality in the United States? How does the United States compare with other industrialized nations in this respect? And has the distribution of income in this country become more or less unequal or has it remained the same over the years? This last question has become one of the most important in the 1980s and pertains to a troubling trend in the nature of inequality in the United States.

Trends in U.S. Income Inequality   We have data showing that income inequality was reduced somewhat during the 1930s and early 1940s due to Depression reforms and full employment during World War II. The most signifi-

TABLE 2-3
MEDIAN INCOME BY OCCUPATIONAL CATEGORY AND EDUCATION, MALE AND FEMALE, 1987

	Median income	
Occupation	Male	Female
Executive, administrative, and managerial	$33,094	19,134
Professional	32,544	19,643
Technical, sales, and administrative support	21,291	10,982
Sales	21,624	6,268
Administrative support and clerical	18,512	12,220
Precision production and craft	20,737	11,758
Operators and laborers	14,850	8,999
Service	8,523	4,714
Farming, forestry, fishing	6,479	2,574
Educational level		
Elementary	9,449	5,033
Less than 8 years	8,488	4,798
8 years	10,933	5,497
High school	18,713	8,112
1 to 3 years	14,158	6,221
4 years	20,314	8,957
College	30,077	15,453
1 to 3 years	24,724	12,468
4 years or more	34,215	18,964
4 years	31,371	16,926
5 years or more	37,640	22,277

Source: U.S. Bureau of the Census. 1989. *Current Population Reports,* "Money Income of Households, Families, and Persons in the United States: 1987." Consumer Income, series P–60, no. 162, pp. 159, 163, 104, 105.

cant change occurred within the top 20 percent and top 5 percent of families, who had their share of income reduced from 54.4 percent and 30 percent, respectively, in 1929 to 44 percent and 17.2 percent by 1945 (Turner and Starnes 1976:51).

As shown in Table 2-4, however, there is again change in the income distribution. There was a slight decrease in income inequality between 1947 and 1975. The percent of income going to the bottom 20 percent of the people increased somewhat, and the percentage of income going to the top 20 percent and top 5 percent of the people decreased. *However,* as noted in the beginning of this chapter, there has been significant change since 1980. There has been a rather rapid and significant increase in income inequality between 1980 and 1988 because, as they say, the income rich have been getting richer while the income poor have been getting poorer. As we see in Table 2-4, the bottom income group now has only 4.6 percent of the income, compared to 5.1 percent in 1980, and the top 20 percent income group now has 44 percent of all income, compared to only 41.6 percent in 1980. And it should be noted that this income

TABLE 2-4

PERCENTAGE OF AGGREGATE FAMILY INCOME BY INCOME FIFTHS AND TOP 5
PERCENT, 1947–1988

Year	Percentage of aggregate income					
	Lowest fifth	Second fifth	Third fifth	Fourth fifth	Highest fifth	Top 5 percent
1988	4.6	10.7	16.7	24.0	44.0	17.2
1980	5.1	11.6	17.5	24.3	41.6	15.3
1975	5.4	11.8	17.6	24.1	41.1	15.5
1970	5.4	12.2	17.6	23.8	40.9	15.6
1965	5.2	12.2	17.8	23.9	40.9	15.5
1960	4.8	12.2	17.8	24.0	41.3	15.9
1955	4.8	12.3	17.8	23.7	41.3	16.4
1950	4.5	12.0	17.4	23.4	42.7	17.3
1947	5.0	11.9	17.0	23.1	43.0	17.5

Source: U.S. Bureau of the Census. 1981. *Current Population Reports,* 1980:63, table 13; U.S. Bureau of the Census. 1980. *Current Population Reports,* Money Income of Families and Persons in the United States: 1978," series P–60, no. 123, table L; U.S. Bureau of the Census. 1989. *Current Population Reports,* "Money Income and Poverty Status of Families and Persons in the United States: 1988," series P–60, no. 166, table 5, p. 31.

inequality is even higher if we use Federal Reserve data, which include more complete income sources than the standard Census Bureau study (Thurow 1987). Using these Federal Reserve data, for example, we find that the top 2 percent of people got about 14 percent of all income.

Figure 2-1 indicates this growing inequality by using these data to construct what is known as a Gini index to measure income inequality. With Figure 2-1 we can see that, since World War II, income inequality in the United States hit its lowest level between 1965 and 1970, but then rose dramatically in the 1980s to its highest point in 1985. In addition to this trend of increasing income inequality in the 1980s is the decline of real income for most Americans since the 1970s. Figure 2-2 shows that real average weekly earnings for Americans (how much money people have after things such as taxes and inflation) increased sharply between 1950 and 1970. *However,* since 1970 we find a sharp drop in real wages for the average American (with most of this drop regained in the late 1980s). What this means is that not only are the poor (as well as the working class and lower middle class) getting less of the income, the income they are getting buys less than it did in 1970.

Another way to consider this growing income inequality is by looking at the percentage change in the number of households at certain income levels as presented for 1987 in Table 2-1. This is done in Table 2-5 for income data from 1970 to 1987. When we look down the column for all families with less than $5,000 annual income we find a slight increase from 3.5 percent in 1970 to 4.4 percent in 1987. But, most interesting, we find a *big decrease* from 1970 to 1987 in the middle-income columns of $20,000 to $35,000: from a total of about 33.3 percent of households in 1970 to only 26.7 percent of households in 1987.

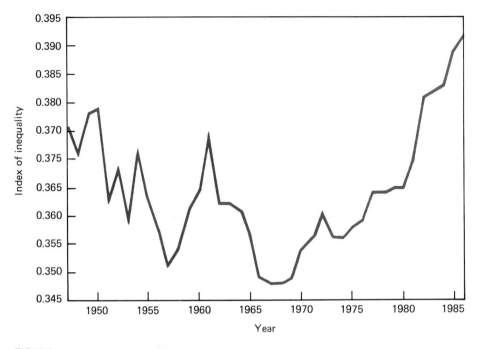

FIGURE 2-1
Family income inequality (Gini index), 1947–1986. *U.S. Bureau of the Census, 1986; Harrison and Bluestone (1988:7).*

That is clearly shrinkage of the middle class in the United States. Then, at the upper income level, we find a rather significant increase in the number of people at the same time the middle is shrinking. The percentage of households in the $50,000 and over column increased from 15.4 percent in 1970 to 22.9 percent in 1987. The middle is falling away, while the affluent and the poor steadily grow more numerous.

The picture for minorities in Table 2-5 is more extreme. For whites we find that people with incomes under $5,000 increased somewhat between 1970 and 1987. However, for blacks and Hispanics, and especially blacks, there is considerable increase in the lowest-income column during this period. The shrinkage of the middle-income class for both of these minorities is somewhat less than for whites (primarily because there were fewer of them there to begin with), but it is also a rather dramatic shrinkage. Then, with the $50,000 and over income column, we also find an increase in the affluence of some minorities. In the case of blacks and Hispanics between 1970 and 1987, compared to whites, the poor were getting even poorer, while the rich were increasing as well.

This is not the place to get into a full explanation of why income inequality has grown significantly in the 1980s, but we can briefly cover some of the most

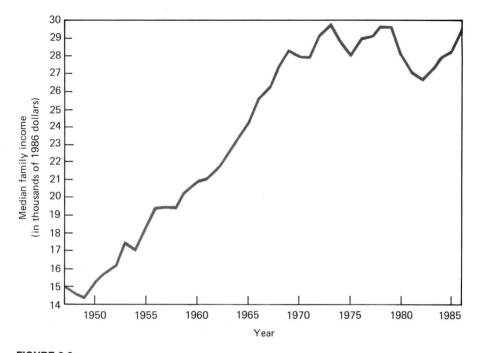

FIGURE 2-2
Real median family income, 1947–1986. *Council of Economic Advisers, Economic Report to the President, 1987 (U.S. Government Printing Office, 1987).*

important reasons. These reasons fall into two main categories: (1) Reagan's political policies, and (2) changes in the U.S. economy. Among the political policies which increased income inequality were changes in tax policies (reducing taxes for the wealthy, while taxes for lower-income groups increased) and cuts in transfer payments such as the means-tested welfare programs for the poor (Harrison and Bluestone 1988). Among the most important changes in the economy has been the reduction in middle-paying jobs in the 1980s (mainly due to the reduced competitiveness of the U.S. economy), while jobs in both the highest-paid and lowest-paid areas of the economy increased (Thurow 1987). This change can be seen in Figure 2-3 for the periods 1963–1973, 1973–1979, and 1979–1986. Further, of all the *new* jobs created in the economy from 1979 to 1986, over 55 percent of these jobs have wages at the poverty level or below (Bluestone 1988).

Comparative Income Inequality Our next question pertains to what the U.S. income inequality looks like compared to other industrial nations. First, we will look at data for the major capitalist nations during the 1960s. Table 2-6 indicates that among these industrial nations the United States was generally ranked about midway in terms of income inequality. France had the highest

TABLE 2-5
DISTRIBUTION OF FAMILIES BY INCOME LEVELS, 1970–1987[*]

Race and Hispanic origin of householder and year	Number of families (1,000)	Percent distribution of families, by income level								Median income (dol.)
		Under $5,000	$5,000–$9,999	$10,000–$14,999	$15,000–$19,999	$20,000–$24,999	$25,000–$34,999	$35,000–$49,999	$50,000 and over	
All families										
1970	52,227	3.5	7.6	9.1	9.9	11.3	22.0	21.2	15.4	28,880
1975	56,245	2.9	8.1	10.0	10.2	10.4	20.9	21.0	16.4	28,970
1980	60,309	3.7	8.2	9.8	10.2	10.2	20.0	20.5	17.5	28,996
1983	62,015	4.8	8.4	10.3	10.1	10.2	19.0	19.2	17.9	28,147
1984	62,706	4.5	8.3	9.7	10.0	9.7	18.4	19.7	19.6	28,923
1985	63,558	4.4	8.0	9.7	9.9	9.9	18.3	19.2	20.6	29,302
1986	64,491	4.5	7.5	9.2	9.6	9.5	17.7	19.8	22.2	30,534
1987	65,133	4.4	7.3	9.1	9.5	9.2	17.5	20.2	22.9	30,853
White										
1970	46,535	2.9	6.7	8.5	9.5	11.3	22.6	22.2	16.4	29,960
1975	49,873	2.3	6.9	9.5	10.0	10.3	21.5	21.9	17.6	30,129
1980	52,710	2.7	6.9	9.2	10.0	10.3	20.6	21.5	18.7	30,211
1983	53,890	3.7	7.1	9.9	10.1	10.4	19.5	20.2	19.2	29,474
1984	54,400	3.4	7.0	9.2	9.9	9.8	19.0	20.7	21.0	30,294
1985	54,991	3.5	6.9	9.1	9.6	10.0	18.8	20.1	22.1	30,799
1986	55,676	3.3	6.5	8.6	9.4	9.5	18.2	20.8	23.7	31,935
1987	56,044	3.2	6.1	8.6	9.3	9.1	18.1	21.2	24.4	32,274
Black										
1970	4,928	9.0	16.7	14.6	14.3	12.0	15.6	12.0	5.7	18,378
1975	5,586	7.4	19.0	15.2	12.2	11.7	16.1	12.5	6.1	18,538
1980	6,317	10.7	18.5	15.1	12.0	9.3	15.6	12.0	6.9	17,481
1983	6,681	13.5	19.2	14.1	11.1	9.4	15.1	10.9	6.9	16,610
1984	6,778	13.3	18.4	14.2	11.6	9.4	14.3	10.9	8.0	16,884
1985	6,921	12.4	16.8	14.1	12.4	8.8	15.0	12.2	8.3	17,734
1986	7,096	13.4	15.9	13.5	10.6	9.7	14.5	13.0	9.5	18,247
1987	7,177	13.5	16.5	12.5	11.8	10.0	13.6	12.8	9.5	18,098
Hispanic[†]										
1975	2,499	5.8	14.9	15.8	13.0	12.2	19.8	12.8	5.8	20,168
1980	3,235	6.5	14.1	15.5	13.5	11.4	17.3	14.1	7.5	20,297
1983	3,788	8.3	16.0	14.1	13.6	11.4	16.3	12.3	7.9	19,313
1984	3,939	8.6	14.5	13.9	12.7	9.9	17.5	14.1	9.0	20,606
1985	4,206	7.4	16.0	14.8	11.7	11.1	16.6	13.0	9.6	20,102
1986	4,403	8.2	14.3	14.8	11.8	10.6	16.1	13.3	11.0	20,726
1987	4,588	8.6	14.4	14.7	11.7	10.2	15.7	14.0	10.9	20,306

[*]In constant 1987 dollars.
[†]Hispanic persons may be of any race.
Source: U.S. Bureau of the Census. 1989. *Statistical Abstracts of the United States, 1989,* table 720.

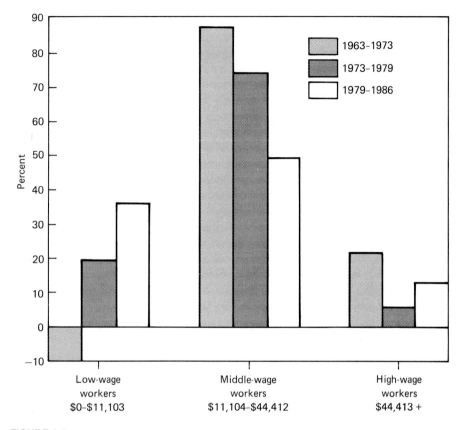

FIGURE 2-3
Net change in employment by wage categories, 1963–1986. *U.S. Bureau of the Census, Current Populations Report, 1964–1987; Harrison and Bluestone (1988:122).*

amount of income inequality, as we can see when we look down Table 2-6 to the share of income going to the top 10 percent and top 5 percent of families compared with income attained by the bottom 10 percent of families. Income inequality, however, was rather similar among all these nations, with Canada, West Germany, England, and Australia showing the lowest levels in the 1960s.

Comparative income inequality for the 1980s, however, shows some very important changes. As we might expect from our above discussion of growing income inequality in the United States, Figure 2-4 now shows that the overall highest level of income inequality is found in the United States, with the lowest level found in Japan (also see Menard 1986; Verba 1987). The gap between the average income of the top 20 percent group and the bottom 20 percent income group in the United States is 12 to 1 (meaning the top average is 12 times that of the bottom), while this same gap is only 4 to 1 in Japan (World Bank 1986:227). What has happened since the 1960s data in Table 2-6 is that, though

TABLE 2-6

PERCENTAGE OF AGGREGATE INCOME BY INCOME DECILES, MAJOR NONCOMMUNIST INDUSTRIAL NATIONS, 1960s

Country	Lowest 10%	10–20%	20–30%	30–40%	40–50%	50–60%	60–70%	70–80%	80–90%	90–100%	Top 5%
					Percentage of aggregate income by*						
Australia	2.4%	4.7%	5.9%	7.0%	8.2%	9.4%	10.8%	12.7%	15.4%	23.5%	14.1%
Canada	2.3	4.4	5.6	6.7	7.9	9.3	10.8	13.0	16.0	24.0	14.1
Denmark	1.4	3.0	4.2	5.2	6.6	8.1	10.0	12.8	17.2	31.5	19.7
Finland	.5	2.2	3.8	5.2	6.5	8.2	10.2	13.0	17.5	32.9	20.9
France	.5	1.8	3.3	4.4	5.8	7.5	9.5	12.5	17.5	37.2	24.7
West Germany	2.6	4.3	5.4	6.6	7.7	9.2	10.8	13.1	16.4	23.9	13.7
Japan	1.0	3.6	5.1	6.3	7.6	8.9	10.6	12.8	16.0	28.1	17.9
Netherlands	1.0	3.0	4.3	5.4	6.6	8.1	9.9	12.4	16.3	33.0	22.0
Sweden	1.3	3.3	4.7	5.8	7.2	8.7	10.5	13.1	16.9	28.5	17.4
United Kingdom	2.3	4.3	5.4	6.5	7.8	9.2	11.0	13.2	16.4	23.9	13.7
United States	.8	3.5	4.9	6.2	7.5	8.9	10.6	12.9	16.4	28.3	17.8

*Data on all countries compiled during the 1960s. All the data are not exactly comparable because some relate to all individuals while others relate to households.

Source: Table constructed from data presented in Jain (1975).

Japan and the United States had similar levels of income inequality before, Japan has had a substantial reduction in income inequality, while the United States has experienced increased income inequality.

The change in the relative income inequality positions of Japan and the United States in recent years presents us with some very important questions about social stratification. Why has this occurred in both Japan and the United States, but in opposite directions? And what are the effects of this change on such things as future economic competitiveness for the United States and Japan? These questions will be considered in several places in coming chapters, and especially in Chapter 13 on social stratification in Japan.

Wealth Inequality

Despite the importance of income inequality in the United States, in some ways wealth inequality is more significant. Most people use income for day-to-day necessities. Substantial wealth, however, often brings income, power, and independence. On the one hand, wealth in significant quantities relieves individuals from dependence upon others for an income. As we will see, the authority structure associated with occupational differentiation is one of the most important aspects of the stratification system in the United States, and the impact of this authority structure is reduced when people have substantial wealth. On the other hand, if wealth is used to purchase significant ownership of the means of production in the society (most importantly stock ownership in

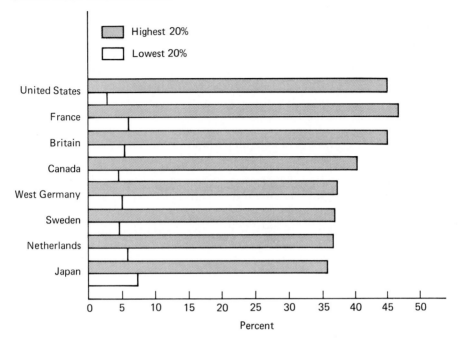

Share of Pretax Household Income

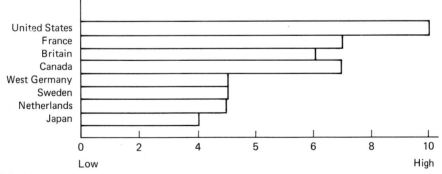

The Ratio between
Highest and Lowest 20%

FIGURE 2-4
Comparative income inequality, leading capitalist nations, 1980s. *World Bank (1986).*

major corporations), it can bring authority to the holder of such wealth (depending on the amount of ownership). Substantial wealth is also important because it can be transferred from generation to generation more easily than income, producing greater inheritance of position and opportunity within the stratification system. This is especially true since 1982 with one of Reagan's tax bills which substantially reduced inheritance taxes in this country.

Table 2-7 reports the 1983 wealth holdings by fifths of the population along with figures on income inequality from 1983. Although income is highly unequal in the United States, these data show wealth to be even more unequally distributed. For example, while the top fifth of the population received 42.7 percent of the *income*, the top fifth held over 78.7 percent of family *wealth* in 1983. Moreover, the top one-half percent of the population controlled 27 percent of all wealth, and the top 10 percent of the population controlled about 68 percent of all wealth according to a study by James Smith (Institute for Social Research 1986). In contrast, while the bottom fifth received 4.7 percent of the income, the bottom fifth held even less of the wealth (−0.4 percent). Considered another way, we find that the top 40 percent of the population held 93.2 percent of the wealth, leaving only 6.8 percent of the wealth for the remaining 60 percent of the population.

As we did with income, we need to consider race and ethnic inequality with respect to wealth. When we do so we find even greater inequality in wealth compared to income. Table 2-8 presents the distribution of U.S. households by net wealth, in categories from zero wealth or less to $50,000 or more in assets in 1984. In the category of zero wealth or less we find 11 percent of all U.S. households, in contrast to 30.5 percent of black households, 23.9 percent of Hispanic households, and only 8.4 percent of white households. As we move up in net wealth to the $50,000 to $99,999 category, the percentage for white households goes up, but the percentage for blacks and Hispanics drops. Also important to consider is the median net wealth for each group. Here we find the biggest disparities. The median net wealth for whites is $39,135, compared to only $3,397 for blacks and $4,913 for Hispanics.

Another way to look at wealth inequality, of course, is by examining the superrich. *Forbes* magazine (Oct. 24, 1988) estimated that there were fifty-one

TABLE 2-7
DISTRIBUTION OF WEALTH AND INCOME BY FAMILY
FIFTHS, 1983

Family fifths	Percentage of total wealth	Percentage of total income
Highest fifth	78.7	42.7
Fourth fifth	14.5	24.4
Middle fifth	6.2	17.1
Second fifth	1.1	11.1
Lowest fifth	−0.4	4.7
	100.0%	100.0%

Sources: U.S. Bureau of the Census. 1989. *Current Population Reports,* series P–60, no. 146. *Note:* Also see footnote 2 below.

TABLE 2-8
DISTRIBUTION OF HOUSEHOLD NET WORTH BY RACE AND SPANISH ORIGIN, 1984

Characteristic	Number of households (thousands)	Zero or negative	$1 to $4,999	$5,000 to $9,999	$10,000 to $24,999	$25,000 to $49,999	$50,000 to $99,999
Total	86,790	11.0	15.3	6.4	12.4	14.5	19.3
Race and Spanish Origin of Householder							
White	75,343	8.4	14.0	6.3	12.2	15.0	20.7
Black	9,509	30.5	23.9	6.8	14.0	11.7	9.3
Spanish origin	4,162	23.9	26.3	7.6	11.4	9.5	13.1

Source: U.S. Bureau of the Census. *Current Population Reports,* Household Economic Studies, "Household Wealth and Asset Ownership: 1984," series P–70, no. 7, 1986:18.

billionaires in 1988. And it was obviously a fine climate for the rich to get richer in the middle 1980s because the number of billionaires *doubled* in two years between 1986 and 1988. Heading the list of billionaires in the United States for 1988 was Sam Walton of the Wal-Mart discount store empire with $6.7 billion. Next came John Warner Kluge of Metromedia Co. with $3.0 billion, H. Ross Perot of Electronic Data Systems with $3 billion, Samuel Newhouse and Donald Newhouse with $2.6 billion each, and Henry Lea Hillman with $2.5 billion. Another sign of the times, however, is indicated by the fact that Americans no longer head the worldwide list of billionaires. Sam Walton rates fifth in the world behind Japan's Yoshiaki Tsutsumi ($18.9 billion), Taikichiro Mori ($18 billion), Canada's Kenneth Cole Irving ($8 billion), and Haruhiko Yoshimoto ($7.8 billion).[1]

Wealth inequality data for the overall population are not gathered as often as for income inequality in the United States, and, before 1983, the last time a complete study such as this was made was in 1962 (U.S. Office of Management and Budget 1973:164). But in contrast to income inequality, at least up to 1983, there has been somewhat less change in wealth inequality compared to the 1962 data.[2] This might seem puzzling until we remember that wealth and income are not the same thing. There has not *necessarily* been an increase in wealth inequality while income inequality has been going higher. The increase in income inequality, as we have seen, has been due to an increase in low-income people, fewer middle-income people, and slightly more higher-income people, though not necessarily more *very* high-income people. And the presence of more people at higher income levels does not always mean they are accumulating more wealth (especially if this money is not being saved or reinvested to accumulate more assets). However, it is most likely that wealth inequality shows only some change when comparing 1962 and 1986, but that there has been more change between these two points in time. As indicated by Table 2-9, the percentage of wealth held by the top was going down at least

TABLE 2-9
PERCENTAGE OF TOTAL WEALTH
HELD BY TOP 1 PERCENT AND TOP
0.5 PERCENT, 1958–1972

	Percentage of wealth held by	
Year	Top 1%	Top 0.5%
1958	25.5%	20.4%
1962	26.2	20.7
1969	24.4	19.3
1972	24.1	18.9

Source: U.S. Bureau of the Census. 1980.
Statistical Abstracts of the United States, table
786, p. 471.

until 1972, and would have had to come back up since 1972 to make the 1962 and 1986 distributions similar. Thus, we probably have been experiencing an upward trend in wealth inequality in recent years, and especially so since 1983 (again, see footnote 2). For example, in 1990 the IRS released new data showing that the number of millionaires had almost doubled (from 475,000 to 941,000) between 1982 and 1986 (see the *Los Angeles Times,* August 23, 1990).

Another important question pertains to the source of wealth for the top wealth holders in the United States. As indicated in Table 2-10, in 1972 both the top 1 percent and top 0.5 percent of the population (in terms of wealth) held a greater portion of their assets in corporate stock. In fact, the top 1 percent and 0.5 percent of the population held 56.5 and 49.3 percent of all personally owned corporate stock in the United States. As noted earlier, and as

TABLE 2-10
TOP WEALTH HOLDERS BY TYPE OF WEALTH, 1972

Assets	Value of gross assets held by (in billions of dollars)		Percentage held by	
	Top 1%	Top 0.5%	Top 1%	Top 0.5%
Total assets	1,046.9	822.4	24.1%	18.9%
Real estate	225.0	150.9	15.1	10.1
Corporate stock	491.7	429.3	56.5	49.3
Bonds	94.8	82.5	60.0	52.2
Cash	101.2	63.6	13.5	8.5
Debt instruments	40.8	30.3	52.7	39.1
Life insurance	10.0	6.2	7.0	4.3
Trusts	89.4	80.3	89.9	80.8
Miscellaneous	83.3	59.5	9.8	6.8
Liabilities	131.0	100.7	16.2	12.5
Net worth	915.9	721.7	25.9	20.4

Source: U.S. Bureau of the Census. 1980. *Statistical Abstracts of the United States,* table
786, p. 471.

will be discussed more fully in later chapters, ownership of corporate stock is most important because such ownership can bring significant economic power. The ownership of real estate, for example, brings certain rights pertaining to how the real estate is used, but significant ownership of corporate stock can influence the overall economy through influence in major corporations in this country. (We emphasize "can" because there are many questions about such influence that must be considered further.)

In another study looking at some other sources of wealth in 1983, the Federal Reserve Board found that the most wealthy 10 percent of the U.S. population held 41 percent of all money in checking accounts, 72 percent of all the corporate stock, 50 percent of all physical property, and 78 percent of all business property (Harrison and Bluestone 1988:136).

Historical Trends in Wealth Inequality   As with income inequality, a major question pertains to the historical trends in wealth inequality in the United States. We saw in Table 2-9 that wealth inequality went down somewhat between 1958 and 1972 (with the holdings of the top 1 percent and 0.5 percent of the population). Table 2-11 shows that the proportion of wealth held by the top 1 percent of the population has mostly been going down slowly since World War II. We do find a significant increase and then drop in the wealth holdings

TABLE 2-11
PERCENTAGE OF TOTAL
WEALTH HELD BY TOP 1
PERCENT, 1922–1972

Year	Percentage of wealth held by top 1 percent[*]
1922	31.6
1929	36.3
1933	28.3
1939	30.6
1945	23.3
1949	20.8
1953	24.3
1954	24.0
1956	26.0
1958	23.8
1962	22.0
1965	23.4
1969	20.1
1972	20.7

[*]Based on wealth held by all persons 21 and over. Figures in Table 2-9 based on wealth held by all persons.
  Source: U.S. Bureau of the Census. 1980. *Statistical Abstracts of the United States,* table 785, p. 471.

of the top 1 percent between 1922 and 1945, which (along with the change in income distribution) is no doubt related to the major changes in this country brought about by the Depression of the 1930s and World War II. But despite these changes since 1922, we have other evidence that the amount of wealth held by the most wealthy 1 percent did not change much between 1810 and 1945 (see Gallman 1969:6).

As noted above, while both wealth and income are distributed very unequally in the United States, wealth is distributed even more unequally. A comparison of wealth and income inequality can be made most strikingly with what is known as a *Lorenz curve*. A Lorenz curve is constructed by indicating how much wealth or income is held by various percentages of the total population. As shown in Figure 2-5, a condition of equality would show a straight diagonal or line across the graph. In other words, 20 percent of the population would receive 20 percent of the wealth or income, 40 percent of the population would receive 40 percent of the wealth or income, and so on. On the other hand, the further the curve from the diagonal, the greater the inequality. Using 1983 data, Figure 2-5 graphically shows the magnitude of both income and wealth inequality in the United States.

Figure 2-5
Lorenz curves on wealth and income inequality, 1983. These curves are estimates from data presented in Table 2-7.

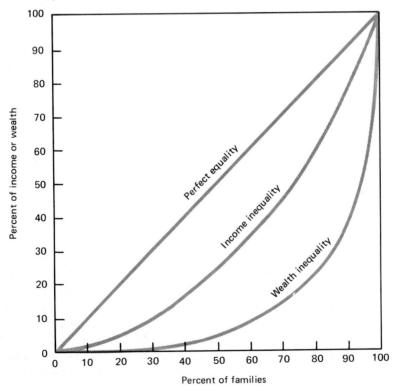

INEQUALITY IN BASIC NECESSITIES

With the extent of income and wealth inequality reviewed above, it would seem quite obvious that other material goods are distributed unequally in the United States. However, there are other issues that must be noted with respect to the distribution of basic necessities. An unequal distribution of income is not always an accurate indication of how basic necessities such as food, housing, and medical care are distributed. There are two reasons for this: First, we must consider the possibility of state subsidies of necessities; and second, we must consider the relative cost of basic necessities.

In considering state subsidies for basic necessities, we need only mention at this point that, contrary to political rhetoric, the United States spends only an average amount for welfare-type programs when compared to other industrialized nations (Wilensky 1975; Nutter 1978). This is the only industrialized nation that does not have a basic guaranteed income program for all families below the poverty level or a comprehensive national health program meeting the medical needs of all families (Moynihan 1973:95; Kahn and Kamerman 1978; Ozawa 1978:39; Harrington 1984). And when families do receive welfare support for basic necessities, the money they receive places them well below the income needed for those necessities. For example, with a median family income of $30,850 in 1987, the median family income for those existing on income from welfare payments was only $7,741 (U.S. Bureau of the Census, *Current Population Reports* 1989:99). We will have much more to say on this subject when we consider poverty in the United States.

Even with a highly unequal distribution of income, the distribution of basic necessities may be less unequal if the cost of such basic items is relatively low. If this is the case, luxuries and savings become most unequal, not basic necessities. But to the extent that this has ever been the case in the United States, it is rapidly becoming less so. As everyone knows, the decade of the 1970s was one of rapid inflation; between 1967 and 1978 the consumer price index almost doubled. But the cost of basic necessities rose 44 percent *faster* than the cost of non-necessities between 1970 and 1976 (Blumberg 1980:182), which means that those toward the bottom of the income scale find it even harder to maintain an adequate standard of living. None of this had improved by the end of the 1980s.

Food, of course, is one of the basic necessities; Duncan (1976) shows that the lowest 10 percent of the population (in terms of income) had to spend over 40 percent of its income for food in the early 1970s. And just between 1972 and 1974, the proportion of this group's income going for food increased from 40.1 percent to 46.6 percent. At the same time, however, the proportion of income going for food among those in the highest income decile increased only from 10.8 percent to 11.4 percent.

A broader picture of the cost of basic necessities in 1974 is given by Nulty (1977), who includes the cost of energy, shelter, and medical care, as well as food. The picture presented in this study is even more striking because it is based on net family income (after taxes, and so on). Although income at the bottom was probably underestimated by this study (see Blumberg 1980:183), it is clear that people toward the bottom of the income scale would need to go into *debt* if they were to buy all necessities in the United States. In contrast to the bottom 20 percent in income who had to go into debt to buy necessities, the top 10 percent in income spent only 38.4 percent of their net income for these necessities.

We will consider health and health care in more detail below, but at this point we can consider housing costs in more detail. One aspect of the American dream is home ownership. And at one time this was a dream most Americans could attain—but no longer. As late as 1970 about 45 percent of all United States families could afford median-priced new homes. But by 1976 only 27 percent of American families could do so (Blumberg 1980:203). In 1966, 31 percent of all new homes were purchased by families in the upper 25 percent income bracket, while 17 percent were purchased by families in the lower third of the income scale. By 1976, however, families in the upper 25 percent income bracket were purchasing 58 percent of all the new homes, while families in the lower third income bracket were buying only 4 percent of all the new homes (Blumberg 1980:204).

Inflation was not a major problem in the second half of the 1980s, but neither was there a change in this ratio of the cost of necessities versus nonnecessities, meaning the cost of all basic necessities remains beyond the reach of the poor and lower classes in this society. What has changed in the 1980s is the number of people who are poor or near-poor and cannot afford these basic necessities. As noted in previous sections, the number of poor and low-income families has increased considerably through the 1980s, while the middle-income families who could afford all of the basic necessities has been reduced.

In conclusion, although it is not always the case in all societies, an unequal distribution of wealth and income in the United States does have an impact on the distribution of basic necessities. With various government programs like Aid to Families with Dependent Children, food stamps, and Medicaid instituted or expanded during the 1960s, few people are now starving or without basic necessities like shelter and medical care. But it must be remembered that most of these poverty programs are rather recent and have experienced large cutbacks in the 1980s (Piven and Cloward 1982). And even with these programs, basic necessities are unequally distributed, with those toward the bottom of the income scale receiving a less than adequate share and goods of much poorer quality. A more detailed description of this condition, however, must be delayed for our chapter on poverty.

HEALTH INEQUALITIES

Good health is an obviously important human condition; but unfortunately for those toward the bottom of the stratification system, good health is to some degree unequally distributed through the stratification system. There are two basic reasons for this: First, adequate health care is unequally distributed; and second, conditions promoting better health are unequally distributed.

Much like income and wealth, health care is in constant demand. People seldom have enough health care; there are often new aches, new procedures, brighter and straighter teeth to attain, and preventive medicine. Thus, because health care is a scarce quantity, as with any scarce quantity, there must be a method of distribution. With health care there are two opposing methods of distribution. On the one hand, health care can be distributed through a pricing mechanism. Those who can afford to pay for it get it; those who cannot afford to pay do without. On the other hand, health care distribution can be based on some principle of need. Those in greatest need get it first; those with less need must wait. Between these opposing methods of distribution, the distribution of health care in the United States is based more on the ability to pay, whereas in virtually all other industrialized nations distribution is based more on need (although no society today is at either extreme).

Since 1915 there have been attempts in the United States to enact legislation establishing a national health care system that would help distribute health care on the basis of need (Morris 1979:77). It was not until 1965 that a small achievement in this direction was gained with the Medicare and Medicaid programs. But the way these programs were designed, and especially so with Medicaid for the poor, it was only a small achievement. In all states in this country Medicaid does not pay for all kinds of medical needs, and what is paid for is done at a reduced level. Hospitals and doctors accepting Medicaid patients must accept a lower fee (for example, 80 percent of standard fees). Studies have shown that with this new program the poor now get more medical care than in the past, but it is care of less quality than that received by the more affluent (Dutton 1978). Health care quality continues to be unequally distributed in the United States through the ability to pay.

The above points were made most clearly by two studies which were widely reported in newspapers during the summer of 1989. The first study found that at least 20 percent of all Americans lack any major coverage for medical care, either through a private insurance company or a government health program, such as Medicare for the elderly (receiving Social Security) or Medicaid for the very poor. Another federal government study released in 1989 found that almost half of all the people unemployed up to nine months had no health care coverage (U.S. Bureau of the Census, *Current Population Reports,* Household Economic Studies 1989:8). This condition has developed because of the growing expense of private medical insurance and the increasing number of people in low-paying jobs who cannot pay for private health coverage, but at the same time do not qualify for government-funded Medicaid. This second condition was caused by the Reagan cuts in the Medicaid program (Piven and Cloward 1982). As with the other welfare programs, such as Aid to Families with Dependent Children, much of the Reagan cuts in Medicaid were made by cutting off the working poor. The Medicaid program (before Reagan's presidency) had coverage for what was called the ''medically indigent,'' which meant that a family which was not ''poor enough'' to receive from other major poverty programs could count their medical bills against their income so that, for eligibility purposes, they would be considered poor enough to receive Medicaid.

If you do not have either government or private medical coverage, how-ever, you will usually receive some medical treatment for serious injury or dis-ease in the United States through "charity hospitals" or county- (or state-) funded hospitals. The problem, as noted above, is this is where the poor, with or without Medicaid, must go, and these hospitals are usually overcrowded, understaffed, and unable to provide adequate health care. This was the theme of the second news story cited above. A study of the major hospitals in the Los Angeles area, for example, found huge differences in death rates for people admitted to the hospitals for the same illness or injury (*Los Angeles Times,* July 7, 1989). And it was the hospitals where the poor must receive treatment that had the highest death rates.

A second reason good health is unequally distributed in the United States is that a low income often means poor nutrition, less sanitary living conditions, and (less important) less knowledge about how to maintain better health. But also, as we are increasingly finding, a lower position in the stratification sys-tem means a more unhealthy work environment. With more and more danger-ous machines and industrial chemicals, the working class must put its lives and health on the line for corporate profits.

The outcome of these two sources for an unequal distribution of good health can be found in a number of statistics. For example, infant mortality is an often-used indicator because it is a condition that can be reduced with better medical care. Government data indicate that the lower the income, the higher the infant mortality rate in the United States (U.S. Department of Health, Ed-ucation and Welfare, 1975). Furthermore, it is important to note that with the best medical technology and knowledge in the world, the United States has a relatively high infant mortality rate among industrialized nations (see Table 2-12). A prime reason for this poor standing by the United States may be that its distribution of medical care is based more on the ability to pay than on need. Studies have shown that it *is* the lack of adequate medical care that explains much of the higher infant mortality rate among the poor in this country (Gortmaker 1979).

The relationship between an unequal distribution of income and health that is given with the figures in Table 2-13 showing that chronic diseases are more prevalent among those with lower incomes is not surprising.

UNEQUAL POLITICAL OUTPUTS

By unequal political outputs, or simply political inequalities, we refer to out-comes of the political process that favor some class interests more than others. In this section our focus is not on inequalities of political power per se, but rather on the outcomes of differing amounts of political power—or the benefits flowing from the attainment of political power. This subject, as one may sus-pect, is rather broad when we consider the extent of government outputs to-day. But our goal at this point is simply to indicate a pattern using a few basic examples.

TABLE 2-12
COMPARATIVE INFANT MORTALITY RATES,
1987

Country	Infant mortality rate (rate per 1,000 live births)
Japan	5.0
Sweden	5.7
Finland	5.8*
Switzerland	6.8
Canada	7.3
Ireland	7.4
Netherlands	7.6
France	7.6
Denmark	8.3
West Germany	8.3
Norway	8.4
East Germany	8.5
Australia	8.8*
United Kingdom	9.1
Belgium	9.7
Italy	9.8
Austria	9.9
New Zealand	10.0
United States	10.1
Israel	11.4*
Greece	12.6

*Rate is for 1986.
Source: United Nations, *Population and Vital Statistics Report,* April 1989.

TABLE 2-13
PREVALENCE OF SELECTED CHRONIC DISEASES BY ANNUAL INCOME

Annual income	Prevalence per 1,000 persons			
	Heart disease (1972)	Diabetes (1973)	Anemia (1973)	Arthritis (1976)
Under $3,000	114.1	45.0	27.5	
$3,000–4,999	78.0	35.9	22.0	218.6
$5,000–6,999	54.5	23.8	17.1	
$7,000–9,999	39.9	17.3	14.3	135.1
$10,000–14,999	32.8	14.4	12.3	91.0
$15,000 or more	35.2	12.9	10.2	79.3

Source: U.S. Bureau of the Census. 1980. *Social Indicators III,* table 2–17, p. 101.

When examining political inequalities, we find that the pattern that emerges is one in which those toward the top of the stratification system receive more of the services or general outputs provided by government agencies. Despite the common misconception of a welfare state, the poor do not receive most government benefits, and the benefits going to those toward the bottom of the stratification system are the ones most likely to be cut back in times of government retrenchment.

The general nature of the state must be noted before proceeding. The state or polity has many functions, and has developed for many reasons. Some of these, related to social stratification, will be examined in the next chapter. At this point, and for our purpose (which is to describe inequality), the state can be considered as a *redistributive institution*. That is, one function of the state is to take from some and redistribute to others.

In this regard, of course, the state is an important mechanism in a system of social stratification. It is based in class conflict to the extent that one class wants to be sure that it gets from the state what has been taken from other classes, while at the same time having to give up as little as possible. There are other functions of the state that are related to social stratification, one of the most important being the maintenance of the class system. Again, however, our focus at present is on the inequality in government outputs.

Taxes

One very important type of political inequality pertains to government tax policies. Government services and functions must be paid for by someone. The question becomes, "Who pays?" As noted above, this is a key question in the class conflict behind the state as a redistributive institution. Because most states in industrialized nations emerged when the old aristocratic privileges of the Middle Ages were under attack, new ideas of democracy and equality (or equality of opportunity) were built into these new states. With respect to government tax policies, this often meant that those most able to pay would pay more in taxes—that there would be progressive taxation. In reality, however, this philosophy is often subverted.

We must begin by noting the sources of total federal tax revenue in the United States. As shown in Table 2-14, money from individuals and families accounts for about 80 percent of tax revenues in the form of individual income taxes and Social Security deductions (called employment taxes). These sources of tax revenue have been increasing most since 1960, while corporate income taxes have been decreasing.

If we look back further than 1960, this pattern becomes even clearer. In 1916, individual and employment taxes made up only 9.4 percent of tax revenues; in 1930, 31.6 percent; and in 1950, 43.6 percent. In contrast, corporate income taxes accounted for 34.8 percent of federal tax revenues in 1930, 27.6 percent in 1950, 15.5 percent in 1979, and as shown in Table 2-14, only 11.6 percent in 1988 (U.S. Department of Commerce, *Statistical Abstracts of the*

TABLE 2-14
INTERNAL REVENUE COLLECTIONS BY SELECTED SOURCES, 1960–1988

Source of revenue	Percentage of total				
	1960	**1970**	**1978**	**1979**	**1988***
Individual income taxes	49.0	53.0	53.3	54.6	43.3
Employment taxes such as old-age and disability insurance, unemployment insurance	12.2	19.1	24.3	24.5	36.5
Corporation income taxes	24.2	17.9	16.4	15.5	11.6
Estate and gift taxes	1.8	1.9	1.4	1.2	0.8
Excise taxes	12.9	8.1	4.7	4.1	3.9

*In 1988, close to 4 percent more came from customs duties, miscellaneous receipts, and Federal Reserve earnings deposits.
Source: U.S. Bureau of the Census, 1980. *Statistical Abstracts of the United States,* table 446, p. 268. U.S. Bureau of the Census. 1989. *Statistical Abstracts of the United States,* table 490.

United States, 1974:222; U.S. Department of Commerce, *Historical Statistics of the United States,* 1960:713).

When we turn more directly to individual and family income taxes a major question, of course, is "Who pays?" And one way we can approach this question is by looking at how the distribution of income is affected by the tax sys-

TABLE 2-15
THE EFFECTS OF TAXES AND WELFARE PAYMENTS ON THE DISTRIBUTION OF INCOME BY INCOME QUINTILES, 1986
(Total Households = 89,479,000)

Definition of income	Lowest quintile	Second quintile	Third quintile	Fourth quintile	Highest quintile
Income before taxes:					
1. Money income excluding capital gains (current measure)	3.8	9.7	16.4	24.0	46.1
2. Definition 1 less government money transfers	1.1	8.2	16.0	25.6	49.2
3. Definition 2 plus capital gains	1.0	7.6	15.1	23.9	52.5
4. Definition 3 plus health insurance supplements to wage or salary income	1.0	7.6	15.0	24.1	52.4
Income after taxes:					
5. Definition 4 less federal income taxes	1.1	8.2	15.7	24.4	50.6
6. Definition 5 less state income taxes	1.1	8.4	15.8	24.5	50.2
7. Definition 6 less Social Security payroll taxes	1.1	8.4	15.8	24.4	50.3

Source: U.S. Bureau of the Census. *Current Population Reports,* Consumer Income, "Measuring the Effect of Benefits and Taxes on Income and Poverty, 1986," series P–60, no. 164–RD–1, 1988:5.

tem. If we have a truly progressive income tax, one in which the rich are taxed at a higher rate than the poor and not so rich, then the after-tax income distribution should be less unequal than the before-tax income distribution. This question is addressed by Table 2-15.

This table shows five income distributions by 20 percent population segments, from the poorest 20 percent of the population to the richest 20 percent of the population. The first line in Table 2-15 shows the distribution of income before taxes, but after government transfers (such as welfare and Social Security payments) are added to income. Thus, the first line shows that the poorest 20 percent of the population receives 3.8 percent of the income, while the richest 20 percent of the population receives 46.1 percent of the income. The next line shows what the distribution of income would look like without the government transfer payments. As would be expected, in this case the income share of the poorest 20 percent is reduced sharply to 1.1 percent, which then leaves more of the total income to go to other groups, with the upper 20 percent group gaining most. The third line adds the value of capital gains to what is counted as income, which of course adds to the income of the rich. The fourth line adds in the value of health insurance supplements by employers, which has only a small effect on the income distribution. Finally, lines 5 and 6 include the effects of federal income taxes and then state income taxes to the distribution of income. We find only a slight effect on the distribution of income because of income taxes. And we find that it is welfare benefits that have most effect on the distribution of income by improving the income of the poorest 20 percent.

We must look further into the effects of taxes on the distribution of income, however, because Table 2-15 includes only income taxes in the analysis. Another form of taxation is a sales tax, which is regressive rather than being even close to progressive, as with income taxes in the United States. Sales taxes are called *regressive* because the less affluent pay more as a percentage of their income than do the more affluent. (For example, if a person with an income of $10,000 and a person with $100,000 both pay a total of $300 in sales taxes in a year, this represents a much greater share of the first person's income.) A study of the effects of all forms of taxes on the distribution of income has found that all forms of taxation taken together actually increase the level of income inequality in the United States (Devine 1983). But, as we saw in Table 2-15, this study also found that government transfer payments to the less affluent reduce income inequality. Thus, the end result was that taxes and transfer payments added together make the level of income inequality what it would have been without either effect by the government.

Much has been said about the tax law changes during the Reagan administration because these changes purposely reduced the tax rates for the wealthy early in the 1980s. Reagan's tax bill certainly did that, but what also happened due to increases in other more regressive income taxes, such as the Social Security payroll tax, is that the overall tax rates for the less affluent and poor actually went up in the 1980s (Harrison and Bluestone 1988).

It was said at the time that this change in the tax rates would finally benefit the poor and less affluent because the benefits given the rich would "trickle down" to those below in the form of more jobs and income when the rich invested this money. As we have already seen with the increasing income inequality and drop in real wages during the 1980s, it did not happen that way. The extra money in the pockets of the rich was not always invested in the economy to produce more jobs and income for those below. A study conducted soon after the tax law changes in the early 1980s found that, in fact, the "trickle-down" effect from increases in the income of the rich has almost never worked to improve the incomes and jobs of the poor (Treas 1983). The only group somewhat improved by this trickle-down effect since World War II has been white males. And not only are women and minorities less helped by investments by the rich in good economic times, they are more harmed in times of economic stagnation (Parcel and Mueller 1989).

Finally, it should be noted that the tax laws were again changed shortly before Reagan left office in 1988, but the effect on income distribution by this last change is expected to be very little. Reagan's first tax law change brought the "possible" tax rate on the highest income group down to somewhat above 50 percent from the earlier rate in the 60 percent range. But we must say "possible" tax rate, because with what are called *tax loopholes* the wealthy seldom would pay this amount, and the real tax rate (effective tax rate) for the highest income group ended up being in the 30 percent range most often (Stern 1973). What Reagan's last tax change did, in effect, was to bring down the top tax rates to this 30 to 35 percent range and do away with some of the tax loopholes. Thus, how taxes were figured changed. Some among the rich gained while others in different circumstances, because of previous favoritism of tax loopholes that were lost, were hurt. The result was that the overall income distribution effect of these tax changes at the end of the 1980s was almost none.[3]

Government Services

In this final section in inequalities we approach a vast subject that can be treated at this point with only a brief description and a few examples. When the subject of government services is raised, welfare for the poor comes to mind most often. But such an image of government services is highly misleading. There is another side of government services that may be called *wealthfare* (Turner and Starnes 1976:89). Most of what government does, it does *not* for the poor, but for the nonpoor. And among the nonpoor, it is often the wealthy and corporations that benefit most. This is yet another aspect of how the stratification system and unequal power affect the state as a redistributive mechanism.

In addition to providing welfare for the poor, consider what else the federal government does. The federal government provides subsidies to many industries like agriculture, research and development that directly benefit major corporations, tariff protection for many industries, regulatory agencies that protect major industries, and other direct services that industries would otherwise have to pay for out of their own profits (such as the Federal Aviation Administration's maintenance of air guidance systems, airport landing systems, and research and development for new airline technology). In addition to all of this, the federal government keeps many large corporations in business through billions of dollars in defense-related contracts (see Turner and Starnes 1976:90).

Let us look at a few examples. About one-half of all 1988 federal spending went for various programs that provide money or services (such as health care) for individuals. On the one hand, most of these programs and money transfers do not go to poor people; on the other hand, most of these transfers are paid for through specific or additional income withholding taxes that operate much like pension programs or insurance programs.

The largest example of federal money going to the nonpoor as well as the poor is Social Security. The Social Security program operates much like a pension or insurance program (that is, workers pay for the system by contributing to a special fund) and it accounted for almost $300 billion, or about 28 percent, of the federal budget in 1988. Another $46 billion went to federal employees' retirement and insurance benefits. In contrast to this total of $346 billion, the federal government spent only about $28 billion on direct-transfer payments to the poor under public assistance programs like Supplemental Security Income (SSI) and Aid to Families with Dependent Children (U.S. Bureau of the Census, *Statistical Abstracts of the United States,* 1989:304). As for other 1988 federal expenditures, about $285 billion went for the military, $27.2 billion for transportation programs, $12.4 billion for commerce and housing credit, $22.4 billion for agriculture, $10.9 billion for scientific and technology research, and $2.7 billion for energy programs, to name only a few.

The main point in presenting the above examples of federal spending is to demonstrate the expanse of government programs and services going to the nonpoor. But the actual benefit these services provided to the wealthy cannot be judged solely in government outlays. A relatively inexpensive government program for price supports, business regulation, or protection from foreign and domestic business competition can result in billions of dollars in greater profits or in transfers from consumers to business.

It can be argued that many of these government services that directly help the wealthy and corporations also help the general public, and hence the working class and poor. The question becomes one of who is helped most, and by how much. If we find that the wealthy and corporate classes have more resources that are used to influence government policies and programs, we must recognize that it is their interests that are probably most directly served. Information supporting such a conclusion is central to the study of social stratification and will be considered in coming chapters. We can conclude this discussion by simply noting again that the *wealthfare* system is equally, if not more importantly, an aspect of the state as is welfare for the poor. Along with the many other inequalities described in this chapter, inequalities in government services must be added.

DIMENSIONS OF INEQUALITY: A CONCLUSION

The design of this chapter has been to present descriptive information on the extent of inequality in the contemporary United States. Toward this end, inequalities in income and wealth, standards of living and health, and taxation and government services were examined. These primarily material inequalities are among the most important, but they are by no means the only important ones.

We have said nothing about educational opportunities and inequalities in the actual attainment of education. Educational attainment, as might be expected, is in many ways linked to divisions in the stratification system—as both an outcome of this system and a means of its maintenance. This subject receives considerable attention later.

Neither have we said anything substantial about inequalities in power and authority. Authority divisions (or institutionalized power) are obvious outcomes of social organization in complex societies with an expanded division of labor. We need not describe the fact that some people give many orders, while others only take orders. And power inequalities per se, or the ability to influence others whether such power is institutionalized or not, are difficult to measure in the absence of a specific context. We have no simple scales with which to rank people in terms of power as people can be ranked in terms of income or wealth. We will consider the importance of inequalities in both power and authority in later chapters.

In addition to the inequalities already outlined, it should now be evident that any material good, condition, or service that people come to value, for whatever reason, may be unequally distributed by or through a stratification system. One such valued condition, of course, is life itself. Those lower in the stratification system, however, are more likely to be victims of violent crime and find they must fight and die for their country, as shown in studies of the Korean (Mayer and Hoult 1955) and Vietnam wars (Zeitlin, Lutterman, and Russel 1973). But there are other inequalities that require brief mention.

Along with various material goods and services, the stratification system also provides an unequal distribution of status or honor, self-esteem or self-evaluations, and social deference. As briefly noted in the previous chapter, because human beings tend to evaluate things, conditions, behavior, and people differently, a status hierarchy will emerge that tends to correspond with hierarchical divisions within a stratification system. Thus, people and groups are ranked by others in terms of status, prestige, or honor. They usually receive social deference from those of lower status rank in ritual interactions, and they tend to rank or evaluate themselves unequally in terms of their positions in a system of social stratification.

Many sociologists, in fact, have argued that this status dimension of social stratification is of primary importance. Among functional theorists (such as Parsons 1951, 1970) there is the view that status inequality produces an unequal distribution of material goods and services as rewards for attaining high status. There is, as we will see, extensive research on the distribution of status within the occupational structure.

For several reasons outlined in coming chapters, however, more sociologists now reject the causal logic of this functional argument. Especially in complex societies, status is considered more a product of unequal power and wealth than a cause. In other words, power and material wealth usually bring status or prestige, not the other way around (see Lenski 1966). But none of this rejection of the functional view of status inequality is to deny its existence or its secondary importance for understanding social stratification.

Status divisions are of considerable importance in understanding the *maintenance* of social stratification. For example, individuals of a particular class often establish status boundaries (based upon lifestyle) to protect their privilege by excluding people from lower-class divisions. Also, there is everyday social interaction that requires prescribed deference rituals among unequal status members. These deference rituals give everyday meaning and reinforcement to the stratification system (Collins 1975:161–215). And finally, such status divisions can lead to differing amounts of self-esteem and differing self-evaluations that lead people to accept their place in the stratification system and to accept the system's legitimacy (Della Fave 1980). These nonmaterial inequalities will be discussed more fully when we have occasion to explain their use in maintaining a system of social stratification.

The point that inequalities of many, many kinds are shaped and produced by a system of social stratification has been made. It is time to consider why and how such inequality is produced. We will first explore how stratification systems have evolved throughout the history of human societies. That is the task of our next chapter.

NOTES

1 It should be noted that between 1985 and 1988 the value of the Japanese yen doubled in value compared to the U.S. dollar and this is part of the reason for the rise of the Japanese on the list of billionaires. But the United States still had the most billionaires in 1988, at fifty-one to Japan's thirty-four. Another important point is that the wealthy in Japan pay much higher taxes on income and have very high inheritance taxes which will make it more difficult to pass this wealth to the next generation. And equally important, the Japanese billionaires have most of their money tied up in corporate assets with more restrictions on what can be done with this money. Other issues, such as why the Japanese still have the lowest rate of income inequality among industrial nations despite having the most wealthy individuals, will be considered in Chapter 13 on social stratification in Japan.

2 Until the early 1980s there had not been a comprehensive study of wealth inequality in the United States since the early 1960s. In the most discussed study of wealth in-

equality in the early 1980s, James D. Smith was able to work with the Internal Revenue Service to collect a random sample of 3,824 individuals, plus 438 individuals among the top wealth holders in the United States (see Smith 1986; Institute for Social Research 1986:3). When this study was released in 1986, most newspapers in the country ran front-page stories about the reported "extensive increase" in wealth inequality between 1963 and 1983 (for the *Washington Post* story, see Berry 1986). For example, it was reported that the top 0.5 percent of wealth holders increased their percentage of wealth from 26 percent in 1963 to about 35 percent in 1983. Many scholars have included these figures in their works on the subject. However, soon after these data were released, the researchers discovered that a coding mistake had inflated the amount of wealth controlled by the top 0.5 percent, and the real percentage was around 27 percent, not 35 percent. Most newspapers reported the mistake (though in back pages) and presented the new figures (for example see the *Washington Post* story by Vise 1986), and the researchers issued the corrected data (Institute for Social Research 1986). But many publications continue to cite the incorrect data for 1983.

3 Information released by the Internal Revenue Service in 1989 shows that, in 1987, 595 individuals with incomes averaging about $600,000 paid no income tax. Another group of 33,805 individuals with income over $200,000 paid their income tax at a rate of less than 15 percent of their income (*Los Angeles Times* Oct. 22, 1989). This is the most recent IRS report and does not reflect the taxes paid on income made in 1987 after Reagan's last tax law went into effect. The next report by the IRS will thus be watched closely for any effect in reducing loopholes in the tax laws which favored these individuals.

SOCIAL STRATIFICATION IN HUMAN SOCIETIES: THE HISTORY OF INEQUALITY

We live in a society with extensive social inequality. The life chances of the rich, middle class, blue-collar worker, and, of course, the poor are separated along a vast scale measuring not only wealth and income differences, but also health, a safe work place, legal justice, and even the chance of death in war. Has it always been so? Is our society more unequal than others? Will it always be so? The last question, no doubt, is among the most difficult to answer. No one is very good as yet in predicting the future with any degree of accuracy. But the first two questions can be answered with some confidence.

In this chapter we will be concerned with the first question. Our subject is the history of inequality and social stratification in human societies. The age in which we find ourselves has been shaped in large measure by the historical hand of many human solutions to the question of who gets what, and why. Thus, in addition to comparing our age with previous ages, we can gain some insight into how we got where we are today. The insight gained will prove invaluable in our later attempts to understand the nature and causes of inequality and social stratification.

At the outset the relative brevity of what we think of as society must be recognized. What can be called hominids (our closest ancestors) have lived on this earth for *at least* 4 million years (see Leakey and Lewin 1977). Human beings began settling down in more or less stable agricultural communities, forming what we can call societies, only about 10,000 years ago. Thus, even from that time (10,000 years ago) to the present represents less than 1 percent of human existence.

What, in general, do we know about the extent of inequality throughout this long history of human existence? In comparison with our present society we can say that inequality most often was less, but sometimes (in the more recent past with fully developed agrarian societies) it was greater. It has been noted (see van den Berghe 1978) that human beings are unique among animals in the systematic coercion of nonkin, in cooperative efforts to exploit others of the species, and in the degree of inequality among our own kind.

But all of this can be found to vary greatly in the history of human societies, and for the most part it is relatively recent. The best evidence, some of which will be examined below, suggests that throughout most of their existence human beings have lived in a state of near equality, in vast contrast to the inequality that is prevalent today. In short, with only a limited surplus, if any, above the minimum necessities of life, our ancestors most often shared what they had with other members of the tribe. They lived in small groups, existed on what food could be gathered in the immediate environment, and moved on when local resources were depleted. No one fared much better than others in terms of material goods, nor could a tribal member hold excessive dominance over others.

Not all types of inequality were absent, nor did all tribes everywhere around the earth live in a similar manner. And times were sometimes hard for these early human beings. But the evidence, as we will see, does point toward a standard of relative equality, even if it sometimes (but by no means always) meant an equality of scarcity.

About 10,000 or so years ago, after many more thousands of years of life in small hunting and gathering societies, something revolutionary began happening. During what may be called the *Neolithic revolution* our ancestors began settling down to an agricultural life, a life of planting crops and herding food animals that increased their output of basic necessities.

In one sense it is incorrect to speak of a revolution. The change was gradual and uneven around the world. But from the perspective of our total previous existence on earth and the changes produced, it was revolutionary. Large cities began emerging and, a few thousand years later, civilizations and empires. No longer was everyone required to work the fields to feed the population. The division of labor increased, and some people were able to pursue science, religion, arts, or military technology. Soon, in relative terms, a cycle of technical innovation producing higher crop yields freed still more people from the land for other occupations (producing even greater technical innovation) and propelled us into the industrial age.

Most people paid a price for this advance. As one observer put it, with only some exaggeration, the process of civilization was also one of enslavement (see Wells 1971:193). When human beings ceased their nomadic ways during the Neolithic revolution, the history of stratification, inequality, elites, and exploitation began (see Pfeiffer 1977:20). The history of civilization *is,* in fact, the history of social stratification. But we are getting far too ahead of our story.

THE EMERGENCE OF INEQUALITY AND SOCIAL STRATIFICATION

It is time to add a more detailed historical dimension to our examination of inequality and human stratification systems. At the outset it must be clear that what follows is only a general outline of this history of inequality. In reality we find no unaltered linear progression from primitive communal societies to industrial class systems; only a general tendency in this direction over the centuries.

Perhaps only at first, as human beings began roaming the earth's surface, did one general type of society exist alone. But as we move through history the picture becomes mixed. We find the living remains of older forms of human organization surviving while new ones ascend to dominance through the world. For example, it is estimated that there are about 300,000 hunting and gathering people today (Leakey and Lewin 1977:176; 1978:95). It is fortunate for us that along with archaeological evidence, and eventually some written records, we have living societies resembling earlier forms with which to expand our knowledge. But although history does not show a step-by-step progression of human organization, we do find the older forms slowly giving way to more technologically advanced societies. We will begin this examination at the beginning, at least as we know it.

Early Human Groups

The most conclusive evidence of early human beings (*Homo habilis*) was located a few years ago by Louis Leakey in the Olduvai Gorge in East Africa. These remains (primarily skull fragments) date back some 3 to 4 million years (Leakey and Lewin 1977:86). From what may be the original sites of human existence in East Africa, the evidence shows steady but slow movement across the earth, beginning about 1 to 2 million years ago (Pfeiffer 1977:53).

By 25,000 to 50,000 years ago *Homo sapiens* had reached the North American continent, spreading southward from their crossing over the then existing land bridge from what is now Russia. This movement across the earth was not what we would consider a planned migration, but movement in search of food. In these very early times, much before the important changes some 10,000 years ago, if food became scarce in one area (because of increased population or poor climate), there was space to move on.

Depending upon how far back in the chain of human evolution one is willing to concede "true" human beings appeared (with *Homo sapiens* or, say, *Homo erectus,* or perhaps *Homo habilis*), we can say that human beings have been on this earth from 500,000 to over 4 million years (see Leakey and Lewin 1977:85; 1978:75). Assuming the most conservative estimate of 500,000 years, we can conclude that for at least 490,000 years human beings survived primarily with what is called a hunting and gathering mode of production.

The general type of social organization based on this level of technology was described in Chapter 1 as primitive communalism. Although geographic and environmental variations helped produce many differences among these primitive communal tribes (such as differences in beliefs about the supernatural, family structure, food sources, and degree of male dominance; see Lenski 1966:101), one characteristic appears quite common—near equality (Lenski 1966:102). And by our definition of social stratification—structured inequalities—it was seldom if ever found.

Several living examples of this type of human existence—such as the Andaman Islanders (Radcliffe-Brown 1948) and the Bambuti Pygmies of Zaire (Turnbull 1961)—have been found to meet this characteristic of equality most fully. What tools and other artifacts they have, the food they find, is either considered common property or divided equally among all members of the tribe. Inequalities of power and influence over others in the tribe have been found at times, but the level of these inequalities tends to be very low. And when inequalities of power are found they usually are based on the experience of age or the status of being the best provider of food. Most common is a decision-making method involving free group discussion by all adult members of the tribe (in some tribes only males are included, however); thus, a form of democracy or equality of influence exists.

Because of their level of technology—that is, their methods of providing the necessities of life—these tribes are generally nomadic or seminomadic. Because they lack knowledge or at least the use of agriculture or animal husbandry, the food sources in their environment are usually depleted through time, and they must move on. This also prevents the accumulation of many personal possessions; they must travel light. The maximum size of the tribe is also strongly related to its level of technology; its method of food production can support only a few people in one area. An examination of living hunting and gathering tribes shows they average only about fifty members (Murdock 1949:81), and that about 90 percent are nomadic or seminomadic (Murdock 1957; see also Lenski 1966:98).

Along with the relationship between their level of technology, tribal size, and nomadic lifestyle, we generally find other characteristics that affect the degree and type of social equality among these people. With respect to the first of these, cooperation versus conflict, the general evidence would suggest that the French philosopher Rousseau was more accurate (though not completely) in his view of early human beings than was Thomas Hobbes (who assumed their life to be "solitary, poor, nasty, brutish, and short"). Hunting, especially, is much more efficient as a cooperative enterprise:

> For early people on the savanna, getting meat was a matter of life or death. Meat was an estimated one-third or more of their diet. They would have soon become extinct if they had not observed and anticipated the movements of prey together, and together planned appropriate strategies. Cooperation could not be a casual, sometime thing. Cooperation was vital after the prey was killed, as well (Pfeiffer 1977:48).

From cooperative food gathering comes the necessity of sharing (Pfeiffer 1977:50). What is gained through cooperation must generally be shared among others in the tribe. If such sharing was not practiced, the incentive to continue the cooperative exchange relationship was probably weakened; thus, all could starve. Moreover, with weapons no more sophisticated than a club or spear, no member of the tribe had the power to forcefully prevent a majority of others from attaining their share of the prey. It simply made sense to work and share together, for in the long run, all were better off for it.

Thus far we have neglected an important biological trait in the long process of human evolution. This biological trait combined with the mode of production among early human beings to produce a sexual division of labor. As Pfeiffer (1977:50) describes:

> The increasing complexity of life on African savannas favored an increasingly complex nervous system, a large memory and a greater capacity for weighing and choosing among an increasing number of alternative actions. This process had major repercussions. The bigger a primate's brain, the more slowly it matures. Mothers were compelled to devote themselves to their infants for longer and longer periods. Monkey infants depend completely on their mothers for about a year, ape infants for more than two years. The hominid infant of millions of years ago, however, was helpless for an estimated four to five years. It was even more helpless than the infants of other primates because, unlike them, it could not cling to its mother as she moved about.

Because of this infant dependency, mothers were required to stay closer to the home base and could not pursue wild game as easily. A division of labor based on sex developed, with men doing the hunting and women taking care of infants and gathering food that could more easily be collected around the home base. A division of labor alone does not necessarily require social inequality. But, in the absence of economic or power concentration, when one occupation comes to be of major importance for the survival of the group, those who are most skilled in this occupation will usually come to be more highly rewarded.[1] In hunting and gathering societies, most goods were in short supply, but status or honor was not. Thus, the skilled hunter came to be more highly honored, and it is here that we find the most important form of inequality in primitive communal societies.

The development of this form of sexual inequality is demonstrated most clearly through an examination of living tribes that vary in their dependence on meat. For example, the Hadza of Tanzania and the Palliyans of southwest India eat little meat. Here the level of status inequality between the sexes is low. However, the Eskimos, the !Kung, and the Bambuti of Africa have a high dependence on meat, and the level of sexual inequality is greater (see Leakey and Lewin 1977:235; 1978:247). Women don't always have low status, nor has biology always placed women in an inferior status. But when physical strength is demanded for tasks very important to group survival (a condition seldom found in modern societies), men usually perform this work and receive more status.

We must note two further aspects of status inequality based on skill. Age ranking is also quite common among primitive communal tribes. Again, this status ranking is based primarily on skill in hunting. The young to middle-aged male is favored. But there is also skill, or rather knowledge, that comes with age. The older tribal members may through experience know where and how best to find food, or their knowledge of tradition, mythology, or any other set of knowledge may be superior. Thus, we may find both age and sexual status inequality.

One of the most interesting systems of age and sex inequality is found with the Masai of East Africa (van der Berghe 1978:148):

> The age-grade system operates somewhat like an American school system, where, at regular intervals, classes get promoted to the next higher grade. The Masai age-grade system extends throughout the entire society and encompasses most of an individual's life time.

As these males move up the age-grade system they achieve increasing status. In the young adult years it is because of their physical abilities; then, in later years, because of their experience, they become respected leaders and decision makers (making decisions through democratic councils based on their age status).

Last, many primitive communal tribes do have leaders in the form of chiefs or medicine men. However, these are part-time leaders (Lenski 1966:100). They cannot accumulate material riches, for there are few. They cannot demand that all others work for their benefit, for there is seldom enough food to relieve people from their daily food-gathering duties. Their part-time leadership status is based on skill, skill in story telling, skill in performing religious rituals, or, again, skill in providing food. Thus, it is based on status gained through function. The advantaged position cannot bring an accumulation of power and wealth to create hereditary inequalities or a system of social stratification. Unlike most later societies, the offspring are not assured their parents' higher place in a stratification system.

Early Social Change The thousands, if not millions, of years between the emergence of human beings and a change away from hunting and gathering or primitive communal tribes is not what is most incredible. What is incredible is that change occurred at all. A cycle existed in which primitive methods of food production required most of the daily energy and attention of every tribal member (Lenski 1966:97). There was no time, energy, or incentive for advancement. And contrary to what is often thought, life for these early human beings was not always "solitary, poor, nasty, brutish, and short." From our evidence of present-day hunting and gathering tribes, tribes isolated from the technical progress of modern society, we often find rather content and happy people. All prehistoric people were not so secure and content, of course. But it took a significant change that affected the lives of many such primitive people to propel our ancestors into a cycle of increasing technological advancement.

The change came for an increasing number of hunting and gathering people about 10,000 to 15,000 years ago. Most archaeologists agree that a primary stimulus for the change was a steady increase in population in many areas, in the face of declining food resources (see Cohen 1977; Harris 1977; Redman 1978:88–112). Population had increased before. But by this time it was more difficult to find new territory not already claimed by others. In addition, some argue that "there was less land as well as more people. Land had been decreasing ever since the height of the last ice age 20,000 or so years ago, when so much water was locked up in polar ice caps and glaciers that the ocean levels stood 250 to 500 feet lower than they stand today" (Pfeiffer 1977:69).

In what were the more populated areas of the world at the time, such as Northern Africa and the Near East, the ever-increasing scarcity of food and land produced more intertribal conflicts (Pfeiffer 1977:33). Change and disruption of some kind seem to account for the violent behavior and high inequality reported in a few living primitive communal tribes (see Skinner 1973). We have some archaeological evidence of this increase in violent conflict. Sites dating back about 15,000 years ago show human remains with arrowheads and other stone projectiles piercing the bones (Pfeiffer 1977:246).

The pressure of less land and more people provided the necessity for change. We will never know with certainty *exactly* where and when human beings found that through settled agricultural methods of food production more people could be fed, but the current evidence seems to show that this happened in the Near East about 10,000 years ago. It is unlikely that someone suddenly discovered that plants could be cultivated—the Eureka theory. It is more likely that the knowledge was already present. As Pfeiffer (1977:70) describes it:

> The basic elements of agriculture were known long before agriculture was established. But domestication makes no sense at all in a normal hunting–gathering context. Wiessner tells of one man in the Kalahari who cleared a plot of land, put a fence around it, sowed corn, and obtained a good crop. At harvest time his relatives came, and all of the corn was consumed in a week. In the winter they tore down his fence for firewood. This premature venture had a sad ending. Next year he refused to share his crop and was forced to leave the band.

What happened was that it became necessary for more and more people to apply agricultural methods. Every one of the tribe was required to participate in agriculture to survive. The pattern of nomadic hunting and gathering was altered for more and more people. Those who did not change did not survive in these highly populated areas. The Neolithic revolution had arrived.

The Neolithic Revolution

Most social scientists regard the Neolithic revolution as the earliest, most important event in the evolution of human societies (see Childe 1952). Not only do we find a change in the technology of food production, we find change in almost every aspect of human organization. The changes, of course, did not come as rapidly as did those during the industrial revolution. Human settlements at this time were more isolated, and transportation and communication were still undeveloped. It took about 5,000 years for agricultural methods to be established firmly with farming villages and irrigation (Pfeiffer 1977:144).

At first, people remained in small tribes, mixing farming with their old hunting and gathering ways. Their first agricultural tools were simple digging sticks. Consequently, their level of food production remained relatively low. But, because of the new agricultural methods, there was at least some surplus of food, a surplus that freed some people from full-time labor producing food.

With the release from food production for some (at least part-time) there emerged artisans, craft workers, a small commercial class, and, most importantly, political and religious leaders. But as yet we find no great distinctions in wealth and power. These leaders are not placed far above common members of the farming tribe. More often we find only a "nominal leader who acts to redistribute food and perform a few minor ceremonial activities . . ." (Wenke 1980:343). As with earlier hunting and gathering tribes, status is the main form of inequality. In the earliest farming tribes the status distinctions may be greater than before, but not yet attached to hereditary wealth and power (Flannery 1972).

Through time, however, especially in the more populated areas such as the Near East, hunting and gathering methods increasingly gave way to full-time agriculture. And our ancestors became better at it. In fact, the population increase that provided part of the stimulus for agriculture was given an even greater boost. It is estimated that during the first 8,000 years of agriculture (beginning about 10,000 years ago, remember) the total human population rose from 10 million to 300 million people (Leakey and Lewin 1977:176). Through hunting and gathering methods of food production it had taken human beings more than a million years to reach a population of 10 million. This relatively rapid population growth, itself an aspect of new agricultural methods, produced further change in human societies.

It is useful at this point to examine some of the data from the first few thousand years of agricultural development that relate to our specific topic of social stratification. We have no written records from these early agricultural tribes and later agricultural settlements, but we do have archaeological data. And what we have shows *increasing social inequality*.

The two main types of archaeological evidence that concern us are burial practices and housing structures. It became common practice to bury personal possessions with the dead: "There were numerous reasons for including valuable goods with burials . . . but in general it indicated a person's wealth or status" (Redman 1978:197). What these burial sites show is increasing inequality with the development of agriculture (Redman 1978:277). Some archaeologists also conclude from the evidence that these inequalities of wealth and power finally emerged as hereditary inequalities. This conclusion is based on findings of children buried in graves rich with material possessions (see Redman 1978:277; Wenke 1980:349). In summarizing the general findings on burial practices, Wenke (1980:349) writes:

Some ancient cemeteries have three or four distinct classes of burials. Some types are well constructed of stone, have rich grave goods, and are centrally located, while others are simple graves with little in them except the corpse. And it is a reasonable inference that these divisions correspond to different economic and social classes.

In addition to the burial data there are indications of growing inequality reflected in housing (see Redman 1978:277; Wenke 1980:346). With the advancement in agriculture we find villages with many simple common houses, but toward the center are often larger, better constructed family dwellings. Pfeiffer (1977:94–95) describes one such site in southern Jordan occupied for many generations:

> . . . a 7000 B.C. occupation level is made up entirely of small houses averaging some 120 square feet, the size of a small twentieth-century bedroom. In the level immediately above a different pattern appears, representing the same settlement no more than a few generations later, the beginnings of a range of hierarchy of house sizes. The village now consisted mostly of small houses distributed around a slightly raised central area, a section reserved for houses three to four times larger than the rest, with large hearths and plastered walls and floors.

Again, as with burial sites, we find increasing material inequality. But evidence of inequality is also found in large religious monuments. An example of such monuments is Stonehenge on England's Salisbury Plain. It is estimated that 30 million hours of human labor were required to construct this monument. A reasonable conclusion is that such an investment in human labor required inequalities of power and sufficient power over others to mobilize such a work effort (Pfeiffer 1977:95).

Having noted the importance of religious monuments we should also note the overall importance of religion in these early agricultural societies. Compared with religion in previous hunting and gathering societies, more systematic and organized religion can be found in these later societies. Marxists, among other social theorists, argue that religion developed along with civilization and new class inequalities (Wells 1971:1974). As agriculture advanced we do find evidence of influential religious elites. Others, however, argue that religion developed before class inequalities (see van den Berghe 1978:246). The dispute is in part due to what one is willing to call organized religion.

But one thing is clear: Religion generally became the most important base of structured inequalities in these early agricultural societies (Lenski 1966:128). It is hard to say which came first, wealth and power inequalities or high status as a religious leader. The two, however, reinforced one another. Religion has often been a useful means of justifying and maintaining power and wealth inequalities (Pfeiffer 1977:104). But this religious base for inequality, as we will see, slowly gave way to more powerful secular political elites with advanced agricultural societies.

The digging stick and hoe gave way to the plow and irrigation by about 5,000 years ago. At this time we find evidence of more stable agricultural settlements able to support greater numbers of people. And with these more advanced methods of agriculture more people were freed to pursue other occupations in the arts, crafts, religion, and warfare. Accompanying these changes were further increases in hereditary inequalities of all types.

While many cities were emerging independently at this time, the first known city was Uruk. This city was in southern Mesopotamia, located between the Tigris and Euphrates rivers, about 5,500 years ago, with an estimated population of 20,000 people. Here again, as in the early village in Jordan reported above, excavations have shown that over the years there were increasing levels of inequality among its inhabitants (Pfeiffer 1977:159). An important base of inequality was slavery, although religion was clearly the most important. Impressive religious temples that contained much of the riches of the city have been uncovered. However, "although the evidence is slight, it is likely that individual families or groups of families rose to positions of wealth and power on the basis of success in agriculture" (Redman 1978:278). Wealthy families independent of religious elites may have emerged at this time, but religious elites often remained primary. But top religious leaders alone could not command such a growing population. Armies and administrative officials developed to tend to the business of social order, construction projects, and taxation.

With respect to the more complex form of agricultural production and the emergence of secular elites, it should be noted that with some agricultural settlements we find the early beginning of what Marx called the "Asiatic mode of production" (see Mandel 1971:116–129; Krader 1975). The development of this Asiatic mode of production is found especially in regions such as China, India, and the Middle East, where agriculture required irrigation. Because irrigation required a higher form of social organization, even though land was often common property, something like a state elite emerged in charge of common projects like irrigation systems. Through time, in places like China and India, this state elite grew to dominate the society in a form of social organization distinct from feudalism (where power was based on land ownership rather than on the political elite positions with the Asiatic mode of production).

Agricultural methods of production alone do not explain the rise of these new cities. There were forces pulling more people into cities, as well as other forces pushing them toward cities. The pull came with city elites looking for more personnel to work on construction projects and to pay taxes. The push came with threats to the security of rural people from armies of other cities (Pfeiffer 1977:165). Throughout this period of urban development an increasing number of city elites often competed for people, land, and other resources. Military conflict thus increased, as is suggested by the often large walls built around these early cities (Redman 1978:266).

As military conflict increased a new type of inequality slowly took hold. For the first time among human societies we find human beings owning other human beings. Slavery did not represent a widespread form of inequality in early agricultural cities, in contrast with later civilizations, but it was almost nonexistent in hunting and gathering societies. The reason for the absence of slavery in hunting and gathering societies is related to their methods of food production. It simply did not make sense to hold slaves when every individual could only produce enough food to feed one person. Slaves, therefore, could not improve economic output for the tribe.

When food production methods advanced to the point where one person could produce a surplus, slavery did develop. And when more and more people were freed from food production, slaves could be used in construction projects more cheaply and efficiently than free labor. The final factor of importance in the development of slavery was, of course, military power. Military power was necessary to hold slaves as well as to attain them.

One other form of inequality deserves mention. We last found women in a lower status position in some hunting and gathering societies (especially in those most dependent upon hunting). Lenski (1966:136), through an examination of living agricultural tribes, finds the status of women in most of these tribes unimproved. Others, however, argue that their status was probably worse in most agricultural tribes (see Pfeiffer 1977:463). For one thing, with simple agriculture and a decline in the importance of hunting, there was more work that could be done by women tending small children. A related and probably more important factor was the emergence of organized warfare. The high status of the hunter shifted to the high status of the warrior. Again, women who more often than today were with small children were at a disadvantage.

It should be clear that agricultural settlements and early cities existed at varying times throughout much of the world. And, of course, in the more undeveloped regions of the world they exist to this day. Their development and existence depended upon a particular method of food production that left a food surplus and a growing population. In the Americas these conditions emerged later, about 3,000 years ago, primarily in Central America. The first large city of about 125,000 people at its high point, Teotihuacán, did not emerge until about 100 A.D. around what is now Mexico City (Pfeiffer 1977:369). Others, for example in the Aztec and Maya civilizations, followed even later and were still in existence during the Spanish conquest.

What is important to note about these early American cities is that extensive archaeological investigation has found the existence and forms of inequality roughly similar to those of early cities in other parts of the world. There were powerful religious leaders, vast material inequalities, and early slavery, and all of these inequalities became hereditary. At this stage of economic development the archaeological data, as well as studies of living human societies, show the first big jump in the level of human inequality (Lenski 1966:154). As we will see, inequality did continue to expand in more advanced agrarian societies, but the *magnitude of the increase* was never as large.

Early Agrarian Empires

Among the developments discussed above, the emergence of a distinct military class and state organization proved crucial for further inequalities of power and privilege. Out of these new means of power agrarian empires developed. The agricultural economic base of these societies expanded, became more complex, more technologically advanced. But it was state organization and military power, along with more rapid transportation and communication (with the use of the wheel and the sail) that could spread this power over wider areas, that produced empires: "For the first time in history, technologically based differences in military might become a basic reality within human societies, and the opportunities for exploitation were correspondingly enlarged" (Lenski 1966:194).

In this section we will briefly consider the nature of these *early* agrarian empires. They began some 5,000 years ago, in places such as Egypt and China, although the height of their development came much later. Of these, the Roman Empire was one of the most powerful, and one of the last in a series. This empire began its ascent around 300 B.C. and its final decline at the hands of invaders (such as Attila the Hun) 1,500 years ago (500 A.D.). What followed was a period of stagnation and decline through much of the advanced world (China's advance was less broken and the Islamic Empire did emerge at this time), until new feudal states emerged during the Middle Ages in Europe (the subject of our next section).

As might be expected, there were many differences among the early empires. Differences can be found as well within the same empire because of its usually long existence. Egypt, for example, never reached the level of state centralization found later in Rome. Greece also was less centralized, with a system of relatively independent city states. Moreover, Greece was more of a republic (until very late in its existence), its leaders were secular rather than religious, and the degree of inequality never reached the level found in Rome. With Greece these differences stemmed in large measure from its different economic base, which relied more on seaborne commerce (Lenski 1966:192).

As for internal variation, the Roman and Egyptian empires, for example, experienced early periods of less inequality and some democracy (especially in Rome). All these societies suffered from chronic warfare, however, and slavery tended to be very important in their economy. These empires were usually conquest states; thus, the ruling class was often in a position of power because of such conquests. And more than anything else these empires approximate slave stratification systems.

Despite the differences in these empires, we find other common characteristics. They generally had centralized governments with political and religious ruling elites who had vast economic as well as political control. The state function was to enforce laws, draft soldiers, levy taxes, and extract tribute from conquered territories. The empires had large populations and wide territories that contained many settlements and cities of various sizes and often distinct economic functions. There was a complex division of labor, with full-time craftsmen, artisans, and merchants, plus the usual religious, military, and agricultural people. The agricultural production that supported these more complex societies had to be more technologically efficient. There were metal plows with animal power to pull them, irrigation, and more high-yield strains of cereal crops.

Human societies generally reached a high point of inequality during this period. At the top of the hierarchy of wealth and power was a small ruling class. In earlier societies (before agrarian empires) the ruler was considered more the trustee of communal property (Lenski 1966:165). Now, however, the property belonged to the ruler. And with this property and surplus production the ruler could buy the loyalty of functionaries who worked to maintain this system of high inequality.

The structured inequalities and hierarchical divisions were not always completely rigid. Although most inequalities of wealth and power were hereditary, there was at least some chance of social mobility. And while there was not a total separation between those on top of the stratification system and the masses, the masses for the most part lived at or close to a subsistence level. Only a small group owned a little land or possessed a skilled trade, placing it between the masses and the ruling class in the stratification system.

Inequality in the Roman Empire   In the space of a brief review of early agrarian empires we cannot hope to give much detail on all, or even a few, of them. What we can do, however, is provide some detail on one of the later, and perhaps most important, empires in this period. And the Roman Empire does provide a more detailed written history to follow.

The Roman republic began its ascent to dominance from the disintegration of the vast empire of Alexander the Great about 300 years before the birth of Christ. During this period Rome is referred to as a republic because in these earlier years there was at least some democracy (patterned somewhat after that of Greece) and the level of inequality was lower. But it did not last. By 59 B.C., with Julius Caesar's rule, the republic had moved to a dictatorship from which it did not escape (Brunt 1971:1). The general reason given for this shift from a republic was the growth of extreme inequality, a level of inequality and exploitation that eventually would help destroy the empire around 500 A.D. (Wells 1971:415; Antonio 1979).

The Roman economy was by this age of human technological development rather diverse. There was much commerce, craft works, even some small-scale industry, and central cities. But the economy remained highly dependent on agriculture (Finley 1973). The ownership of land accounted for most wealth (Jones 1974:35–37). And unlike during the feudal period in Europe, agriculture was oriented primarily toward market exchange rather than local consumption on a manor. In part, the widespread use of money accounted for this market orientation, and for the ability of some to accumulate large financial fortunes.

On top of the stratification system "two aristocratic orders monopolized the most powerful and lucrative social, economic, and political positions" (Antonio 1979:899). One, the "senatorial order," accounted for about 0.002 percent of the Roman population; the other, less powerful "equites" accounted for about 0.1 percent. Wealth was one of the most important requirements for membership in these aristocratic orders. It is estimated that senator status required property accounting for more than 250,000 times a laborer's wage, with about half that required for equite status (Duncan-Jones 1974; Antonio 1979:900).

In the face of this wealth, life was hard for the masses. For them there was stark poverty and the most "unpleasant and dangerous conditions imaginable" (Carcopino 1973:22–51; Antonio 1979:900). And not only material conditions were harsh; the masses were viewed with contempt by the wealthy and forced to show degrading deference to their social "betters." At the very bottom, of course, were slaves. Military conquests greatly expanded the number of slaves and the economy came to depend upon them. But the slave class grew from internal conditions of inequality as well, with strict debtor laws leaving many of the masses in slavery. It is estimated that slaves accounted for about a *quarter* of the population by the later centuries (MacMullen 1974:92).

There was some mobility in Rome, mostly attained through the advanced system of education, and when the person could be of service to the upper classes. But such social mobility was uncommon. In the face of this rigid class system and exploitation, rebellion among the lower orders grew. It brought down the early Roman republic (about 2,000 years ago) and forced social reforms. The tax structure was liberalized, there was again more democracy, and the level of inequality was reduced somewhat. But these reforms did not last (Antonio 1979:899). The old ascribed status positions remained, and in short order the reforms were reversed, with inequality and exploitation reaching even higher levels.

Before proceeding it will be of value to explore the meaning of these lower-class rebellions because such rebellions are encountered again and again with the development of rigid inequalities in human societies. In short, when faced with what lower orders may define as extreme injustice, and with no legitimate way of voicing concern or redressing a felt grievance, political violence is a typical outcome (see Moore 1978). Rebellion, riots, peasant revolts, and other types of political violence may be the only avenues for change open to people with no voice in the political or economic system.

Political violence often fails to achieve lasting change, as it failed during the Roman Empire, but it will be attempted over and over again. Descriptions of the many lower-class revolts during the Roman Empire, as well as throughout earlier agrarian societies, are remarkably similar to those encountered in the late feudal period in Europe (see Rudé 1964; Lefebvre 1973), and even during hard times in the United States (see Garner 1977; Piven and Cloward 1977). These rebellions do not always fail to achieve any reforms or even at times revolutionary change. But the typical pattern when they do win reforms is for these reforms gradually to be lost, with a return to the status quo (see Piven and Cloward 1977).

We find this pattern during the time of the Roman Empire. After a period of weak reforms around the time of Christ, inequality and repression were reinstituted on an even higher level (Antonio 1979:907). The vehicle for increased repression was the development of a strong state bureaucracy. In a very interesting description of this bureaucracy, Antonio (1979) is able to show that with increasing economic problems by 300 A.D. the lower orders were controlled at the expense of the needed reforms to revive the economy.

Rome, as we know, declined and fell by 500 A.D. This fall had nothing to do with the moral fiber of the common people. Rather, the greed and shortsightedness of the wealthy were responsible. The upper classes were concerned only with their short-term profits (Antonio 1979:908). The masses were controlled by the bureaucracy and were thus unable to force needed economic and political reforms. The resulting anger and alienation on the part of the masses resulted in an unwillingness to defend the country. Finally, nomadic raids from such groups as the Vandals and from Attila the Hun usually met with no resistance from the common people of Rome (see Wells 1971:432–433).

Inequalities of wealth and power, even at extreme levels, are not always met with strong resistance from the lower classes. The Roman Empire (earlier a republic, remember) was able to survive for about 1,000 years, much of this time with very high levels of inequality. The Indian caste system survived much longer. A system of social stratification is by its nature an arrangement that functions to maintain inequalities of class, status, and power. It does so, in part, by justifying such inequalities as right and/or useful for the common good, and at times by defining "fair" rules by which those on top achieve their positions.

With very high levels of inequality and very limited amounts of social mobility, however, the status quo is often difficult to maintain, partly because extreme and rigid inequalities seldom can be made acceptable forever and partly because with so much power and wealth in the hands of a few, shortsighted exploitation that harms the overall health of the society is typical. The Indian caste system was remarkable with respect to its survival. The stratification system of the Roman Empire felt the strain and the empire eventually fell, even in the face of strong repressive power from the large state bureaucracy. This sequence of events is not untypical throughout history, before the Roman Empire and after.

Late Agrarian Societies

With the increase of nomadic conquests around 500 A.D. most of the early agrarian empires were in decline. The Western world regressed toward what is known as the Dark Ages. It is true that Attila the Hun and Genghis Khan (who appeared a few centuries later) received a bad press; Western historians have written much about the atrocities of these nomadic invaders, while more often neglecting those of early agrarian empires (Wells 1971). But these societies did enter a period in which art, literature, science, technological innovation, and social institutions in general were in decline. Especially in what was once the northern part of the Roman Empire, and in Europe more generally, people banded together for protection, forming small settlements much like those of earlier agricultural people. For centuries this was the form of social organization in what we call the West.

In the East, China, for example, was able to absorb the nomadic invaders with less social disorganization. And in the Middle East, North Africa, and Spain, the Moslem Empire emerged with the fall of the Roman Empire to bring advance and social order. But not until about 1000 to 1200 A.D. were technological advancement and widespread social–political organization on the advance in the West again. It was in these years that the classical period of feudal or estate societies emerged in Europe. And with these new societies, extreme inequalities reemerged.

Our description in Chapter 1 of the ideal type of estate or feudal system of stratification should be remembered at this point. We need not present a detailed description again. But Bloch's (1961) argument that the feudal period in Europe should be divided into two stages is worth repeating. In the earlier stage, before 1200 A.D., social stratification was less institutionalized; inequalities of power and wealth were supported by tradition and custom. Out of the disintegration of previous civilizations people had grouped together to live and work under the protection of a military nobility. In return for protection the common people followed a new tradition of providing tribute to the nobility in the form of service (such as military duty) and turning over much of their economic surplus. By about 1200 A.D., however, inequality had grown, and the more informal system of social stratification was threatened, both by rebellion from the lower orders and by the gradual emergence of a new class of merchants whose wealth at times equaled that of the nobility.

In a very interesting work, Hechter and Brustein (1980) have provided more detail on the growth of the feudal system and on how the more rigid inequalities of this system later developed. Before 1200 A.D. in Europe there were at least three differing modes of agricultural production and corresponding forms of social organization. Among these, the sedentary pastoral mode involved self-sufficient households linked through kinship. In contrast to the feudal mode there was much more independence and equality. Around the Mediterranean and southern Germany a petty commodity mode of production dominated. Here land was worked in small independent units, with production oriented toward trade to the more numerous towns in the area. There was a higher level of social mobility, with less rigid class divisions.

In other areas around Europe the feudal mode dominated; there was a manor system, with tenants and a landlord. Agricultural production was a more collective and more organized operation. Moreover, in contrast to the other modes of production, land remained in large units over the years because it was not subdivided with each new generation. A result was greater production under the feudal mode, and thus a greater surplus. In part, this was because collective labor on larger units of land was more efficient, especially with new advances in agricultural technology at the time. Because of its greater efficiency, the feudal mode finally came to dominate all of Europe.

At first the feudal system represented many fairly independent manors, with a local nobility dominating each. But as the power and wealth of some landowners grew, they began dominating other landowners. A wealthier and more powerful nobility emerged, producing even greater levels of inequality between the nobility and the common people. To further solidify these inequalities, by 1300 A.D. "modern" states emerged.

Hechter and Brustein (1980) are primarily concerned with why these states developed when and where they did. We saw that during the Roman Empire a strong bureaucracy supported by the upper class developed in response to a rebellious lower class. Something similar occurred in later feudal Europe. But this time it was in response to a two-pronged threat to the upper class (Hechter and Brustein 1980:1085). By the fourteenth century in Europe, peasant revolts were perhaps more widespread throughout Europe than at any other time. At the same time, in the cities, a wealthy merchant class began challenging the power and wealth of the nobility. In response to both challenges, the nobility united in support of new state systems with the power to maintain their positions of privilege.

The key to Hechter and Brustein's argument is in data showing that the feudal zones in Europe, where threats to the privileges of nobility were experienced, were where the modern state grew. With the development of these states across the face of Europe a rigid system of inequality, lost with previous agrarian empires, was restored. For a time there was another period of order, until, as we will see, change again disrupted the rigid inequalities enjoyed by an agrarian-based upper class.

Before turning from the feudal period the reader should be given at least a sense of the inequalities and lifestyle differences of the three major estates, or divisions, in this type of society. In the first estate, of course, is the higher clergy; the second belongs to the nobility. One must not, however, get the idea that the clergy was always most prominent in the estate system. The underlying ideology that God was first in the affairs of people and the divine sanction given secular rulers by the Church accounted for the clergy's position (and throughout most of feudal history in Europe Catholic clergy made up the first estate). Although the Church and nobility often coexisted in a somewhat uneasy relationship, they tended to work together to strengthen and reinforce the position of each other above the third estate (or commoners). This uneasy relationship is nowhere better symbolized than at the crowning of Charlemagne, the first king in early feudal Europe, by Pope Leo III. Although the ceremony did not call for it, the pope placed the crown on Charlemagne's head (to the surprise of the new king). With this act the pope sought to signify what he saw as the authority of the church over the affairs of secular leaders.

Despite vows to be the humble servants of God, the priestly class was extremely wealthy. Priests received much of the surplus produced by laboring classes, and lived in comfort exceeded only by the higher nobility. The most important source of wealth during this period was land ownership. From land ownership came rents, taxes, and other forms of tribute and services. In fourteenth-century England, for example, the Church owned about one-third of all land; the situation was similar in France. Also:

The Church in pre-Reformation Sweden owned 21 percent of the land, while in sixteenth-century Russia, it owned 40 percent or more in certain districts. . . . The Primate of the Spains, the Archbishop of Toledo, is reported to have ranked immediately below the king in point of power, wealth, and the extent of his dominions in the early sixteenth century (Lenski 1966:257–258).

The clergy itself was highly stratified. During this time the main division was between the upper and lower clergy, a division similar to that between the nobility and peasants. The upper clergy were most often recruited from the nobility or governing class and enjoyed a similar lifestyle. The lower clergy, in contrast, was recruited from the common people. It was the job of the lower clergy to serve the common people, to watch over them for the Church and nobility, as parish priests living not much better than commoners (see Lenski 1966:258). We say they were to watch over commoners because for most of these common people in small villages and the countryside, the upper clergy and nobility were far away. But the parish priest was always there. It was the parish priest who could be counted upon to follow the dictates of the Church hierarchy and make sure the common people followed (Le Roy Ladurie 1978:11).

The principal center of wealth and power was found with the nobility, the governing class, and, as more powerful states emerged, most importantly with the king. The lifestyle and riches of this feudal aristocracy are legend, and this wealthy and powerful group was very small. In nineteenth-century Russia (which was still a feudal society at the time) this group accounted for 1.25 percent of the population; in seventeenth-century England it was roughly 1 percent (Lenski 1966:219); and in seventeenth-century France it was about 1.5 percent (Soboul 1974:35).

Despite its small numbers, it did hold most of the wealth. For example, during the thirteenth century, the king of England had an income about 24,000 times greater than the average peasant (Lenski 1966:212). In France during the sixteenth century it is estimated that the nobility—accounting for 1.5 percent of the population, remember—owned 20 percent of the land (Soboul 1974:35). Overall, from his review of many agrarian societies, Lenski (1966:228) estimates that the ruler and his or her governing class usually accounted for about 2 percent of the population, but received about one-half of *all* income.

In contrast with the great wealth of the first and second estates, commoners most often lived in extreme poverty. There were merchants and artisans who did well, and sometimes equaled the nobility in wealth. But for the vast majority life was harsh. We have the following description compiled by Lenski (1966:271):

. . .the diet of the average peasant consisted of little more than the following: a hunk of bread and a mug of ale in the morning; a lump of cheese and bread with perhaps an onion or two to flavor it, and more ale at noon; a thick soup or pottage followed by bread and cheese at the main meal in the evening. Meat was rare, and the ale was usually thin. Household furniture consisted of a few stools, a table, and a chest to hold the best clothes and other treasured possessions. Beds were uncommon and most peasants simply slept on earthen floors covered with straw. Other household possessions were apparently limited to cooking utensils.

For the most part, however, we know relatively little about the common people of Europe during this time. Written records tell us much about religious and secular elites, but more often than not ignore the common people.[2] We do have a remarkable account compiled by Le Roy Ladurie (1978) of one French village, Montaillou, in the fourteenth century, however. Le Roy Ladurie obtained his information from a forgotten Vatican record of an Inquisition that describes in detail the lifestyle, beliefs, and activities of most of the common people in this village of about 200 people.

The diet and possessions of the Montaillou villagers were similar to, but somewhat better than, those described by Lenski above (Le Roy Ladurie 1978:53). Often neglected, however, is the fact that the people of a small village such as Montaillou were themselves stratified, although the inequalities among them were not great. And the record shows that in their daily lives it was stratification within the village of commoners that received most of their attention. It is estimated that there was a wealth difference (primarily in private land) of about 50 to 1 between the wealthiest family and the poorest. The average well-to-do family might own from eight to ten hectares of land, while the poorest had one or two hectares, if any (Le Roy Ladurie 1978:53). What they had to eat, the houses in which they lived, and their daily labor, however, differed only in small details.

Most important for these people was a family system of status ranking. There were strong rivalries for status and family honor, only to some degree centered around material possessions. At times these family rivalries could reach extreme levels. For example, at one point some families were using the Church Inquisition as a means of reducing the status and property of competing families (Le Roy Ladurie 1978:60). Most often, however, family conflicts were not so great. In fact, more common was an atmosphere of cooperation and respect among families—a cooperative spirit resulting in help when needed in the face of life tragedies.

We noted that the important centers of power were usually far away from the small villages of this time, but these centers of power did have representatives in the villages. The representative of the nobility was the bayle (or bailiff), who collected rents, taxes, and other manorial dues; the representative of the first estate was the parish priest, whose duty was to force loyalty to the Church. In stable periods these representatives brought only an accepted burden. Thus, although the life chances of these common people were highly influenced by these important centers of power, they could usually be ignored or tolerated.

But these centers of power were not always far away. The people of Montaillou lived in a time of great inequalities of power as well as wealth. The nobility and religious leaders were obligated by tradition and sometimes law to respect the limited rights and property of the common people, but these elites in large measure defined the traditions and established the laws. Moreover, given the power and wealth of these elites, they could easily ignore the law.

Especially during "hard" times for the nobility or governing class, when it needed more money, it could simply tax commoners more heavily or demand more of the surplus production. Taxes could, and often were, placed on about anything—salt, household goods, livestock, bread and other foods. There was usually a system of tax farming whereby someone wealthy enough to pay for appointment to the office of tax collector could collect taxes from villages, keeping varying amounts above the prescribed tax. Also, as happened from time to time, people were simply pushed off the land in times of change and left with nothing. Lefebvre (1973:14) estimates that during 1788 in France, for example, 10 percent of the total rural population was reduced to begging because of land seizures.

This, for the most part, was the power of the secular elites during the feudal period. The people of Montaillou during the fourteenth century lived at a time when the demands of the king and nobility were not so pressing. They paid their traditional taxes and rents with enough left over to live. They were not, however, as fortunate in their relationship to the Church. The Catholic Church at the time was "concerned" by the many new religious ideas spreading among the common people.

As the reason for the detailed report on Montaillou indicates, the people of this village were subject to an Inquisition. There were 114 people from this village and surrounding areas accused as heretics, 94 of whom actually appeared before the Inquisition. "When the trials were over, various penalties were inflicted: imprisonment of varying degrees of strictness, the wearing of the yellow cross, pilgrimages and confiscation of goods" (Le Roy Ladurie 1978:xvii). Five were burned at the stake. And many of those who were imprisoned, if they came back to Montaillou, found they had nothing left. Such was the power of the Church, which must be added to the power of the state and nobility over the lives of common people during the feudal period in Europe.

The Fall of Feudalism and the Rise of Industrial Societies

The feudal system's fall throughout most of the world has been one of the most intensely studied subjects in the social sciences. Many books by early sociologists were devoted to the subject, and many others were concerned with what was emerging out of the ruins of feudal systems. Interest remains at a high level today. With all that has been written on the subject, we know that it was a complex process of change that varied somewhat from nation to nation.

Most simply, however, the forces of change that were stimulated when human beings first settled down to more stable agricultural villages between 5,000 and 10,000 years ago gradually reached another stage—first in Europe, about the fifteenth and sixteenth centuries. The cycle of better agricultural methods producing an ever-greater surplus, freeing more and more people from the land to expand the level of technology further, had continued (Chirot 1984; 1986). By the sixteenth century in Europe a new industrial system of production was taking root that was to change the nature of society perhaps more rapidly than ever before.

The drama of change varied somewhat from society to society. But in most three principal actors were thrown into conflict by these changes. These three consisted of (1) the old nobility or aristocracy whose profit and influence ultimately depended on land ownership, (2) the political elite whose position came with the large state bureaucracy that (as we have seen) originally developed to protect the interests of the nobility, and (3) a new and increasingly powerful merchant class that depended on the emerging industrial system of production (Bendix 1978). The common people—the craft workers, peasants, bakers, and so on—also played a part in this drama of change. But their role was usually that of pawns—people who, because of their misery in the face of change, rioted, rebelled, or in other ways contributed to a national crisis that was then played out by the three principal actors seeking to turn the crisis to their advantage.

In places like China and India the change came more slowly. A principal reason for this lack of change (until later), it is argued, is that in China and India the form of agricultural production was not exactly feudalism, but an Asiatic mode of production (Mandel 1971; Krader 1975). As with late feudalism, a state structure with powerful political elites developed. However, with the Asiatic mode of production these political elites developed much earlier (with the greater importance of a political elite to oversee irrigation projects and other collective agricultural needs) and grew more powerful.

Also, because land was less often privately owned, and new urban merchants were more dominated by political elites, the power of political elites was not challenged by wealthy landowners or a new merchant class. Thus, the Asiatic mode of production was more stable, lasted longer, and retarded industrialization. But the Asiatic mode of production was eventually forced into change through international conflict with new industrial societies.

The story of these changes is not complete unless we recognize that by the sixteenth century a world economic system was developing that increasingly brought the more powerful nations into conflict in a world economy, often over the question of which powerful nation would exploit which of the less developed nations or regions as colonies (Wallerstein 1974, 1980, 1989; Chirot 1986). As we will see in more detail in our last chapter on this world system, Portugal and then Spain were the first to send many ships all over the world to exploit the riches, cheap labor, and resources of these other world regions. But neither Spain nor Portugal was able to become capitalist industrial powers because of their outdated political systems.

The Netherlands was the first country to become a dominant nation in this modern world system, in large part because the Dutch were the first to have a bourgeois revolution in the 1560s that overthrew the outdated state. It was the old political system dominated by the old landed nobility which prevented the new merchant class from becoming stronger through commerce. England also came to be a dominant nation in the modern world system after the decline of the Dutch because the British landed nobility lost political power as well. In England, however, it was more of a gradual process of a shift from dominance by the landed nobility to dominance by the new merchant class. This occurred because the nobility in England was weaker, unable to prevent the expansion of industrial commerce at its expense, and also sometimes joined the merchant activity.

In other nations such as France and Germany the old nobility was stronger for a longer period of time (Bendix 1978; Schama 1989). Here, feudal interests of the landed nobility were protected by the state—until an economic crisis provoked by international competition became extreme. The economic and political crisis resulted in violent revolution and the emergence of a merchant class (or bourgeoisie) as the class of dominance.

In societies that advanced less rapidly, such as China (with an Asiatic mode of production) and Russia, the economic and political crisis, when it came, followed a somewhat different line. In these nations, the state and the merchant class were both too weak in the face of dominance from the nations (in the world economic system) that had moved to the industrial stage earlier. What happened in these more slowly developing nations was that authoritarian state bureaucracies emerged out of violent revolution, leading to state socialism. (See Moore 1966, and Skocpol 1979, for the best descriptions of the above process of change.)

Of most concern for us is that new industrial societies developed, ranging from capitalist to socialist, with all kinds of mixtures in between. In all these societies, new elites emerged with new bases of power. The differences among these new societies should not be overstressed. Despite differences in political ideology, degrees of democracy, and (to some extent) levels of inequality and social mobility, the new industrial technology and social organization that emerged placed general limits on the type of stratification system that could exist.

THE REDUCTION OF INEQUALITY
WITH INDUSTRIAL SOCIETIES

The history of human societies has been shown to be one of increasing inequalities. We moved from relative equality in hunting and gathering societies, or primitive communalism, to very high levels of inequality in advanced agrarian societies. The life of the common people throughout this progression to advanced agrarian societies improved only slightly, if at all, whereas the wealth and power of elites multiplied rapidly.

With mature industrial societies the trend has been altered. After an initial period of increase in inequalities at the beginning of industrialization for most countries, *inequalities have been reduced.* As we have seen in Chapter 2, a high level of inequality of all types remains. However, the general population has finally achieved some benefits from revolution connected to the expanding output of ever more advanced systems of economic production. And although elites in relatively democratic industrial societies may have lost some of the commanding political power once held by elites in earlier societies, the material advances of the general population have *not* come at the expense of the elites. In other words, as is roughly indicated in Figure 3-1, in industrial societies the lot of the masses has generally improved, but so has that of elites. In fact, it can be said that the economic position of elites in industrial societies has improved in part because that of the masses has also improved. This is not to say that all industrial societies have equally low levels of inequality. Nor is this to say that inequality will not again increase, as it has been doing in the United States in recent years. But compared to preindustrial societies, inequality is generally much lower in industrial societies (Breedlove and Nolan 1988).

Briefly, we can list some of the reasons for this change in the historical trend of growing inequality. All these factors may not be of equal importance and, no doubt, there can be disagreement on which are more important. But all have clearly had a significant impact on the level of inequality in industrial societies (see Lenski 1966:313–318).

1 One of the major characteristics of industrial societies is the complexity of the machine and organizational technology. Elites have found themselves in a position of ignorance about much of this technology. This is because no individual or even small group of individuals can possess the knowledge needed to run the vast industrial enterprise. Thus, elites have had to make concessions to their authority for the sake of efficiency, and these concessions have re-

FIGURE 3-1
The progression of inequality in human societies.

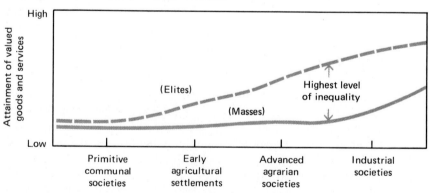

sulted in greater rewards for subordinates. Elites in the economy *do* have final authority, but they have had to delegate at least part of that authority with respect to technical details.

2 Allowing lower classes more of the economic surplus has increased productivity. This is partly because a working class that is less hostile because of increasing personal benefits from the expanding industrial output will be less likely to strike, to stage slowdowns, and to indulge in industrial sabotage. Also, with a rapidly expanding industrial output, if wages were kept on a subsistence level there would be no market for the increase in industrial goods. In short, with a general population having no money to buy goods above the basic necessities of life, increased profits for elites would be difficult.

3 A rapid increase in wealth and material goods soon reaches a level of marginal utility. With an income of several million dollars, another million brings less value. As Lenski (1966:315) writes, "Because elites have multiple goals, and are not concerned with maximizing material rewards alone, they may be willing to make certain economic concessions in a highly productive and expanding economy." These concessions may reduce the dangers of revolution and win some measure of respect from the lower classes.

4 Also important is the reduced rate of population growth in industrial societies, especially for the lower classes. In previous societies, as production increased, so did the population. With the population growing at a rate that closely equaled the increase in production, there was only enough produced to support this growing population without reducing the proportion going to elites. But with production increasing along with a more stable population, there is much more to divide among both the elites and the masses.

5 In the first point it was noted that the increasing complexity of industry has forced elites into a greater reliance on technical experts. But throughout the industrial system much more knowledge and skill is required. A poor and ignorant class of peasants would not be useful in today's industrial society. Again, concessions must be made to ensure a more skilled work force.

6 The spread of a more egalitarian ideology and democratic systems have generally followed industrialization and revolution. In large part, this is because the new class of merchants that replaced the powerful agrarian nobility at the end of feudalism did so only with the help of the masses. In order to ensure the support of the masses in these revolutions, it was necessary to make democratic political concessions. And with at least some voice in the new industrial state, the general population has been able to receive other concessions in the level of inequality.

7 With increasing international conflict and the development of total war, elites could not afford to lose the allegiance of the population. To place one's life in jeopardy for a nation requires a belief that the nation is worth fighting for. Slaves may go to battle, but they may also flee if the chance arises. We have seen how the general population in the late Roman Empire put up little or no resistance to nomadic invaders. The Roman Empire had lost the allegiance of its people in the face of extreme inequalities and exploitation. So concessions had to be made in order for industrial societies to survive in growing international conflicts that often resulted in total war.

8 Finally, while the level of inequality within industrial nations is lower, worldwide inequality is growing rapidly (Nolan 1983a, 1983b; Chirot 1986; Breedlove and Nolan 1988). It may well be that the two are, in fact, related. The division of labor is becoming worldwide with more of the lowest-paying jobs occurring in the less developed nations, while advanced industrial societies benefit from more high tech and higher-paying jobs, and a higher standard of living made possible by the exploitation of cheap Third World labor and resources (Wright and Martin 1987).

The above list of factors that have helped retard the historical trend in inequality is not exhaustive, but it includes the factors generally cited as being among the most important. Whether or not the drop in the level of inequality with industrial societies is, in fact, a trend or is simply a one-time occurrence cannot be answered with any accuracy. We do know that income and wealth inequalities in the United States during this century have gone up and down, and are currently increasing again. And though the United States has the highest level of income inequality of all industrial nations, inequality in the United States is lower than in most preindustrial and developing nations.

It may be that only with some significantly new type of society emerging from present industrial societies will we be able to understand the nature of any trend toward more or less inequality. Many of today's industrial societies are no doubt different in some respects from their earliest forms. Since the beginnings of industrial societies we find further expansion of white-collar labor, a rapidly growing public sector, a growing service economy, more social services, the increased importance of technical knowledge in the production of goods and services, and, as will be examined in detail later, the growing dominance of big industrial firms not so easily controlled by wealthy capitalist families. These changes have led some to announce the arrival of advanced industrial or postindustrial societies (Galbraith 1971; Bell 1976). But with the exception of the last change noted, the overall stratification system has changed very little in industrial nations (Giddens 1973; Miller 1975). And it could very well be that the reduction of middle-paying jobs in the United States and the growth of lower-paying jobs producing more inequality in the past decade and a half is a trend other industrial nations may follow, which is in contrast to the above images of a "postindustrial" society.

CONCLUSION: THE HISTORY OF INEQUALITY

The primary task of this chapter has been to provide the reader with a general idea of what existed before with respect to inequality and social stratification. Of course, our outline of history has been more than descriptive. As with *any* historical presentation, ours has been guided by some general theoretical assumptions. With the outline of history behind us, we can now consider more fully the conflict perspective that has guided our review of history.

The theoretical perspective in this chapter follows to some degree that of Gerhard Lenski (1966), who has reviewed the history of stratification in much more detail than space has allowed here. What Lenski generally found is that the level of inequality in a society is related to (1) the *level of technology* and (2) the *amount of surplus goods* produced by that society. These two factors are usually interrelated. The higher the level of technology, the greater the amount of surplus goods and services produced. From these interrelated factors Lenski (1966:46) predicts that (1) "in the simplest societies, or those which are technologically most primitive, the goods and services available will be distributed wholly, or largely, on the basis of need," whereas (2) "with technological advance, an increasing proportion of the goods and services available to a society will be distributed on the basis of power."

With a low level of technology and, thus, little or no surplus, no one will have the power to dominate the resources of the society. A general level of equality will exist. As technology advances and more surplus is produced, the elites, freed from everyday production, will find ways of dominating the surplus of goods, giving them power over others as well as a greater share of the surplus. The level of inequality generally increases with the advance of technology.[3]

Our review of history has more or less conformed to Lenski's general findings. In early hunting and gathering societies the surplus production of food and other goods was generally low. Along with this, the degree of inequality was also low. With the emergence of agricultural methods of food production the stage was set for ever-increasing levels of inequality. A significant degree of inequality first became widespread in early agricultural settlements about 10,000 years ago. The expansion and growth of these settlements into large civilizations occurred about 6,000 years ago. With more advanced methods of food production we found a further jump in the level of inequality. The highest levels of inequality were then attained with more advanced agrarian societies a few thousand years later. Only since the industrial revolution has the trend reversed somewhat (for the reasons listed at the close of our last section).

A further point about Lenski's perspective and the historical outline presented above is in order. There is no simple path of social evolution that all societies have followed or will follow. There is only a very rough tendency toward ever more complex and technologically advanced societies. Along the way, because of a particular physical, social, and cultural environment, some societies change (or advance) while others do not.[4] This goes almost without saying, given the diversity of cultures in the world today.

Also, when societies change, they do not change according to one established pattern because of a particular physical, social, and cultural environment in which they find themselves. A simple linear model of social evolution, one that sees all societies following a similar path of development, must be rejected (Portes 1976). This is especially true with respect to economic development. For example, as we will see in Chapter 15, on world stratification, unlike the already developed nations, undeveloped and developing nations today must contend with an international system of economic power that often negatively affects their chances of becoming more advanced economically.

The outline of history presented here does, however, provide a general picture of how inequality came to be a pervasive aspect of most human societies. With it we can understand the conflict that usually lies behind systems of social stratification. Inequality doesn't always result in exploitation; nor does social stratification always serve to benefit only the rich and powerful. As we will see, a functional theory of social stratification is able to show that systems of social stratification are mechanisms that help societies solve many problems of survival and advancement. Despite this functional aspect of stratification, the conflict perspective taken here suggests that those most advantaged in a society wish to remain so advantaged, while those below would most often prefer to trade places with the people at the top. In other words, at the root of social stratification, as this review of history has shown, is conflict.

In fact, *the existence of inequality and conflict over scarce resources is what makes social stratification necessary.* Without a system of social stratification we would find perpetual overt conflict and aggression over the question of how scarce resources are to be distributed. Once a system of social stratification is firmly established, however, "little contest need take place concerning the sharing of resources. The contest has already taken place and has been settled—at least for a time" (van der Berghe 1978:54). In other words, the questions of who gets what, and why, have been answered. But, as our historical review of inequality suggests, we must add—"at least for a time."

NOTES

1 Following Lenski's (1966) description of hunting and gathering societies, we are saying that rewards (in this case status) are distributed on the basis of functional contribution to the group. In later types of societies, the concentration of power and wealth in the hands of a few can result in ever-greater rewards going to this small group irrespective of its contribution to the common good. As for the lower status of women in hunting and gathering or primitive communal societies, it is *not* being argued that the child rearing and food gathering done by women were not functional for group survival. But two factors led to lower status with these tasks: (1) They were not tasks that generally required scarce abilities and (2) although one mother may have been especially skilled at caring for children, the payoff would not be seen until the children grew up. With hunting, a rare ability in bringing back meat was more obvious.

2 The list of exceptions to this neglect of the history of common people, however, is growing longer in recent years. This is especially the case among French historians of social history, such as Le Roy Ladurie (1978; 1979), who examine the conditions of common people and their lifestyles through the ages. Another excellent example of

this new work is *A History of Private Life,* a three-volume collection of articles under the general editorship of Philippe Ariès and Georges Duby. This work covers the early Roman Empire to the end of the feudal period in Europe (Veyne 1987; Duby 1988; Chartier 1989).

3 It should be clear that the term *technology* is being used in a very broad sense. By technology we mean everything from stone tools to modern machines, and even the knowledge of various methods of food gathering and other types of production.

4 The review of the history of inequality presented in this chapter has stressed material variables (such as technology) over culture or values in shaping the basic nature of societies and social change. We are *not* suggesting that these material variables explain everything, or that they do not combine with culture and values for specific outcomes. The level of inequality, the power of elites, how inequality is maintained, among many other aspects of society, are all influenced by political ideology, religion, family systems, or, more generally, culture. But in such a general review of human societies as the one presented here, the important factors that affect social organization most widely must be the dominant focus. In a study of 330 existing societies of varying types, Heise, Lenski, and Wardwell (1976) have found that material variables (such as level and type of technology) explain much more of the other characteristics of these societies than values or cultural differences do.

PART TWO

EXPLANATIONS OF SOCIAL STRATIFICATION: STRATIFICATION THEORIES

SOCIAL STRATIFICATION THEORY: EARLY STATEMENTS

From the earliest writings on the human condition we find an interest in inequality and social divisions. Whatever the reason—guilt, curiosity, anger, or justification—the topic has often been one of lively concern. "Some of the earliest records of thought on this subject are found in the writings of the early Hebrew prophets who lived approximately 800 years before Christ. In the writings of such men as Amos, Micah, and Isaiah we find repeated denunciations of the rich and powerful members of society" (Lenski 1966:3). Aristotle as well had much to say about inequality; but for him there was no criticism of this "natural condition." As he wrote in *Politics,* about 350 B.C. (see Dahrendorf 1968:153):

> It is thus clear that there are *by nature* free men and slaves, and that servitude is agreeable and just for the latter. . . . Equally, the relation of the male to the female is *by nature* such that one is superior and the other is dominated. . . .

During the seventeenth and especially eighteenth century the nature and causes of social inequality were the subject of even more lively debate. It was during the Age of Enlightenment that the old inequalities of the feudal period were attacked by such philosophers as Locke, Rousseau, and Montesquieu. Somewhat later, after revolutionary movements had taken their toll on many feudal inequalities, nineteenth-century philosophers such as Bonald, Maistre, and Saint-Simon further developed systematic theories of society, theories in which the nature of human inequalities played a central role (see Zeitlin 1968; Strasser 1976). A science of society emerged from the work of these philosophers. And as with these earlier philosophers, the nature of human inequalities provided the central question for the new science called sociology (Dahrendorf 1968:152).

In this chapter we will examine some of the earliest sociological thought on social stratification. For our purpose—which is to understand the foundations of modern thinking on the subject—the works of Karl Marx, Max Weber, and Émile Durkheim are most important. Beginning with Marx, we will examine the major assumptions behind these theories, as well as show the roots of major contemporary theories of social stratification to be explored in Chapter 5. With each of the three giants from sociology's classical period we will focus also on some key concepts found in their work that have contributed most to our understanding of modern stratification systems.

COMPETING PARADIGMS IN THE STUDY OF SOCIAL STRATIFICATION

Contrary to the idealized view of scientific methods and theory, a scientist's view of the subject matter and the construction of theory are not based simply on a cold calculation of available empirical data. Rather, scientists must, to some degree, work from a set of prescientific and untested assumptions about the phenomena under study. This is true for physical science no less than for social science. As Albert Einstein put it, "For the creation of a theory the mere collection of recorded phenomena never suffices—there must always be added a free invention of the human mind that attacks the heart of the matter" (quoted in Dukas and Hoffman 1979:24–25). At times Einstein went further by *rejecting* the idea that ". . . facts by themselves can and should yield scientific knowledge without the free conceptual construction" (quoted in Clark 1971:63). We can call the general images of reality (which shape more specific theories) *paradigms,* and the assumptions about reality within paradigms can be called *paradigm assumptions.*[1]

Before we consider the most important theories of social stratification in this chapter and the next, it will be useful to begin with a brief examination of conflicting paradigms in the study of social stratification. But two points of caution must first be made:

1 Although we will see that values and politically related assumptions at times have shaped or influenced theories of social stratification, we do *not* find only political debates in the study of social stratification. There is a reality out there, however complex and many-sided it may be, that these theories are struggling to understand. Just as the physical scientist must attempt to understand his or her subject matter by making certain untested or even untestable assumptions, as Kuhn's (1970) work clearly shows, so must the social scientist.[2]

2 Related to this, at the level of general theory or paradigms, we cannot ask whether a paradigm is right or wrong, true or false. Rather, we must ask whether a paradigm is useful or less useful in answering specific questions about the subject matter. All of the paradigms and general theories outlined below lead us to some important insights about the nature of social stratification. But, depending on the questions asked, some may be more useful than others. As will be seen throughout the remainder of this book, if in the study of social stratification we are most concerned with the question of who gets what, and why, it is increasingly recognized in sociology that some type of conflict theory will be able to supply the most useful answers.

Since the earliest years of sociology there have been two main macro level general theories or paradigms which have influenced the development of theories of social stratification. In comparing these two general theories of society we must begin by recognizing the main task of what can be called *functional* and *conflict* theories of society. They are both attempts at answering the most basic question in sociology—"How is society possible?" In other words, with a mass of people in large industrial societies, how is it that most people obey the rules most of the time? How is it that we can have orderly interaction without perpetual disruptive conflict between differing interest groups? From the works of several sociologists (see Dahrendorf 1959; van den Berghe 1963; Horton 1966; Cohen 1968) we can select three main model assumptions found to diverge between functional and conflict paradigms.

1 Functional theorists maintain that society is held together primarily by a general consensus over the major values and norms in the society. People tend to obey the rules because through a long socialization process they have come to accept these rules, so for the most part they live by them. Conflict theorists, on the other hand, maintain that society is held together in the face of conflicting interests because either (a) one group in the society has the power to enforce the rules (and thus make subordinate groups follow rules that may primarily serve the interests of the subordinate group) or (b) there are so many overlapping and divided interest groups that individuals or groups must learn to cooperate. The overall argument made by conflict theorists, however, is that through the structure of conflict in society, order can be maintained in one of these two ways.

2 One reason for the above divergent model assumptions between functional and conflict theorists is that whereas functional theorists tend to focus more on societies as holistic systems (much like biological organisms), conflict theorists tend to focus on parts and processes within what we call societies.

3 It follows from this organic analogy that functional theorists tend to view societies as social systems with specific needs of their own that must be met if the societies are to function properly, and thus survive. Conflict theorists, on the other hand, view societies as settings within which various groups with differing interests interact and compete.

These three sets of divergent assumptions represent two competing models of society that attempt to answer the most basic question of how social order is possible. They are, as we defined paradigms, differing images of the subject matter (society), just as the physicist has an image of his or her subject matter (for example, an Einsteinian image of the universe). These images are not right or wrong, but simply more or less useful in answering specific questions about the subject matter.

Our typology of stratification paradigms is constructed by combining two divergent sets of paradigm assumptions. One set of assumptions comes from those discussed above separating functional and conflict images or models of society. The other set of three assumptions is taken from Lenski's (1966) discussion of conservative and radical value assumptions on social stratification, using more politically neutral terms—what we will refer to as *critical* and *uncritical* value assumptions. Table 4-1 summarizes these two sets of model and value assumptions. Combining these gives us a four-cell typology (Table 4-2) similar to one suggested by Strasser (1976). In the first cell we have what can be called a *critical-order* paradigm; in the second, an *uncritical-order* paradigm; in the third, a *critical-conflict* paradigm; and in the fourth, an *uncritical-conflict* paradigm.

The payoff in constructing such a typology as presented in Table 4-2 is in the understanding or clarification it provides. With this typology we can group specific theories of social stratification having similar properties or explanations. The reason for these similarities is that they share some basic paradigm assumptions about the nature of society and social inequality. The use of such a typology is *not* an excuse for ignoring the finer points of each theory (as they will be presented in this chapter and the next), but a method for furthering a

TABLE 4-1
VALUE AND MODEL ASSUMPTIONS IN SOCIAL
STRATIFICATION PARADIGMS

Value assumptions	
Critical	**Uncritical**
1. Inequality not inevitable (at least to present degrees)	1. Inequality inevitable (little or no criticism)
2. Optimistic view of human nature	2. Distrust of human nature
3. Better, more just, societies the goal of social science	3. Sociology should be value free
Model assumptions	
Conflict	**Order**
1. Society held together by conflict and unequal power	1. Society held together by consensus (norms and values)
2. Focus on parts and processes within the society	2. Holistic view of society
3. Society a setting for struggles between classes or interest groups	3. Focus on a social system with needs of its own

TABLE 4-2
A TYPOLOGY OF SOCIAL STRATIFICATION PARADIGMS

		Value assumptions	
		Critical	Uncritical
Model of Society	Order	Critical-order paradigm	Uncritical-order paradigm Functional theory (Durkheim)*
	Conflict	Critical-conflict paradigm Ruling class theory (Marx)	Uncritical-conflict paradigm Power conflict theory (Weber)

*The placement of specific theorists will be discussed in Chapter 5.
Source: Adapted from Hermann Strasser (1976).

better understanding. Let us now proceed by examining the logic of the paradigms in explaining the nature of social stratification.

We must begin by noting that the first cell of our typology (Table 4-2) remains empty with respect to *recent* theories of social stratification (see Strasser 1976). Although a number of eighteenth- and nineteenth-century theorists can be described as working from a *critical-order* paradigm (such as de Bonald and de Maistre; see Strasser 1976), the most prominent contemporary theories are grouped around the three remaining cells.[3]

In the second cell of the typology we can describe a general *uncritical-order* paradigm. This label indicates a combination of uncritical value assumptions (little or no criticism of the status quo) and an order model of society (Table 4-1). With respect to social stratification, the logic of the assumptions within this paradigm suggests that present inequalities are inevitable because (1) human nature is basically selfish and/or (2) the social system requires inequalities to meet some of its basic needs.

The second point is to suggest that social inequality or social stratification serves some function for the health and well-being of the total society—such as ensuring that the most talented people are motivated to fill the most important positions in the society. Another major tenet of this uncritical-order paradigm is that because human nature is not to be trusted, the needs of society, if it is to survive, require some restraining mechanisms. These mechanisms are usually found with a socialization process and an ongoing legitimation process that maintain consensus around major norms and values in the society. These norms and values justify the existing inequalities as necessary for a society's health and survival, thus preventing those with fewer rewards from threatening the system. The elites must also be restrained, lest they use their favored positions for individual greed.

Last, theorists working within this paradigm tend to view the task of social science as that of making a value-free analysis of society, rather than of attempting to understand how societies can be changed for the better. However, there is a tendency to be at least *relatively* supportive of the status quo, because given selfish human nature and the needs of society, a more equal society (in their view) is unlikely. As we will discuss later, what is commonly called a *functional* theory of social stratification is located within this cell of our typology.

In the bottom right cell of our typology we find an *uncritical-conflict* paradigm of social stratification. This paradigm shares with the uncritical-order paradigm a distrust of human nature and an assumption that inequalities are in large measure inevitable. In one major variant of this paradigm, because society is assumed to be a setting for conflicting interests, it is the power of one group over others that maintains social order. Given the view of human nature inherent in this paradigm, when one group is able to achieve a dominant position in the society, this group will tend to use that position to serve selfish interests.[4]

In addition, as with the uncritical-order paradigm, theorists in an uncritical-conflict paradigm tend to view the task of social science as that of making a value-free analysis of society in order to uncover basic social laws, rather than of attempting to promote social change. From their perspective, a society without some form of class conflict is viewed as impossible, and a more equal or just society is rejected. As will be discussed later, specific theories within this uncritical-conflict paradigm can most commonly be referred to as power conflict theories, although other varieties will be examined.

In the lower left cell of our typology we find what can be called a *critical-conflict* paradigm. This paradigm shares with the uncritical-conflict paradigm an image or model of society that considers conflict and power as the key to social order (at least in present societies). The power of one group—such as an upper class or a power elite—leads to social order. A powerful group is usually able to coerce or manipulate subordinate classes (through force, threat of force, withholding of jobs, or other means) because of the dominant group's influence over basic institutions in the society (such as the economy, government, courts, and police).

But the critical-conflict paradigm combines this conflict model of society with critical value assumptions. Although theorists working under an uncritical-conflict paradigm view power, conflict, and exploitation in much the same way, they are less critical of this perceived status quo. Theorists from an uncritical-conflict paradigm are more accepting of these conditions, not necessarily because they are unsympathetic toward the lower class, but because, given their assumptions about human nature and the inevitability of inequalities, they do not foresee that more just and equitable societies are possible.

Critical-conflict theorists, on the other hand, are more optimistic. Because they view human nature as more altruistic, cooperative, and unselfish, or perhaps simply more flexible (meaning that human beings can be either selfish or unselfish, depending on factors outside themselves), they believe that more equal and humane societies are possible. But if they agree with power conflict or critical-conflict theorists about present social conditions of inequality and exploitation, how do they explain these conditions?

Uncritical-conflict theorists are distrustful of human nature, whereas critical-conflict theorists are distrustful of *restraining social institutions*. According to them, the historical development of present social institutions shapes human behavior in such a way as to lead to exploitation by the powerful. In other words, the role people must play under a particular set of social institutions requires the exploitation. If this historical stage of social development is altered, the new set of social institutions can lead to basically different social relations.

Critical-conflict theorists are, as the label implies, more critical of the status quo because their value assumptions lead them to be more optimistic about future social conditions. And it follows that they are more likely to maintain that the task of social science is to understand present society so as to be able to alter it. Their work is often more historically oriented than that of other theorists. They believe that by examining the historical progression or evaluation of human societies we can better understand how we arrived at our present predicament, and, thus, how we can change the status quo.

Within the critical-conflict paradigm we have just outlined, the most prominent group of theorists can be described as Marxists. For them it is the capitalist *system* and its characteristics that shape present conditions of exploitation and inequality. Clearly, not all theorists working within this critical-conflict paradigm can be described as Marxists. Theorists like C. Wright Mills (1956) and G. William Domhoff (1967, 1970) are equally critical of present social, political, and economic institutions, but their explanations of present social arrangements are not based on Marxian terms; nor do they see a social ideal in a communist state.

We stress that this typology is a simplification. Theories can never be placed into neat either-or categories represented by a dichotomy. For example, with respect to the critical versus uncritical value assumptions described in the typology (Table 4-1), we are not suggesting that all theories are *totally* critical or uncritical of such conditions as inequality. We can speak more accurately of *degrees* of criticism. Many theorists within the uncritical side of the typology may believe that poverty or the extent of inequality found in the society is deplorable. But their criticisms of this situation are less extensive and/or their suggested solutions are less drastic than those of theorists on the critical side of the typology. In essence, this dimension of critical versus uncritical may be viewed as a continuum, with theories most accurately located at different points along the continuum.

THE MARXIAN HERITAGE IN SOCIAL STRATIFICATION: THE DEVELOPMENT OF A CRITICAL-CONFLICT PARADIGM

Our examination of three giants in the development of modern thinking on social stratification will begin with Karl Marx, not simply because Marx was the earliest of the three writers, but also because his works have had the greatest impact throughout the world. Marx's ideas were most influential in early European social science where, as we will see, both Weber and Durkheim in part constructed their theories in reaction to Marx's earlier works. But Marx's influence has been increasingly felt in the United States as well (see Mullins 1973:273), where Marx's general perspective and predictions about some aspects of advanced capitalist societies are becoming more respected today.[5]

Several historians of social thought (see Zeitlin 1968; Gouldner 1970; Giddens 1973; Strasser 1976) have traced the development of modern sociological theory from Saint-Simon, whose ideas date back to the early 1800s. The seeds for both conflict and functional theories were contained in Saint-Simon's works. Durkheim was a principal figure who transferred Saint-Simon's ideas into Western academic sociology in the form of an uncritical-order paradigm. But it was Marx who transferred these ideas into a critical-conflict paradigm. Like perhaps all great theories, Marx's ideas had many predecessors (see Berlin 1963:129). And, clearly, Saint-Simon's view of class conflict and exploitation influenced Marx (Berlin 1963:74–75). With Marx, however, these ideas matured into a complex, critical explanation of class and of class domination as an historical force in the development of human societies.

We need only comment briefly on some of the underlying paradigm assumptions in Marx's work, for these will be evident in the more detailed exploration of his theory that follows. Any examination of Marx's many writings shows that at the base of human societies (at least until the "final" stage of communism) he saw class conflict and domination. Marx's perspective was one of dynamics and change, in contrast to the static and holistic perspective of early functionalists such as Durkheim. In Marx's view, social order exists because one class (the dominant class) is favored by a specific stage of economic development and is, thus, able to maintain social order through its power over the lower classes.

With respect to Marx's value assumptions, he saw the tasks of social science as not only to understand society, but also to change it. He was critical of existing inequalities, conflicts, and exploitation, and believed these conditions could, or more strongly *would,* be changed. Unlike an uncritical-conflict theorist like Weber, Marx was an optimist. He saw the root of these conditions of inequality and exploitation in social structures that had been, and would continue to be, subject to change. These conditions were *not,* according to Marx, explained by "selfish human nature"; "A positive image of man, of what man might come to be, lies under every line of his analysis of what he held to be an inhuman society" (Mills 1962:25). Thus, Marx anticipated more humane social conditions, and saw his task as furthering social change and an objective understanding of the present (see Strasser 1976:108).

Karl Marx was born in Trier, Germany, in 1818. His family lived in relatively comfortable economic conditions, in contrast to Marx's later years of life in London. His father, Heinrich Marx, was a respected lawyer and government servant who was "closely connected with the Rhineland liberal movement'' (McLellan 1973:7; for another interesting biography of Marx, see Berlin 1963). Karl Marx attended the universities of Bonn and Berlin (beginning in 1835), and finished a doctorate of philosophy in 1841. After completing a Ph.D., however, Marx could not find employment in a university, so he turned to journalism, editing several newspapers, first in Cologne and later in Paris.

During the 1840s most of Europe was in political turmoil. Many socialist movements were active, especially in Germany and France, where Marx spent these years. Although not exactly a political activist in the physical sense of participating in street battles of the times, Marx nonetheless supported many of these movements through his journalism. His vocal editorship of newspapers in Germany and France led to trouble with political authorities. He was first deported from Germany to France. Then, after the massive rebellion in 1848 in Paris, he was forced by political authorities back to Germany. But again he was not welcome in Germany, and in 1849 he finally found a home in London.

Marx spent most of his remaining years in London, in desperate poverty because of his inability to find stable work. His family existed through his part-time employment as a newspaper correspondent (he wrote many articles for the *New York Herald Tribune*) and many contributions from his friend and collaborator Friedrich Engels (a wealthy capitalist). Still, his family lived in extreme poverty, often without adequate food, clothing, or medical care. (The death of one of his children is attributed to the family's lack of money to pay a doctor.) The poverty he saw around him and the general conditions of poverty and worker exploitation in England at the time no doubt contributed to his view of capitalism.

Despite his poverty, or perhaps because of it, Marx found time in London to research and write his most important works. He spent most of his days, usually from 9 A.M. to 7 P.M., reading and writing in the British Museum. It was during this time that he completed his three-volume *Capital* and notes for another work that was more than 1,000 pages long, *The Grundrisse,* as well as many other books. During this time Marx also helped establish the Communist International, an organization important in bringing together many communist and socialist leaders throughout the world and shaping the future of communism.

On Understanding Marx

Before turning to some of the key components of Marxian theory it is necessary to consider a few points of caution. At first glance the main ideas behind Marx's theory of society and social stratification are deceptively simple. And, of course, in the brief summary of his theory that follows, the simplicity may seem overemphasized. But Marxian theory is at the same time both simple *and* very complex. Marx began or built his theory of society from a set of very basic concepts. From this base he then expanded with many elaborations, qualifiers, and amendments, thus producing a complex theory contained in many volumes of work written over a period of about forty years. It is important to understand these basic concepts of Marxian theory first, but its richness and complexity should not be overlooked.

In a related point, it should be recognized that there are to this day many confusing debates over what Marx really said. A good deal of this debate can be traced to the complexity of Marxian theory. But there are other reasons as well. As noted in the brief description of Marx's life, he was at the same time a political activist *and* a social scientist. This dual role is found in Marx's works. Some of his works reflect the political activist role; they were written in a simplified form to make their ideas more accessible to the general population. His motive here was to stimulate social action. Included in this category is the famous *Communist Manifesto,* written with Engels during the many socialist revolts in Europe around 1848. To a large degree, it has been argued, *Capital* must be included among his more political works as well (see Bottomore 1973:23; McLellan 1973). Therefore, a problem with understanding the richness of Marxian theory fully is created when the essence of his ideas is taken only from these more politically motivated writings. To do so is tempting because his more political writings are brief and require less intellectual investment (such as his preface to *Critique of Political Economy,* written in 1859; see Marx 1971:14; Harrington 1976:37; Miliband 1977:7). But this problem in understanding his work is compounded by another.

The limited access Western social theorists have had to Marx's complete works provides another obstacle to a full understanding. And the works that have been most accessible, until recently, more often reflect the political side of Marx. It was only in 1953 that a German edition of what has been described as the most complete of Marx's works (*The Grundrisse*) was published; and only in 1971 was part of this work published in the United States (Marx 1971). Research now suggests that Marx himself viewed *Capital* as a more political statement taken from the more general work published later as *The Grundrisse* (McLellan 1973).

The main point of all this is that, for several reasons, social scientists are just beginning to understand the complexity and richness of Marxian theory. This is not to say that most are now convinced Marx was the most accurate social theorist of his time, or that all of his ideas remain useful today. But the old "vulgar" interpretations of Marxian theory must now be rejected. In what follows, we will attempt to respect the complexity of Marxian theory, at the same time trying to be brief.

Basic Foundations of Marxian Theory

As an introduction to the basics of Marxian theory, and to make the above comments about political interpretations of Marx more concrete, it will be useful to consider first what has been described (somewhat inaccurately) as the overall *historical-materialist* and *deterministic* thrust of Marxian theory. Marx (Marx and Engels 1965:27–31) began by stressing that:

The first premise of all human history is, of course, the existence of living human beings. Thus the first fact to be established is the physical organization of these individuals and their consequent relation to the rest of nature. . . . Man can be distinguished from animals by consciousness, by religion or anything else you like. They themselves begin to distinguish themselves from animals as soon as they begin to *produce* their means of subsistence, a step which is conditioned by their physical organizations. By producing their means of subsistence men are indirectly producing their actual material life. The way in which men produce their means of subsistence depends first of all on the nature of the actual means of subsistence they find in existence and have to produce. . . . The nature of individuals thus depends on the material conditions determining their production.

In short, Marx believed that to understand human societies the theorist must begin with the *material* conditions of human subsistence, or the economics of producing the necessities of life. And to understand human societies most fully, the key is the *historical* progression or development of these material conditions of production. Thus, we find the concept of *historical materialism*. All other aspects of human societies—from political organization and family structures to religion and ideologies—are generally (though not always) secondary phenomena. The nature or variety of political organization, political ideologies, religion, family organization, and other factors in specific human societies are generally *shaped* by the particular means of production or economic base in that society. This Marxian or materialist perspective is usually contrasted with that of Weber, who argued, for example, that cultural factors such as religious beliefs could have an equal hand in shaping the economic structure (see Weber's *The Protestant Ethic and the Spirit of Capitalism,* 1958).

This, then, is a key or foundation of Marxian sociology. However, it must be stressed that the *rigid* historical-materialist and deterministic strain is found only in Marx's more political works (those until recently most accessible to Western social theorists). In *The Grundrisse,* for example, this relationship between the material (or economic) to cultural and ideological aspects of society is viewed as less rigid and less deterministic (see Bottomore 1973:18; Harrington 1976:41; and Appelbaum 1978a:78). While understanding that the relationship between what Marx labeled the *substructure* and *superstructure* of society is a key in Marxian theory, one must not overstress a deterministic relationship. Marx clearly recognized that *ideas* or other aspects of the superstructure can at times be of independent importance in shaping the nature of human societies (a view that places Marx much closer to Weber than heretofore recognized).

We must be more specific about what Marx meant by *substructure* and *superstructure.* Following this idea that the nature of human society "depends on the material conditions determining . . . production," he referred to this material and economic base as the *substructure*. Human beings may go about producing what they need for survival simply by gathering what can be found in the forest, hunting, herding animals, planting crops, or working at the most complex method of industrial production. Because of the importance of economic tasks and the amount of time people invest in these activities, each of these differing modes of production tends to influence (or shape within certain limits) other aspects of life in these societies. Thus, the substructure shapes the superstructure.

Following Marxian theory, in agrarian societies or feudalism, for example, we would be surprised to find a democratic political system, a nuclear democratic family structure, the absence of strong authoritarian religious traditions, or an individualistic ideology, because the substructure (or mode of production) found in this type of society would not fit well with such a superstructure (see Figure 4-1).

To make our point clear we must further specify what Marx included within the substructure. Within the *mode of production* that makes up this substructure Marx also distinguished between the means of production and the relations of production. The *means of production* refers most directly to the type of technology used to produce goods (such as hunting and gathering, agrarian methods of varying sophistication, machine technology). As we saw with Lenski's work in Chapter 3, the level of technology has many important consequences for the general nature of the society and the stratification system. But in understanding class divisions Marx also distinguished level of technology or the means of production from the relations of production. This was seen as necessary because differing relations of production can be found within a given level of technology or means of production.

By *relations of production* Marx meant the human relationships within a given means of production. Under capitalism these relationships include (1) the relationships between workers as dictated by the type of production (whether they work together and can interact in a mass production setting

FIGURE 4-1
The Marxian model of social organization. The solid arrow indicates a primary causal relation, and the broken arrows indicate a secondary causal relation.

(Political organization, ideology, religion, etc.)

Superstructure

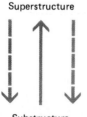

Substructure

(Means and relations of production)

or work in smaller settings or in isolation from other workers), (2) the dominance–submission relationships among workers and authorities, and (3) the ownership and distribution of valued goods in the society. (For a discussion of all of this, see Giddens 1973:85–88.)

Thus, the relations of production are a part of the substructure that can influence the superstructure. For example, how workers relate to machines and other workers can influence their outlook on life or belief systems. The predominant type of authority relation within the economy or production system can shape authority relations within the wider society. Also, how workers are related to machines and each other can affect their family relations, leisure activities, child-rearing practices, and self-esteem. (All of this will be discussed more fully in the chapter on the middle and working classes in the United States.)

Perhaps most important for Marxian theory, however, is the way ownership patterns can shape the superstructure. When one group in the society is able to own and/or control the most important means of production within the society, the power this gives the owner–controller class allows it to shape or maintain aspects of the superstructure favoring its class interests. In a famous phrase Marx (Marx and Engels 1965:61) wrote, "The ideas of the ruling class are in every epoch the ruling ideas: i.e., the class which is the ruling *material* force of society, is at the same time its ruling *intellectual* force."

Marx meant that the dominant normative system or ideology in a society is shaped and maintained by this powerful group because it serves its interests. An example can be found with the extent to which owners or controllers of the means of production in capitalist nations sponsor programs to "educate the public" about the lack of alternatives to capitalism, how capitalism works, and the importance of private property for the "health and well-being of society."

But we must also consider how the political system is shaped by ownership relations. A political system that gives voting rights only to those who own land, for example, may be supported successfully by landowners in an agrarian society, but this political system is likely to be destroyed when the power of factory owners is increased.

Again we must caution that the superstructure is not completely determined, but only influenced or shaped, by the substructure or general mode of production. Marx recognized that in many places the political system or cultural traditions could at times shape or influence the means and relations of production (more generally the substructure) (see Giddens 1973:87; Harrington 1976:43). In the long run the influence of the substructure over the superstructure was seen as primary in Marx's writings, however.

Social Change   Marxian theory is one of dynamics, social change, and conflict, rather than one of social equilibrium and order, as with functional theory. The historical progression of human societies has a major place in the Marxian view of the world. With the stimulus of class conflict and "internal contradictions" within societies "based on the exploitation of one class by another" human societies are seen to evolve through a series of stages to the final communist society. We can now build upon the basic concepts discussed above to understand the Marxian view of social change.

If it is the substructure of society that primarily shapes the superstructure (rather than vice versa), then, from the perspective of Marxian theory, change in the substructure leads to more total or revolutionary social change (see the simplified diagram in Figure 4-2). It is useful to consider first some of the major types of societies described in various places in Marx's writings. Five are given primary attention: primitive communism, ancient society (slavery), feudalism, capitalism, and communism (with another, Asian systems, or the Asiatic mode of production, given less attention).

Each of these types of societies is characterized by a particular substructure or mode of production. In primitive communism (similar to what Lenski described in hunting and gathering societies) most property that exists is held collectively and production of necessities is achieved collectively. There are few, if any, inequalities of power and material goods. Ancient society is based on slave labor, or a mode of production that involves slaves performing much of the necessary labor but receiving only enough to stay alive. In feudalism, the most important means of production is land, owned primarily by the nobility, with serfs working the land and turning over the surplus to landowners.[6] Capitalist society is based on a new substructure; the means of production are primarily industrial, with relations of production characterized primarily by private ownership of the major means of production. Finally, in communist society the means of production remain industrial, but the relations of production have changed to collective (rather than private) ownership of the means of production.

In tracing Marx's logic of social change we can focus briefly on feudal and capitalist societies. The breakup of feudal society is located primarily in the

FIGURE 4-2
The Marxian model of social change.

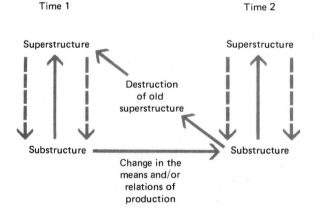

emergence of a new means of production—from production based on land to production based in industry—and relations of production based on new market forces and labor power as commodity (see Giddens 1973:84–85). By the end of the Middle Ages in Europe (around the 1600s and 1700s) factory production was beginning to challenge agrarian production as the most important form of commerce. With this developing change in the overall mode of production, conflict surfaced between two classes with differing interests in these two competing modes of production. The old superstructure (the political, ideological, and religious components) had been shaped by the old feudal substructure, and thus continued to favor the interests of landowners over those of the emerging factory owners. Tax laws, the method of political representation, and foreign policy, for example, were all structured to meet the needs of the dominant class under feudalism.

In this situation, one of two extreme outcomes was possible. As was more the case in England, various compromises were achieved with relatively less violence to transform the superstructure to one more in line with the new substructure. This process began as far back as the Magna Carta in 1215, increased with Cromwell's revolution in the mid-1600s, and continued through the nineteenth century. This less violent change was due in part to the fact that many of the old landowners moved to capitalist forms of trade and agrarian production and invested in industrial production. In essence, the two powerful classes were not always confronted with such mutually exclusive interests.

At the other end of the spectrum, as in France, the strongly opposed powerful classes did not make for such a relatively nonviolent transition. Compromise could not be satisfactorily achieved, and the contradictions between the old feudal superstructure and the emerging industrial, capitalist substructure led to a violent break with the French Revolution of 1789. (For a discussion of the above, see Soboul 1974.) With this break a radically new social order was created; in short order there was a drastic transformation of the state and religious hierarchy that had previously supported the old substructure.

The triumph of capitalism, however, would not resolve forever the conflicts and contradictions between the substructure and the superstructure, Marx believed. With time he saw further change in the mode of production that would lead to the eventual emergence of communism. Change would result not so much from a radical alteration in the technical means of production, as it did with agrarian to industrial production, but from a radical change in the relations of production. Of primary importance would be a change from small scale, individual production to *monopoly capitalism*.

Under monopoly capitalism production is performed collectively in large factories by a mass of industrial workers, while private ownership of the means of production continues. This is because industrial firms grow in size, with a few large firms accounting for more and more of the production. At the same time many former factory owners are "thrown down" to the level of workers (that is, lose their place as industrial owners), and with these large factories workers become more numerous.

A contradiction in the relations of production emerges. Although production capacity expands, with many workers *collectively* producing goods (that is, working together in large factories), private ownership of the means of production remains. Also, the extreme unequal distribution of the fruits of this production (wealth and income) remains.[7] In time, the numerically powerful workers, Marx believed, will recognize that their interests are in opposition to the private ownership of the means of production and the unequal distribution of rewards (profits or surplus). Revolution is inevitable, placing workers in power and resolving the contradiction between *private* ownership of the means of production and *collective* production in favor of collective ownership.[8]

The above description of social change from a Marxian perspective has been brief, and many details have been omitted. In many ways, the materialistic, deterministic side of Marxian theory has been overemphasized. Thus, the full richness of the theory has not come through. However, Marx began from the basic ideas presented above, refining and amending as he shaped his theory. For an understanding of the fundamentals of Marxian theory we have left only his more specific view of class and class exploitation.

The Marxian View of Class   Marx and Engels began their most famous work, *The Communist Manifesto,* in 1848, by writing,

> The history of all hitherto existing society is the history of class struggles. Free man and slave, patrician and plebeian, lord and serf, guild-master and journeyman, in a word, oppressor and oppressed, stood in constant opposition to one another, carried on an uninterrupted, now hidden, now open fight, a fight that each time ended, either in a revolutionary reconstitution of society at large, or in the common ruin of the contending classes.

This statement is powerful and to the point, but, as we have noted, it is more of a political statement than a cautious, scientific one. However, it is clear that class and class conflict run throughout Marxian theory as *the* basic concepts in understanding human societies.

With class divisions maintaining such a central role in Marxian theory, one would expect Marx to have spent much time on a specific definition of the concept. But he did not. Through the many volumes of Marx's writings, class is used in differing, and at times contradictory, ways. When he was finally about to undertake a more detailed and systematic discussion of class at the end of the third volume of *Capital,* he died (see Dahrendorf 1959:8). It was as if Marx saw the concept of class as so basic and important he assumed until the end of his life that it needed no systematic discussion. Although he used the word in different ways and wrote of several different classes in many of his works, his most important general and abstract view of class is relatively clear.[9] And it is here that we will begin.

The key in understanding human societies for Marx was "the material conditions determining their production," that is, the mode of production. It is with *private ownership of the means of production* that class and class conflict begin. In feudal societies based on land and agricultural production, the two great classes are the lord and the serf, or the landed aristocracy and the peasant. The lord or the aristocracy owned the land (the means of production), while the serf and peasant owned little but their labor power.

In capitalist society based on industrial production the two great classes are the *bourgeoisie* (the owners of the means of production or capital) and the *proletariat* (or working class). Marx recognized the existence of the bourgeoisie in the later stages of feudal societies and the continued presence of the aristocracy in capitalist societies. But as noted in the above discussion of Marx's theory of social change, when the dominant means of production shifted from land to industry, it was the bourgeoisie that came to dominate in capitalist society.

Having considered Marx's most general definition of class, it is next important to understand what he saw as the moving force in history—that is, "the history of all hitherto existing society is the history of class struggles," or *class conflict*. The root of class conflict is differing class interests. In class societies, which include, in Marx's view, all existing societies except "primitive communism" and the "future mature communist society," one class owns or controls the means of production. This class dominates and controls the surplus goods produced in that society for its own needs. There is exploitation by one class over another.

Marx was most concerned with capitalist societies, and it was here that he devoted most attention to the details of this exploitative class relation. He proposed a *labor theory of value* to explain the value of all goods produced in a society. As he wrote, "... the magnitude of the value of any article is the amount of labor socially necessary, or the labor-time socially necessary for its production" (see Anderson 1974:16).

The exploitative nature of capitalism, for Marx, is found in the fact that the capitalists (owners of the means of production or the factories) pay workers only a living or subliving wage, a wage below the value workers actually produce. The remainder is "surplus value" that is taken by the capitalist for his or her own profit; "surplus value is nothing but the difference between the value created by the worker and the cost of maintaining him" (see Anderson 1974:18).

The exploitative relationship of capitalism is extended by the production of capital itself. By capital is meant the factories, machines, or any goods used as a means to produce more goods. Thus, "capital is stored-up, accumulated labor" (Anderson 1974:18). This stored-up labor or capital from past workers is used to produce even more surplus value for the capitalists' own profit, taking more and more profit from fewer and fewer workers.

With a reduced need for workers as capitalism advances, more workers are reduced to an *industrial reserve army* living in poverty and able to work only in times of boom or periods of economic expansion. In Marx's poetic terms,

"Capital is dead labor, that vampire-like, only lives by sucking living labor, and lives the more, the more labor it sucks" (Marx 1906:257).

For Marx, then, class and class conflict were the moving forces in history. There is a dominant class that owns the means of production and exploits other classes. But in the face of this exploitation, these other classes find it in their interest to overthrow the dominant class and establish a social order more favorable to their interests when the historical progression of the mode of production allows. With feudalism, as we have seen, the dominant class was overthrown by the bourgeoisie; with capitalism, the dominant class would be overthrown by the proletariat.

This would happen, in part, when the proletariat *recognized* its true interests—moving from a class in itself that has only objective interests in common but does not yet recognize its common interests or act upon them, to a class for itself that does. With the proletariat in power, however, Marx believed that class struggle would end, because he saw the proletariat as the final class in the history of class struggles, with no class below it to exploit. This is why he believed that with the coming of a workers' state in advanced communism, class conflict would end where human society began (with "primitive communism"). But at the end of this class struggle would be an industrial society of plenty so that all could live in comfort.

Concluding Notes

We can conclude our discussion of Marx by again noting the importance of his ideas in the development of social stratification theory. His image of society, or the critical-conflict paradigm he helped develop, is most important. Many of his specific predictions about the future of capitalism we now know are incorrect. The nations that have experienced "communist revolution" (Russia, China, Cuba, Vietnam), contrary to Marxian ideas, were less industrialized, principally agrarian societies. In the most advanced capitalist nations, where he saw communist revolution as most likely, the working class has been less than revolutionary. (Some of the reasons will be taken up in later chapters.)

Marx failed to see how a state coming to power in the name of his ideas could develop into a society far from what he envisioned. (Some of the reasons for this will be considered in the chapter on stratification in Soviet nations.) He also failed to see how a welfare state could develop in capitalist societies to manage some of the conflicts, exploitation, and internal contradictions that he believed would lead to the demise of capitalism. (This will be considered in our chapter on the poor.)

But Marx did see better than most in his time the expansion of "monopoly capitalism." And with the elaboration of Marxian ideas by Lenin, the expansion of capitalism into a worldwide network of class conflict and exploitation was foreseen (to be considered most fully in our final chapter). Overall, while not accurate in many details, the Marxian view of society has been valuable to our present understanding of inequality, class, and social stratification in human societies.

MAX WEBER: AN ALTERNATIVE CONFLICT PARADIGM

In comparison to those of Marx, Max Weber's specific contributions to stratification theory were relatively brief—but no less powerful. Two sets of ideas developed and expanded by Weber have had a particular impact on our understanding of advanced industrial societies. The first, his expansion of Marx's single class or economic dimension of social stratification into a *multidimensional view* (class, status, and party), has provided us with a very useful tool in understanding the complex nature of social stratification. Perhaps most important, however, Weber's writings on the development and growth of large *bureaucratic institutions* has enabled us to understand the nature of power and dominance within advanced industrial societies of all types (whether capitalist or communist) better than any other single idea by a social theorist.

Therefore, Weber's insights into the multidimensional nature of social stratification and the power of bureaucratic institutions will concern us most in this discussion. However, as we have done with Marx, we must look more broadly into the development of Weber's general sociological perspective. In contrast to Marx's critical-conflict assumptions, we find with Weber a set of paradigm assumptions we have labeled uncritical-conflict.

Like Marx, Weber was most consistent in stressing conflict as the human relationship most important in shaping the nature of society although, as we will see, Weber's view of conflict was more encompassing. But even more important, with Weber we find a far different perspective with regard to what we have called value assumptions. While it can be said that Marx was basically an optimist—for be believed that conflict, inequality, alienation, and exploitation could eventually be reduced or eliminated in future societies—Weber had no such hope. As we will see, he was truly a pessimist in his estimate of the potential for more just and humane societies. Especially in his view of the legal-rational mode of social organization (that is, bureaucracies), Weber was pessimistic and even fearful of what he saw as an expanding ''iron cage.''

At the outset it should be noted that Weber's ideas, much like Marx's, have been misunderstood until recently by many social scientists. Weber's work was most often described as primarily a ''debate with Marx's ghost.'' Weber *was* aware of the limitations of a *strict* historical-materialist view of society; thus, he showed (1) how a new value system was also behind the development of capitalism in *The Protestant Ethic and the Spirit of Capitalism* (1958) and (2) that there are dimensions of social stratification other than just material or economic.

But his work was much more than simply an alternative to that of Marx. Rather, in many cases it was an expansion of Marx's ideas. As with Marx, American social scientists have only recently had the benefit of translations (from the German) of most of his work. In addition, the most extensive early interpretations of Weber's work (see Parsons 1937) came from theorists who read into Weber many functional (or, in our terms, uncritical-order) assumptions that simply were found inaccurate upon a more complete analysis (see Cohen, Hazelrigg, and Pope 1975). Thus, overall, we find more agreement between Weber and Marx than was heretofore recognized.

Before proceeding to the more specific value of Weber's insights, it will be useful and interesting to consider briefly the context within which Weber's ideas developed. (For very useful biographies of Weber and his times see Marianne Weber 1975, and Mitzman 1969; see also Gerth and Mills 1946, and Bendix 1960.) Max Weber was born in Erfurt, Germany, in 1864, and died in 1920. His life, therefore, spanned an exciting and challenging period of change and conflict in his homeland. And unlike Marx, it can be said that Weber had a homeland; for he was a patriotic citizen of Germany who sought to understand his society so that it could be strengthened and humanized (much like Durkheim, discussed below). In fact, his earliest professional work was an attempt to shed light on the problems of land ownership and utilization in this country, with special emphasis on the power of the old backward-oriented upper class in Germany at the time (the Junker class).

For brief periods Weber left his academic studies for service to his country—as a hospital administrator during World War I, as a delegate to the peace conference after World War I, and as a voice and consultant on many issues confronting the new German government during reconstruction. But over the years Weber grew more pessimistic with the prospect of reform, especially after the recurring bouts with extreme mental depressions that began with his father's death in 1897. For many years Weber was unable to lecture or write. But his greatest works were completed after his recovery.

Like Marx, Weber grew up in an upper-middle-class family. His father was a lawyer who held several political positions in his life. But unlike Marx, Max Weber primarily pursued the life of a scholar and teacher within the academic hall. He held positions in a number of major German universities and was a central figure in the establishment of sociology as a respected academic discipline.

Also in contrast to Marx, Weber was an early advocate of a value-free orientation in the study of society. That is, Weber maintained that the social scientist's task is to understand human societies without the interference of political objectives. However, as we have discussed in the preceding chapter, very *general* paradigm assumptions about human nature and social organization make a complete value-free analysis impossible.

And although it seems Weber was advocating this value-free stance in order to shelter the new discipline of sociology from the political debates on both the left and the right (see Gouldner 1973:3–26), this value-free perspective guided his work by making him more concerned with *what exists,* rather than attempting to understand what *could be* (in contrast with Marx's attempt to understand how society will change for the better). We can now examine how a particular set of paradigm assumptions we have called uncritical-conflict assumptions informed Weber's work, and through him influenced the development of many modern theories of social stratification.

Weber's Paradigm Assumptions

As with Marx, but not as with Durkheim, the image or model of society that guided Weber's perspective on social stratification was one of conflict. He did *not,* however, view conflict between the owners of the means of production (the bourgeoisie in capitalist societies) and the workers (the proletariat) as the only, or even at times the most important, conflict relationship in the society. For Weber, many varied and differing group or individual interests could form the basis of conflict relationships in human societies. As we will see, he believed these varied conflicting interests could be merged with more specific economic interests, although this is not always so.

Weber's conflict perspective can be understood in contrast with that of functional (order) theorists such as Durkheim. For example, "Weber did not suggest that dominant persons act to integrate collectivities in the interest of effective functioning. Rather, he treated such individuals as acting in terms of their own ideal and material interests as they perceive them" (Cohen, Hazelrigg, and Pope 1975:238). Furthermore, Weber did not neglect the divisions and separate elements of human societies by focusing exclusively on the integration and functioning of the whole. In fact, "A correct understanding of Weber's general sociology is impossible unless founded on a faithful reading of his theory of domination" (Cohen, Hazelrigg, and Pope 1975:237).

As we have suggested, unlike Marx, Weber did not focus only on conflict flowing from the economic relations within society. In Weber's view, the base of conflict relations could be located in many types of differing interests (social, material, political, and so on). But, if any of these can be said to be more important in his interpretations of society, it is political or organizational conflict and dominance; "Weber . . . came very close to what amounted to a transposition of Marx's monistic explanation from the economic to the political realm. One sees this most graphically where Weber describes the ongoing process of centralization of power in all fields of human activity: war, education, economics, religion, and most crucial of all, politics" (Mitzman 1969:183–184).

With respect to what we have described as value assumptions, Weber's view of conflict and domination in human societies converged with his pessimistic view toward the possibility of a more equal and just society. The result was a perspective that saw no end to conflict and domination, only changing forms or bases of conflict.

Much like Pareto, Mosca, and Michels, who also contributed much toward an uncritical-conflict paradigm, Weber saw a society always divided between those who ruled and those who were ruled. But Weber differs from the above theorists by providing a more complex and robust theory of social conflict. The interests behind this conflict and domination are viewed as more diverse, and he recognized that the *means* of domination must be distinguished from the interests or goals of domination.

Finally, Weber was not explicit in charging that continued domination was due to anything like selfish human nature. Whether or not human nature was part of the cause, Weber saw that increasing population density and diversity resulted in the need for organization and coordination. And the most efficient means of achieving this organization was bureaucratic administration. It was for this reason that Weber came to view programs for radical alternatives to the present inequality and domination as hopeless (Mitzman 1969:185).

Multidimensional View of Stratification

Having discussed some of the more general aspects of Weber's work, we are prepared to examine the two aspects of his work most important for modern theories of social stratification. We can begin with his *multidimensional view* of social stratification. Marx, as we have seen, believed the key to social stratification in capitalist societies was the division between those who owned and controlled the important means of production (capitalists, or the bourgeoisie) and those who have only their labor to sell (the proletariat). For Marx, these two groups and their conflicting interests formed the two major classes in capitalist societies (that is, Marx stressed this single dimension of social stratification).

Weber, however, argued that this view of class was overly simplistic for two reasons. First, Weber demonstrated that this class or economic dimension of stratification was in itself too simple. In addition to ownership versus nonownership of the means of production, the social scientist must consider a person's more general *relationship to the marketplace*. Thus, we find Weber's expanded view of economic or class divisions. Second, he maintained that other important divisions exist within society, divisions that are at times independent of this class division. Weber, then, came to stress a *multidimensional* aspect of social stratification; more specifically, the dimensions of *class, status,* and *party* (or power).

With respect to *class*, Weber wrote (see Gerth and Mills 1946:181), "We may speak of a class when 1) a number of people have in common a specific causal component of their life chances, insofar as 2) this component is represented exclusively by economic interests in the possession of goods and opportunities for income, and 3) is represented under the conditions of the commodity or labor markets."

Again, we can see that Weber saw more than ownership behind class divisions, although this ownership of productive forces was primary (see Gerth and Mills 1946:182). There is also the important aspect of opportunities for income. By opportunities for income, Weber meant the skill level possessed by a worker (such as scientist, lab technician, or skilled blue-collar worker). The higher the skill level, other things being equal, the more return (income or wealth) a worker was able to obtain for his or her labor.

Most sociologists today agree that this is an important expansion of Marx's view of class, given the growth of technology—and thus needed skills—in advanced industrial societies (capitalist and communist). Furthermore, this expanded dimension of class stratification, most sociologists stress, is needed in understanding the place of the new middle class in industrial societies. In Weber's view, therefore, in addition to the dichotomy between owners and nonowners of the means of production, there is a dimension of class stratification based on skill level that is more continuous (that is, contains many ranks or levels, rather than only two).

In understanding divisions and inequalities in human societies (or even small social groups) Weber also stressed *status honor* or prestige. "In content, status honor is normally expressed by the fact that above all else a specific *style of life* can be expected from all those who wish to belong to the circle. Linked with this expectation are restrictions on 'social' intercourse" (Gerth and Mills 1946:187).

Divisions based on status honor flow from the ability of someone to live up to some set of ideals or principles held important by the society or some social group within it. As people, we tend to judge and evaluate others in terms of a set of ideals or values. Thus, we commonly find rankings based on these evaluations. Examples may be an old family of wealth able to pursue a life of high culture, movie stars, famous athletes, or famous scientists. This, then, is a more subjective dimension of social stratification, one that has been stressed most often by functional theorists.

Important also within the status dimension are the restrictions on social intercourse. By this Weber wanted to emphasize that status groups tend to draw lines around themselves, restricting intimate social interaction, marriage, and other relations within the status group. Thus, "where the consequences have been realized to their full extent, the status group evolves into a closed 'caste'" (Gerth and Mills 1946:188). Here we find much of the ascriptive nature of class systems, often (but by no means always) based on racial or ethnic divisions. In our discussion of the upper class in the United States we will find how useful this status dimension of stratification is in understanding how powerful upper-class families have been able to keep wealth and power within their own group by status distinctions that hold the new rich at a distance. And when we examine social stratification in Japan we will see how the status dimension of stratification can be very important in a homogeneous society with extensive value consensus (or agreement on major values).

Finally, there is the dimension of *party* or power. Weber (Gerth and Mills 1946:194) wrote,

> Whereas the genuine place of "classes" is within the economic order, the place of "status groups" is within the social order, that is, within the sphere of the distribution of "honor." . . . But "parties" live in a house of "power." Their action is oriented toward the acquisition of social "power," that is to say, toward influencing a communal action no matter what its content may be.

The most important aspect of this party (or power) dimension of stratification is organization, or "rational order," and a staff with which to dominate or influence others for whatever goal. Thus, it is the political party or the bureaucratic form of organization that most typifies this dimension of stratification. Where one stands with respect to the organized forms of dominance or power within the society defines one's position in this dimension of stratification. And, as we will see, Weber came to stress this dimension as increasingly important in advanced industrial societies.

Weber, then, saw all three dimensions as important hierarchies leading to the ranking of individuals or groups in human societies. However, they were not all of equal importance throughout the history of human societies. In the early stages of capitalism the class dimension was viewed as more important. In caste societies, the status dimension remained supreme. And, as we have said, Weber saw that in modern societies the party or power dimension gained importance.

But—and this must be stressed—Weber considered all societies to have divisions based on all three dimensions of class, status, and party. Equally important, Weber saw that normally there would be a *large degree of overlap* among all three dimensions. A person high in one dimension, such as class, would typically achieve a high position on the dimensions of status and party as well. For those on top, of course, this overlap adds to their overall strength within the stratification system (as we will discuss with the upper class in America). It is primarily in times of social change that these three dimensions can diverge most widely, leading to differing arenas (for class, status, and party) in which conflicts for advantage may be brought to the forefront.

With respect to Weber's more general model of society, we can see from the above that he viewed conflict and domination as more pervasive and enduring than Marx did. For Weber, even if one aspect of conflict and inequality could ever be eliminated, others would remain, and perhaps become an even more important basis for inequality and conflict. In short, Weber's view of conflict was broader than that of Marx. It was partly for this reason that Weber was less hopeful than critical-conflict theorists that inequality, conflict, and domination could ever be substantially overcome.

The Rise of Bureaucratic Dominance

It may be that sociologists will soon come to recognize (if they have not already) that Weber's ideas on the bureaucratic form of organization and power have contributed most to our understanding of advanced industrial societies. Currently, we find politicians, business leaders, and the general public from all political perspectives denouncing the growing influence bureaucracies have over our lives. Large bureaucratic organizations are seen as dehumanizing, alienating, inefficient, and encroaching upon valued human freedoms. But behind all the denunciations, complaints, and political rhetoric, no one has been able to do much toward solving the problem.

Everyone seems to want less government, but a wide collection of interest groups also wants a strong military, better economic planning, protection for business in the face of foreign competition, better prices for farmers, less crime, protection from pollution and unsafe consumer products, etc. The sum total of all these interest group demands is more government and bureaucratic regulation. It must be recognized that the many problems flowing from large and complex societies such as ours require some means of corrective action; this invariably results in expanded bureaucracies.[10]

Max Weber, at the turn of the century, clearly recognized the future growth and increasing influence of rational-legal forms of social organization—that is, bureaucracies. By the later 1800s, Weber could already see how the state bureaucracy was growing in response to interest group demands for protection, primarily from powerful capitalists (DiMaggio and Powell 1983). And Max Weber recognized the human costs of this condition. Weber foresaw what he called a growing iron cage that people were building for themselves; but he foresaw no solution to this situation (see Marianne Weber 1975:415; Mitzman 1969:177).

Weber (1947:328) wrote of three principal ideal types of legitimate authority: *rational-legal authority* ''resting on a belief in the 'legality' of patterns of normative rules and the right of those elevated to authority under such rules to issue commands''; *traditional authority* ''resting on an established belief in the sanctity of immemorial traditions and the legitimacy of the status of those exercising authority under them''; and *charismatic authority* ''resting on devotion to the specific and exceptional sanctity, heroism, or exemplary character of an individual person, and of the normative patterns or order revealed or ordained by him.''

Traditional authority was primarily of earlier times, and began falling with the breakdown of feudalism in the face of rising industrialization. Charismatic authority is only temporary; it comes with a revolt against the old status quo led by an influential personality (such as Jesus, Lenin, or the Ayatollah Khomeini). Once a new authority structure is established after successful revolt, charismatic authority gives way to one of the other, more stable, types. Of the three, Weber saw rational-legal authority as the most efficient for modern societies.

We must be specific on what this form of authority and organization entails. Weber (Gerth and Mills 1946:196–198) wrote of six main characteristics of bureaucracy:

1 There is the principle of fixed and official jurisdictional areas, which are generally ordered by rules; that is, by laws or administrative regulations.

2 The principles of office hierarchy and of levels of graded authority mean a firmly ordered system of superordination and subordination in which there is a supervision of the lower offices by the higher ones.

3 The management of the modern office is based on written documents.

4 Office management . . . usually presupposes thorough and expert training.

5 When the office is fully developed, official activity demands the full working capacity of the official. Formerly, official business was discharged as a secondary activity.

6 The management of the office follows general rules, which are more or less stable and more or less exhaustive, and which can be learned.

Weber believed this form of social organization was far superior to any other (in terms of a rational means to goals), and would therefore come to exclude all others. "The fully developed bureaucratic mechanism compares with other organizations exactly as does the machine with the non-mechanical modes of production" (Gerth and Mills 1946:214). The "precision, speed, unambiguity, knowledge of the files, continuity, discretion, unity, strict subordination, reduction of friction and of material and personal costs, and calculatable rules" are all among the reasons cited by Weber for the superiority of the bureaucratic form of organization.

It can be argued that Weber was overstating the efficiency of bureaucratic organizations in the above descriptions; no doubt he was. But we must recognize what preceded this form of organization to understand Weber's point. The list of states that fell to revolutions because of their inability or unwillingness to embrace this more efficient form of organization is a long one (see Skocpol 1979). And it must also be recognized that Weber is referring to the superiority of bureaucracy as a rational *means* of organization. The *goals* for which this means is applied, of course, may be (and often are) irrational with respect to differing interests within the society (see Marcuse 1971).

One final characteristic of bureaucracy described by Weber is important for our consideration: "Once it is fully established, bureaucracy is among those social structures which are the hardest to destroy. . . . And where the bureaucratization of administration has been completely carried through, a form of power relation is established that is practically unshatterable" (Gerth and Mills 1946:228). This "permanence" of bureaucracy, once established, does not mean, however, that it will always be used to serve the same goals or interests. The key, again, is that bureaucratic organization is a *means* of domination; it "is easily made to work for anybody who knows how to gain control over it" (Gerth and Mills 1946:229). The large bureaucratic structures that expanded rapidly in Bismarck's Germany, for example, served liberal governments and Hitler equally well.

Herein lies the primary importance of Weber's view of bureaucratic organization for understanding social stratification. Because bureaucratic organization is a form, or means, of control, it implies the existence of conflict (see Collins 1975:289). If one group, such as an economic class, fascist party, or small communist organization, is able to gain control or influence over established bureaucratic organization, the power of this group is *greatly* increased.

Theorists concerned with political and economic power in advanced industrial societies (that is, the power of those at the top of the stratification system) have all benefited from Weber's ideas. As we will see in our two chapters on the top of the stratification system in the United States, major theorists such as C. Wright Mills (1956) and Thomas Dye (1979), as well as recent Marxian theorists, have come to recognize that the system of stratification in advanced industrial societies cannot be understood adequately without a recognition of this new dimension of power. And as we will also see in the chapter on stratification in communist nations, this bureaucratic means of power can be found in its most developed stages in countries such as the Soviet Union.

It may be useful in concluding our discussion of Weber's work to summarize the important influence he has had on modern thought on social stratification. Functional theorists (or those within what we have called an uncritical-order paradigm) have tended to stress the status dimension of Weber's multidimensional view. Strata or class divisions, they maintain, flow from the need people have to evaluate and rank others in terms of a dominant value system (see especially Parsons 1951, 1970). In addition, functional theorists (among many others) have tended to stress a *continuous* class ranking rather than more rigid class divisions. This means that functionalists have emphasized occupational *status*.

Further, Weber's work has provided a base for the study of *status consistency* or *status inconsistency*. From the functional view of an integrated social system, if the social system is to be healthy, the various dimensions of social stratification should show at least a minimum of convergence. It is believed that if some degree of convergence between stratification dimensions (such as occupational status, education, income) is not achieved, tensions, conflicts, and confusion will be the result—for the general society as well as for individuals within it.

Conflict theorists as well have benefited from Weber's work. For example, theories within what we have called a critical-conflict paradigm have benefited from Weber's critique and expansion of Marx's ideas. While often continuing to stress the importance of class divisions as Marx originally described them and Weber continued to stress as important, these theorists have come to recognize the significance of bureaucratic means of domination.

Thus, we find many contemporary Marxian theorists writing of the importance of the state and other bureaucratic forms of dominance in providing the upper class (in Marxian terms the owners of the means of production) with an added means to maintain their position (for example, see Miliband 1969, 1977; Harrington 1976; Therborn 1978; Wright 1978a).

Finally, theorists working from what we have called an uncritical-conflict paradigm have benefited from Weber's ideas. Many, if not most, of the current theorists within this paradigm have built their theories around the dimension of stratification Weber came to stress in his later years—that is, party, power, or domination by centralized bureaucratic organizations (see Dahrendorf 1959; Collins 1975). While it may be argued that Weber's work is more useful than that of others of his time in understanding the contemporary United States because of his recognition of our particular traditions and values (see Tiryakian 1975), it can equally be argued that Weber's work is most valuable in its recognition of a primary aspect of all advanced industrial societies—the bureaucratic mode of organization.

AN UNCRITICAL-ORDER PARADIGM MATURES: THE FUNCTIONAL THEORY OF ÉMILE DURKHEIM

From the conflict perspectives of Marx and Weber, we turn to the functional perspective of Émile Durkheim. As will be noted in several places, Durkheim's work provided fertile ground for later functional theorists of social stratification. But unlike Marx or Weber, Durkheim himself gave only passing attention to class divisions, class conflict, and even social stratification. His relative neglect of class, and his writing on the subject when it was forced on his attention, however, are most instructive in themselves. The brief treatment given class and social stratification by Durkheim shows how the more holistic perspective taken by functional theorists leads to a world view in which the needs of a social system overshadow those of interest groups or classes within this social system.

In tracing the development of functional theory (or, more broadly, an uncritical-order paradigm) most historians of social thought draw a direct line from Saint-Simon and Auguste Comte, through Émile Durkheim, to modern functional theorists such as Talcott Parsons (see Gouldner 1970; Giddens 1973; Strasser 1976). Saint-Simon, a Frenchman, made some of the first contributions to functional theory in the early 1800s (Zeitlin 1968:58). But it was with Comte that this perspective was carried into the academic hall; and it was with Durkheim that this perspective grew to maturity. And it was with both Comte and Durkheim that this perspective was "relieved of its critical potential" (Strasser 1976:5).

Durkheim called for bolstering the status quo (uncritical value assumptions) around a moral integration of society (order model). For Durkheim, the problems of his era were moral, not material; problems of alienation, exploitation, structured inequalities, or class conflict were due "not to the state of our economy, but rather the state of our morality" (Durkheim 1962:247). But even the solution to this problem of morality should not be in terms of a new morality; this reform "... has for its object, not to make an ethic completely different from the prevailing one, but to correct the latter, or partially to improve it" (Durkheim 1964:35–36).[11]

Our present task will be to consider more fully Durkheim's paradigm assumptions and theoretical statements about social stratification, and contrast them with those of Marx and Weber. We will not take time to consider his many works on such subjects as methods of social research, social causes of suicide, the function and development of religion, or the function of education. But it is clear that all of Durkheim's work contained the consistent theme that social order is possible only when human nature is restrained through a morality represented in the collective force of a dominant normative system.

David Émile Durkheim was born in France in 1858 (for details on Durkheim's life, see Lukes 1973a). His father, grandfather, and great-grandfather had all been respected rabbis in various parts of France. Durkheim's family lived under modest economic conditions, but "he grew up within the confines of a close-knit, Orthodox and traditional Jewish family, part of the long-established Jewish community of Alsace-Lorraine that was notable for providing France with many army officers and civil servants at the end of the nineteenth century" (Lukes 1973a:39). No doubt this strongly knit moral community fed Durkheim with the view of the need for moral integration so evident in his later sociological work. But during his college years, beginning in the École Normale Supérieure, Durkheim came to reject the specific Jewish underpinning of this view of moral integration (but *not* the need for moral integration).

After graduation, Durkheim held teaching positions at Bordeaux (1887–1902) and the Sorbonne (1902–1917), where he held the important position of chair of education and sociology. Through his students as well as his writings Durkheim influenced the development of sociology in France, and later the world. Unlike Marx, and even more than Weber, Durkheim remained for the most part detached from active political involvement. He was concerned about the problems of his country, and the world more generally with the outbreak of World War I. But he saw his role as that of the detached scholar providing ideas toward a future moral integration of the newly emerging industrial society.

A key to understanding Durkheim's sociological perspective, and thus his view of social stratification, is his *organic analogy*. From this perspective, society is considered as similar to a biological organism. There are various organs or parts within this social system that serve different functions for the health and maintenance of the total society—much like the functions served by organs within the human body.

It is easy to see that this organic analogy could lead a social theorist to focus on the social system as a whole (holistic perspective) and on the interrelation of its parts rather than on divisions and opposed interests among groups within the society. For example, one does not usually think in terms of a differing set of "interests" between the heart and lungs, and although we may think in terms of a hierarchy of biological organs—for example, the heart and brain are more critical for the overall survival of the organism than the eyes—all are considered as contributing to the maintenance of the whole. Hence, this organic analogy leads to a perspective on social stratification far different from that of Marx and Weber.

Within the social system, it must be added, Durkheim considered morality to be the major factor contributing to social order and integration. For Durkheim, it has been said, "morality was the centre and the end of his work" (see Lukes 1973a:95). The importance of morality in maintaining social order is related to his view of human nature, as well as his view of the needs of the social system. Much like Weber, Durkheim was distrustful of human nature. Left to themselves, people would be in continuous conflict, selfishly dominating and exploiting fellow human beings for their own narrow interests. In order to save people from social chaos and even individual destruction (that is, suicide), a strong moral order is necessary (Strasser 1976:120).

Unlike Weber, however, Durkheim was optimistic about the ability of new social institutions to continue regulating selfish conflict for the common good. Various social institutions are important in maintaining this strong moral integration—such as religion, the family, occupational associations, and, above all, education. A continuing socialization process is needed so that people can internalize a moral order that could reduce selfish behavior for the collective good.

The Division of Labor and Organic Solidarity

The maintenance of social order (that is, moral integration) was relatively simple in small-scale preindustrial communities. In the idealized view of these preindustrial societies held by Durkheim, Ferdinand Tönnies, and other early sociologists, it was in large part the closeness of interpersonal relations that helped maintain moral integration. But with a change toward large industrial societies, with many social divisions resulting from an expanding division of labor, moral integration was recognized to be increasingly problematic. Thus, the question of social order in industrial societies became central to the work of early sociologists such as Durkheim.

As Durkheim viewed the problem, societies must move from *mechanical solidarity* (the moral order in preindustrial societies) to *organic solidarity* in industrial societies. This organic solidarity was possible, he believed, through occupational organizations or guilds. It was reasoned that within each of the many occupational guilds, moral principles could be established regarding the rights and duties of workers and employers. As with preindustrial societies, this new type of moral order could restrain the selfish interests for the good of the larger society (see Durkheim 1964). Thus, in industrial societies there was need for more social differentiation, but this social differentiation did not have to result in social disorganization.

In the context of Durkheim's thought in *The Division of Labor* (1964) we can gain some insight into his more specific views on inequality and social stratification. But for the most part, as noted above, Durkheim had relatively little to say on the subject. His concern, his model of society, was so dominated by a holistic image that the divisions (such as classes) that may exist within this society were easily neglected. And when they were not neglected, they were given only minor consideration.

The functional theory Durkheim helped establish was to wait almost fifty years before a systematic analysis of the functions of inequality "for the good of the social system" was undertaken (see the discussion of the Davis and Moore theory in the next chapter). However, the early ideas behind this systematic theory of the function of inequality can be found in Durkheim's work.

Principally, Durkheim saw two types of inequality, what he called *external* and *internal* inequality. As he described them in *The Division of Labor,* external inequalities are those imposed upon the individual by the social circumstances of birth, what we have referred to earlier as ascribed status. It was in mechanical solidarity, or preindustrial societies, that these external inequalities predominated. In industrial society, on the other hand, there was a need for internal inequality: "All external inequalities compromise organic solidarity" (Durkheim 1964:371), that is, threaten social order and the proper functioning of the division of labor in industrial societies. Internal inequalities were seen as inequalities based on individual talent, what we earlier called achieved status. For the proper functioning of the industrial system, Durkheim implied, the people with the proper talents must be allowed to move into positions for which their talents are best suited.

What Durkheim anticipated was a "meritocracy" based on equality of opportunity. Inequality there would be, but he believed an inequality based on merit was needed. And although Durkheim's ideas paralleled somewhat those of many modern functionalists, given his overriding concern with solidarity and moral integration in society, his stress was different. The dominance of internal over external inequality, he believed, was most important for the maintenance of social solidarity. If external inequalities were forced upon individuals, "constraint alone, more or less violent and more or less direct, binds them to their functions; in consequence, only an imperfect and troubled solidarity is possible" (see Lukes 1973a:175). Thus, in contrast to Davis and Moore (1945, considered in Chapter 5), Durkheim was more concerned with moral integration and cooperation than he was with the efficient staffing of "important" positions in industrial society.

The Place of Class and Class Conflict in Durkheim's Perspective

As we have suggested, "Durkheim had a strong tendency always to conceive of 'society' as a whole, rather than in terms, say, of a plurality of or conflict between different social groups and forces" (Lukes 1973a:21). It is therefore easy to understand that "the term 'class' ... hardly appears in *The Division of Labor*" (Giddens 1978:36). However, Durkheim was forced to consider the existence of class and class conflict by his consistent critics and by the clear existence of class divisions and class conflict in the expanding industrial societies.

In essence, Durkheim dealt with the existence of class and class conflict by dismissing them as unnatural: "If the division of labor produces conflict, it is either because society is in a transitional state of development, or because of the existence of a pathological condition of social order" (Giddens 1978:114). This pathological condition of conflict existed, in Durkheim's view, because the occupational guilds were not performing their proper function of providing moral order and society was being threatened by selfish individual or group interests. But it never occurred to Durkheim that the whole system of a division of labor in industrial society could be a power structure for the domination of one class by another (as conflict theorists maintain).

Durkheim's view of the state in industrial society can also be considered in this respect: "For Durkheim, the state is above all a moral agency, which concentrates within itself the values of the broader social community. . . . Again, a biological parallel is used: the state is the 'brain,' the coordinating mechanism of the social organism" (Giddens 1978:115). A society was in need of moral organization provided by the state for the good of the total society, and all the people in it. Unlike conflict theorists such as Marx or Weber, Durkheim never considered that the state could be a mechanism for maintaining the dominance of one class over others.

Finally, with respect to dominant norms and values, or the moral order Durkheim held to be so important, it did not occur to Durkheim that this moral order itself could be a mechanism of dominance by one class over others (see Strasser 1976:122). It is here most clearly that we find how paradigm assumptions can shape a theorist's view of society. For Durkheim the moral integration of society served the interests of all in the society. Both functional and conflict theorists recognize the importance and existence of norms and values. But for conflict theorists, these norms and values, when internalized by the lower classes, can work to maintain their support for a system in which their interests are subordinated to the interests of the dominant class. As we have seen, Marx believed that this "normative rationalization" for support of the status quo by workers would be broken when the proletariat changed from a class in itself to a class for itself.

THE CLASSICAL PERIOD OF SOCIOLOGICAL THEORY: A SUMMARY

To summarize the key ideas from the three theorists considered in this chapter, we must remember that Marx began with the assumption that people's material needs are basic. From Marx's perspective, those aspects of society located in the *superstructure* are also important in understanding the nature of society and social stratification; but the *substructure* is primary and, more often than not, shapes the aspects of society he located within the superstructure.

In understanding class divisions and social change, two elements of the substructure must be considered: The *means of production* refer to how people go about producing the necessities of life and the *relations of production* refer to such things as how the fruits of this labor are distributed, how people are related to each other in the production process, and what the authority and ownership relations are within the production process. A change in some aspect of the substructure (means or relations of production) will force changes in aspects of the superstructure. This change may be gradual or violent and revolutionary; but from Marx's perspective, a change in the substructure is the key to moving human societies from primitive communism through feudalism and capitalism to the "final" communist society.

Most important for the study of social stratification, Marx saw all societies (except in the first and last stages) divided between those who ruled and those who were ruled. The key to this division was again the substructure. Those who owned or controlled the major means of production in the society were able to dominate the other classes because the owners of the means of production are able to control the necessities of life. Thus, they can require others to follow their rules to obtain these necessities. Also, the owners' favored position in relation to the superstructure must be considered. The various components of the superstructure (ideologies, political organization, the legal system, and so on) generally help reinforce ruling class dominance.

Finally, Marx viewed the class system as loaded with conflict and exploitation because the favored position of the ruling class, or the bourgeoisie in capitalist society, allows it to extract surplus value from the working class. Marx's labor theory of value considered the value of all things produced to be found in the amount of labor time necessary to produce these goods. But in a class society workers are not given (or paid) the full value of their labor. Rather, they are given only a living wage, with the surplus going to enrich the ruling class. With Marx, therefore, we find the essence of a critical-conflict paradigm.

With the work of Max Weber we do not find such a systematic set of concepts used to construct a basic framework of the total structure of society. But Weber's view of society was no less guided by the overall existence of social conflict. However, because Weber saw conflict as more pervasive and at the very heart of all complex social organization, unlike Marx he held no hope that this human conflict could ever be completely eliminated.

For the study of social stratification, Weber made two most important contributions. *First,* he expanded Marx's class dimension of stratification and added the dimensions of status and party (or power). In addition to ownership of means of production, he saw a person's relation to the market (or level of skill that could bring a greater or lesser return) as leading to a particular class position.

Second, Weber recognized most fully in these early years of sociology the importance of the legal-rational mode of social organization for the nature of social stratification. In fact, it is here that Weber came to stress the party or power dimension of social stratification over the other two. The bureaucratic form of organization made necessary by large, complex industrial societies provided the means of dominance of one group over others. It is also here that we find the essence of Weber's uncritical-conflict paradigm.

Finally, with Émile Durkheim we examined the basic paradigm that was to shape modern functional theories of social stratification. Durkheim himself had little to say about class, conflict, or even social stratification. But his holistic view and organic analogy led to a stress on the needs of a social system, requiring social stratification for the good of the whole. Class divisions and conflicting class interests were neglected from this perspective. And when Durkheim was forced to recognize the existence of such divisions and conflicts, he explained them as unnatural and only temporary conditions. In time, he believed, such conditions would be eliminated or reduced when morality was strengthened in new industrialized societies. With Durkheim we find the essence of an uncritical-order paradigm of social stratification.

Having considered briefly some of the major ideas about the nature of social stratification from three major theorists during the early years of sociology's development, it is time to reemphasize some central points. We have chosen to focus on the works of Marx, Weber, and Durkheim not only because they are among the most respected classical sociological theorists, but also because their ideas helped form the basis of three competing schools or paradigms in the study of social stratification today. By focusing on these three theorists we hoped to enable the reader to have a better grasp of the major contemporary theories of social stratification to be considered in more detail in the next chapter.

NOTES

1 "A paradigm is a fundamental image of the subject matter within a science. It serves to define what should be studied, what questions should be asked, how they should be asked, and what rules should be followed in interpreting the answers obtained" (Ritzer 1980:7). Similar to a paradigm, but more specific as to images and assumptions about the subject matter contained within a paradigm, are what Gouldner (1970:31) calls *domain assumptions,* or what we may also call *paradigm assumptions.* Examples of domain assumptions relevant to the study of society are assumptions of human nature as rational or irrational or as selfish or altruistic and assumptions of whether society is fundamentally stable or changing and based upon unity or conflict.

At the outset, it must be noted that the idea of paradigms behind sociological theory is relatively controversial. Most sociologists do not reject the view that paradigms exist; rather, they disagree about what is contained within paradigms and about the exact number of paradigms that can be located behind competing sociological theories. Since Kuhn's (1962) first work on the subject of paradigms in the physical sciences there have been a number of works applying the idea of a paradigm to sociological theory (for example, see Friedrichs 1970; Effrat 1972; Ritze 1975, 1980). These works have defined a differing number of paradigms, with differing sets of paradigm assumptions and slightly differing views on what constitutes a paradigm.

2 In a fundamental respect, social scientific paradigms must be related to our experience of social phenomena. With respect to social inequality in particular, we can assume that as inequality emerged as an important aspect of society when human beings turned from hunting and gathering or primitive communal societies, people began a struggle to understand and act upon this new experience. Since human beings first learned to express themselves in written records that could be preserved they left evidence of competing assumptions about the nature of inequality that are in some ways similar to current competing assumptions (see Lenski 1966:3–17).

But this story of the development of assumptions about the nature of social stratification requires us to recognize a difference in the nature of social scientific paradigms when compared with physical science paradigms. The struggle to understand social phenomena such as inequality is not only a scientific endeavor; it also has a basis in class or group interests. The advantaged classes, and especially elites, have had (and continue to have) an interest in shaping the understanding of social stratification so that this understanding does not threaten their interests in the status quo.

Elites prefer to think that inequality rests upon the superior qualities of those on top, that it is beneficial for all, and that it is inevitable or necessary. The lower classes, especially when their conditions become unbearable, struggle to understand the exploitative and negative nature of structured inequality so that it can be altered. Because the upper classes have usually had the means to make their view of social phenomena the accepted view (because of their free time to speculate and write, because of their influence over religion and education, and because of their ability to reward or punish social thinkers), the upper-class view of inequality has usually (although by no means always) been the dominant view.

3 It can be argued, however, that Marx's view of the future communist society would fit in this critical-order cell in our typology (see Strasser 1976). With an optimistic view of human nature and a belief that inequality is not inevitable, Marx was critical of capitalist society because he believed that the future mature communist society would be based on cooperation and a lack of major class conflicts. This is in contrast to his view of capitalist societies as based on class conflict and exploitation, thus placing his theory of capitalist societies in the critical-conflict cell of our typology (to be discussed in detail below).

4 There is, however, another major variant within this uncritical-conflict paradigm, one that has been especially predominant in the study of the distribution of political power. This variant of the paradigm differs primarily in one respect from that discussed above. It is assumed in this variant that conflicting interests can be *structured* in such a way as to limit the extremes of conflict and exploitation. If, for example, conflicting interest groups are overlapping rather than superimposed, the society will not represent two exclusive groups in conflict (the haves and have-nots, for example). With overlapping conflict groups it is argued that a "web of conflicting interests" reduces extreme conflict (see Coser 1956, 1967). It is generally held, however, that the overlapping web of conflict can work only to limit to *some degree* the inevitable inequalities. This perspective will be discussed in more detail in our chapter on the corporate class.

5 It is interesting to note in this regard that Appelbaum (1978b:67) found few articles dealing with Marxian ideas in leading sociology journals in recent years. But the number is increasing, especially as Marxian-oriented scholars turn to more empirical methods. Also interesting is a study of introductory sociology textbooks (see Swatos 1980). This study compiled the total number of citations to specific authors found in these texts between 1973 and 1977. In similar previous studies covering the years 1958 to 1972, Marx was seldom mentioned. But in the 1973 to 1977 period, Marx was cited *more than any other author,* followed closely by Weber, then Durkheim.

6 It should be noted that although Marx had less to say about an Asiatic mode of production, many sociologists are recognizing the utility of considering this mode of production as distinct from feudalism (Mandel 1971; Krader 1975). As we saw in Chapter 3, with this Asiatic mode of production as a relatively distinct form of production and social stratification we are better able to understand the agriculturally

based differences in China and India as contrasted with those in Japan and European feudal societies. With an Asiatic mode of production there is less private ownership of land and a stronger political elite that developed with need for collective management of irrigation projects. In time this political elite came to control the surplus production much as the landowners did under feudalism. As with feudalism, the dominant means of production was agriculture, but the relations of production differed. In the Asiatic mode of production the relations of production involved political elite control of production (rather than private ownership of the means of production), with the surplus going to this political elite.

7 Many theorists, especially until recently, stressed that Marx believed the "owners would get richer, while the workers would become progressively poorer" as capitalism advanced. Therefore, this increasing misery would provide the anger necessary for social revolution. However, a more complete reading of Marx shows this "progressive misery" argument is found only in Marx's more political writings. Marx actually gave greater stress to a type of relative deprivation argument (see Davies 1962). He foresaw that the working class could become better off materially as capitalism advanced, but that the gap between the material existence of owners and the working class would increase (see Giddens 1973:34; Anderson 1974:23; Harrington 1976:130). How people judge their condition with reference to others (in this case the upper class) is more important, Marx recognized, and would thus produce anger.

But Marx did predict that the material existence of some within the working class would become worse, thus adding to the anger and conditions promoting revolution. This group he called the industrial reserve army. As fewer workers would be needed in advanced or monopoly capitalism, a large group of poor workers would develop who could find work only in good economic times.

8 In his later years Marx came to believe that violent revolution may *not* be necessary to transform capitalist societies to communism (see Berlin 1963:207; McLellan 1973:444). In one of those contradictions in Marx's writings Marxian theorists today would like to forget, Marx came to recognize that workers may gradually gain power through unions and working-class political parties to transform the state, and through it the economic structure of society to communism. This is one of the main goals of Euro-communist parties today. And many present Marxian theorists such as Erik Wright (1978a) are also coming to stress this possibility.

9 Marx did have a more complex view of class divisions than will be stressed here. For example, Marx did foresee the rapid growth of a middle class in advanced capitalism because of the increased need for technical skills and bureaucratic organization (see Giddens 1973:177). Most Marxian theorists, however, continue to stress that this middle class is an extension of the working class or proletariat (see Anderson 1974:52–56). Also, Marx described the *lumpenproletariat* as an extremely poor urban class that had no function in industrial society. But for the most part, in capitalist societies the bourgeoisie (or capitalists) and the proletariat (working class) were the primary class divisions in Marx's views.

10 Bureaucracies are often inefficient and create further problems. But the point is that all industrial societies have found it necessary to adopt bureaucratic methods of organization as described by Weber. And this includes private as well as public sector organizations.

11 Karl Mannheim (see Wolff 1971:161) best conceptualized this aspect of "conservative thought": "Thus progressive reform tends to tackle the system as a whole,

while conservative reformism tackles particular details.'' In other words, for Durkheim no basic change is needed in the status quo; only small changes are needed to make it work better. This is in contrast to the position of a critical theorist like Marx, who called for a more basic or radical change of the status quo. Using common political descriptions, we can say that Durkheim would be described as conservative, or even liberal, while Marx would be described as a radical.

CHAPTER 5

MODERN THEORIES OF SOCIAL STRATIFICATION

Though today most sociologists consider social stratification one of the most important areas of study, this has not always been the case. In fact, the importance of this subject in understanding society and human behavior has been widely recognized by American sociologists only in the past fifty years, at most. The contrast to European social thought is clear. As we noted in the previous chapter, Marx, Weber, and even those before them such as Comte and Saint-Simon began their studies of society with the nature of class divisions and inequality as central questions (see Strasser 1976). What accounts for this contrast to American sociology? Our answer to this question can in part help us understand the state of stratification theory today.

Sociology as a separate discipline of study in the United States dates back only to about the early 1900s. But in the works of the founders of American sociology (men such as William Graham Sumner, Albion Small, and Edward Ross) we find a rather classless view of American society (Pease, Form, and Huber 1970; for a summary of these works see Gordon 1963; Page 1969). The relative neglect of social stratification is not surprising, however. Unlike in European nations, the old rigid class and estate inequalities were less in evidence. The value system stressed equality of opportunity for all, and at least an appearance of opportunity and democracy was in greater evidence. Not until the Great Depression of the 1930s was this classless image seriously reexamined, and then only by a few social scientists. Even then, many years passed before the study of social stratification was able to make a significant break with American classless mythology.

The first detailed American study in social stratification appeared in 1929 with Robert and Helen Lynd's *Middletown*, followed later by *Middletown in Transition* (1937). This first work was to establish a long tradition of stratification studies of small community life in the United States. But the general conflict perspective of this study was only much later a part of this tradition. The Lynds' focus was on power and economic inequalities, and the overpowering image of equality of opportunity in American society was exposed as a myth (see Gordon 1963:66). With the Depression over, their view of American society was placed on the shelf and all but forgotten.

Of the social stratification research stimulated by the Great Depression, Lloyd Warner's work (in the 1930s and 1940s) had the most significant impact, at least for the next twenty to thirty years. Like the Lynds' research, Warner's many-volume *Yankee City* study (as well as others by his students) was centered on social stratification in small communities. Using various methods of study, from survey research to detailed participant observation, these works sought to examine the extent of inequality and social mobility, as well as the meaning of social stratification for the people involved.

But the Warner school differed from the Lynd tradition in three important ways. Most importantly, the Warner school came to define social stratification in terms of *status* (Weber's second dimension of social stratification). As Warner (and Lunt 1941:82) wrote: "By class is meant two or more orders of people who are believed to be, and are accordingly ranked by the members of the community, in superior and inferior positions." With such a view, inequalities of power and economic dominance were easily ignored, and the dynamics of conflict related to these stratification dimensions were dismissed.

Secondly, the Warner school failed to examine the actual extent of equality of opportunity critically. In the face of contrary experience highlighted by the Depression, this research tradition continued to stress a "reality" of social mobility for all who had the talent and ambition to succeed, a finding now disputed in a reanalysis of *Yankee City* (Thernstrom 1964).

Finally, we find in the Warner school an emphasis on social stratification as *functional* and necessary for complex societies like our own. The conflict, the structured and hereditary nature of inequalities, the harsh conditions for workers, and the extensive poverty all too often found in the expansion of American capitalism were all but ignored.

The primary points are these:

1 During the earliest stage of American sociology the subject of social stratification was generally ignored. With very few exceptions, such as in the work of Thorstein Veblen, it was as if "nasty" conditions of class conflict, hereditary wealth, and race and class exploitation did not exist in the "classless" American society.

2 It took the experience of this country's most severe economic crisis to bring many social scientists to face the reality of rigid class inequalities. But even when this happened, the sobering reality forced upon us by this economic crisis was for most social scientists short-lived.

3 When the study of social stratification was increasingly taken up by American social scientists, the more palatable subject of *status* inequality dominated their work. The praise of America as the most classless of all industrial societies would continue for some time.

All of the above would be worthy of no more than a short footnote in the history of American sociology were it not for the fact that this tradition of stratification research remains to a large degree. As we will see, conflict perspectives have only recently become more widely respected by academic social scientists as a counter to the limited view of functional theories of social stratification. Research continues to be dominated by mobility studies that focus attention on individual characteristics rather than the structured and rigid inequalities of wealth and power (see Huber and Form 1973:36). Our research on poverty, for example, is still struggling to escape the "culture of poverty" perspective that focuses attention on characteristics of the poor (or what is wrong with the poor), rather than directing our attention to the wider stratification system that helps maintain poverty (Kerbo 1981a).

However, a tradition of stratification theory and research was at least begun. The Warner school stimulated many students, and there was soon a wide variety of research on subjects such as differing class values and lifestyles, occupational prestige (if not occupational power), and the degree and causes of social mobility (Pease, Form, and Huber 1970). One review of the early stratification literature found at least 333 research articles and books on the subject published between 1945 and 1953 (Pfautz 1952). By 1954 the first American textbook on the subject was published (Cuber and Kenkel 1954).

The study of social stratification by the 1950s, however, was clearly dominated by a *functional* perspective. It was a perspective more in line with that of Durkheim than Marx or even Weber. Such dominance could not last. As social scientists looked more deeply, the American values of equality of opportunity and free enterprise began to appear as questionable guides to the reality of social stratification in this country.

The break with functional theory came first with Floyd Hunter's (1953) study of community power, then most dramatically with C. Wright Mills' (1956) description of a power elite on the national level. Before Watergate, Vietnam, the energy crisis, and our discovery of poverty and discrimination in the 1960s, these works were ahead of their time. And though they were initially attacked by social scientists (see Domhoff and Ballard 1968, for these attacks), just as Einstein's paradigm-breaking work was originally attacked, they could not long be ignored.

Functional views of social stratification don't have to be completely discarded, and conflict theories don't have all the answers. But functional theories of social stratification are limited. We must turn to some of these theories to see what they do have to offer, and their exact limitations.

FUNCTIONAL THEORIES OF SOCIAL STRATIFICATION

Within the functional or uncritical-order paradigm described in Chapter 4, and following the Warner tradition described above, we find two most prominent modern functional theories of social stratification. The first of these was published by Kingsley Davis and Wilbert Moore in 1945, somewhat amended by Kingsley Davis in 1948, and has come to be known simply as the Davis and Moore theory of social stratification. The theory was "logically" constructed to show why social stratification and inequality are positively functional, and therefore necessary in all but the simplest human societies. The second theory is from the more abstract and general functional perspective of Talcott Parsons. This theory does not contradict that of Davis and Moore, but its focus is on social order more generally and the function of social stratification for the overall maintenance of social order.

The Davis and Moore Theory

Clearly the most noted and most debated theory of social stratification is that of Davis and Moore (1945). A few years after the theory was published it set off a long and sometimes heated debate among social scientists. The controversy surrounding the theory can be understood best by remembering our earlier discussion of paradigm conflicts in the study of social stratification.

The Davis and Moore theory clearly and simply outlined the functional view of social stratification as necessary to meet the needs of complex social systems. In other words, from a perspective that considers society as something like an organism, the theory argued that this organism has needs that must be met if it is to remain healthy. Among these needs is for the most important positions or jobs in the society to be staffed by the most qualified and competent people. Social stratification is considered a mechanism that ensures that the need is met.

The Davis and Moore theory is no *general* theory of social stratification. Its goal is limited to explaining why inequality is necessary to ensure the proper functioning of complex societies. With this in mind we can summarize the basic points of the theory. (The summary is from Tumin 1953.)

1 Certain positions in any society are functionally more important than others, and require special skills to fill them.

2 Only a limited number of people in any society have the talents that can be trained into the skills appropriate to these positions.

3 The conversion of talents into skills involves a training period during which sacrifices of one kind or another are made by those undergoing the training.

4 In order to induce the talented people to undergo these sacrifices and acquire the training, their future positions must carry an inducement value in the form of a differential—that is, privileged and disproportionate access to the scarce and desired rewards the society has to offer.

5 These scarce and desired goods consist of the rights and prerequisites attached to, or built into, the positions, and can be classified into those things that contribute to (a) sustenance and comfort, (b) humor and diversion, and (c) self-respect and ego expansion.

6 This differential access to the basic rewards of the society has as a consequence the differentiation of the prestige and esteem various strata acquire. It may be said to constitute, along with the rights and prerequisites, institutionalized social inequality; that is, stratification.

7 Therefore, social inequality among different strata in the amounts of scarce and desired goods and the amounts of prestige and esteem they receive is both positively functional and inevitable in any society.

Let us now follow the logic of this theory, using the example of two positions, physician and garbage collector, to provide maximum clarity.

1 It can be argued, with somewhat questionable validity, that the job performed by the physician is *more important* than that of a garbage collector. We say the differing importance of these two positions is somewhat questionable because in large urban areas both are important. (The problem of assessing functional importance will be considered below.) One has only to imagine a strike by both physicians and garbage collectors to see the importance of these positions. In either case the city would be in trouble. But the key difference is found in the next point.

2 Davis and Moore assume the task of a physician requires special *talents* that are limited in the population. In addition, to become a physician requires a *long training period* if the special talents are to be developed into the needed skills. No such talents or training period is required for a garbage collector.

3 It is further assumed that some *sacrifice* is necessary to acquire the needed skills of a physician. Such sacrifice would include the time, money, effort, and psychological pressure involved in medical school. The position of garbage collector requires no such sacrifice to obtain training. A key point follows.

4 In order to *induce qualified people* to undergo the sacrifice of obtaining the needed skills to perform as physicians, the future position must bring expected rewards appropriate to the required sacrifice. No such special rewards are seen as necessary to fill the position of garbage collector.

5 Thus, the rewards, of various types, must be attached to or built into the position. In other words, the rewards must not be random (only some physicians highly paid), but *an expected part* of a position as physician for maximum inducement to people with special talents.

6 A result is that the physician and garbage collector have differing access to the basic rewards of the society, and the two positions reflect differing amounts of prestige and esteem.

7 Therefore, social inequality with respect to the positions of physician and garbage collector is both positively functional and inevitable to ensure that the position of physician is filled by the most qualified people.

At face value the Davis and Moore theory of stratification appears a simple, clear, and valid explanation of inequality and social stratification in industrial, if not all, societies. In a sense it is a labor market model analyzing the supply and demand of labor as it relates to rewards for labor. In short, when the supply of skilled labor is low in relation to the amount of labor needed, the employer (in Davis and Moore's perspective, the society) will be required to pay more for this labor. *But* the Davis and Moore view of this labor market model is flawed. And several social scientists have revealed other problems of logic and omission over the years. The Davis and Moore theory doesn't have to be rejected on every point, but it does need to be amended in several respects. Let us turn first to some of the criticisms of the Davis and Moore theory, then go on to some empirical research.

Critiques of Davis and Moore We may begin with one of the most far-reaching criticisms of the implied labor market model behind the Davis and Moore theory. As Collins (1975:420) argues: "Following through the pure market model leads us to a startling conclusion: The system must tend toward perfect equality in the distribution of wealth." This is the opposite of what Davis and Moore suggest with their theory to explain why an unequal distribution of rewards must exist.

One problem with the theory is that Davis and Moore neglect restraints on the labor market in the form of unequal power and influence; that is, conflict assumptions. Without such market restraints there would be a tendency toward equality because where labor is free to move to higher paying jobs, the jobs that pay high wages will attract a surplus of workers, leading to a decline in the income for these jobs. Jobs paying low wages would tend to attract fewer workers. Without market restraints "wherever jobs pay above or below the average, processes are set in motion through labor mobility which eventually bring wages back into line with all the others" (Collins 1975:120).

And if we consider other rewards attached to positions, such as a good working environment or the prestige that comes with greater skill, we might find another result opposite from that predicted by Davis and Moore. Again assuming a free market model, we might find that, using our examples, a physician would be paid *less* (in income) than a garbage collector because of the other rewards (such as prestige and working environment) attached to the position of physician.

Davis and Moore have two lines of defense to the above criticism. Both, however, are weak. On the one hand, Davis (1948) amended the theory shortly after it was published to say that the family structure will create a restraint on equal access to occupations. This is because those families higher in the stratification system will be able to secure better access to education and jobs for their children. Davis argues that their original theory was abstract theoretical reasoning, and in real life other factors will influence the process they described. But, of course, this is the point of critiques from conflict theorists! The question is, how much does the theory vary from real life? The critics argue that real life is far different from the theory.

Davis and Moore, on the other hand, argue in the original theory that not everyone is equally talented or capable of performing the tasks of some very important positions. In this sense they do not acknowledge free labor competition. Many people could collect garbage, but only a few have the talent to become physicians. But again we find a weakness in the theory. Are there really so few people with the talent to make it through medical school and become physicians? The critics' response is no. Many people have the talent to become physicians, but in reality there are limitations on who and how many people can become physicians because of the ability of the medical profession to restrict and limit access to training for the occupation.

Most of the criticisms of the Davis and Moore theory evolve around their neglect of power (see Wrong 1959; Lopreato and Lewis 1963; Cohen 1968:60). As our review of history in Chapter 3 should have made clear, the greater the rewards received by individuals or groups, the greater their ability to make sure they continue receiving such rewards, and even more rewards, no matter what function they serve for the society.

There is also the question of what, in fact, the most important positions in the society are. The critics' response is that those with power are able to influence which positions are defined as most important (see Tumin 1963; Cohen 1968:60; Kerbo 1976a). And some criticism questions the *degree* of inequality necessary among positions in our society. One may grant the assumption that a physician is more important than a garbage collector, or at least that the position of physician requires more training and skill. But, for example, if we find that the physician earns twenty times more income than the garbage collector, can we say that the physician is twenty times more important than the garbage collector? Or do some occupations provide greater control and influence that allow them to demand greater pay?

Other criticisms of the Davis and Moore theory can be found in the literature. But for now it will be useful to summarize what some, and Tumin (1953:393) in particular, have described as the *dysfunctions* of stratification and inequality, in contrast to the so-called functions.

1 Social stratification systems function to limit the possibility of discovery of the full range of talent available in a society because of unequal access to appropriate motivation, channels of recruitment, and centers of training.

2 In foreshortening the range of available talent, social stratification systems function to set limits upon the possibility of expanding the productive resources of the society, at least relative to what might be accomplished under conditions of greater equality of opportunity.

3 Social stratification systems function to provide the elite with the political power necessary to procure acceptance and dominance of an ideology that rationalizes the status quo, whatever it may be, as logical, natural, and morally right.

4 Social stratification systems function to distribute favorable self-images unequally throughout the population. To the extent that such favorable self-images are requisite to the development of the creative potential inherent in people, stratification systems function to limit the development of this creative potential.

5 To the extent that inequalities in social rewards cannot be made fully acceptable to the less privileged in a society, social stratification systems function to encourage hostility, suspicion, and distrust among the various segments of a society and thus to limit the possibilities of extensive social integration.

6 To the extent that the sense of significant membership in a society depends on one's place on the prestige ladder of the society, social stratification systems function to distribute unequally the sense of significant membership in the population.

7 To the extent that loyalty to a society depends on a sense of significant membership in the society, social stratification systems function to distribute loyalty unequally in the population.

8 To the extent that participation or apathy depend upon the sense of significant membership in the society, social stratification systems function to distribute the motivation to participate unequally in a population.

Empirical Research on the Davis and Moore Theory   Although it is often difficult to examine general theories of social stratification empirically, the Davis and Moore theory does make some specific predictions that can be tested. But even here, as we will see, it is most difficult to measure and test all important propositions suggested by the theory.

Abrahamson (1973) has empirically examined the proposition that the most important positions in a society will be more highly rewarded. To measure functional importance, Abrahamson reasoned, periods in which some needs of the society have undergone change can be considered. One such change may be during times of war. In this case, it is suggested, positions in the military would be functionally more important than during peacetime. The implication from the Davis and Moore theory is that during wartime, the pay of military positions would increase relative to comparable civilian occupations.

To test this proposition Abrahamson selected three military positions and three comparable occupations in the private sector (corporal versus factory worker, captain versus public school teacher, and diplomat versus college professor). He then compared changes in the national pay scale of these six positions over a period from 1939 to 1967, which included three wars. Although Abrahamson was able to find adequate data on only about one-half of the comparisons, the Davis and Moore thesis appears supported in eleven out of the twelve comparisons. The negative finding was during peacetime in 1963, when diplomats gained in relation to college professors.

Abrahamson's test of the Davis and Moore theory has received extensive criticism. One serious problem is the lack of adequate data for many comparisons. Leavy (1974) attempted to gather more extensive data to reexamine Abrahamson's findings, and did find complete comparisons on corporals versus industrial workers from 1943 to 1967. The additional data conformed to

Abrahamson's conclusions except in two years, 1943 and 1947. In 1943 (a war year) industrial workers gained in relation to corporals, and in 1947 (peacetime) corporals gained in relation to industrial workers.

However, Leavy remains unconvinced that the study supports Davis and Moore. In addition to neglecting the potential effects of scarcity of qualified workers, the study does not show that more qualified personnel were attracted to these positions when pay increased (a key point in the Davis and Moore thesis). But most importantly, Leavy suggests, many of the industrial workers during the three war periods included in the study were involved in military production, a fact making the comparisons less meaningful.

Several other weaknesses in the Abrahamson study have been noted by Vanfossen and Rhodes (1974). First, they argue that a conflict perspective can equally explain Abrahamson's findings. It may be that during war periods the military has more influence to demand pay increases because of national concern about war. Also, following the Davis and Moore thesis, in times of war higher military officers should be functionally more important than privates. But Vanfossen and Rhodes present data showing that privates gain more in pay than higher officers during war. In fact, the data show higher officers obtained more pay increases during peacetime.

In other research, Abrahamson (1979) found that scarcity and importance of differing positions on major league baseball teams are related to the pay of these positions, as Davis and Moore would predict. But in a study of corporate executive income, Broom and Cushing (1977) found that the functional importance of a corporate executive (measured by how many other workers depend on the executive role) and the performance of an executive (corporate profits and growth) were not related to income. Further, Broom and Cushing (1977) found that corporations that could be assumed to be more important for a society (producing products such as steel, food, drugs, and clothing) did *not* pay their executives more than executives were paid in less functional corporations (such as those producing tobacco, cosmetics, and soft drinks). Again, the Davis and Moore theory is not supported.

A number of empirical studies have shown that the general population in this nation, as well as in others, tends to believe that inequality and social stratification *should* operate in a manner generally suggested by the Davis and Moore theory (for example, Grandjean and Bean 1975; Jasso and Rossi 1977; Alves and Rossi 1978; also see Verba and Orren 1985; Coxon, Davies, and Jones 1986; Vanneman and Cannon 1987). But, of course, this does not mean that the theory fits reality. We have examined some of the limited empirical research on this question, and the overall findings are at best mixed.

Parsons' Functional Theory of Social Stratification

Compared with the Davis and Moore theory, Talcott Parsons' work is much more general and abstract. One of the central figures in modern American sociology, Parsons developed a theory that is often considered the most important functional statement on all aspects of society ever made. But, as stated, his work is so abstract and highly theoretical that few precise empirical predictions can be made or tested from his work (as Parsons admitted, 1977). Nonetheless, Parsons' work has been highly influential in carrying on the tradition of Durkheim and the Warner school of social stratification in American sociology. In this section we will consider briefly the major components of Parsons' theory, then criticisms of this theory, and finally some research attempting to test the validity of some of his ideas.

Parsons' functional theory does not contradict that of Davis and Moore, but the emphasis is different. Following the long tradition of functional analysis, Parsons saw the most important question for sociology as how social order is possible. And following this tradition of sociological analysis, his answer was *norms and values.* The norms and values of a society, generally internalized by individuals through a long and ongoing socialization process, guide behavior and human interaction. In other words, we do what we do, our institutions do what they do, for the most part because of a common value system. (For example, most people do not steal, not because they believe they will be caught and sent to jail, but because they think it is wrong to steal.) Like Davis and Moore, Parsons assumed a society with needs of its own. And one of the most important of these needs is social integration. A common value system operates to serve this need.

From these basic assumptions Parsons argued that two sets of concepts help us understand social stratification. In his first article on social stratification in 1940 Parsons (see 1964:70) wrote that "central for the purposes of this discussion is the differential evaluation in the moral sense of individuals as units." In his subsequent works on social stratification in 1949, 1953, and 1970, this theme was continued (see Parsons 1964, 1970). What Parsons meant by this, as in the Warner school, is that *status* or honor is the most important dimension of social stratification. People are evaluated and ranked by others in terms of how well they live up to the dominant values in the society, whatever these values may be. This means that there will always be a hierarchy of status honor in every society.

Parsons recognized wealth and power differences, but for him these are by definition *secondary.* Writing of wealth, Parsons (1964:83) stated, "In spite of much opinion to the contrary, it is not a primary criterion, seen in terms of the common value system ... its primary significance is a symbol of achievement." Parsons arrived at the same conclusion as Davis and Moore. But for Parsons the common value system helps ensure that the functionally most important roles are filled by competent people through their status striving.

In order to specify the placement of people in the stratification system Parsons had to rank which roles or tasks are the most respected (to the least respected) in the society, which involved getting more specific about the dominant value system. Tackling this task, Parsons first offered his description of the four major *functional subsystems* within a society that are related to the four major *functional prerequisites* that all societies must meet if they are to survive. That is, all societies must solve problems of (1) *adaptation* of the environment, (2) *goal attainment,* (3) *integration,* and (4) *latent pattern maintenance* (or for short, AGIL). The primary "concrete" institutions that usually perform these functional prerequisites for a society are, in order, the economy, the state, the legal system or sometimes religion, and the family, schools, and cultural institutions.

It will be helpful at this point if our earlier discussion of the organic analogy of society is remembered. Like body organs, each of these types of institutions is said to be serving a function for the health of the total organism—that is, society. For example, it is the task of economic institutions to extract resources from the environment and produce needed goods and services. The task of the state or polity is to define goals and provide direction toward these collective goals. Institutions such as law and religion help provide integration of the social system through rules or moral standards. Finally, the family and institutions such as education perform pattern maintenance through training and socializing individual members of the society and serving their personal needs so that they can be functioning members of the society.

The importance of all the above in understanding social stratification, Parsons claimed, is twofold: (1) The differing tasks of these various institutions lead them to stress differing values (or pattern variables). (2) Societies differ with respect to which of the four sets of institutions (adaptive, goal attainment, integration, or latent pattern maintenance) is primary. In a society where one set of institutions is primary (say, goal attainment or the polity), the common value system will be more heavily weighed toward the values most consistent with this institutional stress. *Thus,* the individuals who best live up to the values shaped by the primary institution or institutions will receive more status, as well as the secondary rewards that are tied to high status, like wealth.

Let us summarize these very abstract ideas:

1 A person's place in the status hierarchy (stratification system) is determined by the moral evaluation of others.

2 This moral evaluation is made in terms of a common value system.

3 The common value system is shaped by the institution that is given primary stress in the society (the institutional stress coming from the particular historical and environmental circumstances of the society).

4 Thus, people who best live up to these values or ideas will receive, in addition to high status, other rewards, such as a high income and wealth.

It is also important to note that authority (or power) is attained through an individual's functional position in the occupational structure, which, of course, is gained through status attainment (see Figure 5-1).

We can now briefly consider what the above means for the United States stratification system. It is doubtful that anyone would disagree with Parsons' view that the adaptive subsystem (the economy) is given greatest stress in the United States. This means that the value system in this country is weighted

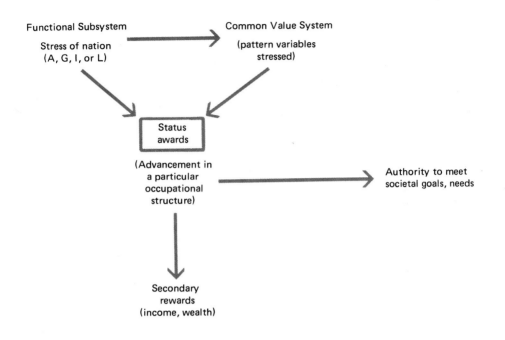

FIGURE 5-1
Parsons' theory of social stratification.

toward performance in the occupational structure (Parsons 1951:399) and that people who meet the performance and achievement ideals in the economic occupational structure will be rewarded with greater status, advancement in the occupational structure, and the secondary rewards of wealth and high income.

By way of contrast, Parsons would argue that a country such as the Soviet Union stresses goal attainment, or political institutions, over economic institutions. The values in this country, following the stress on goal attainment or the polity, are weighted toward leadership ability and commitment to political ideals. The people who most typify these values would receive high status, advancement in the political bureaucracy, and secondary rewards such as wealth and high income. A similar description would be given for societies stressing, say, religious institutions and values (such as Iran since its revolution in 1979 or monks in the closed environment of a monastery).

Parsons' view does not contradict that of Davis and Moore. Only the stress on moral evaluation is different. Parsons still maintains that the most important positions in the society will be most highly rewarded, with status first, and wealth as a secondary reward. What Parsons has done, however, is specify more clearly what the most important positions will be, given a particular institutional stress in the society.

Critiques of Parsons One does not need an empirical study to test Parsons' prediction that top business executives are most highly rewarded in the United States. Nor need we empirically examine the Soviet stratification system to find that top political elites are most rewarded. But one can certainly disagree with Parsons over *why* these people are on top of the stratification system in these countries. In other words, what Parsons leaves out of his analysis, or reduces to secondary importance, is a key to the critics' responses. And because Parsons clearly follows the functional tradition of Durkheim, most criticisms of Durkheim's view noted in the previous chapter apply equally to Parsons.

One of the most prominent criticisms of Parsons' work involves his assumption of a society with needs of its own. From this perspective, people in top institutional positions are doing what they do for the interests and needs of the total society. For Parsons, the interests of individuals and groups within the society are secondary. Like Durkheim, Parsons recognized class divisions, but again, these were seen as less important (Burger 1977).

Take the example of power. Parsons preferred the term *authority* because he viewed power and influence over others as something given to occupants of top institutional positions so that the interests and needs of the total society would be furthered (see Parsons 1964:327; 1960:181). Parsons rejected the notion that power is often used to promote the interests of particular individuals or groups over others. One need only remember our review of history in Chapter 3 to see the problem with Parsons' assumptions about power.

Most enlightening in this respect was Parsons' reactions to C. Wright Mills' famous work *The Power Elite*. Parsons (1968:61) began his criticism of Mills' thesis (that there is a power elite that dominates the country in its own interests) by saying he had very few criticisms of fact, only of theoretical interpretation. In Parsons' (1968:82) view, "The essential point at present is that, to Mills, power is not a facility for the performance of function in, and on the behalf of, the society as a system, but is interpreted exclusively as a facility for getting what one group, the holders of power, wants by preventing another group, the 'outs,' from getting what it wants."

In other words, if you take away Parsons' assumptions that there is a social system with needs of its own and that actors in this system are working to fulfill society's needs rather than their own, Parsons' description of the United States stratification system is close to that in C. Wright Mills' *The Power Elite* (Atkinson 1972:33). This also means that "what was a nightmare to C. Wright Mills, it seems, constitutes perfection of the social system to Talcott Parsons" (Strasser 1976:179).

This view of a society with needs of its own also helps us to understand Parsons' conceptual trick in defining wealth and high income as secondary rewards. Parsons could do this because he believed that people primarily seek status, therefore striving to live up to dominant values. By striving to live up to the dominant values—remembering that Parsons saw the values as shaped by the needs of society—people are serving the needs of society. Parsons did not see people as striving primarily for power and material wealth for *personal interests*. But even if status striving is primary, also neglected by Parsons is that a common value system may be shaped by the interest of those in powerful, wealthy positions in the society.

Conflict theorists like Tumin (1953:393) point out that "social stratification systems function to provide the elite with the political power necessary to procure acceptance and dominance of an ideology which rationalizes the status quo, whatever this may be, as 'logical,' 'natural,' and 'morally right.'" An elite may legitimize its own high status through its influence over people's perspective of what is to be valued. To the extent that this is the case, people may be given status and other rewards *not* because they meet the needs of the overall society, but because they *serve the interests of elites in the society*. More detail on this process will be given in the chapter on legitimation.

Because status striving has a central position in Parsons' theory we must examine this concept more fully. It will be remembered that in Weber's multidimensional view of stratification, status (honor or prestige) was only one dimension, to which Weber added class (or economic inequality) and power (or party). Weber viewed all three as important dimensions or divisions in a society, although in most of his work he tended to view power as increasingly primary in modern society. We must ask what the relationship is among all three of these dimensions. It will be instructive to return briefly to our earlier review of the history of inequality.

We found (following Lenski 1966) that in societies with a low level of technology and thus no or little surplus, goods were distributed on the basis of need. More importantly for our present discussion, we found hunting and gathering, or primitive communal societies, for the most part to have no or few inequalities of wealth and power. But there were usually inequalities of status. Lenski argues that awards of status are based on how well someone serves the needs of the tribe. For example, when a tribe depends primarily on hunting for food, the best hunter is given respect or status by other members of the tribe. Thus, the data we have tend to support much of the functional explanation of stratification *with this type of human group*.

However, we saw that as the level of technology increased in human societies, so did the level of other types of inequality (for example, power and wealth). The best explanation seems to be that as some individuals or groups obtained the resources or means to dominate others—through control of the expanding surplus, free time, new weapons, and so on—they did so with the result of growing inequalities of power and wealth. Status inequalities, of course, continued. But from the conflict perspective the primary base of status had changed. As indicated in Figure 5-2, the primary base or attainment of status comes from power and economic dominance (see Lenski 1966:46, for a

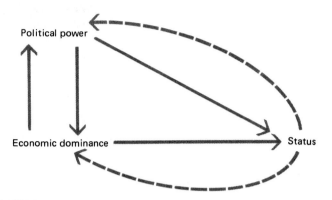

FIGURE 5-2
A conflict view of economic dominance, power, and status. Conflict
theorists, of course, may disagree whether political power or
economic dominance, or neither, is most important.

similar figure). Status as a route to power and economic rewards (the functionalist view) is considered in Figure 5-2 as secondary (as indicated by the broken
line).

Conflict theorists, as indicated by Figure 5-2, do not discount the importance of status inequalities. Nor do they reject the possibility that at times and
under special circumstances status inequality may be a primary dimension of
social stratification. Let us turn to a special circumstance. A study by Della
Fave and Hillery (1980) examined the stratification system in monasteries. The
study was conducted using participant observation (over a seven-year period),
with survey data also obtained form several monasteries across the United
States. The value system of monasteries consciously restricts material inequalities, but power inequalities are also at a minimum. The nominal authority figure in the monastery, the abbot, was found in reality to have very little power
with the decision-making process typically democratic in practice.

But, as we would expect from the evaluating nature of human beings, Della
Fave and Hillery did find inequalities of status. What accounts for these inequalities of status in the face of the egalitarian values of the monastery? The
researchers found no relation between the status ranking shown in questionnaire data and formal positions such as abbot, priest, or brother. Neither was
there a relation between the status ranking and previous family background, or
the differing economic tasks assigned the monks.

Most simply, the data showed the status ranking to be strongly related to
personal qualities of individual monks; that is, those who typified or best lived
up to the religious ideals received higher status. Della Fave and Hillery conclude, however, that Parsons' theory of social stratification has only limited
value. Status inequalities are primary dimensions of stratification *only* when

there is a small community that is *highly integrated* around a strong set of moral principles. We will see in a later chapter that Japan has a stratification system which emphasizes status–honor rewards more than other industrial societies. And we will also see that this is possible because of Japan's homogeneous population making value consensus more extensive.

Other evidence supports Della Fave and Hillery's general conclusion. For example, studies of this kind have been made of the early Israeli kibbutzim (Rosenfeld 1951; Spiro 1970). Around 1910 Jewish intellectuals and socialists began settling in what is now the state of Israel. Bringing with them egalitarian principles and little else, they established small agrarian communes called *kibbutzim*. The settlers intended these communities to be purely democratic, with no inequalities of power and material possessions. For the most part they succeeded, sharing virtually all material goods and using a rotating system of nominal leadership (Spiro 1970). But as we would suspect, they were unable to eliminate inequalities of status. Originally, the value system of these small communities stressed hard work and primarily agrarian labor. Those who were better able to meet these ideals received more status.

Through time, however kibbutzim changed, and how they changed is very instructive. As the original ideals weakened over the years, inequalities other than status emerged. In some kibbutzim there followed an increase in wealth inequalities; in others, power inequalities became most prominent. Rosenfeld (1951) reports that managers (the administrative elite) developed a rigid class system based on inequalities of authority. In addition, these inequalities became hereditary because the children of the manager class were often seen as showing great promise and talent, and given special privilege.

Again we find that in a highly integrated moral community equalities of all kinds except status can be maintained. But as with the kibbutzim, when this moral integration breaks down, other types of inequality soon develop. One can hardly imagine a highly diversified industrial society with many class, race, ethnic, subcultural, and/or religious divisions maintaining the required moral integration of a monastery or kibbutz. Status as a *primary* dimension of inequality seems limited.

In conclusion, Parsons (1977:338) considered his theory to be analytical and not falsifiable. In other words, it is a guide to our understanding of phenomena such as social stratification, rather than a theory with specific hypotheses that can be tested empirically. For the most part Parsons is correct in this view. The theory is so abstract that it can be described more accurately as a paradigm.

But, as we have noted many times, an accumulation of empirical, historical, and other types of data and information can lead us to suggest that one abstract theory or paradigm is more useful or less useful in providing understanding of a particular subject matter such as social stratification. The ideas of Davis and Moore and Talcott Parsons reviewed here are not without value. Societies do, to some extent, operate in the manner described by these functional theorists. However, because of an accumulation of supporting information, a very small part of which is presented here and in other chapters, social scientists are increasingly turning to conflict explanations of inequality and social stratification.

CONFLICT THEORIES OF SOCIAL STRATIFICATION

Among conflict theories of social stratification, unlike functional theories, we find no clear leaders. There are, it seems, two main reasons for this: First, and most important, we find a greater diversity of relevant paradigm assumptions (as discussed in Chapter 4) that influence the construction of conflict theories. Second, the more recent popularity of conflict theories (in contrast to functional theories) in American sociology has provided less time for leadership.

With respect to the first reason for diversity, it will be remembered from our discussion in Chapter 4 that we can identify two major conflict paradigms—uncritical-conflict and critical-conflict paradigms—that influence the development of conflict theories. After noting some of the general differences and similarities in conflict theories, the main tasks of this section will be to (1) outline briefly recent additions to Marxian theory, (2) examine some uncritical-conflict theories (primarily that of Dahrendorf), and (3) provide a general description of the main components of conflict theories (of all types) most useful for understanding the nature of inequality and social stratification in the United States. In effect, this final task will involve something of a synthesis of the main types of conflict theory.

One of the most useful means of understanding some of the main differences between the two conflict paradigms (and functional as well) is to consider the dimension of social stratification stressed by each. From Weber's influential description of stratification systems we recognize the primary dimensions of class, status, and party (or power).

What is interesting about theories of stratification is that there has been a tendency for theorists to stress one of these dimensions most heavily (see Table 5-1). Theories from the uncritical-conflict paradigm have tended to stress

TABLE 5-1
CLASS, STATUS, AND POWER DIMENSIONS STRESSED IN STRATIFICATION PARADIGMS

		Value assumptions	
		Critical	Uncritical
	Order	Empty with modern theories	Functional theory
Model assumptions			**Status–honor** (and occupational status)
	Conflict	Ruling-class theory	Power–conflict theory
		Class	**Power**

power or party as the main dimension of social stratification. For example, these theories focus attention on political power or formalized bureaucratic power and authority (as did Weber) in explaining the nature of inequality and social stratification in industrial societies.

Theories from the critical-conflict paradigm have tended to stress Marx's view of economic or property relations, that is, *class* as the most important dimension. And following our discussion of functional theories, we can see that these theorists have stressed Weber's *status* dimension.

Although functional theorists have also stressed the importance of an occupational structure (the other part of Weber's class dimension) in the nature of inequality and social stratification (especially the Davis and Moore theory), at the base of this occupational structure they stress *status* divisions (as we saw especially with Parsons' theory).

In part, a reason for this difference in stress on the various dimensions of stratification can be found in the divergent paradigm assumptions outlined in Chapter 4. Critical conflict theorists assume that inequality can be significantly reduced and that the major source of inequality in our society is related to the historical development of property relations. If inequality is to be reduced, it must be based on changing property or class relations, rather than on a more general conflict of interests "always found" among human beings.

Uncritical-conflict theorists, in contrast, tend to view inequality and social stratification as based on differing human and group interests in a more general sense. Although not always explicitly stressing this conflict of interests as related to selfish human nature, they assume that some kinds of interests will always be in conflict. In complex societies, therefore, these differing group interests will be reflected in organized power structures (or bureaucratic or political organizations) that are generalized means of furthering group interests of any type.

Uncritical-order or functional theorists maintain that inequality will always be present, but they tend to stress the needs of complex human organizations as the reason for this inequality. Thus, it is the status structure that helps provide social order and results in unequal status ranking in relation to the functional division of labor (or occupational structure necessary in complex societies) that explains social stratification and inequality.

Modern Marxian Theory

We can begin by stating that modern Marxian theorists continue to accept Marx's basic view of social stratification outlined in Chapter 4. We need not repeat that basic outline. The primary concern of modern Marxian theorists has been to apply this Marxian view of society to industrial societies that have experienced change since Marx's time, while also using new methods of social science research to validate some of the principal Marxian concepts. We will consider first the changes in industrial societies that produce apparent problems for Marxian theory. We can approach these changes by focusing on some of the main problems faced by Marxian analysis today.

Among these problems, by far the most serious is the absence of socialist revolutions in any of the advanced capitalist nations. In fact, the working class that was seen by Marx as making such a revolution has become, it seems, less class conscious and less critical of capitalism since Marx's time. Related to the above, capitalist nations have not experienced the crisis periods Marx saw as leading to revolution, or, to the extent that they have experienced such crisis periods, the crisis has so far been managed with less than revolutionary results.

It will be remembered that Marx predicted increasing monopoly capitalism with a more powerful upper class in control of the economy and nation. Something like monopoly capitalism has certainly developed, as we will see in Chapters 7 and 8. But many argue, with some convincing evidence, that an upper class in the traditional sense of wealthy families with ownership of the major means of production in the society no longer exists, or, if it does, it has much less ownership and power.

In addition to the above, we find a relative reduction in traditional working-class occupations in advanced capitalist societies and the emergence of a new middle class to an extent Marx did not predict (Wright and Martin 1987). Finally, there is a serious problem with respect to the reality of communism in nations such as the Soviet Union today. Part of the problem is that nations like Russia and China that claim to be communist did not develop from the breakdown of advanced capitalist nations as Marx predicted. Furthermore, we should add, the communist nations that exist today are far from the ideal that Marx envisioned, even after Gorbachev's reforms and democracy in the Soviet Union.

In the face of these problems, many theorists point out that Marx cannot be held responsible for failure to predict the future in every respect. They also note, with some validity, that Marx was not concerned with formulating exact universal laws, only historical tendencies (see Appelbaum 1978a; 1978b). The basic Marxian view of society, they claim, must not be considered a deterministic model of society, but a guide to our thinking. As we noted in our earlier discussion of Marx, recent Marxian theorists are correct in stating that the political and deterministic-materialistic Marx has been overly stressed in the past. Nevertheless, some specific predictions in Marxian theory have been shown to be incorrect. How are these incorrect predictions dealt with?

With respect to the first major problem, that of no socialist revolution in advanced capitalist nations and little revolutionary consciousness among the working class, some argue that Marx was simply inaccurate in timing. The revolution will come, sooner or later. But even if this is true, it begs the question of why it has taken so long. The Marxian response to this question can be combined with the response to the second question noted above: Why has there been no major crisis in capitalist societies, or why have such crisis periods been managed without revolutionary changes? Two general factors are presented to account for these original inaccuracies in Marxian theory: (1) *the growth and strength of the state* and (2) *unforeseen influences on the working class*.

There has been much recent work by Marxian theorists to correct Marx's neglect of the function of the state in capitalist societies by adding Weber's insights (Miliband 1969, 1977; Harrington 1976; Therborn 1978; Wright 1978a). Another group of structural Marxists even argues that a strong state has developed in capitalist societies with *some* autonomy from upper-class interests (Althusser 1969, 1977; Poulantzas 1973, 1975). This strong state so far has been able to manage the *collective* interests of the bourgeoisie (upper class) to prevent crisis, and manage crisis periods to prevent revolutionary changes. This is done through (1) economic planning and control of conditions (such as a falling profit rate, inflation, reduced demand for goods produced) that could produce crisis, (2) welfare spending to control and appease the poor and unemployed during hard times, and (3) the management of conflicts within the bourgeoisie that could result in economic crisis (such as government regulation preventing competition from getting out of hand and destroying some corporations). In other words, rather than being almost a captive of upper-class capitalists, the state is now viewed by recent Marxian theorists as somewhat autonomous and managing the economy for overall upper-class interests.

In addition to describing how the working class has been pacified by welfare state reforms, modern Marxians cite other factors as reducing revolutionary class consciousness among the working class (see primarily Marcuse 1964; Miliband 1969; Aranowitz 1974). First of all, labor unions are seen as making some material gains for the workers, but at the expense of controlling the working class for long-term capitalist interests. In what is called institutionalization of class conflict, elites in big labor unions are seen as working for capitalist interests by controlling strikes and preventing workers from considering more threatening issues such as worker influence over corporate decision making.

Second, with respect to material gains, the high standard of living achieved by the working class in advanced capitalist nations is seen as co-opting labor. A consumption orientation among workers, promoted by the higher standard of living and mass advertising, was never foreseen by Marx. An outcome has been a willingness on the part of workers to support the basic capitalist system and tolerate alienating work conditions as long as they can share in the material fruits of capitalism (such as cars, boats, campers, and motorcycles).

A third factor often cited for the absence of revolutionary class consciousness is the strength of the legitimation process in advanced capitalist nations (Habermas, 1975, 1984). As noted previously, every stratification system must convince those toward the bottom of this system that their low position is somehow justified. The effects of a mass media unimagined in Marx's day, among other factors such as education (to be described in our later chapter on this process), are cited by Marxian theorists as helping produce acceptance of the capitalist system by the general population.

The expansion of the white-collar class of technical, sales, clerical, service, and bureaucratic workers is also acknowledged by many as unforeseen by Marx. But some Marxian theorists see no serious problem for Marxian theory:

This middle class is simply defined as part of the working class, although serving a different role in the capitalist system (Anderson 1974). More recently, however, the prediction that the growing middle-class jobs have been "deskilled," making them like working-class jobs (Wright et al. 1982), has been refuted empirically (Wright and Martin 1987). There are, in fact, more middle-class jobs which cannot be defined away as "really" working-class jobs. Wright and Martin (1987) argue that this goes against Marxian predictions, but can still be explained in a Marxian framework. What Marx failed to see was that capitalism has become more international, with working-class labor growing and conditions for the working class becoming worse as these types of jobs are exported by the rich capitalist nations to poor countries.

The growth of the middle class in advanced capitalist nations like the United States is also seen as posing another problem for the Marxian prediction of increasing criticism and opposition to the capitalist class in the population. This new middle class is usually rather conservative politically (see Mills 1953 for an excellent analysis), promoting divisions among nonowners below the rank of capitalist class. The divisions are produced because (1) white-collar workers generally have higher status (if not more pay), leading to status divisions; (2) white-collar workers (because of more interaction with capitalists and their managers) tend to identify more with capitalist interests; and (3) the expansion of the occupational structure (more ranks from top to bottom) has promoted more social mobility. In addition to creating more divisions in the working class, the expansion of the occupational structure and the hope of social mobility have reduced class consciousness because of the possibility of escape from "alienating" and low-status blue-collar work.

The charge that an upper class (that owns and controls the major means of production) is no longer present is countered with data to the contrary (see, for example, Zeitlin 1974). These theorists admit that ownership and control are more complex than Marx envisioned, but they continue to argue that such ownership and control by a capitalist class is no less present. Because of the complexity of this issue and its importance for the nature of social stratification in our society, it will be considered extensively in Chapters 7 and 8.

Finally, more Marxian theorists now agree that the Soviet Union has created a form of state communism (some say state capitalism) far from what Marx predicted. A new class of party bureaucrats has taken power in the name of the working class, but rather than working for the working class, this new class is "exploitative in the exact sense that Marx gave the term—the workers and peasants are forced to surrender a surplus to the bureaucracy ... " (Harrington 1976:50).

Generally, the problem with Marxian theory in this respect is that Marx failed to understand the state as a generalized power structure, a power structure that can serve the particular interests of capitalists as well as the narrow interests of some other type of elite (as Weber understood; see Wright 1978a:213). Some argue that a new class of party bureaucrats emerged in the Soviet Union because that country experienced a premature communist revolution. (In 1917 Russia was not an advanced capitalist nation with a strong working class that had sufficient power to maintain its class interests.) But most also agree that Marxian theorists must understand political structures better to prevent the type of bureaucratic dominance found in the Soviet Union (Wright 1978a:219).

In conclusion, it must be stressed that the above is not exhaustive of all the problems recent theorists have recognized in Marx's original work, nor do all Marxian theorists today agree on all points we have described. But the above is a fair sampling of some of the main problems found in Marx's work and of how recent Marxian writers have attempted to deal with these problems. For our concern, the main point is this: Marxian theorists continue to follow the basic guidelines of Marx's theoretical work. With some revision, they find this general theory useful in understanding most aspects of contemporary stratification systems.

Critiques of Marx and Recent Empirical Work   Of course, one may well disagree that current Marxian theory is a useful guide to understanding most aspects of modern stratification systems. A clear problem remains: Marx's writings were at times ambiguous and contradictory. Even today there is much disagreement over what Marx really meant, and almost any criticism can be deflected by Marxists with one or another interpretation of the "true" Marx (a situation not unlike that in functionalism). Until more aspects of Marxian theory are examined empirically and the theory is further refined, problems will remain.

Most recently, however, some interesting empirical research from a Marxian perspective has been attempted with success. The most impressive of these attempts has been Erik O. Wright's empirical work on Marxian class categories (1978a, 1978b; Wright and Perrone 1977; Wright et al. 1982; Wright and Martin 1987). By following Marx's idea that class must be defined in relation to the productive system in the society (that is, by one's relation to the means of production), rather than simply occupational status levels, as functionalists suggest, Wright develops a four-class model. With this four-class model Wright is able to show the usefulness of the Marxian view of class and to explain some of the problems found with functional views of occupational categories.

Defining class in relation to the productive system, we have what Wright calls capitalists, managers, workers, and the petty bourgeoisie. Capitalists own the means of production (factories, banks, and so on), purchase the labor of others, and control the labor of others. Managers merely control the labor of others for capitalists, and sell their labor to capitalists (such as managers of corporations). Workers, of course, have only their labor to sell to capitalists, while the petty bourgeoisie own some small means of production but employ very few or no workers. (This includes, for example, small shop or store owners.) What does this Marxian concept of class help us understand?

Most previous empirical research in social stratification has been done from the functional perspective. Class positions or, more accurately, occupational status positions, are viewed by functionalists as skill and status rankings on a continuum from lowest to highest. Pay, status, and educational levels are all assumed to roughly follow this continuum. In other words, functionalists do not consider class divisions, but rather rankings, as on a ladder. However, these previous functional studies have many problems. For one, research shows no simple relation between these occupational grades and income. Another problem is that education level does not predict income very well (see Jencks et al. 1972 on these problems).

Research by Wright and Perrone (1977) and Wright (1978b) has produced some interesting findings using the Marxian class categories. With national samples of people in the labor force, Wright's research found class position (the four categories above) to be about as good in explaining differences in income between people as is occupational status and educational level. Also interesting is that capitalists have higher incomes, even controlling for (or eliminating) the effects on income from education level, occupational skill, age, and job tenure. In other words, being a capitalist, and especially a big capitalist, irrespective of other factors such as education and occupational skill, brings more income (see also Aldrich and Weiss 1981).

There are other interesting findings. For example, education does *not* on the average help workers attain a higher income, but more education does bring more income for the managerial class. And, examining people *within* class categories, there is not much difference between males and females, and blacks and whites on income. The male–female and black–white overall income differences (males and whites have higher incomes) are due primarily to *class position*. That is, females and blacks have lower average incomes because they are proportionately more often than white males to be in the *working class* (as defined by Wright).

A similar study by Robinson and Kelley (1979) attained similar results using national samples from the United States and England. These researchers also found separate mobility patterns in terms of class position and occupational status. To attain a capitalist class position it is best to be born of capitalist parents; to attain a high occupational position it is best to be born of parents with high education and high occupational position.

What all this means is that a person's relation to the productive system, or means of production, does make a difference that has been ignored by most social scientists in the past. Considered another way, however, the above research shows class position defined in Marxian terms does not explain everything about social mobility and income attainment and Marxian theory alone does not tell us all we need to know about social stratification. We will return to this theme at the end of this chapter.

Let us conclude our discussion by noting a final criticism that brings us to the next group of conflict theories. Perhaps the most important weakness of Marxian theory is the assumption that class or economic conflicts are the only conflicts of interest among people or groups, or at least the most important conflicts. It is because of this assumption that Marxian theorists can foresee equality and harmony (no conflict) when the private ownership of productive forces (capital, factories, and so on) is eliminated. History, at least so far, and except for small, exceptional human groups, suggests this assumption is incorrect. Inequality may be reduced to a degree with the elimination of private ownership of productive forces; but there are other interests in conflict, and other conflict groups in modern societies.

Power Conflict Theories

Other conflict theories of social stratification follow what we have described as an uncritical-conflict paradigm. Most importantly, these theories view conflict as a more pervasive aspect of human beings and human societies, a condition not restricted to economic relations. As Dahrendorf (1959:208) puts it, "It appears that not only in social life, but wherever there is life, there is conflict." Or as Collins (1975:59) tells us, "For conflict theory, the basic insight is that human beings are sociable but conflict-prone animals."

The label "uncritical-conflict theorist" is a bit unfair. We are *not* saying that these theorists are often uncritical of exploitation and inequality, or unsympathetic toward those at the bottom of the stratification system. But these theorists agree that conflict and exploitation, in one form or another and to some degree, will always be found among human beings and in human societies. It is only from this understanding of the conflict in all societies, they argue, that we can ever learn to deal with, and perhaps reduce, inequality and exploitation. Like Weber, however, they tend to be pessimistic about this possibility.

Aside from telling us about the conflict nature of human beings and human societies, what, specifically, does this type of conflict theory have to say about social stratification? Beginning from the assumption that people have conflicting interests of many types, they suggest that a more general view of power and conflict is needed in understanding social stratification. Power may be defined in many ways, but most broadly it means the ability to compel (through force, rewards, or other means) another individual to do what you want, or to give you what you want, even when it is against the other person's interests to do so. Whatever the means of power (economic, political, military, and so on), it is a generalized commodity that can serve many interests or goals. Furthermore, if you want to understand a widespread social arrangement such as social stratification, we must recognize that collectives of individuals can have common interests and work together to meet these common interests. Thus, to understand a *system* of social stratification, we must understand organized class or group interests, rather than random individual conflicts.

Dahrendorf's Conflict Theory One of the most influential conflict theories of social stratification is that of Ralf Dahrendorf (1959). He begins his theory by describing the strong and weak points of Marxian theory, then adds to Marx's strong points what he sees as the strong points of Weber's work. In his review of Marx, Dahrendorf agrees that societies must be viewed from the perspective of conflict and differing interests. Furthermore, he believes that Marx was correct to focus on both organized (or manifest) and unorganized (or latent) *group* interests to understand the more fundamental aspects of social stratification.

In other words, the social scientist must understand not just the organized and manifest group conflicts, but also the manner in which group or class interests are distributed in a society and whether or not a particular group or class recognizes its latent group interests and acts upon these interests. The potential for these latent group interests to become manifest is always present. Finally, Dahrendorf accepts Marx's primary *two-class model*. There are always, from his perspective, superordinate and subordinate classes.

Dahrendorf rejects Marx on other points. For example, he disagrees that revolution will destroy class conflict; class or group conflict is an inevitable aspect of organized societies. Perhaps most importantly, Dahrendorf rejects Marx's view that class conflict in advanced industrial society is based primarily or only on economic interests. He supports his rejection of Marx on this point by arguing that an upper class no longer owns and controls the means of production. Rather, he accepts the managerial control thesis (discussed here in Chapters 7 and 8) that control is divorced from ownership, with nonowning managers controlling the economy. In addition, Dahrendorf believes that the growth of a middle class in industrial societies also has altered the nature of economic divisions as described by Marx.

So where does Dahrendorf locate the basis of class conflict, if not in economic interests defined by Marx? It is at this point that he adds Weber's insights. All industrial or complex societies must have some forms of social organization, what Weber called *imperatively coordinated associations*. These imperatively coordinated associations are like bureaucratic organizations centered around major tasks in the society. They are found in business, government, labor unions, universities, charitable organizations—that is, in all organized social structures. And within these imperatively coordinated associations differing roles or positions are filled by individuals.

Thus, because these imperatively coordinated associations are so pervasive in society, individual and group *interests* are structured by the individual or group relationships to these associations. Within all imperatively coordinated associations there are authority roles of domination and subordination. As Dahrendorf (1959:165) writes, "One of the central theses of this study consists in the assumption that this differential distribution of authority invariably becomes the determining factor of systematic social conflicts of a type that is germane to class conflicts in the traditional (Marxian) sense of this term."

Unlike Marx, Dahrendorf recognizes all kinds of individual or group interests. There are interests in obtaining more material rewards, freedom, status recognition, leisure, all kinds of services from others, and so on. But the main point is that the *means* to attaining these interests are related to authority positions within imperatively coordinated associations. In other words, the *haves* get what they want because they are on top in the association, while the *have nots* find it in their interests to challenge the status quo that assigns them low positions and low rewards (Dahrendorf 1959:176).

Figure 5-3 roughly summarizes Dahrendorf's conflict theory. It is important to recognize that Dahrendorf is referring to imperatively coordinated associations of all sizes, performing all kinds of tasks. Also important to recognize is that individuals have a position in many of these associations at the same time. For example, someone has a position in relation to the government (a political elite or just a citizen), the overall economy (a corporate executive, or, say, a consumer), his or her occupation (manager or worker), as well as some other associations such as a church (high church official or simple member) or university (president or student). Each of these positions represents a different set of interests in relation to the authority or lack of authority maintained. These interests are only latent interests held in common (such as manager versus worker interests) until they become recognized and acted upon by the opposed interest groups (manifest interests).

Summary and Critiques of Power Conflict Theories　Although attention has been focused on Dahrendorf's theory of social stratification, there are others that generally fit within the uncritical-conflict paradigm. In most respects, Lenski's (1966) theory, discussed briefly in Chapter 3, is in this category. We say "in most respects" because with hunting and gathering societies and industrial societies Lenski reverts to a few functional assumptions in explaining social stratification.

More recently, Randall Collins (1975) constructed a conflict theory based on various conflicting interests. Especially interesting and useful with Collins' theory is that he combines microlevel (individual or small-group level) analysis from social interaction theorists such as Goffman (1959) and Garfinkel (1967) with

FIGURE 5-3
Dahrendorf's conflict theory.

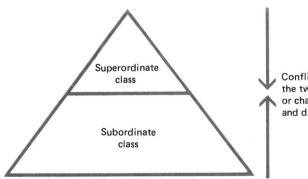

macrolevel analysis. More than other theories, Collins' work is devoted to explaining all types of human behavior (such as family relations, social interaction, and conversation) that is influenced by a system of social stratification.

We do not have the space to consider all the differences and particular characteristics of the various power conflict theories, but we should summarize their common principles. They all begin from the assumptions that (1) theories of social stratification must be grounded in differing individual and group interests, (2) which are varied, and (3) form the basis of class conflict. Most important is how groups come together within organized social structures (what Dahrendorf calls imperatively coordinated associations) that form systems of social stratification.

Most criticisms of this general type of conflict theory are related to the assumptions held by other theorists. The criticisms from functional theorists should be easily understood. For example, they charge that individuals primarily seek status in terms of a common value system, which in turn leads people to ensure that needs of the social system are met. Individual and group conflicts, they argue, are of secondary importance for social stratification. Critical-conflict theorists, of course, tend to stress economic relations as primary. As Marx observed, material conditions relating to the basic necessities of life are at the center of conflicts in human societies. Part of the problem, Marxists argue (Appelbaum 1978a:72), is that Dahrendorf's theory is ahistorical; that is, he has failed to adequately recognize the development of social stratification systems as conflicts over economic resources.

These types of criticisms are predictable and are primarily matters of perspective. But focusing on Dahrendorf's theory, there are more serious criticisms. One involves his very general treatment of imperatively coordinated associations. It may be agreed that these are all structures of hierarchical authority relations, with some people having more authority than others. But considering cross-national and cross-historical comparisons, surely some imperatively coordinated associations are at times more important within a nation than others (Giddens 1973:73). This is not the same as the Marxist critique, because it may be that in some nations economic associations are primary, while in others political, religious, military, or others may be more important in the overall stratification system.

Finally, and most seriously, with Dahrendorf's theory how do we decide who is in which of the two classes? At times this is a simple matter. At General Motors the board of directors belongs to the superordinate class, while a worker on the assembly line is in the subordinate class. But what about engineers, lesser managers, line supervisors? In other words, where do we draw the line between the two classes? Dahrendorf could respond that it depends on the particular interests that are in conflict. This response, however, is too arbitrary. There are degrees of authority, but recognizing that makes the theory much more complex and at times confusing.

Before concluding let us consider a relevant and interesting empirical study. Robinson and Kelley's (1979) study was mentioned above in relation to

Marxian class categories, but it also attempted to measure and test some of Dahrendorf's views of class. The capitalist class (in a Marxian sense) was defined and measured as those who own or control the means of production, while Dahrendorf's class categories were measured in terms of *degrees* of authority (noting the above criticism). Robinson and Kelley measured degrees of authority by how many levels of employees were above and below the individual. As a third definition of ranking they measured the usual occupational status or skill levels. Their data consisted of national samples of employed people in England and the United States.

Robinson and Kelley correlated these differing measures of class and occupational status with three main dependent variables. They found (1) that all three class/occupation measures did about equally well in explaining income differences among individuals in their sample, (2) that all three class/occupation measures helped explain differing class identification in the sample (for example, whether people saw themselves in the upper class, middle class, or working class), and (3) that all three class/occupation measures were related to differing political party voting (that is, voting Democrat or Republican in the United States), except for class position (in Dahrendorf's terms) in the United States.

Finally, as discussed in part above, their findings show that there are distinct lines of class and occupational attainment. For example, having a father with a high class position, in either Marx's or Dahrendorf's definition of class, will provide a better chance for the son to attain the high class position also. At the same time, having a father with a high occupational position as defined by status and skill level will provide a better chance for the son to attain the high occupational position also. But the processes are not strongly related. That is, having a father with a high *occupational* status position will not be of much help for the son in attaining a high *class* position (defined in either of the two ways), and vice versa.

In addition to having some analytical value, Dahrendorf's class theory receives some empirical support. But as we noted in our discussion of recent Marxian theorists, Dahrendorf's theory does not tell us all we need to know about social stratification. We will return to this theme in our concluding section after we examine some relevant information from sociobiology.

A Note on Sociobiology

As described above, stratification theorists in this uncritical-conflict category maintain that conflict and inequality (of some kind, to some degree) will always be found in human societies. While most of these theorists suggest only implicitly that conflict and inequality are related to selfish human nature, others are quite clear in their arguments that selfish human nature is behind much of the inequality and aggression found in human societies (see van den Berghe 1974; 1978). To the extent that this is true, we find further support for at least some aspects of this type of stratification theory. Let us examine some of the evidence.

Sociobiology is a new and very controversial area of study in sociology. Some of the most important works in this area were published by Wilson (1975) and were soon followed by many critical (see Barash 1977; Lenski 1977; Quadagno 1979; Lewontin, Rose, and Kamin 1984) and supportive publications (see van den Berghe 1977, 1978; Ellis 1977; Bolin and Bolin 1980). The main argument for sociobiology is that by relating our studies of society and human behavior to certain biological tendencies within human beings we can increase our understanding of some aspects of this behavior. The counter argument is that although biology can help us understand the behavior of other animals, human behavior is much more complex and almost completely shaped by learning, culture, the social environment, and other nonbiological factors.

A basic assumption of sociobiology is that what Charles Darwin described as the process of natural selection has resulted in the survival of only those human beings most genetically fit for the environment in which they existed. Those who were best equipped genetically to survive in their environment in turn passed their genes on to the next generation of human beings. The process has continued into the present generation. Most important is that (1) it takes many, many generations for a gene pool to be altered significantly; and (2) because over 99 percent of human existence has been in an environment far different from the one that exists in modern societies, the earliest human environment shaped much of our biologically influenced behavior.

What was it about this early environment that shaped the genetically influenced behavior in people? In contrast to advanced industrial societies, it is argued, basic necessities such as food were seldom secure for early human beings. Competition for the resources that did exist was usually great, and more often than not the competition was from other animals as well (see van den Berghe 1978:30). If this is true—and the description does seem reasonable— over the few million years that human beings were developing in this environment the most aggressive and selfish people were the ones who survived. Of this selfish trait in general, van den Berghe (1978:46) writes:

> Animals are selected to behave in ways that increase their fitness, that is, their reproductive success. Increasing one's fitness typically means securing access to valuable resources in competition with other organisms, in short acting selfishly. Animals that behave selfishly tend to have more offspring, and therefore, the genes that predispose toward selfish behavior will tend to increase their portion in succeeding generations. Man, in this respect, is no exception. Indeed, he seems more than averagely aggressive and nasty to his own species.

If all this is true, however, how do we explain the frequent altruistic, generous, and cooperative behavior also found among human beings? Sociobiologists add two additional arguments. As for the first, it is pointed out that survival of a gene pool requires altruistic behavior toward kin (Wilson 1975:117; Bolin and Bolin 1980). That is, if a particular set of genes is to survive, there must be protection or even sacrifice for close kin (especially children). Secondly, it is argued that more general cooperation was also required for survival. This cooperative behavior is especially related to hunting: "For early hominids, solitary hunting or even scavenging was not a realistic possibility ..." (van den Berghe 1978:46). Human beings with a tendency toward this cooperative small-group behavior, sociobiologists conclude, were more likely to survive (Leakey and Lewin 1977:149; Pfeiffer 1977:48).

Sociobiology is a relatively new area of study, and very little of what we can judge to be well-established explanations of human behavior can be found in the literature yet. Even many who support this area of study admit that some writers have been overly ambitious in trying to set biological foundations for human behavior (see Bolin and Bolin 1980). Clearly, even if there are some biologically based tendencies in human behavior, the wide variety of behavior among human societies tells us that most of what we do is shaped by non-biological factors. But the above description of a biological tendency toward both selfish and altruistic or cooperative behavior does seem reasonable.

What do these selfish and cooperative tendencies in human behavior help us understand about social stratification? Probably not much. It is absurd to think that a set of genes leads us to establish feudal systems or caste systems rather than join the Peace Corps. *But* biologically influenced selfish behavior may lead us to maximizing our rewards under certain conditions. And combined with a tendency toward cooperative behavior, people do tend to share with others, at the same time they are cooperating to exploit others. All of these types of behavior are common in human stratification systems.

Under conditions of scarcity, people tend to become more aggressive. In an earlier chapter we examined archaeological evidence for this type of aggressive behavior during the scarcity that led to early agrarian settlements about 10,000 to 15,000 years ago. Under conditions of adequate resources but no surplus, we found, there was evidence of more cooperative and sharing behavior. And under conditions of surplus goods people tend to be more selfish, while cooperating with a few to control the surplus. This is precisely the behavior that many sociobiologists predict (see van den Berghe 1974:785).

But this tells us very little of what we need to know about systems of social stratification. It does tell us that we must recognize a selfish tendency among people, and a tendency to cooperate to exploit others under certain conditions. The task for theories of social stratification is to recognize these tendencies and specify how and when this selfish behavior will be maximized or minimized. Perhaps most importantly, stratification theories must specify how the social structure in a particular society determines which interests (attaining ownership of factories, political power, positions in imperatively coordinated associations, or others) are most important.

THEORIES OF SOCIAL STRATIFICATION: A CONCLUSION

In this chapter and the preceding one we examined some of the leading theories of social stratification. We have noted some of the value in functional theories, but for the most part found them quite limited. We have noted more value in various conflict theories, but again found some weakness. Theories, as Einstein put it, are attempts at simplification. The general task of a theory—any theory—is to evaluate the many factors influencing a phenomenon such as social stratification in order to detect which of the factors or set of factors provides the clearest explanation. It is then the task of social scientists to examine the logic of each theory, balance and weigh the evidence put forth as support for each theory, and make a decision as to which of the competing theories or group of theories is most useful. However, the task is even more complex when we find that some theories answer some questions best while other theories are best in answering other questions.

In the study of social stratification we mainly want to know who gets what and why. Related to this question are others. How are inequalities maintained? Why are inequalities and the groups that receive the most rewards in the society often quite stable over long periods of time? Why do stratification systems change? Upon balancing and weighing the evidence presented in this chapter, in those that follow, and in our review of history, we have concluded that conflict theories are better able to answer more questions about social stratification.

A main assumption is that *stratification systems are attempts to reduce overt conflict over the distribution of valued goods and services in a society.* Once a system of social stratification is established, the manner in which valued goods and services are distributed requires less conflict and aggression, at least for a time. All of this means, of course, that at the base of social stratification we find individual, and most importantly, group conflicts. These conflicts may be more hidden at times, the distribution of rewards may be less contested, the power of those at the top less challenged. But this only shows that the stratification system has, for a time at least, succeeded in regulating and controlling the conflicts of interest. As our review of history has shown, however, the conflicts regulated by a system of social stratification are brought to the forefront again and again.

The question of which conflict theory best explains the nature of social stratification is more complex. Each of the ones we have examined contains weak and strong points. In the face of this situation, and until the Einstein of social stratification comes forth, we have chosen in this work an eclectic approach with respect to conflict theories. We will emphasize what we believe to be the strong points of each. For example, we may agree with Marxian theorists that economic conflicts are among the most important, especially in capitalist societies, but not always. And we question the *degree* to which ownership of the means of production continues to be the principal or only line between conflicting classes. In addition, we question the possibility of completely eliminating conflicts of interest in some future ideal state.

From power conflict theories, or the more general uncritical-conflict paradigm, we accept the assumption that individual and group interests of many kinds are behind systems of social stratification. And we also accept the assumption that these conflicts in advanced industrial societies are most often played out within formal organizations, bureaucracies, or imperatively coordinated associations. But we must recognize that some of these organizations are more important battlegrounds than others, and that there are degrees of authority within each.

We can also accept some aspects of functional theory. We can accept that status distinctions are important, but not that these status distinctions are determined by a common value system unaffected by inequalities of power in large, complex societies. We can accept that there is an occupational structure based on skill level that influences the distribution of rewards, but not that this occupational structure serves the needs of society, unaffected by inequalities of power. A supply-and-demand relation does explain some of the distribution of rewards within this occupational structure, but it is supply and demand in a marketplace that is not always free. Those with power can influence the supply as well as the demand in terms of their interests.

What we have learned so far suggests the rough outline of the process of social stratification presented in Figure 5-4. This figure suggests that theories of social stratification must be based on varied individual interests. Most important, however, is that these individual interests are shared by others in similar positions and situations in the society, and become group or class interests.

Depending on the particular level of technology, historical and cultural influences, the international environment, and other factors that we will include in the influence of social structure, these group interests are contested within one or more substructures in the society. Within one society the property class structure in a Marxian sense may be primary, while in another the political structure may be primary. But we also find that at times more than one may be of prime significance and that these structures are usually in some way interrelated and influence each other. We have excluded from Figure 5-4 other substructures—such as religious, military, or status structures—that may at times be important in smaller or less industrialized societies.

FIGURE 5-4
The process of social stratification.

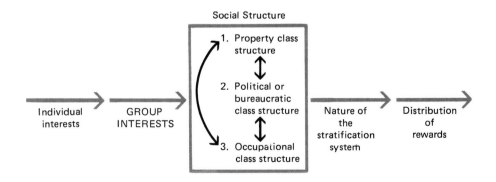

Finally, Figure 5-4 suggests that the conflicts shaped by these substructures influence the general nature of the stratification system in each society, and ultimately the distribution of rewards. How inequalities are maintained and justified, who is on top and for what reasons, the openness of the stratification system—in short, the overall nature of the stratification system—are influenced by these substructures and their degree of importance.

Figure 5-4 is fairly simple, yet has organized much of what we have learned so far. With the various factors helping to shape the nature of stratification systems in mind, we can begin by focusing on the stratification system in the United States. After a general introductory chapter on the United States we can examine the positions of those at the top, the middle and working class, and the poor. But because of the importance of the top of the stratification system—the most powerful individuals, groups, and institutions in our society—we must devote two chapters to this subject. When this is done, more attention will be paid to how inequality—and the stratification system more generally—is maintained through a legitimation process, and how and when there is individual movement within the stratification system.

PART THREE

SOCIAL STRATIFICATION
IN THE UNITED STATES

SOCIAL STRATIFICATION IN THE UNITED STATES: HISTORICAL FORCES AND THE CONTEMPORARY CLASS SYSTEM

We have a great deal to understand about human behavior and social organization, but the relatively short history of empirical research in the social sciences has at least demonstrated the importance of social stratification in much of this understanding. We can't always predict individual behavior or attitudes from class position alone, but the research is consistent in showing that many differences in behavior, attitudes, and other individual characteristics are often associated with positions in the stratification system. Let us consider some specific examples.

Even the most intimate kinds of human behavior can be influenced by place in the stratification system. Using level of education as an indicator of class position, Weinberg and Williams (1980) examined extensive data on many types of sexual behavior from separate studies conducted between 1938 and 1970. They conclude from their examination that throughout this period clear differences are evident between social classes in many types of sexual behavior. For example, among their findings in the 1970 data is that people with less education generally had earlier sexual experiences of various types (from necking to sexual intercourse). However, females with a college education more often responded positively to their initial experience with sexual intercourse, masturbation (by self and opposite sex), and oral sex (Weinberg and Williams 1980:43).

Very general psychological conditions such as happiness and self-respect also have been found to have a significant relationship to social class. For example, Bradburn and Caplovitz (1965) discovered that those higher in the class system were more likely to report being happy. Similarly, Andrews and Withey (1976) have shown that there is a positive relationship between social class and a general sense of well-being. And the important condition of self-worth or self-esteem, which itself has many implications for behavior, has been found to be positively related to social class among adults (Rosenberg and Pearlin 1978).

The stratification system, however, is not limited to effects on *individual* behavior and attitudes. Perhaps more importantly, the stratification system can influence more general social conditions above the individual level. Social institutions such as the family, education, the polity, and the economy, to name only a few, cannot be understood fully without reference to the nature of the stratification system in a particular society (Useem 1979a). Again, let us look briefly at some examples.

There is broad agreement that the federal government has obtained tremendous power over the course of this century in the United States. With a federal budget now well in excess of $1 trillion, federal government agencies of many types are able to influence such things as business practices, home ownership, environmental quality, medical care, sports activities, and the quality and location of schools attended by small children. But many, if not most, of these influences by the federal government are *not* neutral to class interests. Who gets elected to important policy-making positions and the policies they support once in these positions (as we will see in later chapters) are influenced in large measure by the nature of the stratification system.

Before examining the impact of class in the United States, however, we must consider more basic questions. We must first consider some of the main characteristics and nature of the United States stratification system in a general way and then decide on the most meaningful definition of class.

HISTORICAL FORCES AND THE NATURE OF SOCIAL STRATIFICATION IN THE UNITED STATES

In the last chapter we outlined some basic assumptions about the nature of all systems of social stratification. We may assume that people usually attempt to maximize the share of the society's goods and services they receive, as well as those of others to whom they have strong emotional attachments (such as kin). In addition, people often come together with others sharing common interests to collectively further their common interests.

The main goals of this chapter will be to understand (1) the most important ways these common interests are produced and (2) how these common interests relate to objective and subjective class formation (what Dahrendorf referred to as latent and manifest class formation).

But first we must examine *how historical forces have shaped the major institutions in our society*. As was noted previously (see Figure 5-4), it is important to understand how these historical forces have influenced the character of our basic institutions, and thus the class structure in which the most important group interests are brought into conflict. In the United States, three aspects of historical development are most important for our concern: *industrialization,* the *advanced level* of our industrialization, and *capitalism*.

Industrialization

In our review of history (Chapter 3) we followed Lenski's (1966) description of the significant change in the degree of material inequality as societies move from agrarian, or less economically developed societies, to industrial societies. It will be helpful at this point to review more recent empirical studies of this relationship between economic development (that is, level of technology or industrialization) and level of inequality.

Using various measures of economic development and inequality within nations (see Table 6-1 for a cross-national comparison of inequality among noncommunist countries), a number of comparative studies have reached similar results; there is a strong tendency for *inequality to be reduced* once nations

TABLE 6-1

CROSS-NATIONAL COMPARISON OF INCOME INEQUALITY WITHIN NATIONS

Country	Percentage of total household income	
	Poorest 20%	Top 20%
Bangladesh	6.2	46.9
India	7.0	49.4
Kenya	2.6	60.4
Zambia	3.4	61.1
Indonesia	6.6	49.4
Philippines	5.2	54.0
El Salvador	5.5	47.3
Egypt	5.8	48.0
Thailand	5.6	49.8
Peru	1.9	61.0
Turkey	3.5	56.5
Costa Rica	3.3	54.8
Brazil	2.0	66.6
Panama	2.0	61.8
Mexico	2.9	57.7
S. Korea	5.7	45.3
Argentina	4.4	50.3
Venezuela	3.0	54.0
Hong Kong	5.4	47.0
Spain	6.9	40.0
Ireland	7.2	39.4
Italy	6.2	43.9
United Kingdom	7.0	39.7
Netherlands	8.3	36.2
France	5.3	45.8
Japan	8.7	37.4
W. Germany	7.9	39.5
United States	5.3	39.9

Source: Table constructed from data presented in World Bank (1986:226–227). Data are from years between 1970 and 1981.

become fully industrialized (Jackman 1975; Hewitt 1977; Stack 1978a; Weede 1980). Equally important, this relation between economic development and less inequality remains strong even when the possible effects on inequality from other variables (such as type of political system) are eliminated statistically (although, as we will see in the last chapter, a nation's place in the world stratification system does have an effect on inequality independent of economic development; Breedlove and Nolan 1988).

In Chapter 3 we also reviewed Lenski's (1966) description of a number of factors helping to produce less material inequality in industrial societies. One of the most important factors is the changing nature of the *occupational structure*. With industrialization the occupational structure is expanded, creating more occupations in the middle (that is, between the rich and the poor) that require more skills, thus producing a greater range of economic rewards.

What this process of economic development means for us is that, in considering the nature of social stratification in the United States, we must remember that the United States is an industrialized nation. Historical forces have produced a division of labor or occupational structure in this nation that helps us to find out who gets what and why. People who attain a more highly skilled position in the occupational structure will generally receive more rewards. In other words, individual and group conflict over rewards is in part located in the occupational structure. We will have more to say on the specific nature of occupational stratification in the next section.

Before we leave this discussion, however, we must ask if any other factors work along with industrialization and economic development to affect social stratification and thus the degree of inequality within nations. This question is important because one of the most noted studies of the relationship between economic development (using the standard measure of economic development, energy consumption per capita) and less inequality shows the relationship to be curvilinear (Jackman 1974, 1975). More economic development produces more income equality only up to a point; beyond this point it does *not* produce more equality.

But as can be seen in Table 6-1, there are differences (although they tend to be relatively small) between nations in the level of inequality, even at roughly the same level of industrialization. Are there other differences among industrialized nations that can help produce more equality among the population? This question was left unanswered in our discussion of inequality in industrialized nations in Chapter 3.

Most of the speculation about further reduction of inequality in industrialized nations centers around the nature and behavior of the political system. There has been some research on this, but the results are as yet inconclusive. One important characteristic of the political system believed to affect the level of inequality is the degree of political democracy. Jackman (1974, 1975) found no relation between the degree of political democracy and inequality when statistically controlling for the influence of economic development. But this conclusion has been challenged. More recent studies, using more refined measures of the main variables, have found a significant positive relation between the degree of political democracy and less income inequality (Hewitt 1977; Rubinson and Quinlan 1977; Stack 1978a; Weede 1980; Muller 1988).

However, because all three variables (economic development, political democracy, and level of inequality) are interrelated, it remains difficult to determine whether (1) economic development causes both less inequality *and* greater political democracy or (2) political democracy has an effect on inequality *independent* from economic development. Using a method that considers *how long* a nation has had political democracy, Hewitt (1977) presented data showing that political democracy does have an independent effect on less inequality. And this conclusion has been confirmed by Muller (1988), who found that democracy takes about twenty years (on average) to reduce income inequality.

This effect of the nature of the state on more equality is further supported by other studies. For example, Stack (1978a) and Devine (1983) have found that more direct government involvement in the economy (following Keynesian economics) helps produce more equality. In addition, Hewitt (1977) and Tufte (1978) found that socialist governments (communist and democratic socialist) tend to produce more income equality. Thus, the behavior of the state, in addition to the level of economic development, seems to have an effect on the level of inequality in a nation. But we must turn to our next topic to understand how and when this political effect on inequality and social stratification may operate.

The United States as an Advanced Industrial Nation

It is important to recognize that the United States is an industrial nation with a complex division of labor and a multilayered occupational hierarchy; it is also important to recognize that this is an *advanced* industrial nation. Although recent trends show a relative industrial decline for the United States, by the term "advanced" we meant that significant changes have occurred in the industrial structure of the United States since the time this country first could be referred to accurately as an industrial nation.

One important source of change as industrial societies become more advanced occurs in the occupational structure. With the growth of machine technology there is usually a reduction in working-class (manual labor) jobs and an increase in white-collar, or middle-class (nonmanual labor) jobs. Following this change is usually an increase in service jobs in the white-collar sector (jobs in health care, legal aid, tax consulting, etc.). Thus, we would expect an increase in the middle class and a reduction in the working class in advanced industrial societies.

As we will show with census data in our chapter on the middle class and working class, this generally has been the case in the United States. But it is a complex and controversial process of change that goes on in advanced industrial societies. First, not all advanced industrial nations experience the changes equally. For example, we will see in our chapter on Japan that the Japanese occupational structure contained a relatively fewer percentage of working-class jobs from the early stage of industrialization because (1) Japan industrialized late and copied more advanced machinery requiring less human labor from the already industrialized nations; and (2) they have a distribution system (selling goods) that requires more workers in middle-class positions than other industrial nations.

Second, international competition certainly changes the occupational structure of nations in different ways. In Chapter 2 we saw that the number of middle-paying jobs in the United States shrunk, and that this is one of the reasons for increased inequality in this country. These lost jobs are primarily higher-skilled working-class jobs in the making of cars, steel, and other consumer goods. Some countries are losing these jobs relative to other nations (such as the United States), while other countries are increasing their share (such as Japan, South Korea, and Taiwan).

Third, there are conflicting trends of a growth in jobs requiring more skills *and* a growth in jobs requiring less skills. A traditional Marxian assumption has been that there would be more and more people in lower-paid working-class jobs as capitalist societies advanced (Wright et al. 1982). But recent studies have found that this is not the case in the United States (Wright and Martin 1987; Steinmetz and Wright 1989) nor in Canada (Hunter 1988). Jobs are requiring more and more skills and education, rather than less, in contrast to what many people expected to happen with machines presumably making jobs more simple.

However, there is the conflicting trend discussed in Chapter 2 of a big increase in low-skilled jobs which pay wages below the poverty level. It is likely that this latter trend has been occurring in this country because of the large disparities in educational attainment (due to existing poverty and discrimination), leaving many people incapable of taking advantage of the trend in higher-skilled and higher-paying jobs. And because these people exist in our society in large numbers, competition for any job among these low-educated people makes it easy for employers to take advantage of them with temporary low-paying work. But it must be remembered, as noted earlier, that this trend in low-paying service jobs (e.g., serving hamburgers or cutting people's grass) is rather recent (during the 1980s). We need more research (and time) to tell if (1) this is a lasting trend, and (2) if it is confined primarily to the United States, which has been in relative economic decline (losing middle-paying jobs while at the same time remaining in the forefront with many new technologies to keep higher-skilled jobs).

The next set of changes occurring in advanced industrial societies relates to the growth of bureaucratic organizations. Many writers have commented upon the advanced nature of our industrial society (Galbraith 1971; Bell 1976), using terms such as *postindustrial society*. More Marxian-oriented writers prefer the term *advanced capitalist society*. And although these writers stress different characteristics of the advanced nature of our industrial society, they do have one dominant theme—broad *bureaucratization* of most aspects of our society. This is a theme that was introduced most forcefully by Max Weber (and described in Chapter 4). Of course, earlier ages and earlier societies also had bureaucratic organizations. The bureaucratic states in early Rome and during the late feudal period in Europe have already been described. But they were vastly different from today's advanced industrial societies.

Perhaps most important in today's advanced nations is the *extent* of bureau-cratization. Rather than limited state bureaucracy, as in some earlier societies, we find bureaucratic institutions in most sectors of the society—in the economy, education, religion, all levels of government, voluntary organizations (such as the Boy Scouts and YMCA), and professional organizations (such as the American Medical Association). The list could go on and on.

Furthermore, not only the number of bureaucratic organizations but also their *size* is important. In today's advanced societies, the state with its many departments and functions dwarfs previous bureaucratic states. One method of measuring the relative size of state bureaucracies is by examining government expenditures as a percentage of total national income. In the United States, the growth of the federal government has been most rapid since 1929 (in response to the Great Depression and World War II). As can be seen in Table 6-2, total government expenditures as a percentage of total national income have climbed from 12.12 percent in 1929 to 41.90 percent in 1976 (see Nutter 1978:74). Table 6-3 indicates that the United States is not alone among Western industrialized nations in the degree of government spending as a percentage of total national income. In fact, the United States is below average. This is also shown in somewhat different form in Table 6-4. In this table we find the comparative tax revenues (how much money the government takes in), which show the United States even further from the average. Only Japan and Spain are shown to have a lower rate of tax revenues as a percent of GDP in 1984, though this has changed as of 1989 with a new consumption tax in Japan, making Japan's tax revenues as a percent of GDP almost identical to the United States. (It is worth noting that the different ranking for the United States in Tables 6-3 and 6-4 indicates a main problem for the U.S. in the 1980s—huge

TABLE 6-2
UNITED STATES GOVERNMENT
EXPENDITURES AS A PERCENTAGE OF
NATIONAL INCOME, 1929–1976

Year	Total government expenditures per national income, %
1929	12.12
1935	23.70
1940	23.12
1945	51.33
1950	25.82
1955	29.86
1960	33.11
1965	33.19
1970	39.07
1976	41.90

Source: Nutter (1978:74). The original data are from the U.S. Department of Commerce, *The National Income and Product Accounts of the United States* (Washington, D.C., 1977).

TABLE 6-3
TOTAL PUBLIC EXPENDITURE AS A PERCENTAGE OF GDP

Country	1964	1972	1983
Canada	28.9	37.2	46.8
France	38.0	38.3	51.5
Germany	35.9	40.8	48.6
Italy	31.8	38.6	57.4
Japan	—	21.8	34.8
United Kingdom	33.6	39.8	47.2
United States	28.3	32.0	38.1

Source: Table constructed from data presented in World Bank (1986:20).

government deficits from spending at an average rate, while taxing or bringing in government revenues at a very low comparative rate.)

Again, the point of all of this is that the United States government bureaucracy is large. And it is actually larger than most of the other governments listed in Tables 6-3 and 6-4 when we consider that the U.S. GNP and GDP are

TABLE 6-4
COMPARATIVE TAX REVENUES, 1984

Country	Government revenues as % GDP*
United States	29.0
Australia	31.2
Austria	42.0
Belgium	46.7
Canada	33.7
Denmark	48.0
Finland	36.0
France	45.5
West Germany	37.7
Greece	35.2
Italy	41.2
Japan	27.4
Netherlands	45.5
New Zealand	31.0
Norway	46.4
Portugal	32.0
Spain	28.4
Sweden	50.5
Switzerland	32.2
United Kingdom	38.5

*Includes taxes at all levels of government and Social Security contributions. GDP is gross domestic product, which is the value of all goods and services produced in the domestic economy alone, not including foreign production of domestic corporations.
Source: U.S. Bureau of the Census, *Statistical Abstracts of the United States, 1987,* p. 828.

by far the largest in the world, thus actually making dollars spent by U.S. government agencies greater than most nations. (For example, the U.S. GNP is, in fact, twice as large as that of Japan in second place, making U.S. government expenditures much larger than in Japan when figured in actual dollars.)

For the study of social stratification it is most important to understand these bureaucratic institutions as *hierarchies of power and control*. These aspects of bureaucratic organizations are important for two main reasons: (1) the authority divisions that are created *within* the organization, or what Dahrendorf described as class divisions; and (2) the influence these organizations may obtain in other sectors of the society (influence *outside* the particular organization's boundary).

Focusing on the above points, let us consider the two types of bureaucratic organizations most dominant in our advanced society—economic corporations and the state. In contrast to an earlier trend of more and more people working in larger and larger corporations, the percentage of the work force employed in smaller firms actually has been increasing in recent years. This is one of the reasons for the growth of low-paying jobs discussed above and in Chapter 2, because smaller firms usually pay lower wages. About 25 percent of workers are in companies with twenty employees or less, compared to 13 percent of workers in companies where there are 1,000 workers or more. Still, in major industries in the United States most workers are employed by larger companies with huge bureaucracies. For example, the largest 100 industrial corporations (of a total of about 200,000) employ over 70 percent of all industrial workers (U.S. Bureau of the Census, *Statistical Abstracts of the United States, 1987*).

What this means is that these workers are brought into the authority structure of large bureaucratic organizations with many ranks, rules, and much influence over their lives. But the size of our economic bureaucracies also gives them much influence outside their formal boundaries. Their impact on communities is easy to see when so many workers can become unemployed if a corporation moves or discontinues part of its operation in the community. Equally important, however, are the forms of corporate influence on other organizations (such as welfare, education, and cultural organizations), including government policies of many types (a factor considered in detail in Chapter 7). And because size can be an indicator of influence, we must say that these top corporations are potentially more powerful today. In 1950, the top 100 industrial corporations controlled only 39.8 percent of industrial corporate assets. By 1985, the top 100 corporations controlled 70.3 percent of all industrial corporate assets (U.S. Bureau of the Census, *Statistical Abstracts of the United States, 1987*:519).

As for state or government agencies in general, we also find a large work force brought within their bureaucratic boundaries. For example, in 1985 there were over 17 million workers employed by government agencies at all levels in the United States, with over 3 million employed by the federal government alone (U.S. Bureau of the Census, *Statistical Abstracts of the United States, 1987*:280). And we need not detail here the many areas of our society influenced by government agencies and regulations.

In light of our discussion of the growing bureaucratic power of the state, it will be instructive to consider the relation between state influence and the degree of income inequality noted in our description of economic development and inequality. Several studies were mentioned showing that the state *can* work to influence the level of inequality in a society. Large state bureaucracies do have the means to reduce or increase income inequality through redistribution policies (such as income maintenance programs and welfare and health services), progressive income taxes, minimum wage laws, and other interventions in the economy.

In fact, for the most part, the state today can best be understood as a *redistributive organization*; it takes from some groups and gives to others. This makes the state a *focal point for class and interest group conflicts,* with each group trying to ensure that it is the one that receives more than it gives. In large measure, the class interests favored by government policies can be viewed as an indicator of the comparative power of different classes and interest groups (Pampel and Williamson 1985; Kropi 1989).

We can add some life to the above discussion with some results of the actual class struggles in several capitalist industrial nations. The bottom scale of Figures 6-1 and 6-2 indicates the percentage of years that a labor party or socialist party controlled the executive branch of government between 1945 and 1969 in each of the countries. These are all democratically elected governments, and we can assume that these labor or socialist governments were pri-

FIGURE 6-1
Working-class political influence and comparative income inequality. *Source:* Tufte (1978:96).

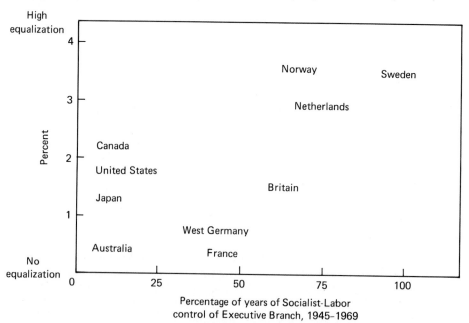

Percentage of years of Socialist-Labor
control of Executive Branch, 1945–1969

marily supported by the working class and middle class. In Figure 6-1 we find that countries with more years of a labor or socialist government tend to have less income inequality. Figure 6-2 also shows that these governments tend to keep the unemployment rate lower as well. Other figures presented by Tufte (1978) show that socialist or labor governments tend to produce somewhat higher government spending as a percent of GNP and slightly higher inflation. This last finding is interesting because we usually find an inverse relation between unemployment and inflation over time (in other words, as unemployment goes up, inflation tends to go down because fewer people have money to spend, therefore keeping prices down). What this means is that socialist or labor governments know that their supporters are more worried about unemployment than inflation (the working class is most likely to be unemployed to bring down inflation). If there is to be a trade-off between unemployment and inflation, they prefer to fall on the side of lower unemployment.

We have one remaining issue pertaining to the growing bureaucratic nature of advanced industrial societies. We have seen earlier that Marx believed there

FIGURE 6-2
Working-class political influence and comparative unemployment rates. *Source:* Tufte (1978:93).

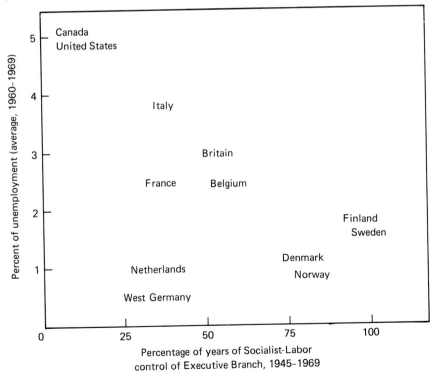

were two main classes in capitalist industrial societies based upon the relationship to the means of production—there are owners of the capital (the upper class or capitalists), and there are the workers who have only their labor to sell. But with the growth of large bureaucratic organizations in the economy and state there is now a new position of controlling or managing the industrial capital, rather than owning it, as well as controlling or managing the state bureaucracy that is owned by others (the taxpayers). This has led some people to claim this creates a new class of controllers of bureaucracies who can have interests in conflict with capitalists or smaller owners of stock in corporations, *and* taxpayers with respect to the "true owners" of the state bureaucracies.

There is no question that this class exists, as we have indicated with our discussion of the equal importance of the bureaucratic authority structure along with the occupational structure and property structure. But some people who stress the importance of this concept of the "new class" claim that this means the new class is in conflict with the interests of the capitalists and taxpayers, leading to the possible exploitation or harm of the economy and taxpayer interests (Kristol 1972; Kirkpatrick 1976; also see Gouldner 1979; Bruce-Briggs 1979).

We will question the basis of this thesis in the next two chapters by considering who has the most power—the capitalist class, managers of major corporations, or the political elites. We will find that the independent power of political bureaucratic elites is limited, though a new corporate class of nonowning elites (managers of major corporations) is very powerful in the economy and state. But we will see that it is questionable that their interests lead them to behave differently than earlier owner–capitalists, and therefore harming the economy as charged by the new class theorists. And as Brint (1984) has shown, this "new class" does not have attitudes or political ideologies indicating opposition to the capitalist private sector of the economy.

In concluding our discussion of the nature of advanced industrial societies, we should note that they are not all becoming similar in every respect (Giddens 1973, 1976). We do find a common characteristic of bureaucratization and the authority relations shaped by this force, but we must remember Weber's insight that bureaucracies are only a *means* of influence. Depending upon the underlying class interests that dominate in a society, these bureaucratic organizations will "behave" differently in different societies. And as Weber also instructed, we must recognize how differing historical traditions may shape the behavior of bureaucratic institutions. Both types of influences on the nature of bureaucratic organizations in the United States must be considered in the light of our history of capitalism.

The Tradition of Capitalism

We may define *capitalism* as an economic system in which the means of production (factories, railroads, banks, and so on) are for the most part privately owned and operated for private profit. It is usually assumed that conditions of free competition will exist, but such an assumption is not a defining characteristic of capitalism. (When free competition is very limited, however, we may speak of monopoly capitalism.)

Capitalism may be contrasted with *socialism*, defined as an economic system in which the means of production are not privately owned. Rather, they are collectively owned and operated, with the profits of the economic enterprise shared collectively. It is most often assumed that the state will be the director of the economic system in the name and interests of the collective (total population). The terms *socialism* and *communism* are sometimes used interchangeably, but most often today socialism is used to mean *democratic socialism*. In democratic socialism the *relative* democratic nature of the state that directs the economic system is emphasized. In communist societies a political elite directs the state and economic system, with less nonelite input.

Of course, both capitalism and socialism as defined above are ideal types. In reality most societies vary somewhat and in differing ways from the ideal typical definitions. But from these definitions it should be clear that the United States is primarily a capitalist society. It was founded on the philosophy and reality of private ownership and profit, with a spirit (if not the complete reality, especially later) of free competition.

For the study of social stratification, the strength of this capitalist tradition and its effect on the solution of who gets what and why must not be forgotten. There are several indicators that capitalist ideology and values of private ownership and free individual (or business) competition in the United States are stronger than in almost all other industrial nations (Putnam 1976). For example, in their study of attitudes about equality held by elites in the United States, Sweden, and Japan, Verba et al. (1987) found much more support for income equality in Sweden and Japan than in the United States. And as we have already seen, income inequality is, in fact, much higher in the United States. In another study by Simkus and Robert (1989) of popular attitudes about issues related to traditional capitalist ideology, again we see the United States is rather different. Table 6-5 indicates much less support for government action to reduce unemployment and income inequality compared to other industrial nations in the sample.

Along with attitudes, we can look to actual economic conditions indicating how "traditional" nations are with respect to some aspects of capitalism. Table 6-6 presents the reality of private ownership in the United States compared with that in other advanced industrial societies. The results are again striking. When we examine the amount of state ownership of the basic industries listed in Table 6-6 we find almost none in the United States, compared to extensive state ownership for other capitalist industrial nations. Japan is the only one close to the United States in this respect, and as of 1989 Japan is actually closer to the U.S. pattern than is indicated in Table 6-6. During the second half of the 1980s Japan privatized most of its telecommunications and railways.

But capitalist tradition and practice in this nation have not survived unaltered. The historical forces already examined, further advances in the techni-

TABLE 6-5
COMPARATIVE ATTITUDES TOWARD INEQUALITY AND GOVERNMENT INVOLVEMENT IN THE ECONOMY TO REDUCE INEQUALITY, 1987*

Question	Hungary	Austria	Italy	West Germany	Switzer-land	The Netherlands	Great Britain	Australia	United States
1. The government should provide everyone with a guaranteed basic income.	77.8	53.6	66.9	50.1	41.6	47.9	59.4	38.1	17.6
2. The government should provide a job for everyone who wants one.	90.0	76.9	82.0	74.3	48.4	73.8	57.9	39.7	44.0
3. The government should provide support for children from poor families to attend college.	71.6	78.3	89.8	84.8	80.7	84.1	82.6	74.0	75.2
4. It is the responsibility of government to reduce the differences in income between people with high incomes and those with low incomes.	76.9	76.7	81.0	55.9	41.1	63.9	62.9	43.8	28.3

*Sample sizes vary from 970 (Switzerland) to 2570 (Hungary).
Source: Simkus and Robert (1989).

TABLE 6-6
CROSS-NATIONAL COMPARISON OF GOVERNMENT OWNERSHIP OF BASIC INDUSTRY

Industry	Percentage of government ownership in														
	Australia	Austria	Belgium	Canada	England	France	W. Germany	Italy	Japan	Mexico	Netherlands	Spain	Sweden	Switzerland	United States
Telecommunications	100*	100	100	25	100	100	100	100	100	100	100	50	100	100	0
Electricity	100	100	25	100	100	100	75	75	0	100	75	0	50	100	25
Gas	100	100	25	0	100	100	50	100	0	100	75	75	NA	100	0
Oil production	0	100	NA	0	25	NA	25	NA	NA	100	NA	NA	NA	NA	0
Coal	0	100	0	0	100	100	50	NA	0	100	NA	50	NA	NA	0
Railways	100	100	100	75	100	100	100	100	75	100	100	100	100	100	25
Airlines	75	100	100	75	75	75	100	100	25	50	75	100	50	25	0
Auto industry	0	100	0	0	50	50	25	25	0	25	50	0	0	0	0
Steel	0	100	50	0	75	75	0	75	0	75	25	50	75	0	0
Shipbuilding	NA	NA	0	0	100	0	25	75	0	100	0	75	75	NA	0

*The approximate percentage of the industry government control in each nation. NA = not applicable or negligible production.
Source: Adapted from *The Economist* (December 30, 1978).

175

cal means of production, and expanding bureaucratic organization have produced significant changes. These changes will be described in more detail in our next two chapters, but a summary will be helpful at this point.

First, as several theorists (see Galbraith 1971; Bell 1976) have noted, the importance and even power of technological knowledge has increased (an aspect of the expansion of the occupational structure in a technical sense). The management of major corporations is no longer solely in the hands of capitalists (owners) or even top executive officers of corporations. This is in part because the broad technical knowledge needed for such management is seldom in the possession of one, or even a few, individuals. It can be argued that capitalists, along with top managers, do have the final or the most important say in how a corporation is operated, but that authority is more widely delegated than it was in the past.

Second, the trend of bureaucratization has also affected the capitalist structure in two ways—*externally* and *internally*. With respect to *external* effects, the growth of the state with expanded bureaucratic means of influence has provided some state control over the economy in general, and individual corporations in particular. Whether this state influence has harmed or furthered capitalist and corporate interests (and if either, to what degree) is an important question that will be given more attention.

With respect to *internal* effects, expanding bureaucratic organization is associated with the growth of individual corporations. An important consequence of this growth on the nature of capitalism is reduced corporate competition. Also, the combination of growth and the increased importance of technical knowledge has produced a more complex pattern of control of corporations. The increasing size of corporations has (1) resulted in a wider distribution of stock ownership in most corporations and (2) made necessary an expanded managerial elite to manage the day-to-day operation of the giant firms. These changes have also given rise to the debate (examined in following chapters) over whether major capitalists or a managerial elite (without significant ownership) is primarily in control of major corporations.

However, despite these changes (and the degree and significance of these changes must be considered later), for the study of social stratification it must be recognized that private ownership and control (whether by capitalists or managers) of the means of production remain firm. The economy is still based on private profit. The United States continues to be a *capitalist* nation. The process of industrialization has shaped the stratification system as in other nations; but in this nation the process also had a strong tradition of capitalism that shaped class interests, and to a great extent it remains with us.

The Institutional Structuring of Class Conflicts: A Summary

Our discussion of industrialization, the process of bureaucratization, and the tradition of capitalism does not imply that these forces alone have shaped the nature of inequality and social stratification in the United States. Reality, as always, is more complex. For example, it can be argued that the timing of the American frontier experience helped produce relatively greater support for equality in the early United States, in contrast to new industrial societies in Europe that emerged from a stronger tradition of feudal inequalities. As Lenski and Lenski (1982:215) note, "Frontier conditions often broke down the sharp inequalities and exploitative patterns that characterized all traditional agrarian societies . . ." and "by creating a more egalitarian class system, the frontier prepared the way for the more open and fluid class systems of modern industrial societies."

However, the strong tradition of individualism that accompanied our frontier experience had a later effect of reducing popular support for government programs to reduce inequality in the United States (as we will see in Chapter 10). Furthermore, we must not neglect the early system of slavery in the United States or the tradition of sexual inequality inherited from earlier societies when considering the nature of social stratification in this country. But despite these other influences, the structure of social stratification in the United States must be examined with the three major institutional forces outlined above in mind.

To understand the nature of social stratification in a particular society, we must understand more than the tendency for people to come together in groups to further collective interests. As was outlined in Figure 5-4 at the end of the previous chapter, we must also know how the institutional structure in the society has both *shaped these interests* and provided the battlegrounds in which they *may be contested*.

In this section we have examined how, in this country, (1) industrialization has influenced inequality and created an expanded occupational structure, (2) the advanced nature of industrialization has resulted in the bureaucratization of most of our major institutions (especially the state and the economy), and (3) the continued tradition and reality of capitalist property relations remain important. These historical forces, separately and in combination, have shaped the nature of social stratification in the United States. The *occupational structure*, the major *bureaucratic organizations*, and *capitalist property relations* in the economy provide important battlegrounds in which group interests are brought into conflict. But we have a final question to consider: How are we specifically to define class in relation to these historical forces? We now turn to this question.

THE BASES OF CLASS STRATIFICATION AND CLASS LOCATION

Considering the theoretical controversies in the study of social stratification, a controversy might be anticipated over how class can be defined most meaningfully as well. In large measure the controversy follows the theoretical debates (functional versus conflict theories) over which dimension of social stratification is most important (Weber's class, status, or power). Other assumptions, however, are also involved in the debate over the most useful conceptualization of class.

Dennis Wrong (1959, 1964), for example, outlines what he calls *realist* versus *nominalist* definitions of class. The realist places emphasis on clear class boundaries—people identifying themselves as members of a particular class and interacting most with others in the same class; in other words, forming distinct social groupings based on class divisions. For the nominalist, most important are the common characteristics groups of people may have that influence their life chances and share of valued rewards in the society, such as education level, occupational position, or bureaucratic power position. People are then placed in class categories in terms of these common characteristics, whether or not they are aware of these characteristics and associate with others in the same class.

Similar to the above are *subjective* versus *objective* definitions of class. With the subjective view the emphasis is on whether class has meaning to the people said to be in a particular class, while the objective view stresses particular life chances or economic characteristics people may have in common. Some theorists use the term *class* to cover both views, reserving subdefinitions of class for the objective and subjective aspects. Examples would be Marx and Dahrendorf, who refer to a class in itself and latent interest groups on the objective or nominalist side of the debate, while using the terms class for itself and manifest interest groups on the subjective or realist side.

Another definitional issue is whether *continuous* or *discontinuous* class rankings are most evident. The continuous view is that class or strata should be considered as ranks on a scale; there are positions from high to low, with numerous grades in between. From the continuous view it therefore becomes difficult, or even meaningless, to determine specific class boundaries. The discontinuous view, in contrast, is that there are fewer class divisions, that we can find class divisions with distinct boundaries, and that the divisions between classes are more important than differences within class divisions. Conflict theorists tend to favor the discontinuous and objective views, while functionalists tend to favor the continuous and subjective views (the second leading a few recent functionalists to suggest that the concept of class only weakly applies to the United States; see Nisbet 1959).

We will to some degree take sides in the above debates, by referring again to what may be considered the most important question in the study of social stratification, "Who gets what, and why?" When attempting to answer this question we are directed to *objective class divisions* that people may commonly share. Class in a subjective sense (whether people recognize these conditions, interact with others having similar objective interests, and collectively act upon these interests) is important but may or may not exist, depending on conditions that must be explored later.

To identify some of the most important objective factors behind class location, and before we offer a specific definition of class in the United States, we must return to the institutional structures shaped by the historical forces discussed in the previous section—that is, we must consider the *occupational structure,* the *bureaucratic power structure,* and the *capitalist property struc-ture.* We must understand how people's life chances are affected by these structures, separately and in combination, and, for our present purpose, how people are ranked in each. When we do this, we will also find that the debate over how class should be viewed (continuous versus discontinuous, objective versus subjective) differs to some extent with respect to which of the three structures is seen as shaping class interests. After examining the divisions created by these three structures we can discuss how these divisions converge on what is commonly referred to as the upper, middle, working, and lower classes in the United States.

Occupational Structure

By position in the occupational structure we are referring to one's relation to the market, as Weber, in part, referred to economic class. (The other economic class ranking Weber used was similar to Marx's ownership of the means of production.) In other words, within the occupational structure, people are ranked in terms of skill level and tend to receive greater rewards (such as income) with higher skills. (The exact relationship between rewards and skill level will be examined later.) Thus, with the occupational structure we are stressing objective class factors and a continuous ranking. We are not saying that these rankings are determined and rewards given because of the contribution to the needs of society made by a person in his or her occupation, or that status is received primarily because a certain occupation or skill level meets society's needs. Rather, we are suggesting that rewards are given because the jobs are more or less important to the people (economic or bureaucratic elites) more in control of the rewards to be given. This, of course, is the conflict position.

We can agree to some extent, however, with the Davis and Moore (1945) theory (discussed earlier) that there is something like a competitive market that operates in the occupational structure. People generally are competing to obtain higher skills (usually through the educational system) so as to achieve higher rewards by moving up the occupational structure. But—and this is a key point—it is often not a free competitive market. Access to highly rewarded positions can be restricted, occupational associations may operate to fix prices, or the control over the market by monopolistic industries may allow them to pay their workers higher wages in the face of union power (an outcome of the dual economy described later).

Most previous work on occupational ranking or occupational prestige has been done by functional theorists. We must examine some of their work because even with our different assumptions about the underlying conflict nature of the occupational structure some of this work is of value for us.

Studies of Occupational Prestige   The vast majority of people in industrial societies depend on income from a job to meet their needs. That often makes the occupational structure the most visible form of stratification, in contrast to property relations or power differences. Functional theorists suggest that this visibility leads to extensive agreement among the population on relative ranks in the occupational structure, what they claim are ranks based on status or prestige. Let us examine the evidence.

In 1947 (North and Hatt 1947), 1963 (Hodge, Siegel, and Rossi 1964), 1971 (Siegel 1971), and then again in 1989 (Nakao and Treas 1991) similar studies were conducted to access occupational prestige rankings in the United States.[1] In the 1989 study a total of 740 occupations were ranked by subjects in a national sample, with a focus on a core of 40 well-known occupations. The responses given by the national sample for each occupation were transformed into a ranking for each occupation that ranged from a possible high of 100 (all excellent responses) to a low of 0 (all poor responses).

Table 6-7 lists the rankings for a sample of forty occupations from the study conducted in 1989. At the top of this list is "department head in a state government," which received a ranking of 76, with "filling station attendant" receiving the lowest rank (21). The occupation of physician received the highest ranking overall (86) but is not included in Table 6-7 because this occupation was not included in the list of occupations ranked by everyone in the national sample.

What is rather remarkable is that all three occupational prestige studies found very similar rankings by national samples. For example, there was a correlation of .96 to .97 (1.00 being a perfect correlation) between the 1963 and 1989 occupational rankings (Nakao and Treas 1990). There have been a few differences; for example, in 1947 only 49 percent of the respondents claimed to know what a nuclear physicist was and it was ranked below seventeen other occupations. By 1963, 90 percent claimed to know what a nuclear physicist was and only two occupations received a higher rating. In the 1989 study, service occupations in general had a relative increase in ranking, with professional positions remaining about the same compared to 1964. Again, however, the differences in order of rank were minor in all three studies.

There is other evidence of strong agreement on occupational rankings. Hodge, Siegel, and Rossi (1966) also compared the 1947 and 1963 national studies to more limited studies done in the United States in 1925 and 1940. Again strong consensus was found, with correlations of $r = .93$ and $r = .97$ to the 1963 study. Furthermore, Hodge, Treiman, and Rossi (1966) compared the 1963 national ranking with similar studies conducted in twenty-four other nations. Correlations to the 1963 United States study ranged from a low of $r = .62$ with Poland to a high of $r = .95$ with New Zealand. And a recent study has found similar occupational prestige rankings in urban China (Lin and Xie 1988). The most comprehensive comparison, however, was made by Treiman (1977), who was able to find extensive agreement on occupational prestige in sixty nations around the world. A reasonable conclusion from these various studies is that people do, in fact, agree widely on the relative standing of occupational positions in this society, as well as across most industrial nations. But we can question the reasons for such wide agreement on occupational ranks, and will do so after considering the development of stratification scales.

TABLE 6-7
OCCUPATIONAL PRESTIGE SCORES IN THE UNITED STATES, 1989

Occupation	Prestige score
Department head in a state government	76
Lawyer	75
Chemist	73
Medical technician	68
Clergyman	67
Accountant	65
Public grade school teacher	64
Banker	63
General manager of a manufacturing plant	62
Musician in a symphony orchestra	59
Policeman	59
Superintendent of a construction job	57
Airplane mechanic	53
Farm owner and operator	53
Locomotive engineer	48
Manager of a supermarket	48
Insurance agent	46
Secretary	46
Bank teller	43
Welder	42
Post office clerk	42
Travel agent	41
Barber	36
Assembly line worker	35
Baker	35
Cook in a restaurant	34
Housekeeper in a private home	34
House painter	34
Shipping clerk	33
Cashier in a supermarket	33
Bus driver	32
Logger	31
Gardener	29
Lunchroom operator	27
Bartender	25
Bill collector	24
Saw sharpener	23
Janitor	22
Telephone solicitor	22
Filling station attendant	21

Source: Nakao and Treas (1991).

Socioeconomic Status Scales   Given the importance of social stratification in understanding much of human behavior and given functional theorists' stress on the occupational status dimension of social stratification, there was a clear need to devise a simple and useful method of measuring socioeconomic status for empirical research. Since the early history of American sociology, class position or socioeconomic status has been measured in a number of ways. One of the first measurements was developed by people from the ecological school. Focusing much of their research on the population of Chicago (the ecological school was dominated by sociologists at the University of Chicago), they employed a *residential approach* with the assumption that people from different social classes live in different parts or zones of the city. Thus, a person's class position could be indicated by area or residence (see, for example, Zorbaugh 1929 and Frazier 1932). There were obvious limitations to this approach. The correspondence between class and area of residence is not always close, and severe restrictions are placed on research conducted across several cities.

A new trend in class measurement began with Lloyd Warner's *Yankee City* studies. Focusing on small communities and using extensive observational techniques, Warner developed a *reputational method* of class identification. This method relied primarily upon the *status* judgments of people made by others in the community (see Warner 1953). From this method Warner concluded that there are six distinct class positions based on status:

1 Upper-upper (1.4 percent of the community)
2 Lower-upper (1.6 percent)
3 Upper-middle (10.2 percent)
4 Lower-middle (28.1 percent)
5 Upper-lower (32.6 percent)
6 Lower-lower (25.2 percent)

The upper-upper included rich and old, well-established families in the community. The lower-upper class included the new rich who did not yet have the respect and lifestyle of older rich families. The upper-middle class represented successful (but not rich) families in business and the professions. The lower-middle class was made up of the small business families and what we would call lower white-collar occupations (such as sales clerks and teachers). The upper-lower class were strong, "moral" members of the community, but were not economically well-off. Finally, the lower-lower class included the poor and unemployed with "low moral standards" who were looked down upon by those in the community.

Besides the fact that this technique of class measurement employed by Warner is time-consuming and would be difficult to use with studies examining stratification in more than one small community, there are other problems. One of the most critical is that studies of other communities using the same technique have found differing numbers of class positions (see Lynd and Lynd 1929, 1937; West 1945; and Hollingshead 1949). And, of course, there is the problem of basing class position exclusively on status judgments as described in the preceding chapter.

A breakthrough in class or prestige measurement came with the first study of occupational prestige in 1947. However, a problem remained; rankings were obtained for only ninety occupations. If this ranking was to be widely useful for studies of social stratification it had to be extended. The problem was solved in part with the development of *Duncan's Socioeconomic Index* (see Reiss et al. 1961). This SEI scale was constructed by weighting a person's education level and income so that a ranking of occupations could be made resembling that found in the 1947 occupational prestige study. The method was then able to expand the original ninety occupations ranked in 1947 to a set of 425 occupations.

An even simpler method of measuring socioeconomic status (though with less direct relation to the occupational prestige studies) was developed by Hollingshead (see Hollingshead and Redlich 1958; Miller 1977:230). Referred to as *Hollingshead's Two Factor Index of Social Position,* this scale gives differing weight to a respondent's type of occupation (from a simpler listing of occupations) and education level to indicate a respondent's class position.

Both of these scales are now used widely and have become standard methods of measuring social class in studies of the relationship between social stratification and such factors as attitudes, political behavior, psychological conditions, sexual behavior, and deviance (see Miller 1977:215–216, 231–233, for a listing of these early studies). In fact, it was not until these scales were developed that extensive empirical research in social stratification emerged. These scales are based primarily on the underlying assumption that prestige is the most important aspect of divisions in the occupational structure. The problem with this prestige or status assumption will be described below. However, the prestige assumption is not necessary, and the scales remain a useful tool in stratification research no matter which theoretical perspective is accepted.

Critique of Occupation as a Status Hierarchy   Studies of occupational prestige demonstrate a high rate of agreement in this country and in others on the relative rankings of different occupations. But do these studies show that the agreement is based on status or prestige rather than other factors about an occupation? One study (Balkwell, Bates, and Garbin 1980) showed that people carry in their minds similar concepts of occupational ranks, although there is no doubt that people judge *many* factors about an occupation when ranking occupations (see Baker 1977).

Conflict theorists claim these rankings are made by people in terms of the income and power of the occupation ranked, with status factors secondary (see Gusfield and Schwartz 1963; Lenski 1966:431). Functional theorists seem to have ignored the fact that when respondents in the original 1947 study were asked *why* they rated an occupation high, the most important reason listed was that "the job pays well" (see Heller 1969:120).

Studies have indicated that occupational status research has not adequately recognized the class differences in ranking occupations (Guppy 1982; Coxon, Davies, and Jones 1986). One study has shown that there is significant disagreement on the ranking of occupations between people of different class, race, and education who are asked to rank the occupations (Guppy and Goyder 1984). And it seems that education is one of the most important factors leading raters to agree or disagree on the level of status for particular occupations. The higher the level of education of the raters, the greater their agreement, indicating that learning is perhaps leading to similar ratings. And, finally, Hope (1982) has presented data indicating that the economic rewards of the occupation are as important as the social importance of the occupation in the minds of raters when they rate an occupation as high or low in status.

Other conflict theorists argue that even to the extent that prestige or status is a factor in making such occupational rankings, a person's concept of which jobs are more important and honorable can be influenced by inequalities of power. For example, status judgments can be shaped by (1) the ability of those high in the stratification system to obtain higher income because of their power, and reward with higher income those occupations serving elite interests (income is related to prestige judgments, remember); and (2) the ability of elites to influence what we think about different occupations through their influence over the dominant values in the society (see Kerbo 1976a). There is some support for both arguments in the cross-national prestige comparisons. It was noted above that Hodge, Treiman, and Rossi (1966) found much agreement on cross-national studies of occupational prestige. But there was some variation, with least agreement found between Poland (a communist country) and the United States.

It is interesting in this regard to look more closely at studies conducted in the United States and in communist countries. Yanowitch (1977:105) describes similar occupational prestige studies conducted in Russia, while Parkin (1971) also describes such studies conducted in Poland and Yugoslavia. These studies from communist countries show a consistent difference from those from the United States; working class or manual labor occupations in communist nations are ranked significantly *higher* than in the United States (higher even than many white-collar or nonmanual occupations).

A conclusion is that a communist ideology that praises the working class, an ideology maintained in part to justify elite dominance, has had an influence on the population's concept of occupational prestige. This conclusion is further supported when we find that occupations in *industries* (such as heavy production) that are given more recognition by the communist elite (by stressing rapid economic development) receive more occupational prestige, even compared with the same occupation in less favored industries (Yanowitch 1977:107).

In addition, the income influence on occupational prestige is shown, because working-class or manual jobs receive more pay than most low-level white-collar or nonmanual jobs in Russia (Yanowitch 1977:30). Furthermore, manual jobs in industrial sectors stressed by the communist elite receive more pay than the same manual jobs in industrial sectors not stressed (Yanowitch 1977:32).

We can conclude from all of the above that continuous occupational divisions do exist in industrial societies, and that people in these societies have a remarkably similar conception of these occupational rankings. We must question, however, the degree to which these occupational divisions are based on status or prestige, rather than on economic market forces (many of them not free market competition). The status dimension can be very important in small communities (as we saw with Warner's studies, and studies of the kibbutzim and monasteries in Chapter 5). As we will see in Chapter 7, status is an important dimension in placement in the upper class in this country. But the information we have examined and will examine later suggests that with the occupational structure, occupational skill level, income, and power in the marketplace (as Weber described) are most important in affecting life chances.

Divisions Within Bureaucratic Power and Property Structures

In contrast to the occupational structure, there is less empirical research on how class is related specifically to the bureaucratic power and property structures, or how divisions within these structures influence behavior and attitudes. There certainly has been no shortage of theoretical work in this area, much of it examined in the previous chapter. Because we are concerned in this section with class divisions or class placement, and because empirical work on this subject (in contrast to occupational prestige studies and scales, reviewed above) is limited, this section will be brief. But the research we do have is leading us to understand that divisions within these two structures are equally important in shaping the nature of class and the overall stratification system in this society.

Bureaucratic Authority Divisions   With bureaucratic organizations we are concerned with organized authority or power structures. As Weber (1947:325) observed, "the imperative coordination of the action of a considerable number of men requires control of a staff of persons"; that is, divisions formed in relation to bureaucratic authority (formalized, legitimated power).

The number of staff and their exact function vary across different organizations, but there are usually top positions such as president, chairman of the board, chief executive officer, and vice-president. Below this level we may find many staff positions in charge of more specific functions or departments within the organization, such as assistant secretaries in the federal government, or deans within a university. Below these typically many-layered authority positions, and closer to the simple employees at the bottom, we usually find supervisory positions. These include such positions as plant foreman, department chairperson in a university, and employee supervisors in a state agency. Finally, at the very bottom are employees performing various types of labor within the organization—assembling cars, sending bills to customers, watching over welfare recipients and determining eligibility for public assistance, and so on.

In Dahrendorf's theory of power within imperatively coordinated associations a class dichotomy was assumed that divided those with authority from those without authority. But, as many have pointed out (see Collins 1975; Robinson and Kelley 1979; Robinson and Garnier 1985) and our above description of staff positions suggests, this dichotomy is too simple. We must recognize *degrees* of authority in terms of how many people are above and below a particular staff position. Those people at the top are in such a position because there is no one else *within the particular organization* they must answer to. People immediately below these top positions must answer to those at the top, but at the same time are in positions of authority over many people below. And so it goes, with more and more above, and fewer and fewer below, until we reach the very bottom of the organizational hierarchy.

The above description has stressed official positions *within* particular organizations, because, of course, when we recognize authority links *between* bureaucratic organizations the pattern becomes more complex. For example, the president of a state university holds the top position in that particular organization, while also being subordinate to the board of regents, the state legislature, and/or governor. Similarly, the president of a corporation may be subordinate to top officers in another corporation that has a controlling interest in the first corporation, and/or dominant stockholders. The examples could go on, but the point is that we must recognize degrees of authority relative to an organizational complex or interorganizational network.

Finally, although most people have specific positions within a bureaucratic organization—for example, with a job—the influence of these organizations does not always stop with these formal positions. We are subject to the authority of many state agencies (such as the legal system, Internal Revenue Service, and the Division of Motor Vehicles), and with increasing economic concentration, although formal authority may be lacking, corporate power as well.

As all of our discussion thus far should make clear, a general scale ranking everyone in terms of bureaucratic power is impossible. But divisions or ranks in this sense cannot be ignored if we are to understand fully the nature of social stratification in advanced industrial societies. However, such measurement is possible in relation to specific research questions. We can examine some examples of such research.

Kalleberg and Griffin (1980) examined the effects of bureaucratic power divisions on income and job fulfillment. In this study they were concerned with bureaucratic authority divisions in both capitalist sector organizations (corporations) and noncapitalist organizations (such as government agencies and educational and civic organizations). To measure bureaucratic authority divisions Kalleberg and Griffin (1980:737) asked two questions of respondents in their sample: (1) Are they self-employed? (2) Do they supervise anyone as part of their job? "Individuals who responded 'yes' to both were defined as *employers.* Individuals who responded 'no' to both were defined as *workers. Managers* were those who responded 'no' to the first and 'yes' to the second."

The researchers admit that this is a very rough measurement of authority divisions, and their findings are probably weaker than if more precise measures were possible. It may also be added that degrees of authority are missed in these measures. But the findings are significant; there were clear income differences between these divisions, even after controlling for the influence on income from job tenure, work experience, educational level, occupational skill level, and mental ability. And although the income of people in capitalist sector organizations was greater, the income differences in relation to authority divisions were significant in both capitalist and noncapitalist sectors examined separately. Finally, the higher the position in the authority structure, the greater the job fulfillment claimed.

In a similar study (described in part in the previous chapter), Robinson and Kelley (1979; see also Robinson and Garnier 1985) also examined the effects of authority divisions on income, as well as on a person's class identity. However, measures of bureaucratic authority were used that distinguish more precise *degrees* of authority. Respondents were asked (Robinson and Kelley 1979:44): (1) Do you have a supervisor on your job to whom you are directly responsible? Does that person have a supervisor on the job to whom he or she is directly responsible? (2) In your job, do you supervise anyone who is directly responsible to you? Do any of *those* persons supervise anyone else?

With these measures Robinson and Kelley found significant income differences (higher income to higher positions), even after controlling for the effects on income of ownership versus nonownership of the means of production and occupational prestige positions. As for class identification—that is, a tendency for people to identify themselves as upper, middle, working, or lower class—educational level, occupational status, ownership versus nonownership, and bureaucratic authority position all contributed about equally to predicting the class identification made.

Empirical research in this area of social stratification, as noted, is limited. It is only recently that studies such as the two described above have appeared. There is much work to be done, and measures of degrees of authority must be refined. However, such research shows great promise in further demonstrating the importance of authority divisions in helping us understand much class-related behavior and attitudes, as well as the general nature of structured inequality.

Divisions Within the Property Structure   In a Marxian sense it is the property structure that creates a primary division between those who own the major means of production and control both the use of this property and the profits derived from it, and those who fit none of these conditions. In reality, of course, the advance of industrialization under capitalism has created a property structure that is no way simple.

However, neither was it simple when Marx produced his major works; and as previously noted (in Chapter 4), many differing levels and descriptions of what he called class can be found in these works. But central to the concept of class for Marx was how people are tied to the productive forces (the means of production) in the society—in other words, the relations of production.

Marx stressed the main class relation as that between capitalists (or bourgeoisie) and workers (or proletariat). But at other times he identified other classes or divisions, such as the commercial laborer (that would include must of the middle class today; see Anderson 1974:54), and peasants (whose relation was to an agricultural mode of production).

Marx even further identified divisions within the dominant class; in contrast to the active bourgeoisie (who are actually engaged in production), Marx wrote of the intelligentsia (whose job it was to rationalize and justify the rule of the bourgeoisie; see Marx and Engels 1965:48), and the financial aristocracy ("who is not interested in producing wealth, but only in confiscating it"; see Anderson 1974:57). Then, also, there is the industrial reserve army (which is able to work only in times of full employment), and the lumpenproletariat (who Marx despised as vagabonds, discharged jailbirds, swindlers, brothel keepers, and so on; see Anderson 1974:54).

What should be clear from these examples is that although the bourgeoisie and proletariat constituted the main classes, Marx followed no specific set of class categories; rather, he defined class categories as his interests moved from one issue to another. But behind all of these classes is one main idea; that is, *class must be defined by the relationship people have to the primary means of production* in the society—what we can simply call the property structure. For, as Marx stressed, it is whether or not people own this property (or capital), control it, help manage it, or simply work for others who do, that affects their life chances. However, in contrast to a traditional Marxian perspective, we have stressed that other characteristics of the stratification system, and, in particular, divisions in the occupational structure and bureaucratic authority structure, interact with a property class structure to influence life chances, behavior, and attitudes.

A primary question remains: What is the most useful means of defining property relations or divisions for our present purpose? Following the main idea that class (in this sense) must be defined in the context of people's relation to the means of production in a society, Erik O. Wright's (see Wright and Perrone 1977; Wright 1978a) work described in Chapter 5 is a useful guide.

Wright defined *capitalists* as those who own the means of production and employ many others; *managers* as those who work for capitalists and control the labor of others; *workers* as those who simply sell their labor to capitalists; and the *petty bourgeoisie* as those who own their means of production but employ few workers. With this definition Wright was able to show significant income differences between class categories, and differing effects of education in obtaining more income (such as managers receiving a greater return from more education).

In a similar study, using similar measures of property class positions, Robinson and Kelley (1979) found much the same effect on income (along with the independent effects on income from degrees of bureaucratic authority). And another empirical study has further shown the value of these property class categories in predicting income and satisfaction with work (see Kalleberg and Griffin 1980).

The Convergence of Occupation, Power, and Property on Class Stratification

Thus far we have examined divisions or ranks in what many consider three of the most important institutional structures in our society. Not only do these three hierarchical structures help shape the interests of major divisions or classes within the population, for the most part they also provide the setting in which conflicts (sometimes overt, sometimes hidden) over valued rewards take place.

But, as was suggested in the previous chapter (see the discussion of Figure 5-4) other historical and contemporary forces shape the nature of social stratification. Included among these are age, sex, and race discrimination. These aspects of inequality will be examined in coming chapters. These sources of inequality are to a significant degree also influenced by the three structures we have examined in detail.

A Working Definition of Class   It is time to provide the working definition of *class* that will guide the remainder of our examination of class stratification in the United States. One goal of this chapter has been to demonstrate why we must reject any definition of class based on a single dimension of inequality (whether this is occupational status, bureaucratic power, property relations, or anything else). However, in the face of such complexity, how can class be defined so as to capture the many divisions and rankings we have outlined? As noted in beginning this work, we can define a class as a group of people who share common objective interests in the system of social stratification.

A second goal of this chapter has been to specify these important objective interests. We are *not* suggesting that there are three (or more) separate class systems (occupational class, bureaucratic class, and property class systems). Rather, these three structures tend to converge, producing groups or classes that have common interests with respect to all three structures. In the contemporary United States more often than not the *interaction* or *convergence* of all three influences life chances and rewards, or who gets what and why.

In identifying classes in relation to the convergence of the three institutional structures we have thus far examined, we will use the rather standard labels *upper class, middle class, working class,* and *lower class* (or the poor). In addition, we have inserted between the upper and middle classes a group that will be called the *corporate class.* As is suggested in Table 6-8, members of the

TABLE 6-8
THE CONVERGENCE OF OCCUPATIONAL, BUREAUCRATIC, AND PROPERTY DIVISIONS ON CLASS CATEGORIES

Class categories	Positions in three main types of institutional structures		
	Occupation	Bureaucratic authority	Property relation
Upper class	High	High	Owner
Corporate class	High	High	Nonowner
Middle class	High to mid-level	Mid-level	Nonowner
Working class	Mid-level to low	Low	Nonowner
Lower class	Low	Low	Nonowner

upper class tend to have high positions in the occupational structure and bureaucratic authority structure and are primary owners of the means of production. Those in the corporate class are high in both the occupational and bureaucratic authority structures, but lack significant ownership of the means of production. Those in the middle class are high- to mid-level in occupation, mid-level in specific bureaucratic structures (when not self-employed professionals), and nonowners. Those in the working class are mid-level to low in occupation, low in specific bureaucratic organizations, and nonowners. Finally, those in the lower class are low in occupation and bureaucratic authority, and, of course, nonowners.

The class divisions outlined in Table 6-8 represent something of a synthesis of the three main paradigms of social stratification described in Chapters 4 and 5 (see especially Table 5-1). Remembering that functional theorists focus on occupational status, power conflict theorists focus on authority divisions, and Marxists or ruling-class theorists focus on property class divisions, it can be seen that all three sets of divisions have been included in Table 6-8. However, two points must be stressed: first, we have rejected the functional view of occupational status ranks in favor of Weber's view of occupational competition through skill or relation to the marketplace; and second, we have stressed the convergence of the occupational structure, authority structure, and property structure.

This typology of objective class positions is not all-inclusive. There are people or even categories of people that provide problems of placement in the typology. However, it is the function of a typology, as with a theory, to provide some understanding in the face of apparent complexity. The value of understanding class with respect to positions in the three main institutional structures we have examined should be evident in coming chapters. But before turning to these chapters we have one final issue that as so far been avoided. We are now prepared to consider the complex question of class identification, or the subjective dimension of class.

A Concluding Note on Subjective Class Identification

In our discussion of the various views over how class is to be defined, part of the debate centered on the question of continuous versus discontinuous divisions. By defining class in terms of the convergence of three hierarchical structures, we have suggested that classes are divided to some extent with respect to both continuous divisions (occupation and, to some extent, bureaucratic power) and discontinuous divisions (ownership of the major means of production). But the combination of these three structures tends to produce somewhat distinct class categories, as outlined above.

However, with respect to another major debate, we have thus far focused on *objective* rather than subjective divisions. The perspective stressed is that clear objective forces determine people's share of valued rewards and life chances, whether or not people always recognize these forces and identify with others having common interests in relation to these forces.

The debate over the extent to which subjective class identification exists, however, *is* an important question. When the degree of class identification is high in a society, class conflict can be more intense, resulting either in a change with respect to how rewards are distributed or more force by those on top to maintain the existing distribution of rewards.

Marx, of course, predicted that as capitalism progressed there would be more class conflict as class consciousness also increased. An elementary aspect of class consciousness is simple subjective class identification. We have discussed earlier why many of Marx's predictions about increasing class conflict have failed to materialize. It is time to address the more elementary question of class identification. And we will do so by first examining some of the empirical research.

One of the earliest empirical studies of class identification in the United States was conducted by Richard Centers (1949). Previous research (for example, see *Fortune* 1940) had found that by asking people whether they could be placed in the upper, middle, or lower class, the vast majority (79 percent in the *Fortune* study) said they were middle class. It was interpreted to mean that this is primarily a middle-class nation where class divisions are of little significance (since most people are middle class).

But when Centers simply added the category of working class in a national study, there was an important change in the responses; 51 percent identified themselves as working class, and 43 percent identified themselves as middle class. Furthermore, about three-fourths of the business, professional, and other people with white-collar occupations responded that they are middle or upper class, while four-fifths of the manual laborers responded "working class." Centers' conclusion was that class is a meaningful concept to most people, and does correspond to a large degree with objective class divisions (at least with occupational divisions that were stressed by sociologists at the time).

The Centers study has since been challenged as containing some limitations, at least with respect to the conclusions he attempted to draw from his data. For example, Gross (1953) found that when people are given no fixed choices on a questionnaire (such as upper, middle, working, lower class), but simply asked to name their class position, 39 percent responded that they belong to no class or do not know. Only 31 percent responded "middle class," and 11 percent "working class." (Other responses were 1 percent upper class, 3 percent lower class, and 15 percent some other class.) When people are asked how many classes there are in the United States, Kahl and Davis (1955) received responses ranging from two classes (10 percent), three classes (42 percent), four classes (20 percent), five or more classes (5 percent), no concept of a class order (12 percent), to explicit statements that class does not exist (6 percent).

Despite these criticisms, it is clear that the concept of class *does* have meaning for most people (Vanneman and Cannon 1987). In the Kahl and Davis study, for example, a total of only 18 percent either denied the existence of classes or did not understand the concept. Given the "classless" ideology of individualism in this country, what is surprising is that only 18 percent failed to provide an opinion of how many classes exist. Furthermore, when sociologists cannot agree among themselves upon the most meaningful number of class categories or the exact class boundaries, it would be unreasonable to expect the general population to do so.

Extensive research has shown recently that the most widely accepted class labels (upper class, middle class, working class, lower class) do show a reasonable correspondence with objective class indicators such as income, education, occupational skill level, and manual versus nonmanual jobs (Hodge and Treiman 1968b; Vanneman and Pampel 1977; Kluegel, Singleton, and Starnes 1977). And Vanneman (1980; Vanneman and Cannon 1987) has found that although people in England were usually assumed to have more class consciousness and class identification than people in the United States, there is virtually no difference in class identification in these two countries among manual and nonmanual workers.

There is one new trend in the research on class identification which is worth mention because it relates to issues in stratification theory and research that will be considered in many places throughout coming chapters. The primary issue relates to how we should consider the place of women in the class system. In the past it was assumed that class placement of women would be determined by the position of their husbands in the occupational, authority, and property structures of the stratification system. With most married women now employed in the labor force, this assumption is no longer unquestioned. Some sociologists argue that the standard of living, income, and property are still distributed through the family unit, and because males continue to have the longest working careers and higher incomes compared to their wives, the class placement of women continues to be determined by the male head of household (Curtis 1986; Goldthorpe, Llewellyn, and Payne 1987). However, there have been a number of new studies on subjects such as social mobility to see if there are differences between the experiences of men and women on these aspects of social stratification.

There is also more recent information on the subject of class identification. Do we find that class identity of women is primarily shaped by the objective class position of their husbands? Or, when they themselves are employed, do we find that women define their class position in terms of their own job, income, and education? Approaching this subject with new data, Davis and Robinson (1988) find that, compared to the 1970s, women in the 1980s increasingly identified their class position with their own occupation and education. And it is interesting that men were doing the same—that is, identifying their own class position with reference to their own occupation, income, and education rather than considering their wives' class position as well. Findings such as these give reason to focus more attention on the possible separate realities of class position for men and women, in addition to the combined realities for the family unit.

The complex nature of hierarchical divisions (rather than a single class structure) in this country produces no clear and unambiguous concept of class for most people. Differences in occupational, bureaucratic, and property positions, as well as income and education level, may all be important dimensions to people, but they do not always correspond (although they are significantly related; see Wright and Perrone 1977; Wright 1978a; Robinson and Kelley 1979; Kalleberg and Griffin 1980). A person may be high with respect to some dimensions and low with respect to others.

Furthermore, while some of these divisions can be viewed as continuous (occupation, income, education, and, to some extent, bureaucratic authority), others are more discontinuous (the property class structure). And *all* of these rankings have been shown to be *separately* related to class identification (Robinson and Kelley 1979). While some people may identify with the middle class because of their position in the occupational structure, others may identify with the middle class (or working class) because of their position in the bureaucratic structure, and so on with all the divisions.

It therefore becomes a complex task for people to choose whether to place themselves in the upper, middle, working, or lower class. But *objective class divisions* are still important in the distribution of valued rewards and life chances among people. As the information we have presented and will present shows, these divisions are important both singly and in combination.

Thus, although the terms *upper class* (and *corporate class*), *middle class, working class,* and *lower class* (or the poor) mask important separate divisions and interests between groups in our society *and* do not show a simple or unambiguous relation to subjective class identification, the terms remain useful. These class terms are useful both because they seem to have the most meaning for the most people and because they are to a large degree related to the convergence of divisions in the occupational, bureaucratic, and property structures stressed in this chapter. Our next task, to specify further the value of these class divisions, will be tackled in the next four chapters.

NOTES

1 The 1989 occupational prestige study was again planned and started by Bill Hodge, but was taken over by the co-directors of the research project, Keiko Nakao and Judith Treas, upon his death in 1989. At this writing many aspects of the study remain to be analyzed, but Professor Nakao was kind enough to release some of the core results to be included here.

CHAPTER 7

THE UPPER CLASS

Consider the following situation: Someone from a distant culture or, say, a distant planet, wishes to gain enough knowledge of the present United States to understand its major political and socioeconomic institutions. Having no prior information, this person would be faced with an almost insurmountable task. Numerous complex social and economic forces affect the major institutions in this society. But if this individual concentrates on the forces that are of major importance in shaping the basic features of our society—those features that most influence how people live, die, earn their living, educate themselves, or exist in peace or war—the scope of the task can be narrowed.

To understand these basic features this individual must begin by examining the nature of social stratification. Furthermore, the top of this stratification system commands the greatest attention. The institutions, men and women at the top of this stratification system are not all-powerful. They don't even always influence major events in the direction they may desire. But, in the words of C. Wright Mills (1956:28), who in his time understood better than most the potent new forces developing, "given the enlargement and the centralization of the means of power now available, the decisions that [the power elite] make and fail to make carry more consequences for more people than has ever been the case in the world history of mankind."

In this chapter and the next we will examine the top of the system of stratification in this country. We will begin by considering the nature and means of influence held by an upper class of interrelated families. Then, in the next chapter, we will consider the nature and means of influence held by what we have called a corporate class. To be sure, there is some overlap or interrelationship between the upper class and the corporate class. But as the size and complexity of major corporations increase in capitalist societies, some argue that the corporate class is emerging out of the old upper class of family wealth to maintain dominance. Still, even to the extent that this corporate class is emerging with greater power, the upper class continues to share the top of the stratification system, and the base of power created by upper-class wealth was what made a corporate class possible.

LOCATING THE UPPER CLASS

Probably one of the most used, and abused, terms referring to the people in a position of superiority in the society is the *upper class*. In everyday language the term can be found describing a wealthy small-town merchant, higher professional people such as physicians, celebrities, and movie stars, or anyone with wealth or income substantially above the average. Most likely, however, none of the above categories would qualify as truly upper class.

The "true" upper class is so removed from the experience of most people that for them local physicians or current movie stars become the only candidates for the position of upper class. But wealth, power, education, or fame by themselves (or in combination, for that matter) will not assure one of upper-class status. So exclusive is this group that only from 0.5 percent to 1 percent of the population in this country would qualify.

Names such as Du Pont, Mellon, Rockefeller, Vanderbilt, and Carnegie may come to mind as signifying the upper class. Most of those who are members today, however, are unknown outside of this exclusive social circle. In fact, many of the names identified with upper-class membership were at one time excluded from this social circle. The "original" Rockefeller, John D. Rockefeller who made the family millions (later billions) in oil during the late 1800s, was rejected by some in this social circle as a gangster (see Lundberg 1968:343). Even former Presidents of the United States are usually of questionable material for upper-class membership.

Clearly, therefore, such criteria as wealth, fame, and power do not assure upper-class status. More important is the kind of wealth and how old it is, a certain lifestyle rather than celebrity recognition, and the source of power rather than power per se. It will be remembered that Max Weber described three dimensions of stratification as class, status, and party (or power). These three typically converge, with upper-class families usually at the top on all three dimensions. Simply affecting a certain lifestyle, however, would not be enough. Being involved in the social institutions of the upper class, such as social clubs, expensive private schools, exclusive summer resorts, debutante balls, high-status charities, and cultural events that promote a certain lifestyle, is most important.

The United States has never had an aristocracy in the true sense of the word. As a new nation, born in an age of revolt against European traditions of aristocratic rule, the United States proved to be less than fertile ground for a well-developed royalty. A nineteenth-century Frenchman, Alexis de Tocqueville (1969), marveled at the spirit of equality that seemed to thrive in this new nation at the time of his visit in the early 1800s. But old cultural traditions, even when transmitted from abroad, die hard. Before the wounds of the Revolutionary War had healed, the founders of this new nation were considering whether or not the position of President should be hereditary and what the proper title should be. (Should it be "His Highness the President of the United States," "His Serene Highness the President of the United States," or, thought Washington himself, "High Mightiness"? See Amory 1960:61.)

And the urge to establish some kind of aristocratic tradition, even if it lacked legal support, as in Europe, did not stop with the nation's leadership positions. Attempts to establish exclusive societies signifying a family pedigree and hereditary social status emerged quickly. First there was the Society of Cincinnati (having nothing to do with the city), founded in 1783, which originally included Washington, Hamilton, and Knox as members (Amory 1960:41). There was also the First Families of Virginia (Amory 1960:43), mentioned by Max Weber as an example of a status group established to restrict social intercourse within a circle of acceptable hereditary families. But this nation was to wait about 100 years before anything resembling a national aristocracy could emerge.

It is time to offer a concise definition of upper class. E. Digby Baltzell (1958:7), one of the most quoted researchers in this area of study (a sociologist, and himself a member of the Philadelphia upper class), offers the following:

> The *upper class* concept . . . refers to a group of families, whose members are descendants of successful individuals (elite members) of one, two, three, or more generations ago. These families are at the top of the *social class* hierarchy; they are brought up together, are friends, and are intermarried one with another; and finally, they maintain a distinctive style of life and a kind of primary group solidarity which sets them apart from the rest of the population.

There are several components of the concept of upper class as defined above that need further explanation and detail. First, we find a stress on families who have *descended* from successful people (usually successful in terms of making a great fortune). New money is always suspect. It is assumed (and at times it is a well-founded assumption) that great wealth generated over a short period of time is somehow dirty money. Members of the upper class often view the new rich as gangsters who have acquired great wealth through illegal or immoral means (forgetting, of course, that their inherited wealth originally sprang from similar methods). For example, the Kennedy family has only recently become secure in its upper-class status because the father (Joseph Kennedy) of John, Robert, and Teddy Kennedy was believed to have acquired the family millions in illegal whiskey deals during Prohibition.

Tied to the requirement of descendants of success and wealth, upper-class members must cultivate a "distinctive style of life." This cultivation takes time, and few new rich are able to make it. One must be involved with the arts and the right charities, and acquire a whole host of proper manners and traits to be displayed among high society. The crude Texas millionaire, though he or she may try, will usually find that his or her efforts in cultivating the proper style of life are judged unacceptable.

And there are the women who usually must attach themselves to their husbands' success if they are to break into the upper class. The wife is an equal partner in displaying the proper lifestyle to gain acceptance. She must be involved in the right charity work and community organizations to enhance the status and power of the upper class in general, as well as the position of her husband (Ostrander 1984). Many years ago Thorstein Veblen (1899), in his famous work, *The Theory of the Leisure Class,* also noted the importance of women in displaying a lifestyle that would make one an acceptable upper-class member.

The men, of course, must display a lifestyle that only great wealth can bring. But much time and effort in this display is required—time and effort that men busy managing their wealth may not have time to pursue. Also, there is the display of wealth in the style of dress that business dress codes often (especially in earlier days) prohibited. Thus, it falls with the women to involve themselves in activities that only great wealth (and servants at home) will allow, and to show their great wealth in expensive dress and jewelry.

We also find that, according to Baltzell's definition, the upper class tends to be "brought up together, are friends, and are intermarried one with another." Among other things, this suggests that there is a *class consciousness* or group unity among the upper class. Several social scientists (such as Mills 1956; Baltzell 1958; Domhoff 1970, 1974, 1983) argue that the upper class shows a higher degree of class consciousness and unity of action with respect to common political and economic interests than any other class in the United States. An important reason for this is that the upper class, due to its close interaction in early school years and later in life, has created a strong "we" feeling.

This social solidarity is furthered by several important social institutions of the upper class. As Domhoff (1967:16) describes it, "Underlying the American upper class are a set of social institutions which are its backbone—private schools, elite universities, the 'right' fraternities and sororities, gentlemen's clubs, debutante balls, summer resorts, charitable and cultural organizations, and such recreational activities as foxhunts, polo matches, and yachting." Through the life cycle from childhood to adulthood the upper class experiences these social institutions, which help promote class consciousness and unity.

In the earliest years, the young child is brought into an advantaged world of the upper class that provides many unique learning experiences and an early socialization into the world outlook and values of this class. But the formal upper-class institutions begin with the prep schools or private boarding schools. These schools are most important in transmitting the traditions and values of the upper class, as well as in forming the early friendship ties that remain in later years (Mills 1956:65; Lundberg 1968:338; Cookson and Persell 1985). Not all children of upper-class, or prospective upper-class, parents attend these boarding schools, and more recently these schools have opened their doors to a few bright students who are not upper class.

A small number of highly exclusive schools (such as Groton, Choate, and St. Andrew's) are commonly listed as most important (see Domhoff 1983:44–46; Cookson and Persell 1985:43), and old school ties formed at such schools seem more important as an identification of upper-class status than those formed at the elite universities attended in later life. The girls of the upper class have their elite prep schools as well. These girls' schools have not been given equal importance and the standard list is somewhat larger, but they serve the same basic functions for the transmission of upper-class traditions and social ties later in life. (It should be noted, however, that some of these schools have become coed or have merged with other schools to become coed in recent years.)

The next stage in the life cycle, especially for the upper class, leads to college. With a high degree of regularity the graduates of exclusive prep schools attend a handful of rather exclusive Ivy League colleges, such as Harvard, Yale, and Princeton (see Domhoff 1983:27). But here there is an increasing problem of upper-class identification; more and more, these institutions have opened their doors to "commoners." This is one reason that the prep school ties have become more important. The problem is not great, however, because within these Ivy League colleges, most important for upper-class identification are exclusive fraternities, sororities, and eating clubs, which become the most important badges of upper-class standing. For example, As C. Wright Mills (1956:67) noted, there are actually "two Harvards":

> The clubs and cliques of college are usually composed of carry-overs of association and name made in the lower levels at the proper schools; one's friends at Harvard are friends made at prep school. That is why in the upper social classes, it does not by itself mean much merely to have a degree from an Ivy League college. That is assumed: the point is not Harvard, but which Harvard? By Harvard, one means Porcellian, Fly, or A.D.: by Yale, one means Zeta Psi or Fence or Delta Kappa Epsilon: by Princeton, Cottage, Tiger, Cap and Gown, or Ivy.

By the college years the exclusive social circles maintained by fraternities and sororities are important not only for their influence on later social and business ties, but also for regulating the marriage market. Debutante balls serve this function earlier; however, the college years remain critical. Each of the exclusive fraternities for men have their counterpart in equally exclusive sororities for young women of the upper class. Dating ties are maintained between upper-class fraternities and sororities, and criticism is often brought to bear on someone from one of these exclusive clubs dating outside this network. In this way the marriage market is restricted, and it becomes more certain that someone from the upper class will marry within the upper class—preventing "tragedies" such as the one depicted by Erich Segal in *Love Story*. As Baltzell (1958:26) puts it, ". . . the democratic whims of romantic love often play havoc with class solidarity." It is always well received when, for exam ple, a Mellon marries a Du Pont, for tremendous fortunes are merged and the unity of upper-class interests is increased. Increasingly, however, this inter-marriage has become more difficult and occurs less often (Domhoff 1983:34–36).

The next set of upper-class institutions said to promote unity and class consciousness are the exclusive men's social clubs. According to Dye (1979:184) and Domhoff (1970:22–26) the most important upper-class male social clubs are:

Arlington (Portland)
Bohemian Club (San Francisco)
Boston (New Orleans)
Brook (New York)
Burlingame Country Club (San Francisco)
California (Los Angeles)
Casino (Chicago)
Century Association (New York)
Chagrin Valley Hunt (Cleveland)
Charleston (Charleston)
Chicago (Chicago)
Cuyamuca (San Diego)
Denver (Denver)
Detroit (Detroit)
Eagle Lake (Houston)
Everglades (Palm Beach)
Hartford (Hartford)
Hope (Providence)
Idlewild (Dallas)
Knickerbocker (New York)
Links (New York)
Maryland (Baltimore)
Milwaukee (Milwaukee)
Minneapolis (Minneapolis)
New Haven Lawn Club (New Haven)
Pacific Union (San Francisco)
Philadelphia (Philadelphia)
Piedmont Driving (Atlanta)
Piping Rock (New York)
Racquet Club (St. Louis)
Rainier (Seattle)
Richmond German (Richman)
Rittenhouse (Philadelphia)
River (New York)
Rolling Rock (Pittsburgh)
Saturn (Buffalo)
St. Cecelia (Charleston)

St. Louis Country Club (St. Louis)
Somerset (Boston)
Union (Cleveland)
Woodhill Country Club (Minneapolis)

These clubs provide a social setting within which their typically upper-class members can share their ideas about common political and economic concerns and maintain social and business ties. Also important are the multiple-club memberships of upper-class people that help transform the upper-class network into national proportions (Mills 1956:61). Becoming a regular member of one of these clubs is no easy task. They pride themselves on being exclusive, and to a large degree view their task as gatekeepers of the upper class.

In his research on San Francisco's Bohemian Club, Domhoff (1974:48–49) reports the following membership procedures:

1 Membership is by invitation only.
2 The potential member must be nominated by at least two regular members.
3 The prospective member must then fill out application forms and list at least five club members as references.
4 Personal interviews are conducted by a membership committee.
5 A list of prospective members is then given to all regular members of the club for their opinions.
6 Finally, the prospective member must pass a vote of the membership committee.

On top of all the socializing, drinking, sporting events, and other types of recreational activities, club participation is a serious matter. As would be suspected, many business deals are made. And as Amory (1960:212) reports through one of his informants, the more important the club the bigger the business deals: "At the Metropolitan or the Union League or the University . . . you might do a $10,000 deal, but you'd use the Knickerbocker or the Union or Racquet for $100,000 and then, for $1,000,000 you move on to the Brook or Links."

Mingling with and hearing politicians is no less important. Besides the usual discussion of various political and economic issues facing big business and the upper class, at clubs like the Bohemian, Domhoff found, noonday speeches brought together top business leaders and high government officials. Although the government officials are often not of membership caliber, they are invited to club outings. The list of political figures who *are* members includes George Bush, Ronald Reagan, Gerald Ford, Richard Nixon, George Shultz, Caspar Weinberger, Henry Kissinger, and James A. Baker III (Domhoff 1981).

Finally, we move to an "institution" that has a most interesting place in the history of the upper class in this country. In the second half of the nineteenth century, with new wealth emerging quite rapidly, it became increasingly difficult to determine who was in and who was still out of respectability among the upper class. A score card was needed—a list that could be referred to when giving a party or deciding who should be invited to any type of social event. In a rather informal way, the *Social Register* was brought into existence.

Founded in 1887, and dominated by Mrs. Edward Barry for many years, the *Social Register* is nothing more nor less than a listing of families who are acceptable members of high society or the upper class (Amory 1960:3–7). Much of the responsibility for deciding who was listed (or dropped) was retained by Mrs. Barry (and later the other "secretaries"). To become listed a prospective family must submit five reference letters from families already included in the *Social Register*.

The listings are still controlled by a few people, and there is always much speculation among the upper class as to why someone is dropped or included. For example, as Domhoff (1983:23) found, names are dropped for such reasons as "scandal, divorce, marrying outside of one's social class, marrying a movie star, and so forth." Perhaps for this reason, the *Social Register* has lost some of its authority today as a gatekeeper of upper-class membership. Still, several studies have shown that these volumes remain rather reliable lists of the old families that make up the center of the upper class (see Domhoff 1983:21). At its high point in 1925 the *Social Register* was published in twenty-five cities, but then that number was reduced to twelve. Since 1976 (when publication was taken over by the Malcolm Forbes family), however, the *Social Register* has been consolidated into one large book (Domhoff 1983:20–21).

To the extent that the upper class exists today, it is at the summit of all three dimensions of social stratification (class, status, and party) described by Weber. In the above discussion we have focused most on the dimension of social status or esteem. This dimension is by no means the most important in determining the place of the upper class in the overall stratification system in this country, for in the final analysis wealth and political power are primary. But the social esteem dimension is important in maintaining the upper-class unity and class consciousness that in the long run affect the dimensions of economic and political power.

UPPER-CLASS DOMINANCE TODAY?

Most social scientists agree that the power of wealthy upper-class families was very extensive at the turn of the century in this country. No one believes that the upper class completely dominated the country economically and politically; there were conflicts within this group (as there are today), and there have always been other economic and political contenders able to prevent complete dominance by one group. But compared with that of other groups in the country, the economic and political dominance of the upper class was most pervasive. We find much less agreement today on the current place of an upper class in the overall stratification system.

Several changes, some say, have reduced the power of wealthy upper-class families in the second half of the twentieth century. Most importantly, the large industrial and financial corporations once under the control of these wealthy families *may* now be more directly controlled by a new group of corporate managers. In addition, it is said, the federal government has grown more independently powerful since the Great Depression of the 1930s, thus reducing upper-class power. And, it is charged, the upper class is no longer playing as important a role within government as it once did. Finally, some argue, the upper class is no longer as unified as it once was.

On the other hand, additional changes have occurred that may have *increased* upper-class power. For example, it is argued that individual wealthy families own less stock in *particular* corporations today. But it may be that they still have enough stock ownership to control these corporations, while at the same time they own a lot of stock in each other's corporations. This collective ownership by the upper class may, in fact, produce greater common interests and unity. Finally, it is charged that the upper class has retained its influence over the federal government through new means, and with the expanded powers of the federal government this political power of the upper class has increased.

In this section these various beliefs will be considered. We will begin with an examination of information suggesting continued upper-class dominance. In the next chapter we will consider contrary evidence and the emergence of new contenders for power.

The Upper Class as a Governing Class

G. William Domhoff (1967, 1970, 1974, 1979, 1983) is among those most actively attempting to demonstrate that an upper class of wealth remains dominant in the United States. He uses the terms *governing class* and *ruling class* to indicate that this social upper class, through various means of influence in the economy and political system, does in fact govern the country. Two major steps are involved in Domhoff's research approach: (1) he attempts to show that the upper class continues to exist and that there is enough unity among the members of this class, and (2) he presents evidence showing that this class is a governing class through its various means of influence over the economy and political system.

In part, the second step relies on what Domhoff calls a *sociology of leadership method* to indicate that people from the upper class (measured in the first step) hold important positions within the major economic and political institutions in the country. Recently Domhoff (1990) has also focused on how the policy-forming process in the government and economy is shaped by upper-class influence, whether from the direct involvement of the upper class in institutional positions of power or from other, more indirect, means of influence.

In his first works (*Who Rules America?*, 1967; updated in *Who Rules America Now?*, 1983; and *The Higher Circles,* 1970) Domhoff included information on both the unity among the upper class and how it is able to dominate economic and political institutions. In a subsequent work (*The Bohemian Grove,* 1974) Domhoff provided some very interesting inside information on upper-class unity and consensus-forming processes in social clubs and retreats. And in still other works (*The Powers That Be,* 1979, not to be confused with Halberstam's book of the same name, *The Power Elite and the State,* 1990) he provides more detail on various processes employed by the wealthy in influencing government policy.

At the outset, however, it must be stressed that much like C. Wright Mills (1956) and even more Marxian-oriented theorists, Domhoff does *not* argue that this upper class or governing class completely dominates or rules the country politically and economically. Given the many interest groups that exist and the complexity of advanced industrial societies such as ours, no one group can be completely dominant. But when important decisions are made (involving such things as how to deal with inflation, foreign trade problems, and becoming involved in foreign conflicts), and especially when these decisions may affect the interests and well-being of the upper class, Domhoff believes that this class has more influence than any other group. Researchers in this area of study are concerned with relative *degrees* of dominance by one group or another. Reality, especially with the present subject matter, never fits nicely into clear-cut categories. For this reason, as should be evident in what follows, researchers in such an important area of study remain divided over many conclusions.

Indicators of Upper-Class Membership   To begin, Domhoff must show that an upper class does continue to exist, and that this class maintains sufficient unity and interaction to act upon common interests. Isolated people or even small groups may try to influence events on a national (or local) level. But it is most unlikely that these people will have much impact until they are united in such numbers that their power outweighs that of other groups. The wealthy, of course, have vast political and economic resources that can be mobilized to influence national events. But even the resources of these wealthy people are usually not enough, operating alone. Thus, unity and consensus are critical if they are to have an impact on major events.

As already discussed, there are several types of upper-class institutions (ranging from elite prep schools and social clubs to listings of upper-class status in such books as the *Social Register*). Having participated in these institutions and/or a listing in the *Social Register* would seem to indicate upper-class membership. Possessing great wealth is also considered a criterion of upper-class membership, but if you are a member of a social club or listed in the *Social Register,* for example, you are assumed to be wealthy. To be specific, Domhoff (1970:21–27) lists five major indicators of upper-class membership (also see Domhoff 1983:44–49):

1 A listing in one of the various blue books or the *Social Register*

2 Any male member of the family attending one of the exclusive prep schools (such as those listed in Domhoff 1970)

3 Any male member of the family belonging to one of the exclusive social clubs (see Domhoff 1970)

4 Any female member of the family belonging to an exclusive club or attending an exclusive prep school or

5 Upper-class membership is assumed if the "father was a millionaire entrepreneur or $100,000-a-year corporation executive or corporation lawyer" *and* the person attended an elite prep school or belonged to an exclusive club on an *extended* list of these schools and clubs.

Identification with any one of these five categories places a person on Domhoff's list of upper-class membership.

In developing these indicators Domhoff relied on several previous studies of upper-class institutions (such as those of Baltzell 1958, and Amory 1960). He also interviewed and communicated with a number of upper-class people and local newspaper editors in charge of reporting high-society events. Domhoff claims that these various people confirmed the validity of the indicators used above in locating upper-class membership. Moreover, he claims that these various indicators are interrelated, so that, for example, if someone is found to have attended a prep school such as Choate in his early years, he is most likely to be listed in the *Social Register* and to be a member of an exclusive social club such as the Knickerbocker in New York City. Domhoff admits that the interrelationship among these indicators is far from perfect. However, his effort does provide the most extensive support thus far for the existence of an upper class as defined at the beginning of this chapter.

Upper-Class Unity   The existence of upper-class unity or cohesiveness is of central importance for those who argue from a ruling-class or governing-class position. But it is extremely difficult to demonstrate. And it is here that Domhoff has been most criticized. It can be assumed that some unity exists when we find that the upper class tends to go to the same few prep schools and its members belong to the same few exclusive social clubs. But such evidence is not enough. For one thing, the upper class as defined by Domhoff is not a small group. Relative to the total population the upper class represents only about 0.5 percent of the people. That, however, still amounts to more than 1 million people. And, of course, there is the question of *how much unity* is necessary for this upper class to act together on its common interests, or even recognize that it has common interests. Must its members simply know, or know of, a large number of other upper-class families? Or must they interact on a regular basis with many other upper-class people, discussing their common interests often and deciding on action to ensure that their common interests are protected?

Some historical case studies of the upper class indicate extensive upper-class unity in some parts of the country. E. Digby Baltzell (1958), for example, has studied the Philadelphia upper class and found that the tendency of the upper class to attend the same schools, belong to the same clubs, and frequent the same resort areas leads to much unity, class consciousness, and organized political and economic activity. (For similar findings in five other cities, see Ingham 1978. And for an interesting study of the community upper-class institutions and status ranking in New Orleans, see Raabe 1973.) We find major limitations with this type of research, however, the most obvious being that this is only a local examination of the upper class. If it is a national upper class and this class is able to maintain some level of unity and concerted action on a national level, the type of research done by Baltzell is not adequate. To date, Domhoff is one of the few who has attempted to demonstrate the existence of upper-class consensus and unity on a national level.

Domhoff's most interesting study of upper-class unity is contained in his book *The Bohemian Grove* (1974). The Bohemian Grove is a summer retreat north of San Francisco primarily for members of one of San Francisco's most exclusive social clubs, the Bohemian Club. For two weeks every summer these members (still all male at the Bohemian Club, which is fighting laws requiring them to open their doors to women) come together for relaxation, drinking, and amateur theatrical performances, among other things. Aside from the serious subject matter of the book, Domhoff paints an interesting picture of an upper-class lifestyle, which, despite the wealth and power, is not in every way far removed from that of the middle class.

In some ways the retreat is like a Boy Scout summer camp. This image comes across most directly in the annual opening ceremony, called the *Cremation of Care* (Domhoff 1974:1–7; also see Domhoff 1981). But of course, these men are not Boy Scouts. Rather they are people from wealthy and powerful families, major corporate executives, and political leaders. And despite what is suggested in the Cremation of Care ceremony, these men do not forget their worldly business while at the two-week retreat. Through inside informants, a study of guest and membership lists, and a list of the actual activities during this retreat, Domhoff found that much serious work is accomplished.

In examining this retreat it is important to be specific about who is involved. Reviewing the membership list of the Bohemian Club, Domhoff (1974:30) found that 27 percent of the members are also members of the exclusive Pacific Union Club of San Francisco. In addition, he found 45 percent of the 411 nonresident regular members (members living outside California) listed in various upper-class blue books such as the *Social Register*.

Finally, Domhoff (1974:31) interprets as a tie to the corporate elite figures showing "that at least one officer or director from forty of the fifty largest industrial corporations in America were present" at the Bohemian Grove retreat in 1970, along with directors of twenty of the top twenty-five banks, twelve of the top twenty-five life insurance companies, ten of the top twenty-five in transportation, and eight of the twenty-five top utilities. In total, 29 percent of the top 797 corporations in the United States were represented at just *one* two-week retreat by at least one officer or director! Domhoff (1983:70) again examined the list of those attending the 1980 Bohemian Grove retreat and found very similar figures on corporate elite participation.

Other important research on upper-class unity is focused on more quantitative indicators; for example, measures of association between various clubs and other policy-forming organizations to which the upper class often belongs. This type of research attempts to show that upper-class members interact extensively with one another, creating a network for cooperative political and economic activity, along with upper-class unity. In one study Domhoff (1975) was able to show that *673* of the top 797 corporations in America have at least one corporate executive represented in *just 15 clubs and policy organizations* (such as Links, Bohemian Club, and Council on Foreign Relations, and the Business Council). In Domhoff's words (1975:179), "This finding is even more impressive when we consider only the top 25 corporations in each category. Here we see that 25 of 25 industrials, 25 of 25 banks, 23 of 25 insurance companies, 24 of 25 transportation, 24 of 25 utilities, 19 of 25 retails, and 18 of 25 conglomerates are connected" by these 15 clubs and organizations.

Upper-Class Economic Power

If we have an upper class in this country that, because of its power, can be described as a governing class, by what means does it govern or dominate? As noted, theorists such as Domhoff consider the upper class dominant in both the economy and politics. But precisely how is this dominance achieved? We will examine first how the upper class is said to have extensive influence over the economy through stock ownership, then turn to the question of economic power through extensive representation in major corporate offices.

Stock Ownership As some argue, the most important means of upper-class economic power lies in its ownership of the primary means of production. The upper class has power over our economy because of its control of the biggest corporations through stock ownership. (We will discuss in more detail in the next chapter the importance of the tremendous size and concentration of major corporations today, which make such ownership even more significant.)

Legally, the ultimate control of corporations is found not with top corporate executives, but with major stockholders. In a sense, top corporate executives and boards of directors are charged with managing these corporations for the real owners—the stockholders. Stockholders have the authority to elect corporate directors who are to represent stockholder interests. These directors are then responsible for general corporate policy, including the task of filling top executive positions. The day-to-day management of the corporation is in turn the responsibility of the executive officers, who must generally answer to stockholders and their representatives on the board of directors.

Assuming for now that corporate authority actually operates this way (questions about this ideal power arrangement will be considered below), the largest stockholder or stockholders in a corporation should be in control. Thus, if we find that upper-class families have extensive stock ownership and that this stock is in major corporations, we can say that upper-class families dominate the American economy

It is clear, as described in Chapter 2, that wealth is very unequally distributed in this country—more so even than family or personal income. One of the most important categories of wealth (because of its usual high return on investment) is corporate stock. We have seen that 1 percent of the people in this country owned *56.5 percent* of the privately held corporate stock, and only 0.5 percent of the people owned *49.3 percent* of the privately held corporate stock in the United States. Thus, from 1 to 0.5 percent of the people in this country (roughly equal to the number Domhoff believes is in the upper class) hold most of the privately owned corporate stock.

This concentration of private stock ownership is even more striking when we find that most of the remaining stock is controlled by large financial corporations (see U.S. Senate Committee on Governmental Affairs 1978a, 1980; Kerbo and Della Fave 1983, 1984). To the degree that the upper class also has a lot of influence over these financial corporations (such as banks with large amounts of stock control in other big corporations), the actual stock control of the upper class is much greater (for example, see Figure 7-1, showing upper-class stock ownership in corporation B plus ownership in corporation A, which also controls stock in corporation B).

In reality, adequate data pertaining to actual stock ownership in specific corporations in this country are very hard to obtain. Many government agencies and congressional committees have attempted to obtain this information with less than complete success (for the latest, most successful, attempt, see U.S. Senate Committee on Governmental Affairs 1978a). Large amounts of stock held by a family afford economic power in many ways, but the most extensive power flowing from stock ownership comes when this stock is concentrated in a corporation to a sufficient degree to ensure control over the corporation. The amount of stock owned brings an equal number of votes toward electing the board of directors (who can hire and fire the managers) and deciding major issues that come before stockholders. Thus, it becomes important to

FIGURE 7-1
Upper-class economic power through stock ownership and control.

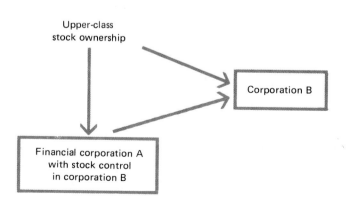

know how much stock individuals or families hold in each major corporation in determining the control of that corporation.

In the early stages of industrialization in this country the control of corporations was fairly easy to estimate. Most corporations were owned, and thus controlled, by specific families. We knew, for example, that the Rockefeller family controlled Standard Oil, the McCormick family controlled International Harvester, the Mellon family controlled Aluminum Company of America, and the Morgan family controlled Morgan Bank by virtue of their extensive stock ownership of these companies. But this concentration of stock ownership by specific families in one or a few corporations has changed greatly in recent decades. Few clearly family-controlled corporations such as the Ford Motor Company (with the Ford family owning 40 percent of the stock) are found today.

Because of the wide distribution of stockholders in most corporations, government agencies and researchers agree that 5 to 10 percent ownership in a particular company by a family will often result in control of that company by the family.

A government study, however, found only thirteen of the top 122 corporations in this country to be clearly controlled by one family (see U.S. Senate Committee on Governmental Affairs 1978a:252). But we must emphasize *clearly* controlled. One of the problems in determining control is that the ownership of stock in specific corporations is often hidden. For example, the owner of stock may be listed under meaningless names (such as street names) or under trusts and foundations (Zeitlin 1974). To make the situation even more complex, corporations (especially banks) control stock in other corporations.

Consider the following situation: A family owns about 2 percent of the stock in corporation A with other families also owning about 2 percent each. In turn, this original family owns, say, 5 percent of the stock in corporation B (a bank) and 6 percent in corporation C (an insurance company). We find upon further investigation that company B (the bank) controls 4 percent of the stock in corporation A, and corporation C (the insurance company) controls 7 percent of the stock in corporation A. Who controls corporation A?

It *may* be that our original family does, through its stock in corporation A, as well as B and C. But other families own stock in A who in addition have much stock in corporations D and E. And (you are probably ahead of me), corporations D and E also control stock in corporation A! This example is not an exaggeration, as anyone will see in examining the data on stock ownership published in a Senate study (U.S. Senate Committee on Governmental Affairs 1978a, 1980). In the face of this complexity of wide stockholdings many researchers simply conclude that top managers of a corporation control by default (for example, Berle 1959; Galbraith 1971; Bell 1976). But, as we will see below, this generalization also has many drawbacks.

In terms of upper-class dominance in the economy through stock ownership, all we can say is that its stock ownership is very extensive. But we cannot as yet arrive at firm conclusions about upper-class control of specific corporations. The data are hard to obtain, complex, and sometimes of questionable quality. Therefore, the arguments by ruling-class or governing-class theorists that an upper class dominates the economy through control of stock in major corporations cannot be completely confirmed.

One argument by ruling-class theorists is given more support; the upper class today has more extensive *common economic interests* than it once had. Rather than each family owning and controlling one corporation, today the families more often have extensive ownership in many corporations. They don't own each corporation in common, but they do have extensive common interests throughout top corporations in this country. There is a bond of common economic interests that helps cement a unity in defense of the top corporate structure as a whole.

Upper-Class Backgrounds of Economic Elites   Aside from actual stock ownership there is another possible means of upper-class leverage over the economy. After the authority of stockholders in a corporation we find the board of directors and top executive officers. We will call these people *economic elites.* The family backgrounds of these economic elites may be important in how they think, whom they trust, and what group interests they serve while making decisions in their positions of authority in the corporate world. Ruling-class theorists such as Domhoff believe that these economic elites often come from, or have backgrounds in, upper-class families. Thus, even if upper-class families may not own enough stock to control many corporations, their people are there in important positions of authority.

Using the indicators of upper-class membership outlined earlier, Domhoff (1967) has examined the directors from many top corporations. He has found (see Table 7-1) that of the top twenty industrial corporations, 54 percent of the board members were from the upper class; of the top fifteen banks, 62 percent were upper-class members; of the top fifteen insurance companies, 44 percent were upper-class members; of the top fifteen transportation companies, 53 per-

TABLE 7-1
UPPER-CLASS FAMILY BACKGROUNDS OF
CORPORATE ELITES

Type of corporation	Upper class, %
Domhoff's study (corporate directors)	
Top 20 industrials	54
Top 15 banks	62
Top 15 insurance	44
Top 15 transportation	53
Top 15 utilities	30
Dye's study (upper-class membership indicated by exclusive club membership)	
Top 201 corporations (all types, directors and top officers)	44

Sources: Domhoff (1967:51); Dye (1979: 184).

cent were upper-class members; and of the top fifteen utility corporations, 30 percent were upper-class members. Clearly we find much overrepresentation by the upper class on these boards of directors when it is noted that the upper class accounts for only about 0.5 percent of the population.

In another study Soref (1976) took a random sample of board members from the top 121 corporations in the United States. Using Domhoff's definition of upper class, he found upper-class board members had more board positions in other companies (average of 3.49 for upper-class directors, 2.0 for others), and were more often members of board subcommittees that made important long-range decisions in the company. In a similar study of corporate directors who were also college trustees (thus the sample is somewhat limited), Useem (1978, 1984) found that the directors who were wealthier and also members of elite social clubs (indicating upper-class membership) had more directorship positions in corporations than directors who were not upper class.

Finally, in a massive study of institutional elites, Thomas Dye (1979, 1983) obtained background information on the boards of directors *and* top executive officers of the top 201 corporations in 1976 (those corporations controlling 50 percent of the assets in each type of corporation—industrial, financial, insurance, and utilities). This sample included 3,572 people who by our definition were economic elites. Using a list of 37 upper-class social clubs from Domhoff's work, Dye (1979:184) found that *44 percent* of these 3,572 economic elites were members of one or more of these upper-class clubs (see Table 7-1). Thus, by Domhoff's definition, 44 percent of these people were members of the upper class.

In conclusion, we find some evidence supporting the argument that the upper class is able to dominate the economy through positions of authority in major corporations. But this evidence is far from conclusive. A primary reservation raised by Dye (1983) pertains to the validity of upper-class indicators such as elite social clubs. It may be that many economic elites gain club memberships only after they become economic elites. To the extent that this is true, we cannot always say club membership indicates upper-class background or upper-class membership.

There is also the question of whether upper-class members act exclusively to protect the interests of the upper class when in positions of corporate authority. In part, this second reservation pertains to the strength of upper-class unity and consciousness discussed earlier. It is clear that corporate elite membership in social clubs and interlocking directorates through multiple board memberships help unify the structure of large corporations today. However, the question of whose interests (an upper class or corporate elites themselves) are served by this unified corporate structure remains inadequately answered.

Upper-Class Political Power

The next questions of importance for ruling-class or governing-class theorists are the degree and means of political power exercised by the upper class. The significance of the state, and especially the federal government, on domestic affairs in this nation has increased rapidly since the 1930s. We find today a federal government with an annual budget well over $1 trillion, with programs designed for such things as regulating the economy as well as its traditional job of managing foreign affairs.

The potential impact of the federal government upon upper-class interests is clear. If the upper class is to maintain a position of dominance in the nation it is imperative that it have influence over the state as well as the economy. In this section we will consider evidence suggesting upper-class influence over the government through (1) direct participation by the upper class in politics, (2) the selection of government leaders, (3) the activities of lobby organizations, and (4) organizations established to shape the development of government policy.

Upper-Class Participation in Government   Research on direct participation by the upper class in government is focused heavily on the President's cabinet. Cabinet members are under the direction of the President, but because of the President's many concerns and lack of time in gathering all the needed information in making policy, the President must rely heavily upon cabinet members for advice and information. If these cabinet members represent the interests of the upper class, they can provide the President with information to guide his policy decisions in a way that will ensure that upper-class interests are maintained.

We will consider shortly research that directly attempts to measure the upper-class membership of cabinet members. But at this point it will be interesting to examine briefly how cabinet members may be selected. Jimmy Carter's cabinet is of special interest. As the first President *elected* after Watergate, Carter presented himself as a political outsider who would represent the people, in contrast to previous Presidents, who were among the inner circle of old-guard politicians and big business.

However, even before Carter became a candidate for the presidency he was associated with upper-class circles. Carter was recommended by J. Paul Austin (chairman of the board of Atlanta-based Coca-Cola) for membership in a new upper-class organization called the Trilateral Commission. The Trilateral Commission was established in 1972 by David Rockefeller, with the assistance of the Council on Foreign Relations and the Rockefeller Foundation. "The Trilateral Commission is a group of corporate officials of multinational corporations and government officials of several industrialized nations who meet periodically to coordinate economic policy between the United States, Western Europe, and Japan" (Dye 1979:60).

The Trilateral Commission is today a rather weak arm of the Council on Foreign Relations (an upper-class organization, by Domhoff's definition; over one-half its members have upper-class backgrounds; Domhoff 1967). But in its early days there were big plans for the Trilateral Commission to be a mechanism for coordinating the economic activity of multinational corporations.

What is most interesting about the Trilateral Commission at this point, however, was its membership. In addition to David Rockefeller and Jimmy Carter we find Zbigniew Brzezinski (then executive director of the Trilateral Commission),

Harold Brown (then president of Cal Tech), Hedley Donovan (editor of *Time* magazine), Werner Blumenthal (president of Bendix Corporation), Cyrus Vance (Wall Street lawyer), and Walter Mondale (United States senator).

All these people later became members of Carter's cabinet, special advisers with cabinet level status, or, in the case of Walter Mondale, Carter's choice for vice-president. We see, therefore, that the close association Carter had with an organization sponsored by the upper class formed a network of relations that Carter would turn to later for his close advisers while President.

All cabinet members do not have upper-class family backgrounds. But even where upper-class background is lacking, cabinet membership may be attained through the sponsorship of upper-class circles. Henry Kissinger's rise from Harvard professor to Nixon's cabinet was strongly influenced by the Council on Foreign Relations (and the Rockefeller family), as was Zbigniew Brzezinski's rise to Carter's cabinet (Dye 1979).

In contrast to Carter, who was supported by the liberal wing of the upper class and corporate class, Reagan was seen as the President of the very conservative new rich. When we look at Reagan's early supporters from California there is strong evidence for this description (Brownstein and Easton 1983). And like Carter, before being elected to the presidency Reagan was associated with an organization sponsored by the corporate elite (Committee on the Present Danger), though in this case, of course, it was a right-wing political organization devoted to reviving the cold war against the Soviet Union (see Domhoff 1983:140). But, like Carter again, Reagan selected thirty-two members of this organization to serve in his new administration.

At the beginning of the Reagan administration there was the idea that the old upper class had been thrown out of power by Reagan's right-wing new rich supporters. However, when we examine Reagan's top political appointees we get a somewhat different picture. The rich were certainly there: Reagan's top five political appointees (Vice-President, attorney general, secretary of state, secretary of defense, and secretary of the treasury) were all multimillionaires, and over 25 percent of the top 100 appointments that Reagan made were of millionaires (Brownstein and Easton 1983:xv). But there was a mixture of the old establishment rich and the new rich. Of his 90 top appointees, 31 were members of the upper-class Council on Foreign Relations and 12 were members of the Trilateral Commission (Domhoff 1983:140). As for his most important selections, the cabinet, 10 had elite "Ivy League" university degrees, 11 had been executives or directors of major corporations, and 8 were members of the Council on Foreign Relations (Dye 1983:74).

And then Reagan's Vice-President became President himself. But unlike any President since John F. Kennedy, Bush not only selected top advisers from the corporate class and establishment upper class, he *was* old-line upper class. Bush's parents were members of the New England upper class, where Bush attended an elite prep school (Phillips Andover Academy) and then graduated from Yale (where he was a member of one of the most elite fraternities). After college and World War II Bush took some of his father's support and money to Texas (where new money at the time was being made in oil) to start his own company in the oil industry and make his own fortune (Dye 1983:74). But during this time he kept his upper-class ties through membership in the Bohemian Club, Council on Foreign Relations, and Trilateral Commission, among other organizations.

It is time to present some evidence of the upper-class and corporate backgrounds of cabinet members in general. Using his definition of upper-class membership outlined earlier, Domhoff (1967:97–99; see also Kerbo and Della Fave 1979:7) examined the backgrounds of secretaries of state, the treasury, and defense between 1932 and 1964. He found that 63 percent of the secretaries of state, 62 percent of the secretaries of defense, and 63 percent of the secretaries of the treasury could be classified as members of the upper class before assuming office (see Table 7-2 below). As Domhoff admits, the above represents only a small part of the cabinet for a period of a little more than thirty years. But with these positions we find the upper class represented in proportions far greater than their 0.5 percent of the population would suggest.

Since Domhoff's earlier work an extensive study of cabinet members has been conducted by Beth Mintz (1975). Using Domhoff's indicators of upper-class membership, Mintz (1975, along with Peter Freitag, 1975) undertook the massive job of examining the backgrounds of *all* cabinet members (205 people) serving between 1897 and 1973. Her most interesting finding at this point is that *66 percent* of these cabinet members could be classified as members of the

TABLE 7-2
UPPER-CLASS ORIGINS OF GOVERNMENT ELITE

Position in government	Upper class, %
Domhoff study	
Cabinet (1932–1964)	
Secretaries of state	63
Secretaries of defense	62
Secretaries of the treasury	63
Mintz study	
All cabinet (1897–1973)	66
Democratic cabinet (1897–1973)	60
Republican cabinet (1897–1973)	71
Dye study	
Top government elite (1970)*	6
Top military elite (1970)	9

*Dye's government elite includes the cabinet and an extended list of top executive government and congressional officeholders.

Sources: Domhoff (1967:97–99); Mintz (1975); and Dye (1979:184).

upper class before obtaining their cabinet positions (see Table 7-2). Also interesting is that the number of cabinet members coming from the upper class is fairly consistent between 1897 and 1973, suggesting that Baltzell (1964) is incorrect in his belief that the upper class is not participating in government as much as it once did. And in case anyone believes that the wealthy and upper class strongly favor Republicans over Democrats, Mintz's data show that Republican presidents chose over 71 percent of their cabinet members from the upper class, while Democratic presidents chose over 60 percent from the upper class.

In her background research on these cabinet members Mintz also included information pertaining to the previous occupations of these people. Along with Freitag (1975), she reports that over 76 percent of the cabinet members were associated with big corporations before or after their cabinet position, 54 percent were from *both* the upper class and top corporate positions, and *90 percent* either came from the upper class or were associated with big corporations. Focusing on corporate ties of cabinet members. Freitag (1975) shows that these ties have not changed much over the years, and vary only slightly by particular cabinet position. In fact, even most secretaries of labor have been associated with big corporations in the capacity of top executives, board members, or corporate lawyers.

Most ruling-class or governing-class theorists consider the cabinet to be the most important position for direct government participation by the upper class. The cabinet allows easy movement into government and then back to top corporate positions. As might be expected, Mintz (1975) found most cabinet members between 1897 and 1973 coming from outside of government, rather than working their way up within government bureaucracies. The United States and England are unique in this aspect of top government elite recruitment. Putnam (1976:48–49) has found that in most other Western industrial societies the top political elites (with positions comparable to those in the United States cabinet) are more likely to come from within government bureaucracies, working their way to the top in a line of career promotions. In the United States and England, this atypical method of political elite recruitment affords the upper class and corporate elite opportunities for political influence lacking in these other industrial nations.

In a massive three-volume work by Burch (1981) examining elites throughout American history, we find that the rich and corporate elite have always dominated the top federal government positions. From 1789 to 1861, 96 percent of the cabinet and diplomatic appointees "were members of the economic elite, with a great many landowners, lawyers, and merchants in the group" (Domhoff 1983:142). Then from 1861 to 1933 the percentage was 84 percent, with more of these people now coming from major corporations that did not exist before 1861.

There are other political positions of importance. The heads of various government agencies (such as the Federal Aviation Agency), Supreme Court justices, members of the Federal Reserve Board, and top senators and congressmen all represent positions of influence within the government. Although one may agree with C. Wright Mills and others that the cabinet offers more opportunities to influence policy within the federal government, these other positions are of considerable importance. But there is one difference. These other government positions are more often headed or staffed by career bureaucrats or politicians. Thus, they are less open for members of the upper class, who are more often wealthy business leaders.

For an indication of the background differences of these top government officeholders we have Dye's (1979) previously discussed study of elites in the United States. In addition to including cabinet members in his sample of top government officials for 1970, Dye (1979:12) included "the president and vice-president . . . under-secretaries, and assistant secretaries of all executive departments; White House presidential advisors and ambassadors-at-large; congressional committee chairpersons and ranking minority committee members in the House and Senate; House and Senate majority and minority party leaders and whips; Supreme Court Justices; members of the Federal Reserve Board and the Council of Economic Advisers." In all, Dye's sample of nonmilitary government elites included 286 people, along with an additional group of fifty-nine top military officials. Using a somewhat more limited indicator of upper-class membership (membership in a list of thirty-seven exclusive social clubs from Domhoff's work) Dye presents findings on the upper-class affiliation of these government officials.

As might be expected from our discussion of upper-class recruitment of cabinet members in contrast to other government elites, Dye (see Table 7-2) finds that only 6 percent of the nonmilitary government elite and 9 percent of the military elite were members of these exclusive social clubs. This compares with 44 percent of the top executives and board members of the 201 largest corporations who were members of upper-class clubs. We find, therefore, that few government officials outside of the cabinet can be described as upper-class members. The 6 percent Dye found belonging to these upper-class clubs were most likely cabinet members (although Dye's data are not broken down in a way that allows us to consider the cabinet members for 1970 separately).

Political Campaign Contributions Today it costs money, lots of money, to obtain a major elective office. In 1972, for example, Richard Nixon spent $60 million to win reelection, while his opponent spent $30 million. Since this time there have been limits placed on presidential campaigns, but House and Senate campaigns have not been so restricted. In the 1978 U.S. congressional elections, special-interest groups alone contributed $35 million to candidates. This figure increased to $55 million in 1980, and to $150 million in 1988! The average Senate campaign in 1988 cost $4 million.

In his famous work on the power elite just a little over thirty years ago, C. Wright Mills had relatively little to say about campaign contributions. But the subject can no longer be neglected. Especially in an age when political campaigns are won more through presenting images than issues, the image-creating mass media are extremely important and costly. Most presidents and congressional officeholders are wealthy, but they are not super-rich. With a few rare exceptions they cannot afford to finance their own political campaigns. Who, then, pays for these campaigns? Thousands of contributors send $25 or $50 to favored candidates. For the most part, however, the money comes from corporations and the wealthy.

With the nationwide reaction against Watergate and the many illegal campaign contributions to Nixon's reelection committee in 1972, some election reforms were undertaken by Congress in 1974. Among these reforms was the creation of a voluntary $1-per-person campaign contribution from individual income tax reports. A Presidential Election Campaign Fund was established to distribute this money to the major parties and candidates during an election year. In addition, a Federal Election Commission was established to watch over campaign spending, and people were limited to a $1,000 contribution in any single presidential election, with organizations limited to $5,000. Perhaps these reforms contributed to less spending in the 1976 presidential election (Dye 1979:90); Carter and Ford spent a combined total of about $50 million in 1976, compared with Nixon and McGovern's $90 million in 1972. But $50 million continues to be a substantial investment, and requires large contributors.

An interesting outcome of the campaign reform law of 1974 is that much of the illegal activity in Nixon's 1972 campaign was *made legal* as long as correct procedures are followed. For example, organizations are limited to $5,000 in political contributions per election. However, if there are more organizations, more money can be contributed. And this is precisely what happened by 1976. There was an explosion in the number of political action committees (PACs) established by large corporations and their executives, an increase far outnumbering those established by any other group, such as labor unions (Domhoff 1983:125). By the 1980 congressional elections, 1,585 corporate, health industry, and other business PACs contributed $36 million to candidates, while $13 million was contributed by 240 labor union PACs.

Furthermore, the idea of letting each taxpayer contribute $1 of his or her taxes to a presidential campaign fund appears a nice way of producing more democracy in campaign contributions. But this pool of money is given out to candidates as matching funds. In other words, candidates are given this tax money in proportion to the amount they can raise by traditional methods. For example, Morris Udall had 3,000 *more* campaign contributors than did Carter in 1976, but Carter received $3.5 million of the tax money compared with $1.9 million for Udall (Domhoff 1979:152). Although Udall had more campaign contributors in 1976, Carter's were wealthier and gave more money. In essence, this campaign reform amounts to a *subsidy for the rich*; the more the rich give to a particular candidate, the more the Federal Election Campaign Fund must give.

Campaign contributions, therefore, continue to be an important means of political influence. The wealthy are not assured that their interests will be protected by those they help place in office, but they obviously consider the gamble worth taking. Usually, it is hoped that these campaign contributions are placing people in office who hold political views that lead to the defense of privilege when unforeseen challenges to upper-class interests occur along the way.

For example, it seems that campaign contributions by oil companies to congressional candidates paid off in 1979 when 95 percent of the people receiving this campaign money voted for the bill sponsored by the oil industry challenging President Carter's windfall profits tax on oil companies. The oil industry investments in campaign contributions will bring a sizable return in increased profits over the years.

Since the early 1970s a number of studies have been done on this subject (Mintz 1989). For example, Allen and Broyles (1989) examined data pertaining to the campaign contributions of 100 of the most wealthy families (629 individuals) in the United States. They found that about one-half of these individuals made large contributions. And it was the more "visible" and active rich who made these large contributions. By this they mean that the rich were more likely to make contributions if they were corporate directors or executives, listed in *"Who's Who,"* and/or directors of nonprofit foundations. These people were more likely to contribute to Republicans, and this was especially so with the new rich, non-Jews, and people with extensive oil stocks. In a similar manner, Burris (1987) found a split between the old rich (Yankees) and the new rich in who they supported with their money (new rich were more likely to support Republicans). Burris also found that the rich were more likely to make large campaign contributions if their company did business with the federal government (such as a defense contractor) or was in some way regulated by the government.

In another study, Boies (1989) examined the top 500 companies in the United States between 1976 and 1980 to determine what explains the varied size of the money they contribute through PACs. As we might expect from what has already been discussed, he found that companies with more material interests in the outcomes of government policy were most likely to contribute huge amounts through PACs. Specifically, they were more likely to contribute large amounts if the company was a top defense contractor, if they were trying to get the government to approve a new corporate merger, or if they were the subject of some kind of criminal investigation by the government. And in another study of PAC contributions by big corporations, Clawson, Newstadtl, and Bearden (1986) found extensive consensus by big corporations on the "best" business candidates to support: When looking at individual campaigns, they found that in 75 percent of the cases one candidate received nine times more of the corporate PAC money compared to the political opponent.

Congressional Lobbying   If the interests of the wealthy are not ensured by their direct participation in government, and if those the wealthy helped put in office seem to be forgetting their debtors, a third force can be brought into action. The basic job of a lobbyist is to make friends among congressional leaders, provide them with favors such as trips, small gifts, and parties, and, most importantly, provide these leaders with information and arguments favoring their employers' interests and needs. All of this requires a large staff and lots of money.

Oil companies in the United States are among the largest corporations, with Exxon (the largest), Mobil, Texaco, Standard Oil of California, Gulf, and Standard Oil of Indiana holding six of the top ten positions in terms of industrial assets. It may not be surprising, then, that oil companies pay the lowest taxes on profits of all major corporations (Sampson 1975:205). In 1972, for example, Exxon paid *6.5 percent* of its net profits in income taxes, Texaco paid *1.7 percent,* Mobil paid *1.3 percent,* Gulf paid *1.2 percent,* and Standard Oil of California paid *2.05 percent.* The actual corporate tax rate in the United States was *supposed* to be 48 percent in 1972. But, as a whole, the nineteen top oil companies paid an average of 7.6 percent of profits to taxes in this year (Blair 1976:187). This compares with an actual federal income tax rate of about *20 percent* for the average-income family in the United States at the time (Turner and Starnes 1976:94).

In one of the first empirical studies of the effects of certain characteristics of corporations on government policies toward these corporations (such as tax policies), Salamon and Siegfried (1977) found that the size of the corporation showed a strong inverse relation to the amount of taxes paid by the corporation. And this inverse relation between size of the corporation and the corporation's tax rate was especially upheld when examining the oil companies and including their state as well as federal taxes paid (Salamon and Siegfried 1977:1039). Thus, the bigger the corporation, the less it tends to pay in corporate taxes.

Later studies have confirmed this relationship between size (and power) and corporate tax rates. Jacobs (1988), however, measured the concentration of powerful corporations within each type of industry. The findings were similar: The more corporate concentration (meaning the size of the firms in the industry and their dominance in the industry), the less the taxes for the corporations in that industry. In examining how this is done in the oil industry and health-care industry, Laumann, Knoke, and Kim (1985) studied 166 government policy decisions relating to these industries, and interviewed 458 lobbyists for these industries. They found that there are leading corporations in these industries which have a reputation for being most politically active in influencing government for the overall industry, and that this reputation is very accurate when measuring their lobbying activity. Finally, in an historical study of industrial corporations between 1886 and 1905, Roy (1981) reached similar conclusions. He found that the size of the corporation, the volume of its exports, and its political activity were related to the extent of favorable treatment it received in government policy decisions.

It is clear that these special favors are secured in part through lobby organizations. And to use the example of oil companies again, they are noted for the strongest lobby organizations in Washington. The oil lobby's most important successes have been in securing and maintaining a depletion allowance that allows them tax breaks on investments and foreign tax credits that allow them to write off any taxes they must pay abroad in obtaining, selling, or shipping oil (Blair 1976:189–199). The latter tax break has resulted in paper adjustments of profits so that most of the profits seem to come from overseas operations, resulting in reduced taxes in this country.

It is the main job of a lobby to convince Congress that the special favors it asks for its employers are needed to keep the industry strong and benefit the country as a whole. And those who have the most resources at their disposal have the best chance of getting their views on this matter accepted by Congress. With our example of the oil industry, their main argument has been that they need more profits and less tax to find and produce more oil for the country. One of their greatest successes in convincing Congress of this was in 1974. At that time the oil industry secured a bill allowing the price of new oil to increase, with the argument that it needed the increased profits to find and produce more oil. While the industry was making this successful plea, however, Mobil was bidding $500 million of its profits to buy Montgomery Ward and Gulf was trying to buy Ringling Brothers, Barnum and Bailey Circus (Sampson 1975:267). And with a higher price for new oil obtained after 1974 bringing higher profits to oil companies, the actual production of oil in the United States went *down* (Sampson 1975:305).

Lobby organizations, therefore, can be of major importance in ensuring that the special interests of a wealthy upper-class and corporate elite are served. If special favors are not completely ensured through direct participation in the cabinet and campaign contributions, the powerful lobby organizations may then move into action. The upper class and big business are not the only groups that maintain lobby organizations in Washington. The American Medical Association, the National Rifle Association, the Milk Producers Association, and many others have maintained successful lobby organizations. But when considering the big issues such as how to deal with inflation, tax policy, unemployment, foreign affairs, and many others that broadly affect the lives of people in this country, the corporate and upper-class lobbies are most important. Of the lobby process, Domhoff (1970:337) writes, "The effects of lobbying are hard to assess, for the process is more subtle than it supposedly used to be. However, it is certain that various business groups and their Washington lawyers are the most prominent lobbyists, even when they do not bother to register as such."

Shaping Government Policy   Of the various means of upper-class and corporate political influence, the type least recognized by the general public is referred to as the *policy-forming process* (see Domhoff 1979:61–128, 1983:98–112, 1990; Dye 1983:237–264). As scholars believe, in the long run this means of political influence is perhaps one of the most important. The basic argument is this: The federal government is faced with many national problems for which there are many possible alternative solutions. For example, consider the problem of inflation. The possible government means of dealing with this problem are varied, and a key is that different solutions to the problem may favor different class interests. Some possible solutions (such as wage and price controls) are believed to favor the working class, and thus are pushed by labor unions. Other possible solutions (such as restricting the money supply and raising interest rates on loans) favor the interests of corporations and the upper class and contribute to higher unemployment for the working class. One important means of ensuring that the federal government follows a policy that is favorable to your class interests is to convince the government through various types of research data that one line of policy is the overall best policy. Generating the needed information and spelling out the exact policy required take a lot of planning, organization, personnel, and resources. And there must be avenues for getting this policy information to the attention of government leaders. It is no surprise, ruling-class theorists argue, that the upper class and its corporations are able to achieve the above and guide government policy in their interests.

Far from the eyes of the general public there is a little-known policy-formation process that goes on in this country. The federal government cannot always use its massive resources to generate the information needed in developing policy alternatives with respect to many issues. A mostly private network has developed over the years, supported with upper-class and corporate money and personnel to provide government input when important decisions are to be made. Domhoff (1979:63; also see Dye 1983:240) has charted this process, as shown in Figure 7-2.

At the heart of this process are (1) upper-class and corporate *money and personnel* (2) that fund and guide *research* on important questions through foundations and universities, (3) then process the information through *policy-planning groups* sponsored by the upper class (4) that make direct recommendations to government, and (5) influence the opinion-making centers, such as the media and government commissions, which in turn influence the population and government leaders in favoring specific policy alternatives.

We will consider briefly the more important steps in this policy-forming process and some of the supporting evidence obtained by various researchers. It is significant to note that although this policy-formation process fits neatly into the ruling-class or governing-class theory, we find much agreement on this process even among these rejecting a ruling-class argument (such as Dye 1983).

Many writers in sociology, political science, and economics have come to stress the increased importance of information and ideas generated through research in guiding the economy and government in advanced or postindustrial societies (see Galbraith 1971; Bell 1976). As a consequence, some writers argue that an upper-class or wealthy elite is no longer in control of the economy or political system because the ideas and specialized knowledge are in the hands of a new group of elites—strategic elites or technocrats (see Galbraith 1971; Keller 1963).

Others, especially ruling-class theorists, counter by charging that the knowledge and information behind the operation of the economy and govern-

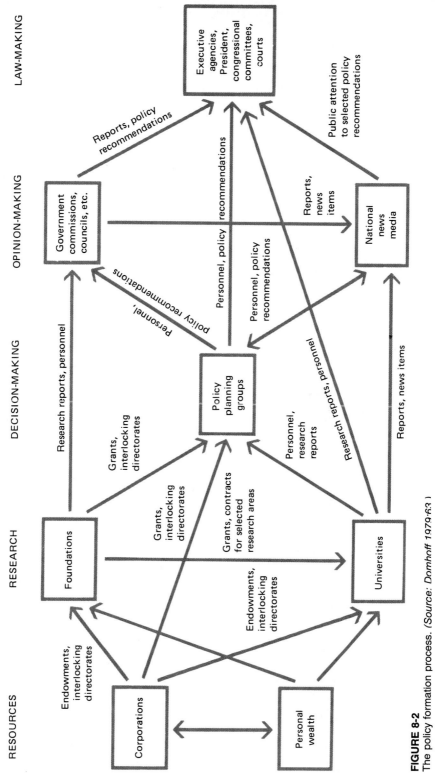

RESOURCES   RESEARCH   DECISION-MAKING   OPINION-MAKING   LAW-MAKING

Executive agencies, President, congressional committees, courts

Government commissions, councils, etc.

National news media

Policy planning groups

Foundations

Universities

Corporations

Personal wealth

Reports, policy recommendations

Public attention to selected policy recommendations

Personnel, policy recommendations

Personnel, policy recommendations

Reports, news items

Personnel, policy recommendations

Research reports, personnel

Research reports, personnel

Reports, news items

Personnel, research reports

Grants, interlocking directorates

Grants, interlocking directorates

Grants, contracts for selected research areas

Endowments, interlocking directorates

Endowments, interlocking directorates

FIGURE 8-2
The policy formation process. *(Source: Domhoff 1979:63.)*

FIGURE 7-2
The policy-formation process. *Source:* Domhoff (1979:63; Dye 1983:240).

ment today are not always neutral. Much of this knowledge is generated through upper-class sponsorship, and thus favors its class interests. Increasingly, knowledge needed by corporations and government is generated through research conducted at major universities. Scientific research requires a lot of time, money, and personnel. The upper class and corporations, it is argued, influence the research process through funding and authority positions in major research-oriented universities.

A major source of funds for research is large foundations. These foundations possess extensive wealth that is given to fund research projects (see Lundberg 1968:498–505) that directors of these foundations judge to be important in generating information needed in guiding political and economic decisions. In most cases, these large foundations were established by wealthy people as a means of reducing taxes. But these families often maintain control of the foundations, influencing their funding policies (see Dye 1979:120).

For example, the largest foundation, the Ford Foundation, lists a board of directors containing many upper-class and corporate leaders. Among them are Walter A. Hass (president of Levi Strauss and Co. and director of Bank of America), Edward H. Land (former president of Polaroid Corp.), John H. London (former chairman of Shell Oil), and Robert S. McNamara (former president of Fort Motor Co. and secretary of defense under Kennedy). Henry Ford II himself maintained an active role in this foundation. Among the directors of the Rockefeller Foundation we find the familiar names of John D. Rockefeller III, C. Douglas Dillion, Cyrus Vance, and W. Michael Blumenthal. In a study of top foundations (those with over half the assets held by all foundations) Dye (1983:143) found that 50 percent of the directors of these foundations were members of upper-class social clubs.

Also important in the research process are the major universities in which much of this research is conducted. Among these universities, for example, are Harvard, Yale, Chicago, Stanford, the Massachusetts Institute of Technology, and the California Institute of Technology. In these universities faculty are often released from their teaching responsibilities to devote most of their time to conducting research sponsored by large corporations and foundations, as well as the federal government. One means of upper-class and corporate influence, therefore, is through guiding what type of research is conducted by the faculty.

We have only a few studies of the exact impact of funding sources on this research, but what we do have is enlightening. For example, Useem, Hoops, and Moore (1976) have found that there is a relationship between members from the upper class on a university's board of trustees and obtaining more funds from corporations and foundations. As to the effect of these funds on the direction of research conducted, Useem (1976a, 1976b) obtained answers to questionnaires from 1,079 professors in anthropology, economics, political science, and psychology. A majority of these professors admitted that their research plans (what type of research they could do) were influenced by the policies of funding agencies (in this case, the federal government). In other words, they were doing the research the funding agency thought was most important, not what they or their scientific disciplines thought most important. This study by Useem involved only social science research. But it can be suggested that the influence of these funding agencies is even more extensive in other branches of science, where corporate and foundation funding is more extensive.

Finally, there is the more general influence over university policy that may be exercised by corporations and the upper class. Most universities are governed much like a corporation. Above the executive officers (such as presidents and vice-presidents) is the board of trustees (resembling a board of directors in a corporation). This board of trustees has broad authority in governing the university and its general policies. Thus, it is often deemed important to understand the outside interests of the university board of trustees.

In Dye's (1983) massive study of elites he examined the backgrounds of presidents and trustees of the top twelve private universities (such as Harvard, Princeton, and MIT). He found that *62 percent* of these university trustees were members of just 37 exclusive upper-class clubs. Much of the research sponsored by corporations and the upper class is in state-sponsored universities not included in Dye's sample. But other research indicates that the trustees of these universities are also dominated by corporations and the upper class (Domhoff 1967:77–79; Dye 1983:157–160).

In this policy-forming process the next important link is through what has been called *policy-planning groups*. The corporate elites and upper class come together in these groups, discuss policy, publish and disseminate research, and, according to Dye and Domhoff, arrive at some consensus about what should be done in the nation. The most important of the policy groups are sponsored directly by the upper class for the purpose of linking the research information discussed above to specific policy alternatives and making certain these policy alternatives find their way to government circles.

Perhaps the most has been written about the Council on Foreign Relations (CFR) and the Committee on Economic Development (CED). Both groups are clearly upper-class institutions (as defined by Domhoff), the former specializing in foreign policy and the latter specializing in domestic issues. The Council on Foreign Relations was established shortly after World War I by upper-class members with the direct intent of influencing the United States government with respect to their business interests overseas (see Shoup 1975). Among the CFR's early successes were to have the government define Japan as an economic threat by 1940, to establish some of the ideas behind the development of the World Bank and the United Nations, and to motivate the government to define certain parts of the world as important areas of economic interest (multinational corporation interests). Membership in the CFR is limited to 1,400 people, half of whom are members of the upper class (Domhoff 1983). The Committee on Economic Development emerged out of the Business Advisory

Council in 1942 to continue the input into government by the upper class that began with this earlier organization in the 1930s (Domhoff 1970:123–128, 1979:67–69; Collins 1977).

It is often believed that the upper class and big business are extremely conservative politically and in opposition to all government involvement in the economy. But this image is formed primarily by such groups as the vocal and less powerful National Association of Manufacturers, which is backed primarily by small business (Burch 1973). These biggest of businesses will accept government involvement on some issues when there is strong disruptive pressure from workers or minorities, but they fight very hard against support for labor unions, expansion of welfare programs, and policies to significantly reduce unemployment.

We do not have studies of the overall membership of the CED, the way we do with the CFR. Dye (1983:255), however, has traced the backgrounds of directors of both the CED ($n = 61$) and CFR ($n = 22$), finding them to be strongly upper class. There was an average of 4.1 corporate directorships among CED directors (3.2 for CFR) and an average of 1.0 government offices held (such as cabinet, 3.0 for CFR), 72 percent belong to upper-class clubs (64 percent with CFR), and 62 percent went to elite universities (such as Harvard, Yale, Princeton; 82 percent for CFR). With respect to research on major universities, 67 percent of CED directors and 68 percent of CFR directors were also trustees of major universities.

A number of other organizations have been investigated and located among these policy-planning groups sponsored by the upper class. These include the Trilateral Commission (discussed above), the Brookings Institution, the RAND Corporation, and the Business Council. A number of these have been shown sharing memberships with upper-class social clubs on the East and West Coasts (Domhoff 1974:105). The exact influence of these organizations is hard to estimate. Their goals are to decide among themselves what government policy should be and then get the government to adopt the policies. This is a behind-the-scenes process that can be measured only by its outcomes.

Dye (1978) has investigated the major policy goals set by the CFR and CED in the early 1970s. For the CFR these were (1) an international campaign for human rights, (2) finding alternative approaches to nuclear stability and nonproliferation, (3) restricting international arms sales, (4) finding new approaches to relations between rich and poor nations, and (5) recognition of and economic cooperation with the People's Republic of China. For the CED the major policy recommendations were (1) energy independence through conservation and fuel-rationing authority for the President, (2) more government programs to create jobs, and (3) welfare reform along the line of an income-maintenance program.

What is most interesting about these policy recommendations by the CFR and CED is that in the later 1970s *all* of them were adopted with few revisions by the Carter administration (Dye 1978:318–325). Carter seemed to take the nation by surprise with the full recognition of China, his international human rights campaign, and his energy policy (in 1977, before the big gas lines in 1979). But these policies were no surprise to the members of the policy organizations that had been working to establish them even before Carter assumed the presidency.

We have finally to mention briefly the other parts of the policy-forming process described in Figure 7-2. Various government commissions are established from time to time to make recommendations on such things as civil disorders, the conduct of the CIA, and energy (to list some recent examples). These commissions make public the recommendations of these upper-class policy groups and provide their members with a semiofficial position in the government.

As for the national news media, they are often said to have a liberal slant in their views and to possess much power in shaping public and government opinion. Recent investigations have given some support to these charges (Halberstam 1979; Dye 1983). But the moderate conservative wing of the upper class and corporate leaders most influences the media. The major television networks, magazines, and newspapers are highly concentrated and tied to corporations (see Dye 1983:120). In terms of the backgrounds of top leaders in the national media, Dye (1983:210) found 33 percent had previous careers in big corporations and 44 percent were members of upper-class clubs. Their upper-class backgrounds are not as extensive as those of corporate leaders, but neither are the top media leaders from humble origins.

The backgrounds of media directors, the extensive corporate influence through ownership, and the huge funding from advertising all contribute to making mass media organizations cautious in presenting views that may be overly critical of the upper class and corporate interests. Information critical of these interests is not ignored by the mass media. The upper class might not even want this information to be ignored, for corrective action is often needed to prevent economic problems and corporate abuse from getting out of hand and requiring more drastic solutions that may harm more general corporate interests.

The news media are in part a policing agency involved in calling attention to problems that need correction. It is not what is criticized as much as how it is criticized, where blame is placed, and what possible solutions are offered. John Chancellor, for example, would not lose his job if he criticized Exxon; but what would happen if he were to suggest that socialist-type economic controls are needed or that the federal government should nationalize oil companies?

One final point requires emphasis. Few theorists writing in this area (on the upper class or, more specifically, on upper-class influence in the mass media) suggest that the upper-class or corporate elites completely control the mass media in the country. Neither do most writers in this area believe that there is some kind of upper-class secret conspiracy to control the mass media—or anything else in the country, for that matter. Rather, they are trying to call attention to an economic structure that allows more influence (in the many ways outlined above) to fall into the hands of groups like the upper-class and corporate elites. Each class or economic interest group tends to have a world view or way of perceiving reality that has been shaped by its own economic and political interests. When one group has more influence over the major means of conveying information, its view of reality often comes to be accepted by more people.

In summarizing the total policy-forming process, we find an underground network in this country that is highly influenced by corporate and upper-class institutions. The federal government and Congress have the authority to adopt or reject the policy recommendations flowing from this process, but most often they accept them, leaving the government to decide exactly how the policy will be carried out (Dye 1979:226).

Sometimes differing factions of the upper-class and corporate elite disagree over correct policy, and their views may change with differing circumstances. It is clear that the moderate conservative wing of the upper-class and corporate elite dominated policy formation in the 1960s and early 1970s. But with changing economic and international problems in the latter 1970s and 1980s, a more conservative orientation has emerged. The liberal solutions to protecting upper-class and corporate interests are being rejected.

The policy-formation process has not changed (although some conservative policy research institutions like the Hoover Institute and the American Enterprise Institute [Domhoff 1983:90] are receiving more recognition); it has only responded to new needs and concerns. The more liberal solutions fed to the Carter administration and the conservative solutions adopted by the Reagan and Bush administrations have emerged through the same policy-formation process; the process has not changed as much as the views of many behind the process have.

THE UPPER CLASS: A CONCLUSION

We can conclude this chapter by briefly restating what has been presented. The main arguments of the ruling-class thesis have been outlined, along with bits of data often used to support their case. We began by considering the evidence relating to the existence and unity of the upper class, then approached the question of how this class is able to dominate the economy and political system.

We have found some support for the existence of upper-class unity through interaction patterns in prep schools, social clubs, policy-formation organizations, and multiple corporate board positions. We have also found evidence of upper-class influence in the economy through stock ownership and membership on corporate boards. And we have found evidence of upper-class political influence through direct participation in government, campaign contributions, lobby organizations, and a policy-formation process. Upper-class interests are said to be maintained through these means of influence in the economy and the political system.

We have seen a few of the criticisms directed toward the ruling-class thesis along the way, but we have yet to look at these criticisms and others in a more systematic manner. The basic task of this chapter has been to present the ruling-class view for what it has to offer in understanding our current system of stratification. But along with other theories attempting to explain this most difficult area of research in social stratification, the ruling-class view leaves many questions unanswered or answered less than adequately. Much information needed in resolving the many debates about the power of an upper class is simply lacking. The wealthy and powerful guard much of the needed information closely because of the legal, political, or economic interests they have at stake. In Chapter 8 we will critique the ruling-class arguments more systematically, then present some alternative perspectives, with a focus on what can be called a corporate class.

THE CORPORATE CLASS

The previous chapter presented some of the major arguments by those who believe that an upper class of wealthy families is at the top of the United States stratification system. The convergence of economic power, political power, and high social status is seen as assuring this class of its place of dominance. Because the dimensions of the top of the stratification system in this country are so important in understanding the many other characteristics of this society, as well as the life chances of others and future trends, this chapter will analyze this top layer in more detail.

We will begin with a critique of ruling-class theory, suggesting where some of the arguments are weak and where some continue to receive support. Primarily, in what follows we will build on ruling-class views by amending weak points and retaining those judged stronger. In brief, we will examine arguments suggesting that a somewhat different class can now be described as at the top of the stratification system in this country.

The *corporate class,* as it will be called, retains many of the same characteristics as the upper class; but its basis of power lies not with ownership of the means of production, but rather with *control* of the major means of production (big corporations) in this advanced capitalist society. This analysis of the power of this corporate class that will be presented below does *not* rest with a conspiracy theory that sees evil forces or evil people at work in the world. What must be understood is a social structure that provides a group of otherwise normal people with the power to protect and maintain its particular economic and political interests, even when these interests are in conflict with others in the society. In concluding the present chapter, therefore, we will be

in a better position to understand the overall stratification system in this country and the place of other classes within it.

THE UPPER CLASS AS RULING CLASS: A CRITIQUE

According to the ruling-class perspective, at the top of our stratification system can be found a group of families dominating the country through their
ownership and control of the most important sources of wealth (the means of
production or the major corporations). This class is seen as extending its economic dominance into the political sphere through direct participation in government (for example, in the President's cabinet), selection of other major government officeholders (through campaign contributions), extensive lobbying in
Congress, and shaping of the policy-formation process.

The ruling-class perspective, thus, views the upper class as at the top of the
stratification system in terms of its class or economic position and its position
of political power. But the upper class is also a social group. It is able to maintain itself at the top status ranking by creating something like a caste division.
A system of upper-class institutions such as prep schools, elite social clubs,
and the *Social Register* defines who are, and who are not, acceptable members
of the upper class. There are also differing traditions, a lifestyle, and a manner
of presenting the self that are a part of this upper-class status display.

Ruling-class theorists, however, view this status division as more than a
means of maintaining status boundaries. It is also a means of promoting class
unity, organization, and political and economic consensus. A united front is
thus achieved that helps this upper class work together to protect its common
interests as a class. A class with great economic wealth and political influence,
when united in this manner, comes to dominate the most vital aspects of our
society. If the major task in the study of social stratification is to answer the
questions of who gets what and why, then upper-class theorists such as
Domhoff have supplied one systematic answer.

There are, however, other answers. But before we turn to these it is helpful
to consider some of the main weak points in the ruling-class answer. The
ruling-class view has been attacked on many points, although the criticisms
most recently have centered around two fundamental themes. The first is directed toward the question of whether or not the upper class even exists as an
identifiable group with unity and class consciousness.

As noted briefly in a few places in the previous chapter, this question is of
major importance because only if this class identifies itself as a class with common interests can it work together to achieve the tremendous power claimed
by ruling-class theorists. There is no question as to the existence of wealthy
families who tend to belong to elite social clubs, frequent the same resorts, be
listed year after year in blue books such as the *Social Register,* and send their
children to exclusive prep schools. But do they form a united class? If they do
not, then the findings indicating upper-class dominance of corporate positions
and the cabinet, for example, have less significance.

One charge is that too many people are considered to be members of the upper class for it to have much overall unity and organization (see Hacker 1975; McNall 1977). Related to this is the charge that ruling-class theorists have not shown enough overlap among the indicators of upper-class membership. Are people who attend the prep schools also listed in the *Social Register* and do they belong to the same exclusive social clubs? Last, there is the question of whether membership in elite social clubs and/or a listing in the *Social Register* indicates upper-class family backgrounds or simply represents high institutional position (in the economy, government, foundations, and so on). In other words, does one have to be from an old wealthy family to belong to exclusive clubs and obtain a listing in the *Social Register* today? One study has suggested that intraclass marriage is less frequent among the upper class and listings in the *Social Register* are less restrictive today (Rosen and Bell 1966).

The significance of all these criticisms is that there is not enough unity among the upper class to claim that it is a ruling class. The question of how much unity is enough, however, is not a question that can be answered with any degree of confidence. We are speaking of matters of degree; other things being equal (such as the amount of wealth), the greater the unity and cooperation to meet common interests are, the greater the dominance of this class will be. But the point at which an upper class ceases to be a ruling class because of disunity cannot be specified.

The second fundamental set of criticisms directed toward the ruling-class view pertains to upper-class ownership and control of the means of production; that is, major corporations. This is perhaps the central criticism, because ruling-class theorists claim that the basis of upper-class power lies with its ownership and/or control of corporations. Wealth alone brings little power. One could have $100 million but remain relatively powerless if this $100 million were in a blind trust or simply sitting in a bank.

It is how money is used in influencing people and institutions that is a key to great power. If this $100 million is used to buy stock, *and* through this stock controlling interest in a major corporation, then in addition to the $100 million there is control over vast assets of the corporation. This massive corporate institution and its resources are now more or less at one's command to influence other corporations, the United States government, consumers, and even foreign governments. Given the size of our major institutions today (to be discussed in more detail below), no one is really powerful without a command position that is attached to one of those institutions. The wealth of individuals or families is dwarfed alongside the assets of these institutions.

We have already considered the difficulty, in contrast to that during previous decades, in determining the ownership and control of major corporations today. The most recent attempt by Congress (U.S. Senate Committee on Governmental Affairs 1978a, 1980) concluded that only thirteen of the top 122 corporations were family controlled. Ruling-class theorists counter, and will no doubt continue to for some time, that there is much hidden stock control that if uncovered would show that families continue to control most corporations.

We are left again with an unanswered question with respect to the validity of the ruling-class perspective. It can only be concluded that at present the ownership and control of most corporations by an upper class are doubtful. But if this argument is so central to the ruling-class theory, must the whole theory and all the arguments covered in the previous chapter be thrown out?

One group of scholars answers yes. Since the early writings of Berle and Means (1932) the concept of a managerial revolution has gained popularity. And until recently this view had come to dominate the thinking on the subject in the social sciences (Zeitlin 1974). The managerial revolution or managerial-control thesis claims that today the control of each corporation is found with the top corporate executives. The old wealthy families, they claim, have lost their control of corporations because of the wide distribution of stock ownership in most corporations. In fact, it is believed, the stock ownership in most corporations is distributed among so many people that they cannot effectively unite in confronting the authority of corporate management. The top executive officers of the corporation are thus free to run the corporation as they see fit. The basic perspective presented by most who accept the managerial-control thesis is one of many separate corporations, each with its management in control, competing among themselves for a share of the market in the economy. But there are several weaknesses in this managerial-control view.

For one, the evidence strongly favors a conclusion that major corporations are not so separate and competitive economic units. We live in a period of a few corporate giants who among themselves account for a majority of the corporate assets in the present economy. In addition, various interests tie these corporations together, reducing competition (though seldom completely) and magnifying their collective means of dominating the economy.

And there is a problem with the view of managers in control of each corporation *without* major interests from outside the corporation looking over their shoulders as they run the corporation. Although the board of directors, the body that legally has authority over management, may not represent the interests of major stockholders as much as it once did (because of the wide distribution of stockholders), there are new interests represented on the board. These interests are from other corporations that may have business interests at stake or banks with financial interests at stake.

These ties and outside interests will be described in more detail in this chapter. For now it must be pointed out that a new thesis has emerged. In this view a group that can be referred to as a *corporate class* (see Useem 1978, 1979b, 1984) is considered at the top of the present stratification system in the United States. The group is called a *class* because it has economic interests in common, possesses enough unity and intraclass organization to recognize these common class interests, and has the means to dominate the economy and political system.

In essence, this corporate class is in many ways similar to an upper class. Its power, however, lies not with the ownership of the means of production but with *control* of the collective means of production. This corporate class is also similar in some ways to the managerial elite described by those accepting the managerial revolution view. But this corporate class is above the interests of separate, competing corporations; rather, it unites them into a complex of interrelated corporate bodies. Finally, this corporate-class perspective forces us to *retain many of the arguments from the ruling-class theory* about the overall dominance of the economy and political system by one class.

In what follows we briefly consider the evidence showing the economic concentration within our society today. We will then outline the place of the corporate class within this structure of economic concentration, along with its means of influence over the political system.

THE STRUCTURE OF CORPORATE CONCENTRATION: FOUNDATION FOR A CORPORATE CLASS

We may define a *corporate class* as a group of people holding key positions of authority in major corporations. They form a network of associations, much like old upper-class families, that crisscross these major corporate institutions, creating an interpersonal web of relations at the top of these institutions. Their influence is not found in personal wealth, although many are wealthy, but in *control* of corporate resources.

These people are chief executive officers or board members of a major corporation, and at the same time board members in other corporations. And they are not unfamiliar in the halls of government, with many in the corporate class having moved in and out of government in various capacities such as advisers, cabinet secretaries, or special committee members. Their personal as well as class interests lie not just with one corporation, but with the structure of corporate concentration as a whole. Again, much like the old upper class, they are often members of exclusive social clubs, frequent many of the same resorts, and send their children to exclusive prep schools. But unlike the old upper class, their ranks are permeable. There is at least some room at the top for those who win the recognition of members of this corporate class (Alba and Moore 1982).

Because the base of corporate class power is located in a structure of corporate concentration, we must begin with an examination of this concentration. If the economic concentration were lacking, this corporate class would be reduced to a managerial elite (as described by Berle and Means 1932) with little influence beyond its own individual corporate hierarchy. It is one thing to be chief executive officer of a major corporation in tough economic competition with other large corporations, but it is quite another to be a member of a corporate class sitting astride many corporate hierarchies, each tied together in various ways. The interests of such a corporate class lie not in individual corporations; they lie in a structure of corporate concentration that is at the heart of the economic system of advanced capitalism as a whole.

At the very least the economic concentration found today is based on:

1 The size of major corporations and their ability to dominate the market for their particular industrial products or services.

2 The economic diversification of many large corporations into a multitude of products and services, thereby broadening their economic base and stabilizing their place at the top of the corporate structure.

3 The concentrated control of stock in major corporations by other corporations (mostly large banks and insurance companies).

4 The network of interlocking directorates that ties top corporate personnel together, distributing their loyalties from individual corporations to the corporate structure as a whole, and making possible coordinated activities, more influence in government, and planning.

Corporate Size and Concentration

One of the most important characteristics of our economy is the increasing size and market control of major corporations. There are about 200,000 industrial corporations operating in the economy today, but more than 70 percent of all the industrial corporate assets are in the hands of 100 (0.0005 percent) of these corporations. Most of the 200,000 are small local enterprises that come and go from year to year. For these lesser firms the old capitalist ideal of competition is alive and deadly.

But in the upper ranks, the old capitalist ideal is more dogma than reality. Their size and market concentration have largely (though not completely) removed them from the ordeal of competition within national boundaries. And it is here that we find a key to their growth and stability. The rapid growth of major corporations has been a phenomenon of industrialization throughout this century. There was even recognition of this trend in the later 1800s. At this time federal government concern was expressed through passage of the Sherman Antitrust Act of 1890, achieving its first major action in 1911 with the breakup of Rockefeller's Standard Oil. Later, C. Wright Mills (1956) saw the expansion of economic institutions laying the foundation for what he called the power elite. The growth of corporations has proceeded much faster since Mills' time.

Corporations are usually grouped by function into several categories. Among these are industrial corporations (producing or mining a product); transportation, utilities, and communication corporations; commercial banks; and insurance companies. Of the industrial corporations we find that just 100 corporations out of 200,000 in 1985 controlled over 70 percent of the industrial assets in the country (see Table 8-1). As an indication of growth we may consider the share of industrial assets held by the top 100 corporations since 1950. In 1950, it was 39.8 percent; in 1955, 44.3 percent; in 1960, 46.4 percent; in 1965, 46.5 percent; in 1970, 52.3 percent; in 1980, 55 percent; and by 1985, over 70 percent.

Commercial banks represent another sector of corporate concentration. Here we find the largest grouping of corporate assets overall. There are 14,659 commercial banks in the nation, just fifty with total assets of over a trillion dollars. But thirty banks account for 50.7 percent of all banking assets, with only fifteen banks accounting for 41.1 percent of banking assets (see Table 8-

TABLE 8-1
LARGEST 100 INDUSTRIAL CORPORATIONS BY SIZE OF ASSETS, 1989

1989 rank	Name of corporation	1989 assets (billions of dollars)
1	General Motors	173.3
2	Ford	160.9
3	General Electric	128.4
4	Exxon	83.2
5	IBM	77.7
6	Chrysler	51.0
7	Mobil	39.0
8	Philip Morris	38.5
9	Nabisco	36.4
10	Du Pont	34.7
11	Chevron	33.9
12	Amoco	30.4
13	Xerox	30.4
14	Shell Oil	27.6
15	Texaco	25.6
16	Time Warner	24.8
17	Kodak	23.7
18	Atlantic Richfield	22.3
19	Dow Chemical	22.2
20	Occidental	20.7
21	Westinghouse	20.3
22	USX	17.5
23	Tenneco	17.4
24	Procter & Gamble	16.4
25	Weyerhaeuser	15.9
26	Pepsico	15.1
27	United Technologies	14.6
28	Textron	13.8
29	McDonnell-Douglas	13.4
30	Boeing	13.3
31	International Paper	11.6
32	Alcoa	11.5
33	American Brands	11.4
34	Phillips Petroleum	11.3
35	Caterpillar Tractor	10.9
36	Unisys	10.8
37	Digital Equipment	10.7
38	Allied-Signal	10.1
39	Hewlett-Packard	10.1
40	Minnesota Mining & Mfg.	9.8
41	Berkshire-Hathaway	9.5
42	Unilever U.S.	9.4
43	Unocal	9.4
44	Deere	9.2
45	Anheuser-Bush	9.0
46	Rockwell Int'l	8.9
47	Coastal	8.8

TABLE 8-1 (*Continued*)
LARGEST 100 INDUSTRIAL CORPORATIONS BY SIZE OF ASSETS, 1989

1989 rank	Name of corporation	1989 assets (billions of dollars)
48	Sun	8.7
49	Monsanto	8.6
50	Union Carbide	8.5
51	Baxter International	8.5
52	Bristol-Myers Squibb	8.5
53	Goodyear	8.5
54	Pfizer	8.3
55	Coca-Cola	8.3
56	Johnson & Johnson	7.9
57	Motorola	7.7
58	Seagold Vineyards	7.6
59	Champion Int'l	7.5
60	Temple Inland	7.2
61	Georgia Pacific	7.1
62	Amerada Hess	6.9
63	Lockheed	6.8
64	Merck	6.8
65	Cooper Industries	6.7
66	General Dynamics	6.5
67	Sara Lee	6.5
68	LTV	6.3
69	Black & Decker	6.3
70	Stone Container	6.3
71	Hoechst Celanese	6.1
72	Eli Lilly	5.8
73	Hanson Industries	5.8
74	Scott Paper	5.7
75	American Home Products	5.7
76	PPG Industries	5.6
77	Ethyl	5.6
78	W. R. Grace	5.6
79	Pitney Bowes	5.6
80	James River Corp.	5.6
81	Reynolds Metals	5.6
82	Emerson Electric	5.4
83	Whirlpool	5.4
84	Raytheon	5.3
85	TRW	5.3
86	Honeywell	5.3
87	Litton Industries	5.3
88	Dana	5.2
89	Owens-Illinois	5.1
90	American Cyanamid	4.9
91	Kimberly-Clark	4.9
92	Penzoil	4.9
93	Abbott Laboratories	4.9
94	Borden	4.8

TABLE 8-1 (Continued)
LARGEST 100 INDUSTRIAL CORPORATIONS BY SIZE OF ASSETS, 1989

1976 rank	Name of corporation	1976 assets (billions of dollars)
95	Texas Instrument	4.8
96	Bethlehem Steel	4.8
97	Coca-Cola Enterprises	4.7
98	Archer Daniel Midland	4.7
99	Bayer USA	4.6
100	NCR	4.5

Total industrial asset of top 500, 1988 = $2,078.8 Billion.
Percentage held by top 100 = 74.1%

Source: *Fortune*, April 23, 1990; U.S. Bureau of the Census, *Statistical Abstracts of the United States*, 1989.

2). The top five banks (BankAmerica Corp., Citibank, Chase Manhattan, Manufacturers Hanover, and Morgan Bank) are corporate giants with broad influence in the economy. We will consider in some detail below the importance of these large financial institutions in the overall corporate structure. Finally, we can consider insurance companies. Of the approximately 1,790 insurance companies in the nation, only eight control 50.3 percent of the assets. Furthermore, the top eighteen insurance companies control about two-thirds of the assets (65.7 percent).

The size of major corporations in our society is only one aspect of economic concentration, though a very important aspect. What this size indicates is that the overall economy is dominated by a mere handful of corporations. This gives these corporations the ability to have an enormous effect on the economy (as well as politics) by the decisions they make or fail to make. Their performance as corporations, their profits, losses, and layoffs, affect the lives and well-being of millions of people. And, as we have noted previously, research has shown that the size of corporations is related to the amount of influence they may have over government policy (Salamon and Siegfried 1977; Jacobs 1988).

The importance these corporations have in the economy is also indicated by the cases in which financial problems threaten their existence. Government officials are well aware of the consequences for the economy of the bankruptcy of one of these corporations. Thus, Lockheed was guaranteed $250 million in loans from the government when it was in trouble in 1971, Chrysler (the third largest auto maker) could seriously ask the government for $1 billion in help through loan guarantees in 1979 (with Carter finally approving $1.5 billion), and Continental Illinois Bank could get loan guarantees of more than $4.5 billion in 1984.

Another important aspect of this concentration is market control. When, for example, only three large firms are producing the vast majority of the automo-

TABLE 8-2
LARGEST 30 COMMERCIAL BANKS BY SIZE OF ASSETS, 1988

1976 rank	Name	1988 assets (billions of dollars)
1	Citicorp	207.6
2	Chase Manhattan Corp.	97.5
3	BankAmerica Corp.	94.6
4	J. P. Morgan & Co.	83.9
5	Security Pacific Corp.	77.9
6	Chemical Banking Corp.	67.3
7	Manufacturers Hanover Corp.	66.7
8	First Interstate Bancorp.	58.2
9	Bankers Trust New York Corp.	57.9
10	Bank of New York Co.	47.4
11	Wells Fargo & Co.	46.6
12	First Chicago Corp.	44.4
13	PNC Financial Corp.	40.8
14	Bank of Boston Corp.	36.1
15	Bank of New England Corp.	32.2
16	Mellon Bank Corp.	31.2
17	Continental Bank Corp.	30.6
18	NCNB Corp.	29.8
19	First Fidelity Bancorp	29.8
20	Suntrust Banks	29.2
21	Fleet/Norstar Financial Group	29.1
22	First Union Corp.	29.0
23	Shawmut National Corp.	28.4
24	Marine Midland Banks	26.0
25	Barnett Banks	25.7
26	NCNB Texas National Bank	25.6
27	Banc One Corp.	25.3
28	Republic New York Corp.	24.5
29	First Bank System	24.2
30	NBD Bancorp	24.2

Top 30 percent of total banking assets = 47%

Source: Fortune, April 23, 1989; U.S. Bureau of the Census, *Statistical Abstract of the United States, 1989.*

biles in the country, the competition to reduce costs and provide more safety is diminished. And even when there are more than three corporate giants in a particular market, their size and other relationships among them (discussed below) may lead to less competition.

A final aspect of economic concentration is the number of people who play key roles in the economy. Of *all* the corporations controlling 50 percent or more of the corporate assets among the types of corporations considered above (industrial, transportation, utilities, communication, banks, and insurance corporations), only about *3,500 people* (presidents and board members of these corporations) exercise formal authority over half the nation's corporate assets in these areas (Dye 1979:19).

Concentration Through Diversification

In recent times we find a rapidly growing movement toward product and service diversification among large corporations. The outcome is corporate conglomerates producing everything from bread and soft drinks to clothing and oil products. The diversification movement has led to economic concentration, with the large corporations gobbling up smaller and medium-size firms, expanding the control of large corporations over the economy in general.

In addition to increased assets, profits, and economic power, conglomerate status produces security and stability. With adequate planning and intelligent decision making the large corporation can spread its assets in a wide range of products and services. It can take losses when needed (at times purposely, to reduce taxes), cut its losses when it wants by reducing production in falling markets, and expand its production into new growth markets. In short, the conglomerate is no longer at the mercy of the market and is afforded more control in its pursuit of profits.

By way of example, International Telephone and Telegraph owns, among *many* firms, Hartford Fire Insurance, Aetna, Continental Banking Co., Hancock Industries, Sheraton Hotels, Avis Rent-a-Car, and Bobbs-Merrill Book Co. (Sampson 1973). Other examples include Pepsico's (Pepsi-Cola) ownership of Frito-Lay, Wilson Sporting Goods, and Lee Way Motor Freight; J. C. Penney's ownership of Thrifty Drugs and Great American Reserve Insurance; and Mobil Oil's ownership of Montgomery Ward, Marcor Inc., Beefeater Restaurants, Golden Bear Family Restaurants, and Jefferson Stores (U.S. Senate Committee on Governmental Affairs 1978a).

An important outcome is that those on top in the corporate world are able to stay on top in part through their wide range of subsidiaries. In the past there was movement among the top 100 corporations. Of the top 100 corporations in 1909, for example, only twenty-four remained in the top 100 by 1960. But this has changed. Mermelstein (1969), in a study of the changes among the top 100 corporations since the early 1900s, found the top to be much more stable in recent years. In another aspect, the top 100 are becoming more equal in size (Collins and Preston 1961). Thus, through mergers and diversification the top corporations have achieved broad economic influence and the necessary stability to maintain this influence.

Concentration of Stock Control

One of the most important means of influence within a corporation is the ownership or control of a large amount of stock in that corporation. Stock ownership usually brings votes in the affairs of that corporation in direct proportion to the amount of stock owned. The individual or family ownership of stock in major corporations today has become dispersed rather than concentrated. Fewer individuals or families own large amounts of stock in *particular* corporations.

But emerging is a new form of stock control. With growing funds from pension programs for workers and other large trust holdings, large *institutional investors* have increasing control over stock in major corporations. These institutional investors, such as banks and insurance companies, do not own these massive concentrations of stock, but *control* them. As the U.S. Senate Committee on Governmental Affairs (1978a) found, these institutional investors are given the voting and selling rights to this stock by the true owners. The result is control of the stock by large institutional investors.

The above-mentioned Senate study examined the stock control patterns in the nation's top 122 corporations. As an indication of the size of these 122 corporations, their stock accounted for 41 percent of all the common stock issued in the United States at the end of 1976. The study was most concerned with investors who held one of the *top* five stock-voting positions in these 122 corporations. The study attempted to identify the investor controlling the most stock (or stock votes) in each corporation, the investor controlling the second highest amount of stock (or stock votes), and so on. It should be noted that while some changes in the *exact* stock control figures for *particular* companies have occurred since 1976, the overall structure of corporate stock control has not changed significantly.

With 122 top corporations in the study there are 610 top five stock-voting positions (5 × 122 corporations = 610). The most interesting finding from this study is that just *twenty-one investors* accounted for more than *half* of all these top five stock-voting positions (325 of the total 610 top five positions). These twenty-one investors include eleven banks, five investment companies, four insurance companies, and one family group (the Kirby family). The most important investor was Morgan Bank, with one of the top five stock-voting positions in almost *half* of these top 122 corporations. Morgan Bank was the number one stock voter in twenty-seven of these corporations, the number two stock voter in eleven, number three in eight, number four in seven, and number five in three (see Table 8-3).

Large banks make up the most important group of stock voters in these 122 top corporations. Who controls the stock in these banks? In the U.S. Senate Committee's words (1978a:260), "the principal stockvoters in large banks are—large banks" (see Table 8-4). Of the top five banks in the nation (Bank of America, Citibank of New York, Chase Manhattan, Manufacturers Hanover, and Morgan) we find that in 1976 Morgan was the number 1 stock voter in Bank of America, Citibank, and Manufacturers Hanover. Morgan was also the top stock voter in Chemical Bank (the sixth largest in 1976) and Bankers Trust (the seventh largest in 1976). Chase Manhattan was the only one that varied from this pattern; the Rockefeller family was the number 1 stock voter in Chase Manhattan. Given the prominence of Morgan Bank among these other

TABLE 8-3
MORGAN BANK'S STOCK-VOTING POSITION IN 56 LARGE CORPORATIONS, 1976

Company in which Morgan has stock control	Morgan Bank's stock-voting rank among all stockholders in listed corporation*	Percentage of total stock controlled in each corporation by Morgan Bank
1. American Airlines	1	6.05
2. American Express Company	1	5.22
3. Bankamerica Corp.	1	2.88
4. Bankers Trust New York Corp.	1	1.67
5. Burlington Northern	1	4.03
6. Chemical New York Corp.	1	3.72
7. Citibank	1	3.26
8. Connecticut General Insurance	1	7.25
9. Consolidated Freightways Inc.	1	5.27
10. Federated Department Stores Inc.	1	3.45
11. General Electric Company	1	1.30
12. Goodyear Tire and Rubber Company	1	5.94
13. International Business Machines (IBM)	1	2.53
14. International Telephone & Telegraph (IT&T)	1	2.13
15. K mart Corp. (Kresge Co., S. S.)	1	4.63
16. Manufacturers Hanover Corp.	1	3.88
17. Mobil Corporation	1	2.46
18. Norfolk and Western Railroad Company	1	1.62
19. Pepsico Inc.	1	6.59
20. Santa Fe Industries Inc.	1	2.87
21. Sears Roebuck and Company	1	2.02
22. Southern Co.	1	0.58
23. Southern Railway Co.	1	4.38
24. UAL Inc. (United Air Lines)	1	6.73
25. Union Carbide Corp.	1	2.46
26. U.S. Steel Corp.	1	2.40
27. Westinghouse Electric Corp.	1	1.62
28. Caterpillar Tractor Co.	2	1.66
29. Continental Illinois Corp.	2	3.35
30. Exxon Corp.	2	1.09
31. Eastman Kodak Co.	2	1.55
32. General Motors Co.	2	1.13
33. General Public Utilities Corp.	2	0.30
34. Mellon National Corp.	2	1.86
35. Missouri Pacific Corp.	2	2.02
36. Penney Inc, J.C.	2	3.06
37. Procter & Gamble Co.	2	2.41
38. Travelers Corp.	2	3.36
39. American Broadcasting Companies Inc.	3	2.65
40. Bethlehem Steel Corporation	3	1.89
41. Coca-Cola Co.	3	2.84
42. Du Pont de Nemours Co.	3	1.02
43. Ford Motor Co.	3	1.74
44. Rio Grande Industries Inc.	3	4.39
45. Standard Oil Co. of California	3	1.27

TABLE 8-3 (*Continued*)
MORGAN BANK'S STOCK-VOTING POSITION IN 56 LARGE CORPORATIONS, 1976

Company in which Morgan has stock control	Morgan Bank's stock-voting rank among all stockholders in listed corporation*	Percentage of total stock controlled in each corporation by Morgan Bank
46. Union Oil Co. of California	3	1.63
47. Continental Corp.	4	1.14
48. Gulf Oil	4	0.93
49. Middle South Utilities Inc.	4	1.78
50. Northwest Airlines Inc.	4	3.74
51. Northwest Bancorporation	4	2.61
52. Reynolds Industries Inc., R.J.	4	1.49
53. Texaco Inc.	4	0.92
54. Consumers Power Co.	5	0.37
55. Public Service Electric & Gas Co.	5	0.59
56. Southern Pacific Co.	5	0.90

*A rank of 1 means that Morgan Bank controls the most stock and stock votes of all the stockholders in the particular corporation. For example, Morgan Bank is stock-voter number 1 in American Airlines with 6.05 percent of the total stock votes in American Airlines.
Source: U.S. Senate Committee on Governmental Affairs (*Voting Rights in Major Corporations,* 1978a:280–281).

banks, we need to know who dominates Morgan Bank. In short, the other banks dominate. The top stock voters in Morgan Bank were Citibank, Chase Manhattan, Manufacturers Hanover, and Bankers Trust.

The proportion of total corporate stock held by individuals or families in this country is declining steadily. At present personal or family-owned and -controlled corporate stock accounts for about 50 percent of the total. In 1956 institutional investors controlled about 25 percent of the total stock; in 1976 their control was more than 40 percent; and by 1986 institutional investors controlled 50 percent of the total stock in the United States (U.S. Senate Committee on Governmental Affairs 1978a:593). Thus, the importance of family-controlled stock is declining both in proportion to the total United States stock and in proportion to the stock held in particular corporations. Corresponding to this decrease is the increase in stock controlled by the institutional investor both in proportion to the total United States stock and in proportion to the stock held in particular corporations.

The precise meaning of this shift is in dispute. One the one hand it is charged that institutional investors are not actively involved in using their mass of stock votes to influence the behavior or practices of corporations whose stock they control (Herman 1975). On the other hand there is more evidence to suggest that these institutional investors do use their power from stock control to influence these corporations from time to time in various ways.

These corporations communicate frequently with the institutional investors, ask their advice, and consult with them before major issues (such as the elec-

TABLE 8-4
STOCK-VOTING POSITIONS IN TOP 5 BANKS HELD BY OTHER TOP BANKS

Rank of bank by bank assets	Name	Stock-voting rank held in the bank by other top banks*	Percentage of total stock votes held by other banks
1	BankAmerica Corp.	1 Morgan Bank	2.88
		2 Citibank	2.47
		4 First National, Chicago	1.08
2	Citibank	1 Morgan Bank	3.26
		2 First National, Boston	2.65
		3 Harris Trust & Savings	1.59
3	Chase Manhattan Corp.	1 Rockefeller Family	1.85
4	Manufacturers Hanover	1 Morgan Bank	3.88
		3 Hartford National Bank	1.09
		4 Bankers Trust	0.80
5	Morgan Bank (J.P. Morgan & Co.)	1 Citibank	2.63
		2 Chase Manhattan	1.43
		3 Manufacturers Hanover	1.42
		4 Bankers Trust	1.10

*List of stock-voting positions held by other banks only; for example, stock voter number 3 in BankAmerica Corp. is not a bank and thus is not listed. The exception is that the Rockefeller family is listed as No. 1 stock voter in Chase Manhattan Corp.

Source: U.S. Senate Committee on Governmental Affairs (*Voting Rights in Major Corporations,* 1978a:260).

tion of board members) come before the stockholders (see the study by Julius Allen in U.S. Senate Committee on Governmental Affairs 1978a:559–799). The exact amount of influence these institutional investors (such as banks) exert over corporations whose stock they control is unclear. But the potential for influence is present and recognized by the corporations. This in itself can lead to a relationship in which corporate management is in contact with large institutional investors to make sure it has their confidence—and votes.

One major implication of the increasing importance of institutional investors in top corporations is the additional concentration of economic power in our society. This form of concentration must be added to the concentration due to the size of major corporations and their share of the market flowing from diversification and conglomerate-forming mergers. The economic concentration resulting from the rise of institutional investors comes primarily because these major corporations are less and less independently functioning units. Through ties to a few major institutional investors the top companies form blocs of related economic systems, with banks often at the center of these blocs through stock control.

Using Morgan Bank as an example, we find that American Express, Bank of America, Bankers Trust, Chemical Bank, Citibank, and Manufacturers Hanover have a relationship through Morgan as their number 1 stock voter. With industrial corporations, we find that General Electric, Westinghouse Electric, Mobil, Exxon, Standard of California, Union Oil, Gulf, and Texaco (to name only a few) are all related because Morgan is one of their top five stock voters (see Table 8-3). Through this mass of corporate relations due to stock votes we find one common denominator; the banks have a lot of influence. But it is not independent influence by a particular bank, because they all have stock-voting influence over each other. And if this were not enough to create a concentrated web of corporate connections, there is another web—interlocking directorates.

Interlocking Directorates and Economic Concentration

The highest position of authority within a corporate hierarchy is represented by the board of directors. As a body averaging about twelve people per corporation, this group has the authority to hire and fire management and set broad policy. Its members come from both inside the corporation management (its top managers, such as president and vice-presidents) and outside the corporation. Most of the board members in big corporations are top executive officers (management) from other top corporations (see Warner and Unwalla 1967; Allen 1978).

The board members are charged with representing the interests of stockholders in the corporation but, as we have shown earlier, the controllers of stock are often other corporations. Also, most individual stockholders are, widely dispersed throughout the nation and have relatively minor amounts of stock. The result often is that interests within the corporation and other large corporations that have interests in the corporation (through control of stock, business deals, and financial holdings) gain representation on the board of directors.

The amount of time board members devote to the duties of directing a corporation varies widely by corporation, the number of problems occurring at particular times, and the involvement in subcommittees within the board. Most often the board members come together several times a year to make judgments on issues presented by the management of the corporation. Thus, because the position of board member is not a full-time job these people are free to participate in other activities, such as memberships in other corporate boards and positions as executives of other corporations.

Interlocking directorates can be defined as the linking of two or more corporations through at least one of their board members. For example, a member of the board of directors of corporation A is also a member of the board of directors of corporation B. Corporations A and B are said to be linked through their board of directors. Though not exactly within this definition, corporate interlocks through a corporate executive (such as a president) who is a board member of another corporation are considered equally important by most researchers. Another relationship has received increasing attention by researchers and government agencies. This relationship of *indirect interlocks* is defined as two corporations tied by their board members through a third corporation. Two corporations are indirectly interlocked when a board member from corporation A is linked to a board member from corporation B because both board members come together on the board of directors of corporation C. The relationship between corporations A and B in this case is less than with a direct interlock, but because some of the same outcomes may be achieved (discussed below), it is also considered important. We may add that indirect interlocks have received increasing attention because direct interlocking directorates between competing corporations (such as GM and Ford) are illegal. But such competing companies often are found with extensive indirect interlocking directorates, which as yet have not been made illegal (although this has been suggested; see U.S. Senate Committee on Governmental Affairs 1978b).

It is generally assumed that corporate interlocks are important because they (1) reduce competition among corporations in general, (2) represent outside influences over the corporation, (3) provide a means of sharing information about corporate plans and operations, (4) help provide unity among top corporate officials in the economy (much like social clubs), and (5) thus help provide unity in corporate dealings with the government.

In his detailed study of the corporate class in the United States and England, Useem (1984) found that the most important reason for interlocking directorates was to gain information from other corporate leaders that could be used for economic advantage, what he called "business scan." Galaskiewicz et al. (1985) found that interlocks were more common with chief executive officers from the biggest corporations and that high-status people who would likely have more information were sought out for these interlocks, thus seeming to confirm Useem's (1984) idea. But others have found additional reasons for these interlocks. For example, Galaskiewicz and Wasserman (1981) found that corporations often seek out directors from financial institutions to secure good relations with possible sources of capital. Burt, Christman, and Kilburn (1980) compiled data on interlocks which suggest many interlocks are for the purpose of maintaining or creating market relations with other firms.

Perhaps most important, however, these interlocks create another layer of *economic concentration* in addition to those already discussed through corporate size, diversification, and stock control. And with respect to the second point above, some researchers argue that interlocking directorates provide another means (in addition to stock control and credit) for board influence by large banks over other corporations (Mintz and Schwartz 1985; Mintz 1989). In concluding its detailed study of interlocking directorates, a recent Senate committee (U.S. Senate Committee on Governmental Affairs 1978b:281, 279) summarized the dangers by suggesting:

> Such interlocking directorates among the nation's very largest corporations may provide mechanisms for stabilizing prices, controlling supply and restraining competition. They can have a profound effect on business attempts to influence Government policies. They can impact on corporate decisions as to the type and quality of products and services to be marketed in the United States and overseas. They can influence company policies with respect to employee rights, compensation and job

conditions. They can bear on corporate policies with respect to environmental and social issues and, possibly, control the shape and direction of the nation's economy. ... From the study, the staff has concluded that American business is highly concentrated across industry lines—perhaps more concentrated today than it was in 1913 when Louis Brandeis wrote of the "endless chain," and in 1955 when C. Wright Mills spoke of the "power elite."

Having discussed why interlocking directorates can be important sources of corporate concentration and power, it is time for us to consider some of the evidence indicating the extent and patterns of such interlocks. We can begin by describing the overall magnitude of interlocking directorates among top corporations. In a study of interlocks among the top 250 corporations in 1970, Allen (1974) found these corporations to have an average of 10.41 interlocking directorates each. And among these corporations, financial institutions (primarily banks) had the highest number, with an average of 16.92 interlocking directorates.

In a similar study of the 250 top corporations, Dooley (1969) found a similar pattern, but with a further interesting dimension. Dooley found that the number of interlocking directorates increases with the size of the corporation. There was a range of 6.0 average interlocks with corporations having less than $0.5 billion in assets to an average of 23.7 interlocking directorates for corporations with more than $5 billion in assets. Thus, the bigger the corporation, the more ties to or interlocking directorates with other corporations it has.

The most detailed study of interlocking directorates comes from recent Senate investigations (U.S. Senate Committee on Governmental Affairs 1978b, 1980). In this study the Senate committee included information on 130 top corporations in the United States (115 of the 122 corporations included in the previous Senate study on the control of stock, 1978a). Overall, each of 123 corporations (excluding seven investment corporations) were directly or indirectly interlocked at least once with an average of sixty-two of the other 122 corporations (1978b:280). Nine of these corporations had from ninety to ninety-nine direct *or* indirect interlocks with the other 122 corporations, twenty-two had from eighty to eighty-nine interlocks, and twenty-two others had from seventy to seventy-nine such interlocks.

Special attention was given by this Senate committee to the thirteen largest corporations. These thirteen had ties with *70 percent* of the other 117 corporations through 240 direct and 5,547 indirect interlocking directorates. Among themselves, with the exception of the BankAmerica, these thirteen corporations were *all* directly or indirectly interlocked. And Morgan Bank (previously found to have the most stock control in the top corporations) had the most interlocking directorates of all 130 corporations. Table 8-5 provides a list of the corporations *directly* interlocked with Morgan Bank as an indicator of the general status of these interlocked corporations. Finally, the most heavily interlocked group among these 130 corporations included Citibank, Chase Manhattan Bank, Manufacturers Hanover, Morgan Bank, Prudential Life Insurance, Metropolitan Life, AT&T, Exxon, and General Motors. The financial corporations in this group were, of course, among the most important institutional investors listed in the previous section on stock control.

We may cite one final aspect of the Senate study of interlocking director-ates. As noted above, direct interlocking directorates between competing com-panies are illegal. But the Senate was interested in the extent of *indirect* inter-locking directorates among competitors. Each type of industry (such as auto producers, banks, and energy corporations) was examined and found to con-tain extensive indirect interlocks.

We will take the example of banks, due to their importance in the economy. With the exception of BankAmerica to Bankers Trust and Western Bancorp to Chase Manhattan Bank, all top ten banks in the country were indirectly inter-locked (see Table 8-6). These indirect interlocks ranged from a low of only one between Western Bancorp and Bankers Trust to a high of forty-two between First Chicago Bank and Continental Illinois. Others of importance include thirty indirect interlocks between Morgan and Citibank, twenty-five between Morgan and Manufacturers Hanover, twenty-seven between Manufacturers Hanover and Chase Manhattan, and twenty-six between Manufacturers

TABLE 8-5
DIRECT INTERLOCKING DIRECTORATES FROM MORGAN BANK
DIRECTORS TO OTHER TOP CORPORATIONS, 1976

Corporation	Number of direct interlocks
Aetna Life	1
Bethlehem Steel	2
Burlington Northern	1
Continental Corporation	1
Du Pont de Nemours	1
Eastman Kodak	1
Federated Department Stores	1
Ford Motor Company	1
General Electric	3
General Motors	3
International Business Machines (IBM)	1
John Hancock Life	1
Metropolitan Life	1
Missouri Pacific Corporation	1
New York Life Insurance	1
Procter & Gamble	1
Prudential Insurance	1
Santa Fe Industries	1
Sears Roebuck	1
Southern Railway	1
Union Carbide	1
Western Electric	1
Total direct interlocks	27

Source: U.S. Senate Committee on Governmental Affairs (*Interlocking Director-ates Among the Major U.S. Corporations,* 1978b:935–936).

TABLE 8-6
NUMBER OF INDIRECT INTERLOCKING DIRECTORATES AMONG TOP 10 BANKS

Rank	Bank	Bank by rank									
		1	2	3	4	5	6	7	8	9	10
1	BankAmerica Corp.		3	2	2	2	2	0	3	6	7
2	Citibank	3		18	26	30	24	14	8	10	6
3	Chase Manhattan	2	18		27	17	16	7	6	10	0
4	Manufacturers Hanover	2	26	27		25	32	11	4	8	3
5	J. P. Morgan	2	30	17	25		15	6	6	9	1
6	Chemical Bank	2	24	16	32	15		24	13	15	3
7	Bankers Trust	0	14	7	11	6	24		4	5	1
8	Continental Illinois	3	8	6	4	6	13	4		42	2
9	First Chicago Corp.	6	10	10	8	9	15	5	42		3
10	Western Bancorp	7	6	0	3	1	3	1	2	3	

Source: U.S. Senate Committee on Governmental Affairs (*Interlocking Directorates Among the Major U.S. Corporations,* 1978b:120).

Hanover and Citibank. If indirect interlocks have the potential for restraining competition, increasing economic concentration, and increasing influence over the government, as is suggested by the Senate committee, we certainly have the potential for financial corporate dominance in our society.

Thus far we have been concerned primarily with the overall extent of interlocking directorates among major corporations. There is one final aspect of the patterns presented by these interlocks that deserves discussion. Many studies have examined these interlocks in terms of the interlocked *groups* of corporations that may be found. Of all the mass of interlocks some corporations are more tightly grouped together in cliques. Much like work that has been done by sociologists on individual relationships within work groups or peer-group relations within a classroom, we can group corporations together through an examination of the ties they have with one another. And with this method we can identify central members of a group and "social" isolates.

This type of research with corporations has been done by Dooley (1969), Sonquist and Koening (1975), Mariolis (1975), Allen (1977), Roy (1983), and Mintz and Schwartz (1985). These researchers have identified varying numbers of cliques among corporations, depending on the number studied and the density (or the number of interlocks) used to define the cliques. But one finding is rather consistent; at the center of these corporate cliques big banks are usually found. In other words, the big banks gather around themselves clusters of other corporations through interlocks (Mintz 1989).

Allen (1977) has found these banking cliques to be less concentrated in 1970 than in 1935, but they remain important. The clustering of corporations through interlocks with banks in central positions is consistent with the findings above, showing banks to have more interlocking directorates than other types of corporations. And it is also consistent with other indicators of the central importance of banks, such as their control of stock in other corporations. All these findings seem to suggest that banks play an important function in uniting and centralizing the concentrated corporate structure in the United States today.

We can provide two further examples of the importance and power of large banks in the U.S. economy. Today, the largest bank in the United States is Citicorp (the parent company of Citibank of New York). We have already seen that, like Morgan Bank, Citibank controls the stock votes of many of the largest companies in the United States. Table 8-7 lists some of the corporations in which Citibank is among the top five stock voters. Also included in Table 8-7

TABLE 8-7
CITIBANK INTERLOCKS AND STOCK CONTROL

Citibank stock control in:*	
Atlantic Richfield	First Bank System
Texaco Inc.	Morgan Bank
Continental Oil	BankAmerica Corp.
Exxon Corp.	First Chicago Corp.
Phillips Petroleum	J.C. Penney
Caterpillar Tractor	Sears Roebuck
Eastman Kodak	Federated Department Stores
Duke Power Co.	K mart Corp.
General Electric	Southern Pacific
GT&E	American Express
Coca-Cola Co.	Du Pont
Burlington Northern	

Citibank interlocks†	
Beatrice Foods Co.	Bethlehem Steel
NCR Corp.	U.S. Steel
AT&T	Gillette Co.
Ford Motor Co.	Macy and Co.
General Motors	CBS
Kraftco Corp.	NBC
Pepsico Corp.	Exxon
Ingersoll-Rand Co.	United Technologies
Metropolitan Life	Eastman Kodak
Aetna Life	Kennecott Copper
Mutual Life Insurance	IBM
Equitable Life Assurance	Xerox Corp.
New York Life Insurance	General Electric
Mobil Corp.	Boeing Co.
Dow Corning Corp.	J.C. Penney
Procter & Gamble	Sears Roebuck
Du Point	

*Some of the companies where Citibank is among the top five stock voters.
†This includes only the interlocks with companies listed in the Senate (1978) study.
Source: U.S. Senate Committee on Governmental Affairs (1978a:267–268; 1978b:413–426).

are some of the corporations where members of Citibank's board of directors have other board positions, creating interlocking directorates with Citibank.

The other example relates to the federal government loan guarantees of about $4.5 billion dollars to save Continental Illinois Bank in 1984. This money was not actually loaned to Continental by the federal government but by other banks. This at first sounds rather curious given Adam Smith's view of capitalism because the other banks should not be loaning money to a competitor but cheering when there is reduced competition for them as the competitor goes under. But when we consider some of the details of the bailout by the other banks in light of some of the data we have discussed above, it becomes less curious. There were sixteen banks that came together to loan this $4.5 billion to Continental Illinois Bank. Citibank was among these banks loaning money to save Continental, but the leader of these sixteen banks to save Continental was none other than Morgan Bank (*Wall Street Journal,* May 16, 1984), the number one stock voter in Continental Illinois Bank and Citibank.

Finally, we need to note how the reality of the massive number of direct and indirect interlocks is often difficult to imagine. Figure 8-1 may be of some help in this regard. In Figure 8-1 we find only the four largest New York banks and *some* of their interlocks with the corporations included in the U.S. Senate studies (1978, 1980) discussed above. These lines in the figure represent one direct interlock each to the corporations listed on the right side of the figure. Also remember, however, that these lines are multiplied many, many times as they result in indirect interlocks among all of the corporations listed in Figure 8-1.

The Inner Group of the Corporate Class

Evidence such as that above leads many researchers to suggest that economic institutions are far more concentrated than in the past. A relatively small number of corporate giants with various ties among themselves have come to dominate the economy, and through this domination have obtained tremendous political influence as well. What these corporations do, or fail to do, has major consequences for millions of people in this country and throughout the world. Other major institutions—such as the family, education, the polity, even religion—cannot fully be understood in isolation from these powerful economic institutions (see Useem 1979a).

In one sense, it may be said that these economic institutions themselves represent the top of the stratification system. In response to some writers such as Domhoff and Dye who ask "Who rules America?" or "Who's running America?" others have asked "What rules America?" (Hacker 1975). It is true that these institutions seem to gain an existence separate from individuals who may have some ownership or positions of authority within them. The people come and go, but Bank of America, General Motors, and Exxon live on and on.

IT&T, for example, continues to function with its own set of economic interests of profit and growth even through Sosthenes Behn (the founder) and

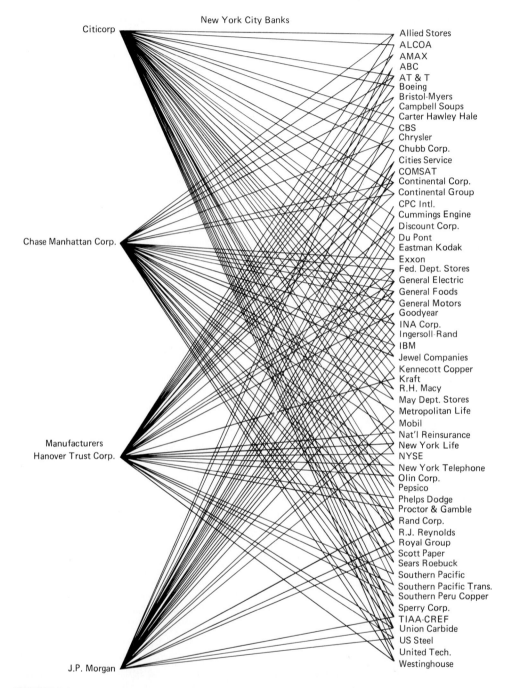

FIGURE 8-1
Some of the corporate interlocks from the largest four New York banks. *Source:* U.S. Senate (1980).

Harold Geneen (the most famous chief executive officer and board chairman) are gone. Ruling-class theorists resist the idea that these economic institutions are independent of the upper-class people or families who own and, in their view, control these corporations. But in the view of others, the concentration of economic resources and collective independence of these institutions have created a new class. This new corporate class owes its position at the top of the stratification system to the power of these corporate institutions. It consists of the board members and executive officers charged with making the decisions and carrying out the activities that give these institutions life.

We began our discussion of this corporate class by suggesting that it was made up of people holding positions of authority in major corporations. But among these board members and top corporate officers there is a group that some suggest represents an even more elite group—the inner group of the capitalist class or corporate class. What are the characteristics of this inner group and of the people who are in this inner group? What function does this inner group serve for the overall dominance of large economic institutions? A good place to begin in our search for this group is among the mass of interlocking directorates already identified at the top of these corporate structures. Much research remains to be done, but we do have some recent information that proves very interesting.

At the outset it is important to recognize that of the mass of interlocking directorates previously discussed, most interlocks are accounted for by a relatively small number of people. For example, in a study of the biggest 797 corporations in 1969, Mariolis (1975) found that of 8,623 board members of these corporations, 7,051 had only one board position (that is, were not interlocked with another corporation). The interlocks were therefore accounted for by the 1,572 remaining board members.

What are the characteristics of this unique group of multiple board members? Allen has compiled interesting information on board members who had four or more director positions in the 250 top corporations in 1970. As we might expect from data on banks discussed earlier, a rather high number of these multiple board members were executive officers from large banks (27 percent). But also interesting is that 81.4 percent made their careers by coming up within a corporation, rather than having much inherited wealth. Another 4.3 percent gained their high status by founding a successful business. Only 14.3 percent of these multicorporate directors were members of the upper class as defined by Domhoff.

In similar research, Useem (1978) also found that executives from large financial institutions (such as banks) had more board memberships. And within each corporation Soref (1976) found that board members who are outside directors (that is, those who are not managers from within the same corporation) tended to have more board positions in other corporations. In addition, it will be remembered from Dooley's study that the larger corporations had more interlocking directorates with other corporations. We can therefore conclude that board members from larger corporations have more board positions. Finally, as with Allen's study, Dye's (1979:179) research indicates that 89 percent of top executives and board members of the largest 201 corporations (of the types noted above) worked their way up the corporate ladder to these highest positions.

A growing number of researchers maintain that the old upper class made up of wealthy families is less important than it once was (Alba and Moore 1982; Barton 1985). The above study by Allen (1978) showing few upper-class multiboard members in 1970 (14.3 percent) seems to confirm this belief. But there is conflicting evidence. In a study of top corporate board members who were members of two or more boards *and* an executive officer of one major corporation, Useem (1978, 1984) found that those with more positions in corporate boards were more likely to be members of upper-class social clubs.

In another study, using a sample of board members from fifty-one of the top 121 corporations, Soref (1976) found that upper-class board members had a greater number of board memberships than board members who were not upper class (average of 3.49 for upper-class people, 2.0 for the others). What this conflicting evidence appears to suggest is that, as Allen found, few of the board members come from *family backgrounds* of great wealth, but they do have a tendency to belong to upper-class social clubs (as Useem and Soref have found). It seems, therefore, that these upper-class social clubs are more open to corporate-class members who lack upper-class family backgrounds than in the past. The importance of these social clubs and other organizations previously seen as upper-class institutions will be considered below.

We have finally to discuss a very useful study by Useem (1976b) that, in addition to identifying this inner group, helps us understand something of its function for corporate for corporate-class unity and influence. Useem began with the 8,623 directors of the top 797 corporations in 1969 compiled by Mariolis (1975). Useem grouped these corporate directors by the number of director positions held by each one (from one to four and more). He found that the more corporate director positions held, the more likely the person was (1) to be a director of a nonprofit organization (such as a large foundation or a university), (2) to serve on an advisory commission or agency in the federal government, and (3) to be a member of important business organizations such as the Business Council or the Council on Foreign Relations.

In summarizing these findings on the inner group of the corporate class we discover that members of this group:

Tend to have more positions on corporate boards.

Are more likely to be board members of larger corporations.

Often represent large banks on corporate boards.

More often belong to elite social clubs.

Have worked their way up the corporate ladder to top positions rather than started at the top from wealthy family backgrounds.

Represent general corporate interests in other institutions such as foundations, universities, and the government.

Within the corporate class (as defined above), therefore, we find an elite group that makes up an inner circle having more corporate contacts. But is there any special significance in this inner group of the corporate class, or does it simply represent the most respected members of the corporate class? Useem (1978, 1979b, 1984), for one, argues that this inner group has an important function for the structure of corporate concentration today. Most importantly, this inner group functions to tie the large corporations together more. To the extent that these large corporations have common economic interests, the inner group of the corporate class helps unite these corporations so they may act upon their common interests.

One set of common interests, of course, is the political environment. When members of this inner group find their way into positions of political authority (such as the President's cabinet or advisory agencies) they are more able to speak for the interests of large corporations as a whole, rather than the separate interests of one corporation. Also, this inner group may be able to coordinate corporate activities in combating challenges to the common interests of large corporations.

Whitt (1979) has found, for example, that corporations have organized their activities to confront popular referendums to establish such things as mass transit or regulate pollution. When one effort was made to fund mass transit in California, major oil companies together spent thousands of dollars to defeat the referendum. What is interesting about this coordinated effort is that the oil companies contributed to this fund in direct proportion to the amount of gas they sold in the state. Someone, in other words, was able to unite these oil companies to the extent that a detailed plan for defeating this mass transit issue established what they saw as a fair method of funding the campaign.

In another example, Whitt found major banks in California coordinating their activities to defeat a mass transit issue in the same manner. It was somehow determined that $10,000 was needed and banks were assessed a certain amount so that the exact total was obtained. We have no information on who was responsible for the coordination among these banks and oil companies, but it seems clear that members of an inner group with wide corporate ties were in strategic positions to achieve this coordination.

The unity and coordinating functions of social clubs and business organizations must also be considered. In our earlier discussion of these social clubs and business organizations the views of Domhoff and others were presented on the importance of these organizations for upper-class unity and coordination. But whether or not Domhoff is correct about the continued existence of a powerful upper class, it should be recognized that these social clubs and business organizations are able to perform the same coordinating functions for a corporate class as well. And as we have found with studies of the inner group of this corporate class, they, too, are frequent members of these organizations.

In fact, as Domhoff's (1974) study of the Bohemian Grove indicates, the participants at the retreat were more often corporate leaders than upper-class members. Thus, no matter whether an upper class or corporate class is seen as more important in the economy, these social clubs and business organizations (such as the Council on Foreign Relations and the Committee for Economic Development) may perform the same functions of unity and coordination for either group.

THE CONCENTRATION OF ECONOMIC AND POLITICAL POWER: SO WHAT?

Thus far we have been concerned with one basic question: Do we find that economic and political power in the United States is concentrated primarily in the hands of one particular class or group? In answering this question we have examined the arguments and data presented by two general perspectives. The first views economic and political power in the possession of an upper class; the second believes this power has passed to a new group—people with positions of authority in the highly concentrated corporate structure.

There are many variations among those who accept one of these two perspectives, and even some who argue that the old upper class and top corporate officials have merged into a unified capitalist class (Useem 1978, 1979b). Neither side claims an upper class or corporate elite has *complete* power or runs the nation's economy and government single-handedly. What they do claim is that either an upper class, corporate elite, or capitalist class, when compared with other interest groups, is better able to ensure that its interests are protected even in the face of opposition to these interests.

We do have something of a democracy in this country. When a strongly united population (something only rarely found) opposes the interests of a powerful group such as an upper class or corporate class, this population will be able to win concessions. But at the same time, because of the power of those on top, elites are able to minimize their losses and, in the long run, maintain their positions of dominance.

Now that we have examined in some detail the question of who or what group can be considered at the top of our system of stratification, we are left with a very important question that has been largely ignored. This question is "So what?" More precisely, if the various researchers followed above are correct in their assessments of the power of either an upper class or a corporate class, what does this mean for the more general society? What does this mean for the other 240 million people in the country? In what ways are their lives affected by the concentration of economic and political power?

There are, of course, the many aspects of inequality described early in this text. But we need to consider more directly the relation between these inequalities and the patterns of power outlined above. Upon closer examination it becomes evident that the relationship is not altogether clear. We may be able to obtain information suggesting that because one group, such as a corporate class, is able to achieve its goals, others are disadvantaged. For example, because of their power large corporations pay less to the federal government in taxes (see Salamon and Siegfried 1977; Jacobs 1988). But does this mean that individual taxpayers lose by having to pay more taxes? In the short run this conclusion may be accurate. One group of theorists, however, claims that in the long run the reduced taxes corporations may pay help economic expansion, resulting in higher wages and more jobs.

In attempting to answer the questions related to outcomes of political and economic concentration one of the main difficulties is accurate information. Too often we are forced to ask "what if" types of questions; we are required to estimate the life conditions for people in this nation "if" economic concentration in the hands of a small group of people in dominance did not exist. But as difficult as this type of analysis may be, there is a further problem. Because the issue of powerful elites so directly confronts our values of democracy and equality of opportunity in this society, the debates over the outcomes of this condition have often been clouded by these values. For the above reasons, as one might expect, there is much disagreement over the outcomes of elite concentration.

From our earlier discussion of general theories of social stratification in Chapter 4, it will be remembered that two basic perspectives have dominated. On the one hand we find functional theories that view stratification as necessary and in the best interests of the overall society. On the other hand we find one type of conflict theory that views stratification as a system resulting in the exploitation of one group by another.

As might be expected, we find the same perspectives divided over the question of elites (see Mintz 1989:222–225). *Functional elite* theories agree that elites of some type are able to dominate the economy and politics in advanced capitalist societies. But because of the nature of these societies they view elites as necessary and in the best interests of society as a whole. *Critical elite* theories also agree that elites of some type dominate. But in opposition to functional elite theories they argue that these elites work for their own selfish interests and to the detriment of classes below.

Not all writers who, because of the general thrust of their views, can be said to have one or the other perspective agree with each other on all points. Any categorization such as that between functional and critical elite theories creates an oversimplification on other points. But for our present purpose the dichotomy does serve to accent the differing views on the outcomes of elite domination. We will consider briefly each of these two perspectives on elites before examining a third—the pluralist view.

Functional Elite Theory

At the risk of some oversimplification we can summarize the major thrust of the views held by functional elite theorists. Most important, in their estimation, all societies have had some type of elite. And because societies have become larger and more complex, the need for elites has increased. As for political organization, the problems of maintaining order and governing an increasingly diverse population require an efficient group of governing elites with wide authority.

Gone are the days when citizens could gather and decide collectively what should be done; there are too many people with diverse interests for this method of governing to be realistic. What is needed, in their view, are strong elites with wide authority to subordinate the more diverse separate interests within the society to the more general, long-range interests of the society as a whole. Also, to deal adequately with the challenges confronting advanced societies, experts with wide knowledge are needed in decision-making positions. As for the economy, highly technical systems of production and the large organizations needed to manage this production also require expert knowledge and people with wide authority for the efficient operation of these huge systems. Again, some type of elite is needed.

We find much consensus about the level of complexity and problems faced with managing large political and economic organizations in advanced industrial societies. But on the need for elites with much *independent authority* to make these decisions we find less agreement. The general assumption held by functional elite theorists is that these elites will usually make decisions that benefit society as a whole rather than the narrower interests of one group.

This point is stressed by one of the leading functional theorists in response to C. Wright Mills' *The Power Elite:* "The essential point at present is that, to Mills, power is not a facility for the performance of function in, and on behalf of, the society as a system, but is interpreted exclusively as a facility for getting what one group, the holders of power, wants by preventing another group, the 'outs,' from getting what it wants" (Parsons 1968:82). For Parsons (1970:27), "the prevalence of large scale organization certainly makes for inequalities in authority and power." Parsons does not quarrel with Mills' "facts," it is only the way Mills interprets these "facts" that bothers Parsons (1968:61). Elites are needed and benefit all in the society.

Parsons (1960:241) goes even further: "We must have a stronger government than we have traditionally been accustomed to, and we must come to trust it more fully." As Strasser (1976:178–179) puts it, "Parsons calls for a strengthening of the elite classes. ... What was a nightmare to C. Wright Mills, it seems, constitutes perfection of the social system to Talcott Parsons." In Parsons' (1970:55) own words, what is needed is a "functional equivalent of aristocracy."

Another theorist who can generally be placed in the functional elite category is Suzanne Keller (1963). Following Parsons, she also sees elites as necessary and beneficial for all in advanced industrial societies. What she calls *strategic elites* have "superior ability" (1963:66), are more "responsible" (1963:51), and work harder than other people (1963:58). These strategic elites are made up of people in positions of authority in a number of important institutions in the society. They must have much independence in making needed decisions in the society, although their independence should be checked by other elites (not from classes below).

Like Parsons, Keller (1963:26) accepts most of the "facts" presented by C. Wright Mills, but disagrees with his interpretation of them. The power possessed by modern elites is functional for all in the society, not just for elites (1963:263). Keller (1963:184–185), however, adds a new dimension in justifying elites in modern society: "If strategic elites are rich, honored, and admired, other members of society by virtue of their psychological identification with them also feel rich, honored, and admired. To oversimplify the point, the social superiority of their elites boosts the egos of the mass of men." What assurances does the society have that their elites will not work only for their own interests? As we have noted, Keller believes in part that other elites, not the classes below, will keep elites honest. But in the end, as Bachrach (1967:64) concludes, "Keller falls back on the conscience of the elite to refrain from abusing its privileged position."

We should mention the work of one other functional elite theorist. E. Digby Baltzell (1958, 1964) is interesting at this point because he diverges somewhat in his description of the type of elite he sees dominating the present United States. Where Parsons and Keller describe a new type of elite based on positions of authority in large political and economic institutions, Baltzell continues to regard the old upper class based on family wealth as primary. For Baltzell, a "Protestant establishment" or ruling class is in firm control in the United States and this is as it should be. Like other functional elite theorists, he feels these elites (upper class) have generally superior abilities.

But more important for Baltzell, the country needs elites who have "moral responsibility" so they will not abuse their power. For the upper class, this moral responsibility is taught in the upper-class institutions such as the elite prep schools. In Baltzell's (1958:60) words, "In any complex society, the problem of the individual abuse of power is a perennial one. Among other things, a sense of honor and morality, even a sense of *noblesse oblige,* serve to check the abuses of power." From this he concludes (1958:63), "The lesson of history then is the fact that a strong and autonomous upper class . . . is one of the important bulwarks of freedom against an all-inclusive totalitarian power." Thus, we must rely on the upper-class tradition of service and moral responsibility to keep us free.

The functional elite theorists seldom cite specific examples of why we are better off with independent elites in control of the country, other than to mention social and political stability. Often, however, the fact that this country has one of the highest standards of living is offered as an outcome of dominance by an elite with superior abilities. The strength of the economy, the economic power of the nation abroad, and our high level of technology are also seen by some as evidence of the benefits of our present system of economic concentration.

Critical Elite Theory

A key in understanding the principal differences between functional and critical elite theories is found with their assumptions about human nature and society. As discussed in an earlier chapter, functional theorists tend to assume that a strong moral order is at the root of social and political stability. This moral order helps restrain naked self-interest. Thus, we find Parsons, Keller, and especially Baltzell stressing that elites in part work for the common good because of their traditions of service and social responsibility.

For Baltzell, the upper class is particularly well suited to rule the country because of the traditions of responsibility acquired in the upper-class social-ization process. Critical elite theorists, on the other hand, reject the idea of a moral order that can restrain individual or group self-interest, especially in a capitalist society that is based on principles of individual profit. It is not that they see human nature as necessarily greedy and selfish, but that people under present conditions have come to internalize these selfish motivations (see Mills 1962:39; Atkinson 1972:36).

Because of these assumptions, contrary to functional theorists, critical elite theorists view society not as an integrated whole but as a setting for conflict and domination. They view societies as divided into classes that have basic interests that are in conflict. The result is that when one class is able to dom-inate it will work primarily for its own narrow interests. Elites, of course, do not always find they must make decisions that lead to benefits for themselves only. In many cases the good of the nation as a whole (themselves included) is furthered by elite activities. But when the interests of elites are in conflict with those of other groups, unless the other groups can mobilize an unusual amount of counterpressure, the interests of elites will win the day. In short, critical elite theorists are skeptical of power and influence overly concentrated in the hands of one or a few groups.

In the works of critical elite theorists such as Mills, Domhoff, Harrison and Bluestone (1988), Blumberg (1980), and more Marxian-oriented writers such as Bottomore (1964, 1966), Miliband (1969, 1977), and Anderson (1974), the an-swer to the question "So what?" leads to a long list of social and economic problems. The consequences of elite domination for other classes range from poverty, poor health, more industrial accidents, and worker alienation, to the energy crisis, war, and pollution. The validity and details of these charges will be considered at many points in the following chapters. The outcomes of eco-nomic concentration in this country and in the world for developing nations (or the Third World) will also be taken up in our final chapter on world stratifica-tion. But at this time we can consider briefly a couple of examples of economic concentration in general.

With regard to economic concentration in general, critical elite theorists can argue that important outcomes have been lower productivity and less effi-ciency in industry and an increasingly lower level of industrial technology in the United States when compared with that of other nations. We have noted above that economic productivity, research and development spending by cor-porations, and our country's share of the world market have all gone down in recent years as economic concentration has increased (Blumberg 1980; Bowles, Gordon, and Weisskopf 1983; Etzioni 1984; Harrison and Bluestone 1988). It is reasonable to ask if this corporate political power and corporate concentration in the United States are somehow related to the following con-ditions: The United States has one of the highest rates of workers killed among industrial nations; workers have less say about how U.S. corporations are run than in any other industrial nation; workers in this country have fewer benefits such as health care and sick leave; it is easier to lay off workers in this country compared to others (Magaziner and Reich 1982); corporations in the U.S. have a lower tax rate than in most other nations and lower than in any other time in U.S. history; and the income gap in the United States between executives and new workers in basic industries like the auto industry is 37 to 1 compared to 7 to 1 in Japan (Abegglen and Stalk 1985:192; *Wall Street Journal,* April 18, 1984).

The oil and energy crisis that first burst into the national consciousness in the early 1970s, which will no doubt return, and its relation to pollution and the environmental crisis of today provides us with an interesting example of some outcomes of corporate power and concentration.

In our discussion of this case we must be relatively brief, considering the amount of information now available. We can, however, cover some of the most important points raised by writers critical of the oil corporations' role in what is called the energy crisis and pollution. In short, these critics argue that the energy problem stems from (1) the power of the oil industry in the economy, (2) its historical influence over government policy, and, thus, (3) its ability to make sure that its interests are met even when these interests conflict with the long-run interests of the nation as a whole. (For a summary of these points from a critical elite point of view, see Harrington 1976:236–264.) From the perspective of short-term profit maximization, the economic interests of oil corporations are to create a public dependence on their product and to control both supply and prices.

With respect to the United States' dependency on oil, it is important to recognize that this nation uses more oil and has fewer alternatives in doing so than any other industrial nation. In part, our higher consumption of oil products is related to our high standard of living. But critical elite theorists charge that this is only part of the explanation. More important for our present examination has been the ability of oil corporations (often working with mutually concerned corporations such as auto manufacturers) to create a national dependency on oil.

Several methods have been used to create this dependency. One has been to prevent the federal and local governments from funding adequate mass transit systems. If funded on a large scale, mass transit would reduce our dependency on oil, as it has in all other industrial nations. The most significant example of industry action in this area occurred in the early 1950s, when the federal government was faced with the alternative of funding mass transit systems around the country or putting these funds into a program to further develop a large system of interstate highways. At this time the oil and auto industry lobbies were able to use their resources to push the federal government toward the second alternative (Harrington 1976).

In an even earlier case, other methods were used in limiting mass transit. In the 1930s Los Angeles had what was described as one of the best mass transit systems in the country. But it was closed before the end of the 1930s. In a 1974 Senate antitrust investigation it was found that shortly before this mass transit system was closed it was bought jointly by Chevron, General Motors, and Firestone (see Sampson 1975:154). In years since, the voters in California have been given the chance to support state-funded mass transit. But in almost every case massive funding by large corporations (primarily oil companies) in support of campaigns to block mass transit has contributed to the defeat of these propositions (for details, see Whitt 1979).

Other examples often cited as contributing to our dependence on oil include the oil companies' substantial ownership of alternative energy sources (such as coal, which has not been fully utilized) and their reluctance to develop energy-saving devices. An end result of all this has been a high dependence on oil that has assured the oil industry its product will remain in high demand *even when the price of oil is high.*

The next step in the process for oil companies has been to acquire control over the supply of oil. From the time of John D. Rockefeller's rise in the oil industry it was recognized that the oil business was risky without adequate control of the supply. If too much oil is discovered or produced, the market is flooded and the price of oil will go down. To guard against this problem the oil industry worked very early to limit oil by secret agreements among its members.

Before World War II, for example, the major oil companies agreed to limit the production of Middle Eastern oil to keep the supply low (see Sampson 1975:131; Blair 1976:34–49). As a further step in this process, the major oil producers in the industry have consistently worked to reduce competition and therefore control prices and limit production by keeping other companies out of the rich oil fields in the Middle East (Sampson 1975:60–79). And as in other industries, there have been a number of government regulations that have helped the oil industry by limiting the supply of oil (see Blair 1976:152–171, for a list of these regulations).

The above examples of activity to maintain our dependency on oil and control both the supply and prices help us understand in part why the oil industry was able to achieve more than a 300 percent increase in gasoline prices without a significant consistent drop in consumption during the 1970s. One must also consider the part played by the oil-producing nations through OPEC. The oil companies, however, are not without blame in this respect. For one thing the price of oil sold in this country has gone up much *faster* than OPEC price increases (Blair 1976). But more importantly it seems the oil industry contributed to a situation making OPEC actions possible.

Many writers have argued, and OPEC nations have admitted, that it is only because an oil cartel was developed by the major oil companies to begin with that OPEC nations were able to step in and control this oil cartel for their own interests (see Sampson 1975; Blair 1976). Our dependency on Middle East oil stems in large measure from the industry's pursuit of quick profits while ignoring the long-run danger of this dependency. The early high profits in this area of the world were the result of the oil companies' ability to influence both

Middle Eastern leaders and our own to establish policies that kept production costs low.

An important part of the process occurred on our side of the world when the federal government (on the urging of the oil and gas lobby) began allowing oil companies in the 1950s to count fees paid to foreign governments as foreign taxes to be subtracted directly from the oil companies' federal taxes (Sampson 1975:110; Blair 1976:199). During the 1970s, for example, oil companies paid less federal income tax than all other corporations. The top five oil companies in this country at the time made about 60 percent of their profits abroad. None of this profit was subject to federal taxes (Sampson 1975:110–111).

As a result the return on investments with foreign operations by oil companies was higher than with any other industry (Sampson 1975:232). It became *much more profitable* for oil companies to produce and explore for oil in the Middle East than in our own country. Our dependency on foreign oil increased over the years as other sources of oil and other types of energy were neglected. Thus, critics of the oil companies charge that because of the pursuit of quick profits the stage was set for OPEC action in the 1970s that further increased our energy crisis.

In conclusion, critical elite theorists can charge that the power of a corporate class working for its own narrow interests produced a situation that has not been in the interests of the nation as a whole. It is true that the oil industry created something of a problem for itself by provoking the OPEC reaction. But it can also be argued that this problem is relatively minor, and in fact may be turned into an advantage. With oil company profits increasing more rapidly than OPEC price increases, with the price of oil produced in this country now allowed by the government to rise to the OPEC price level, and with other types of support coming from the government to stimulate domestic production, the oil companies have been able to turn a crisis into another advantage for themselves.

For the rest of the country the result has been higher home heating and gasoline prices, lines at gasoline stations, reduced pollution standards, more overall inflation, and higher unemployment due to a recession in 1979–1983 that has been attributed in part to the energy problem. Added to the list is the U.S. involvement in war in the Middle East in the 1990s to protect oil supplies. Had the oil companies not been able to pressure the government into adopting the policies noted above, had there been more *effective* control with the interests of the nation as a whole in mind, and had the oil companies not possessed such economic power in general, critical elite theorists argue, the energy crisis might not have developed.

The Pluralist Response

Thus far we have considered only elite theories in describing the outcomes of elite concentration in this country. But there is another perspective that rejects critical elite and functional elite explanations by arguing that an elite (whether an upper class, corporate class, or some other type of elite) does *not* have dominant and independent power in the United States. Pluralists agree that there are important leaders who have more authority and extensive influence, but they see these leaders as responsive to many organized interest groups from below.

Before we describe the pluralist perspective in more detail it will be useful to compare this perspective to critical and functional elite theories in response to three key questions. Table 8-8, which represents the disagreements among the three perspectives on these key questions, is not meant to suggest that these are the only points of disagreement, or that all the theories fit neatly into the categories listed. But it does help us understand some of the major issues dividing these theorists.

Among the issues dividing theorists on the top of the stratification system are the following:

1 Are powerful elites of some type necessary for stability and efficient economic and political organization in advanced industrial societies? Or can complex industrial societies operate effectively with a relatively high degree of democracy, allowing major input into the decision-making process from interest groups below the elite level?

2 Do powerful elites (of any type) usually lead to exploitation because the interests of those in control are served at the expense of the interests of other groups? Or can the total society, under certain conditions, benefit more by a rule of responsible elites?

3 Are advanced industrial societies such as the United States presently dominated by some type of elite or elites?

Referring to Table 8-8, we find that critical elite theorists generally agree that (1) dominant elites are not necessary in advanced industrial societies, (2) powerful elites are by nature exploitative and work primarily for their own narrow interests, and (3) we presently find some type of elite dominating in the United States. Functional elite theorists generally agree that (1) some type of

TABLE 8-8
THREE PERSPECTIVES ON THREE QUESTIONS ABOUT ELITES

Three general issues in the debate	Critical elite theories	Functional elite theories	Pluralists
1. Are powerful independent elites needed in advanced industrial societies?	No	Yes	No
2. Do powerful and independent elites necessarily lead to exploitation?	Yes	No	Yes
3. Is the United States presently dominated by some type of elite (or elites)?	Yes	Yes	No

elite is needed in advanced industrial societies; (2) powerful elites are not by nature exploitative, but can contribute to the overall well-being of all or most in the society; and (3) we presently find elites of some type with extensive power in the United States. Pluralists generally agree that (1) an all-powerful ruling elite is not necessary or inevitable in advanced industrial societies, (2) ruling elites (that is, elites *not* restrained by pressure groups from below) are by nature exploitative of other groups and classes, and (3) we do not presently find elites in dominant power in the United States.

Thus, while pluralists tend to agree with critical elite theorists that elites are not inevitable and that they are by nature exploitative of other groups, they disagree with critical elite theorists over their estimation of the present independent power of wealthy, corporate, and/or political elites in this country. Pluralists and critical elite theorists *may* agree on the type of political and economic organization viewed as ideal in serving the best interests of the society as a whole. We say *may* agree, for there are a number of concepts of an ideal society, ranging from the old concept of *laissez-faire* political democracy and individualistic capitalistic competition to democratic socialism with the state (though a state that is more responsive to wider interests in society) having more influence over the economy in the interests of the nation as a whole.

Pluralist theory has been one of the longest accepted explanations of political and economic stratification among sociologists and political scientists in the United States. The key argument is that although there are elites in authority positions in the economy, politics, the courts, education, and all other institutions in society, these elites do not have independent power. Their activities and decisions are restrained not so much by traditions of service and honor as by the counterpressures from organized groups below the elite level.

All collective interests that a group of people may have can be represented through interest groups or voluntary associations. Of these voluntary associations, Arnold Rose (1967:247) writes, through them "the ordinary citizen can acquire as much power in the community or the nation as his free time, ability, and inclination permit. . . . Political power, or influence, in the United States is not concentrated in the government, but is distributed over as many citizens, working through their associations, as want to take the responsibility for power."

Another pluralist, Robert Dahl (1958, 1961, 1967) describes the significance of what he calls *political resources* in the operation of power in the United States. Political resources include anything that can be used to gain influence, such as money, credit, control over jobs, control over information, group solidarity, time, and numbers of people (Dahl 1961:226). Most important, these political resources are described as *dispersed inequalities,* meaning that no group is without any of these and that those groups better off with respect to some political resources have few of other types.

Having summarized a few of the main points of the pluralist perspective, we must note that this perspective has lost the overwhelming acceptance it once had in sociology and political science. There is still support for this theory in its application to community power structures, but on the national level pluralists have mainly remained silent or moved to one of the elite perspectives in recent years. Since 1967 (with the work of Dahl and Rose) we find few major works from the pluralist perspective.

In the early 1960s there was a revival of pluralism, mainly as a response to C. Wright Mills' view in *The Power Elite* (as Rose 1967:39 states in beginning his book). But for at least two reasons this revival of pluralism, at least in describing the national levels of power, has weakened. For one thing, the political mood of the country, which affects social scientists as well as the general population, has changed. With events such as Vietnam, Watergate, the energy crisis, and numerous other political scandals and investigations during the 1980s, people are beginning to consider the question of elites more seriously (see Theodore Lowi 1973:ix).

The second reason pertains to the amount of empirical evidence slowly building on the nature and existence of powerful elites in this country. No doubt stimulated by the political scandals and mood of the country, several kinds of research have made it difficult to deny the power of corporate and political elites in the United States. Thus, the pluralist position has not been given undue attention in our discussion of the top of the stratification system.

Still, the pluralist perspective has provided us with many valid insights into the operation of power and influence in the United States. It is clear that economic or political (or any other type) elites in this country are not all-powerful. Their influence is countered from time to time by interest groups from below the elite level. All elite theories in varying degrees admit this influence from below.

And most elite theories have made concessions to the pluralists' arguments in recent years (see Kerbo and Della Fave 1979). But though they agree on some details, the overall thrust and implications of functional and critical elite theories differ significantly from those of pluralists. Elite theorists recognize that power is complex and that many interest groups are contending for power and influence in many social, political, and economic arenas in this country, but when considering the most important issues that face the nation and looking beyond the day-to-day power struggles that always continue, they see some type of elite or elites having the most influence over what happens in this nation.

In other words, when looking above the smaller conflicts to the big decisions that in the long run affect strongly how wealth is distributed or how people live and earn their livings, functional and critical elite theorists see an upper class, corporate class, strategic elites, or some other powerful group in dominance. (For an excellent critique of pluralism in these terms from a ruling-class perspective, see Domhoff 1983:203–210.)

THE CORPORATE CLASS: CONCLUSION

The primary task of Chapters 7 and 8 has been to describe the structural base of elite power and privilege in the stratification system of the contemporary United States. Much of the description applies to other noncommunist industrial societies (see Scott 1979), although the unique aspects of each nation must not be overlooked. For example, there is evidence to suggest that corporate elites are more independently powerful in the United States. We saw in Chapter 6 (see Table 6-4) that private ownership (in contrast to state ownership) and control of large corporations are much more extensive in the United States. In addition, corporate elites are more likely to participate in the highest levels of government in the United States.

Despite political rhetoric, it is also evident that state regulation of the economy and restraints on corporate elites are greater in other industrial nations (Thurow 1980). This was especially true with the Reagan administration, which was one of the most favorable to big business in United States history. And it must be recognized that the United States is virtually alone among industrial societies in the absence of worker representatives on major corporate boards of directors (Magaziner and Reich 1982). Finally, as we will see in Chapter 10, the United States is far behind other industrial nations with respect to welfare reforms benefiting nonelites. But given the present lack of cross-national research on elite power, the conclusion that corporate elites are more independently powerful in the United States must be tentative.

To summarize briefly what has been shown in Chapters 7 and 8: The basis of corporate and upper-class power in the United States rests upon:

1 Private (including intercorporate) ownership and control of major means of production (that is, large corporations).

2 The tremendous growth and size of these major corporations.

3 The extensive intercorporate network (based upon intercorporate stock control, interlocking directorates, and social ties among economic elites).

4 The influence these economic elites have in political institutions (through campaign contributions, lobby organizations, the policy-formation process, and direct participation in government).

Another very important means of economic elite influence is found in the legitimation process, which, because of its importance, will be discussed separately in Chapter 12.

In the earlier history of capitalism in the United States it was clear that wealthy upper-class families dominated major corporations. Today, such upper-class family dominance is less clear. The present chapter has provided evidence suggesting that a new group, a corporate class, has now become dominant at the top of the stratification system.

In reality, of course, there are upper-class families with continued ownership and influence in major corporations alongside the new corporate class. Historical trends, however, seem to favor the increasing dominance of a corporate class. But the *means* of influence held by an upper class are still operative. A corporate class can easily step into power on a foundation established by earlier upper-class family dominance.

After noting the (at least partial) shift from upper-class family dominance to the emergence of corporate-class dominance it is fair to ask whether it makes any difference for the more general society which of the two classes dominates.

Recent evidence seems to suggest that it doesn't. It was once believed that upper-class family control had given way to managerial control of rather independent corporations. A result of this new managerial control, it was argued, were corporations less concerned with maximizing corporate profits at the expense of other classes and social concerns (''soulful corporations''; see Berle and Means 1932; Burnham 1941).

However, when comparing corporations still owned and controlled by family interests with corporations not controlled by family interests, research shows these corporations do not differ with respect to profit-maximizing behavior (Larner 1970; James and Soref 1981). The managerial-control thesis neglected the extensive intercorporate ties and continued stress on profits that would force managers of each corporation to drive for profits and growth or be fired. The rules of the corporate game are the same, even if old upper-class families have lost some control to a corporate class.

Finally, what is most important for our present discussion is that whether a corporate class, upper class, or mixture of the two is on top of the stratification system in this country, we must understand the structure of corporate capitalism if we are to have an adequate understanding of the nature of social stratification in the United States. This structure of corporate capitalism and the power of those at the top affect the life chances of those below the top— the middle class, the working class, and the poor.

Those below the top are not totally powerless (as we will see), but there is an underlying relationship of class conflict that limits the individual and collective objectives of those below the top. Having examined the top in some detail, we must now move down the stratification system one step at a time to examine the place of the middle class, the working class, and the poor.

THE MIDDLE AND WORKING CLASSES

In the eyes of nineteenth-century Europeans, the founding and survival of the United States of America seemed one of the most radical developments in the history of human societies. True, some nations, like France, had embarked upon their road to "equality and fraternity" with revolution. But by the early 1800s the French Revolution of 1789 had grown cold. The new dictatorship of Napoleon Bonaparte was in many ways a major reversal for these egalitarian principles—a reversal that would last for many years.

So it was that the Frenchman Alexis de Tocqueville was "startled" by what he saw as a condition of "equality" in this new country of America. From his travels throughout the United States in the 1830s he wrote the famous work *Democracy in America,* which began with the words, "No novelty in the United States struck me more vividly during my stay there than the equality of conditions" (1969:9). Somewhat later in this work he wrote, "Men there are nearer equality in wealth and mental endowments, or, in other words, more nearly equally powerful, than in any other country of the world or in any other age of recorded history" (1969:56).

In one sense, de Tocqueville's observations were quite correct. The United States was among the industrializing nations in which the level of inequality found in feudal societies was being rapidly reduced. Furthermore, in the United States this process of industrialization was proceeding without the strong tradition of aristocratic inequality found throughout Europe. One purpose of de Tocqueville's writing was to warn his European contemporaries of the "hidden dangers" of this new "equality"; that is, of the "tyranny of the majority" and the "restlessness in the midst of prosperity." This theme of the "excesses of equality and democracy" led some writers, such as Baltzell (1958), to defend upper-class traditions and power once they were established in this country.

In another sense, de Tocqueville's observations were misleading. These observations of equality and democracy were made through the eyes of a man accustomed to rigid and still quite pronounced class inequalities in Europe. Although there was a greater *degree* of equality and democracy in this new country, the inequalities of wealth and power were still there. The wealth of our Founding Fathers is well known and, as many have argued, our federal government and Constitution were constructed in such a way as to protect the economic interests of wealthy planters, financiers, and merchants (see Morgan 1956 for a summary of this argument). Perhaps most important, as we saw in Chapter 7, by the later 1800s a national upper class emerged in this country that in many ways resembled the European upper class based in aristocratic traditions.

In direct contrast to de Tocqueville's observations is a Marxian perspective on the growth of capitalism in the United States. As we have seen, a wealthy and powerful upper class did develop based upon ownership of the most important means of production—quite in line with Marxian analysis. The stark contrast between the living conditions of this relatively small group of propertied families and those of the rapidly growing industrial proletariat was all too clear.

However, neither is this historical analysis of the United States without inaccuracies. It is true that ownership and power became more concentrated through time, but the industrial proletariat (or working class) did not grow to the point of including the vast majority of people in this country, nor did their material conditions always grow steadily worse. There was another process at work, one that led to a large new middle class of white-collar workers as a buffer between the two main classes in Marxian theory.

The present chapter will examine the place and life conditions of the two *numerically* dominant classes in the United States system of stratification. As is typical in writings on the American class system, much of this chapter will be devoted to the standard of living, lifestyle, attitudes, and social behavior of these two classes. Equally important, our task will be to locate and describe the position of these two great classes in the more general system of power and social stratification in this country. By doing so we will be able to understand better the forces producing differences in lifestyle, attitudes, and social behavior.

Before proceeding it is important to note why two chapters have examined the top of the stratification system and only one has been reserved for the vast majority of middle- and working-class people in this country. It is because we must fully understand the most powerful upper and corporate classes, their positions, and their interests if we are to understand the present subject. The middle and working classes are not totally powerless, and we are not saying that "whatever future they have will not be of their own making" (Mills 1953:ix). Collectively, the middle and working classes do make history, and much of what the dominant classes do must be done with the potential power of these two classes in mind.

In other words, contrary to mass-society theory, which maintains that the majority of people in our society are shaped and molded in a rather passive manner by the power elite, we must recognize that although the agenda for action is usually set by the dominant classes, the two great classes are not idle bystanders. How they respond, how they (at times) collectively react to challenge events set in motion by the dominant classes, is important in understanding the nature of these events and their outcome in this nation.

There is yet another reason for examining both the middle and working classes in the same chapter; in some ways they are becoming more similar. Although this point should not be overstressed, there are twin processes, usually referred to by the heavy terms *embourgeoisement* and *proletarianization,* that are pushing the middle and working classes together. Embourgeoisement means that in some ways the working class is becoming more like the middle class, while proletarianization means that in other ways the middle class is becoming more like the working class. Again, these twin concepts must not be accepted without criticism, although they do have some validity (as shown below).

With these introductory statements in mind we may proceed by examining first the place of the middle and working classes in occupational, authority, and property structures that shape the nature of stratification in the United States. In doing so we will examine also the size and distribution of resources among these two classes. Then we will describe the growth of the middle class, the change and stability of the working class, and some of the most important nonmaterial consequences of their class positions (such as attitudes toward work, lifestyle, political involvement, and subcultural characteristics). Last, but certainly not least important, we will consider the position of people in these two classes with respect to the overall system of power stratification (with a focus on economic and political conflict in this country).

THE MIDDLE CLASS AND WORKING CLASSES IN THE SYSTEM OF SOCIAL STRATIFICATION

In Chapter 6 (see Table 6-8) the place of the middle and working classes in the overall system of stratification was outlined with reference to the occupational, bureaucratic authority, and property structures in this society. At this point we must expand upon this outline, as well as note the diversity within these two classes. We can begin with the middle class.

With respect to the *occupational structure,* the *middle class* is located within a range of occupations ranked (in terms of complexity and skill) from the highest (such as the traditional professions of doctor and lawyer, accountants, architects, higher-level scientists, and engineers) to mid-level (such as public school teachers, insurance agents, sales clerks, and office workers). There is a wide range of income and education levels within this grouping of occupations, but they do have some important common characteristics.

One of these is the general type of work performed, which can be described as *nonmanual,* in contrast to manual or physical labor. These people are typically involved in less strenuous or less physically demanding labor, labor that involves working with symbols or abstract ideas or talking with people. Because it is not "dirty work"—that is, working with oily machines, digging ditches, or constructing buildings—it is often labeled *white-collar* work. And white-collar labor does have a higher status. In part, most people feel they have higher status when they leave for work wearing a suit rather than overalls or "work clothes."

Another common characteristic of white-collar labor is a requirement of average to above average education (that is, from a high school to a college-level education). To perform white-collar labor means using abstract ideas or numbers or writing reports—in short, using skills that must usually be obtained through the educational system (in contrast to physical skills, which may often be learned in short periods of time).

A wide range of skill levels is used in white-collar labor, and some manual-labor tasks demand a skill and knowledge higher than those demanded by lower-level white-collar occupations (for example, compare office jobs involving nothing more than adding a few simple numbers with manual jobs requiring an extensive knowledge of electricity; Wright et al. 1982). But despite the wide range in job complexity and a small overlap with some manual-labor occupations in terms of skill level, the nonmanual versus manual distinction remains useful.

Before turning to working-class positions in the occupational structure, let us note the useful distinction commonly made between upper-middle-class and lower-middle-class occupations. The upper middle class is at the very top of the occupational structure, with jobs bringing high rewards and requiring higher levels of education (such as a postgraduate college degree). In one sense the distinction between upper- and lower-middle-class occupations is a matter of degree, but the boundary (though somewhat arbitrary and often difficult to specify) is useful.

As we will see below, characteristics other than income and education level tend to differentiate upper-middle- and lower-middle-class people. And what was called the corporate class in the previous chapter may also be located toward the top of the occupational structure. However, the corporate class can be distinguished from the upper middle class in terms of position in the bureaucratic authority structure (with the corporate class on top) and control of the most important means of production.

Working-class people occupy mid-level to low positions within the occupational structure. Working-class occupations are characterized by relatively low skill level, lower education, and a lower degree of complexity, as well as manual instead of nonmanual labor. Working-class people are factory workers, truck drivers, plumbers, gas station attendants, welders, and so on. Their jobs are for the most part lower paying, less secure, and more physically demanding and dangerous.

As with the middle class, a further distinction is often made within the working class, about equally dividing it between skilled and unskilled working-class occupations. The more skilled jobs require more training (usually on the job or as an apprentice), are usually better paying and more secure, and provide higher job satisfaction. In contrast, unskilled jobs are less complex, require little training, are less secure, and are less rewarding both materially and psychologically. Of those who work in our society, the unskilled laborer is on the bottom of the occupational structure.

It must be remembered that the occupational structure is one of conflict and competition within the marketplace. In general, the greater the skill possessed by a worker, the greater the return in terms of material and psychological rewards. And as we will see below, a person's position in the occupational structure is related to many other aspects of his or her life.

Clearly, the occupational structure represents a system of continuous rankings (in terms of skill and job complexity) in which it is difficult to draw firm lines around upper-middle-class, lower-middle-class, and skilled and unskilled working-class occupations. The manual versus nonmanual distinction is less difficult to make, although even here there are a few relatively ambiguous occupational roles (such as computer repair). But we do find it useful to identify class positions, in part, through positioning in the occupational structure.

For most people, occupation influences much about what happens in their life, how others view them, and how they come to view themselves. However, there is another predominant social structure that produces social divisions and shapes the general nature of the stratification system in this country. People are also divided with respect to positions within *bureaucratic authority* structures.

The middle class usually occupies positions toward the middle of authority structures. Its members receive orders from above while giving orders to those below. In the large corporation they are the mid-level to lower-level managers who receive orders from the corporate elite, then pass along orders to lesser managers or workers on the shop floor. In government agencies they are the bureaucrats who receive orders from political elites and pass along orders to lesser bureaucrats or whatever type of low-level worker is associated with the government agency.

There is no simple congruence between position in the occupational structure and position in authority structures. Some workers are self-employed, and the nature of some authority structures leaves mid-level workers (in terms of occupation) on or close to the bottom of the authority structure. Examples of the latter would be legal secretaries in a law firm, case workers in a state welfare department (if we choose to assume that welfare recipients are not part of the work-oriented aspect of this authority structure), and teachers (again, if we choose to assume students are in some ways not part of this authority structure).

The working class usually occupies positions toward the bottom of all authority structures. Its members receive orders from many layers above and are seldom in a position to give orders to others. They are told what work to do, how it should be done, when, and how fast.

The middle and working classes are quite similar in their relation to the *property structure*. Their ownership of the major means of production in the society ranges from insignificant to totally nonexistent. (The vast majority of privately owned corporate stock is held by the most wealthy in our society.) There are two slight exceptions to this rule. Some who may be considered in the middle class own their own means of production—such as small store owners and owners of small repair shops, construction firms, or small factories. As we will see, however, what may be called the *petite bourgeoisie* can also be self-employed workers who own their tools and other machines. But when we consider the overall productive forces in the society, these self-employed workers are hardly significant in the economy.

And in one sense many in the middle and working class may have technical collective ownership of stock in major corporations. This technical ownership is in the form of accumulated pension funds that are often invested in corporate stock. For example, the California Employees Retirement System owns 0.27 percent of the stock in Exxon and 1.29 percent of the stock in BankAmerica (see U.S. Senate Committee on Governmental Affairs 1978a).

However, most important is that workers do *not* have control over this stock (that is, how the stock proxies are voted and the buying or selling of this stock). Most often the pension funds are managed by investment firms or bank trust departments. The increasing amount of stock owned by worker pension funds *may* represent potential influence in the property structure, but at present this potential influence is very seldom used by workers.

A rough estimate of the class distribution of the population in terms of the class categories employed in the present work is given in Table 9-1. From studies of the upper class and corporate class reviewed in previous chapters we can conclude that both these classes together represent about 1 percent of the population. Current studies of poverty in this country (reviewed in the next chapter) suggest that about 13 percent of the population is living in poverty and can thus be called the lower class. And census data suggest that about half the remaining population is middle class and about half working class; thus, about 43 percent of the population is middle class and 43 percent working class.

In estimating the class distribution of the population sociologists generally assume the class distribution of *families* by the occupational position of the

TABLE 9-1
ESTIMATE OF THE CLASS DISTRIBUTION OF
THE POPULATION

Class	Percentage of population
Upper class	0.5
Corporate class	0.5
Middle class	43
Working class	43
Lower class	13

head of the household (usually male; Curtis 1986). Traditionally this has presented few problems because only a small percentage of married women were in the labor force. However, this labor-force participation by women is changing, with about 60 percent of married women of working age now in the labor force; and women more often consider their own occupation when defining their class position (Davis and Robinson 1988). Given this change and the increasing recognition of sexual inequality, it is useful at this point to consider briefly the class position of women who are in the labor force, as well as that of minorities. The subject of female and minority-class inequality will be examined more fully later in this chapter.

Considering the racial and sexual distribution by *occupation*, Table 9-2 shows that employed women were in the middle class in 1988 more often than employed white men. However, within the middle class, women are more often in lower-middle-class occupations (such as clerical workers). Males, as seen in Table 9-2, were more often in the working class (by occupation).

Considering the racial and sexual distribution of class in terms of authority positions, Table 9-3 shows that black males, white females, and black females are all more likely to be found in Wright and Perrone's (1977; also see Wright et al. 1982) working-class category (that is, nonowners with no authority). This is especially so with both black and white females, since Wright and Perrone's working-class category includes clerical and services workers who have no subordinates on the job. Generally, Robinson and Kelley (1979:46) found the same low authority position for women.

We can conclude from Tables 9-2 and 9-3 that although women have somewhat higher occupational positions (due to more lower-level white-collar occupations for women) they have less authority than men. Minorities (both male

TABLE 9-2
OCCUPATIONAL DISTRIBUTION BY SEX AND RACE IN 1988

Occupation	% of employed					
	All	**Male**	**Female**	**Whites**	**Blacks**	**Hispanic**
Managerial & professional	25.4	25.5	25.2	26.5	15.4	13.2
Technical, sales, & administrative support	30.9	19.7	44.6	31.2	27.8	25.0
Total white-collar	56.3	45.2	68.9	57.7	43.2	38.2
Service	13.3	9.6	17.9	12.1	23.1	18.9
Production, craft, and repair	11.9	19.7	2.3	12.3	8.8	13.5
Operators and laborers	15.5	20.9	8.9	14.7	22.9	23.9
Farm, forestry, and fishing	3.0	4.5	1.1	3.2	1.9	5.4
Total blue-collar	43.7	54.7	30.2	42.3	56.7	61.7

Source: U.S. Bureau of Labor Statistics, *Handbook of Labor Statistics,* 1989, Table 17, p. 78.

TABLE 9-3
WRIGHT AND PERRONE'S CLASS DIVISIONS (AUTHORITY AND OWNERSHIP) BY RACE
AND SEX

Class	White males, %	Black males, %	White females, %	Black females, %
Employers	10.9	6.6	3.0	0.0
Managers	42.9	36.8	27.7	22.9
Workers	41.5	55.3	66.6	77.1
Petite bourgeoisie	4.6	1.3	2.7	0.0
Total	100	100	100	100

Source: Wright and Perrone (1977:49).

and female) on the other hand, have both lower occupational positions and lower authority. Finally, white females, black females, and black males are all less likely to be employers (own their own means of production and employ others).

THE MIDDLE CLASS AND WORKING CLASS: RECENT HISTORICAL CHANGES

Class relations are seldom static. If nothing else, an historical analysis of inequality can make this observation obvious. From the vantage point of the present we find striking differences when looking back to, say, the Roman Empire or European feudalism. The overall nature of social stratification may be quite similar—that is, those on top receive more rewards and maintain their advantaged positions in some familiar ways and those on the bottom are viewed as inferior, lazy, immoral, and deserving of their status. But we often find a differing number of classes, laboring under diverse conditions, with an upper class holding its position for different reasons (such as ownership of land, ownership of industrial capital, control of the organized means of violence, or control of religious hierarchies).

When comparing the present with more recent history, however, differences are often less obvious. Except for periods of violent upheaval, as in revolution, class systems normally change slowly. But they do change. The past 100 years or so of United States history has shown some significant, though not often obvious, changes with respect to class distribution. In the present brief section we must review some of the recent changes as they relate to the middle and working classes. By doing so, we should make present conditions and consequences of class position more apparent and understandable.

At the outset we can examine how the occupational composition of the class system has changed. As is indicated in Table 9-4, in terms of occupation, the civilian labor force in this country has become substantially more middle class since 1900. Whereas 18 percent of the labor force was in white-collar occupations and 83 percent in blue-collar occupations in 1900, by the 1970s this

TABLE 9-4
OCCUPATIONAL DISTRIBUTION OF CIVILIAN LABOR FORCE, 1900–1979

Occupation	1900, %	1920, %	1940, %	1960, %	1979, %
Professionals	4	5	7	11	15
Managers	6	7	7	11	11
Sales	5	5	7	6	6
Clerical	3	8	10	15	18
Total white-collar	18	25	31	43	50
Crafts	11	13	13	13	13
Operatives	13	16	18	18	15
Laborers	12	12	9	5	5
Service	9	8	12	12	14
Farmers˙	38	27	17	8	3
Total blue-collar	83	76	68	56	50

˙Because some farmers own extensive farm property, it is somewhat misleading to place all farmers among blue-collar workers. However, as all farmers accounted for only 3 percent of the civilian labor force in 1979 the overall conclusions of this table are not altered.
Source: U.S. Bureau of the Census, *Historical Statistics of the United States, Colonial Times to 1970*, p. 139; U.S. Bureau of Labor Statistics, *Handbook of Labor Statistics*, 1980, Table 7, p. 20.

distribution had changed to about 50 percent white-collar and 50 percent blue-collar. But as we have already seen, there is increasing inequality in the United States, in part because of changes in the occupational structure. While the percentage of working-class jobs has been declining overall (Wright and Martin 1987), there are important changes within the working-class category. There has been a substantial decrease in the higher-skilled working-class positions and an increase in the lower-paying working-class positions not adequately represented in Table 9-4 (Thurow 1987).

Table 9-4 also does not indicate change with respect to authority positions, though the expansion of bureaucratic organizations and the positive relationship between occupational position and authority position (shown above) lead us to conclude that there has been an accompanying increase in mid-level authority positions since 1900. That is, with more bureaucratization, there are more people watching over and giving orders to others. We do have detailed studies showing that the percentage of the work force holding managerial and supervisory positions has grown steadily since 1960 (Wright and Martin 1987).

The New Middle Class

C. Wright Mills' (1953) description and analysis of the new middle class continues to be the best sociology has to offer. Mills' work is not without criticism; times have changed even since 1953. But most of what can be criticized in Mills' work pertains to his overly positive view of the old middle class and his overly negative view of the new middle class. The alienation of the new middle class is no doubt less than Mills described, while times were often hard for the old middle class.

Mills also stressed a condition of mass society with the new middle class—a condition of political powerlessness and self-alienation—that will be critiqued in the final section of this chapter. It was Mills' style of presenting his subject that led to a focus on extremes. But his style provided us with a vivid picture of historical contrasts that makes his work of continuing value.

The description *new middle class* presumes there was or is an old middle class. The small business person, shop owner, family farmer, and self-employed professional typify the old middle class. Some major characteristics of the people in these occupations include (1) freedom in the sense that they are their own boss, (2) the small size of their business, and (3) their ownership of tools, buildings, and so on that are used to produce their livelihood.

"The most important single fact about the society of small entrepreneurs was that a substantial proportion of the people owned the property with which they worked." Mills (1953:7) estimates that in the early 1800s about "four-fifths of the free people who worked owned property." This was a society that reflected the United States' ideology of individualism and free competition. The small entrepreneur remains, but for the most part that society is gone. It was taken over by the giant factory, the chain store, the hospital complex, the big law firm, and agricultural corporations.

In short, what has occurred is the concentration of the means of production, greater technical complexity of production, and increased size of production units. These forces have reduced the ranks of the old middle class relative to other occupations and greatly increased the size of the new middle class (though recent data indicate a slight increase in the self-employed, old middle class in the 1970s and 1980s; Steinmetz and Wright 1989). The new middle class emerged because of the need for technical specialists (lab technicians, engineers, computer operators, and so on), managers to organize and regulate the work of others in the bigger production and sales units, and clerks to manage and do the paperwork required by such large organizations.

In contrast to the characteristics of the members of the old middle class, the members of the new middle class do not own the means of their own livelihood and they lack freedom (they are not their own boss) and control over major decisions that affect their economic security and daily routine. A psychological outcome for the new middle class is stressed by Mills (1953:xii):

> The twentieth century white-collar man has never been independent as the farmer used to be, nor as hopeful of the main chance as the businessman. He is always somebody's man, the corporation's, the government's, the army's; and he is seen as the man who does not rise. The decline of the free entrepreneur and the rise of the dependent employee on the American scene has paralleled the decline of the independent individual and the rise of the little man in the American mind.

One may object to the negative psychological picture presented by Mills. Of course "He is always somebody's man." So what if he is not "hopeful of the main chance" to substantially improve his position in life? The vast majority of Americans work for somebody, must follow their rules, must move when the company believes it is necessary. Besides, the white-collar worker has a safer, cleaner, and, for the most part, more respected occupation than the blue-collar worker. But what Mills is trying to present is a picture of life now familiar to a major segment of our population, a way of life that is taken for granted.

Mills can also be accused of romanticizing the old middle class; it worked hard, the hours were long, the rough competition produced many failed businesses. Life, however, was different; there was a sense of self-worth and independence in contrast to the anonymous and conforming existence described by Whyte's (1956) organization man. It is this difference that must be grasped in Mills' descriptions (1953:189, 169) of "the enormous file" and "the great salesroom." Mills' work is the sociological analysis of the world of the new middle class, of Willy Loman in *Death of a Salesman*.

One important aspect of middle-class life, old and new, is that it has always been held in contrast to working-class life. For example, white-collar work is seen as more interesting and rewarding, and with higher status. But many, and not only Marxian theorists, have come to question the reality of this difference. The rise of the new middle class has brought with it the rather cumbersome concept of *proletarianization*—in short, the idea that the middle class has in many ways come to resemble the working class. Three major changes in white-collar labor are seen as producing proletarianization: lack of ownership, lack of independence on the job, and routinization of white-collar labor (see Giddens 1973:193; Wright et al. 1982). The lack of ownership of the means of production and independence in work we need not reemphasize. But the routinization of white-collar labor requires further comment.

A condition assumed characteristic of manual labor is alienation from work. With industrialization the blue-collar worker has for the most part lost control over the process of production, the assembly line has broken down work tasks into their simplest and most boring elements, and the worker can no longer identify and take pride in the finished product. A result is alienation from work activity that no longer has positive meaning in and of itself or intrinsic value; work has become only a means of earning an existence.

It is clear that the conditions of work for most nonmanual laborers are closer to the above description than they once were. However, whether or not a psychological condition of alienation is a result is a complex question involving many assumptions about the meaning of work that will be examined later in this chapter. But the main point at present is that along with less ownership of their means of production and less control over their labor, conditions believed to be conducive to alienation are also present among an increasing number of white-collar laborers.

We can consider an example. The recent widespread introduction of video display terminals (or VDTs) in office work has led to much discontent among office workers. In 1980 the president of Working Women from the National Association of Office Workers called for congressional hearings on the human impact of this new machine (see the *Los Angeles Times*, November 16, 1980).

In their view, the jobs of secretary and office clerk have been broken down into simple repetitive elements and the pace of work is now controlled by the machine; the results are boredom, lower job satisfaction, and alienated and frustrated employees.

In the past, a secretary would type, take dictation, file reports, answer the phone, arrange meetings, and handle many other tasks. But with the introduction of new automation in the office (like VDTs), each of these tasks is assigned to a different person, who does only one task all day. The result is a work situation that in many resembles blue-collar work on an assembly line.

The proletarianization thesis suggests more than that the working conditions of the middle class are becoming more similar to those of the working class. For the two classes, significant differences in political participation, child socialization, and general lifestyle (among other things) remain. But the rise of the new middle class as represented by changing occupational positions and conditions of work has been an important change for the understanding of class relations and the consequences of class in this country. We will examine some of these consequences after a brief look at the recent history of the working class.

Stability and Change in the Working Class

Although the rise of the new middle class came late in the process of industrialization, the industrial proletariat or working class was born with the industrial revolution. "The modern working class is the product of the machine. . . . It is the creation of the machine—to be exact, of the mechanical tool. No machines would mean no working class" (Kuczynski 1967:51).

The rise of the industrial working class was the product of a dual process: the spread of agrarian capitalism, which pushed peasants off the land, and the growth of urban industry, which brought work to some of the landless peasants. This dual process, as it began in Western Europe, first brought work mostly to women and children. The novels of Charles Dickens, such as *Oliver Twist,* are all too accurate on this point. For example, in the British cotton industry in 1835, 74 percent of the labor was made up of women and children below the age of eighteen (13 percent of the labor force was younger than thirteen).

Comparable figures are found for the United States in 1831: 60 percent of all laborers in the cotton industry were women (Kuczynski 1967:62–63). Factory owners preferred the labor of women and children because they were considered more docile and easily controlled. But as the pool of unemployed males increased, as child labor laws were enacted, and as industrialization spread to other types of production, the industrial labor force became predominantly male.

Since the early stages of capitalism in the United States, as we have seen, the percentage of working-class jobs has been slowly shrinking. And since the 1970s, an important change has been the reduction in skilled working-class jobs while the number of low-skilled working-class jobs has increased. But one of the most important changes not yet discussed has been in the percentage of the labor force represented by a labor union. With the increase in skilled working-class jobs and large corporations in this century, the percentage of the labor force in unions was increasing. But there has been a rather dramatic change downward in the percentage of the labor force represented by unions in the last two decades, which requires more analysis later in this chapter.

Another change deserves more extensive comment at this point. The growth of major corporations, their control over the market, and the concentration of workers in these big corporations are relatively recent phenomena. Such concentration remains unequally distributed throughout industrial sectors. What can be called a *dual economy,* or, from the worker's perspective, a *dual labor market,* exists. In brief, the dual economy means that industries (groups of corporations with the same economic functions, such as producing steel, producing electric power, or merchandising) are divided between *core* and *periphery* industries (see Beck, Horan, and Tolbert 1978; Tolbert, Horan, and Beck 1980).

Some characteristics of core industries include (1) a high concentration of corporate assets within the industry (a few large corporations do most of the business), (2) higher productivity, (3) higher profits, (4) more capital-intensive production, and (5) less economic competition (that is, the industry is more like a monopoly). The periphery industries fall toward the opposite of all five of these characteristics. (In reality, we can look at the core and periphery characteristics as opposite poles of a continuum.) Examples of core industries are petroleum, auto production, and primary metal production (such as steel). Examples of periphery industries are general merchandising (department stores), service stations, and restaurants (see Tolbert, Horan, and Beck 1980:1109).

Most important for our present discussion are the differing outcomes for workers employed in either core or periphery industries in the dual economy. In the core industries in the United States, as well as in other advanced capitalist industrial societies such as Japan (Kalleberg and Lincoln 1988), we find (1) higher wages, (2) better-than-average working conditions, and (3) more fringe benefits. Core industries are in a better position to provide higher wages and better benefits because they have less competition and more profits, and are able to pass higher labor costs to consumers. Also, workers in core industries are more unionized and, thus, are more successful in pressing their demands.

We must note, however, that with more foreign competition affecting especially core industries, and the relative U.S. economic decline, the income advantage of U.S. core workers compared to periphery workers has been reduced since the 1960s (Tigges 1988). And with the other changes we have already discussed in the labor force during the 1980s (the growth in low-skilled labor and shrinkage of high-skilled blue-collar labor), there are probably trends in core versus periphery labor not yet considered in the research on the dual economy. Specifically, because the skilled, better-paying blue-collar jobs that have been lost are more likely to exist in core industries, there is no doubt a reduction in the percentage of the labor force in the core. Related to this, those jobs in the low-skilled employment sector that have been increasing are more often in periphery industries; thus, we expect an increase in periphery employment.

Finally, we must consider the embourgeoisement thesis. The basic idea is that the diverse changes experienced by the working class have made them more like the middle class in many ways (for example, in terms of income, political attitudes, family structure, and lifestyle). In other words, this thesis is that the working class has moved up to become more like the middle class, rather than the middle class moving down to become more like the working class in many characteristics.

Before the 1980s there was some support for this thesis of embourgeoisement: Now there is much less. Again, this is related to recent changes in the U.S. economy, increased foreign competition, and the general relative decline of the U.S. economy. (As should be realized by now, this relative decline of the U.S. economy has affected many things about social stratification in the United States.) The embourgeoisement thesis best fits the changes that were going on among those people in higher-skilled working-class positions, especially in the core industries. But unfortunately for U.S. workers, those jobs are now found more often in several other countries such as Japan, South Korea, and Taiwan.

SOME CONSEQUENCES OF CLASS POSITION

Whether or not they recognize precise class divisions or even the general nature of social stratification in this country, most people are at least vaguely aware of many class differences. They may know, for example, that working-class people tend to live in neighborhoods different from those of the middle class, or that working-class people tend to favor country and western music, or that political candidates often appeal to different classes.

Various class differences are presented every night on the TV news, and we read about them in our newspapers. And most people have a general expectation of income differences between working-class and middle-class families, an expectation that makes exceptions to the tendency worth considerable comment. (How often do we hear about garbage collectors who make more money than teachers?)

For example, *NBC Nightly News* broadcast the following story confronting class expectations. During an especially cold winter day, office workers in a New York City skyscraper overlooking a construction site held a sign to their window reading "It's 78° in here." The freezing construction workers responded with a sign reading, "It's $15.00 an hour out here."

The point is, even when these class differences are recognized, they are not always accurately perceived; nor is the range of the differences fully appreciated. Perhaps most important, the *reasons* for these differences are seldom understood. In this section our task will be to examine some of the consequences of class position for the middle and working classes. We will begin with income differences, then consider differences related to working conditions and attitudes toward work. Last, general cultural and lifestyle differences between the middle and working classes will be explored.

Income Distribution by Class

The most commonly recognized class inequality is income. The usual assumption is that working-class people receive below-average incomes, the middle class receives average incomes, and the upper-middle-class professionals and managers receive above-average to high incomes. Recently, these assumptions have been confronted by highly publicized cases of construction workers, garbage collectors, plumbers, and so on receiving substantial or at least above-average incomes.

The more traditional assumptions about class income inequality are much closer to reality. The belief that working-class people have made substantial income gains relative to the middle class is usually incorrect in three respects: (1) The publicized cases of high working-class incomes are atypical. (2) The hourly wages of some blue-collar workers may at times be high, but the work is usually insecure or seasonal. For example, workers making $15.00 or more an hour on a construction site are often out of work several months between jobs. (3) As we have already seen, the number of higher-paid working-class jobs have been shrinking through the 1980s.

Still, it must be recognized that there is no simple relationship between income and class position because of the many variables that help determine income attainment. One problem has been that, in the past, occupational status or occupational skill level alone was assumed to indicate class position. But as we have already seen, bureaucratic authority and ownership and control of the means of production must also be considered in locating class. The standard United States census data, such as that presented in Chapter 2 (Table 2-3), is based on standard occupational divisions. This type of data consistently shows middle-class occupations (or white-collar laborers) with higher income than working-class occupations (or blue-collar laborers). But this type of data, while useful, masks important income differences *within* occupational categories.

Studies, such as those by Wright (1978a, 1979; Wright and Perrone 1977), Robinson and Kelley (1979), and Kalleberg and Griffin (1980), have examined income inequalities produced by the property and authority structures (as well as occupation) in the stratification system. For example, Wright and Perrone (1977:48) found an average income (in 1969 dollars) for big employers (those owning their means of production and hiring ten or more employees) of $19,188, an average income for small employers (with less than ten employees) of $12,915, an average income for managers of $9,226, and an average income for workers (those with no ownership of the means of production and no subordinates) of $6,145. (Remember, these are 1969 income figures, in contrast to the later income figures in Table 2-3.) And as Robinson and Kelley (1979) found, significant income differences between these class categories (defined by ownership and authority position) remain when controlling for the effects of occupational skill level.

Another source of unequal income related to the nature of the stratification system is worth discussion. It will be remembered that the development of a *dual economy* has direct bearing on middle- and working-class income. But in this case, the major effect of interest to us is how the dual economy produces income inequality *within* class and occupational divisions.

Studies by Beck, Horan, and Tolbert (1978; also Tolbert, Horan, and Beck 1980; Bloomquist and Summers 1982; Jacobs 1982, 1985; Kaufman 1983), among others, have shown that workers in core industries receive higher wages than those in periphery industries, even when controlling for the effects on income from occupational level, education, age, hours worked, job tenure, and union membership in the industry. It was estimated by Beck, Horan, and Tolbert (1978:716) that in dollar terms (for 1976 income), males who are employed full-time in periphery industries have an annual income loss of $4,097.51 because of periphery rather than core employment. Moreover, Parcel (1979) has found that the positive income effect of core industry extends to the wider geographical area in which core corporations are located. That is, even the wages of workers in periphery corporations are higher when periphery corporations are located near core industries.

As noted above, a primary reason core wages tend to be higher is that core industries have less competition and thus higher profits. Core industries are able to pay higher wages because, with less competition, the core industries can more easily pass higher labor costs on to consumers. Another reason for higher wages in the core corporation is related to its greater size. With increased size, corporations have more hierarchical ranks, each higher rank tending to provide more authority and income (Beck, Horan, and Tolbert 1978; Stolzenberg 1978; Baron and Bielby 1984).

Class Effects on Race and Sex Income Inequality

Before turning from the subject of class income inequality it is important that we note the effects of class on race and sex income inequality. No doubt much of the income inequality between men and women and whites and minorities can be explained by historical conditions of racism and sexism in our society (England et al. 1988). However, much of this race and sex discrimination *operates through the established class system.*

Several studies described above have shown that in addition to occupational skill level, income inequality in general is related to positions within authority structures, ownership of the means of production, periphery versus core employment, and unionization. Thus, if we find sex and race differences in relation to these other factors affecting income inequality in general, we have located other sources of sex and race inequality operating through the class system. Several studies show this is in fact the case.

In Table 9-3 it was shown that women and minorities tend to be lower in authority and ownership of the means of production than white males. Several studies have shown that less authority and ownership explain a significant amount of the lower income for females and minorities (Wright and Perrone 1977; Kluegel 1978; Wright 1978b, 1979; Wolf and Fligstein 1979; Treiman and Roos 1983). With respect to the dual economy, other studies have shown that females and minorities have less income, in part, because they are more often employed in periphery industries (Beck, Horan, and Tolbert 1978; Tolbert, Horan, and Beck 1980; Kaufman 1983). Finally, the dual-economy research indicates that unionization is a factor in less female and minority income, with other studies more directly showing that females and minorities are more often employed in industries that are less unionized (Beck, Horan, and Tolbert 1980).

Other studies, however, indicate that more traditional factors like simple discrimination account for sex inequalities in income. These studies take into consideration all of the factors such as authority position, job tenure, education level, and so on that can account for sex and race income inequalities. They still find income differences which must be attributed to racism and sexism (England et al. 1988; Parcel and Mueller 1989). One detailed study has shown that jobs labeled *women's work* bring less income despite education level, occupational skill level, authority, and other factors that are usually associated with income attainment (McLaughlin 1978). And another study has found that even when men and women do the same job, women are often given a different job title with less pay (Bielby and Baron 1986).

With respect to sex inequalities, there are some signs that these inequalities will be reduced further in the future. Just between 1982 and 1987, the male/female income ratio improved significantly, from 61 percent to 70 percent (U.S. Bureau of Labor Statistics 1988). Affirmative action and civil rights laws are showing some effects. Other signs are found in the big increase in women holding jobs traditionally seen as men's jobs. Perhaps more significant, there have been very important changes in the fields of study chosen by college women (U.S. Bureau of the Census, *Male-Female Differences in Work Experience, Occupation, and Earnings,* 1987). No longer do we find women studying only for degrees in education, home economics, recreation, or social work. Many women now study law, medicine, engineering, accounting, and other majors traditionally seen as male-dominated. For example, in 1970 women accounted for only 8 percent of the medical degrees conferred that year. By 1980, however, the percentage of medical degrees going to women had increased to 23 percent. The increase in law degrees going to women in this ten-year period increased from 5 percent to 30 percent, and doctors of philosophy from 13 percent to 30 percent (Taeuber and Valdisera 1986).

Conditions of inequality for blacks and Mexican-Americans, however, do not continue to show the same improvement. And in this respect, whites continue to have very inaccurate beliefs about these conditions, generally thinking there has been much improvement and that there is less race and ethnic inequality than actually exists (Kluegel and Smith 1982). We have already seen the income inequality figures in Chapter 2, which show improvement in the 1960s and 1970s, but then increasing inequality again in the 1980s. The rate of

unemployment and underemployment for blacks has been moving higher relative to the white rate in recent years (Lichter 1988). In the next chapter we
will see that the black and Mexican-American rate of poverty continues to be
much higher compared to whites. And in Chapter 11 we will see that between
1960 and the middle of the 1970s there is evidence that a black middle class
emerged that was able to pass advantages on to their sons and daughters so
that they could remain in the upper middle class as whites have done. But we
will also see that this was less the case in the 1980s. We have seen figures on
the shrinking middle-income families in the United States, but we have also
seen that it is black middle-income families that are shrinking most rapidly.

Despite these worsening figures for blacks, many sociologists maintain that
the problem is in large part related to class, not just racism. In a now-famous
book, *The Declining Significance of Race,* Wilson (1980) argues that, like
whites, when blacks are in the lower class it is hard to move out, as we will see
when we consider the subject of social mobility in Chapter 11. The problem, of
course, is that because of past racism and discrimination, there are relatively
more blacks in the lower class who find it difficult to move out. The main point
is that both race and sex income inequality are in large measure explained by
class, although racism and sexism do continue to play a part.

Conditions of Work

For the big capitalist and the corporate class the conditions of work could seldom be better. In addition to their greater financial resources, the upper and
corporate classes have more interest, respect, and diversion in their jobs; they
have a sense of doing something important, of controlling their own lives; and
they have the resources of the institutions they head—the private jet, vacation
resorts, expense accounts, and the services of many people. What is more,
they have a lot of occupational freedom. If their job is a burden, they can move
on to another. If they prefer to leave their private sector job for a top government job (like a cabinet position), they can do so with the knowledge that suit-
able work (if work is even needed) will be found after the cabinet post is gone.

As with income, the conditions of work are stratified. Those on top are generally better off, while those in the middle can look down upon those at the
bottom with a feeling that their own condition could be worse. In this section
we will examine two important aspects of the conditions of work. The first is
the satisfaction or fulfillment that work may or may not bring. The second has
to do with the physical conditions of work—its safety and physical demands.

Work Satisfaction and Alienation   In Marx's (see Marx 1964:124–125) view,
the alienation of labor comes when work becomes "external to the worker,"
when "it is not his own work but work for someone else," or when work is
"only a *means* for satisfying other needs." There is an underlying assumption
in Marx's view that human nature requires us to have meaningful work, work
that can be identified as an extension of ourselves, to fulfill psychological
needs. When the conditions of labor remove this identity with work, when the

worker has no control over the work process, the result is unfulfillment and alienation.

C. Wright Mills (1953:215) had a different assumption about the meaning of work, but arrived at a similar conclusion about the contemporary conditions of work for most workers: "Neither love nor hatred of work is inherent in man, or inherent in any given line of work. For work has no intrinsic meaning." Because, in Mills' view, work has no intrinsic meaning, the meaning it has comes from our beliefs about work. And for today's worker, an ideology placing value on the type of work most people do is lacking.

What we have is a view of work inherited from a previous age—the age of the old middle class and independent artisan. The kind of work that is most valued is work that results in an identification with what is produced or accomplished, work that is an extension or expression of the self, work that is controlled by the worker. This low value of most contemporary work, Mills (1953:227) believed, holds for both blue-collar and white-collar work.

For many, an important outcome of this alienation from work is the segmentation of their lives. There are hours of work, and there are the hours away from work. It is often difficult for us to understand that in the past work more often provided an identity, a meaningful life in what was accomplished, and that one's life was so much a part of work that lives were less segmented between working hours and leisure hours.

Given the chance, most people today prefer the latter hours, or work of a different type. But given that a different type of work is usually not attainable, work is something that must be tolerated; for there is also an important new longing for consumption and expensive leisure activities that must be paid for by work. In Mills' (1953:237) descriptive words, "Each day men sell little pieces of themselves in order to try to buy them back each night and weekend with the coin of 'fun.'"

There are many detailed examinations of the lives of individual workers with varied occupations. Most of these examinations attest to the alienation from work described by Mills. Such studies include Studs Terkel's (1972) *Working,* Sennett and Cobb's (1973) *The Hidden Injuries of Class,* and Lasson's (1971) *The Workers.* And there are the social scientists who have temporarily left their university jobs to understand the meaning of work by working in a factory themselves (for example, Pfeffer, 1979, *Working for Capitalism*; Kamata, 1982, *Japan in the Passing Lane*).

There are some exceptions to these descriptions of work alienation and discontent—for example, Le Masters' (1975) *Blue-Collar Aristocrats.* But studies that find lower-level workers with positive feelings and identity with work are exceptions. Le Masters' research was with skilled blue-collar workers who work under conditions more like those of the independent artisan. These workers were better able to control their own conditions of work and identify and take pride in a finished product.

Problems do arise with these qualitative examinations of work in that the bias of the researcher can present an overly negative image of work. But there are also problems with quantitative studies that attempt to measure attitudes toward work with a few simple questions that are unable to measure the meaning of work in a deeper sense. Both types of studies, however, indicate that satisfaction with work is positively related *to one's position in the stratification system*. There is more satisfaction and fulfillment with work and less alienation the higher we go in the class system. The relation is not a simple one, for the meaning of work is a complex issue with many factors combining to produce a feeling of satisfaction or alienation. To provide a better understanding of the relation between class and the sociopsychological conditions of work let us turn to some of the empirical research.

We can start with the rather simplistic concept of satisfaction with work. Studies of this type generally begin by asking workers some variation of the following questions: "Do you find your work satisfying?" "Would you get into this line of work again if you had to do it over?" "Would you recommend the type of work you do to friends or relatives?" Others may use some variation of questions to get at the feeling of finding work fulfilling.

In summary (see Jencks et al. 1972:247–252), several studies have found that work satisfaction is positively related to occupational status, income, education level, and general occupational categories (such as manager, professional, clerical worker, skilled laborer, unskilled laborer, service worker). The relationship between occupational divisions and work satisfaction found in these studies is not especially strong, however, because other dimensions of class have not been directly measured.

A more recent study by Kalleberg and Griffin (1980) examined the relationship between other dimensions of class and job satisfaction (or rather, feeling fulfillment with work). Following our perspective of the most important structures or divisions that determine class position—occupational skill level (rather than occupational status), authority position (following and/or giving orders), and ownership—these researchers were able to specify more exactly how class position influences job satisfaction (or fulfillment).

We note first that Kalleberg and Griffin found only a weak relationship between job fulfillment and the functional view of occupational status in their national sample of 1,569 workers. But when class position was defined in terms of ownership and control over the work of others (employers), control over the work of others without ownership (managers), and having no ownership and no control over the work of others (workers), they found significant differences in job fulfillment. Employers felt the most fulfillment in work, then managers, and workers felt the least fulfillment.

The positive correlation between class and fulfillment was maintained even when controlling for the effects of occupational census titles (such as clerk, professional, or sales worker), and when considering separately capitalist (private business) and noncapitalist (such as government) employment sectors (with the manager and worker-class positions). Finally, by defining ranks in the occupational structure in terms of skill level and job complexity (as we have done), they found a greater relationship to job fulfillment than with occupational ranking defined in terms of status (that is, the greater the skill needed and the complexity of the job, the greater the fulfillment).

We have yet to consider empirical research on the complex concept of alienation. Marx wrote of two aspects of alienation—loss of control over the *products* of one's labor, and loss of control over the *process* of labor. Most research has been concerned with the loss of control over the process of labor in highly industrial societies.

To empirically test the relation between alienation and class position, Kohn (1976) examined a national sample of 3,101 people in the civilian labor force. Kohn examined alienation in relation to ownership or lack of ownership of the means of production, position in the authority structure, and degree of occupational self-direction (that is, closeness of supervision, routinization of work, and complexity of work). He found that the lack of occupational self-direction was most strongly related to four psychological measures of alienation (see Kohn 1976:119). This suggests that alienation is mostly the product of work that provides little control over the process of work, as Marx in part defined alienation. Work performed most by the lower middle class (clerks, clerical workers, lower sales positions) and the working class is most conducive to alienation.

Comparative studies on Japan and Japanese management techniques support these conclusions. However, in contrast to the image of Japanese workers often held by Americans, all Japanese are not content, unalienated, and happy workers. Alienation is produced by the machine pace and how workers are treated by management in Japan, just as in the United States (Kamata 1982; Naoi and Schooler 1985). Workers in Japan tend to adjust to this alienation or learn to live with it as they get older, just as in the United States (Loscocco and Kalleberg 1988). However, an important difference is that, more often in Japan than in the United States, management does try to implement policies and management styles that allow for more worker input and more human contact between management and workers. This to some extent reduces the alienation of work (Dore 1987). However, it is likely that the 7 to 1 income gap between top managers and workers in Japan, compared to the 37 to 1 income gap in the United States (Abegglen and Stalk 1985), is the most important factor reducing labor–management conflict in Japan (Dore 1987).

Comparative studies have shown that these management styles can to some extent work to reduce alienation in the United States (Lincoln and Kalleberg 1985). This is perhaps a primary reason why, in Japanese companies established in the United States, workers have not voted for labor unions. It has been suggested in the mass media that unions are to blame when they lose a vote for union representation in the Japanese factories in the United States. Maybe it should be noted that this shows the success of management relations in these factories in contrast to the traditionally American-managed factories.

The stratification system has profound effects upon the conditions of work in our society. Depending on one's position in the stratification system, work can be satisfying and fulfilling or unsatisfying, unfulfilling, and alienating. Given that a great portion of most people's lives is spent in work, these effects of class position on the psychological conditions of work are truly significant. Furthermore, it must be recognized that these psychological conditions are carried into other aspects of life—family relations, overall self-esteem, mental health, and one's outlook on life in general. With some knowledge of this impact of the stratification system on the material and psychological conditions of work, we can gain a better understanding of the class differences in lifestyle, family relations, political and religious attitudes, and leisure activities to be examined below. But before we do so it will be useful to consider briefly the physical conditions of work.

The Physical Conditions of Work   By the physical conditions of work we refer to the work environment in terms of its safety, health, or physical stress. Along with the psychological aspects of work, we find that physical aspects of work are influenced by one's position in the stratification system. And when we consider physical safety and health conditions of work, the dichotomy of manual versus nonmanual labor becomes most important.

White-collar workers may suffer alienating psychological conditions or lack of job satisfaction in common with blue-collar workers. But white-collar work is generally safe in a physical sense. Few white-collar workers are subject to health hazards, injury, or death in the work place. (Exceptions may be lab technicians or scientific workers who work with dangerous materials.) For blue-collar workers, the work is often dangerous. They do the dirty work, the dangerous work, the work that few people want, the work the blue-collar worker may be unable to avoid if food is to be kept on the table.

Blue-collar labor often need not be so dangerous, but it can be more profitable for corporations to continue exposing their workers to a dangerous work environment than to change it. And given the power of corporations in our society, they are able to resist pressures from government and labor unions to change these conditions (see the many accounts of this in Mintz and Cohen 1976:422–431; Caudill 1980; Epstein 1980). Thus, the unsafe conditions of work for manual laborers are related to the impact of stratification in two ways—the power of corporations to resist change and the lack of alternatives blue-collar workers may have for other lines of work.

Exact estimates are usually hard to obtain, but in 1972 the Secretary of Health, Education and Welfare estimated that occupational diseases kill "as many as 100,000" workers annually, and newly disable "at least 390,000." At about the same time, the Secretary of Labor in the United States estimated that work accidents annually account for about 14,200 deaths and 2.2 million temporarily or permanently disabling injuries (Mintz and Cohen 1976:422–423). The main dangers are machines, hazardous chemicals, and unsafe environments (such as mines).

With new dangers of work being discovered at an increasing rate and old dangers coming to light all the time, we can list only a few specific examples. One of the best known conditions of unsafe work is found in United States mines. By their nature, mines are dangerous places in which to work. But they need not be as dangerous as they are in the United States. The record of death and injury in United States mines is much worse than in Europe (McAteer 1971; Mintz and Cohen 1976:423–424; Caudill 1980).

Each year it is estimated that in the United States about "200 miners are killed and thousands more injured by accidents in the mines. Additional thousands are exposed to the risks of various types of lung disease, the most widely known of which is black lung" (Mintz and Cohen 1976:423). The above works by McAteer, Caudill, and Mintz and Cohen list many things that could be done to reduce the death, injury, and disease in our mines, but are not done in the name of higher productivity and profits (see also Pearson 1978).

Another example of danger in the work place is the now highly publicized danger of asbestos. President Carter's first secretary of HEW estimated in 1978 that 8 to 11 million United States workers may have been exposed to this cancer-causing substance since World War II (Epstein 1980:164). And not only workers, but their families have been victims of cancer caused by asbestos brought home in workers' clothing. A recent study of 354 families of asbestos workers showed 35 percent (far higher than the general population) had lung abnormalities, most likely due to asbestos exposure (Mintz and Cohen 1976:427). Part of the problem is that the working-class environment at work is more dangerous than that of other workers. But the dangers from asbestos have often been covered up, and needed changes in the work environment have been resisted.

Finally, we may cite the traditional problem of unsafe factory machines. With the example of metal press workers, in 1974 the Occupational Safety and Health Administration (or OSHA, the agency under attack by business for "placing too many restraints on business") estimated that three out of every 500 workers lose a hand or portion of a hand every year. In Michigan alone in 1973, these workers suffered 307 amputations of hands (Mintz and Cohen 1976:429). Again, the story is one of reforms being pressed by unions and government agencies like OSHA, with these reforms being blocked or made ineffective by counterpressure from business groups. For example, the U.S. Department of Labor estimates that a law requiring locks on machinery so that power is cut off during maintenance and repairs could "prevent 60,000 injuries a year, 28,000 of them serious ones such as loss of limbs or crushed bones" (*Los Angeles Times,* September 3, 1989, pp. 32–33).

There was some improvement in the figures on work-related deaths and injuries by the late 1970s, but the 25 percent cut in the budget of OSHA made by the Reagan administration did not keep the trend going down. In 1988 there were an estimated 10,700 work-related deaths (not counting work-related motor vehicle accidents or diseases caused by the work environment) and 70,000 who were permanently disabled due to direct physical injuries. In 1988 the U.S. Department of Labor estimated that this U.S. record of death in the work place was thirty-six times higher than in Sweden, nine times higher than in England, and four times higher than in West Germany or France (*Los Angeles Times,* September 3, 1989, September 4, 1989).

As noted at the beginning of this discussion, our intent is merely to describe briefly the physical dangers of labor for the working class. The dangers for workers are not equally present in every industry; nor are reforms always successfully resisted by business. One study of the dangers of radiation in uranium mines found that reforms were made when the need for uranium was somewhat reduced, the hazard became clearer, and the industry became larger and more stable (thus, profit stability allowed change without hurting business; see Pearson 1978). But the main point is that the conditions of labor for the working class are often dangerous and the class position of these workers gives them less ability to avoid or change these dangers.

Class Subcultures and Lifestyles

Income inequalities, job satisfaction, conditions of work, and differing amounts of political and economic power (discussed in the next section) are clearly among the most important consequences of class in the United States. But they are not the only consequences of class; nor always the only ones of considerable importance. There are other sometimes obvious, sometimes subtle, sometimes very important differences between classes that must also be understood as consequences of class position.

Under the general concept of *class subcultures* we may consider beliefs, world views, values, and behavior associated with these attitudes that may differ with class position. We use the term *subculture* rather than *culture* to suggest that whatever differences found are usually variations within a more dominant culture that most members of a society tend to share.

Under the concept of a *lifestyle* we include tastes, preferences, and general styles of living that are more superficial in nature—that is, not necessarily related to important value differences or having important consequences in and of themselves. These lifestyle differences, however, can also often be traced to experiences and problems that vary by class.

Almost any casual observation of people in different sections of a city can turn up differences of class lifestyle. Some of these differences may reflect variations in economic resources, while others reflect differing tastes. For example, let us imagine that an upper-middle-class person goes shopping in an unfamiliar working-class section of a city. As this person looks around the stores he or she may soon have a sense that the people are somehow different. The clothing or hairstyles may stand out as different from those of people in the more familiar upper-middle-class milieu. Closer observation may reveal speech differences or differences in body language.

Consider another example—say, of driving through different class neighborhoods of a city. Some differences are striking. The sizes of houses and the space between them may differ considerably between upper-middle-class and working-class neighborhoods. But other differences may become apparent as well. The style of the homes may be noticeably different. In upper-middle-class areas we may find more modern, stylish-looking homes (the kind we see in magazines like *Better Homes and Gardens*) or very old, well-preserved homes (in an old city like New Orleans). In working-class areas we may find simple frame or stucco homes of box shape. A closer look may reveal differences in landscaping, fewer cars, more of which are foreign, in upper-middle-class areas, or more children playing in the street in working-class areas. (In upper-middle-class areas the children are usually off to piano, dancing, or some other kind of lessons.)

Some of the differences between classes may seem trivial or unimportant, although interesting at times. These differences may simply *reflect* the particular daily routines, concerns, or life choices available to class members. For example, the country music that is more often preferred by working-class people tends to stress themes of everyday problems (family stability, unemployment, relations on the job), male strength and aggression, or "Americanism" (for example, in "Okie from Muskogee" the traditional deviance of drinking "white lightnin'" is good and marijuana is bad).

Other class differences may not only reflect particular class experiences but also *reinforce* class inequalities and class boundaries in complex ways. For example, research by Ellis (1967) found that subjects selected for the study were often able to identify the class position of unseen people correctly simply by listening to short recordings of standard sentences. This suggests that there are some class differences in speech patterns and pronunciation. But what is equally interesting is that subjects in a similar research project (see Harms 1961) rated higher-class speakers as more credible, and in Ellis' (1967) study as more likable. As Ellis suggests, these findings have strong implications for hiring practices and employee performance ratings, and for how lower-class people are respected.

Class differences in lifestyle, attitudes, and behavior are only tendencies. Wide variations are sometimes found *within* class categories, and the mass media have greatly homogenized modern people to an ever-increasing extent. But differing class experiences and life chances, among other things, have prevented a completely undifferentiated mass population.

Sociability and Community Participation The early concern in sociology with community organization and social networks has resulted in a wealth of research on class differences in community involvement, neighboring, and friendship ties outside the nuclear family. Such research has been consistent in showing that the middle class is generally more involved in the community and less tied to extended family relations than the working class. For example, there is a direct relationship between class position and joining voluntary associations (for example, the PTA, VFW, Lions Club, or sewing clubs; see Hodge and Treiman 1968a; Hyman and Wright 1971).

In contrast, members of the working class, when they are involved in relationships outside the home, are more likely than the middle class to be involved with their extended family (visiting with parents, grandparents, and more distant relatives; see Komarovsky 1962; Cohen and Hodges 1963). Also, among the working class, husband and wife tend to have separate friendship patterns. The husband goes out with his friends (usually from work) and the wife with hers (usually from the neighborhood). And when people in both the middle and working classes are involved in associations or with friends outside the home, they are class-specific relationships; that is, they tend to associate with people of similar class backgrounds.

What is it about the class system that produces these differing tendencies among the middle and working class? First, members of the middle class are more mobile. Their jobs require them to relocate more often, and they commonly live in communities other than the ones in which they lived as children. In contrast to members of the working class, they are more often away from extended family members. Second, as described earlier, middle-class occupations tend to produce less alienation. And with less alienation there is a greater sense of being a part of the larger community, and thus there is more participation in it. Third, "the greater resources of the higher classes help account for their wider social participation" (Collins 1975:80). It is easy to forget that it takes money and time to become involved outside the home. Fourth, there is a differing world view that is shaped by the occupational structure. What can be called *cosmopolitanism* is the product of a greater variety of interactions and more communications with people from diverse backgrounds. It creates the sense of a wider social environment that affects one's life.

Conversely, the less the cosmopolitan orientation, and "the less the variety of communications, the more one thinks in terms of particular persons and things, short-term contingencies, and an alien and uncontrollable world surrounding familiar local circles" (Collins 1975:75–76). This sense of a wider community or cosmopolitanism is related to the occupational structure, because the higher the occupation, the more interaction there is with diverse people; the working-class person "regularly deals with few besides his boss and a little-changing circle of friends and family" (Collins 1975:64).

Childhood Socialization   Of all the contrasting class characteristics, childhood socialization or child-rearing practices have received the most attention from social scientists. One reason for this attention is the importance of child rearing for the future of children *and* the maintenance of class boundaries. To the extent that childhood socialization varies by class, these class differences may in some way help retard intergenerational mobility in the class system. That is, it may be that *to some degree* working-class children are raised to be working class, while middle-class children are raised to be middle class.

As we will see in Chapter 11 (where the subject of social mobility will be considered in more detail), child-rearing differences alone cannot explain the pattern of social mobility whereby most working-class children remain working class in their adult life. Rather, there is a cycle of variables operating, and childhood socialization is only one link, although an important one, in this cycle.

A number of specific child socialization experiences have received extensive empirical examination. Most importantly, the research shows that middle-class children experience child-rearing methods that stress initiative, self-reliance, an emphasis on ideas and people, achievement of higher occupation, and more deferred gratification. Working-class socialization tends to stress external conformity to rules, less self-reliance and creativity, and working with things rather than ideas (see Kohn 1969).

Most of the research has been directed toward the important contrast between socialization for self-reliance in middle-class families and conformity to external rules in working-class families. For example, when middle-class children are punished there is usually greater stress on why rules should be followed or why some rules are important, rather than simple conformity to all external rules. It is argued that the former type of punishment leads to more self-reliance and a personal code of what is right or wrong rather than to a simple conformity to rules, whatever they may be.

Using 1964 data, the most comprehensive study of this type showed that middle-class fathers do stress self-reliance for their children, whereas working-class fathers stress conformity to external rules (Kohn 1969). A replication of this study by Wright and Wright (1976) supports Kohn's findings (for both fathers and mothers), although it found somewhat less difference between the middle and working class on this aspect of child rearing. The above research findings have been replicated in other countries (see Pearlin 1971; Olsen 1973; Slomczynski, Miller, and Kohn 1981; Naoi and Schooler 1985; Schooler and Naoi 1988).

Findings showing different socialization patterns by class do not suggest that working-class parents have less concern for their children or are harder on their children. For example, it was often thought that middle-class parents are less likely to use corporal punishment. One study indicates that this view is incorrect (Erlanger 1974). Also, one should not get the idea that working-class parents are less concerned about their children's future. What the studies do indicate is that middle-class parents are more concerned with higher-level occupational attainment for their children, while working-class parents are concerned with their children's well-being without reference to occupational level per se (see Keller and Zavalloni 1964; Turner 1970).

As with other characteristics found to differ by class, it is important that we understand why these differences exist. We can conclude by examining a key class difference in child socialization—the differing stress on self-reliance and conformity. Most researchers refer to the importance of parents' occupational status and position in authority structures as producing these child-rearing contrasts (Kohn and Schooler 1982). For example, working-class parents are lower in authority structures and have occupations that require greater conformity to external rules and unquestioned obedience. This experience is reflected in how they treat their children (Kohn 1969). This conclusion has received support from an interesting study by Ellis, Lee, and Peterson (1978) with data from 122 cultures. In this cross-national study they found that the greater the supervision over parents in important aspects of life (like work) the greater the stress on conformity in child socialization.

Political Values and Behavior   A number of generalizations can be made with respect to class and political values. Most generalizations, however, must be qualified, given the complex relationship between political values and class position. We may begin with the relationship between class and party voting. In party voting in the United States, the usual assumption is that voting Democratic means a more liberal political orientation, while voting Republican means a more conservative political orientation. As shown below, there are problems with the above assumption, but party voting does give us some indication of liberal versus conservative political values.

Studies have been quite consistent in showing a strong relationship between class and party vote in the recent history of the United States (Hamilton 1972; Knoke and Hout 1974; Levison 1975). The upper middle class is most conservative and most likely to vote Republican. As we move down the class system from the lower middle class through skilled blue-collar workers to unskilled blue-collar workers, we find a greater tendency to vote Democratic. This relation between lower-class position and voting for liberal parties is found in most Western industrial societies (see Szymanski 1978; Tufte 1978), and often more so than in the United States (Vanneman 1980).

However, the relationship between class and party voting is only a tendency (although a strong one) and may vary under certain conditions. For example, with higher than normal unemployment and high inflation with a Democratic President in office between 1976 and 1980, the working-class vote was split about fifty-fifty for Reagan and Carter in the 1980 election (*Newsweek,* November 17, 1980). Of course, during the 1980 election more working-class voters than ever rejected all choices and did not vote. About half of all voters (53 percent) voted in 1980; thus, Ronald Reagan was elected by about 25 percent of the voters. Roughly the same situation occurred with the Bush election in 1988, but in this case even fewer people bothered to vote (less than one-half of those eligible to vote).

In reference to actual voter participation in the United States, which is lower than in other industrial democracies, we also find class influences. The lower we go in the stratification system, the lower the percentage of eligible voters who participate in elections. This is not the case in other industrial democracies, where the lower classes vote in much higher numbers (Zipp, Landerman, and Luebke 1982). Table 9-5 lists the percentages of voting in the 1984 and 1988 presidential elections by income. In 1984 only 37.5 percent of those with less than $5,000 annual income voted, compared to 75.6 percent of those with $50,000 annual income or higher. In 1988 the percentage of low-income people voting was even lower, 34.7 percent.

There are many reasons for the nonparticipation of the lower classes in elections in this country, such as the length of time between registering deadlines and voting, lack of transportation, and inability to leave work (Burnham 1974; Piven and Cloward 1988). It has been estimated that we could increase the number of working-class people voting with some simple changes such as voting on a Saturday instead of always on a Tuesday. Research has indicated that the rate of lower-class voting could be increased significantly if political parties simply tried to get these voters out (Zipp, Landerman, and Luebke 1982). But also central to this lack of voter participation among working-class people is their sense of alienation from the wider society. This feeling of alienation is higher in the lower classes. As we saw above, the working class is less in-

TABLE 9-5
VOTING RATES BY INCOME, 1984 and 1988

Family income	Percent voted	
	1984	1988
Under $5,000	37.5	34.7
$5,000–9,999	46.2	41.3
$10,000–14,999	53.5	47.7
$15,000–19,999	57.1	53.5
$20,000–24,999	61.1	57.8
$25,000–34,999	67.0	64.0
$35,000–49,999	72.9	70.3
$50,000 and over	76.0	75.6

Source: U.S. Bureau of the Census, Current Population Reports, *Voting and Registration in the Election of November 1988.* Series P–20, no. 440, 1989, p. 4.

volved in voluntary associations and in the community in general. This sense of alienation is more often accompanied by a feeling of powerlessness compared to those in higher-class positions. This feeling was demonstrated by Lane's (1962) in-depth study of working-class men who felt they had little ability to influence events.

Whatever the reasons are for a low rate of voting among the lower classes, the outcome is clear. We have seen in Chapter 6 that in countries where there is an active party representing the lower classes there are important outcomes such as lower income inequality, more welfare support, and higher taxes on the rich. Given the political opinions of the working class on these subjects in the United States (Form 1985), we can say similar outcomes would be found in this country if voter participation were equal all through the class system. The United States especially would follow significantly different policies in many areas related to economic issues (Zipp, Landerman, and Luebke 1982). Which is, no doubt, one of the most important reasons little is done by political elites to increase the voter participation of the lower classes.

In beginning this discussion of class political values we noted that party voting is only a rough indication of political orientation. A more precise understanding of political orientation can be gained by examining some specific issues. With respect to economic issues (such as the role of government in the economy and government redistribution to the lower classes) the lower middle class and working class tend to be more liberal (Lipset and Raab 1970; Hamilton 1972).

With respect to civil liberties and support for minority programs, while the lower middle class and upper middle class tend to be more liberal, the working class tends to be more conservative (that is, less supportive of minorities and civil liberty issues; Lipset and Raab 1970; Hamilton 1972). However, lest we foster the old stereotype of a bigoted working class (as shown in the character of Archie Bunker on television), it is important to examine the working-class views on race further.

What more detailed studies of working-class attitudes toward racial issues and civil rights seem to indicate is that working-class people are often angered by changes favoring minorities because they feel their own hard work has left them in no better an economic position than that of minorities (Ransford 1972). And as Hamilton (1972) shows, less civil rights tolerance among the working class is influenced by more religious fundamentalism (shown to be related to less support for minorities; Lipset and Raab 1970) and region (the Southern working class is much less supportive of minorities).

The question of working-class intolerance and lack of support for civil liberties is related to a much wider debate in the social sciences, a debate stimulated by Lipset's (1960) famous work on working-class authoritarianism. The idea of working-class authoritarianism stems from earlier research by Adorno et al. (1950), who saw an authoritarian personality as primarily responsible for anti-Semitic beliefs. The authoritarian personality is typified by the person who is intolerant and repressive to subordinates and views the world in rigid black-and-white terms.

Borrowing from this concept, Lipset (1960:89) argues that the "lower class way of life produces individuals with rigid and intolerant approaches to politics." Included among the factors said to produce working-class authoritarianism are low education, low participation in the community, little reading, isolation, and authoritarian child rearing (similar to that described above for the working class).

While Lipset and others have presented some evidence claimed to support his view of working-class authoritarianism, there is much counterevidence. For example, the fascism scale used to measure authoritarianism has been questioned as a valid measure for less educated people (see Miller and Riessman 1961; Lipsitz 1965). With respect to working-class intolerance on racial issues, Hamilton (1972:408) concludes, "Were we to take the non-South white Protestant majority and exclude the Southern-reared segment, it is clear that the relationship shown . . . would be shifted in the direction of greater working-class tolerance." Finally, other studies have shown that there is no significant difference between the working class and others on racial intolerance per se (Campbell 1971), and that support for the Vietnam war (suggested by some as linked to working-class authoritarianism) was not greater among the working class (Patchen 1970; Wright 1972).

As with other debates in the social sciences, the controversy over the existence of working-class authoritarianism is no doubt related to the complexity of the issue involved. But it seems reasonable to conclude that overall the working class has no greater personal predisposition toward intolerance or racism than others in our society. When we do find a tendency for the working class to be less supportive of change favoring minorities we must remember the class position of blue-collar workers. It is easy for higher-class people to support civil rights; their interests are less threatened. As Ransford (1972:345) writes, "A lack of decision-making power on the job, the fact of hard earned dollars going for tax programs to aid blacks with no comparable programs for working class whites, a power structure unresponsive to the needs of the working man—these stresses probably affect working class anger as much as personal prejudice.''

Also, to the degree that we find any working-class authoritarianism and racial intolerance, this psychological state must be related to structural conditions that lead to insecurity and scapegoating. Leggett (1972:26) has charged that Lipset failed to distinguish between ''1) workmen found in relatively isolated enclaves marked by economic insecurity and 2) working class populations located in circumstances characterized by maximal contact with the middle classes and minimal economic insecurity.'' When such a distinction is made, Leggett argues, the economically insecure workers are found to be more intolerant and may direct their resulting psychological insecurity and hostility toward underdog minorities in the form of scapegoating. Leggett's empirical work lends support to this view, which may help to explain those studies that do report evidence of working-class authoritarianism.

Middle-Class and Working-Class Subcultures: Conclusion Subcultures imply different values, attitudes, outlooks, and behavior that are contained within a larger culture. The middle and working classes are more alike than they are different. There are two primary reasons for this similarity: The members of both classes are equally products of Western and particularly American culture and both classes are toward the middle of the stratification system. With respect to the latter reason, many of the differing class characteristics can be viewed as lying upon a continuum. The greater differences are found between the extremes—say, between the upper class and the poor. Considering the middle and working classes alone, we find greater differences between upper-middle-class professionals or managers and unskilled laborers.

Another point needs emphasis. Although the two groups have some differences, one is not necessarily ''better'' than the other. We may identify with, and be more familiar with, one class subculture, but we must not let this bias our view of others. Because most social scientists are upper middle class (at least in education and occupational status, if not always income), in the past they have tended to present an overly negative picture of the lower middle class and working class. The working class especially has been viewed as authoritarian, bigoted and harsh with its family. More recent research increasingly rejects these negatives images. But, of course, there are differences. And as we have shown with the above examples, for the most part these differences can be understood with respect to differing positions in the overall class structure.

MIDDLE-CLASS AND WORKING-CLASS POSITIONS IN THE STRUCTURES OF ECONOMIC AND POLITICAL POWER

A central premise in the conflict perspective of social stratification is that groups with strong common interests will, when these common interests are recognized and when possible, work together to ensure that these common interests are attained and maintained. This is no less true for those groups on the bottom as for those on the top. *But* this is true only to the extent that a group with common interests is able to recognize its common interests, and has resources (such as money, numbers, organization, and time) with which to attain its common interests.

As should be evident from our discussion of the upper class and the corporate class, those on top of the stratification system are usually favored in both respects. However, those below the top are not totally powerless, passive, or nonparticipants in the conflict process of reward distribution in the society. Too many theories and too much research on power elites (see Mintz et al. 1976; Whitt 1979) have assumed that they are.

Rather than viewing those below the top as completely powerless, it is imperative that we recognize the part they play in the process of conflict over the distribution of resources in the society. For example, if we acknowledge that conditions are at least to some extent better for the working class today and if we assume that the working class is powerless, we are forced to make the rather dubious assumption that things are better because those on top of the stratification system decided it was fair to give the working class a better life.

True, the working class *is* better off, in part because of changes associated with industrialization. However, with a powerless working class the fruits of industrialization could just as well have gone exclusively to the upper class. When middle-, working-, or lower-class gains are attained, it is more reasonable to assume that they are attained as concessions in the process of conflict. The Southern textile firm of J. P. Stevens did not suddenly grant higher wages and union representation to its workers in 1980 after seventeen years of struggle because J. P. Stevens decided it had been unfair to workers.

Labor Unions

When thinking of labor unions most people think of working-class influence in economic authority structures. Political and economic influence, however, are inevitably linked when we recognize that political and economic elites often work together. Our main focus in the present section is the influence of unions in economic authority structures, saving the political impact of unions for the next section.

We may begin by noting that the history of union activity in this country has three primary lessons for understanding the place of workers in the economic power structure. First, gains were seldom made by workers until they were able to organize effectively. This is the essence of power or *party* as defined by Weber. Before effective union organization, workers were low in all three of Weber's dimensions of social stratification—class, status, and party.

Second, the greater power of capitalists (in class, status, and party) enabled them to prevent the more extensive change sought by labor. In other words, although changes were made (such as higher wages and shorter working hours), these changes represented only relatively small concessions that kept the more important issues—such as corporate control of profits, economic decision making, and control of the work place—from successful challenge. In effect, it is argued, the recognition of labor unions strengthened corporate capitalism (Aronowitz 1974).

Third, and perhaps most important in showing the conflict relationship between capitalists and labor, we find that workers are able to win some demands primarily when political or economic conditions are such that the bargaining position of labor is strengthened. For example, although workers had been struggling for years, legal rights for collective bargaining were not won until 1935 (Griffin, Wallace, and Rubin 1986). It took a major economic crisis to (1) provide more worker unity of action, (2) make the political and (some) economic elites realize that major reforms were needed, and (3) present Franklin Roosevelt with the need for working-class support to achieve economic reforms. All of these factors led to the successful push for union recognition.

Since the routinization (legalization) of labor conflict, we find a similar pattern of some successful labor demands when political or economic conditions provide labor with a better bargaining position. It is commonly thought that strikes occur when conditions are worse for workers. Rather, when unemployment is low and the economy is in general healthy (for example, output is higher), workers can better afford to strike, and capitalists are more hurt by strikes (Snyder 1975).

Furthermore, as the dual-economy research shows, the working class gets better wages in core industries, where union organizing is made easier (Beck, Horan, and Tolbert 1978; Form 1985; Rubin 1986), and in larger factories and cities in which workers are more concentrated and more easily organized (Lincoln 1978). Finally, research on farm laborers shows that after years of struggle they were able to achieve union recognition and improved wages in the 1960s, when they obtained outside support from liberal organizations and politicians (Jenkins and Perrow 1977).

Thus far our discussion has been concerned only with working-class unionization, primarily because middle-class unionization remains very limited. A brief explanation of this limitation is in order. It is understandable that the upper middle class is not inclined toward unionization—for the most part it is part of management or consists of free professionals. As Collins (1975) notes, the more one gives orders in the name of the organization and the closer one is to upper management (or can realistically face the possibility of moving into top management), the more one identifies with the organization and its ideology. Upper-middle-class people working in large organizations have on occasion participated in strikes (take, for example, doctors in large hospitals). But the lower middle class often works under conditions similar to those of blue-collar workers, whom we expect to be more unionized. Still, white-collar unionization remains, in this country at least (Giddens 1973:188), quite limited.

There seem to be several reasons for this limited and uneven white-collar, or lower-middle-class, participation in unions. As Mills (1953:305–308) pointed out thirty years ago, white-collar unionization is limited because white-collar employees often feel they have a greater chance to move into higher occupational positions, are closer and identify more with management, and are less exposed to union organizing, which is usually directed toward blue-collar workers. One reason union organizing is less often directed toward white-collar employees is that these employees are more often women, who are seen as being in the labor force temporarily (Aronowitz 1974:297). Also, white-collar workers are less often employed in concentrated, homogeneous work settings where labor organization is less difficult (Giddens 1973:191).

The bigger question, however, pertains to the shrinking level of unionization for all levels of workers, especially the working class. From a level of about one-half after World War II, by 1975 only 28 percent of workers were union members (U.S. Bureau of the Census, *Statistical Abstracts of the United States 1987*). At the end of the 1980s the level of union membership had fallen to about 18 percent. We see in Table 9-6 that this rate of union membership is much lower than for any other capitalist nation.

Among the most important reasons for this recent reduction is the change in the occupational structure; again, it is that shrinking of middle-paying jobs in this country. It is the workers in precisely these jobs who have had the highest rates of union membership. The big increase in low-paying jobs, on the other hand, is found in those periphery industries that are the most difficult for labor unions to organize.

Even before this change occurred in the occupational structure, the level of union membership in this country was low compared to other nations. Political elites in the United States have never been as tolerant of unions as have other industrial nations (Form 1985). We must remember that it was not until 1935 that workers were even given the legal right to call for a vote of workers to establish a union without being fired from their jobs, or being subjected to other forms of repression. An impressive research project has now shown that it was primarily organized efforts by corporate and political elites that were successful in keeping unions from organizing and establishing themselves in the United States (Griffin, Wallace, and Rubin 1986).

Middle-Class and Working-Class Political Influence

The extent and means of political influence by the upper class and the corporate class have been examined in detail in Chapters 7 and 8. In light of our

TABLE 9-6
COMPARATIVE RATES OF UNION MEMBERSHIP, 1986

Country	Rate of union membership, %
United States	18.0
Japan	28.2
England	52.0
West Germany	40.8

Source: Keizai Koho Center, *Japan, 1988: An International Comparison.* Tokyo: Keizai Koho Center, p. 73.

previous discussion, we need only brief examination of middle- and working-class political influence here. One means of political influence is voting. But as we have noted, this means of influence is limited because (1) those candidates who are more acceptable to the people who provide campaign funds (most often the wealthy) usually have a greater chance of being elected, and (2) once a candidate is elected, his or her behavior in office is often strongly influenced by those able to afford extensive lobby organizations. Also, as we have noted, the lower the class position, the less likely one is even to vote. Perhaps one reason for this lack of voter participation by the lower classes is a recognition of the political influence of the wealthy, but more likely it is related to the greater alienation from the society found among the lower classes.

However, voting is not meaningless, and some influence is gained by the middle and working classes through voting. In 1932 and 1980, for example, the United States experienced huge voter shifts by the middle and working classes that put a new party in office. In 1932 it was the Depression that led to voter rebellion; in 1980 it was primarily inflation and unemployment. In 1932 some reforms (although limited) were forthcoming that helped the middle and working classes. The effects of the 1980 election, however, brought increased inequality, tax breaks for the rich, welfare cuts, and policies attempting to reduce union influence. The fear of economic crisis in the late 1970s was exploited with promises of a trickle-down effect, which historically has not occurred significantly (Treas 1983), nor did it in the 1980s.

What happens is that on occasion, when economic or other conditions that widely affect middle- and working-class people are worsening, these conditions are politicized by elites of the other party so as to win an election. Another faction of the political elite achieves power (with the backing of another faction of the business elite). The political rhetoric used to gain popular support in the election may lead to some reforms in the interests of lower classes, but such reforms are usually limited, and at times harmful to lower-class interests, as in the 1980s.

Besides political influence through electing candidates believed to favor particular class interests (by voting and/or campaign contributions), there is the possibility of political pressure on government officials already in office. We need not review again the most consistent form of this type of political pressure, but we do need to note how those below the upper and corporate classes may be able to use this form of influence.

Most importantly, this form of political influence requires a strong central organization that can (1) pool resources and (2) keep track of the decisions that are being made and need to be made that affect the interests of those represented by the organization. In order to get resources for effective political pressure, a strong organization is needed in order to convince or even coerce those who would benefit from the political pressure to contribute resources for doing so.

Most broad-based interest groups (such as those with common class interests) usually find it very difficult to form effective political lobby organizations. For members of the working class or middle class who are unionized, labor unions do represent a form of organization that may be able to pool resources and overcome the free-rider problem for effective political pressure. Unions have been active with political action committees (PACs) in making campaign contributions (though much less so than corporations).

Also, unions have been active in lobby activities of various kinds. Evidence of this is found in interesting research by Hicks, Friedland, and Johnson (1978). Noting that the lower classes (whether working class or poor) have common interests in greater government redistribution policies to the lower classes, these researchers examined the differing power bases of the corporate class versus the working class in individual states to see if there was a tie between the relative strength of these class power bases and state government redistribution policies. They found that the more big corporations are headquartered in a state, the less a state's redistribution policy helps the lower classes (in such things as welfare spending). In contrast, the more union headquarters, union locals, and union membership found in the state, the greater the state government redistribution to the lower classes. They interpret these findings to mean that the relative strength of corporate to union elites leads to government policies that favor the class interests of the stronger.

The Middle and Working Classes in the Power Structure: Conclusion

There are other means of middle- and working-class political influence, such as lawsuits, information provided to the mass media, and, in some states, political referendums. However, for all of these to be effective, it takes organization and resources, as described above. From time to time an issue will create enough class unity for effective organization and pooling of resources to achieve some change favoring the interests of the lower classes. But because of the many problems noted above, such influence by the lower classes is rare. And when it does exist, the greater power and resources of the upper classes enable them to reduce the impact of the changes that may be forthcoming—to cut their losses.

However, the lower classes do have some influence in economic and political structures. Their place in the overall power structure in a society must be recognized by theories of social stratification. Rather than dismissing the power of the middle and working classes, as mass-society theories have done (for example, Mills 1953, 1956), we have tried to present a picture of *power stratification* (rather than one of power versus powerlessness).

Along with other resources, the power to achieve differing class interests is unequally distributed—but it is distributed. And this is the essence of class conflict. If there is to be a process of active class conflict, the power to achieve class interests must not be in the sole possession of only one class. This is what makes the dynamics of class conflict and change in the United States a reality.

From year to year, from decade to decade, the changes relevant to differing class interests are usually difficult to see (except in time of revolution). This is especially true because in the short run we seldom find a consistent line of change—that is, over (say) a decade, particular classes may win some struggles but lose others. From the perspective of a century or more, however, the class structure may reveal a more consistent pattern of change. We can say with hindsight that the working class has achieved significant change in its favor in the past century. But as our review of the history of social stratification has shown (in Chapter 3), a century of slow improvement for a particular class may or may not be repeated in the next.

10

THE POOR

The United States is in many ways a nation of contrasts and contradictions. Despite Japan's growing economic power, the United States continues to have the world's most powerful economy in terms of the overall size of GNP. American multinational corporations circle the globe in search of profits, while U.S. economic elites live with material comforts beyond the hope of fifteenth-century kings. Yet within the United States we also find much poverty. We have already seen that the United States has the highest level of income inequality among industrial nations. But we can also say that the United States has a greater percentage of its people living in poverty than does any other capitalist industrial nation (George and Lawson 1980).

The contrasts of wealth and poverty are nowhere more striking than in many of the great cities of this nation, perhaps in New York City more than anywhere else. New York City is the financial capital of the nation and in some zip code areas of New York City we find an average income higher than anywhere else in the United States, and probably the world. But New York City also contains the greatest concentration of the nation's welfare recipients. In 1981 it was estimated that each night 36,000 people in New York City had to sleep on the sidewalks, in parks, or over subway vents (see *Newsweek,* March 23, 1981, p. 72). In 1983 this estimate went up to 50,000 with the highest unemployment since the Great Depression of the 1930s. And as we have already seen, recent evidence indicates that the homeless now include a much larger percentage of children and whole families than at any time since World War II.

The 1980s were bad years for the poor in New York City, and across the nation. As we will see below, poverty in the United States went up considerably in the early 1980s, and did not go back down to the levels of the 1970s by the end of the 1980s. And the poor in the 1980s were poorer than before. Those people at the top of the poverty population were further from the income of the average American by the mid-1980s than at any other time since consistent poverty figures have been compiled. Among the poor themselves, a larger percentage were below 75 percent of the poverty line than ever before (*Focus* 1984:7). We will also see that many more children are included in this group of poor people than ever before (*Focus* 1986:6).

With big increases in the number of poor people in the 1980s, we might expect an increase in hunger in the United States. Hunger was brought down in the late 1960s and 1970s, but it was back up in the 1980s. A study by the Harvard Medical School Task Force on Hunger estimated that by the mid-1980s, 12 million children and 8 million adults in the United States could be considered hungry by a standard medical definition of hunger and malnutrition (Brown 1987). One reason for this increase in hunger is that fewer people were getting food stamps after the Reagan cuts in the food stamp program. But even among those who received food stamps, a U.S. Department of Agriculture study found that 80 percent of these people were not getting adequate nutrition to maintain long-term health (Brown 1987:40). This is hardly surprising when we realize that food stamp recipients are given only 49 cents per meal.

The Reagan cuts in welfare during the early 1980s resulted in about 400,000 people being pushed off the welfare rolls totally, with another 300,000 facing sharp reductions in how much money they could receive from welfare (*Focus* 1984:4). Also, in 1976, 75 percent of the unemployed were receiving income assistance. By 1982, however, only 42 percent of the unemployed were receiving unemployment checks. And while the Reagan policies reduced taxes for the rich, the taxes paid by the poor actually *increased*. By the mid-1980s, a family of four living at the poverty line (about $11,000 for a family of four) paid about $1,000 in federal income taxes (*Focus* 1984:5).

Poverty, of course, must also be considered in a relative sense. There is absolute poverty in the United States—a poverty due to lack of basic necessities which is life-threatening. The homeless in the United States dying in the cold winter of 1989 were just as dead as the people who starved to death in Third World countries in 1989. But many considered poor by the material standards of the United States would not be considered poor if living under the same conditions in nations such as Chad, the Philippines, or India. In China, for example, in the 1980s a "highly paid" factory worker bringing home the equivalent of $93 a month in wages, and living with other family members in a 600-square-foot apartment that has no hot water or refrigerator, would not consider himself or herself to be poor by Chinese standards (see the *Los Angeles Times,* December 7, 1980).

The point is that poverty cannot simply be considered relative to the material existence of people throughout the world; in many important ways it is *relative to the society in which the poor find themselves.* In large part this is because the self-worth, the aspirations, and the expectations of people are shaped by the relative position of others in the society. While the poor in rural India may feel no shame or deprivation living in a poverty that has existed throughout the centuries, poverty in the United States will create more psychological damage, shame, and/or discontent in the context of the affluence of many others in the country. This is not to say that poverty is less "bad" or less harmful in India; absolute deprivation, hunger, and homelessness hurt the same anywhere. But there is a psychological aspect of poverty amidst plenty. This difference between *poverty* per se and *inequality* (that is, the gap between the rich and poor in a community) is indicated by studies of the relationship between poverty, inequality, and crime or political violence. Studies of inequality and poverty in American cities show that poverty alone is not related to more crime in the city (Blau and Blau 1982; Williams 1984); the level of inequality usually shows a stronger relationship to crimes like murder. In a similar manner, studies have found that the number of police (per population) hired by a community is related to the level of inequality in the community, not simply the rate of poverty in the community (Jacobs 1979). The same can be said internationally. The murder rate in a country and the level of political violence (such as riots, terrorist activity, violent protest) are related to the level of inequality in the country rather than simply the rate of poverty (Messner 1982; Muller 1985).

Thus, although poverty is an economic condition, it is also more than that. In a complex society such as the United States it means living at the very bottom of the occupational, authority, and property structures of the system of social stratification. Within the occupational structure it means, when work can be found, doing the dirty routine work no one else will do. But most importantly, it means seldom being able to find secure work at all. And in an industrialized nation where no work means either getting no food or receiving welfare, such a prospect is frightening.

In the present chapter our examination of the bottom of the stratification system will focus on the following questions:

1 Who are the poor? Our concern will be to examine the methods used to estimate the existence of poverty in this country and then to examine the distribution of poverty among subgroups in the society.

2 What are the causes of poverty? In this section we will review some of the most noted theories of poverty, examine some of the empirical evidence related to these theories, and offer conclusions on the value of each theory.

3 What has been done about poverty in this country? Our concern will be the various welfare programs designed to meet the needs of the poor or reduce poverty, the history of these poverty programs, some of their outcomes, and how these programs are related to assumptions about poverty contained in the theories previously reviewed.

4 What is the nature of the welfare state and what is the position of the poor in the power structure of this country? As we will see, these two questions are of necessity related. We want to know the main functions of the welfare sate (as it relates to the lower class), the degree to which the United States has a welfare state, and why and when it was developed. Finally, as we have done with our examination of other classes, we want to examine the position of the poor in relation to the overall power structure in our society. In contrast to what is often stated, the poor are not completely powerless, for although the traditional means of influence in the society are often closed to the poor, they have, at times, gone outside these traditional means of influence to effect social change.

COUNTING THE POOR

As most people recognize, the poor in this country are primarily those with limited job skills, inadequate diet, substandard housing, low education, inadequate medical care, a shorter life expectancy—the list goes on. All of these things, of course, are important outcomes of living at the bottom of the stratification system. However, our major task is not to describe all the negative consequences of poverty; rather, it is to understand the existence of poverty in highly industrialized and affluent countries like the United States. It would be helpful to begin by describing briefly who the poor are.

Counting and identifying the poor are typically accomplished by establishing a *poverty line*—that is, an *economic definition* of poverty. Living at the bottom of the stratification system and the primary dimensions that make up this stratification system mean having limited economic resources to meet family needs. The Bureau of the Census arrives at its estimate of poverty through a determination of what it costs a family (of a certain size and place of residence) to buy food, housing, and other necessities.

Criticisms of the Poverty Line

As might be expected, much controversy is created when attempting such an estimate, and most social scientists argue that the poverty line is established too low. The government estimate does not consider poverty to exist when a barely adequate standard of living is maintained; the standard of living has to be considerably less than adequate. With respect to food, for example, the official definition of living in poverty means spending less than one dollar (in 1990 dollars) per meal per person and having a diet that is not adequate to maintain long-term health (see Miller 1971:119; Rein 1971; Blumberg 1980:94).

It is also important to note that the official measure of poverty considers only pretax income (*Focus* 1984:1). That is, when the Census Bureau determines whether or not a family is considered to be living in poverty, all of their cash income is totaled to see if the family is above or below the poverty line without subtracting how much of that cash income is taken away by taxes. It was noted above that at the poverty line the average family would have paid about $1,000 in income taxes in the mid-1980s, not even counting other types of taxes such as sales taxes.

Criticisms of official poverty statistics, therefore, include the obvious charge that poverty is underestimated in this country. But also, the critics charge, a poverty line should consider the *relative* aspects of poverty—that is, because poverty is not only a material condition, we should consider poverty to exist when people are far below the average standard of living in the country. Some suggest that a relative poverty line could be drawn at about half of the average income of the population. Danziger, Haveman, and Plotnick (1986:54), for example, used another method to measure relative poverty by comparing the gap between the poverty line and median income in 1965, then projecting the same gap into the future. If the gap had been the same in 1983, poverty would have been 18.6 percent instead of 15.2 percent as the official figures show.

In addition to indicating the relative, and thus social and psychological, aspects of poverty, a poverty line drawn in this manner would keep pace with the average standard of living in the society. At present, although the official poverty line is revised each year to account for increases in the cost of living, it has tended to fall further and further behind average family income over the years (Blumberg 1980:100).

In a relative sense, the poor today are poorer than they were twenty or thirty years ago. But poverty is a political issue, with each political administration having an interest in putting forth the most favorable image of its accomplishments. Furthermore, a redefinition of poverty could cost millions in federal grants that are tied to the estimated level of poverty.

By the late 1970s, and especially during the early years of the Reagan administration, a different critique of the official Census Bureau's estimate of poverty emerged. In this case it was argued that the amount of poverty is overestimated in the United States. This argument was not so much that the poverty line itself is determined inaccurately, but that the measures of income used by the Census Bureau should be expanded. With the standard Census definition of poverty, all cash income is considered when placing a family above or below the poverty line. Cash income includes all money from any source—a job, investments, rent, royalties, welfare payments, pension benefits, and so on. However, since the 1960s, there has been relatively more government welfare aid in the form of "income-in-kind" benefits, such as food stamps and health care (Medicaid). Thus, the argument is that the value of these kinds of aid should be added to a family's cash income when determining the rate of poverty. With this argument some supporters of Reaganomics went so far as to say there was *no longer* poverty in the United States when you totaled the value of all aid going to the poor during the late 1970s (Harrington 1984:77–79; see, for example, Anderson 1978; Gilder 1981:111–112). Beside the fact that walking around a low-income area in any major American city would show the absurdity of such a claim, there are other obvious problems with such a statement that we must consider below.

As can be seen in Table 10-1, the rate of poverty is somewhat lower when considering income-in-kind as well as cash income, while using the same def-

TABLE 10-1
TRENDS IN THE RATE OF POVERTY WITH THREE
DEFINITIONS OF POVERTY

Year	Census income,* %	Adjusted income,† %	Pretransfer income,‡ %
1965	17.3	16.8	21.3
1966	14.7	—	—
1967	14.2	—	19.4
1968	12.8	—	18.2
1969	12.1	—	17.7
1970	12.6	—	18.8
1971	12.5	—	19.6
1972	11.9	—	19.2
1973	11.1	—	19.0
1974	11.2	—	20.3
1975	12.3	—	22.0
1976	11.8	—	21.0
1977	11.6	—	21.0
1978	11.4	—	20.2
1979	11.7	9.0	20.5
1980	13.0	10.4	21.9
1981	14.0	11.7	23.1
1982	15.0	12.7	24.0
1983	15.2	13.0	24.2

*Includes income from all private sector sources (such as employment income, royalties, investment) as well as government cash transfer payments (such as Social Security and welfare cash payments).
†Includes all income sources in the census income column, plus the value of income-in-kind transfer payments.
‡Includes only private sector cash income sources (such as employment income, royalties, investment income).
Source: Adapted from Danziger, Haveman, and Plotnick (1986:54).

inition of poverty (the poverty line). For example, in 1983 the standard income definition (Census definition) showed the poverty rate at 15.2 percent, whereas the adjusted income definition (including income-in-kind) showed poverty at 13.0 percent of the population (see Danziger, Haveman, and Plotnick 1986:54).

There are, however, several problems with establishing the value of income-in-kind benefits and using this to estimate the rate of poverty (*Focus* 1982). For example, how do we value the medical benefits from the Medicaid program for the poor? If we simply total the dollar amount of the medical care the poor have been given, one could become nonpoor simply by becoming very ill and receiving much medical aid from the government. We could attempt to determine what the poor would pay for medical care through a private insurance program (which is what the Census Bureau has done), but this remains misleading in many ways (see Harrington 1984:85–86).

Some people within the Reagan administration (see Anderson 1978; Gilder 1981:111–112) were arguing that the value of all types of programs for the poor should be included as income to the poor (an argument not accepted by the

Census Bureau and not estimated in Table 10-1). By this argument we might say the poor are no longer poor because the government has hired social workers to watch over them and built buildings to house the welfare offices where welfare checks are processed (which does account for over half of the welfare spending).

There is the additional problem that all the poor do not receive equal benefits from the income-in-kind aid programs, and many of the poor actually receive nothing. For example, to receive money from the largest welfare program (AFDC, Aid to Families with Dependent Children) and therefore qualify for many of the income-in-kind benefits as well, most states require a person to have an income much lower than the poverty line.

Finally, this argument also assumes that all the money for income-in-kind programs actually goes to the poor. Again, this is wrong because (1) more than half of this money goes to administer the programs (to pay welfare workers, maintain welfare offices, etc.) and (2) most of this aid in some of the income-in-kind programs goes to the aged, who are less likely to be poor today (Harrington 1984:81–87).

If we are going to include income-in-kind in the income measure to determine poverty status, we should be consistent and subtract taxes paid by the poor. Currently, this is not done even though families with income about equal to the poverty line pay about 10 percent of their income to federal taxes alone (*Focus* 1984). Michael Harrington (1984:81) has estimated that if the poverty line were drawn where it should be to indicate real economic deprivation due to lack of money for an adequate amount of necessities (that is, a poverty line higher than is estimated by the Census Bureau), we still had more than 15 percent of the U.S. population living in poverty in the mid-1980s, even if income-in-kind sources of income are included. Despite these and other criticisms of the official poverty line, all extensive and yearly estimates of poverty are based upon this method of defining poverty, and it is this method that must be used as we now discuss how much poverty we have, have had, and who is included in this group.

The Extent of Poverty in the United States   In estimating the level of poverty in the United States for 1987 the U.S. Bureau of the Census considered a nonfarm family of four to be poor if its yearly income fell below $11,611. Using this estimate we find that about 13.5 percent of the United States population was considered poor in 1987, as shown in Table 10-2. Comparing the estimated amount of poverty in this country over the past few years, Figure 10-1 shows that the percentage of poor dropped during the 1960s (from about 22 percent in 1959 when the poverty figures were first estimated), then leveled off in the 1970s to about 11 or 12 percent. During the 1980s, however, the rate of poverty went up again, reaching a high point of 15.2 percent in 1983, before slowly moving down again to the 13 percent range by 1989.

Changes in the Rate of Poverty   While our attention is on Figure 10-1 and Table 10-1 we should consider some of the reasons *why* the rate of poverty

TABLE 10-2
EXTENT OF POVERTY FOR SELECT CATEGORIES OF THE
POPULATION IN 1987

	Percentage of group at poverty level
Total United States population:	13.5
Whites	10.5
Blacks	33.1
Spanish origin	28.2
Aged (65+)	12.5
Under 18	20.6
Female-headed households with children:	46.1
White	38.7
Black	59.5
Spanish origin	60.7
Residence	
Inside metropolitan areas	12.5
In central cities	18.6
Outside central cities	8.5
Outside metropolitan areas	16.9
Region	
Northeast	11.0
Midwest	12.7
South	16.1
West	12.6

Source: U.S. Bureau of the Census, *Money Income and Poverty Status of Families and Persons in the United States: 1987.* Current Population Reports, 1989, series P–60, no. 163, table 20, p. 33.

moved up and down as it did between 1959 and 1989. The drop in the level of poverty between 1959 and 1970, and the continued lower level of poverty through the 1970s, was primarily the result of expanded welfare benefits beginning in the second half of the 1960s (Blumberg 1980:100). It must be stressed that welfare benefits alone would very seldom bring a person or family out of poverty. For example, in 1983 only 3.4 percent of the poor were removed from poverty by welfare benefits in cash (such as AFDC) and another 9.2 percent were removed by the income-in-kind benefits (Danziger, Haveman, and Plotnick 1986:65). What happened in this time period was that more of the working poor were allowed to receive some welfare benefits, which, combined with their job income, brought them above the poverty line. This manner of reducing poverty can be seen rather easily from Table 10-1. Remember that the three columns in Table 10-1 represent three different definitions of income. The first includes income from a job, investments, etc., and cash income from government welfare programs (or transfer payments, as they are often called). The second column includes this income plus the income-in-kind cash value discussed above. But the third column includes only "market income"; that is, only private sector income from sources such as a job, and excludes all government aid. It is important to note that from 1965 to 1980 the

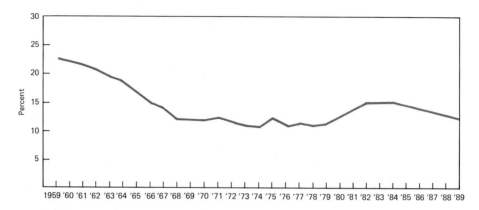

FIGURE 10-1
Percentage of population living in poverty according to official government statistics, 1959–1980.
Source: U.S. Bureau of the Census, *Money Income and Poverty Status of Families and Persons in the U.S.: 1978*, Current Population Reports, 1979, Series P-60, No. 120, and U.S. Bureau of the Census, *Population Profile of the United States: 1989*, Current Population Reports, Series P-20, No. 363, 1989.

rate of poverty measured by this market income or pretransfer definition of income changed very little (staying around 20 percent, where it was in 1959 when we first started measuring poverty in this society). It is only with the two income definitions that include government aid (columns 1 and 2) that we find a reduction in poverty. Thus, poverty was reduced by government aid in this period, not by more jobs, or better-paying jobs. This also helps us understand why poverty stayed down in the 1970s despite the fact that the United States had a higher level of unemployment.

Why did poverty shoot up again in the 1980s? Following the above description we can see that poverty went up in part because of Reagan's cuts in the welfare programs (in other words, poverty was brought down by welfare benefits previously, then brought back up through the cutting of these programs). And in the opposite way from how poverty was reduced in the 1960s and 1970s, by allowing many of the working poor to receive some welfare benefits, poverty was increased by Reagan's welfare cuts, primarily by making the working poor ineligible for welfare benefits (Piven and Cloward 1982; Danziger and Haveman 1982; Dunn 1984).

But as you can see in the third column of Table 10-1, during 1980 to 1982 poverty was going up even by the market or pretransfer definition of income. The early 1980s brought very high unemployment during a time when welfare was no longer as likely to keep the unemployed out of poverty. More importantly, however, the increased poverty of the late 1980s was caused by the changing economy we have described in previous chapters. More inequality *and* poverty were produced in the late 1980s because of fewer jobs paying middle-income wages and more jobs paying poverty wages (*Focus* 1984:10; Thurow 1987).

Movement Into and Out of Poverty   Until there was more extensive research on the subject of poverty, it was commonly assumed that once a person falls into poverty, or especially if they are born into poverty, their chance of moving out of poverty was very low. We now know that this assumption was inaccurate for many of the poor. From a series of studies (see Evanson 1981; Wilson 1987:174–178) the rather optimistic conclusion is that there is rather extensive movement out of poverty. But there is also the less pleasant finding that more people in this country experience poverty at least sometime in their life than was previously thought. Also, the first set of findings must not be seen as totally positive, because those who do move out of poverty seldom move very far above it, with a tendency to fall back into poverty sometime in their life.

Levy (1977), for example, has found that only 43 percent of those who were poor in 1967 continued to be poor for five of the next seven years, and that only 5 percent of the U.S. population was poor for at least five of the seven years (compared to 12 percent of the population poor in any one year). Coe (1978) found that only 1 percent of the U.S. population was poor nine out of nine years included in his study. And Hill (1981) found only 0.7 percent of the U.S. population poor for the full ten years in her study. However, Hill (1981) found that 24 percent of the U.S. population were poor at least one year of the ten years under study, and Coe (1978) found that 25 percent of Americans were poor at least one year in a nine-year period. Thus, while there is movement into and out of poverty, (1) from 43 percent to 60 percent of the poor do not move out (*Focus* 1984:8; Wilson 1987:176), (2) when they do move out they do not move very far above poverty or stay out, and (3) about one-fourth of the U.S. population experience poverty for at least one year during any given ten-year period.

The Distribution of Poverty   In estimating the extent of poverty it is also useful to compare the existence of poverty across subcategories of the population. When doing so we find that the chances of living in poverty are not randomly distributed in the society. For example, as indicated in Table 10-2, minorities, children, and female-headed households had a greater chance of being poor in 1987. Also of note is that of family heads of poor families, about 48 percent were employed at least part-time. Employment, therefore, is not a guarantee of nonpoverty status.

Such a nonrandom distribution of poverty raises questions about the nature of poverty. What characteristics do people who have a greater chance of being poor have that helps produce their poverty? More importantly, what is it about the nature of our society that helps produce greater poverty among some groups of people? With these questions in mind we may ask whether the characteristics of the poor or the characteristics of our society are more important in explaining the existence of poverty. As we will see, the characteristics of the poor have most often been held responsible. But the nature of class conflict in our system of social stratification suggests otherwise. It is time that we examine these questions about the causes of poverty by reviewing some of the most noted theories of poverty.

THEORIES OF POVERTY

When, toward the middle of this century, it finally became apparent to most social scientists that poverty was a pervasive and continuing feature of our society, poverty was singled out as an important social problem worthy of special study. One outcome of this recognition has been special theories devoted to understanding this particular condition.

The separate status of poverty theories is worth noting because it tells us something rather curious about how the subject matter of poverty has been treated by social scientists. It suggests that although one set of processes was believed to help explain ''normal'' inequality and class divisions, the existence of poverty in our affluent society is somehow different. Some of the special theories of poverty examined below provide valuable insights, but we can best understand the existence of poverty as we have class divisions in general—that is, with a conflict (or structural) theory of social stratification.

Blaming the Poor

Before turning to the various theories of poverty, it will be helpful to discuss the belief in or social value of *individualism* in this country. By doing so we can understand better (1) how the general population tends to view the poor in our society, (2) what some of the particular problems faced by the poor are, (3) how our present welfare system is designed, and (4) what some of the main points of the first group of theories examined below mean.

Individualism may be defined broadly as the belief that the individual is more important than the social group (see Lukes 1973b). For those who are a product of the American culture this may seem an unquestionable statement; but in many non-Western cultures it is not. In other cultures the individual is often of secondary importance; the collective is given precedence over the needs and particular interests of the individual (see Dumont's 1970 discussion of India).

This general value of individualism has very wide implications for the society. It usually means, for example, that government should not infringe upon the rights of individuals—giving us our value of *freedom*. Individualism suggests the importance of free competition in business affairs and of having government not interfere in ''free'' economic pursuits (that is, a laissez-faire view of government). Individualism also conveys the ideal of equality of opportunity (not equality per se), whereby people should have the opportunity to better themselves, or to be upwardly mobile and prosper as their talents and motivation allow.

Most important for the present discussion, individualism can mean that people are held responsible for their lot in life. For many, the logic of this value is that because equality of opportunity is supposed to exist, those who are poor have only themselves to blame for their poverty. There are special circumstances in which a person is relieved of responsibility for his or her poverty; to some degree our society has been willing to recognize the unique problems of poverty for the elderly, the disabled, and children. These people make up the "deserving poor." But for the most part, the poor without such "excuses" for their poverty are held in contempt by the general population.

The above description and implications of a strong belief in individualism are somewhat overstated. General social values are never completely accepted by all in the society; nor are they always interpreted in exactly the same way by everyone. And historical change, the realities of a new age, must erode the original strength and meaning of traditional social values.

To the degree that our individualistic tradition was shaped by our frontier era, early Protestant beliefs, and the view of this country as a place where immigrants of the eighteenth and nineteenth centuries could find a new, prosperous life, we might expect this traditional value of individualism to have lost some of its strength. The evidence confirms this, but only to a small degree (Bellah et al. 1985). The continued effect of this value is in part reflected in the operation of our social welfare system and in the beliefs held about the cause of poverty in this society. Let us examine the latter in more detail.

Many studies have examined popular beliefs about poverty in the United States. For example, a national sample of 1,017 adults were asked by Feagin (1972, 1975) to respond to a series of eleven statements about the causes of poverty in our society. The first four statements were designed to assess the degree of individualistic explanations for poverty held by people. In response to these four statements, a majority felt "lack of thrift" (58 percent), "lack of effort" (55 percent), and "lack of ability" (52 percent) by the poor were *very important* reasons for poverty; and a near majority (48 percent) thought "loose morals and drunkenness" were very important. Clearly these statements are in the individualistic tradition of viewing the poor as responsible for poverty.

As we move down the list of statements from 1 to 10, we move from strong individualistic statements about the causes of poverty to structural statements (low wages, lack of jobs, discrimination), suggesting that some aspects of the society (outside of the poor) are responsible for poverty. (Statement 11 shows a fatalistic view of poverty—"just bad luck.") And as we move down the list of statements the percentage of people responding "very important" drops substantially.

It is interesting to examine various subcategories of Feagin's sample for their differing responses about the causes of poverty (see Feagin 1975:99). When doing so we find that individualistic responses are related to age; those over fifty are most likely to have strong individualistic explanations (62 percent) and those under thirty less likely (42 percent). Individualistic responses generally decrease with higher levels of education (42 percent for those with at least some college). Whites are more likely to hold strong individual explanations than are blacks (56 versus 45 percent), and Protestants are more likely to do so than other religious groups (for example, white Protestants, 59 percent; Jews, 35 percent).

Perhaps most interesting is that all income categories examined by Feagin were about equally likely to hold strong individualistic explanations for poverty (51 percent for those with under $4,000 a year family income to 50 percent for those with $10,000 or more family income). This is especially significant when we consider that the vast majority of those with family incomes below $4,000 a year (at the time of the study) would themselves be considered poor.

Other studies of the poor and welfare recipients (Cole and Lejeune 1972; Kerbo 1976b) concur in showing that the poor themselves are often likely to hold the poor responsible for poverty. These findings clearly attest to the strength of individualistic explanations of poverty when even some poor can be convinced the poor are to blame (Ryan 1971). These beliefs about poverty held by the poor themselves have important implications for social stability, the self-concepts of the poor, and the perpetuation of poverty.

Finally, this discussion of the dominant views of poverty must not neglect the effect of these views upon theories and research in the study of poverty. Most social scientists do not blame the poor for poverty, but an individualistic view of poverty has been implicit in much of the past research. For example, a content analysis of research papers pertaining to the subject of poverty published in the top five sociology journals between 1965 and 1975 (see Table 10-3) shows that most have focused in some way on the "characteristics of the poor" in examining poverty (Kerbo 1981a; see also Huber and Form 1973). Most of these social scientists do not accept the idea that the characteristics of

TABLE 10-3
GENERAL SUBJECT AND FUNDING OF POVERTY RESEARCH IN MAJOR SOCIOLOGY JOURNALS—1965 to 1975*

Primary subject of research article	Total by category	Percentage of all poverty articles	Total in each category receiving government or foundation funding	Percentage of total funding going to category
1. Amount of poverty	1	2	0 (0%)	0
2. Individual characteristics of the poor	39	58	18 (46%)	55
3. Political or economic causes of poverty	7	10	2 (29%)	6
4. Poverty programs	19	28	13 (68%)	39
5. General or theoretical discussion	1	2	0 (0%)	0
Totals	67	100	33	100

*The total number of research articles on the subject of poverty between 1965 and 1975 found in *American Sociological Review, American Journal of Sociology, Social Forces, Social Problems,* and *Sociological Quarterly.*
Source: Table constructed from Kerbo (1981a).

the poor are totally responsible for poverty; but such research at least implies that individual characteristics such as present-time orientations, aspirations, or child-rearing practices are important for perpetuating poverty.

What accounts for this focus on the characteristics of the poor in much of the past social science research? First, it must be recognized that social scientists, like anyone else, are often influenced by the dominant values of their society. Second, there has long been a sociopsychological focus in most empirical social research (McCartney 1970; Liska 1977; Mayhew 1980, 1981). When conducting empirical research it was often easier (and thought more scientific) to measure and statistically manipulate data on individual characteristics. Third, and perhaps most significant, research funding is often necessary for extensive social research.

Several studies have shown that the most important agencies financing social research (such as the federal government and private foundations like the Ford Foundation) have a clear bias toward funding research that measures and implies that individual characteristics are involved in social problems such as crime and poverty (Galliher and McCartney 1973; Useem 1976a, 1976b; Kerbo 1981a). Such a funding bias is related to the inaccurate assumption that sociopsychological level research is more scientific, and also to the less threatening nature of such research to the status quo.

The importance of research funding can be seen in Table 10-3 when we note that most of the funding for research on poverty in these top sociology journals went to research dealing with the characteristics of the poor. The implications of this cannot be overstressed. What we think and do about poverty is to some degree related to what scientific research suggests about the nature of poverty. Thus, there is a cyclical process in which our cultural views about poverty help produce research that subsequently helps support this cultural bias. Thinking that we then know the true nature of poverty, the government designs poverty programs that try to change the characteristics of the poor. But as we will see later, these poverty programs have often failed in part because of this cultural bias (Miller 1969).

Three Kinds of Poverty Theories

It is time to take a closer look at some of the theories developed to explain poverty. Three types of categories will be examined. The first has the longest history in sociology, and in large measure suggests that the characteristics of the poor help cause poverty. Although a *culture-of-poverty theory* is now soundly rejected by most recent research, it must be examined to understand why it is inaccurate (as well as why the common myths about poverty are wrong). The second group of theories we can call *situational theories,* and the third is the *structural* or *conflict perspective*.

At the outset, Figure 10-2 may be helpful in summarizing some of the most important differences among the three types of poverty theories. Beginning with Figure 10-2a, we find a representation of the dominant culture or popular

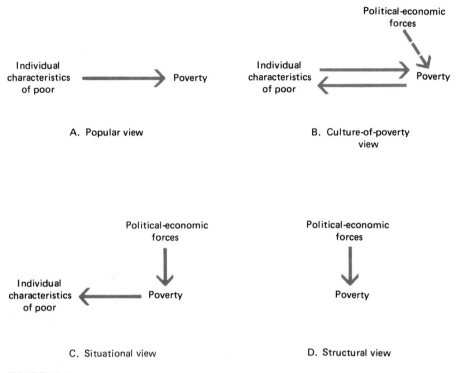

FIGURE 10-2
Causes of poverty assumed by theories of poverty and the general population.

view of the causes of poverty. In short, the poor and their characteristics cause poverty. Figure 10-2b represents the main points of the culture-of-poverty view. This theory (weakly) suggests that social conditions originally helped produce poverty (the broken line in Figure 10-2b); but, most importantly, this theory argues that poverty produces people with unique personal characteristics that in turn help ensure that the poor—and their children—remain poor.

Situational theories of poverty, as represented in Figure 10-2c, place more stress on social conditions as causing poverty. However, they do suggest that poverty produces people with particular characteristics, although these characteristics are not viewed as a compounding cause of poverty. Finally, Figure 10-2d represents a structural or conflict view of poverty. There is almost complete stress on the political and economic forces in the society that produce and maintain poverty.

A Culture of Poverty?

The study of poverty, unfortunately, has been dominated by three questions: (1) Are the poor different from other people? (2) If so, how different are the poor? and (3) How deep are these differences? The dominance of these questions is unfortunate, not because they lack any significance, but because they have deflected interest from more important questions about the nature of our society that helps produce poverty. For example, despite the abundance of research showing that the vast majority of poor, like anyone else, would rather have a decent job than receive welfare, research funding continues to go to studies that find (surprise!) that the poor prefer jobs over welfare. The abundance of such research tells us more about our social myths than about the poor.

The most noted *culture-of-poverty* theory is that of Oscar Lewis. A social anthropologist, Oscar Lewis conducted his research through detailed and lengthy personal observations of families living in poverty. His books, such as *Five Families* (1959), *La Vida* (1966), and *The Children of Sanchez* (1961), make interesting reading—full of sex, violence, and drama—and are more like novels than scientific reports. In these works Lewis attempted to show the existence of a culture of poverty that produces personality and value differences among the poor. There are five major points in this theory:

1 Because of the conditions of poverty, the poor are presented with unique problems in living (compared with the nonpoor).

2 In order to cope with these problems, the poor follow a unique lifestyle.

3 Through collective interaction and in the face of relative isolation from the nonpoor, this unique lifestyle becomes a common characteristic of the poor, producing common values, attitudes, and behavior. A common culture (or, more accurately, a subculture) is developed.

4 Once this common subculture of poverty has become, in a sense, institutionalized, it is self-perpetuating. In other words, it becomes relatively *independent* of the social conditions of poverty that helped produce the subculture. The values, attitudes, and behavior that are a part of this subculture are passed on to the children of the poor—that is, *the children are socialized into this subculture of poverty*.

5 Because this subculture is believed to shape the basic character and personality of people raised in poverty, even if opportunities to become nonpoor arise, the poor will retain the traits that allowed them to adjust to the original conditions of poverty. Thus, the poor will *not be able to adjust to the new situation* through values and behavior that will allow them to take advantage of new opportunities to become nonpoor.

Many characteristics of a culture of poverty have been listed by social scientists (see Lewis 1966:xlv–xlviii). For example, on a community level, there is a lack of participation in the institutions of the wider society (except for contact with the criminal justice system and welfare institutions). On a family level, there is the absence of a long childhood, "early initiation into sex, free unions or consensual marriages, a relatively high incidence of the abandonment of wives and children," and female-centered families. And on an individual level, the poor are believed to have "strong feelings of marginality, of helplessness, of dependence, and of inferiority." Other individual characteristics are believed to be a weak ego, lack of impulse control, "a present-time orientation with relatively little ability to defer gratification and to plan for the future," a sense of fatalism, a value stress on male superiority, and "a high tolerance for psychological pathology of all sorts."

Social scientists have developed considerable attention to the "trait" of a present-time orientation, or an inability to delay gratification. This trait is said to be a coping mechanism, for example, because it would be psychologically damaging to continually worry about and plan for a future that holds no promise of a better life or more opportunities. In short, the poor must learn to live for today.

This "cultural trait" is also seen as important in perpetuating poverty and preventing upward mobility out of poverty because the poor "learn not to delay gratification or plan for the future" and are unable to take advantage of new opportunities. More specifically, the existence of this trait is taken to mean that if new educational or job-training opportunities become available, the poor would be unable to make the sacrifice in time and energy needed to get the job training.

In concluding this summary of the culture-of-poverty theory we would like to point out that the theory is logical, clear, and, perhaps most important, fits nicely most of the common stereotypes of the poor held by the dominant society. It is easy to see why government officials and welfare administrators favor this theory, for although it fits these stereotypes of the poor, it maintains the liberal tradition of ultimately seeing society as part of the problem.

However, this theory is not overly critical of social institutions, because even when some small (nonradical) reforms have been made in the society (as reformers may claim have been made) the poor inevitably continue to exist, with their poverty now seen as their own fault. The goal then becomes one of changing the poor (rather than aspects of the society) so the poor can become "more like us."

The Culture of Poverty: A Critique Despite this theory's wide appeal and logic, it contains serious shortcomings, especially when applied to the United States (Wilson 1987:182–183). In the first place, Oscar Lewis himself never suggested that the theory had wide relevance in the United States (see Valentine 1971:215). As he made clear in one of his most noted works (Lewis 1966:li),

> Because of the advanced technology, high level of literacy, the development of mass media and the relatively high aspiration level of all sectors of the population, especially when compared with underdeveloped nations, I believe that although there is still a great deal of poverty in the United States . . . there is relatively little of what I would call the culture of poverty.

Many people, especially earlier social scientists, government officials, and welfare administrators, have chosen to ignore Oscar Lewis on this point. Accepting this theory is difficult to resist, given our cultural assumptions about the poor.

More specifically, the culture-of-poverty theory can be questioned on several grounds. First, even to the extent that we do find behavioral differences among the poor this does *not* mean that the *values* of the poor differ. As other evidence suggests, because of their conditions of poverty the poor may not be able to live up to an ideal they value equally with the nonpoor (see Rainwater 1969; Gans 1969).

Second, in common with functional theory in general, the culture-of-poverty theory assumes an overly uniform view of culture and values in industrial societies like the United States (Gans 1969). We can assume the existence of some very abstract ideals, such as the individualism discussed above, but even these abstract ideals are viewed and applied differently by different segments of the society. When we focus on more specific values and actual behavior, like deferred gratification and child rearing, we find wide variance among many groups in the society. The poor may differ in some respects, but so do many other people. If we can speak of a subculture of the poor, we can also speak of a subculture of college students, professors, salespeople, politicians, and so on. With many relatively minor differences among many segments of the population, any differences that may exist among the poor must not be overemphasized.

Third, in the previous chapter we saw that various classes may have differing tendencies with respect to such things as political attitudes and community participation. However, these differences *reflect* rather than cause class position. For the most part, this line of reasoning in the culture-of-poverty theory is incorrectly reversed—value and lifestyle differences are said to help cause lower-class placement.

Fourth, direct attempts to measure significant value differences among the poor have for the most part not supported the culture-of-poverty theory (see Ryan 1971; Miller, Riessman, and Seagull 1971). With respect to work values, many have long assumed, following a culture-of-poverty perspective, that the poor value work less than other people do. Several empirical studies of work attitudes have soundly rejected this idea (Goodwin 1972; Kaplan and Travsky 1972). In research on actual behavior, income-maintenance experiments, offering the poor government aid only slightly below what they could receive working, have shown that the poor continue to seek and accept employment (Wright 1975; Rossi and Lyall 1976).

Fifth, and perhaps most important, contrary to the culture-of-poverty view, the poor do not constitute a homogeneous group. More directly to the point of a culture of poverty which is said to keep people in poverty, we have already seen that there is rather extensive movement out of poverty. Remember that only about 1.0 percent of the population in the United States has been found to stay in poverty for nine years in a row. The culture-of-poverty theory, of course, stresses that it is the children who have grown up in poverty who are most likely to have this culture of poverty which keeps them there. But again, the studies do not show much support for this idea. For example, Levy (1977) found that "only three of every ten young adults reared in poverty homes, compared to one of ten reared in nonpoverty homes, set up poverty households on their own" (Wilson 1987:175). And even when blacks are reared in a poverty, welfare-supported, female-headed household, the probability of a young woman setting up her own poverty home was found to be only about one in three.

None of the above, however, is meant to suggest that the culture-of-poverty theory is useless in helping us understand anything about poverty. Sociologists have now begun to use the term "the underclass" (Auletta 1983), the "hard core poor," or "the truly disadvantaged" (Wilson 1987) to describe a relatively small percentage of the poor whose values, lifestyles, and personality problems make them seem close to those said to be affected by a culture of poverty. This group may include only 20 percent of all the poor (or perhaps only 2 percent of the U.S. population), but they make up a larger percentage of the persistent poor (Auletta 1983:37; Wilson 1987:176).

The Situational View of Poverty

As a group the poor do differ from the middle class on some characteristics, such as family stability and work history, and other studies have found the poor to have somewhat lower aspirations for education, occupation, and income (Della Fave 1974a). If these characteristics and behavior are not due to significant value differences, how are they to be explained? What can be called a *situational view* of poverty offers a realistic explanation.

The situational view argues that the poor may sometimes behave differently or have different lifestyles and preferences *because* they are poor, lack secure jobs, or simply lack opportunities to live up to values held by most in the society. In other words, the poor may be reacting realistically to their situation. Thus, although the situational view of poverty may agree with proponents of the culture-of-poverty theory that the poor may at times differ in behavior when compared with the middle class, the situational view *rejects* the idea (1) that the poor would not prefer to live up to most values held by a majority in the society or (2) that the differences found result from deeply held values.

Let us look at some examples. The suggested importance of an inability by the poor to delay gratification has been noted. Even to the extent that this does exist among some of the poor, it may simply stem from a realistic estimation that delaying gratification may not be rewarded. Valentine (1968) uses the example of "free unions and consensual marriages" found to be more prevalent among the poor and said to reflect value differences by the culture-of-poverty theory. In contrast to the culture-of-poverty view, Valentine (1968:132) suggests that "consensual unions provide a flexible adaptation that is functional under conditions in which fluctuating economic circumstances, actual or threatened incarceration, and other external conditions often make it advisable for cohabitating pairs to separate either temporarily or permanently and contract alternative unions, again either temporary or lasting.''

Hyman Rodman (1963) has introduced the concept of ''lower-class value stretch'' to explain how, although the poor may recognize and accept dominant values of the society, they learn to accept behavior that does not meet these ideal values. As Rodman (1963:213) writes, ''Lower-class persons . . . do not maintain a strong commitment to middle-class values that they cannot attain, and they do not continue to respond to others in a rewarding or punishing way simply on the basis of whether these others are living up to middle-class values.'' They have learned they must tolerate deviations from middle-class ideals. ''The result is a stretched value system.''

Following the idea of a lower-class value stretch, Della Fave (1974b) adds the concepts of value preferences, expectations, and ''tolerance.'' He argues that although the poor may prefer to live up to certain values, when their own expectations of being able to do so are low because of their poverty, they learn to tolerate less than preferred behavior. We can use the example of educational aspirations. The idea of a lower-class value stretch suggests realistic expectations may be that (given their circumstances) a college education is unlikely. Thus, they may come to tolerate or strive for less—say, completing high school or a trade school.

Differences between the culture-of-poverty theory and the situational view of poverty may seem trivial, but they are not; they view the causes of poverty in a very different light. For the culture-of-poverty theory the characteristics of the poor are part of the problem; for the situational view of poverty, although the poor may have some differences from the middle class, the differences are not part of the causes of poverty—only a reflection of their situation. And where the culture-of-poverty theory suggests that the poor must be changed if we are to reduce poverty, the situational view suggests that if the situation of poverty is changed, if there are opportunities and jobs, any differing characteristics of the poor will not prevent them from taking advantage of new opportunities. For example, when a present-time orientation or lack of delayed gratification is no longer a functional response to poverty, the poor will respond to new opportunities by investing time and energy for future rewards.

Both theories do have one similarity; they are primarily concerned with the individual characteristics of the poor. The culture-of-poverty theory is concerned with these characteristics because it sees them as part of the problem of poverty, while the situational view is concerned with these individual characteristics more to show that the culture-of-poverty theory is incorrect.

Though theorists following the situational view of poverty recognize that structural conditions, or political and economic forces, are the most important causes of poverty, they have been less concerned with these structural conditions than with showing why the culture-of-poverty theory is wrong. If we want to understand the causes of poverty better we must focus on these structural conditions. That is our next goal.

A Structural View of Poverty

Considering the inadequacies of the culture-of-poverty theory and the incomplete nature of situational views of poverty, Rossi and Lyall (1976) question the existence of a satisfactory theory of poverty. The absence of such a *specific* theory of poverty, however, is perhaps as it should be. If a focus on group conflict and unequal resources of political and economic power can help us understand social stratification and inequality in general, it can also help us understand poverty. We need not neglect the characteristics of the poor (the preoccupation of the above theories), but this is a secondary question, as it was with the individual characteristics of the working class, middle class, and upper class.

Poverty and the Occupational Structure We can begin a structural-level conflict view of poverty by considering the position of the poor in the *occupational structure*. As noted in earlier chapters, Weber viewed the occupational structure as a situation of conflict and competition in the marketplace. Those with greater skills—skills that are in demand and are relatively scarce—can demand and receive higher wages for their labor and maintain more secure jobs. The poor, of course, are at the bottom of the occupational structure. They have few skills, or only skills that can be easily learned by almost anyone (such as how to pick tomatoes or grapes or assemble a part on a gadget moving along an assembly line). The large number of people competing for such jobs reduces their chances for secure jobs as well as their wage levels even when jobs are found.

One of the biggest pools of poor and unemployed people in our society is made up of former agricultural workers and their sons and daughters (Piven and Cloward 1971). We have seen the figures on the reduction of farm labor in the previous chapter. Many people were needed to work the fields thirty or forty years ago, but, increasingly, machines are doing the work. Since World War II about 20 million people have left farm employment in the United States (Piven and Cloward 1971:214). Some of the former farm laborers and their offspring have moved into well-paying blue-collar and white-collar jobs, but many have been unable to do so.

And this brings us to the story we have seen many times already. The once-growing, well-paid blue-collar jobs that Americans could reasonably expect to get even if they did not have a good education are shrinking. Taking the place of these well-paid blue-collar jobs increasingly are the low-skilled jobs paying poverty wages. More than half of all new jobs created in the 1980s were unskilled jobs paying wages below the poverty line (Harrison and Bluestone 1988).

We may ask why those people displaced by a changing technology or the reduction of well-paid industrial jobs have not learned new skills. Many have. But there are at least two primary difficulties with learning new skills. People who have had low skills to begin with—people who have been near poverty most of their lives—must usually attempt to learn new job skills that do not require a high educational background or much investment of time. (It is most difficult for an adult with children to sacrifice desperately needed income, even when such income does exist, to obtain higher job skills.) The problem then becomes one of tough competition to obtain other jobs that require low skills. The experience of many job-training programs in the 1960s was that when the poor were trained for these low-skill jobs, the job market was soon flooded and the poor were still unemployed. Also, the offspring of the poor and unemployed find many obstacles to remaining in school, much less trying to obtain a higher degree. (This will be discussed in more detail in the next chapter.)

A structural feature of capitalist industrial societies that helps produce and maintain poverty is related to the "necessity" of business cycles. No one has yet found a way of preventing the cyclical movements between economic expansion and retraction, or economic boom and bust, in a capitalist economy; it is probable that no such prevention exists short of a rigid state-regulated economy. Unemployment, therefore, is increased in times of a business downturn, then somewhat reduced in times of business expansion. (Of course, there are many hard-core unemployed who are not directly affected by either economic shift.)

It is important to recognize that the cyclical changes in unemployment are *not* always an unintended effect of the business cycles of boom and bust. Inflation, it is believed, can in part be produced by a boom that lasts too long. (Whether or not this is a major cause of inflation can be questioned, but most political and economic elites believe it is an important cause of inflation.) Thus, unemployment is often *consciously* produced by government economic policies as a by-product of a planned economic slowdown intended to reduce inflation.

A result of the above is the existence of what Marx called an *industrial reserve army* that is functional for the well-being of the corporate economy (or at least functional for the elites and more affluent in this economy). The industrial reserve army consists of those people on the bottom of the occupational structure who can be laid off to protect corporate profits in times of economic stagnation, then rehired when needed for increased profits in times of economic expansion.

In other words, the industrial reserve army of low-paying and unskilled labor is the cushion used by the upper class and corporate class to maintain long-term profits. (This industrial reserve army is disproportionately made up of minorities due to their past dependence on farm occupations and the history of discrimination in this country. Because of this, minorities are often last hired and first fired.)

Another feature of our advanced capitalist industry that affects poverty is related to economic concentration and the resulting dual economy described in the previous chapter. As dual-economy theorists have found (see Beck, Horan, and Tolbert 1978; Tolbert, Horan, and Beck 1980), wages are lower and employment is less secure in periphery industries, because bigger corporations in core industries have less economic competition and more control over their market, which for core industries results in more stable profits. So wages for workers in the core are usually higher and jobs are more secure. But for workers in periphery industries, wages are so low at times that many full-time unskilled workers continue to exist below the poverty line, and jobs are less secure. (Again, this is related in part to greater poverty among minorities because we find minorities disproportionately employed in periphery industries.)

One additional aspect of our economy is important in producing poverty. Because industrialization is unevenly spread across the country, there are pockets of poverty where jobs are scarce and prospects for industrial development (or redevelopment) are low. The most visible pockets of poverty can be found in many of our old urban centers where, for a variety of historical reasons—such as the migration of discarded farm workers or coal miners—a high concentration of unskilled unemployed has developed. Because most of these unemployed lack skills, and because many social problems like crime often accompany high concentrations of the long-term unemployed, industries are hesitant to move into or stay in these areas. There have been a few attempts to stimulate industrial growth in such areas, but most so far have failed.

In other areas, pockets of poverty are produced by changing industries. When a city, state, or even whole regions of several states have been so dominated by one or a few related industries, a sudden change in the nature of the industrial base of the area can throw many people into persistent poverty. At least three types of changes are important in this respect: (1) An industry may find it cheaper to move (to the South or to Third World nations) where energy and labor costs are lower. (2) An industry may find demand for its product reduced and be forced to close plants. (3) An industry may become more capital-intensive, with new machines replacing workers. The future for many workers in the industrial cities of the Northeast and North Central United States does not appear bright for all three (and especially the first two) reasons above. Farm workers have already been seriously affected by the third type of change.

In some areas where one or more of the above changes have taken place there is hope that new industries will emerge to take advantage of the pool of available workers, but in other areas the prospect is not very bright. This is especially true in an area so completely dominated by an industry that the resources needed for redevelopment are lacking. If there is no tax base to provide adequate transportation, water, electricity, schools, or other resources needed by new industries, the chances of attracting new industries to the area are poor.

The persistent pocket of poverty in the Appalachian Mountain region of the United States can be used to illustrate this problem. In this region coal has been king, with most of the big mining companies owned, and the mineral rights held, by big corporations (especially oil companies) located in other states (see Caudill, 1962, for a detailed description of what follows). During the early history of the coal industry coal was in greater demand and this industry was more labor-intensive.

But two related processes began during the 1930s: The demand for coal was reduced and somewhat later the mechanization of mining was expanded. Both events produced high unemployment. Because mining so dominated the region both politically and economically and because unemployment was so high, there was no tax base to provide regional development of roads, water, electricity, schools—the things required to attract other industries into the area to relieve the high unemployment. Most importantly, the tax base was, and remains, low because the mining companies have had the political power to keep their state taxes very low.

One result has been that the profits of the mining companies have gone to enrich the regions of the industrial Northeast where the corporations are head-quartered. Thus, many people remain unemployed, and those with better skills or at least more hope have moved to northern industrial areas (where many who knew only unskilled labor in the mines formed white ghettos in northern cities). With the price of oil substantially higher since the early 1970s there are better prospects for the coal industry. However, the industry today is even more capital-intensive (mechanized), resulting in very few new jobs even with a greater demand for coal.

Poverty and the Property Structure   All of the above structural explanations for poverty are related more specifically to the economy and occupational structure in this country. But the nature of poverty can also be understood in relation to what we have described as the *property structure*. It is obvious that most poor and unskilled workers own little, and in most cases no, capital. But it can easily be forgotten that this makes them dependent upon others for their jobs and livelihood. In the past in this country the poor could often move West to claim unused land to provide a living; in other words, there was a chance that the poor could own their own means of production in the form of land. Today, when the prospects for employment are reduced—as with farm workers, coal miners, and skilled laborers in industries such as auto production and steel production—the poor are left with no resources.

The significance of being located at the bottom of both the occupational and property structures can be examined by comparing recent economic figures for blacks and native Americans. As noted earlier, blacks have a high rate of poverty and a very low average income compared with whites. Discrimination and a past dependence on farm employment help explain much of the poor economic standing of blacks.

For native Americans the history of race exploitation also helps explain their poor economic standing. As late as 1969, native Americans continued to be the poorest minority group in the United States, with a lower per-capita median income than even that of blacks or Mexican-Americans. But there has been a recent and surprising change in the overall economic statistics for native Americans. As of 1975, they had a higher per-capita median income than that of blacks or Mexican-Americans (see U.S. Commission on Civil Rights 1978:50; *U.S. News and World Report,* May 28, 1979). The 1975 per-capita median income of native Americans was still far below that of whites ($2,453 as against $4,333), but significant gains had been made.

What has happened with native Americans? In part, they have been moving to cities where employment prospects are better, and extensive government grants and tribal money have been used to obtain better educational opportunities (Havinghurst 1978; Sorkin 1978; Tax 1978; Kerbo 1981b). This has had some effect on their occupational prospects. However, much of the improved economic situation for *some* native Americans is related to property ownership and control of this property. Although most land was taken from native Americans long ago, some tribes were able to hold on to some land, and a few tribes have recently won legal battles to reclaim land illegally taken.

Most importantly, many native American tribes have learned to maintain control of this land and its mineral rights for the collective benefit of tribal members (see *Newsweek,* March 20, 1978). For example, rather than allowing mineral rights to be taken at a very low price (as the early Oklahoma Cherokee had done with their oil lands; see Wax 1971), many tribes now have their own lawyers and business advisers to ensure that a fair price is obtained.

And rather than allowing outside business interests to establish tourist attractions, fishing, or logging companies to exploit the natural resources of native American lands, other tribes are beginning to establish their own companies (*U.S. News and World Report,* May 28, 1979). By doing so, they can reinvest the profits of these tribal corporations for greater future profits, and tribal members are paid through jobs, stock, and stock dividends. In short, many tribes are learning the "white man's game" of business so as not to be taken advantage of as in the past.

Most native Americans remain extremely poor. There continue to be areas of extensive poverty on Indian reservations: many native Americans continue to live in nonreservation rural areas of poverty; and not all the land they were able to retain was of much value. However, some native Americans have retained or reclaimed valuable land resources, and along with other native Americans who have moved up the occupational structure, they have improved the overall economic statistics for native Americans. Their overall extent of poverty and average income remain worse than those of whites, but they have now moved ahead of other minorities, such as blacks and Mexican-Americans.

The point is that some native Americans, although they were, and for the most part continue to remain, low in the occupational structure, were better off in relation to the property structure. When they learned to use this property to their advantage their economic standing improved. Blacks continue to be relatively low in the occupational structure, and their status is compounded by a low position in the property structure. They continue to be at the greater mercy of others, who own the jobs, whereas some native Americans have come collectively to own their own jobs or their own means of production.

Poverty and Authority Structures Now we must consider the position of the poor with respect to *authority structures* in the society. The poor are almost exclusively located at the bottom of economic or occupational authority structures—when they are even subject to these authority structures through employment. They are among the unskilled laborers who give orders to no one; and when they do work, the poor are more likely to work in nonunion industries.

But equally important, the poor are found toward the bottom of the wider power structures of the society. Politically, the poor can be considered the most powerless of classes. As noted in the preceding chapter, the lower the position in the stratification system, the less likely people are to vote, contribute to political candidates, be represented by lobby organizations, or participate in voluntary organizations of many types that may be able to represent the rights and interests of their members.

However, the poor are not completely powerless. As with the middle class and working class, the upper classes must at times reckon with the influence of the poor, as they have on occasion throughout the history of stratification in human societies. At times the poor become politically active, as many poor blacks have done in some cities. Some of the poor, at least for a time, have formed social movement organizations, such as the National Welfare Rights Organization (see Piven and Cloward 1977).

When the poor have had influence, such political influence was often gained outside the normal channels of political influence—that is, through social movements and riots rather than traditional party politics. But because of their limited means of influence the poor have usually won only small and often short-lasting concessions in the conflict over who gets what in the society. As we will see in the final section of this chapter, these concessions have usually been in the form of welfare benefits that keep the poor alive but do not change their prospects of getting out of poverty. These welfare benefits and programs are seldom threatening to the overall stratification system, and in fact help maintain this system.

A system of social stratification based on group conflict does *not* require the extremes of wealth and poverty that exist in the United States. Social stratification means that some people are on top while others are on bottom, but it does not require those on top to be extremely advantaged while those on bottom are extremely poor. In fact, such extremes may be detrimental to a society and produce overt class conflict (in the form of crime and political rebellion), as we saw in our review of the history of stratification in human societies.

In the face of the *overt* conflict sometimes produced by such inequality, all industrial societies have developed welfare reforms to manage these conflicts. Some industrial societies, as we will see, have gone much further than others with these reforms. In the next section we will examine the nature and operation of welfare reforms, primarily in the United States. After this discussion we can conclude with a detailed description of the political and economic conflict that helped shape these welfare systems.

CLASS CONFLICT AND THE WELFARE STATE

The term *welfare state* is often used to describe a society in which the state has taken rather broad responsibility for social problems and providing some basic necessities for lower-class people. However, as noted in many places earlier, what can be called the welfare state (or *wealthfare state*) usually does much more than this; it also helps the rich and middle class in many more ways than it does the poor. But it does help meet some of the needs of the poor.

Throughout the history of the United States, at least until very recently, help for the poor was not considered a proper function of the state. Some poor were seen as "deserving" of aid, such as children, the sick, the blind, and perhaps the aged; but aid even to these categories of people was usually seen as the task of private charity agencies (such as religious groups and other private aid societies) and local communities. It was not until the 1930s that resistance to government welfare programs for the poor was broken, at least in a limited way.

Welfare in the United States

In the face of widespread turmoil and unemployment coming out of the Great Depression of the 1930s, Franklin Roosevelt established many reform programs to regulate the economy and help the unemployed (see Patterson 1986). Most welfare programs for the unemployed did not survive, and were cut back or eliminated before unemployment was substantially reduced. Those that did survive, however, were to establish the basic welfare system that we have today.

The most important foundation of our present welfare system is contained in the Social Security Law of 1935. This law created what is commonly called Social Security, which is a program that collects money from workers and employers primarily to pay benefits to those workers (who pay into this system) who retire or become disabled. However, because the Social Security system was not to begin paying benefits until the 1940s, and because people must work for an employer from whom Social Security deductions are withheld to be eligible for Social Security benefits (this program is primarily for the nonpoor), the Social Security Law of 1935 established another aid program for the poor.

What is commonly called *public assistance, categorical assistance,* or just *welfare* was also established by the Social Security Law of 1935. This is the main-line welfare program that remains in only slightly altered form today. However, public assistance or welfare is usually *not* for all the poor—it is for the "deserving poor." This is why it is often called categorical assistance

(Handler and Hollingsworth 1971:16); it helps only certain categories of the poor.

The original (1935) categories of people considered deserving of public assistance were children under Aid to Dependent Children (ADC), the blind and disabled under Aid to the Blind and Aid to the Disabled (AB and AD), and the aged (those over 65 and not eligible for Social Security) under Aid to the Aged (AA). In the 1950s it was recognized that aid to children could not be achieved unless an adult could survive to help the children, so ADC was expanded to Aid to Families with Dependent Children (AFDC). However, "families" meant children and *one* adult who was not judged able to work (usually the mother). If the family was intact—that is, the mother and father were both present—even if such a family was poor it was not eligible for AFDC as long as the "man of the house" was not disabled and therefore should be working.

In the 1960s AFDC-UP (AFDC-unemployed parent) was added in about half the states (see Piven and Cloward 1971; Steiner 1971:35), although even in many of these states AFDC-UP remains very limited. Under AFDC-UP some families can now receive welfare aid when the father is present but unemployed, as long as he is looking for work, in a job-training program, or disabled. In 1972 there was also a change in the welfare system that combined AA, AD, and AB into Supplementary Security Income (SSI) under more direct control of the federal government (with the states left with shared federal-state control of AFDC).

Finally, there is another aid category called General Assistance (GA) that is under almost total control of local governments. This program sometimes amounts to a catchall category for people in need of assistance who do not fall within the other categories. However, because funding of General Assistance is the responsibility of individual states and local government, coverage is uneven across the United States and the aid the poor can receive under General Assistance is usually very limited.

In addition to the categorical restrictions defining who can receive welfare described above, there are many eligibility rules that further limit who can receive welfare. And because individual states have primary authority to establish these eligibility rules (under AFDC and GA), there is much diversity across the United States as to who can receive welfare and how much they can receive. The most important eligibility rules pertain to income and property. For example, "earned" and "unearned" income is considered in determining eligibility and assistance levels (how much a person can receive in aid), as is the ownership of any kind of property (such as a home, a car, or a boat).

In the United States, states go to great lengths to make sure only the "deserving poor" receive welfare aid. Most welfare recipients are children, with only about 1 percent of welfare recipients considered "able-bodied males" (Feagin 1975:104). There are other types of aid programs (such as food stamps and Medicaid), but these programs also have many eligibility rules (although somewhat less restrictive) that limit assistance to the "deserving poor," and these other aid programs were extensively reduced under the Reagan administration. A person must be *very* poor (significantly below the poverty line) to receive welfare in the United States, and even many of the very poor do not receive welfare because they do not fit into the aid categories that define the "deserving poor."

This is in vast contrast to almost all industrial societies that guarantee at least a minimum standard of living for *all* citizens. Furthermore, as can be seen in Figure 10-3, when the poor do qualify for public assistance payments, the level of aid received is very low, usually well below the poverty line. Each state is able to set the level of welfare benefits it is willing to give under the basic welfare program AFDC, as well as decide how many people will get this aid (then the federal government provides about half of the funding). The food stamp program, however, is a federal program with nationwide standards specifying who qualifies and for how much. But the amount of food stamp aid given depends on the family's income, and because an AFDC check is counted as income, the states providing more AFDC cash reduce the amount of food stamp eligibility to some extent. As can be seen in Figure 10-3, however, the food stamp aid by no means evens out the combined amount of aid each state gives to the poor, nor brings the combined amount of aid above the poverty line in all but a very few cases.

It was recognized that welfare in the United States only keeps recipients alive and does nothing to reduce poverty or get those who are poor out of poverty, and increasing concern about poverty in the 1960s (for reasons considered later) resulted in President Johnson's Great Society Program, or War on Poverty. Working from assumptions about the causes of poverty in the culture-of-poverty theory, the War on Poverty programs attempted to reduce poverty by making the poor upwardly mobile (Patterson 1986). There were many specific programs designed to change the characteristics of the poor—to provide motivation, better educational opportunities, and job training, to make welfare mothers "better mothers," and so on.

But the stress on rehabilitation of the poor proved less than effective in reducing poverty, in part because the nature of poverty was misunderstood. The culture-of-poverty view led to a war on the characteristics of the poor rather than a war on the structural conditions producing poverty in the United States. Many War on Poverty programs were of value, for they did provide additional aid to those living in poverty. But even to the extent that poverty was reduced during the 1960s and 1970s, the reduction was primarily due to additional aid, not employment (Blumberg 1980:100). After President Nixon was elected in 1968, many of Johnson's War on Poverty programs were reduced or eliminated, with even more extensive reductions and eliminations under the Reagan administration.

Despite less popular concern about poverty in the 1970s and 1980s, there has been more recognition that the problem of poverty in this society is related to structural conditions limiting employment opportunities. Rather weak attempts to create jobs for the poor have come from both liberal and conserva-

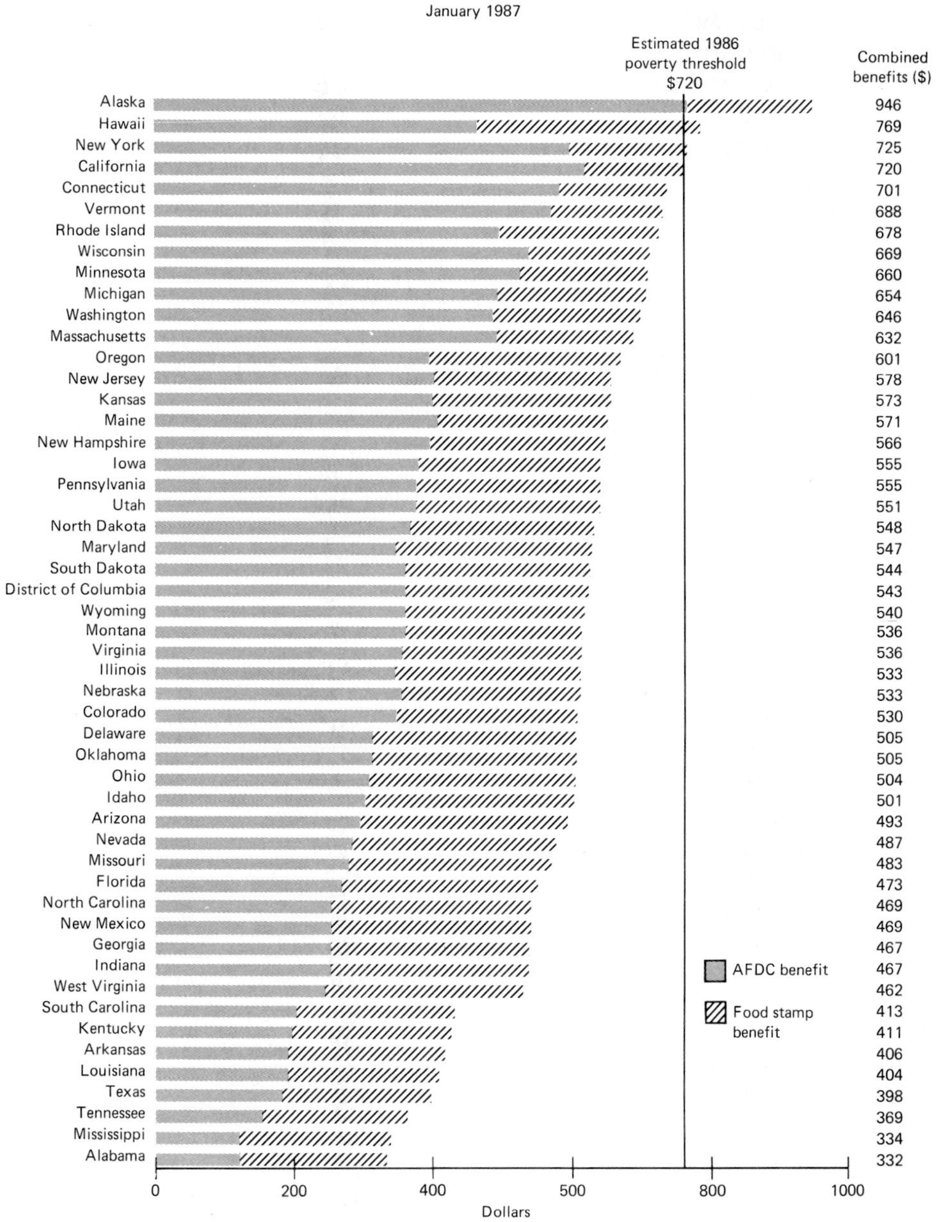
January 1987
Estimated 1986 poverty threshold $720
Combined benefits ($)
Alaska 946
Hawaii 769
New York 725
California 720
Connecticut 701
Vermont 688
Rhode Island 678
Wisconsin 669
Minnesota 660
Michigan 654
Washington 646
Massachusetts 632
Oregon 601
New Jersey 578
Kansas 573
Maine 571
New Hampshire 566
Iowa 555
Pennsylvania 555
Utah 551
North Dakota 548
Maryland 547
South Dakota 544
District of Columbia 543
Wyoming 540
Montana 536
Virginia 536
Illinois 533
Nebraska 533
Colorado 530
Delaware 505
Oklahoma 505
Ohio 504
Idaho 501
Arizona 493
Nevada 487
Missouri 483
Florida 473
North Carolina 469
New Mexico 469
Georgia 467
Indiana 467
West Virginia 462
South Carolina 413
Kentucky 411
Arkansas 406
Louisiana 404
Texas 398
Tennessee 369
Mississippi 334
Alabama 332
AFDC benefit
Food stamp benefit
0
200
400
500
800
1000
Dollars

FIGURE 10-3
A comparison of monthly state AFDC payments and food stamp benefits, 1987. *Source: CRS Review* (1987).

tive government administrations, although their approaches and philosophies have differed in basic ways. The liberal approach more often involves direct government spending to create jobs, while the conservative approach involves providing incentives to private industry to create jobs.

An example of the liberal approach is the Comprehensive Employment and Training Act (CETA), which was expanded during the Carter administration. Under this program, private industry and local government agencies were given federal money to pay part of the cost of hiring the unemployed. But although CETA was the biggest program of its type during the 1970s, the high level of unemployment during the later 1970s made the approximately 0.02 percent of the federal budget going for CETA far from adequate. And during Ronald Reagan's presidency, of course, there were extensive cuts in the CETA program and eventually it was eliminated.

The type of job program historically favored by conservative politicians and business leaders is one in which tax incentives or tax breaks go to private business so they can "create more jobs," at times with special tax breaks for jobs created in poverty areas in particular. Such an approach, as might be expected, has strong appeal in a society dominated by a "free enterprise" ideology, and at face value seems a more efficient and direct method of creating jobs.

In the past, however, this method of creating jobs has been simply a promise offered to quiet the poor when welfare cuts are being made—a promise that is carried through, if at all, with only enough attention to allow politicians to say a program exists. Richard Nixon did fund a few small programs to give tax incentives to business creating jobs in low-income areas like Watts, but after ten years these programs showed almost no success (see the *Los Angeles Times,* December 7, 1980).

Ronald Reagan's approach to fighting poverty was big tax cuts for corporations and the wealthy. With more profits for business and with more money in the hands of the rich for investments (tax breaks to the less wealthy "would only be spent, not invested"), there is supposed to be a "trickle-down" effect to the poor in the form of more jobs. But there is no guarantee that the increased corporate profits and tax cuts for the rich will go to job-producing investments. And if it is invested in industry, it is most likely to be invested in more profitable capital-intensive industries, producing fewer jobs than promised, and only jobs for higher-skilled workers who do not represent the long-term unemployed. Miller (1976:136) predicted that the "free-enterprise" approach to creating jobs (what could now be called the Reaganomics approach) will only create more inequality. As we have already seen, he was correct. Inequality grew in the 1980s because of a small increase in high-tech, high-paying jobs, a significant decrease in middle-paying jobs, and a big increase in jobs paying poverty wages with no future of advancement. And subsequent research we have already discussed has indicated the same by suggesting that the trickle-down effect never came for most poor Americans with this "free-enterprise" approach (Treas 1983).

A Cross-National Perspective on Welfare

From the political rhetoric of the 1970s and 1980s one gets the idea that the United States has the most extensive and costly welfare system in the world—with the exception of England, which is always used as a negative example of how the United States may end up if the spread of the "welfare state" is not stopped. But comparative data show that this idea is, in fact, only political rhetoric. To begin with, of the sixty-three most industrialized nations in the world, *only one nation* does not have some form of guaranteed income program for all families in need. That one exception is the United States (Moynihan 1973:95; Kahn and Kamerman 1978:153; Ozawa 1978:39). The United States is also the only one of these sixty-three industrialized nations without some form of comprehensive national health system for all citizens (Kahn and Kamerman 1978:153).

Comparative statistics on welfare spending show roughly the same picture. Table 10-4 shows the rank of fifteen capitalist industrial societies in terms of their overall welfare spending (transfer payments) as a percentage of their national income. We find that the United States is ranked higher than only Australia and Japan in welfare spending (see Wilensky 1975, and Burtless 1986, for similar rankings). But also interesting is a new ranking of nations with respect to a ratio of welfare spending as a percent of national income compared to each country's relative need for welfare spending (that is, need for welfare spending given the amount of poverty and percentage of elderly people who must be cared for in the society). Using this welfare need/spending ratio, the

TABLE 10-4

TRANSFER PAYMENTS AS A PERCENTAGE OF NATIONAL INCOME IN 15 NONCOMMUNIST INDUSTRIAL NATIONS

Rank	Country	Transfer payments as a percentage of national income
1	Netherlands	29.01
2	France	24.17
3	Norway	21.88
4	Sweden	21.54
5	Italy	19.90
6	Belgium	19.54
7	West Germany	18.59
8	Denmark	17.49
9	Austria	17.31
10	Switzerland	14.17
11	England	13.40
12	Canada	12.85
13	United States	11.88
14	Australia	9.65
15	Japan	6.95

Source: Table constructed from data supplied by Nutter (1978:58–75). Data are for either 1973 or 1974.

position of the United States goes up (with a smaller list of capitalist industrial nations) to about a middle rank. Most striking, however, is the change for Japan. As we will see in Chapter 13, Japan has the lowest level of poverty and unemployment of any industrial nation; thus, when this is considered in the ratio of welfare spending per need we can understand why Japan moves to the top position even though Japan spends relatively little on welfare (see Gilbert 1987).

Table 10-4 also presents interesting, although not conclusive, information against the argument that extensive welfare spending always harms an economy (one of the basic arguments of Reaganomics in the 1980s, see Piven and Cloward 1982). Using economic data for the 1970s, data that would relate to the welfare spending data in Table 10-4, we find in Table 10-5 that Japan had some of the strongest economic indicators in the 1970s, as now. The United States, on the other hand, had the worst indicators of economic growth listed in Table 10-5. Both Japan and the United States, however, were toward the bottom with respect to welfare spending. And other countries do not line up on welfare spending and economic performance as is suggested by the Reaganomics argument. For example, West Germany was much higher on welfare spending than the United States or Japan, but the West German economic performance was almost as good as Japan's. Then England, higher in welfare spending than the United States, but lower in welfare spending than most Americans realize, had an economic performance only somewhat better than that of the United States in this time period. Burtless (1986:46) has suggested the same conclusion from a larger list of nations over a longer time period. In short, welfare spending and economic performance do not seem related at levels represented by the fifteen nations included in Table 10-4.

What these figures suggest is that the United States is far behind most industrialized nations in welfare spending, and does have the capacity to increase welfare support for the poor and unemployed substantially. And given

TABLE 10-5
COMPARATIVE INCREASES IN GNP AND
PRODUCTIVITY, 1970s

	% increase in GNP 1973–1979	Average % increase in productivity 1972–1977
Japan	3.4	3.5
West Germany	3.2	3.5
France	2.7	3.1
Italy	1.6	1.0
Canada	0.4	0.8
United Kingdom	0.3	1.2
United States	0.1	0.6

Source: *Economic Report of the President 1980*, p. 85, *Joint Economic Report 1979*, p. 58.

the strong economy of some of these nations, an increase in welfare support need not necessarily damage the United States economy. (We need more precise comparative research to determine the exact relation between government spending and economic performance.)

The major question at this point is why the United States lags far behind so many nations in welfare spending. But a question that must be answered first is what accounts for changes in the level of welfare-type spending in the United States. As we have already noted, United States welfare spending showed major increases during the 1930s and 1960s. To help answer these questions we must return to some of the characteristics of class conflict in our system of social stratification.

The Welfare State as Conflict Management and the Lower Class in the Power Structure

It is often assumed that the following two factors are most important in explaining differing welfare commitments among industrial nations. First, it is often assumed that mutual aid is a "human drive" (see Friedlander 1968:9); that is, people have a noble side to their character that produces a desire to help less fortunate members of society. Such an assumption is speculative; but, as noted in our review of the history of inequality, we do find some evidence for this "drive." However, the evidence also suggests that such a human tendency toward sharing is found primarily in very small human collectives with close social relations. A human drive toward mutual aid seems much more difficult to maintain over a large, diverse population in complex societies, especially when it means giving up relatively scarce resources to strangers.

Second, following the first assumption, it is usually believed that when the resources of the society are greater, more will be devoted to the welfare of the less advantaged. (This can be referred to as the *state modernization* thesis; see Isaac and Kelly 1981.) Our earlier review of history suggests that this assumption is faulty. As Lenski's (1966) research shows, when societies are able to produce a greater economic surplus, this surplus most often goes to the more affluent. More specifically, with data from twenty-two nations Wilensky (1975) found that the level of economic resources of a society is not directly related to differing levels of welfare spending.

We must return to the conflict perspective that has guided our understanding of social stratification more generally if we are to understand the nature of welfare state development. We can suggest again that the question of who gets what in a society is related to political and/or economic power. This in turn leads us to suggest that since welfare spending in the United States increased substantially (compared with other years) during the 1930s and 1960s, something must have happened to increase the influence of the poor. How can this be when the poor are so powerless in the society? The poor are generally at the very bottom of the occupational, authority, and property structures in the society. In the political arena, where welfare questions are decided, they are less likely to vote, less likely to make political contributions, and less likely to have any kind of lobby organization.

As we found in our review of history, however, when the traditional avenues of power and influence in a society are less accessible to the lower class, they have at times gone outside these traditional avenues. This usually means using the disruptive tactics of social movements and collective behavior in obtaining influence. If the lower classes are strong enough, or, in other words, if the lower classes can cause enough disruption in the society, the elites and more affluent may be willing to give them concessions in order to remove this threat to the overall status quo.

In reality, political elites usually employ two tactics in managing disruption by the lower class. These tactics are often referred to as *two-war strategy* (see Miliband 1969; Oppenheimer 1969:164). On the one hand, force is used to arrest, imprison, or kill primary participants in rebellious activities. On the other hand, this tactic is usually accompanied by reforms to convince less rebellious factions of the lower classes not to join the rebellion. Reforms are intended to show that things will be better, and that therefore there is no need to join the rebellion.

What the above is meant to suggest is that like the working class, the poor are not completely powerless. Power, of course, is unequally distributed, and the poor have less of it than other segments of the society. When social order is strong and when the poor are relatively weak in numbers, a rebellious call for more jobs, social justice, and a decent standard of living is answered (if at all) by welfare. Gains may be made, but welfare, as should be evident, is not the most ideal gain.

Our remarks thus far have been speculative in nature. It is time to add data to these ideas about the conflict nature of the welfare state. We will turn first to the influential work of Piven and Cloward (1971), then to more empirical tests of their thesis of welfare development and growth.

The Functions of Public Welfare   Piven and Cloward (1971) maintain that public welfare serves two primary functions in industrial societies such as the United States. First, during periods of social stability, the welfare system functions to *enforce work norms* and *maintain low-wage labor*. As industrial societies become more affluent it becomes more and more difficult to keep the lowest paid workers content doing the dirty, dangerous, and low-paying jobs. But when welfare (the other alternative besides starvation) is rendered highly degrading and recipients are stigmatized, the near poor are more willing to maintain employment in the worst jobs in the society.

As Piven and Cloward (1971:3) put it, ''Some of the aged, the disabled, the insane, and others who are of no use as workers are left on the relief rolls, and their treatment is so degrading and punitive as to instill in the laboring masses a fear of the fate that awaits them should they relax into beggary and pauperism.'' For the most part, the attitudes we hold toward the poor, and especially welfare recipients, help maintain the stigma of welfare status. The strength of this stigma directed toward welfare recipients is shown when even the poor themselves (Feagin 1975), and welfare recipients in particular, tend to hold these views (for research on these views held by welfare recipients see Briar 1966; Handler and Hollingsworth 1971; Cole and Lejeune 1972; Kerbo 1976b).

Second, Piven and Cloward maintain, during periods of social disruption and turmoil created by the poor and unemployed the welfare system functions to *restore social order*. Social order is restored in part by expansion of the welfare system so as to take care of some of the basic needs of the poor. Also, however, social order is furthered because once on welfare the poor can be controlled better, watched over, and the threat of withholding benefits can be used to keep the poor in line. When social order has been restored, Piven and Cloward argue, the welfare system is again restricted, pushing as many of the poor as possible off the welfare rolls.

The view of welfare put forth by Piven and Cloward may seem depressing and pessimistic to those concerned with the well-being of the poor; but it is supported by much empirical evidence (reviewed below). This view of the functions of public welfare may also seem to contain a conspiracy view of history, wherein elites are working behind the scenes to exploit the poor, to keep them poor and in low-wage work to benefit the rich (see the critical debate in Trattner 1983). That may be the outcome of welfare, but it is less a conscious conspiracy than a result of the system of power stratification in the society.

We can focus on our major concern at present, the welfare function of restoring social order (the second function above), to show that Piven and Cloward's thesis does not rest upon a conspiracy view of history. Consider the position of a United States senator. From what we have already reviewed about the influence of the stratification system on the political process in this country, we can understand some of the pressures on this senator. Federal government funds are always restricted because demands for funding and services by various interest groups are always greater than the amount of funds available to the government. Thus, the groups who have contributed (and most likely will contribute) to this senator's campaign for election, the groups that can pay for lobby activities to influence this senator, and the groups that are more likely to vote in elections are the groups most likely to get the government attention and support they are seeking.

The poor have few of these traditional means of political influence, so their needs are ignored more often than the needs of more influential groups. But when the poor revolt, when they threaten social order, the situation changes somewhat. This senator may now recognize that there is a problem in the country. Some of the demands by other groups are resisted by this senator, who is now more willing to vote for bills in the Senate designed to help the poor.

When social order is restored, when the poor stop rioting, it is back to business as usual. The order of priorities in the political system is shifted back to the more influential interest groups in the country. As Piven and Cloward

(1971:338) end their book, "A placid poor get nothing, but a turbulent poor sometimes get something."

Protest Movements and Welfare: Empirical Evidence   A brief review of welfare changes in the United States will give concrete meaning to the above thesis. It must first be recognized that the United States has had many periods of very high unemployment. But during these periods when the poor and unemployed needed help the welfare system was seldom expanded. For example, although there were periods of relatively high unemployment in 1893–1894, 1914, and 1921, welfare aid was not substantially institutionalized and expanded until the Depression of the 1930s.

True, the Depression of the 1930s was worse than the others. However, as Piven and Cloward show with historical evidence: (1) the Depression of the 1930s per se did not force welfare expansion; rather, it was the rebellion that followed; and (2) welfare has also expanded in times of lower-class rebellion when there was no change in the level of poverty and unemployment (as in the 1960s).

Figure 10-4 presents data which tend to confirm the Piven and Cloward thesis of welfare expansion due to protest by the poor rather than because of increasing need for welfare benefits. Three variables are plotted in Figure 10-4: the rate of unemployment, amount of protest by the unemployed, and a rough indicator of welfare spending by the federal and state governments (for more details on how these variables were measured and sources of data, see Kerbo and Shaffer 1986a, 1986b; Shaffer and Kerbo 1987). We can see that though

FIGURE 10-4
Relationship between unemployment, protest, and welfare expansion, 1890–1990. *Source:* Adapted from Shaffer and Kerbo (1987).

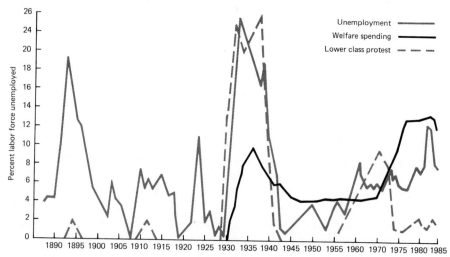

unemployment was high several times before the 1930s (reaching a level almost as high as the 1930s in 1894), welfare spending did not increase significantly until the 1930s. And, of course, protest by the unemployed was very low until the 1930s, when massive protest occurred with the first year of rising unemployment in 1930, creating a political crisis that helped convince political elites to support welfare expansion (see Jenkins and Brents 1989).

We also see in Figure 10-4 that welfare spending went down with falling protest in the late 1930s and during World War II, but many of the welfare programs begun in the 1930s continued to operate, though at lower levels of support. Welfare spending went up dramatically again in the 1960s; this time, however, without the huge increase in unemployment as in the 1930s. But consistent with the 1930s, the 1960s brought high levels of protest in the streets by the poor and minorities.

More extensive empirical research attempting to assess the validity of the Piven and Cloward thesis has focused on the post-World War II period of United States history. In the 1950s the welfare rolls in the United States increased by only 17 percent. But during the 1960s the welfare rolls increased by 225 percent, with most of the increase coming after the major urban riots which began in 1964 (Piven and Cloward 1971:341). These urban riots did not end until 1968, after more than 300 major urban riots had occurred in this five-year period, with 220 people killed and more than 8,000 injured (Downes 1970; Salert and Sprague 1980). Betz (1974) has examined changes in the welfare rolls of major cities that experienced riots compared with changes in cities that did not experience riots. This study showed a significant increase in the welfare rolls of riot cities about one year after a major riot.

In the most extensive empirical examination of the Piven and Cloward thesis, Isaac and Kelly (1981) compiled relevant data covering a period between 1947 and 1976. Most importantly, Isaac and Kelly found that the frequency and severity of riots were directly related to welfare expansion after controlling for (or ruling out the significance of) many other variables which may have been factors in producing the welfare expansion. For example, neither changes in the unemployment rate nor an increase in female-headed families (which could make more people eligible for welfare) were found to be related significantly to an increase in the number of people receiving welfare. Since this major study by Isaac and Kelly (1981), several others have strongly confirmed their conclusions for the 1960s (see Schram and Turbett 1983; Jennings 1983; but for a critique of the Piven and Cloward thesis as it applies to the earlier 1900s, suggesting these authors neglected the importance of state modernization, see Orloff and Skocpol 1984; Quadagno 1984; Skocpol and Amenta 1985; as well as the research more supportive of Piven and Cloward by Jenkins and Brents 1989).

As described above, welfare is a means of placating a rebellious poor that is cheaper and less threatening to the status quo. In other words, little is given up by the more affluent in granting the poor welfare—it is the line of least resistance. Providing jobs and other opportunities for the poor will be most difficult because unless a substantial increase in the number of jobs is forthcoming, it will mean jobs must be taken from the more advantaged.

A recent study by Kelly and Snyder (1980) supports this view. Using national level data, they found that the frequency and severity of riots in the 1960s did *not* create (1) changes in the black–white income ratio, (2) black gains in occupational status, or (3) a reduction in the black unemployment level. Also, Isaac and Kelly (1981) did *not* find that the frequency and severity of riots in the 1960s produced increased benefits from welfare. That is, the riots did not increase the amount of money going to each welfare family; they only produced an increase in the *number of people* receiving welfare benefits.

We can conclude this discussion of historical trends in welfare spending in the United States by noting the welfare cutbacks in the 1980s under the Reagan administration. Piven and Cloward (1971) ended their book by predicting welfare cuts in coming years with a downturn in protest by the poor and minorities (however, see Piven and Cloward, 1982, for their view of why the cuts in welfare were not as much as Reagan had hoped for). Cutbacks in welfare programs of various kinds were not immediate, but the accuracy of their prediction is no longer in question. The 1980s went back to the work-enforcing function of welfare through degrading welfare recipients and outcries against those who seek welfare who are not "truly needy."

Turning to cross-national comparisons, we find a much more complex situation with many possible national differences potentially related to varying welfare commitments. In a limited study examining the cross-national differences in welfare spending among twenty-two industrial nations Wilensky (1975) found that the age of the population was most important in explaining these differences. What this seems to indicate is that with a higher proportion of older people in Western European societies, we find more political power in the hands of the elderly pushing for more support for programs similar to Social Security in the United States. And given that the biggest welfare budget item in most countries is aid for the retired elderly, this political force by the elderly could have the biggest impact on overall welfare spending.

No doubt other cross-national differences relate to differing levels of welfare spending for the poor in general (not just the aged), but adequate research is lacking. However, with a focus on the low welfare commitment in the United States compared with that in most Western European nations and given what we have learned about welfare development in this country, we can suggest the importance of other variables producing cross-national differences in welfare spending.

1 Given the relation between lower-class protest and welfare expansion in this country, we can suggest that a longer history of more intense class conflict in the nations of Western Europe is in part responsible for greater welfare spending in these nations.

2 As Wilensky (1975:65) and Pampel and Williamson (1985; 1988) suggest, a longer history of more extensive political organization among the lower classes in some industrialized nations may produce higher levels of welfare spending (also see Korpi 1989).

3 The lower classes in most Western European countries are more likely to participate in elections (Piven and Cloward 1988). A multiparty political system, in contrast to our two-party system, seems in part responsible. Thus, politicians may be more likely to work for lower-class votes by providing more benefits for the lower classes (Tufte 1978; Pampel and Williamson 1988). We have similar research showing that cross-state differences in welfare benefits in the United States (see Figure 10-3) are related to conditions of political competition that make the votes of the poor more important in some states (Tompkins 1975).

4 Social services are more widely distributed among various classes in many industrialized nations (Kahn and Kamerman 1978). In contrast to the United States, a number of countries provide various state social services such as medical assistance, housing programs, and child-care centers that benefit many above the level of poverty (including the working and middle classes). Because those above the poverty line are more politically active, they are more likely to defend and support these programs (see *Time,* January 12, 1981).

5 Despite Wilensky's findings, it remains likely that differences in the political ideology and political systems of nations help produce differing levels of welfare spending. For example, other studies (see Hewitt 1977; Rubinson and Quinlan 1977; Tufte 1978) have shown that more support for democratic socialist parties and greater political democracy in general are related to less inequality in a nation. Less inequality does not always mean more social welfare spending in industrial nations, but it is likely that less inequality is usually achieved through an expanded welfare state.

Although much more research is needed, it can be suggested that cross-national differences in welfare spending are related to the nature of class conflict. When the poor and lower classes are better organized to further their common class interests, when the poor and lower classes have a longer history of political protest and rebellion, welfare benefits are expanded. The lower classes have not always been passive in the United States (Garner 1977), but the more turbulent class conflicts in the history of most Western European nations throughout the past 200 years certainly overshadow lower-class rebellion in the United States.

Class Conflict and the Welfare State: A Conclusion

The development of the welfare state, like the existence of the poor it is meant to control, can be understood most fully with reference to the nature of class conflict. The state has become a central institution with the task of redistribution. Resources are taken from some and redistributed to others. Those classes with more power are able to ensure that they receive more from the state than is taken by the state. Such a result should be evident from our discussion of the upper class and corporate class in earlier chapters.

But contrary to usual assumptions, the poor are not totally powerless. When the poor achieve some influence, when the poor become turbulent and demanding, they may get government redistribution in the form of welfare. The upper classes, of course, continue to receive the greater benefits of state redistribution policies, although in the interest of maintaining social stability, concessions to the poor are made. Such a result rests not upon any conscious organized conspiracy by the upper classes, but upon a multitude of contested policy decisions (the long-range implications of which are seldom fully recognized at the time) that add up to government policy that expands aid to the poor primarily when the poor become disruptive.

It would be nobler, of course, if the existence of welfare programs were mainly the result of our humanistic desire to help those in need. But the evidence, unfortunately, does not support such a view. Many people do have a humanistic desire to help those in need. But when people are able to act upon their humanistic values to provide the poor with goods and services made available by the society, they are able to do so most often because of social forces they are unable to control. The social worker, the humanistic government bureaucrat, the person volunteering time to work for a welfare agency are all participating in attempts to aid the poor set in motion by political forces that have led to the development and expansion of the welfare state.

11

SOCIAL MOBILITY: CLASS ASCRIPTION AND ACHIEVEMENT

In a highly competitive capitalist society, in a society that stresses universalistic success norms, it is hardly surprising that the question "Who gets ahead?" has received much popular attention. Early in this century the attention was expressed through the wide appeal of "the Horatio Alger stories of the news-boy who 'made it' by reason of personal virtues" (Mills 1953:337). More recently this popular attention is expressed through the many bestselling books describing how success can be achieved through intimidating others, dressing right, investing in real estate, getting right with God, or getting right with your psyche.

In the sociological literature, the study of social mobility and status attainment is most related to this popular concern. *Social mobility* research concentrates on the extent and patterns of vertical movement up and down the occupational structure. That is, compared with our father's position, we want to know how many people moved up or down or were immobile in their adult lives. In a related area of study, *status attainment* research asks why such mobility does or does not take place. What factors account for the patterns of vertical mobility or lack of mobility? In other words, we want to know "Who gets ahead and why?"

As is common in all industrial societies, class attainment in the United States is based on both ascription and achievement. But given our social value of equality of opportunity we are concerned with the exact mixture of ascription and achievement. We want to know the extent to which success or failure is related to personal qualities such as talent, motivation, and hard work, in contrast to ascriptive qualities such as family background, sex, race, or ethnic status. Equally important, because mythology has it that this is the land of opportunity, we want to know how the present United States compares with its past and with other industrial nations in terms of social mobility.

With reference to our success values, the long-standing sociological interest in the study of social mobility can be understood. Until recently, however, this sociological interest brought more theoretical speculation than detailed empirical research. The first real breakthrough in social mobility research came with Rogoff's (1953a) study of movement in the occupational structure using measures of occupational status (see Tyree and Hodge 1978). But Blau and Duncan's (1967) work brought a virtual explosion of research in this area. Blau and Duncan were able to compile a massive set of data on the subject with the help of the U.S. Bureau of the Census, and through new statistical methods of causal analysis produced a work that has become the model for almost all subsequent works on the subject.

Since the 1960s it can be said with only some overstatement that the empirical study of social stratification *is* the study of social mobility and status attainment. As described in the previous chapter, our rediscovery of poverty and inequality in the 1960s, combined with the new empirical methods of social research, brought many attempts to explain the existence of extensive and persistent inequality. The major sociology journals became filled with research on social mobility and status attainment (Pease, Form, and Huber 1970; Huber and Form 1973).

As research conducted in preparation for this text shows, of all articles (2,487) published in five major sociology journals between 1965 and 1975, 453 (18 percent) were primarily concerned with some aspect of social stratification.[1] Table 11-1 lists the distribution of these 453 social stratification articles within ten broad subject areas.[2] A total of 143 (or 32 percent) were mainly concerned with some aspect of social mobility or status attainment. Furthermore, as shown in Table 11-1, these published works on social mobility and status attainment usually included quantitative empirical research (94 percent included statistical analysis of data) and received the most support from government research grants. This pattern of government research funding, it will be remembered, is similar to that discovered in our discussion of poverty.

Research on the subject of inequality of opportunity, whether the focus was on poverty or class inequality in general, was in demand. This was especially true for research with an individualistic rather than a structural focus (see Kerbo 1981a). The individualistic bias in most status attainment research demands further comment later in this chapter.

The rather recent and rapid development of social mobility and status attainment research is clearly impressive. Much of the detail we have about these subjects has come from research that began only about twenty or thirty years ago. But, as will be seen in this chapter, we have much to learn. Much of what explains class attainment remains unspecified. And only recently has the individualistic or sociopsychological bias in status attainment research been widely recognized. The past five years or so have brought new structurally oriented research that shows great promise in expanding our knowledge of the subject further.

TABLE 11-1
THE DISTRIBUTION OF SOCIAL STRATIFICATION ARTICLES IN FIVE MAJOR JOURNALS
BY SUBJECT AND GOVERNMENT FUNDING, 1965–1975

Subject	Number	% of total	Number funded	% of total funded	Empirical research
1. General subject of social stratification	35	8	7	3	15 (43%)
2. Elites (community and national)	51	11	10	5	33 (65%)
3. Poverty	67	15	33	15	56 (84%)
4. Mobility/status attainment	143	32	92	42	135 (94%)
5. Social and political participation	8	2	2	1	7 (88%)
6. Class ideology/values	50	11	26	12	48 (96%)
7. Class lifestyles/subculture	44	10	24	11	42 (95%)
8. Occupational prestige	14	3	7	3	14 (100%)
9. Status inconsistency	37	8	16	7	28 (76%)
10. Income/wealth distribution	4	1	2	1	4 (100%)
Total	453	101	219 (48%)	100	382 (84%)

The first task of the present chapter will be to present a summary of what we have learned about social mobility in the United States. We want to know how much vertical movement there is within the class system, what the nature of this mobility is, and the extent of class inheritance. As much as possible, the present patterns of social mobility in the United States will be compared historically and cross-nationally. Next we will consider the recent status attainment research for what it has to offer in explaining who gets ahead in the United States. The research on social mobility provides clues to who gets ahead and why, but status attainment research is more directly related to such questions. Last, current status attainment models will be examined critically and more recent theory and research will be presented that add to our knowledge of who gets ahead and why.

SOCIAL MOBILITY

Social mobility can be studied from several different vantage points. A first major distinction is made between horizontal and vertical mobility. *Horizontal mobility* is movement from one position to another of equal rank in the occupational structure. For example, an electrician employed by General Motors who leaves his or her job for a similar position with Boeing would be considered as horizontally mobile in the occupational structure. In another case we may consider a move from electrician to railroad engineer. Because both occupations are ranked equally in prestige this again would be horizontal mobility (also referred to as a move from one *situs* to another when different but equally ranked occupations are involved; see Sorokin 1959:7; Hauser and Featherman 1977:217).

Of primary concern in the study of social stratification, however, is vertical mobility. *Vertical* mobility may be defined as the movement from one occupational position to another of higher or lower rank. An example of upward vertical mobility would be movement from police officer to public school teacher. From studies of occupational prestige (see Nakao and Treas 1991) we find the occupation of police officer given a score of 50, whereas that of a public school teacher is given a score of 64 (see Chapter 6). An example of downward vertical mobility would be movement from the position of police officer (scored 50) to barber (scored 36).

It should be easy to understand why vertical mobility is of special concern in the study of social stratification; the overall extent of vertical mobility can tell us something very important about the class system. The greater the degree of vertical mobility, the more open the class system, and the more class inequality is based upon achievement rather than ascription. In other words, the greater the degree of vertical mobility, the closer the society may be to the value of equality of opportunity.

A final distinction must be made between intergenerational and intragenerational mobility. *Intergenerational* mobility is studied by comparing the occupational position of parents with that of their offspring. For example, we want to know if a son has achieved a higher, lower, or equal occupational position in comparison with that of his father. *Intragenerational* mobility is studied by comparing the occupational position of a person over an extended period of time. For example, we want to know if the occupational status of a person's first job is higher, lower, or equal to that of the person's second, third, or fourth job—or if the occupational status of a person has changed after, say, ten or twenty years.

Both intergenerational and intragenerational mobility may be able to tell us something about the degree of openness in the stratification system. Most often, however, the focus of research has been on intergenerational mobility because the inheritability of occupational status from parents to offspring is considered a key indicator of ascription versus achievement.

Before we proceed to our main objective, an outline of mobility patterns in the United States, a brief note on how mobility studies are conducted is in order. It is important to recognize first that current mobility and status attainment studies are grounded mainly in measures of *occupational prestige*. From our discussion in Chapter 6 it will be remembered that occupational prestige is based on the assumption (from functional theories of social stratification) that the key dimension of class is occupational *status*. Following the studies of occupational prestige (such as that of Hodge, Siegel, and Rossi 1966), different occupations have been ranked from high to low with respect to the amount of status associated with a particular occupation. Studies of status attainment (discussed later) use a direct variation of such a status ranking of occupations, whereas mobility studies traditionally employ a cruder ranking such as upper nonmanual, lower nonmanual, upper manual, and so on (or professionals, managers, clerical workers, operatives, and service workers).

But, as already discussed in Chapter 6, such a status ranking creates problems for an adequate understanding of social stratification in industrial societies. On the one hand, we have argued, the status of an occupation may be less important in determining who gets what in the society than the skill level, complexity, or marketability of the occupational skill. The idea of a status ranking neglects the conflict nature of the occupational structure as well as restrictions on free competition in the occupational structure. On the other hand, in addition to divisions in the occupational structure, we have shown the importance of divisions with respect to authority and property. These divisions are not always measured adequately in current studies of social mobility and status attainment.

The biggest problem, however, is found with studies of status attainment because of their more direct use of occupational prestige measures. To the extent that divisions in the occupational, authority, and property structures overlap, the cruder occupational distinctions used in studies of social mobility create fewer problems. But, most importantly, focusing on the occupational structure as it is measured in mobility studies means that the very top of the stratification system in the United States is inadequately represented. In other words, the mobility that is measured in these studies is *mobility below the very top*.

Another introductory note is important before examination of social mobility patterns in the United States. Most studies of social mobility are based on data from employed males. Women have usually been excluded from these studies because it is assumed that (1) the family is the most important unit in social stratification, (2) males determine the status of the family, and (3) the status of women is determined by the status of their husbands. These assumptions have been questioned on several grounds (see Acker 1973), most importantly because there are more women in the occupational structure and more female-headed families. Although most of the research is focused on males, when possible we will present data on female patterns of social mobility.

Social Mobility in the United States

The most impressive studies of social mobility in the United States have been conducted by Blau and Duncan (1967), and more recently by Featherman and Hauser (1978). Blau and Duncan's mobility data were collected with the help of the U.S. Bureau of the Census in 1962, with detailed information on the family backgrounds, educational experience, and occupational history of over 20,000 males in the labor force. Without a doubt, Blau and Duncan's study (*The American Occupational Structure,* 1967) must be considered the landmark study of social mobility in the United States. The Featherman and Hauser study (*Opportunity and Change,* 1978) was designed as a replication of this landmark study, with a similar sample of over 30,000 employed males in 1973. Hout (1988) has updated this research with new data from 1972 to 1985.

Among the important tools of mobility research are *inflow* and *outflow* tables of intergenerational mobility. An inflow table identifies the occupational family backgrounds of people recruited into various occupational positions. For example, an inflow table shows the family origin of people now in upper-middle-class occupational positions, identifying how many of the people in upper-middle-class positions came from families in which the father was upper middle class, lower middle class, and so on. An outflow table, in contrast, gives us a more accurate picture of where sons with various family origins are located in the occupational structure. For example, with an outflow table we can see how many sons of upper-middle-class fathers are themselves upper middle class, as well as how many are in lower occupational positions. A primary focus of outflow tables is the degree of occupational inheritance, while a primary focus of inflow tables is the degree of occupational recruitment from other occupational origins.

The value of inflow and outflow mobility tables can be understood by examining some of the data. Table 11-2 compares the outflow mobility from a father's (or family head's) occupational position to a son's current occupational position for 1962 and 1973. This table combines the original data from Blau and Duncan's study with Featherman and Hauser's replication of this

TABLE 11-2
OUTFLOW MOBILITY FROM FATHER'S (OR OTHER FAMILY HEAD'S) BROAD
OCCUPATION GROUP TO SON'S CURRENT OCCUPATION GROUP, 1962 and 1973

Father's occupation	Son's current occupation					
	Upper nonmanual	Lower nonmanual	Upper manual	Lower manual	Farm	Total
1962 (*n* = 10,550)						
Upper nonmanual	56.8%	16.7%	11.5%	13.8%	1.2%	100%
Lower nonmanual	43.1	23.7	14.6	17.0	1.7	100
Upper manual	24.7	17.0	28.3	28.8	1.2	100
Lower manual	17.9	14.8	21.9	43.4	1.9	100
Farm	10.3	12.3	19.3	35.9	22.2	100
Total	24.5	15.9	20.2	31.7	7.7	100
1973 (*n* = 20,850)						
Upper nonmanual	59.4%	11.4%	12.8%	15.5%	0.9%	100%
Lower nonmanual	45.1	16.6	16.4	20.7	1.2	100
Upper manual	30.9	12.2	27.7	28.1	1.2	100
Lower manual	22.9	12.1	23.9	40.1	1.0	100
Farm	16.4	9.0	22.9	37.1	14.5	100
Total	31.2	11.8	21.9	31.0	4.1	100

Source: Featherman and Hauser (1978:89). The samples include American men in the experienced civilian labor force aged twenty-one to sixty-four.

study with 1973 data. The occupational divisions compared (upper nonmanual, lower nonmanual, upper manual, and lower manual) are similar to what we have defined earlier as upper middle class, lower middle class, skilled blue-collar workers and unskilled blue collar workers (with the added category of farm workers). Overall, Table 11-2 shows that occupational inheritance was quite similar in 1962 and 1973.

Within Table 11-2 it is interesting to note the occupational inheritance of each occupational category. This can be done by looking down the diagonals for both years. For example, we can compare how many upper nonmanual fathers produced sons who are also upper nonmanual, lower nonmanual fathers who produced sons who are lower nonmanual, down to farm-worker fathers who produced sons who are farm workers (moving down the diagonal).

We find that upper nonmanual occupations had the highest degree of occupational inheritance in both 1962 and 1973 (56.8 percent and 59.4 percent, respectively). The lowest rate of occupational inheritance is found among farm workers in both years (22.2 percent and 14.5 percent, respectively).

Regarding the low rate of occupational inheritance among farm workers, it is clear that much of this is due to the fact that farm-labor positions are becoming scarcer with farm mechanization; that is, the sons of farm workers must move up the occupational structure or out of it altogether into unemployment. Regarding the higher rates of occupational inheritance with upper nonmanual and lower manual occupations, we find that the occupational structure is more rigid toward the top and bottom (Featherman and Hauser 1978:179). Sons of both upper nonmanual and lower manual fathers are more likely to end up with occupations similar to their fathers'. No doubt this is a pleasing state of affairs for upper nonmanual sons, but not so pleasing for lower manual sons. However, there is substantially less occupational inheritance between these extremes (Featherman and Hauser 1978:180).

Table 11-3 presents the data on inflow mobility for 1962 and 1973. The focal point of this table is the origin of recruitment into various occupational positions. Origin of recruitment can be seen by moving down the columns in the table (when the totals move down, notice that the total of 100 percent is at the bottom of each column). Again, we find that occupational recruitment was very similar in 1962 and 1973.

We can begin by looking at recruitment into upper nonmanual occupations; in both years the rate of "self-recruitment" (25.4 percent and 29.3 percent) was higher than recruitment into upper nonmanual occupations from other occupations. However, there was a significant amount of recruitment into upper nonmanual positions from the lower positions (16.7 percent of those occupying upper nonmanual positions in 1973 came from lower nonmanual origins, and 20.2 percent came from upper manual origins).

The highest rate of self-recruitment in both years is found with farm occupations. Table 11-3 shows that in 1962, 85.7 percent of those in farm-worker positions were from farm-worker origins, with only a slightly lower percentage (80.7) in 1973. It is instructive to compare these inflow figures for farm workers with the outflow figures shown in the previous table (Table 11-2). For ex-

TABLE 11-3
INFLOW MOBILITY TO SON'S CURRENT OCCUPATION FROM FATHER'S (OR OTHER
FAMILY HEAD'S) OCCUPATION, 1962 and 1973

Father's occupation	Son's current occupation					
	Upper nonmanual	Lower nonmanual	Upper manual	Lower manual	Farm	Total
1962 (*n* = 10,550)						
Upper nonmanual	25.4%	11.6%	6.2%	4.8%	1.7%	11.0%
Lower nonmanual	23.1	19.6	9.5	7.0	2.9	13.1
Upper manual	19.0	20.2	26.3	17.1	2.9	18.8
Lower manual	20.1	25.6	29.7	37.6	6.8	27.4
Farm	12.5	23.0	28.3	33.6	85.7	29.7
Total	100%	100%	100%	100%	100%	100%
1973 (*n* = 20,850)						
Upper nonmanual	29.3%	14.8%	9.0%	7.7%	3.2%	15.4%
Lower nonmanual	16.7	16.2	8.6	7.7	3.3	11.5
Upper manual	20.2	21.0	25.8	18.5	5.8	20.4
Lower manual	21.8	30.5	32.6	38.5	7.0	29.7
Farm	12.1	17.5	24.0	27.5	80.7	22.9
Total	100%	100%	100%	100%	100%	100%

Source: Featherman and Hauser (1978:91). The samples include American men in the experienced civilian labor force aged twenty-one to sixty-four.

ample, in 1973, although there was little occupational inheritance (14.5 percent) for farm workers (in Table 11-2), there was a high degree of occupational recruitment (80.7 percent) from farm workers into farm work (in Table 11-3). What this indicates is that the supply of farm-worker sons was much greater than the demand for farm workers. Only 14.5 percent stayed farm workers, but the sons of farm workers made up 80.7 percent of farm workers in 1973. Again, farm-worker sons had to move up or face the likelihood of unemployment.

Another conclusion gained from Table 11-3 is that there was a higher rate of upward mobility than downward mobility in both years. This can be seen by noting the higher figures below than above the diagonals. For example, with upper manual sons in 1973 (the midpoint in the occupational categories), moving down the column we find more upper manual sons came from lower than higher occupational origins. Only 9.0 percent of the upper manual sons came from upper nonmanual origins in 1973, but 32.6 percent and 24.0 percent came from lower manual and farm origins, respectively.

The same pattern is generally found with all the broad occupational categories in Table 11-3. The exception is with upper nonmanual (or upper-middle-class) sons who could not move up in the occupational structure. (Higher positions in authority and property structures, or with the corporate class and upper class, are not precisely measured in these studies.)

There are two main explanations for the higher rate of upward than downward intergenerational mobility in both 1962 and 1973 (Featherman and

Hauser 1978:217). One factor is the changing occupational structure. There were more jobs being created toward the top of the occupational structure than toward the bottom as our society became more advanced technologically. Thus, relatively more people are needed toward the top. Combined with this, because of class fertility differences, we find that families have slightly more children as we move down the occupational structure. Thus, with the lower-occupation families producing more children and with the relative number of lower occupations being reduced, there is less room at the bottom and more room toward the top of the occupational structure.

The overall intergenerational mobility figures for 1962 and 1973 can be summarized (Featherman and Hauser 1978:93). There was slightly more mobility in 1973 than in 1962. The movers accounted for 66.9 percent of the sample in 1962 and 68.1 percent of the sample in 1973. However, there was slightly more downward mobility in 1973 than in 1962. In 1962, 15.3 percent of the sample were downwardly mobile and 57.6 percent upwardly mobile, but in 1973, 17.2 percent of the sample were downwardly mobile and 50.9 percent upwardly mobile.

The two years can also be compared in terms of structural and circulation mobility. *Structural* mobility can be defined as the amount of mobility accounted for by changes in the occupational structure (for example, relatively more jobs created at the top than at the bottom). In 1962 the rate of structural mobility was 22.0 percent; in 1973 it was 18.8 percent. *Circulation* mobility is the amount of mobility explained by exchange movements up *and* down the occupational structure. In 1962 circulation mobility was 44.9 percent. Putting these figures together for 1973, of the total sample (100 percent) we find 31.9 percent were nonmobile, 18.8 percent were mobile due to structural changes, and 49.3 percent were mobile due to exchanges or circulation mobility.

We noted in beginning this discussion of social mobility in the United States that the 1972 data has been updated, though to date we do not have research as comprehensive as that by Featherman and Hauser (1978). In previous chapters we have seen changes in the American occupational structure and level of inequality that have most likely affected the pattern of social mobility since 1972. Specifically, in the 1980s we have seen the growth of upper-middle-class jobs, the shrinkage of middle-paying jobs, and a bigger increase in jobs paying poverty wages. These changes in the occupational structure and the related increase in inequality must have some effect on the patterns of social mobility, primarily the rate of structural mobility. In contrast to the time period covered in the Featherman and Hauser (1978) study, when the occupational structure was growing more at the top than at the bottom, the 1980s most likely brought structural mobility in a downward direction. Circulation mobility, however, may or may not be affected, because this is the rate of equality of opportunity for all to move either up or down (exchanging positions intergenerationally, so to speak), after the effects of structural mobility have been considered.

Our speculation as to the trends in social mobility for the 1980s can be partially supported by research reported by Hout (1988). However, the period of time included in this study was 1972 to 1985, thus covering more years in the 1970s than 1980s, and not showing the full impact of the changes in the 1980s.

But this research does indicate that the patterns of social mobility are changing in the direction we have suggested. For example, Hout (1988) found that the overall rate of social mobility is slowing for the first time in the years we have data on the subject. He also found that, while there was still more upward than downward social mobility, the upward social mobility had slowed. Again, we can suggest that complete data for the 1980s would likely show much more slowing in upward mobility, and perhaps even more downward than upward mobility.

Social Mobility at the Top   As already noted, traditional mobility studies have been unable to provide us with an adequate picture of the top of the stratification system. By the top of the stratification system, we are referring to the upper and corporate classes. The upper class is defined primarily by property relations; it consists of the families who own large amounts of the major means of production in the society. The corporate class is defined primarily by authority relations; its members are the top corporate officials who control the major means of production. When referring to the corporate class, it will be remembered, we are referring to the top corporate officials in *major* corporations (that is, the 250 to 500 biggest corporations in the United States).

Standard mobility studies (such as those reviewed above) include the corporate class in the upper nonmanual or managerial and professional categories. However, such categories are rather broad, including everyone from the chairman of the board at BankAmerica to doctors, lawyers (wealthy and poor), and managers of small local factories. The corporate class, though extremely powerful, accounts for only a small proportion of those in upper nonmanual positions. Thus, traditional mobility studies provide no insight into mobility patterns at the very top of the stratification system.

Along with the mobility data already described, what we want to know is (1) the extent of inheritability of upper-class and corporate-class positions, and (2) the extent of recruitment into these positions from positions below the top. It is generally assumed that for both of these top classes (and especially the upper class) inheritability is quite high and recruitment from below is severely restricted. Unfortunately, however, research pertaining to mobility at the very top is limited. But we do have some research that, though by no means conclusive, is suggestive.

We can begin with the upper class. One reason mobility into or out of the upper class is assumed to be very low is that by their very nature, upper-class institutions are designed to prevent such mobility. As described in Chapter 7, upper-class institutions such as the *Social Register,* elite prep schools, and exclusive social clubs function to restrict the membership of upper-class circles (see Baltzell 1958, 1964; Amory 1960; Domhoff 1967, 1970, 1974). They are designed to keep the new rich, until they "qualify," from penetrating the upper class, and to ensure that upper-class members marry within the upper class. Debutante balls and exclusive upper-class clubs in elite universities also operate to further class intramarriage. Thus, to the extent that upper-class institutions operate as they are designed to operate, mobility into or out of the upper class is severely restricted.

We have a number of descriptive studies by insiders that indicate these upper-class institutions do operate in such a manner (for example, Baltzell 1958, 1964; Amory 1960). Also, studies suggesting extensive overlap in membership patterns in prep schools, the *Social Register,* and upper-class social clubs provide indirect evidence of continuing restrictive boundaries around the upper class (Domhoff 1967, 1970). We do hear of many complaints by upper-class members that upper-class membership is not as restrictive as it should be or once was (Amory 1960)—although this seems to be a constant complaint of upper-class members in the past 100 years or so.

Finally, we do have some direct research on upper-class intramarriage. Blumberg and Paul (1975) studied upper-class wedding announcements and found a high degree of upper-class endogamy. Using the Philadelphia *Social Register* as an indicator of upper-class membership, Rosen and Bell (1966) found 31 percent and 21 percent of all upper-class marriages were within the upper class in 1940 and 1961 (that is, both marriage partners were listed in the *Social Register*). These figures are lower than might be expected, given the description of Baltzell (1958) and others, but it must be recognized that the marriage partners not listed in the Philadelphia *Social Register* could have been from outside the city (and on another *Social Register*) or simply from another upper-class family not listed in a *Social Register.*

That the marriage partner not previously listed in the Philadelphia *Social Register* was usually acceptable to the upper class is indicated by the finding that only 13 percent in 1940 and 11 percent in 1961 were not included in the Philadelphia *Social Register* the following year. This could mean that the previously unlisted marriage partner was already in the upper class (and simply not listed in the *Social Register*), or that marriage is a means of breaking into the upper class. Baltzell's (1958) qualitative research would indicate the former is more typical, although more research is needed.

The above studies are concerned with social indicators of upper-class membership. Wealth, and especially old wealth, however, is also an important criterion of upper-class membership. More extensive data are needed, but figures on the most wealthy families in the United States show that today most inherit their wealth. For example, of the sixty-six wealthiest people in 1970, 82 percent were from upper-class origins (Dye 1983).

Estimating inheritance and recruitment into the corporate class presents more complex problems. Most importantly, problems stem from a lack of clear agreement on what constitutes corporate class boundaries. A summary of relevant studies indicates that when a broad definition of the corporate class is assumed, recruitment into the corporate class from below is higher than if more restrictive boundaries are assumed (Kerbo and Della Fave 1979). That is, if *all* corporate officers of, say, the biggest 500 corporations are assumed to be members of the corporate class, there is more mobility into the corporate class than if the boundary is only *top* corporate officers of the biggest 200 corporations. Another problem is that previous research has seldom made a distinction between the upper class and the corporate class (as was made in Chapters 7 and 8 above). Despite these problems, let us turn to some of the research to see what, if any, conclusions can be made.

Thomas Dye (1983) has collected background information on the presidents and directors of the nation's 201 top corporations (3,572 people). Dye's (1983) research indicates that 30 percent of the corporate class had upper-class origins (roughly including the 1 percent of the population in the upper class and corporate class as defined above) and another 59 percent had upper-middle-class origins (roughly equal to the upper nonmanual occupations in Featherman and Hauser's research). These data are similar to those found in an inflow mobility table (that is, they indicate recruitment into the corporate class).

We can combine the above figures to suggest that almost 90 percent of the corporate class had family origins at or close to the top of the stratification system. For a better understanding of corporate-class mobility patterns we would also like to see data similar to those found in an outflow mobility table (showing the rate of intergenerational corporate-class inheritance), but no such data are presented.

Other studies have suggested that the corporate class has even more restricted class origins. For example, Domhoff (1983) examined the family origins of the directors of the top twenty industrial, top thirty financial, and top thirty transportation and utility corporations. In each case he found that more than 50 percent had upper-class origins. Using Domhoff's indicators of upper-class membership, Mintz (1975) found that 66 percent of all cabinet members between 1897 and 1973 show evidence of upper-class origins. (About 75 percent of these cabinet members were also officials of top corporations at some point; Freitag 1975.) And research by Useem (1978, 1979b, 1984) and Soref (1976) shows a significant relationship between multiple corporate directorships and upper-class origins.

In summary, the available studies leave us with no firm conclusions about intergenerational inheritance or recruitment into the corporate class. A rough estimate that corporate-class inheritance is substantially higher than the 59.4 percent found by Featherman and Hauser (1978) for upper nonmanual occupations in 1973 seems reasonable. And a rough estimate that recruitment into the corporate class is more restricted than that of upper nonmanual occupations found by Featherman and Hauser also seems reasonable.

As noted above, Dye's (1983) study found that about 90 percent of the corporate elite came from origins at or above the nonmanual level. A rough estimate is usually better than none, but more research is needed for any firm conclusions. Clearly, intergenerational mobility into the corporate class from below does exist, and it is no doubt greater than mobility into the wealthy upper class. But it also seems clear that corporate-class recruitment from below is much more restricted than with upper nonmanual positions in general. And it should be remembered that Featherman and Hauser (1978) found upper nonmanual positions the most closed of those they studied.

Black Mobility Patterns   To what degree do the mobility patterns of blacks resemble those of the general population? More specifically, what effect has racism and a history of discrimination had on the chances of blacks to be upwardly mobile? Equally important, when blacks have achieved some success in the occupational structure, to what degree have they been able to pass occupational advantages on to their offspring? These questions are of critical importance in understanding racial class inequality in the United States. The studies conducted by Blau and Duncan (1967) and by Featherman and Hauser (1978) contain information relevant to these questions.

Table 11-4 presents standard outflow mobility data for blacks in 1962 and 1973. These data show the class system to be *much more rigid* for blacks (especially in 1962) than for the general population. Table 11-4 can be compared with Table 11-2, which shows the intergenerational movement from father's occupation to son's current occupation for the general population (which, of course, is primarily white).

Beginning with the 1962 data, Table 11-4 shows that occupational inheritance at the top was severely limited for blacks. For example, black fathers who had attained upper nonmanual positions were seldom able to pass this advantage on to their sons. Among blacks in 1962, only *13.3 percent* of the sons who had fathers with upper nonmanual positions were able to attain such a

TABLE 11-4

OUTFLOW MOBILITY FOR BLACK MEN FROM FATHER'S (OR OTHER FAMILY HEAD'S) BROAD OCCUPATION GROUP TO SON'S CURRENT OCCUPATION GROUP, 1962 and 1973

Father's occupation	Son's current occupation					
	Upper nonmanual	Lower nonmanual	Upper manual	Lower manual	Farm	Total
1962						
Upper nonmanual	13.3%	10.0%	13.7%	63.0%	0.0%	100%
Lower nonmanual	8.3	14.0	14.0	63.7	0.0	100
Upper manual	8.2	10.9	10.9	67.0	3.0	100
Lower manual	6.7	9.1	11.1	71.0	2.1	100
Farm	1.2	5.4	7.1	66.3	19.9	100
Total	4.5	7.7	9.4	67.9	10.5	100
1973						
Upper nonmanual	43.9%	11.8%	8.3%	36.0%	0.0%	100%
Lower nonmanual	19.5	20.8	13.4	45.5	0.8	100
Upper manual	16.3	13.9	15.8	53.7	0.2	100
Lower manual	12.1	12.2	13.7	61.0	1.0	100
Farm	5.1	6.8	16.5	63.2	8.4	100
Total	11.6	10.8	14.7	59.4	3.5	100

Source: Featherman and Hauser (1978:326). The samples include American black men in the experienced civilian labor force aged twenty-one to sixty-four.

position. This compares with a 56.8 percent inheritance rate for upper non-manual positions in the general population (see Table 11-2).

With lower nonmanual positions, the black inheritance rate was 14.0 percent in 1962, compared with 23.7 percent rate for the general population. What is more significant, in the general population 43.1 percent of sons with lower nonmanual fathers moved *up* to upper nonmanual positions. For blacks, this rate of upward movement was only 8.3 percent.

Where, then, did the sons of black upper nonmanual fathers go? For the clear majority, the movement was *down*—way down. In 1962, *63.0 percent* of black sons with upper nonmanual fathers moved all the way down to lower manual positions. The same figure for the general population was 13.8 percent. What this means is that when a black did make it in the occupational structure, say to a doctor or lawyer, unlike whites this black father was seldom able to pass his success on to his children. In the white world this would be comparable to 63 percent of the children of doctors ending up on an assembly line doing unskilled blue-collar labor.

These findings describe one of the most tragic conditions for blacks since slavery in the United States, and help us in part to understand why blacks for the most part have remained poor and in the worst jobs, when not in the unemployment lines. Unlike white ethnic groups who often came to this country in poverty, blacks have not had a second and third generation that substantially moved out of poverty. In short, the 1962 figures show almost no accumulated advantages for blacks. A black middle and upper middle class does exist, but these figures demonstrate in part why it has remained very small.

Returning to the 1962 data in Table 11-4 for a moment, we do find greater occupational inheritance for blacks in relation to whites in one part of the occupational structure—at the bottom. For black sons with lower manual fathers, 71.0 percent remained in lower manual occupations. The comparable figure for the general population (primarily white) was 43.4 percent. In fact, what Table 11-4 shows is that *no matter what the father's occupation* a majority of black sons ended up in lower manual or unskilled blue-collar work.

Moving to the 1973 figures for blacks in Table 11-4, we find at least one significant improvement. At the top of the occupational structure intergenerational inheritance has increased. For example, in 1973, 43.9 percent of the black sons with upper nonmanual fathers were able to inherit their father's occupational advantage (this compares with 13.3 percent for blacks in 1962). Blacks remain behind the 59.4 percent upper nonmanual inheritance for whites, but a 30 percent improvement is quite significant. Hout (1984) has updated these data to the end of the 1970s and we continue to find an improved position for stability in this black middle class. Less corresponding improvement for blacks is shown for other occupational positions in 1973, but there has been some improvement.

Comparing 1962 with 1973 in Table 11-4, we find a bit more occupational inheritance for blacks in lower nonmanual and upper manual positions, with somewhat less inheritance in lower manual positions. In essence, the black doctor and black teacher were better able to give their sons an occupational boost in 1973, although they remained less able to do so than whites.

The 1973 figures indicate that barring major setbacks, *at least those blacks able to break into higher occupational positions* will be able to form a more stable black middle class. In contrast to the past, middle- and upper-middle-class status may not be a fading dream for *some* blacks.

No doubt some of the improvement for blacks between 1962 and 1973 was due to better economic conditions. But we have had better economic conditions in other periods without significantly improved mobility patterns for blacks. Thus, it seems clear that at least part of the improvement was due to legal action and government-sponsored minority programs outlawing employment and educational discrimination (with the black civil rights movement a stimulus to such action).

However, as we have seen with the earlier success in reducing poverty in the 1960s and 1970s, the gains made by blacks and other minorities with respect to educational and occupational attainment were eroded in the 1980s. For example, while the percentage of whites (twenty-five years old or older) who have completed four years of college was 23 percent in 1987, it was only 11.4 percent for blacks and 8.7 percent for people of Hispanic origin (U.S. Bureau of the Census, Population Characteristics, 1988). More important for our present point is that this rate has dropped slightly for blacks from the high point of 13 percent in the mid-1970s, and even more for people of Hispanic origin from the high point of 11.1 in 1985. The decline for blacks is even more striking when we consider the percentage of high school graduates going on to college. In 1975, 50.3 percent of black male high school graduates went on to college, as did 46.1 percent of black females (for whites it was 56.6 percent and 49.1 percent). By 1985, however, the figures were 43.5 percent and 43.9 percent for blacks, compared to 55.5 percent and 55.2 percent for whites (U.S. Bureau of Census, *Statistical Abstracts of the United States, 1987,* 1988:137).

The improvements just described for the period before the 1980s may seem in contradiction to the continuing high rate of black to white income inequality, black unemployment, and the poverty described in the previous chapter, but they are not. Table 11-4 shows only a little of what is happening because for the most part poor and unemployed blacks are not found on this table (Willhelm 1979).

But even in Table 11-4 we continue to find a much higher concentration of blacks in lower manual occupations. Reading down the lower manual column in Table 11-4 for 1973, and comparing this to Table 11-2 for whites, we find that blacks were still *much* more likely to fall into lower manual occupations no matter what their fathers' occupation. For black sons with higher occupational fathers there was less downward mobility in 1973; but when they were downwardly mobile, they fell much further than whites. Also, the figure for lower manual inheritance for blacks remained substantially higher than that for whites in 1973 (61.0 percent versus 40.1 percent). As for whites and blacks in 1973, the class structure for blacks in even more rigid at the top and bottom—although for blacks it is even more rigid at the bottom.

In essence, despite the continuing high rates of black–white income inequality, black unemployment, and black poverty, Table 11-4 shows the existence of a relatively small black middle class in 1973. The black middle class has benefited most from social change stimulated by the civil rights movement of the 1960s. As noted in Chapter 10, lower-class blacks got welfare and little else. Black inequality is still a racial issue, but it is increasingly a class issue as well. The anger of lower-class blacks is as likely to be directed toward middle-class blacks as toward the white power structure in the next round of riots, which are sure to come if political and economic conditions for lower-class blacks remain the same in coming decades.

Mobility Patterns among Women As with blacks, our main question at present is whether the mobility patterns observed for women differ from those for white males. Because of the availability of data, our focus must be on white women. In beginning our examination of social mobility we noted that most studies have been concerned with men. More recently, however, this concern has shifted to the extent that some reasonably firm conclusions can be made with respect to the mobility patterns of white women.

We will begin with a comparison between men and women who are in the labor force. One of the first studies of this type (De Jong, Brawer, and Robin 1971) found the mobility patterns of women quite similar to those of men. That is, comparing their occupations with those of their fathers, women had patterns of occupational inheritance and recruitment very close to those of men shown in Table 11-2.

However—perhaps because it was one of the first studies of this type—there is wide agreement that several major problems were contained in the study (see Hauser and Featherman 1977:195). One problem was created because there was no indication of which job (first, second, or third) was being measured for women. Careers do change, and the data must be comparable in this respect. A person's first job is often of lower status than later jobs.

The most important problem, however, involved the broad occupational categories employed in the study. As noted in an earlier chapter, because women tend to be concentrated in particular occupations (such as clerical workers), broad occupational categories (such as lower nonmanual and upper manual) are not able to detect important differences between the mobility patterns of men and women.

When examining mobility patterns using eighteen occupational categories (rather than the five in Table 11-2) several significant differences between men and women are found. For example, Tyree and Treas (1974) found that daughters of professional fathers were more likely to be in white-collar occupations than sons of professional fathers. Also, daughters of farm workers were more likely to be in white-collar occupations and less likely to be in blue-collar occupations than sons of farm workers. Further, Hauser and Featherman (1977:204) found that, overall, working women are less likely to be in an occupational status close to their father's when compared with men.

As might be expected when comparing the different occupational distributions of men and women (noted in Chapter 9), most of the difference in mobility patterns between men and women is due to this differing occupational distribution (Hauser and Featherman 1977:203). Following the previous statement that working women are less likely to keep their fathers' occupational status than men, this is because women are both more downwardly *and* more upwardly mobile (compared with their fathers) than men are.

Women are more concentrated in lower nonmanual or lower white-collar occupations, such as clerical workers. Thus, no matter whether their fathers are higher or lower in occupational rank, women are frequently pushed up to, or down to, the lower white-collar positions. There is a sex as well as a race bias in the occupational structure. Black men, it will be remembered, are often pushed down to lower manual positions no matter what the occupational position of their fathers.

There are, however, two mobility patterns among women. Thus far, we have considered only the intergenerational mobility patterns of women in the labor force. But as noted above, the status of women in the stratification system has traditionally been assumed to follow that of their husbands. With more than 50 percent of married women now in the labor force, this assumption must increasingly be questioned.

In also means, however, that slightly less than 50 percent of married women are not in the labor force. To the extent that the occupational structure shapes life chances and the distribution of rewards in the society, the occupational structure more clearly affects this second group of women through the occupational attainment of their husbands. In this case we can consider the intergenerational mobility patterns of women with reference to the occupational position of their fathers vis-à-vis that of their husbands.

Such a mobility analysis of married women not in the labor force has been conducted by Chase (1975), Tyree and Treas (1974), and Glenn, Ross, and Tully (1974). In this respect the intergenerational mobility patterns of women were found to be much closer to those of men. In other words, women tend to marry men who hold occupational positions close to those of their brothers more than they tend to enter occupational positions close to those of their brothers (when women are employed). Put another way, father–son mobility patterns are closer to father–husband mobility patterns than to father–daughter mobility patterns (Hauser and Featherman 1977:197). Thus, for a significant number of women the marriage market more closely reproduces the intergenerational mobility patterns of men.

However, these studies have found some differences between the mobility patterns of women (through their husbands) and those of men. One important difference is that mobility for women through marriage remains slightly greater than mobility for men through occupation. It was commonly believed that

women had more upward mobility through marriage than did men through occupations (Glenn, Ross, and Tully 1974)—the old story of the poor but attractive girl marrying a rich man. On the contrary—women are as likely to marry
down as marry up. The overall effect is slightly more intergenerational mobility for women through marriage than for men through an occupation, but the
mobility goes both up and down (Chase 1975).

Social Mobility: Historical and Comparative

Having examined the more contemporary patterns of social mobility in the
United States, we have two remaining questions of considerable importance.
First, we want to know how the patterns of social mobility described above
compare with those in earlier periods of United States history. Our traditional
ideology claims that this is a country of opportunity. At least with respect to
the occupational structure, and at least with respect to positions between the
very top and bottom, there is at least some support for this ideological claim
among white males. Although most mobility is short range (that is, not far from
occupational origins), the 1962 and 1973 data show that mobility does exist and
that there is more upward than downward mobility. What we now want to
know is whether it has always been so in the United States. In the past, has the
extent of social mobility been less, greater, or the same?

Second, the ideological claims in this country suggest that the United States
has more opportunities for people than other countries do. This is one reason
so many immigrants came to this country in the past and why so many refu-
gees from countries such as Mexico, Cuba, Vietnam, Cambodia, and Haiti
continue to view the United States as the most inviting country among industrialized nations. To what extent are these views correct? Currently, does the
United States have more social mobility than other industrialized nations such
as England, France, Germany, and Japan?

Historical Patterns of Mobility in the United States   We do have some evidence of the extent of social mobility in earlier periods of United States history, although the evidence is less systematic and extensive than that gained
from recent studies. The sociological study of social stratification did not even
exist before the late 1800s in the United States; and even before the mid-1900s
empirical investigation of mobility patterns was almost totally neglected. Thus,
researchers have been forced to design indicators of earlier mobility patterns
from various types of historical records. Some of this research is quite inge-
nious, but it must also be accepted with caution.

In a study concerned with one of the earliest periods of United States history, Thernstrom (1970) examined social mobility in Boston during the second
half of the 1800s using census records, marriage license applications, and tax
records. Thernstrom's data show that of sons born between 1850 and 1879, 36
percent of their fathers were in white-collar occupations, while 56 percent of
the sons ended up in white-collar occupations. This may indicate more upward

than downward mobility. In terms of occupational inheritance, sons of white-collar fathers were about twice as often found in white-collar occupations as were sons of blue-collar workers. Thus, the sons of white-collar fathers were advantaged, but in the face of extensive European immigration, so were the sons of white Anglo-Saxon Protestants no matter what their fathers' occupations.

The most extensive study of early social mobility in the United States was conducted by Rogoff (1953a, 1953b). In this study, Rogoff compared mobility patterns in Indianapolis between 1910 and 1940 using a sample of about 10,000 marriage license applications. At this time, the marriage license applications required a listing of the male's occupation and that of his father. Rogoff's findings were that intergenerational mobility was very similar in 1910 and 1940. More specifically, the rate of occupational inheritance was about the same in both years, and when changes in occupational distribution are considered (some jobs were reduced, others increased), upward and downward mobility was about the same in both years.

Rogoff's data have been subjected to extensive reanalysis by Duncan (1966) and Hauser and Featherman (1977) using more sophisticated statistical methods. Both studies have concluded that the mobility patterns between 1910 and 1940 were quite similar, although there were some minor variations not detected in Rogoff's analysis. Furthermore, Tully, Jackson, and Curtis (1970) have provided more recent mobility data for Indianapolis. Comparing the years 1910, 1940, and 1967, these researchers again conclude that the pattern of social mobility in Indianapolis has varied only slightly over these years.

Guest, Landale, and McCann (1989) were able to estimate the patterns of social mobility during the late 1800s in the United States through innovative use of the census data. From the 1880 census and the 1900 census they were able to match information from the fathers' 1880 occupational positions to that of 4,041 of the sons' in the 1900 census. Using these matched cases they found that upward mobility was lower, and occupational inheritance was higher, in the late 1800s when compared to the 1962 and 1973 data studied by Blau and Duncan (1967) and by Featherman and Hauser (1978). However, when restricting the analysis to nonfarm families only, Guest, Landale, and McCann (1989) found only small differences in the amount of upward mobility and occupational inheritance during the late 1800s and 1962 or 1973.

Another method of detecting possible changes in mobility patterns over the years is *cohort analysis*. Using this method we compare different age workers to see if their mobility patterns have differed. Duncan (1965) has used such an analysis to compare workers entering the labor force between 1942 and 1952 and between 1952 and 1962. Hauser and Featherman (1977) have extended this analysis to workers entering the labor force between 1962 and 1972. These studies have indicated a slight increase in upward mobility since World War II, primarily due to an increase in higher-level occupations compared with lower-level occupations. This trend in the occupational structure, as we have seen, has reversed in the 1980s, leading to the speculation that upward mobility has decreased and downward mobility has increased even further than Hout (1988) had found up to 1985.

It will be remembered that traditional mobility studies do not give us an accurate picture of the top of the stratification system. There have been a few historical studies of the business elite that continue to show that mobility into the very top is quite restricted. For example, Mills (1963) examined the family backgrounds of the nineteenth-century business elite using biographical sources. He found that only 9.8 percent of the business leaders born before 1907 were from blue-collar origins, while 13.2 percent of the business leaders born between 1820 and 1829 had blue-collar origins.

In her sample, Keller (1953) found that only 3 percent of business leaders born around 1820 had lower white-collar or blue-collar origins. In another study, Bendix and Howton (1959) found that only about 1 to 2 percent of business leaders born between 1801 and 1890 had working-class origins. And in a massive study of the upper class in six steel and iron industry communities (Philadelphia, Bethlehem, Pittsburgh, Wheeling, Youngstown, and Cleveland) at the turn of the century, Ingham (1978) found mobility into the upper class almost nonexistent. All these studies were limited to small samples or local areas, but it is reasonable to conclude that mobility into the top of the stratification system has been very restricted over the years, especially for those below the upper nonmanual level.

Comparative Mobility Studies The primary task of cross-national studies of social mobility is to compare the differing rates or patterns of social mobility among nations. We want to know, for example, if the United States has more or less social mobility than France, Germany, or any other nation. Such a task would seem quite simple, involving nothing more than measuring the overall amount of social mobility in each country, then ranking the countries in terms of these measures. But the task is not so simple.

To begin with, comparative social mobility can be measured in many ways, with each measure telling us something different about the subject. There is little agreement as to which of the measures are most useful, or even which questions are most important to ask. Furthermore, if we are to compare nations with respect to movement up and down ranks in the occupational structure, the occupational structure of each nation must be somewhat comparable. If one nation has more occupational ranks than another or if the gaps between ranks in one nation are larger or smaller than in another, a simple indicator comparing movement up and down the occupational ranks in two nations will be misleading (Matras 1980:413).

Finally, traditional mobility studies, and especially comparative studies (Matras 1980:408), are concerned with movement in the occupational structure. The assumption is that the occupational structure of each nation is equally important in the stratification system, that the conflict over valued resources in each society is focused on the occupational structure. Such an assumption, however, is not necessarily valid. Societies may differ with respect to how the distribution of rewards depends on a mixture of political authority, the ownership of property, racial caste, and occupational position. For example, in Chapter 13 we will find that in Japan, income is more related to a person's age and size of the company where employed, and less related to education and occupational status, compared to the United States.

Comparative studies of social mobility, therefore, must be interpreted with caution. The task is somewhat simplified when restricted to Western industrial nations with roughly the same level of economic development, but even here some tough questions remain. Can we say the physician's occupational position in the United States is comparable to that of a physician in England when their economic rewards differ greatly? Would intergenerational movement from college professor to physician in the United States and West Germany be considered upward mobility in both countries? And this is even a bigger question when comparing Japan and the United States. Physicians have similar incomes in Japan and the United States, but the income of college professors is much lower in Japan. However, the status of and respect for of a college professor in Japan are much higher. Thus, should we consider the son of a physician in Japan who became a college professor to have experienced upward or downward mobility?

Comparative mobility studies are not meaningless. They can tell us something about stratification and social mobility in the United States compared to other industrial nations. For example, they can tell us if there is or is not a common pattern of social mobility shaped by the process of industrialization. They also can tell us if things can or cannot be done to influence the rate and direction of social mobility in the society to create more equality of opportunity. These types of questions can be answered with at least some degree of confidence with new studies of comparative social mobility published in the 1980s.

Some of the earlier, cruder comparative studies simply compared the overall rates of social mobility for countries, or compared rates of movement in and out of certain occupational positions in the society (for example, Miller 1960; Fox and Miller 1965; Lenski 1966). We know now, however, that we must adjust for differences in the level of economic development and differing shapes of the occupational structures. For example, countries in later stages of development tend to have fewer working-class positions and more upper-middle-class positions to move into, thus affecting mobility chances and rates.

Correcting for these differences, however, we can learn some important things about comparative rates of social mobility, as was done by Ishida, Goldthorpe, and Erikson (1987) in their study of the United States, Japan, and Western Europe. For example, they found that Japan has a higher rate of upward mobility out of the working class, and less downward mobility into the working class, than the United States or European countries. Most different was the rate of working-class occupational inheritance for Japan (that is, the number of people who must stay in the working class when born there). The figure of working-class inheritance was only 21 percent in Japan, compared to 39 to 78 percent inheritance for the European countries. The overall rate of circulation mobility was not substantially different between Japan and the

United States, even though there were differences at specific places in the occupational structure. We need to know why a greater percentage of working-class offspring in Japan move to higher positions, and will examine the influence of the educational system in Japan (among other things) on opportunities for the working class in our later chapter on social stratification in Japan.

Much of the comparative mobility research in the 1980s was directed toward the "Featherman-Jones-Hauser hypothesis" that nations at roughly similar intervals of economic development also should have similar circulation rates of social mobility once adjustments are made for differences in their occupational distributions (see Featherman, Jones, and Hauser 1975). What this hypothesis claims is that social mobility rates and the chance for people to move up or down are generally the same in all industrial nations, and these chances and rates of circulation mobility are shaped almost exclusively by aspects of industrialization.

Using data from fifteen industrial nations, Hazelrigg and Garnier (1976) at first found some weak support for this hypothesis. Another study by Tyree, Semyonov, and Hodge (1979) also found only weak support for the hypothesis that rates of circulation mobility are similar in all advanced industrial nations. And their findings also made them suggest that wealth and power inequalities that differ among industrial nations may affect circulation mobility rates more than the Featherman-Jones-Hauser hypothesis would indicate. More extensive studies in the 1980s led to a further rejection and modification of the Featherman-Jones-Hauser hypothesis of similar patterns of circulation mobility (Grusky and Hauser 1984; Slomczynski and Krauze 1987; Hauser and Grusky 1988). More specifically, these studies have found that the level of democracy and level of inequality can have more effect on the rates of circulation mobility than most sociologists had believed in the past. The important implication is that political action and government policy can create more equality of opportunity and that higher levels of inequality impede circulation mobility.

The United States has the reputation of being the land of opportunity among many people in the world. The above studies, however, indicate that the United States is only about average with respect to its rate of circulation mobility, or equality of opportunity in general. In fact, none of the advanced capitalist societies are radically different with respect to their overall rates of circulation mobility. But in some places in the stratification system, especially toward the bottom, the chances of moving up are below average for the United States. In one sense, though, people who view the United States as the land of opportunity are correct: More than in most industrial nations we can say that outsiders can get into this country to compete for the chance of upward mobility.

Social Mobility: A Conclusion

Our concern in the first half of this chapter has been social mobility—the pattern of vertical movement up and down the occupational structure. The importance of the subject cannot be overstressed, for the dynamics of class tell us a good deal about the mixture of ascription and achievement operating in a society. The social values of this country prescribe that achievement is good, and thus extensive mobility (when based on achievement) is good.

An examination of world history can also suggest that a relatively open society is usually good because it helps maintain social stability. Even extreme inequalities and class exploitation may be endured by those at the bottom when there is hope for a better future, if not for oneself then at least for one's offspring. When inequality is high, the loss of such hope can have violent consequences, as it has throughout history. With hope, those at the bottom are encouraged to work for individual solutions to their misery.

When hope of individual mobility is reduced, those at the bottom may conclude that the solution to their misery is found with collective challenge to the overall system of stratification, and violent class conflict may be the result. Therefore, social mobility, especially below the elite level, is functional for those at the top. Without it, their positions and rewards may be threatened.

We have noted that social mobility is somewhat extensive—at least in the occupational structure, and at least in the middle of the occupational structure—in virtually all Western industrial societies. A major part of this mobility is upward rather than downward, another condition that is productive of social stability. So far, most industrial societies have continued to expand and advance economically, so that changes in the occupational structure (more jobs created at the top) have produced more upward than downward mobility (Matras 1980:412). Marx's prediction of the destruction of capitalism, at least so far, has been most incorrect on this point. But with inequality quite high in these capitalist societies, widespread and long-term economic stagnation leading to a sharp reduction of mobility could be dangerous, and we have noted that the United States may be moving in this direction, though very slowly at present.

A short summary of what we have discovered about social mobility in this country is now in order.

1 Occupational inheritance in the United States is fairly high at the top and bottom of the occupational structure. Between these extremes, inheritance is less and intergenerational mobility relatively higher. But even at the top, movement (or recruitment) into the top occupational positions exists in the face of inheritance. This is because the positions toward the top are increasing (though not as much as positions at the bottom in recent years), with fewer offspring at the top helping produce more room for those below. Overall, most social mobility in the United States, both up and down, is short-range mobility. That is, when people are mobile, they usually rise or fall only to positions close to those of their family origins. This helps explain, for example, why those who move into the top positions are more likely to be close to the top in their origins.

2 We have very limited and inadequate information on mobility patterns at the very top. This lack of research seems surprising until we recognize that the bias of mobility research has led to a focus on occupational status, neglecting the importance of positions of ownership and/or control of the dominant means of production in the society. And the research we do have is sometimes contradictory because of conflicting indicators of elite positions. There is some agreement that inheritance is very high among the upper and corporate classes, but the extent of recruitment into these classes below the elite level is in more dispute.

Whatever the rate of recruitment into the very top, it is no doubt what Domhoff (1967, 1970) and others call *sponsored mobility*. That is, recruitment is very selective to ensure that those brought into the very top will be supportive of the class inequalities and privilege attached to top positions. (Put another way, we would expect to find few top officers at General Motors who are in favor of extensive equality and restrictions on corporate-class power.)

3 Extensive data from 1962 and 1973 suggest that the mobility patterns for white males have been very stable in this time period. Less extensive data also suggest that mobility patterns have been rather stable for at least fifty to perhaps 150 years. The major exception to this stability has been with farm occupations because they have been reduced sharply over the years. A slight exception to this stability was the very slow increase in upward mobility over the years. During the 1980s, however, this pattern was changing with the shrinkage of middle-level jobs, and the most growth occurring in lower manual and low-paying jobs. This indicates that social mobility most likely slowed in the 1980s, and there actually may have been more downward than upward mobility by the end of the 1980s.

4 The patterns of mobility for blacks and women have diverged from those of white males. The occupational structure has been much more rigid at the bottom for blacks. Occupational inheritance at the bottom has been the rule, but with extensive disinheritance at the top for blacks. But the 1973 figures did show some change, so that the offspring of blacks at the top have a better chance to stay at the top, although still not as good a chance as whites. Again, however, recent data indicate that black improvements found in the late 1960s and 1970s were slowed or reversed in the 1980s.

Until recently, women have been neglected in mobility studies. But we now have more research showing that two mobility patterns must be distinguished for women. On the one hand, when considering women in the labor force, their mobility diverges from that of white males because women are concentrated in lower nonmanual occupations. No matter where women originate (in terms of their fathers' occupations) they are likely to move up or down to lower nonmanual positions. On the other hand, when we consider the occupational status of women to follow that of their husbands, the intergenerational mobility pattern is more similar to that of white males. The exception is that there is slightly more upward and downward mobility through marriage for women than through occupation for men.

THE ATTAINMENT PROCESS

The primary focus of mobility research is the amount and patterns of movement in the occupational structure. The studies, however, raise very important questions that cannot be answered directly through examination of mobility patterns alone. For example, in Blau and Duncan's study, what distinguishes the 56.8 percent who inherited their fathers' upper nonmanual positions from the 43.2 percent who were downwardly mobile? What distinguishes the 43.1 percent of sons with lower nonmanual fathers who moved up to upper nonmanual positions from those not upwardly mobile? In other words, what factors account for the attainment of positions in the occupational structure? We can conclude from many of the data presented in the preceding section that family background contributes a good deal of occupational attainment. But what is it about family background that influences attainment? And because it seems clear that family background factors alone do not determine attainment, what other factors influence attainment?

These questions are the province of what is usually called *status attainment* research. The focus, again, is on the process of attainment in the occupational status structure, although the attainment of income and education is included in much of this research. Common knowledge may tell us that educational attainment, intellectual ability, motivation, and the economic and educational standing of one's parents help influence occupational attainment. But we want to know which of these factors, among others, are more important. And the question becomes extremely complex when we find that most of the significant factors—such as family background, education, performance on achievement tests, and aspirations—are interrelated.

Status Attainment Models

In addition to achieving a breakthrough in mobility research, Blau and Duncan (1967) contributed much to our understanding of the process of status attainment. They did so primarily by employing a method of data analysis (path analysis) that allows us to disentangle the direct and indirect effects of a number of interrelated independent variables.

In this research Blau and Duncan were most concerned with the effects of father's education, father's occupation, and the son's education and first job on the occupational status of their respondents in the massive data collected in 1962. In summary (see Figure 11-1), Blau and Duncan (1967:170) found that (1) father's education affects son's occupation through the son's educational attainment, (2) father's occupation also affects son's occupation through the son's educational attainment and the son's first job (with father's occupation having a small independent effect on son's 1962 occupation), and (3) of all the variables, the son's educational attainment produced the strongest effect on the son's 1962 occupation (partially through the effect of the son's education on the first job attained).

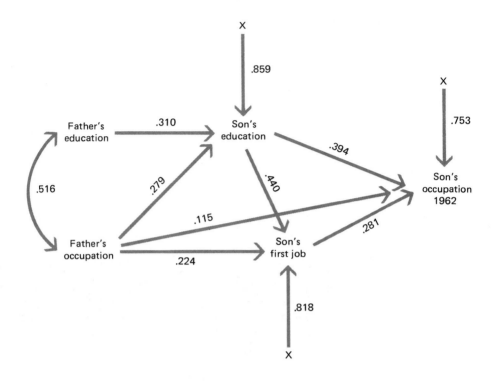

Blau and Duncan's path model for the process of occupational status attainment. *Source:* Blau and Duncan (1967:170).

In other words, fathers were able to influence their sons' 1962 occupation primarily by influencing their sons' educational achievement, and the sons' educational achievement also had a strong independent effect (independent of family background) on their 1962 occupational status. But note that in Figure 11-1 the residual path from x to 1962 occupation is high (.753), indicating that much of the variance in occupational status is not explained by the four independent variables in the model. Together, the four independent variables explain about 43 percent of the variance in sons' 1962 occupational status. (About 57 percent of the variance in sons' occupational status was not explained.)

Although Blau and Duncan's research on the status attainment process represented a significant breakthrough, much was left unexplained. For example, we want to know how father's education and occupation affect son's education, and we want to understand the other factors explaining respondent's occupational status and education that were not included in the model. The Blau and Duncan model was soon expanded with what has come to be known as the *Wisconsin model* of status attainment.

The Wisconsin Model   The Wisconsin model of status attainment adds several psychological variables to the original Blau and Duncan model. The addition of these sociopsychological variables can be seen as an attempt to specify how family background affects educational and occupational achievement, as well as an attempt to explain the model more fully. More specifically, these sociopsychological variables include the son's educational and occupational aspirations and the influence of significant others on these aspirations. Also included in the Wisconsin model are indicators of mental ability and academic performance.

Figure 11-2 represents the most cited path model of the Wisconsin school (see Sewell and Hauser, 1975, for the complete study). Several important findings are worth noting. First, in this model all the effects of the parents' socioeconomic status (SES) on the son's educational and occupational attainment operate through other variables. Most important, the parents' SES affects the son's significant others (for example, peer relations), which in turn strongly affect the son's educational (path = .508) and occupational (path = .441) aspirations.

Occupational aspirations have a weak effect on occupational attainment (path = .152), but educational aspirations have a strong effect on actual educational attainment (path = .457), with educational attainment having a strong direct effect on occupational attainment (path = .522). Also of note is that mental ability has a strong effect on academic performance, with academic performance directly (though more weakly) affecting aspirations and actual educational attainment. Overall, the model explains about 40 percent of the variance in occupational attainment and 57 percent of the variance in educational attainment.

Several studies using differing samples from this country and others have generally confirmed the basic findings described above (see Wilson and Portes 1975; Alexander, Eckland, and Griffin 1975). In summary, what these studies indicate is that there is a mixture of ascriptive and achievement factors that helps explain educational and occupational attainment. The ascriptive effect of family SES works most importantly through significant others on aspirations, while aspirations, in turn, directly affect educational attainment. But educational attainment has the strongest effect on occupational attainment, and educational attainment, it is argued, is in part an achievement variable (not completely determined by family SES).

Studies from the Wisconsin tradition of status attainment research have made important contributions to our understanding of how significant others influence who gets ahead. Also, the importance of educational and occupational aspirations in the process of status attainment has been demonstrated by this research tradition. However, the status attainment perspective in general contains several shortcomings, many of which are related to the individualistic perspective of the tradition (Horan 1978). The status attainment perspective has neglected the extent to which the structure of unequal opportunity sets limits on achievement, and researchers from this perspective have often un-

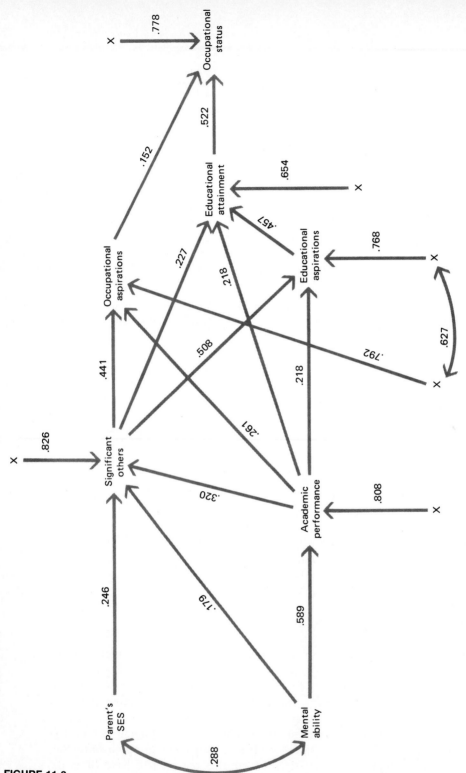

FIGURE 11-2
Path model of status attainment process from the Wisconsin school. *Source:* Sewell, Haller, and Ohlendorf (1970:1023).

derestimated the full effect of ascriptive factors such as family background. In addition, status attainment models have been very weak in attempts to explain income attainment (see Sewell and Hauser 1975).

As for the underestimation of ascriptive factors in the attainment process, a reanalysis of several studies from the status attainment perspective found that family background, in fact, explains almost *50 percent* of the variance in occupational status attainment (Jencks et al. 1979:214–217). In addition, this reanalysis of the data suggests that education is not the great avenue of achievement in our society the status attainment perspective would have us believe (see Jencks et al. 1972:135; 1979:225). In summarizing all their findings from reanalysis of status attainment research, Jencks et al. (1979:82) wrote, ''If we define 'equal opportunity' as a situation in which sons born into different families have the same chances of success, our data show that America comes nowhere near achieving it.''

Before pursuing a more general critique of status attainment research we need to give more attention to education as a mediating structure in the attainment process. By doing so we can see how some of the education-related factors found important by the status attainment perspective operate and how educational attainment helps further inequality and class inheritance in our society.

Education as Mediating Structure

All sides in the debate agree upon the importance of education both in promoting achievement and in reproducing class inequalities through inheritance. They also agree that education is becoming more important for both achievement and ascription as our society becomes more advanced and the education level of the general population increases (Featherman and Hauser 1978:227–233). In this section we will examine briefly some of the factors that influence educational attainment, beginning with the earliest years of schooling and following this process through the college years.

The Early Years of Schooling   The road to higher educational attainment begins very early. Children from higher-class families are more likely to have a home environment that provides the intellectual skills they need to do well in school (Jencks et al. 1972:138; Mercy and Steelman 1982). They get toys and books that give them an early advantage, and they are more likely to see their parents engaged in activities like reading and writing—thus, the image that these are valued skills. Because of all this, studies indicate, middle-class children are already ahead of lower-class children in intellectual ability before the first year of school (Jencks et al. 1972). Intellectual capacity (as distinguished from educational achievement), is to some degree biologically inherited, but the best estimate is that only about 45 percent of IQ is biologically determined, and IQ is only weakly related to social class (Jencks et al. 1972:65, 81).

By the time children are in school the process of separating the winners from the losers becomes even clearer (Jencks et al. 1979). An important factor in this process is teacher expectations; several studies have shown teachers expect more of children from higher-class backgrounds, and the differential treatment of children in terms of teacher expectations leads to better performance among these children (Rosenthal and Jacobson 1968; Rist 1970; Stein 1971; Good and Brophy 1973). There have been some negative reports on the importance of teacher expectations in children' performance (see Claiborn 1969), but the weight of evidence remains in favor of this argument.

Perhaps more important in separating the winners from the losers in the early years of schooling is the practice of tracking. Even though tracking may be more extensive in European nations with long histories of class restrictions on educational attainment (Rubinson 1986), it has been estimated that about 85 percent of the public schools follow the practice of placing children in different tracks that prepare some students for college and others for vocational skills that do not lead to college (Jencks et al. 1972:33).

There have been numerous studies on both the factors that influence track placement and the outcomes of track placement. As for the factors that help determine track placement, it was commonly believed that track placement is directly influenced by the class background of children. But such a direct influence of class must be rejected as overly simple. Measured intellectual skills have been found to be most responsible for track placement (Jencks et al. 1972:35; Heyns 1974), although class background is also involved to some extent (Alexander, Cook, and McDill 1978:65). But the effect of track placement, because cognitive skills and academic performance are influenced by class background, is the same; tracking tends to separate children by class background and race (McPortland 1968; Jencks et al. 1972:35).

Many outcomes of track placement have been found. Some studies indicate that children in the college preparatory track, or higher track, improve in academic achievement over the years, while those in the lower track perform at lower levels (Rosenbaum 1975; Persell 1977; Alexander and Cook 1982), although a few studies show that this is not always the case (see Jencks et al. 1972:106–107). But also important, children in the higher track are less likely to drop out of school (Schafer and Olexa 1971; Gamoran and Mare 1989), have higher educational aspirations (Alexander, Cook, and McDill 1978), and are more likely to attend college (Jencks et al. 1972:34; Alexander, Cook, and McDill 1978). In conclusion we can say that tracking works to reinforce class differences and has an independent effect of further differentiating children in terms of family background (Alexander, Cook, and McDill 1978:57; Gamoran and Mare 1989).

Finally, much has been written about the importance of school quality on later educational attainment. The assumption has been that lower-class children more often attend schools of poor quality that prepare them less well for higher educational attainment. This assumption, however, has been challenged with Jencks et al. (1972) famous study. The study showed that a number of quality indicators—such as per-pupil spending, teachers' pay, and teachers' qualifications—did not show significant relationships to outcomes such as test scores and later college attendance.

School quality, however, is difficult to measure with much precision. A more recent study did find some difference in occupational and income attainment due to school quality. Griffin and Alexander (1978) conducted a 1970 follow-up study of 947 males originally studied in 1955. They found school quality accounted for 11 percent of the variance in occupational attainment and 15 percent of the variance in income attainment among the sample. But even these findings are relatively weak. Thus, until more precise studies of school quality are conducted, we must conclude that school quality alone has only a very small effect, if any, on class differences in educational attainment.

Family Background and College Attendance   With access to higher occupational positions becoming more dependent on educational attainment (Featherman and Hauser 1978:227), college attendance is a key mechanism of class achievement or ascription. Those who finish college have a 49 percent occupational advantage over those who do not, while those who finish high school have only a 15 to 29 percent advantage over those who do not (Jencks et al. 1979). The most important question becomes what influences college attendance and college completion.

Several of the class-related factors described above are important in college attendance. However, as the Wisconsin model of status attainment indicates, much of the effect of class background on college attendance is through educational aspirations. Sewell and Hauser (1975:186) found that sociopsychological variables such as aspirations explain about 60 to 80 percent of the relationship between class background and educational attainment.

Educational aspirations, which show an important relationship to college attendance, are influenced by parents and significant others such as the peer group. Higher-class parents are more likely to encourage their children to go to college and provide role models leading to higher educational aspirations (Sewell, Haller, and Ohlendorf 1970). But close in importance to parents in influencing educational aspirations is the peer group (Sewell 1971). When the peer group is made up of children whose parents are doctors, lawyers, and other higher professionals, the higher aspirations of this peer group will affect others in the group. Thus, access to privileged peers is almost as important as access to privileged parents in educational attainment.

If college attendance were based primarily on intellectual skills there would be much less class inheritance than exists today. But class inequality operates to retard the relationship between intellectual ability and college attendance. In a study of 9,007 high school students, Sewell and Shah (1968) found that 91.1 percent of the students with high intelligence *and* high-class backgrounds attended college. However, only 40.1 percent of the students with high intelligence but low-class backgrounds attended college.

Looking at the other end of the intelligence rank, 58 percent of the students with low intelligence and high-class background attended college, but only 9.3

percent of those with low intelligence and low-class background attended college. No matter what their intelligence, 84.2 percent of the students from higher-class backgrounds attended college, and only 20.8 percent of those with lower-class backgrounds attended college. In other words, class background is strongly related to college attendance (Featherman and Hauser 1978:309).

A final question pertains to college completion. A good indicator of completing college is a student's college grade point average (GPA) (Barger and Hall 1965; Stanfiel 1973). Several studies, however, have found class background to be a very weak predictor of college GPA (Barger and Hall 1965; Bayer 1968; Labovitz 1975). In fact, these studies have found high school GPA and college entrance exam scores to be about the only, though weak, predictors of college GPA, even when a number of psychological scales are included in the research (Himelstein 1965).

In contrast to its importance in earlier years, the reduced importance of class background in predicting college GPA and ultimate college completion is due to the rather homogeneous class background of college students (most are middle class). Whatever factors do produce higher college GPAs and college completion, the low effect of class background at this level seems to indicate that achievement is more important than ascription on the college level. And it is perhaps at this higher level of education that class ascription is prevented from being higher than it otherwise would be.

The achievement effect of college (in contrast to an ascription effect) is also produced because the type or quality of college attendance does not show a strong relation to later income attainment (Sewell and Hauser 1975:141) or occupational attainment (Jencks et al. 1979:226). In short, class background is very important in determining who goes to college; but once a student is in college, class background gives little assurance of college completion. And it must be remembered that completing college is much more important in occupational and income attainment than simply having attended college (Jencks et al. 1979:223).

A Conflict Perspective of Education   We have seen that education can promote both ascription and achievement. Functional theory stresses the achievement aspect of education whereby important skills are attained by the most talented, who are then prepared to fill important positions in the society (Davis and Moore 1945). The full validity of this functional view of education must be questioned, however, when we find (as noted above) that the offspring of higher-class families are much more likely to go to college no matter what their intellectual ability. Furthermore, the functional view must be questioned when we find that getting a college degree is much more important than attending college in attaining higher occupational status and income. In other words, it is highly questionable that the most important function of college is providing skills when we find that the final year of college completed is much more important for occupational attainment than the third or second year of college.

Finally, Collins (1971) has provided evidence showing that the educational upgrading of occupations over the years is not explained by any increase in the technical requirements of these occupations. Thus, more education is needed to obtain most jobs, but this is not explained by the technical requirements of the job. What, then, is most important about college completion?

A conflict view of education is partially supported by the research showing that higher-class offspring are much more likely to go to college. This may indicate that education is a means of class conflict; that is, in the conflict over valued rewards the higher-class members are better able to ensure that their offspring win through education.

Furthermore, following the data on educational upgrading of occupations over the years, Collins (1971) argues that education is a means of maintaining class boundaries. For example, in the past, when college degrees were much more limited and the middle class typically had only high school degrees, middle-class occupations required a high school degree. But as more of the middle class obtained college degrees and more of the working class obtained high school degrees, middle-class occupations were typically upgraded so that a college degree was required for employment. Thus, the class boundaries of middle-class occupations were maintained through an upgrading of educational requirements.

Collins' data indicate that the same process has occurred with working-class, upper-middle-class, and elite occupations. As might be expected, this process of educational upgrading of occupations has produced a reduction in the occupational and income return for each year of education (Featherman and Hauser 1978:223; Jencks et al. 1979:228). Whereas a college degree once brought an elite occupational position with elite pay, it now brings a middle-class position with middle-class pay. From the conflict perspective, education is more a certification of class membership than of technical skills.

However, even to the extent that some lower-class offspring are upwardly mobile through education, the conflict view of education may be supported when we consider what the educational system does. If the educational system does not function primarily to teach occupationally related skills, as the data indicate (Diamond and Bedrosian 1970; Jencks et al. 1972:187; Rawlins and Ulman 1974), it certifies that people have learned to respect the authority and accept the values, ideals, and system of inequality in the occupational structure (Bowles and Gintis 1976). As Collins (1971:1011) puts it, "Educational requirements for employment can serve both to select new members for elite positions who share the elite culture and, at a lower level of education, to hire lower and middle employees who have acquired a general respect for these elite values and styles."

Education does provide some knowledge and skills, and the knowledge obtained is important. But because the educational system requires some conformity to authority, those who succeed in the educational system—no matter what their class background—are certified as potential workers who can respect authority divisions in the occupational structure. Thus, education provides two important services for higher-class members; it is a means of class inheritance and a means of selecting responsible new recruits for higher occupational positions.

The Conflict Perspective: A Critique and Reinterpretation of Status Attainment Research

We began this chapter by noting the relatively short history of status attainment research. Since the early 1960s much progress has been made; but since the mid-1970s critical research also has increased rapidly. The general critiques of status attainment research fall into four main (though overlapping) categories: (1) Status attainment models have limited explanatory power. (2) They attempt to explain the wrong thing (that is, occupational status). (3) They are focused on individual characteristics or "human capital" variables rather than equally important structural variables. (4) Most of the findings from this research can be better (or at least equally) explained by a conflict (or allocation) perspective rather than a functional theory of social stratification. We will consider each of these general critiques in turn.

Limited Explanatory Power As noted earlier, in his now famous work Jencks brought together data from several status attainment studies. Jencks' (see primarily Jencks et al. 1972) reanalysis of the combined data stressed how little we really know about the process of getting ahead in the United States. The limited explanatory power of status attainment models was shown in two ways. First, taking the current methodological perspective of these models, combining all the variables explains only about 50 percent of the variance in occupational status and 40 percent of the variance in income attainment. Second, from another methodological perspective, when we compare the variance in intergenerational attainment *within* occupation and income divisions, the data show almost as much variance within categories as between categories.

The first point is not difficult to understand, but an example of the second point may be helpful. Consider the general occupational categories of upper nonmanual and lower nonmanual. What Jencks' research shows is that the family backgrounds and current income of those *within* upper nonmanual positions differ almost as much as the backgrounds and income *between* upper nonmanual and lower nonmanual position holders.

In his most recent work (Jencks et al. 1979) Jencks reanalyzed additional data to conclude that almost 50 percent of the variance in occupational status is explained by family background alone. Still, much of what we know about who gets ahead is unexplained. In the face of this lack of explanatory power, Jencks first emphasized (Jencks et al. 1972) that luck is very important in attaining occupational status and income. In his second major work (Jencks et al. 1979:306–311), Jencks has admitted that structural economic forces not measured in his work may help explain much of the inequality in occupation and income, although luck in a limited sense is again given some credit.

The process of attainment is very complex, involving much of what can be called luck on a personal level. We can use the example of two brothers, both with a college degree. One brother finishes college to become a low-level manager in a firm that goes out of business in a couple of years, leaving him unemployed for a time and forced to take a lower-level job. The other brother has difficulty finding a job at first, but happens to hear about a possible job opening as a low-level manager with a rapidly growing firm. In the interview for this job the second brother finds the boss to be from his old college fraternity. This brother's luck again holds out when he unknowingly says the right things to impress his future boss during the interview. This second brother gets the job, and because of the rapid expansion of the firm, is soon promoted to fill a mid-level management position in a new factory opened by the firm. A few years after graduating from college, the first brother has a low-status job making $19,000 a year, while the second brother has a mid-level management position paying $55,000 a year.

In a very general sense we might say that these two brothers are separated by luck—luck in joining the right firm, in saying the right thing during an interview, and in one having a boss that respects the old school ties. Many such factors beyond the control of specific people can influence occupational and income attainment. However, if we move from the individualistic focus of current status attainment models, we find political and economic forces that can be measured and that can help us explain more of the variance in occupational and income attainment.

In other words, luck may lead a person to be in the right place at the right time to land a job with the right firm. But when we move from an individual level to a higher level of sociological analysis, various structural variables can help us explain more of the variance in occupational and income attainment. These other structural variables will be considered below. But first there is a problem with the traditional focus on occupational status that leads to limited explanatory power in status attainment research.

The Limitations of Occupational Status   Earlier chapters have noted the problems associated with the functional theory's concept of occupational status or prestige. These problems have two main roots.

1 Within the occupational structure, status ranks do not always correspond to more important ranks based on job complexity or skill and authority (Wilson 1978; Spaeth 1979; Robinson and Kelley 1979; Lord and Falk 1980; Kalleberg and Griffin 1980). Also, the functional view of stratification based on status ranks assumes a free, open market (see, for example, Davis and Moore 1945). But as Horan's (1978) critique demonstrates, such an assumption must be questioned. For example, two occupations may be ranked equally in terms of status, but competition in one may be restricted, making it more difficult to enter the occupation and making it higher paying.

2 Previous chapters have stressed that the stratification system includes inequalities based on authority and property as well as occupation. Thus, even to the extent that status attainment models have furthered our understanding of attainment with respect to the occupational structure, authority and property divisions have been neglected. The neglect of these other divisions is important because they, too, have an influence on income and occupational attainment.

Considering the first problem, we can begin by noting that in one sense it can be quite misleading to suggest that intergenerational mobility has occurred when a son moves from his father's upper manual or skilled blue-collar position to a lower nonmanual or lower white-collar position (Willhelm 1979). The son's lower nonmanual or white-collar position may very well be lower in job complexity, authority, and pay than the father's upper manual or skilled blue-collar position. True, the lower nonmanual position is most likely ranked higher in prestige; but there is much more to occupational divisions than prestige. Let us look at some recent research.

Spaeth (1979) measured vertical occupational divisions in three ways—occupational status, job skill level or complexity, and authority. He found that the authority and complexity measures were more strongly correlated to each other than to occupational status. Thus, occupational status cannot be assumed to be an indicator of job authority or skill level. More specific to the process of educational attainment, Spaeth (1976) has also shown that father's job complexity has an important independent effect on the educational attainment of offspring.

Other research has examined how the traditional focus on occupational status has resulted in an inability to explain much of the variance in income attainment. The full Wisconsin status attainment model presented by Sewell and Hauser (1975) could explain only a very small part of the variance in income. If occupational status is very important, including occupational status in the model should explain a good deal more than 7 percent of the variance in income. In a more limited study, Wilson (1978) constructed an index of *occupational power* and an index of education based on the curriculum needed to attain positions of occupational power (rather than occupational status). Using these new measures Wilson was able to explain 46 percent of the variance in income in his sample.

We noted the research by Kalleberg and Griffin (1980), Robinson and Kelley (1979), and Wright and Perrone (1977) in a previous chapter. These studies examined the relationship between income attainment and stratification divisions based on occupational authority and ownership of the means of production (property relations), as well as occupational status. All these studies showed that we can explain much more of the variance in income attainment by including authority and property divisions, although more than half of the variance in income remains unexplained by all of these factors. Equally important, Robinson and Kelley (1979) found that the variance in occupational authority attainment is explained more by the father's level of occupational authority than the father's occupational status. In other words, the process of occupational authority attainment and the process of occupational status attainment are not identical. The same conclusion was supported when this study was conducted in France (Robinson and Garnier 1985), and also when

Kerckhoff, Campbell, and Trott (1982) examined the multidimensional aspects of status attainment in England. Attainment in occupation, education, authority position, and capitalist property ownership were affected by different combinations of factors, and this was especially so for the attainment of property. And finally, in a five-nation study by Robinson (1984) we find that status attainment differs for each of the class categories described by Wright (1978). For example, education is important in attaining occupational authority, but education is not much help in attaining ownership and control of property or a position in the petite bourgeoisie.

Finally, other research (Wright 1978b; Wolf and Fligstein 1979; Treiman and Roos 1983) has shown that the process of income attainment for women and blacks differs from that of white males in part because of the effects of occupational authority. Even when women and blacks have occupational status equal to that of white males, their income tends to be lower because their occupational authority tends to be lower. With respect to education, equal amounts of education (compared with that of white males) gained less occupational authority for women and blacks.

Economic Structural Influences on the Attainment Process   It was noted earlier that Jencks (Jencks et al. 1979) to some degree now recognizes the impact of economic structural variables on the attainment process; Hauser (1980) has also admitted as much, at least for income attainment. In our imaginary example of two equally educated brothers, part of the luck that separated these brothers was in being employed by different firms; one firm did well, the other went under. The dual-economy research discussed in previous chapters is directly relevant to income attainment, as is recent research on the differing organizational structures of specific firms.

The problem with standard status attainment models in this respect is that they are focused on personal characteristics. The human capital resources of people—such as job skills, education, experience, intelligence, and perhaps even aspirations—are assumed by these models to be the most important, if not the only, factors relevant to the attainment of occupational status and income (Knottnerus 1987). But impersonal economic forces beyond the control of most people have a hand in determining the payoff of human capital resources. For example, Grusky (1983) has shown that regional economic differences can produce differences in the occupational attainment process.

Briefly reviewing the dual-economy research, corporations can be divided roughly between core and periphery organizations. The core firms are bigger, make more profits, have more control over their markets, pay higher wages, and are more likely to be unionized than periphery firms. The dual-economy research has found that workers with the same occupational status may receive differing incomes, depending upon core or periphery location, even when other human capital variables such as education and experience are controlled (see Beck, Horan, and Tolbert 1978; Tolbert, Horan, and Beck 1980; Beck, Horan, and Tolbert 1980). Also, this research has shown that education brings different amounts of income, depending upon core or periphery location, and that movement from periphery to core employment is restricted if the family background and/or a person's first job is located in the periphery sector (Tolbert 1982; Jacobs 1983).

Other research has shown that characteristics of individual firms besides core or periphery location have an impact on the occupational and income attainment process (Stolzenberg 1978; Baron and Bielby 1980, 1984). One important difference between firms is the degree of bureaucratization. When firms are more bureaucratized there are more occupational ranks from top to bottom, thus allowing an employee to move further in terms of occupational and income attainment (compared with someone in a less bureaucratized firm).

With respect to income and occupational attainment, Baron and Bielby (1980) suggest that at least five levels of analysis are important—the general economy, the industry sector (for example, the core–periphery division), individual firms, specific occupations across firms, and individual workers. At each level of analysis above individual workers there are influences that can affect the occupational income and income attainment of employees independent of their human capital resources. The conclusion is that much of the unexplained variance in occupation and income found by traditional status attainment research is due to these structural-level variables.

Figure 11-3 summarizes what a number of studies have shown to be important in helping to explain income attainment. Other factors have been suggested as important, but research is still lacking. Functional theory and status attainment models have focused only on occupational status, resulting in an inability to explain much of income attainment. An individualistic bias in these models has led to an inadequate view of income attainment and social stratification in general. The other variables in Figure 11-3 have all been shown to be about equally important as or more important than occupational status in

FIGURE 11-3
Structural and individual variables affecting income attainment.

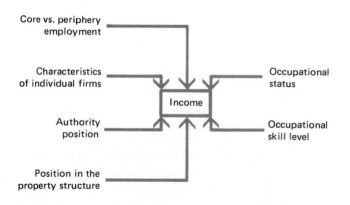

explaining income attainment. Further research is needed that combines the effects of all these variables on income attainment, but the development of research critical of status attainment models has yet to reach this stage.

A Conflict Perspective: Allocation Versus Attainment A final critique of status attainment research is more general. In this critique the findings and variables included in status attainment research are less the issue than the *interpretation* of the findings. From the perspective of status attainment research, the individual is considered "relatively free to move within the social system, his attainments being determined by what he chooses to do and how well he does it" (Kerckhoff 1976:369; also see Knottnerus 1987; Kerckhoff 1989).

This assumption is directly confronted by a conflict perspective that considers *allocation* rather than attainment to be the most important process: "An allocation model views the individual as relatively constrained by the social structure, his attainments being determined by what he is permitted to do" (Kerckhoff 1976:369). The most important aspect of social structure that constrains the free movement of people is the corporate structure (Collins 1975; Willhelm 1979; Beck, Horan, and Tolbert 1980). The needs of this corporate structure and capitalism, rather than the desires of individual actors, determine what positions require occupants, and people are selected in terms of what is needed in filling these positions (Goldman and Tickamyer 1984). Put another way, the focus of the allocation perspective is on control by dominant agencies; the selection process is based upon their needs.

Related to the above, others have charged that the standard status attainment view includes the mass society assumptions of classlessness. The view is of increasing universalism, meaning that class boundaries are less and less relevant to where a person ends up in the stratification system (Knottnerus 1987).

Another argument usually associated with the allocation perspective pertains to the criteria relevant to the selection process. Status attainment models stress that occupational attainment is based on marketable skills obtained through the educational system (although, of course, occupational status is measured in this research). The allocation perspective, in contrast, stresses that selection is based upon class cultural criteria.

As Collins (1975:452) puts it, "The conflict model proposes that careers take place within an ongoing struggle of cultural groups to control positions by imposing their standards upon selection. Success comes to individuals who fit into the culture of those who hold the resources to control old positions or create new ones." Class inheritance in the occupational structure doesn't always prevail. The mobility data would not support such a view. Rather, Collins is saying that when upward intergenerational mobility does occur, it is because the mobile person fits the cultural criteria of the higher-class position.

The most important certifying agent in this process is the educational system. As we saw earlier, the conflict view is that success in the educational system comes not solely with cognitive ability, but also with the ability to learn higher-class values and lifestyles. As Collins (1975:454) again puts it, "The evidence best fits the interpretation that education is important, not for providing technical skill but for membership in a cultural group which controls access to particular jobs'' (also see Collins 1971).

Thus, occupational inheritance is relatively high because the offspring of higher-occupational fathers are better able to succeed in the educational system. But upward mobility does occur, and it is because some of the lower-class offspring have been able to acquire higher-class cultural traits through the educational system. Both the status attainment and allocation perspectives agree that education is the key to occupational inheritance and mobility—but for different reasons.

We can now point up the differing perspectives with an example. Consider the case of a young man whose father is an unskilled factory worker. This young man was able to work his way through college to attain an advanced degree and a job as a chemical engineer. The status attainment perspective would view this case as one in which social mobility occurred because of the aspirations and talent of this young man. In other words, through free competition the motivation and talent of this individual led to his success.

The allocation perspective, in contrast, would argue that the corporate structure at the time had a need for chemical engineers. This young man was selected for the position because he was able to show acceptance and conformity to the dominant class values through success in the educational system. His entry into this particular occupational career was influenced because, while in college, he recognized that he could make a living by pursuing this career rather than one as a social worker. Social workers were not needed at the time because the poor were not rioting and the welfare system was contracting. Thus, the needs of the corporate structure strongly influenced the occupational career of this young man, and the class system and its criteria influenced the selection of this young man.

In an excellent summary of the status attainment and allocation perspectives, Kerckhoff (1976) has shown that to a large degree both perspectives fit the existing *individual level* data generated by the status attainment research. As noted in our earlier discussion of social scientific paradigms, social reality is complex, and it is the purpose of theory to explain as much of this reality as possible. We have described the many problems associated with the status attainment perspective. Because of these problems, and because of the additional research reviewed above, the allocation perspective contained within a conflict theory of social stratification has been favored.

The Conflict View of Attainment: A Conclusion

In the second half of this chapter we have reviewed one of the most impressive bodies of empirical research in the study of social stratification. In the past thirty years or so our knowledge of who gets ahead has grown rapidly. Most of this impressive growth in knowledge has come through the use of causal analysis by researchers concerned with building models of the status attainment process. This development was first stimulated by Blau and Duncan (1967), but it was later expanded by the Wisconsin school through the addition of sociopsychological variables that linked family background variables to educational and occupational attainment. The Wisconsin model of status attainment stresses that significant others, ability, and aspirations link family background to educational and occupational attainment.

The Wisconsin model, however, was shown to have limitations. First, its stress on occupational status creates problems in that status is not most important in the occupation structure. Second, the Wisconsin model has limited explanatory power. Much of this problem results from a stress on individual-level human capital resources. The effects of the corporate structure (such as the dual economy and authority relations) are also necessary in understanding occupational and, especially, income attainment.

At present much more research is needed that combines the variables traditionally included in status attainment models with these structural effects. When such research is done, we would expect that much more of the variance in occupational and income attainment can be explained. Luck is doubtless a factor in who gets ahead, but a good deal of this luck can be explained by a more careful consideration of structural features in our stratification system.

Finally, we described how an allocation perspective based on a conflict view of social stratification can explain the data generated by status attainment research. Because the status attainment perspective is based on a functional view of social stratification and because a functional view has been shown to be inadequate in several other respects in previous chapters, we have concluded that the allocation perspective should be favored.

People do compete for and achieve some success through their motivation and abilities. But it is competition for success structured by the needs of the overall corporate structure. From a more individualistic level of analysis, both achievement and ascription can be found. In his analysis of attainment research, however, Jencks et al. (1979) concluded that almost 50 percent of the variance in occupational attainment is explained by family background. In the process of getting ahead, those with parents already ahead have the edge.

Chapters 7 through 10 examined the characteristics, structural bases, rewards, and power of the major class groupings in the United States. The present chapter examined the dynamics of class in this country—the amount and means of class inheritance and mobility. We have a final important point to examine about our class system and social stratification in general. We need to know how class inequalities are maintained. The question becomes important when we find that those on top receive a highly disproportionate share of the rewards and are in a much better position to ensure that their offspring inherit their favored position. What prevents those toward the bottom from resisting such a state of affairs? What prevents them from trying to achieve a basic change in the stratification system? We will turn to these questions with a review of the legitimation process.

NOTES

1 The five journals examined were the *American Sociological Review*, the *American Journal of Sociology, Social Forces, Social Problems*, and *The Sociological Quarterly*. Determination of the main subject of each article was made through reading the abstract (or the article itself, if no abstract was included or if the classification was problematic). The article was coded as a social stratification article only if some major issue in social stratification was the primary subject of the article. For example, if the subject of an article was the causes of crime, and poverty or class inequality was examined as related to crime, the article was not coded as a social stratification article.

2 Subareas in the study of social stratification can be grouped in many ways. Previous studies have examined fewer subareas (Pease, Form, and Huber 1970; Huber and Form 1973), and no doubt many more than ten could have been examined here by dividing some of the ten categories further. A few subjects that could be considered subareas of social stratification were excluded because of the difficulty in judging the main focus of the article (for example, race, sex, and age inequalities). Research on racial and sex differences in status attainment and social mobility was included in category 4. Studies of mental and physical health differences by class were not included, however.

THE PROCESS OF LEGITIMATION

Imagine a society with an extremely high degree of inequality—much higher than that in the United States. Imagine further that within this society those at the bottom of the stratification system are extremely deprived both materially and psychologically. This low-status group lives in the worst conditions with respect to basic necessities, and is allowed to perform only the dirtiest and most degrading jobs (such as collecting and disposing of human feces in baskets).

In addition to having poor material conditions, this group is held in extreme contempt by the rest of the society. Its status is such that its members are considered socially unclean and prohibited from almost any contact with respectable members of the society (that is, everyone except members of their own status group). They cannot be under the same roof as respectable members of the society, much less eat or work in their presence. When passing respectable people on the street they must hide or, if this is not possible, bow with their face in the dirt. Finally, imagine that the members of this unclean lower-status group have no hope of ever leaving their low status—at least in their lifetime.

Given Western assumptions of human nature we might except this low-status group to reject its status and, when possible, rebel. We might assume that its condition is so unbearable and without hope its members would be extremely discontent, reject the system of social stratification that led to their position, and collectively attempt to change this system.

All these assumptions may be false, however. The conditions described above are comparable to those experienced over the centuries by untouchables in India. For the most part these untouchables accepted their status (Dumont 1970), and Barrington Moore (1978:62) has found no historical records of any revolts by these untouchables before the twentieth century. As noted in an earlier chapter, it was primarily the incredibly strong cultural and religious reinforcement of the Indian caste system that brought about such stability and passive acceptance of extreme inequality.

The Indian caste system may be an extreme example, but history records many cases of passive acceptance in the face of extensive inequality and what we would consider social injustice (see Moore 1978). There are prisoners who passively accept confinement and even identify positively with their captors; there are societies where members accept their own deaths as noble human sacrifices. In more recent examples we have Aleksandr Solzhenitsyn's (1973) description of how Soviet citizens often passively accept arrest and confinement in Russia's system of prison camps and the mass suicide and murder of over 900 followers of Jim Jones's People's Temple in Guyana.

The willingness of most people throughout history to accept a less than equal share of goods and services requires no further comment at this point. But it will be useful to describe another outcome of inequality in more detail— the willingness of most people to follow commands given by authority figures.

Inequalities in material goods and inequalities of power and authority (that is, legitimated power) are key elements in a system of social stratification. If the stratification system is to remain stable, inequalities of both types must be accepted, at least to some degree. The extent to which people follow commands from authority figures can be seen everywhere in everyday life.

Our introductory point can be made most dramatically, however, by examining the extent to which people often follow orders that may result in violence to other human beings. We know that in times of war many, and perhaps most, people will kill others upon command. And we know that people can go as far as to participate in war atrocities such as the My Lai incident during the Vietnam War or Hitler's extermination camps. Are these examples simply extraordinary consequences of wartime fear? In one sense they are not. At least the capacity to follow such orders is an outcome of a socialization process that leads most people to respect inequalities of authority. Let us examine some evidence.

With laboratory experiments Stanley Milgram (1974) examined the extent of obedience to authority among people who were led to believe that such obedience would harm another person. Disguising the research as an experiment in learning behavior, volunteers (subjects) were told to give electric shocks to another "subject" (the "learner") when the "learner" failed to provide the correct answer in a word association test.

The learner was in fact part of the research team and no electric shocks were actually given. But the key is that subjects in the research (given the role of teacher) believed electric shocks were being received by the learner when they (the subject and teacher) pulled a switch. On a desk in front of the teacher was a series of switches labeled 15 to 450 volts (thirty switches in all, with the last six marked *danger: severe shock*). The so-called teacher was asked to pull a progressively higher switch (in voltage) each time the learner gave an incorrect answer. In a major part of the research, the teacher and learner were separated by a wall but could communicate verbally.

With the research in progress, there was a prearranged response pattern to the shocks "received" by the learner. For example, with the lower voltage shocks there was simply an "ouch" that got louder with higher voltage (see Milgram 1974:56). But at 150 volts the learner would plead, "Experimenter! That's all. Get me out of here. I told you I had heart trouble. My heart's starting to bother me now. ..." This type of prearranged response continued through 330 volts, at which point the learner became silent, not screaming or responding to questions through the remaining voltage levers.

The main question is how many subjects or teachers will continue through all switches to 450 volts. How far will subjects go in following the orders of an authority figure (the psychologist)? After the cry of protest from the learner at 150 volts almost none of the subjects wanted to continue shocking the learner. But they were told to do so by the authority figure.

In this variation of the research, over *60 percent* of the subjects actually followed these orders, however reluctantly, through *all the switches to 450 volts*. In another variation of the research the learner and teacher sat next to each other. Here the teacher was required physically to place the learner's hand on the shocking device. Even in this case, 30 percent of the teachers went through all the switches to 450 volts.

Milgram's research subjects represented people from all walks of life— housewives, students, business people, and so on. Few if any of these people enjoyed hurting others. They resisted giving further shocks, but most followed orders to do so. By what process are people led to such obedience in possibly harming others, depriving themselves, and submitting to a distribution of goods and services that is far from equal?

Force is sometimes a factor; but in the long run force is inefficient and costly. A minority in strong opposition to authority and the status quo has often been the target of force throughout history; but force in the face of widespread and strong opposition will not be successful in maintaining the status quo for long.

In addition to force there are material incentives for obedience and support of the status quo. This method is most common, but it also has limitations. What prevents nonelites from deciding that their obedience is bought too cheaply? What happens when material incentives become limited for a time? And what prevents nonelites from deciding that other elites with a new status quo can provide more material incentives?

The point is that force and material incentives as methods of promoting obedience and maintaining the status quo have serious limitations. The most efficient means for the job involves somehow convincing nonelites that inequality is morally right, and that those most advantaged are justified in giving orders and receiving a greater proportion of valued goods and services. This method of maintaining obedience and structured inequality can be referred to as the *process of legitimation*.

The task of legitimation, however, is more complex than simply justifying the rewards and function of a particular set of elites or inducing people to respect authority and submit to their commands. Moving from the more specific to the more general we can identify legitimation of inequality and authority with respect to (1) individual elites and their status, (2) a particular regime in power and its authority and policies, (3) a particular system of social stratification or political economy, and (4) stratification and inequalities of wealth and authority in general (see Della Fave 1974c, 1980).

For example, a population may come to reject the legitimacy of particular elites, perhaps because they are considered incompetent, but the population may still accept the policies favored by these elites. It simply feels someone else can serve its interests better. Equally possible, a population may come to reject particular elites and their policies, while the more general economy (say, capitalism or socialism) remains legitimate. And, of course, elites, their policies, and the general form of social stratification or political economy may all be seen as illegitimate, while *some* form of authority and structured inequality is not questioned.

The present chapter will examine the process of legitimation on two levels. First, we will consider the micro-level legitimation process. Our concern will be the sociopsychological processes that produce legitimacy for inequality and authority divisions in a more general sense. Second, we will consider the more macro-level or social-level legitimation process. Our concern at this point will be the process by which particular elites gain legitimacy for their policies and the particular political economy they represent. The first process is more basic, for only if social stratification and inequality in general enjoy support can particular elites and a particular political economy hope to maintain any allegiance.

Before turning to the micro process of legitimation it is worth noting that all theoretical perspectives in the study of social stratification recognize the importance of a legitimation process (Della Fave 1980, 1986). What were described as theories from functional, uncritical conflict, and critical conflict paradigms of social stratification agree that some process of legitimation is required for social order. They agree that norms and ideologies must produce allegiance to elites or some form of social organization if society is to be possible.

These theoretical perspectives, however, part ways on the question of the outcome and exact nature of the legitimation process. For functional theory, social stratification and elite legitimacy are considered necessary and beneficial for all in the society. For uncritical conflict theory, elite legitimation is a means of elite dominance that is not always beneficial for all in the society. And for critical conflict theory, legitimation is a means of elite dominance that prevents acceptance of a political economy resulting in much less inequality and exploitation.

THE SOCIOPSYCHOLOGICAL PROCESS OF LEGITIMATION

It is seldom easy to separate sociopsychological processes totally from more general or macro sociological processes. Society is a collective of actors who are individually shaped and influenced by group forces, while themselves contributing to these group forces. When the level of analysis (or study) is the individual—his or her behavior, self-concept, belief system—a more general level of analysis is also implied. When the level of analysis is the general society or some structural aspect of the society—of a concentration of power—a sociopsychological level of analysis is implicit.

In the first case, because we are social animals, we must recognize that the group or society has a hand in shaping individual behavior. In the second case, because society is a collection of individuals, any collective process must be grounded in individual understandings and motives. But we can choose to focus on one level while holding the other level implicit. When we want to understand a more general-level phenomenon, such as inequality and social stratification, we benefit most from a macro-level analysis. From time to time, however, we can also benefit from touching base with a more sociopsychological level of analysis. In examining the maintenance of social stratification such an analysis will be helpful.

Let us begin by restating two basic questions: Why do some people often willingly accept a smaller share of goods and services than others in the society? And why do people often willingly accept the legitimacy of authority figures and follow their orders? We must emphasize *willingly* in these two questions because our concern is behavior in the absence of direct coercion.

A conflict relationship may be at the heart of social stratification, but when societies are relatively stable, when overt conflict does not threaten major rebellion and social change, this conflict relationship is pushed into the background. What the above questions ask, in short, is how such conflict is pushed into the background. The first half of this chapter will examine how basic legitimacy is maintained through norms of distributive justice, self-evaluation, and ideology (more specifically, equality of opportunity).

Norms of Distributive Justice

As we saw in our review of the history of inequality, there is evidence that most people came to accept social and material inequality as small agricultural settlements emerged about 10,000 to 15,000 years ago (Wells 1971:193; Pfeiffer 1977:21). As one theory has it, when food became more difficult to find or produce, a norm of distributive justice emerged along with human societies (Pfeiffer 1977). The idea is that because human beings must somehow cooperate when conditions force them to live in close proximity, a sense of elementary justice or fairness in sharing goods and services will be established to reduce overt conflict. One way of establishing fairness is to sanction greater rewards for those who contribute most to the well-being of the collective. We can imagine that in the earliest societies the best hunter or the person believed able to influence supernatural forces was given greater rewards for his or her greater contribution.

From another perspective, many social scientists have argued that because people strive for cognitive consistency (Festinger 1957) they will develop principles of fairness, such as distributive justice, that maintain that rewards should be proportional to investments and contributions. This psychological need for cognitive consistence present in all human beings accounts for the apparently universal norm of distributive justice (Homans 1961, 1974).

But there appears to be another side to human psychology that has an effect on distribution norms. Because of our ability to understand the feelings of others, to understand their suffering and needs, there is at least some support for distribution based on need. Thus, Moore (1978:37) argues that all societies have distribution norms based on both need and contribution.

There is abundant evidence for the existence of norms of distributive justice. Most evidence has been obtained with research on small groups (see Ofshe and Ofshe 1970; Homans 1974; Leventhal 1975). A typical pattern in this research is to bring several subjects together to do some collective task. The task is structured in such a way as to make it evident that one person contributes most in completing the task, others about equally, and still others contribute least. When subjects are asked how rewards should be distributed among the members of this small group they consistently opt for rewards distributed in terms of contribution (see Leventhal, Michaels, and Sanford 1972).

In other research, subjects have been asked to judge the fairness of income distributions when given descriptions of various individuals and families (Jasso and Rossi 1977; Alves and Rossi 1978). The findings are that people make judgments in terms of both merit and need, and there is some consistency in the judgments among research subjects.

For example, in terms of merit, those with a higher-level occupation and education are judged to deserve more income. In terms of need, those with a larger family are judged to deserve more income. The research subjects also show some agreement upon the fairness of maximum and minimum income levels. Computing the maximum and minimum levels for a husband-and-wife household with lowest need and merit to the highest need and merit, Alves and Rossi (1978:557) established an average fairness judgment that ranged from $7,211 to $44,466 in yearly income—an income distribution, they note, that was much narrower than the level of income inequality at the time.

What can be concluded from such evidence? The most obvious conclusion is that norms of distributive justice do exist, and that there is at least some agreement among people with respect to these norms. Evidence from other industrial societies makes such a conclusion even stronger (Grandjean and Bean 1975). In the context of the present discussion, there is support for inequality based on norms of distributive justice. But despite some wide agreement, there are differences among people in applying the justice norms. For example, Alves and Rossi (1978:559) found that those higher in the class system tend to focus more on merit when making fairness judgments, while those lower in the class system tend to focus more on need.

A fundamental problem with the idea of distributive justice, however, is that such norms are rather ambiguous in concrete application. The task of defining *which* contributions are most important and the *degree* of reward justified for particular contributions remains. Among small groups this problem is minimized. But in large societies, where contribution can seldom be judged with much accuracy, the problem is extensive. There is the potential for elites to manipulate judgments of contribution so that their greater rewards seem justified (Moore 1978:40; Della Fave 1980:960). Thus, while we do find support for "fair" inequality with norms of distributive justice, we must look further to understand how extensive inequality comes to be accepted by many people.

The Socialization Process and Self-Evaluation

One of the most basic sociopsychological theories of legitimation has been outlined by L. Richard Della Fave (1980, 1986). Following what we know about socialization and the development of a self-concept, we can understand how a person's *self-evaluation* is constructed so that a person comes to view himself or herself as one who deserves a higher or lower position in the stratification system. And within more specific social contexts (or positions) we examine how a person comes to have a higher or lower view of his or her abilities and is or is not deserving of more rewards (Stolte 1983).

From the work of George Herbert Mead (1935) we recognize that a self-concept is first developed through interaction with significant others, and later through interactions with members of the wider society. In essence, we become aware of what others expect of us by how they react to us. "People, in general, see us as bright or dull, attractive or ugly, strong or weak, capable or incapable. This amalgam of perceived generalized expectations and reactions constitutes the generalized other" (Della Fave 1980:959). Thus, through this generalized other we come to define who we are; this constitutes our self-evaluation. The key is that those toward the bottom of the stratification system usually come to have a lower self-evaluation; they come to view themselves as less deserving. Let us consider how a low self-evaluation is produced.

Beginning with our earliest socialization experiences, we described in Chapter 9 how child-rearing methods differ by class. Working-class children, for example, are more likely to be taught to respect authority per se, without questioning the reason or purpose of commands from authority. Middle- and upper-middle-class children are taught by their parents to be more self-reliant, to have greater self-confidence in themselves and their abilities.

When children reach school age, the self-concept and self-evaluation are developed further by a wider social circle. We have described in Chapter 11 how the educational system tends to treat children differently by class background. How the peer group and teachers react to children, their track placement and other such experiences, all help to foster the self-evaluation process of children. The status attainment research described in the previous chapter shows how class background shapes educational and occupational aspirations through the influences of significant others. But aspirations are only one outcome of this process; self-evaluations are another outcome.

The self-evaluation process does not end when a person completes his or her education; it is an ongoing process that continues throughout life. One of the most important sources of feedback from others in the self-evaluation process during adulthood is the occupational structure. A person's relation to authority, how he or she is treated by the boss and co-workers, contributes to the self-evaluation. Research has shown that class position is more strongly related to self-esteem or self-evaluation in adults than in children (see Rosenberg and Pearlin 1978; Demo and Savin-Williams 1983). This seems a result of the adult's contacts with a wider range of other class members, making their own class position more significant. Children, in contrast, are more likely to interact with children from the same class background because of class-segregated neighborhoods and schools. Thus, an adult's occupation and education come to have an important effect on his or her self-esteem (Jacques and Chason 1977).

More specific to authority relations in the work place, qualitative studies suggest that when workers are treated in a dependent and degraded manner, when work is organized so that workers cannot come to feel self-reliant, self-esteem among the working class is low (Sennett and Cobb 1973; Pfeffer 1979). Those in higher authority seldom assume that workers can be counted upon to perform their work obligation properly and that they have the intelligence or good sense to perform their jobs without consistent supervision; the workers are therefore treated like dependent children. Thus, the lower we move down occupational authority ranks, the lower the self-evaluations.

When we move from the family and work relations to the wider society, we find other sources of feedback that contribute to a lower self-evaluation as we move down the class system. Here the feedback becomes more generalized in depicting images of class members as a group. From the mass media, from movies, news stories, and television, people pick up the general images of class members held by the more general society.

We have already seen how the degrading views of welfare recipients and the poor help contribute to their low self-concept (see Piven and Cloward 1971; Kerbo 1976b). Others have argued that the working class also receives negative images of itself through the representation of working-class characters in films (Miliband 1969; Aronowitz 1974:108; Gitlin 1979). For example, television and movie heroes are seldom from the working class or lower class, and when working-class and lower-class members are presented they usually conform to dominant stereotypes that lead to low self-evaluation.

Thus far we have focused upon the self-evaluation of people in positions toward the bottom of the class system. However, the self-evaluation of those toward the top can be understood as a complement of this process. While those in lower-class positions usually receive more negative feedback, those in higher-class positions usually receive more positive feedback simply because they are in higher positions.

But there is an added ingredient. Those in higher-class positions usually have a wider audience from which to receive feedback contributing to their self-evaluation. They have a wider audience through interacting with more people in their occupation and with more subordinates below them, and they are likely to be more widely known in the community (or even nation). This wider audience may appear to be made up of more objective outside observers than more immediate significant others. In other words, your family, friends, and peers may provide positive feedback, but you can seldom escape the feeling that these significant others have a positive bias. Thus, the more positive feedback obtained from a wider audience can contribute even more to a person's self-evaluation (Della Fave 1980:962).

Higher-status people have another advantage in the self-evaluation process. From the work of symbolic interaction theorists such as Goffman (1959) we can view the interaction process as similar to a stage production. Various stage props and image-creating mechanisms are used by people to form the best possible presentation of the self to others. Interaction rituals can also be viewed as a conflict relation, with each party attempting to present a more favorable view of the self, but with the higher-status person having greater power and resources to do so (Collins 1975:115).

For example, the wealthier can display higher status in personal appearance and in the setting in which encounters take place (such as in the home or office; see Della Fave 1980:963). Higher-status people are better able to give the appearance of being calm and in control (Hall and Hewitt 1970). There is the power to dictate explicitly or implicitly where a meeting will take place. Equally important, the superior often requires the subordinate to wait, signifying that his or her time is more important than that of the lower-status person (Schwartz 1974). All this means that a higher-status person can usually manage a better performance, contributing to a higher self-evaluation (Della Fave 1980:963).

In large societies people are often required to make status judgments of someone else with only a few clues to the status of the other person (Berger et al. 1972; Webster and Driskell 1978). The interaction rituals described above, therefore, become even more important in enhancing the status of higher-class members in the eyes of lower-class members. If greater rewards are to be justified, following the norm of distributive justice described above, a person must be seen as making a greater contribution to the society. But because higher-status people have more resources to make a favorable impression, *their contribution can appear to be greater.* "What is crucial is that the entire process through which the appropriate level of reward is determined is *circular,* in that the very fact of being wealthy or powerful influences our assessment of 'contribution' and, on the basis of such assessment, we judge that person worthy of such a high reward" (Della Fave 1980:961).

It is time to summarize how the process of self-evaluation and self-efficacy contributes to a legitimation of inequality in a very general sense. It is important to remember that at this point we are not concerned with the legitimation of a particular political economy, specific policies, or specific elites, but simply inequalities of wealth and authority in and of themselves.

Della Fave's (1980:962) primary proposition is as follows: "The level of primary resources that an individual sees as just for him/herself, relative to others, is directly proportional to his/her level of self-evaluation." That is, when a person, for all the reasons noted above, comes to have a lower self-evaluation, *he or she will come to view his or her own low rewards and the high rewards of others as just.*

In relation to the wider society, "The strength of legitimacy of stratification in any society is directly proportional to the degree of congruence between the distribution of primary resources and the distribution of self-evaluations" (Della Fave 1980:962). In other words, taken as a whole, *when the people with fewer rewards are generally those with lower self-evaluations, social inequality is more likely to be viewed as legitimate.*

The Effects of Equality of Opportunity

It is often difficult for people in modern industrial societies to appreciate the powerful influence our belief in equality of opportunity can have in maintaining the class system. Modern people are so accustomed to the ideology that a society without such a belief system is hard to imagine. But such societies have existed, and in fact only a very small proportion of the societies that have ever existed have had a value of equality of opportunity.

In those societies without this revolutionary new ideology, the maintenance of class inequalities fell to other ideologies—religion in the hands of political and economic elites tended to be the most favored. But once these old ideologies were broken in that turbulent period between feudal and industrial societies, the belief in equality of opportunity proved a new and powerful tool for the legitimation of inequality.

This new belief in equality of opportunity, however, provides both a strong support and a danger for higher-class privilege, because the value must have at least some basis in reality if it is to legitimate the class system. With the hope and expectations of a population raised, if reality does not appear to show at least some support for this value the consequences could be revolutionary.

As we found in the previous chapter, thus far industrial societies have been expanding at a rate that provides generally more upward than downward social mobility. Where the modern idea of equality of opportunity has been exported to underdeveloped nations with more rigid class boundaries the consequence has usually been more overt class conflict. And where the value has less basis in reality for minorities in modern industrial societies, like the United States with respect to blacks, a consequence has been more overt class conflict along racial lines.

Our discussion of equality of opportunity has yet to consider the sociopsychological effect on class legitimation. This is our present task, which can be accomplished with reference to Lane's (1962) now classic study of working-class men in a Northeastern industrial city. In Lane's detailed interviews with fifteen white blue-collar workers he found a strong belief in equality of opportunity that had profound effects on what these men thought about their position in life. Perhaps the most important effect of this belief is that it leads people to *find some defect in themselves* when explaining their relatively low status. Lane (1962:59) found that these men felt they had more opportunities than they were using; in short they felt they had let opportunities slip away.

The importance of education, of course, is a key ingredient in the belief in equality of opportunity in the United States. As one man stated, "If I had gone to college . . . I would be higher up in this world" (Lane 1962:70). But it was an opportunity he believed was wasted. The low self-evaluation of these men, at least with respect to educational opportunities lost, helps them explain their low status. But it does so with some face-saving as well; "at least it is only the fault of an irresponsible youth, not a grown man" (Lane 1962:71).

Another key in understanding the acceptance of inequality among these men is that they have much invested in the present system. They may be relatively low in the class system, but they feel they have worked hard for what they have achieved. They have had some opportunities for more pay and security they believe their fathers did not have; so although they are not on top, neither are they on the bottom.

In this respect we can understand why these men even fear greater equality (Lane 1962:73). These men may gain with more equality, but they believe all their life's hard work would be of little value if the poor below them, whom they view with contempt, were given equal rewards. Which returns us to a point noted in the chapter on poverty in the United States. When the poor are viewed with contempt, this abstract category of the "undeserving poor" serves the function of legitimating inequality by making those just above the poor feel better about their own low rewards (Gans 1972).

A final aspect of the world view of these men is worth exploring. For the most part these men are distrustful of human nature. If all in the society were assured equal rewards, they have the feeling there would be no incentive; there would be nothing to work for and the "lazy" side of human nature would prevail (people, they believe, would not "put forth their best efforts," Lane 1962:76). Thus, they see equality of opportunity as a fair and necessary policy in providing incentive, which is to say their world view is close to the ideal put forth in the Davis and Moore (1945) functional theory of social stratification.

What is interesting, however, is that none of these men ever considered the idea that inequality could be reduced from its present levels (Lane 1962:78) with no adverse effects. The ideological debate has been safely limited to inequality versus equality. A more reasonable controversy over *degrees* of inequality is not on the agenda, in large measure because of the manner in which their world view has been shaped by wider forces in the society. (We will consider such forces in the second half of the present chapter.)

It was noted above that every society must provide some legitimating ideology for inequality if the stratification system is to remain stable. It seems reasonable to conclude that historical circumstances have led the United States to stress the mythology of equality of opportunity more than other nations. Although more comparative data are needed for any firm conclusions in this respect, we do have data comparing British and American views of inequality.

Robinson and Bell (1978) found acceptance of inequality similar in both nations. But they conclude that this acceptance is in part related to differing ideological supports. In England people are "taught at an early age to reconcile themselves to their lot in life" (Robinson and Bell 1978:141); their historical traditions have led them to a greater acceptance of ascription (Turner 1960). But in the United States, our historical traditions preclude aristocratic privilege, and ascription must be denied with the belief that anyone can achieve success through hard work (Lipset 1963). Thus, although in England people are taught to accept inequality more often, in the United States people come to accept inequality because an ideology of equality of opportunity has led those less successful to partially blame themselves for their lower position.

Before concluding this discussion of the micro supports for inequality we must mention briefly the sociopsychological effects of solidarity rituals. Our concern at this point is the emotional support for society's basic institutions and values gained through collective rituals. For many years social theorists (most notably Durkheim) have recognized that collective emotional rituals can strengthen social bonds and provide an almost godly respect for human institutions. In the face of such strong emotional support, traditions of unequal power and wealth may come to appear almost sacred in nature. It becomes most difficult for someone to question the legitimacy of these conditions while continuing to desire membership in the surrounding community.

Raising the idea of emotional rituals brings religion to mind. Religion has often been used to support inequality, as Marx was one of the first to stress. But, as noted earlier, such a view is overly simple, because religion can be used equally to support or challenge inequalities of power and privilege. One of the most interesting examples in this respect is the mixing of fundamentalist Christian ideals and socialism by the rural poor in Oklahoma protesting exploitation by wealthy landlords between 1912 and 1920 (Burbank 1976).

In the United States the mixture of religion and Americanism often provides emotional support for the basis of inequality. Religion in the United States has come to be a civil religion (Bellah 1970) in praise of country, the flag, anticommunism, and Americanism, as much as any pure religious ideals. Even before the rise of the Moral Majority during the 1980 presidential election this quality of American religious beliefs was widely recognized by sociologists (see Herberg 1960).

An outcome of this civil religion or the mixing of religious ideals with Americanism is that national values and institutions are sometimes given emotional support to such a degree that to question such values and social arrangements is kin to immorality. The Moral Majority was not supported by everyone, and many highly religious people do not equate religion with unquestioned acceptance of American institutions. But civil religion in the United States must be recognized as making a significant contribution to the legitimation of inequality and authority.

The source of ritual solidarity must be considered when we recognize its existence in virtually all human societies. Because human beings can think abstractly they seek meaning in the world; a meaningless world is an insecure world. Thus, there is a social construction of reality that becomes possible and is maintained through collective rituals (Berger and Luckman 1966).

Emotional collective rituals are important because such emotional arousal makes the reality people seek more meaningful or unquestioned (Collins 1975:153); their reality comes to seem more transcendental rather than simply man-made. It is understandable that when collective rituals take place people emphasize their commonality—the social values, institutions, and social relations they have in common. What this means for the legitimation of power and inequality is that the form of social stratification the society has developed, for whatever historical reasons, can be given positive meaning through rituals of solidarity.

Elites often seek control of solidarity rituals for obvious reasons (Collins 1975); but control by elites is not always necessary. If power and privilege by an elite are a firm aspect of the common reality, they will most often be supported as the overall social reality and given legitimacy through rituals of solidarity. But if the power and privilege of elites are threatened or weakening, a call for support through rituals is a useful tool. This call is most often made by finding or manufacturing some threat to the general society. One of the most soundly supported sociological ideas is that out-group conflict tends to produce in-group solidarity (Coser 1967). In some capitalist societies, communism is as functional as the devil was for highly religious societies, while communist elites often find their capitalist imperialists or "capitalist roaders" of equal value.

The Basis of Legitimation: A Summary

Thus far we have found that norms of distributive justice, the process of self-evaluation, solidarity rituals, and the ideology of equality of opportunity in this country help provide an underlying base for the support of inequality. The main focus has been on people and the factors leading them to reason that the pattern of inequality in a society is somehow fair and necessary.

Our major concern, of course, has been the micro process of legitimation among nonelites, although we did consider how those high in the class system may come to have a higher self-evaluation (and thus feel justified in receiving greater rewards). The legitimation process among elites needs less explanation—because they are most advantaged in the stratification system, legitimation is less problematic at this level.

One point requires restatement. Up to this point we have considered only sociopsychological processes that lead to *a tendency to accept inequality in a very general or abstract sense.* Many social scientists make the claim that inequality exists in all societies, except perhaps the most elementary, and assume that some startling fact has been revealed. But the issue of real importance is not the simple existence of inequality, it is the extent of differential rewards and the span of inequality that exists within societies. What we have examined above helps us understand a tendency to accept inequality in principle. It does not help us understand the *degree* of inequality that can be maintained, or its exact form. To understand the degree and form of inequality that may be maintained we must look to how elites build upon this sociopsychological base to establish legitimacy for themselves and the particular political economy they represent.

A related point requires emphasis. The processes and factors described above only help to produce tendencies to accept inequality. There is no automatic acceptance of inequality by everyone; neither is everyone willing to accept the same level of inequality or accept inequality for the same reasons. It will be remembered that Alves and Rossi (1978) found higher-class people more willing to accept inequality based on merit, while lower-class people are more willing to accept inequality based on need. In another study of the acceptance of inequality, Robinson and Bell (1978) found that in the United States the young, minorities, and those lower in occupational status are more likely to favor greater equality. This suggests that it is more difficult to convince those toward the bottom of the stratification system that the present level of inequality is just.

The tendency to accept inequality in a particular society may also be related to a person's *perception* of the degree of inequality that exists in that society. In other words, people may believe the level of inequality that exists is legitimate because they underestimate the degree of inequality in the society. Bell and Robinson (1980) have found perceptions of inequality to vary. For example, in both the United States and England, minorities are more likely to perceive greater income inequality, and in the United States there is more overall variance in the perception of income inequality than in England (people more often differ in their estimates of inequality in the United States). What this says is that many people in the United States may accept the present level of inequality because they do not recognize, or have been misled about, its extent. The misconception of the extent of inequality is a subject we must examine in our next section.

There are at least four levels on which legitimation may vary (Della Fave 1980, 1986). The acceptance of inequality or social stratification per se is most abstract. We become more specific as we consider the legitimacy of a particular system of political economy (such as capitalism, democratic socialism, or communism), a particular group of elites and their policies, and particular elites themselves (for example, their honesty or competence).

The sociopsychological tendency to accept inequality we have examined pertains primarily to inequality on an abstract level. Inequality per se may be accepted, but this does not mean that more specific kinds of inequality will be accepted. For example, studies have found that the working class may accept inequality in principle, but it often objects to exact levels of income inequality and particular authority relations (Liebow 1967; Sennett and Cobb 1973).

Because inequality and social stratification in principle are usually accepted, elites are able to achieve legitimacy for their particular place in a particular system of social stratification. Without the legitimacy of inequality, if even only in principle, they would have no hope. However, this also means that if elites seek legitimacy for their particular rule within a particular system of social stratification *they must work for it*. There is no automatic acceptance. How do elites work for legitimacy on a more specific level? What means do elites have for maintaining such legitimacy? It is to these questions that we now turn.

THE MACRO PROCESS OF LEGITIMATION: BUILDING SUPPORT FOR SPECIFIC FORMS OF INEQUALITY

From a sociopsychological base, helping to make the acceptance of inequality among the general population more likely, the job for elites begins. Their task is now to turn the general or abstract acceptance of inequality into the specific acceptance of their high rewards, the policies that favor their interests, and the general political and economic system that provides their base of power and privilege.

In short, an abstract legitimacy for inequality is only a beginning. The next step requires what can be called a *macro* process of legitimation—macro in the sense that elites must move beyond a sociopsychological tendency for the acceptance of inequality to legitimation of social arrangements that lead to their power and privilege. For example, if capitalism is the base of elite power and privilege, the population must be convinced that private ownership and private profit are just and in the best interests of all in the society. If communism is the base of elite power and privilege, the population must be convinced that this political economy is just and in the best interests of all in the society, if not at present, then at least when a mature communist state becomes reality, after present sacrifice.

With respect to more specific policies, a particular foreign policy or economic policy to fight inflation may be in the best interests of economic elites. But because alternative policies (all equally possible within a given political economy) may be employed, and because other policies may favor the interests of nonelites, the task becomes that of creating acceptance for the policy that favors economic elite interests.

To maintain their power and privilege elites have learned to use the norms of distributive justice by convincing nonelites that (1) elite contributions to the society are in proportion to the rewards they receive and (2) the abilities of elites are superior to those of nonelites (Moore 1978:40). To put it crudely, in the case of clear exploitation by elites, the legitimation process resembles a con game or sting operation. The trick is to exploit nonelites without their realizing they are being exploited. In the terminology of the con artist, this requires "cooling out the mark." More typically, where elites do perform some important function for the general society, the task becomes one of convincing nonelites that this function is even more important than it actually is, thereby justifying a greater "take" of valued goods and services than would otherwise be possible (except, of course, by overt force).

Throughout history, we have noted, some form of ideology has been used to justify elite privilege. Most often, past elites have used some religiously based ideology (Pfeiffer 1977:21, 104). A case in point was the use of religion to justify slavery in the southern United States (Aptheker 1963:57). Ideological legitimation, however, tells us little about the *process* of legitimation. Ideologies are not automatically accepted, and any particular ideology can be used to justify other elites and different policies. Thus, we must look further. In what follows we will consider how legitimacy is maintained through the educational system, the mass media, and opinion-influencing organizations. Our focus will be on the United States in particular, although most of what we consider applies to industrial societies in general.

In beginning this examination we must acknowledge that by considering each of the means of legitimation separately we are oversimplifying the overall process of legitimation to some extent. The various means must be considered in concert; they tend to overlap and reinforce each other. To use functional terminology, the process of legitimation is an interrelated process or system. If one part of the system is not performing, the whole process may be weakened; it becomes more difficult for each part to serve its overall function. If the parts are all functioning well, the task becomes easier for each part. For example, if the educational system is performing its legitimation function adequately, it becomes much easier for the mass media to serve their legitimation function. If this overall process is kept in mind, however, examination of each part separately presents less of an oversimplification.

Another issue must be clarified before proceeding. When we say that the educational system is or the mass media are performing a legitimating function, we are suggesting that they are passing on information that helps support a particular set of elites, their policies, and/or a particular system of political economy. To put it bluntly, we are saying that these institutions are involved in propaganda and indoctrination.

Americans don't like these words—"that's something communists do." But by propaganda, or persuasion if you will, we simply mean the practice of convincing others of your particular point of view. We are not saying that the information offered is inaccurate, although it is often biased or slanted to favor the view and interests of those providing the information. Most simply, it must be recognized that the act of attempted persuasion implies a conflict relationship. And as we have suggested throughout previous chapters, human organization is full of conflict relations. For example, there is often an immediate conflict relation between parent and child. The parent wants the child's behavior to conform to his or her expectations, but the child may have other ideas. Parents use propaganda and indoctrination to make the child conform. Propaganda and indoctrination are not unique to any political or economic system.

The Legitimation Function of Education

Our schools perform much more than a legitimation function (for inequality, capitalism, democratic principles, or particular elites) by passing on important knowledge of all kinds. But schools do provide a legitimation function. Consider a most blatant example. At the beginning of each school day, teachers in virtually every school conduct the flag salute and pledge of allegiance. Five days a week throughout the school year, at about 8:30 or 9:00 in the morning, visualize millions of children standing, placing their right hands over their hearts, facing the flag, and reciting "I pledge allegiance to the flag of the United States of America. . . . " This is a political ritual designed to maintain political legitimacy. Few if any people object to this elementary form of indoctrination. The general political economy is considered legitimate by most Americans; the legitimation process has been successful.

Consider, however, a more controversial practice that exists, or existed, in most American schools—the morning prayer. This practice is more controversial because the Christian religion is not accepted, or considered legitimate in a personal sense, by all Americans. Jews, Muslims, atheists, and so on, all may object to Christian religious rituals in public schools. The issue has been oversimplified purposely to make a point; the legitimation of our political economy is accepted by most as an important function of public schools because our political economy itself is accepted by most adults. And most adults, if even in a vague way, recognize the legitimation function of public schools. This is why there is so much conflict over what is taught in schools and what books are used. Adults want to make certain that their values are taught, or at least not rejected.

In the previous chapter we suggested how the educational system helps support the stratification system by teaching children to respect authority and accept their places in the stratification system—a function that contributes to the self-evaluation process described earlier. Our concern in this section, however, will be the content of information obtained in the educational system. Many studies of textbooks have been conducted (for example Kane 1970; Bowker 1972) that consistently show the views of upper-middle-class whites to dominate these works, while those of minorities are almost totally neglected.

But for the present discussion what is most important in terms of content requires no systematic study to detect; the American past and its institutions are idealized. School children are seldom told of our almost successful attempt to exterminate native Americans in our early history (see Brown 1970) or of the total brutalizing effects of slavery. Children may read about early communist influence in labor unions, but little of the systematic and violent attempts by the state and corporations to prevent union organizing. If civil disorder is given any attention, children do not learn that most violence has come not from demonstrators or social movement members, but from authorities against those who voice dissent (Gamson 1975; Stohl 1976).

Children do read about a few political and corporate scandals, but these scandals are portrayed as isolated products of greedy men rather than as any system defects. They are unlikely to read about the support for fascism by some big business leaders (Sampson 1973) before World War II or the congressional evidence suggesting that some business leaders were planning to seize the government illegally during Franklin Roosevelt's early years as President (Archer 1973) because they thought he was turning to communism.

None of this is very surprising, and we do not need more examples. Throughout history all children have been socialized to accept the dominant values and institutions of their society. Once a political economy has been established, the socialization process gives it momentum. But the legitimation process is not ignored by those most advantaged in the society. Legitimacy can be eroded over time, and in the event of a major crisis, the extent of political legitimacy can be an insurance policy preventing basic change. Because of this, elites have often taken steps to ensure that the educational system is performing its legitimation function "properly" (Wells 1971:718).

This is especially true since societies have become more secular and the major task of shaping loyalty has been transferred from the churches to the public schools (Collins 1975:378). As we will see below, economic elites in this country have not been willing to assume that the educational system is doing its job in teaching the "proper" views of our economic system. They have spent millions to train teachers and provide books and teaching aids (Domhoff 1979).

Although the effect of education on political attitudes and legitimacy is often difficult to determine directly, we do have some evidence that more education tends to produce more conservative political views. For example, national surveys have shown that people's attitudes on specific issues are related to education levels. During the Vietnam conflict, the more educated were more likely to support our government's involvement in Vietnam (Patchen 1970). Also, the more educated tend to support the government's position on the expansion of nuclear energy (*Gallup Opinion Index* 1979).

The relationship between education and conservative attitudes, however, is not always consistent. As we noted in a previous chapter, the less educated are more likely to blame the poor for poverty and hold negative welfare stereotypes (Feagin 1975). This attitude is no doubt related to the need for working-class people to feel better about their own low status. But on more general political views, Huber and Form (1973) have found that those with lower incomes (and presumably less education) are more likely to believe that a power elite is in control of the country and less likely to believe that personal attributes account for wealth. Throughout noncommunist industrial nations, the more educated most often reject leftist political parties (Szymanski 1978:248).

A problem with studies such as those cited above is that we cannot say confidently that more support for elite policy is shaped directly by the educational system. But in a unique study by Cummings and Taebel (1978) we do have a bit more confidence about the direct efforts of education. In this study 370 school children were questioned to see if their support for dominant capitalist ideology increased as they advanced in grade level.

The findings show that increasing support does occur, sometimes dramatically. For example, on the issue of state intervention in the economy (along the lines of democratic socialism), 66 percent of the sixth-grade students favored such intervention, but by the twelfth grade only 31 percent did. With respect to private ownership of major corporations, only 25 percent of the sixth-grade students thought this was right, while 63 percent of the twelfth-grade students thought it was proper. Finally, only 29 percent of the sixth graders expressed negative views toward unions, although by the twelfth grade 59 percent expressed such views.

Thus far we have considered schools in general. Perhaps special mention is necessary for higher education. The information is quite clear that the corporate class and upper class dominate formal positions of authority in most universities. In addition, the biggest and most respected universities depend on the wealthy and corporations for their funding (Smith 1974).

For example, in the thirty top universities in the nation, one-third of their trustees were listed in the *Social Register* in the mid-1960s, and 45 percent were corporate directors or executives. About one-half of the largest 200 industrial and financial corporations had a representative among the trustees of these thirty leading universities (Domhoff 1967:79). Many of these top thirty universities are not state supported. However, trustees of state-supported universities are no less corporate and upper-class members. For example, of the twenty-four trustees of the University of California's multicampus system, four are public officials. But the other twenty appointed regents are represented on sixty major corporate boards (Dye 1979:135).

As suggested in an earlier chapter, major universities serve important functions for the corporate class and upper class by conducting valuable research and formulating ideas for government policy (Domhoff 1979; Dye 1983). But many theorists also argue that the funding and formal positions of authority in universities held by the wealthy and corporate leaders have a significant, if not always immediate, influence on the ideas that reach students.

Universities, above all, are seen as institutions in which the marketplace of ideas should be open. Limits are enforced from time to time, however. Trustees have the power to call for dismissal of university employees, and funding by the wealthy and corporations can be withheld. There are enough known cases in which members of the faculty have been fired for teaching "radical" ideas or funding is threatened because "antibusiness speakers" have been brought on campus to make universities cautious (Szymanski 1978:251). The control of "acceptable" materials of instruction is less in universities than in secondary and elementary schools, but there are limits on what can be taught, and these limits are sometimes enforced. The instruction provided in universities is supposed to be balanced and objective. But definitions of what is balanced and objective are certainly in dispute.

The Legitimation Function of the Mass Media

The role of the mass media in the process of legitimation is difficult to demonstrate directly (Domhoff 1983), in part because long-run effects on public opinion are most important, and these are difficult to measure in the face of other influences on public opinion. The most important role of the mass media in supporting overall legitimacy and elite policy, it is argued, is found with (1) supporting new government policy directly by "getting the word out" (Domhoff 1977; Dye 1983), (2) shaping more general world views favorable to the dominant political economy, and (3) ridiculing alternatives to the present political economy (Miliband 1969; Domhoff 1970, 1979, 1983). The first function was considered in some detail in Chapter 8. Thus, at this point, our focus will be on the latter, more abstract, functions.

The mass media in the United States are not censored, nor are they completely controlled by corporations and the wealthy. This somewhat free environment within which the mass media operate, it is argued (Miliband 1969:219), produces more acceptance for what is presented. There is, in other words, a critical line that must be recognized. Media that are totally independent and unbiased may undermine legitimacy for elites and the political economy, but media that are overly controlled by elites may undermine the legitimacy of the media itself.

Much like universities, many of the mass media are under the influence of the wealthy and corporate class. And as with universities, the several means of influence are not always noticed in the day-to-day operation of the major mass media. But such influence is in the background to be used when limits are violated. And there are enough instances in which this influence has been used to keep the media aware of the limits (see examples in the *Los Angeles Times,* February 3, 1980). We can begin by considering some of the means of influence over the media held by corporations and the wealthy.

The three major television networks in the United States are privately owned. The precise stock control by the top six institutional investors in these networks is listed in Table 12-1. As noted in Chapter 8, with a wide distribution of corporate stock (most importantly among institutional investors), the U.S. Senate Committee on Governmental Affairs (1980) suggests that these top six institutional investors have extensive political influence in these television networks. This is especially important considering the estimates that most Americans (perhaps 90 percent) get their news information from the three TV networks (Dye 1983:122).

Table 12-2 lists *some* of the corporations that were directly interlocked through directors of the three major networks (or RCA Corp., which owns NBC). The *total* number of direct interlocks with other corporations was fifty-one for RCA, thirty for ABC, and twenty-four for CBS (U.S. Senate Committee on Governmental Affairs 1980:354, 397, 582). Also of note is that ABC had 275 indirect interlocks (corporate linkage through board membership in an intermediate or third corporation), CBS had 270 indirect interlocks, and RCA had 300 indirect interlocks with the top 100 corporations included in the Senate study (1980:88).

In the print media there are many more newspapers and magazines, with less concentration of ownership and domination of the total United States market. One way of considering concentration of newspaper circulation, however, is by the number of newspapers in competition in each major city in the United

TABLE 12-1

TOP SIX INSTITUTIONAL INVESTORS AMONG THE THREE MAJOR TELEVISION
NETWORKS IN THE UNITED STATES

	Institutional Investor (% stock controlled)		
	ABC	**CBS**	**NBC (RCA)**[*]
	1 Capital Group Inc. (3.77%)	1 Prudential Insurance (4.77%)	1 Morgan & Co. (4.59%)
	2 Equitable Life (3.69%)	2 State Street Research & Management (4.35%)	2 TIAA/CREF (4.57%)
	3 Lumberman's Mutual & Casualty (3.27%)	3 BankAmerica Corp (2.91%)	3 Chase Manhattan (1.92%)
	4 Donaldson Lufkin Jenrett (2.61%)	4 Morgan & Co. (2.41%)	4 Delaware Management (1.54%)
	5 BankAmerica Corp (2.08%)	5 TIAA/CREF (2.10%)	5 First Union Bancorp (1.43%)
	6 Maryland National Co. (1.89%)	6 Bank of New York (1.69%)	6 Maryland National Co. (1.03%)
Top six total stock control	17.31%	18.24%	15.08%

[*]NBC is owned by RCA Corp.
Source: U.S. Senate Committee on Governmental Affairs (1980:88).

States. The following figures show that the percentage of large United States cities with two or more independent newspapers has dropped rapidly in this century: 57.1 percent had two or more in 1910, 21.5 percent in 1930, and 4.1 percent in 1970 (Mintz and Cohen 1971:96).

TABLE 12-2

SAMPLE OF DIRECT INTERLOCKS BY TOP CORPORATIONS AMONG THE THREE MAJOR
TELEVISION NETWORKS IN THE UNITED STATES

Company interlocked

ABC	CBS	NBC (RCA)[*]
Bethlehem Steel	American Electric & Power Co.	Atlantic Richfield Co.
Citibank	Atlantic Richfield Company	Charter New York Co.
Manufacturers Hanover Corp.	Citibank	Chemical Bank
Metropolitan Life	Eastern Airlines	Citibank
General Motors	Manufacturers Hanover Corp.	Marine Midland Bank
IBM	Metropolitan Life	Metropolitan Life
Morgan & Co.	New York Life Insurance Co.	Security Pacific Corp.
	Pan American World Airways	U.S. Steel
	Union Pacific Corp.	

[*]NBC is owned by RCA.
Source: Table constructed from data presented by the U.S. Senate Committee on Governmental Affairs (1980).

Also of importance is that many of the top newspapers in the country are owned by companies that own several other major newspapers, magazines, and local television stations. For example, the New York Times Company owns nine other newspapers; the Washington Post Company owns *Newsweek* plus five TV stations; and Time Inc. publishes *Time* magazine, *Sports Illustrated, Fortune, People Weekly, Life, Money,* and *Discover* (Dye 1979:99; *Wall Street Journal* February 20, 1981). With newspapers specifically, the ten largest newspaper chains account for about one-third of the newspaper circulation in the United States (Dye 1979:110).

It is widely recognized and admitted that our major mass media make news in the sense that they select *what* will be presented and *how* it will be presented (Gans 1979; Lester 1980; Dye 1983). Thus we get a view of our nation and the world that is structured by media elites. As noted above, the mass media are free in the United States, but there are limits. With the potential corporate influence described above, and with their operating funds coming primarily from corporate advertising (Marger 1987:220–224), the media cannot afford to alienate major corporations.

The media must report corporate and political scandals, but they must be careful to be "objective" (as this is defined by those in power), or not to present these events "too extensively" or in such a way as to challenge the more general political economy. Put another way, Dan Rather must report that the airline industry or oil companies have been involved in price fixing; but he must be careful not to say something like "This is another example of greed that can result from the structure of corporate concentration unrestrained by government regulation."

In an extensive examination of how the media elites are led to censor news and slant what is presented to protect corporate and upper-class interests in the United States, Herman and Chomsky (1988) studied major news stories, and others that were not presented as major news stories by media elites. For example, they wanted to know why it was more "newsworthy" (that is, much more news coverage given) when a religious leader was killed by government officials in Poland during the early 1980s than when many, many more religious leaders were killed during the same time period by government officials in Latin American countries supported by the U.S. government (Herman and Chomsky 1988:40).

In their examination of many cases such as the above, Herman and Chomsky (1988) have developed a model focusing on five factors which create a slant in the news favoring U.S. corporate and government interests.

First, they note, as we have above, how much of the news media in the United States are owned by the upper class and major corporations, and are directed by interests of profits.

Second, because the major mass media are primarily dependent upon advertising to stay in business, this leaves the media open to pressure from corporate elites who can withdraw this economic means of the media's existence. Herman and Chomsky (1988) cite many cases throughout their book of when this has happened. For example, in 1985, when a public TV station showed a documentary called "Hunger for Profit" which was critical of specific U.S. multinational corporations' activities in Third World countries that helped to produce more hunger in these countries, Gulf & Western complained that the program was "virulently anti-business if not anti-American" and cut all funding previously given to the station (Herman and Chomsky 1988:17).

Third, Herman and Chomsky (1988:2) note that "the reliance of the media on information provided by government, business, and 'experts' funded and approved by these primary sources and agents of power" leads to limits placed upon information we receive, and a slant toward supporting the interests of these powerful groups in the news that is presented.

Fourth, there are "flak-generating" organizations that will create so many problems for the media if they present information which corporate and top political elites find "objectionable," that mass media organizations learn what must be "self-censored." Again, Herman and Chomsky (1988) describe many actual cases where this has happened in the 1980s and before, and list organizations which have established these "flak-producing" agencies. For example, in the 1970s and 1980s, "the corporate community sponsored the growth of institutions such as the American Legal Foundation, the Capital Legal Foundation, and Accuracy in Media" (Herman and Chomsky 1988:27), among others, to intimidate the mass media through lawsuits and publicity campaigns attacking the media if they disliked its presentation of the news.

Finally, in many news stories of foreign events and U.S. foreign policy studied by Herman and Chomsky (1988:2) they found that "anticommunism" is like "a national religion and control mechanism" which can be used to mislead the public and justify what is done in U.S. corporate and government interests.

Concerning all five of these "filters" on the news, Herman and Chomsky (1988:2) write that "the elite domination of the media and marginalization of dissidents that results from the operation of these filters occurs so naturally that media news people, frequently operating with complete integrity and goodwill, are able to convince themselves that they choose and interpret the news 'objectively' and on the basis of professional news values." However, the "constraints are so powerful, and are built into the system in such a fundamental way, that alternative bases of news choices are hardly imaginable."

In the context of the above it is interesting to examine the Soviet news media. It will probably come as a surprise to most Americans, influenced by the U.S. news "filters" described above, that Dan Rather, Peter Jennings, and Tom Brokaw's counterpart in the Soviet Union, Vladimir Dunayev, does not have his news scripts approved by the state before his evening news broadcast (*Time*, June 23, 1980:58). Mr. Dunayev, of course, is not free to say anything he likes; neither, for that matter, are Rather, Jennings, and Brokaw. They all know the limits, and they all want to keep their jobs. But it is more complex than this because they have all learned to respect what it means to be "professional" and "responsible." That is one reason they are at the top of their profession. They all work within the norms of their profession that prescribe limits. These limits are developed through a history of events that have brought pressure to bear from the state, courts, and private citizens or corporations when the limits were seen as violated.

We think that the Soviet news media are not free because of state domination. This is more clearly the case with books and magazines, for which state review before publication is the norm (though even this was reduced by Gorbachev). For the most part this is accepted. (See Solzhenitsyn's very interesting description [1980] of the battles by the magazine *Novy Mir* to get his works published in the Soviet Union.) But professional journalists in the Soviet Union think that the United States news media are not free because of corporate domination.

The point is that the news media in both nations work within differing sets of influences and limits they have generally come to view as legitimate (Hopkins 1970:109–110). As Dunayev states, "The most important thing is to be objective, not for the sake of objectivity—I am a Communist and believe in my ideals—but because we have to prepare people for the real facts" (*Time*, June 23, 1980, p. 58).

The "real facts," of course, are subject to interpretation. And they are interpreted through differing world views established through the process of legitimation in both countries. In both countries the top media professionals, because they are a part of their society and its world view, practice self-censorship (consciously and unconsciously).

Also, the marketplace of ideas in the United States is free to the extent that you have money—lots of it. Major corporations can buy advertising time to tell us how good their companies are and what they are doing to help the country. We continually hear how oil companies are helping us by finding oil with "inadequate" profits, how chemical companies are giving us better lives and how safe all their products are, and so on. Corporate advertising is designed to sell their view of economics as well as their products (Miliband 1969:215).

In addition to the ad campaigns by individual corporations, the Advertising Council is an arm of major corporations that attempts to present a favorable image of corporations in general and influence public opinion about economic issues. A good example of this is the Ad Council's radio and television advertising campaign to "upgrade" the public's "economic quotient" by showing how "free enterprise really works in the best interest of the country" (see Domhoff 1979:183–191). Of course, in none of the Ad Council's advertisements do we find out about the extent of market concentration, the concentration of corporate ownership, interlocking directorates, or other such matters.

In considering the ability of television to shape world views we must remember that most of what people see is not news or advertising, but entertainment programs. And Cerulo (1984) has found that the images and symbols presented in all the major forms of mass media have become more standardized since World War II, primarily because of television's becoming widespread in the 1950s. The exact influence of these programs is most difficult to measure, but many social scientists have argued that what people see works to emphasize class stereotypes, degrade minorities, make "radical" ideas appear ridiculous, and praise dominant American values (Miliband 1969:228; Sallach 1974; Gitlin 1979; Dye 1983). The heroes almost never express unaccepted political and economic ideas; in fact, they are usually "antiradical." And the working-class characters are usually unintelligent, bigoted, and superpatriotic. Archie Bunker, of course, is meant to present a satire. But Vidmar and Rokeach (1974) found that people who enjoy watching the show tend to be more rather than less prejudiced, and few people realize that Archie was being made fun of; many simply believe Archie is telling it like it is (Dye 1979:109).

The mass media cannot be accused of dominating or constructing world views for the public in favor of accepted corporate values. The mass media are only part of the legitimation process, and they are as much a product of the legitimation process as they are a part of it. If the mass media step out of line in presenting views critical of the corporate structure, America in general, or major values held by the population, they must answer to influential corporations as well as the public.

The legitimation process is a cyclical process, and the public that has come to accept the legitimacy of our political economy expects to see it supported by the mass media. The mass media can support specific issues or policies, as when the Time Inc. publications (*Time, Life, Fortune, Sports Illustrated, People, Money,* and *Discover*) all ran special issues one week on the theme of American renewal, implicitly endorsing much of what President Reagan was beginning to push with his new government policies (see *The Wall Street Journal,* February 20, 1981). But they cannot present an overly critical view of the political economy and remain accepted by most of the public or keep their business advertising.

Opinion-Influencing Organizations

The educational system and the mass media are the most recognized means of shaping opinions, but many organizations are formed by interest groups to get their point across to the public. The struggle for minds is carried on by many voluntary organizations that use the media, distribute books and pamphlets, and sponsor discussion seminars.

When an interest group has wealthy backers or a very wide following among the population it can usually get plenty of money for such activities. When an interest group does not have wealthy backers and only a relatively small following (or even a large following of relatively poor people) it is at a disadvantage. When the latter is the case, however, there is at least some hope of getting the point across by "using" the media. Demonstrations, sit-ins, marches, and so on will often bring media attention, although there is a chance of discrediting the aims of the group by using such tactics.

There is also a strong possibility that a group going against the power structure will be discredited through the activities of government agencies. Such activities include planting false information about the group in the press, using blackmail, planting false information within the group to promote in-fighting, and using agent provocateurs to create violent incidents that are blamed on social movement members. The CIA and the FBI have admitted doing all these things in the United States (see Gary T. Marx 1974; Mintz and Cohen 1976:367–385; Domhoff 1979:196).

The concern at this point is opinion-influencing organizations supported by corporations or agencies of the federal government that attempt to support the status quo. We will begin by examining corporate and upper-class organizations. In Chapter 8 the functions of the Council on Foreign Relations (CFR) and Committee for Economic Development (CED) were described. It is the job of these organizations to influence government policy. But these groups also have affiliations that attempt to shape public opinion.

For example, with the CFR there is the Foreign Policy Association (FPA), whose directors are mostly CFR members and corporate officials (Rosenau 1961; Domhoff 1970:151). The Foreign Policy Association sponsors World Affairs Councils, discussion groups, and speakers for local gatherings (like the League of Women Voters) to discuss the views of corporate leaders on matters of world affairs.

The CFR also sponsors Committees on Foreign Relations in over thirty cities that meet about once a month to hear speakers provided by the CFR or the government (Shoup and Minter 1977; Domhoff 1979:174). The goal of Committees on Foreign Relations is to inform local community elites on the CFR's view of foreign affairs so these local elites can in turn inform citizens in their communities. In addition to these activities, the Foreign Policy Association and CFR are linked with the American Assembly and the United Nations Association, which organize discussion groups around the country and foreign affairs institutes at universities to "spread the word" (Domhoff 1979:176).

With respect to domestic economic issues, the CED, like the CFR, has affiliated organizations that attempt to influence opinion on economic questions. Remembering our discussion of the importance of public schools in shaping ideas about economic issues, it is perhaps understandable that the CED formed an organization to make sure students are "properly taught."

The Joint Council on Economic Education was formed in 1949 by the CED with funding by the Ford Foundation (Schriftgiesser 1967). "Its biggest donors in 1975 were the American Bankers Association, AT&T, International Paper Company Foundation, the J. M. Foundation, Northern Natural Gas Company, The Sears Roebuck Foundation, the Sloan Foundation and the Department of Health, Education and Welfare" (Domhoff 1979:180). The joint Council conducts minicourses and summer workshops to train teachers in economics (with 19,500 participants in 1974), and helps develop textbooks and curricula to be used by teachers (Domhoff 1979:181). Through activities such as these corporate leaders can influence public school teachers, and through them, their students.

Another opinion-influencing organization is the aforementioned Advertising Council, formed in World War II to help the war effort, which today helps finance advertising on all kinds of issues it deems important (Domhoff

1979:183). In addition to TV advertising, it sponsors ads on the radio, in newspapers, and on billboards. With television advertising the Ad Council "utilizes 80 percent or more of the public-service advertising time that television networks must provide by law" (Domhoff 1979:188).

The Ad Council promotes economic information, such as its campaign to increase the public's "economic quotient" (that is, to present its idealized view of free enterprise), but also information on social issues. For example, one of the most famous cases is its work to reduce racial tensions during the riots of the 1960s. What is most important to recognize is that the directors of the Ad Council decide which publicity campaigns will be sponsored. Once they do so the campaign is turned over to a Madison Avenue advertising agency that does the work at no charge.

Although the Ad Council sponsors ads on social issues that affect the total society, there is the charge that its efforts are directed toward making corporations look better. For example, in its ad campaign on pollution the theme is, "People start pollution; people can stop it." Hirsch (1975) argues that the goal of this ad campaign is to direct responsibility for pollution away from corporations and to the general public. The Ad Council's advisory committee gave explicit instructions that the ads "should stress that each of us must be made to recognize that each of us contributes to pollution, and therefore everyone bears responsibility" (Hirsch 1975:69).

We have no direct research on the outcome of ad campaigns, discussion groups, seminars, teacher training, or books and pamphlets sponsored by the above groups. We must assume that corporations and wealthy families believe they have some effect, because they continue to spend millions of dollars on such efforts. These organizations are only one part of the legitimation process geared toward specific issues and support for the general political economy. But they are most likely an important part. Corporate elites cannot simply hope that support for their views will be forthcoming. They must work for support, and do so through a large network of organizations that lead from corporate boardrooms to the general public.

The federal government also attempts to influence opinion. At the higher levels of government the means of such influence is readily at hand because what they do makes news. Top officials know how to use the press with "news leaks" and press conferences. Top cabinet officials and major agencies of government also have press secretaries or other people employed to manage the information they want made public. But there is also a covert means of influencing public opinion that has been well known only since a number of congressional investigations in the 1970s. Covert influence over public opinion is the job of the FBI and CIA.

One means of influencing information is through publishing books. In one of the more famous instances, the CIA helped finance a book by Walt Rostow (*The Dynamics of Soviet Society*) through the MIT Center for International Studies (Marchetti and Marks 1974:175–181; Mintz and Cohen 1976:283). The

U.S. Senate Select Committee on Intelligence Activities found that the CIA has helped publish over 1,000 books—over 200 in 1967 alone. In other specific cases the CIA has attempted to influence public opinion on foreign issues such as the Vietnam conflict, our military involvement in the Dominican Republic, and our relations with the Soviet Union and China through funding book publications (Marchetti and Marks 1974; Mintz and Cohen 1976:283–284).

The CIA has also been engaged in efforts to influence opinion through the news media (Mintz and Cohen 1976:285). For example, in congressional hearings the CIA has admitted employing over fifty United States journalists, and in 1966 it secretly established a news service (Forum World Features) based in London to feed the news media with stories unfavorable to other nations and favorable to the United States foreign policy (sometimes true, sometimes false). Most of these efforts were designed to influence the opinions of people in other countries, although the stories did reach United States newspapers. Marchetti and Marks (1974:156–181) have described some of the false stories that were planted by the CIA that later became important news items in United States newspapers, although other cases were omitted from their book because of court action by the CIA.

There is other information to suggest that CIA ties to the major news media are even more extensive. For example, Carl Bernstein (the investigative reporter who helped break the Watergate story) claims that informants from the CIA acknowledge that about 400 United States journalists have worked with the CIA, from organizations such as *The New York Times,* CBS, and Time Inc. (Bernstein 1977; *The New York Times,* September 12, 1977). One job of these journalists is to pass information to the CIA, but we have other reports of cooperation in planting news stories to influence public opinion (Bernstein 1977:57; Leggett et al. 1978:55–57). In the case of the CIA-originated news stories designed to bring down the Allende government in Chile, *The New York Times* has admitted being a party to publishing these stories (*The New York Times,* December 25, 1977; Leggett et al. 1978:56–57).

Another operation by the CIA to influence public opinion is described by Domhoff (1970:257–259; see also Marchetti and Marks 1974:47–48). Without the knowledge of most of its members, the National Student Association received about $4 million during the 1960s from the CIA. The National Student Association is the national link of college student organizations on campuses throughout the country. The CIA money was used for student meetings, international programs, and educational material. The CIA hoped its efforts would help counter the growing criticism of the United States by foreign students in the 1960s, but remember that it was a major United States student organization that was used as a propaganda device.

We have no way of knowing the impact of activities such as those described above. But the goal is to shape public opinion with respect to various issues and counter criticism of the status quo in this country and abroad. It is one link in the process of legitimation, and when all these opinion-influencing organizations are recognized, it seems reasonable to conclude that their impact is significant.

The Macro Legitimation Process: A Conclusion

It would be incorrect to view the legitimation process in the United States as a simple conspiracy. There are, of course, behind-the-scenes plans to induce the public to accept what elites are doing or plan to do. But it usually falls short of what we generally think of as a conspiracy for several reasons. First, in contrast to the situation in the Soviet Union, the *overall* process of legitimation in the United States is unplanned. There is planning on specific issues and policies—to maintain public acceptance of military and economic intervention in other countries, of specific economic policies in this country, of nuclear energy, of pollution policies, and so on—but such planning is usually uncoordinated.

Second, no overall plan is accepted by all elites because there are often divisions among elites (as noted in Chapters 7 and 8). One segment of elites may strongly favor a specific policy (for example, foreign intervention supported by multinationals and defense industries) while other elites have less interest in the policy or even oppose it. In such a case elites may compete for public favor. There are issues on which all elites agree, such as private profit and support of the overall political economy, but even here they may disagree on how the issues should be defended or even if a defense is needed.

Third, the process of legitimation for specific issues usually falls short of what would be called a conspiracy because most of the process is not secret. Most people are unaware of the process, but the information on what is being done by elite organizations is obtainable. There are cases of hidden operations, as with the CIA's work to legitimate foreign policy or with undisclosed corporate organizations intended to mislead the public on certain issues. Elites do plan behind the scenes to manipulate public opinion. But the process cannot usually be described as a conspiracy, even though it is often quite effective and unrecognized by the public.

It would also be incorrect to assume that elites can make anything they do legitimate in the eyes of nonelites. There are limits, although these are seldom clearly defined and unchanging (Moore 1978). Cultural and historical forces operate to establish limits, but these forces are subject to change. During the late 1960s and early 1970s, for example, big tax breaks for corporations and drastic cutbacks in government social spending would have been difficult to defend. But as we now know, the 1980s brought new limits in this respect. An enlightened elite learns to work with cultural and historical forces in its favor. When the public is ready for some kind of change, elites will be ready with the changes they want and will attempt to make the changes appear to be in the national interest.

Finally, we must recognize that everything done by elites need not be accepted as legitimate. On the one hand, most of the public is often unaware of what is being done by elites. In this respect, a highly informed public would be threatening to elites—despite elite rhetoric to the contrary. From the perspective of rational self-interest, the game is to keep as much information from the public as possible, especially if the information might be controversial. And when pressed for information by the public, the game is to let out as little information as possible (Schattschneider 1960).

On the other hand, even when a policy that goes against public opinion is known by the public, unless there is a strongly organized interest group or social movement to challenge such a policy, elites will be able to continue the policy. The task for elites in this case is to prevent an organized challenge by discrediting their opponents, creating confusion, and/or discouraging the hope that change is possible.

For the most part, however, the public is apathetic unless it recognizes that an issue affects it strongly. We have seen evidence indicating the general public favors much more income equality than presently exists. But more income equality would most benefit relatively powerless groups and harm the interests of relatively powerful groups, which means most of the population remains apathetic. Besides, efforts to reduce income inequality can be opposed by elites on procedural issues. A bill may be introduced in Congress to reduce income inequality, but before it passes (if ever) it will be so altered as to render it ineffective.

In the second half of the present chapter we have examined how legitimacy for specific policies, for specific elites, and for a specific form of political economy can be maintained. Building on a sociopsychological base of acceptance for inequality in general, the educational system, the mass media, and specific opinion-shaping organizations can work to legitimate more specific forms of inequality. The overall process operates in the manner outlined in Figure 12-1. The trick is for elites to use the sociopsychological process of legitimation to their advantage. They learn to play upon the public's acceptance of inequality in an abstract sense to make what they do acceptable. They usually do this by making what elites do appear to be in the interests of nonelites and by making their contributions appear to be greater than those of others.

All of what has been described in this chapter implies that a delegitimation process can occur as well. The legitimation process is an ongoing process that

FIGURE 12-1
The interaction of micro and macro processes of legitimation.

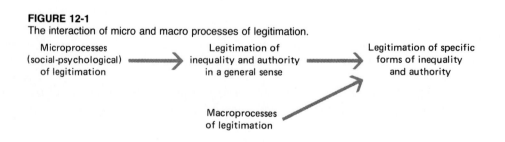

can be weakened or reversed. The legitimation of inequality and stratification in general is simpler to maintain (Mann 1970; Della Fave 1980); but, as described, there are at least four levels of legitimation, and delegitimation at lower levels of abstraction may coexist with legitimation on a higher level.

For example, the failure of elites to maintain social order or economic well-being *may* produce delegitimation at progressively higher levels (Mankoff 1970; Della Fave 1980). Disorder (political and/or economic) may result in a loss of legitimacy for specific elites and their policies if not corrected. And through time, if other elites and new policies cannot restore order, the political economy itself may lose legitimacy, with the population willing to support a new form of political economy (for example, socialism or fascism). We say disorder *may* result in a loss of legitimacy because for at least a period of time elites may be able to successfully blame outside forces for the disorder. Perhaps for this reason there is a natural tendency for all elites to seek scapegoats.

Even on a sociopsychological level the self-evaluation process may break down so that some people come to evaluate themselves equally with, or above, those higher in the class system (Della Fave 1980:967). For example, this appears to be the case with blacks in the United States. Earlier studies found that blacks had lower self-esteem than whites (see Pettigrew 1964; Grier and Cobbs 1968). But more recent studies have found that this is no longer the case (Baughman 1971; Rosenberg and Simmons 1972; Jacques and Chason 1977). Thus, blacks have come to see their lower overall status as illegitimate.

Throughout history inequality has generally been accepted. But it is not always accepted, especially on lower levels of abstraction. As we saw in our review of inequality in the history of human societies, elites are rejected from time to time, as are particular forms of social stratification. As we also saw at many points in earlier chapters, the level of inequality is quite high in the United States. Given this high level of inequality, the biggest question is not why people rebel, but why people rebel so seldom. In the present chapter we have attempted to provide some answers to the second question.

PART FOUR

SOCIAL STRATIFICATION BEYOND THE UNITED STATES

CHAPTER 13

SOCIAL STRATIFICATION IN JAPAN*

Throughout previous chapters we have seen how the level of technology in a society, or, more generally, the material base of the society, shapes the basic nature of social stratification in that society. Past theories have claimed that most aspects of a society are determined primarily by cultural values rather than concrete material conditions or even social organization. Extensive evidence has been provided (primarily in Chapter 3) which indicates that through history we do, in fact, find that the type of social stratification in a society is primarily shaped by material conditions and level of technology. When considering industrial societies, however, the earlier theories and historical studies indicating that the level of technology was most important in shaping the class systems of the first industrial societies had to be taken with caution. At that time *all* industrial societies had developed in societies with roughly similar Western cultural values. Still, there is only one fully advanced industrial society which has developed without a Western cultural tradition—Japan. Has Japan's Eastern, collectivist cultural tradition led to the development of a significantly different class system during its process of industrialization? This question and others like it are very important for our understanding of social stratification in modern industrial societies, and it is for this reason that we now take up the subject of social stratification in modern Japan.

Ranking in Japan: Some Preliminary Observations

A Western traveler to Japan encounters a country that at first sight seems like any other modern nation. True, the written language on the signboards and

*I would especially like to thank John McKinstry, Meika Sha-Clucas, Keiko Nakao, Keñichi Tominaga, and Lonny Wiig for their comments on various parts of this chapter.

trucks is certainly different than that found in any other advanced industrial society; and everything seems somehow smaller to Americans—the trucks, the rooms, portions of food in the restaurants, and even the people (at least the older people). Still, the people go about their work much like we would expect in other industrial societies (through it is true that they generally do more of it, and for longer hours). They talk about marketing, problems with financing, the technical problems associated with designing a new product, conflict between management and labor in wage discussions, and the ever-present, advanced-society problems such as traffic, pollution, smog, and urban crowding.

Upon closer analysis, however, there are what some people might see as puzzling aspects of the society. With respect to our subject of social stratification, for example, it is interesting to note how the Japanese seem fascinated with ranking and hierarchy (Woronoff 1980; Christopher 1983; Taylor 1983:42). Corporations are ranked; universities are ranked; all education programs are ranked; in fact, almost anything which can be ranked is ranked, with magazines and newspapers reporting on the ranking. One of the first things a foreigner may learn to say is "*ichi ban*," which means, roughly, "number one"!

This stress on ranking and hierarchy is not limited to things and institutions—it carries over to people. There is concern with a relative status ordering of people which makes it difficult for Japanese people to interact with each other as equals (Woronoff 1980:23–25). It is quite true that Japanese people are unable to sit, talk, eat, or drink with other people until the relative ranking order of those present has been reasonably ascertained. Within this social context the practice of exchanging business cards (or something like them) called *meishi* has developed (Nakane 1970:30). There is a ritual involved with the exchange of these *meishi* so that no one will be offended by someone who does not take due regard of the status cues on the card. (One of the next things a foreigner is likely to learn to say is "*Watashi no meishi des.*" "Here is my business card.") Once the status-relevant markers such as age, sex, education, occupation, and place of employment have been established among all present, then the business of eating, talking, drinking, or whatever can proceed in an orderly manner that is unlikely to offend someone who expects greater status deference.

It is to be expected that in such a society the language will be well developed to express deference, respect, and informality or formality as the situation calls for. There are, in fact, few languages that are as extensive as Japanese in allowing people to express levels of status, respect, and formality (Miller 1967; Goldstein and Tamura 1975). It is not an overstatement to say that almost every word uttered by one Japanese person to another indicates some aspect of their relative status ranking (whether that ranking is superior. inferior, or equal to the person spoken to).[1]

With this concern for ranking and formality that could easily disorient a laid-back Californian, we might expect Japan to be a society with a high degree of inequality in every aspect of life. But such expectations are far from accurate. You may remember from Chapter 2 that we have found Japan to have the lowest level of income inequality of all major industrial societies. We saw that while the average income gap between the top 20 percent and the bottom 20 percent of people in the United States is about 12 to 1, this same gap in Japan is about 4 to 1. In the corporate world these figures are even more profound: In the major corporations of Japan the pay gap between top executives and the lowest-ranked workers is around 8 to 1 (Abegglen and Stalk 1985:191). This same figure in the United States is about 37 to 1. As we will see in the coming pages, this relative equality in Japan is not just limited to income. While rising land prices in the 1980s and 1990s have produced growing real estate–based wealth inequalities, most basic necessities and services, from housing to access to education and medical care, are more equally distributed in Japan than in most other industrial societies.

It is tempting to conclude that the primary difference with Japan is simply that the Japanese have a tradition of unequal status ranking, but with more equality in material things. We must not, however, be tempted to draw such a conclusion. Yes, the language showing deference and status ranking has developed over the centuries, but the income inequality figures for Japan were rather different less than 100 years ago. Going back only to the 1920s we find not an 8-to-1 gap within major corporations in Japan, but a 100-to-1 gap (Abegglen and Stalk 1985:191). During the 1930s in Japan, about 16 percent of the people had over 50 percent of the income, and the top .0019 percent of the people had 10 percent of all income (Hane 1982:11).

One of the main tasks of the present chapter is to uncover a logic to this apparently puzzling system of social stratification in Japan. There are certainly different features of the nature of social stratification in Japan, as there are in all societies when we start comparing them (though we may admit that Japan has more than its share). But following the primary principles of social stratification as we have done in previous chapters, we can make sense of the stratification system in this Asian industrial society as well.

A HISTORY OF SOCIAL STRATIFICATION IN JAPAN

There are six main topics that we must cover in this brief review of Japanese history. We must understand how Japan's collectivist culture orientation developed and the effects of this culture on social stratification. We must examine Japan's relative isolation until the late 1800s, as well as the particular type of feudalism that developed. We will note the rigid stratification (somewhat like a caste system) which was institutionalized during the Tokugawa shogunate (1600s to mid-1800s). We will also assess how Japan developed and modernized from the Meiji restoration beginning in the second half of the 1800s, and the post–World War II changes in Japan pushed by the U.S. Occupation Forces that led to the nature of social stratification and economic power in contemporary Japan.

Asian Collectivism Historical and comparative research have generally shown that the major values of a society are shaped by a long history of coping with, and learning to adapt to, a particular material environment (for example, see Gouldner and Peterson 1962; Heise, Lenski, and Wardwell 1976; Lenski 1978; Lenski and Nolan 1986). For most Asian countries it is argued that a long history of rice cultivation (in contrast to the cultivation of cereal crops such as wheat in Western civilizations) helped establish a *collectivist* value orientation. This collectivist value orientation means that the group is given greater importance and protection in comparison to individual needs and desires. A primary reason for the development of a collectivist orientation in most Asian societies was the need for much greater group cooperation in growing rice, if the group and individuals in the group were to survive. Thus, out of necessity, values favoring group unity and control over the individual developed through the centuries.

Not all Asian societies, of course, have developed this collectivist value orientation equally. Most important for our investigation is the fact that Japan did develop this collectivist value orientation, but not to the same degree or in the same way as China. Because of the far-greater abundance of water coming down from the mountains in Japan, wet rice farming did not require large group projects or large groups working together as in China (Reischauer 1987:17). Thus, Japan did not have the early development of a state structure to organize irrigation projects which resulted in a powerful political elite as in China. These "hydraulic empires," as we pointed out in Chapter 3, in contrast to what has been called "hydroagriculture" in Japan (Wittfogel 1957), led to more rigid social stratification and a political elite based upon land control that, in recent centuries, blocked changes needed for industrialization.

Japan's Isolation   Japan began industrializing only a little more than 100 years ago. When China was already an old agrarian empire at about the time of Christ, Japan was just emerging from a simple horticultural level of technology (Bendix 1978; Befu 1981). And in contrast to other recently industrialized societies like the United States, Japan's industrializing culture was not transported from an already industrialized nation through colonization. Thus, compared to other industrial nations today, Japan has traveled from simple horticulture to industrialization in a relatively short time, and in a more independent manner. Japan has borrowed some of its culture from China and Korea, while a limited amount of European contact influenced Japan from the 1600s (Reischauer and Craig 1978; Reischauer 1987), but more than other major nations today, Japan was relatively isolated until the 1850s (Yanaga 1949). In the roughly 1500 years that Japan has existed as a country, until the 1800s foreigners had penetrated the country only three times for brief periods (the Chinese twice, and Europeans in the 1600s; Bendix 1978:65).[2]

The most important effect of this isolation has meant that Japan continues to have a homogeneous culture and race to a greater degree than any other developed nation—97 to 98 percent of the Japanese are racially and culturally similar. The roughly 2 to 3 percent who are not ethnically Japanese are Koreans, Chinese, and the native Ainu in northern Japan. This extremely homogeneous culture creates a sense of in-group versus out-group and an internal unity to an extent found in no other large nation today.

Japan's Feudal System   We can be brief on this subject given what we have already covered above. Without a hydraulic empire as in China, and with more small-group rice cultivation, Japan's feudal system by 700 A.D. was more like that of Europe in the middle ages than that found in many other Asian nations (Bendix 1978; Reischauer 1978:52; Reischauer and Craig 1978). There was usually less control by a central government, which means more local autonomy, and most land was not owned by the state or a national elite. For most of Japan's preindustrial history this meant a less rigid feudal system of social stratification with some chance of social mobility, individual autonomy, and competition by the local landed aristocracy (*daimyo*), and the lack of a powerful central state that could prevent social change seen as a threat to its rule.

The Tokugawa Shogunate   What we have just said above, however, was not the case with the Tokugawa period in Japan. The term *shogun* refers to the leader of a military clan which had achieved dominance over most of Japan, backed by the lesser landed aristocracy (*daimyo*), with the emperor serving as only a figurehead. The Tokugawa period was the last of the shogunates, and lasted from the early 1600s until it fell soon after Japan was forced by the United States to open the country in the 1850s. It was a long period of peace for Japan, during which time significant changes occurred in the nation's social structure and value system, as well as in the earlier, less rigid feudal system of stratification.

During this period the ruling shogunate instituted a rigid stratification system that in many ways resembled the Indian caste system we have examined in earlier chapters.[3] There were rigid ranks with very little chance of mobility, a concern with ritual purity, a requirement that people must display their caste positions in their clothing and on their homes (Benedict 1946:61), and a group of people very much like the untouchables of India at the bottom of this caste system. A primary difference compared to the Indian caste system, however, is that the Tokugawa caste system was never as institutionalized nor as accepted by the lower castes as in India. From time to time there were revolts against the upper caste, mainly by peasants. In fact, as many as 2,800 such revolts were recorded between 1590 and 1867 (Hane 1982:7).

At the top of Japan's castelike system were, of course, the shogunate warrior-bureaucrats, their samurai military elite, and the higher aristocracy (*daimyo*) in control of the local areas. Together they accounted for about 6 percent of the population and directly owned about 25 percent of the land (Reischauer and Craig 1978:81). The power of these elites was immense. For example, the samurai were the only people allowed to carry swords and had the right to kill anyone of lower rank if they showed the slightest disrespect. Next in rank came the peasants in a theoretical position of honor due to their social responsibility of feeding the rest of the population. In reality, this group was the poorest and most exploited, except for the outcastes. In a third position of status were the artisans, and last (again, except for the outcastes) were the merchants, "whose contribution to society was least valued" (Reischauer and Craig 1978:87).

In reality, however, members of the merchant caste were sometimes wealthy and its accumulation of wealth by the sixteenth century was one of the reasons the Tokugawa shogunate instituted this caste system. Because of trade and contact with European merchants at this time the shogunate and *daimyo* felt threatened. The response was that the Europeans were expelled (except for some Dutch on an island off Nagasaki), the Japanese islands were closed (few people could get in or out), and Japanese merchants were rigidly controlled and repressed.

Finally, in the bottom position, and actually completely outside of the system (thus, the term *outcastes*) were people called *eta* or *hinin* at the time, and later (and more commonly today) referred to as *burakumin,* who made up about 2 percent of the population. (The term *eta* means roughly "heavily polluted," while the term *hinin* means "nonhuman." The term *burakumin* has the least degrading meaning, "people of the hamlet"; Hane 1982:139–140.) These *burakumin* "seem to have originated in pre-Tokugawa times from persons defeated in warfare, criminals, and groups whose professions, such as butchery or leather work, were considered demeaning since they violated Buddhist dictates against the taking of animal life" (Reischauer and Craig 1978:88). This last characteristic again shows a strong resemblance to the untouchables or outcastes of India. As we will consider in more detail later, this group of *burakumin* are today still discriminated against even though these people are very difficult to identify. And even though these people cannot be identified as looking "non-Japanese," many Japanese still believe these people are from an "inferior race," perhaps Korean in origin (Hane 1982:139).

Before concluding this discussion of the Tokugawa period, it should be noted that the upper-class samurai subculture at the time became heavily influenced by a conservative form of neo-Confucianism imported from China. A respect for order, self-sacrifice, the family, male dominance, and ranking is central to this religious philosophy. During the Tokugawa period this belief system was not dominant throughout the society, but when the new social order was shaped by the lower samurai who took power in the 1860s at the fall of the last Tokugawa shogun, this Confucian belief system was built into many of the new laws of Meiji Japan as the country industrialized (Hendry 1987:22). As we will see, these values and laws continue to influence Japanese society and are the center of conflict as women and minorities try to reduce what they see as discrimination based upon these laws and values.

The Meiji Restoration   By the middle of the nineteenth century the United States was in a position to copy the European powers (at least a little) by obtaining colonies, or at least some areas in the world, for economic dominance. In Asia, Japan was one of the few places not already dominated by, or in the process of being dominated by, European powers. Thus, in 1858 about one-quarter of the U.S. Navy with its superior weaponry was sent to Japan to tell the Japanese government to open up to U.S. trade "or else" (Reischauer 1987:78). They opened up. But in the process of doing so, the already weakened Tokugawa shogunate "lost face." Criticism of the Tokugawa policy of isolation and lack of development was already building among the few groups who had much knowledge of the outside world. This criticism came mainly from a segment of the samurai, especially the lower-ranked samurai among the military elite.

What followed by 1868 was the *Meiji Restoration,* a revolt by this lower samurai military and scholarly elite that overthrew the Tokugawa shogunate and took control of the new government. It was in essence a top-down revolution which followed (Bendix 1978:482), though it was called a "restoration," because this new elite claimed that the emperor's power was wrongly taken by the Tokugawa shogunate 200 years ago, and that they would restore the emperor's rule. It was in reality the lower samurai who took power and held it for many years, as indicated by the fact they soon accounted for about two-thirds of all top government positions (Bendix 1978:482).

Economic development and capitalism were achieved in a rather different way in Japan during the Meiji Restoration, a way that, in fact, was state-sponsored capitalism (Clark 1979:25). The state began by creating government-owned and -controlled industries. However, as the government needed money for more industries, it sold the already established companies to wealthy merchants and other Japanese from the old elites at remarkably low prices. This practice quickly created a powerful upper class in the Marxian meaning of that term (Halliday 1975). This capitalist class soon formed into what was then and is now called the *zaibatsu,* or interlocked groups of major corporations centered around the most powerful capitalist class members, usually controlling major banks. A few (but very few) of these powerful wealthy family interests existed before this time, such as the still-active Mitsui group (Reischauer and Craig 1978:97), but most of the powerful Japanese corporations known today (such as Mitsubishi, Sumitomo, Fuji, Hitachi, etc.) were formed in this manner during the Meiji period.

Another important feature of the rapid industrialization produced by the Meiji government was extensive exploitation of peasants and the new working class. An important cause of increased misery for the peasants was taxes. About half of all taxes to fund the state-sponsored capitalism and make the *zaibatsu* rich came from the poor peasants (Clark 1979:20). Taxes took about 35 percent of the crop in the early Meiji period, and rents paid to landowners took another 50 percent. It became a widespread practice in rural areas for farmers and peasants to sell their daughters into prostitution in the cities, where, at least, parents assumed their daughters could eat. It is fairly easy to understand that labor unions were not allowed to grow during this time, though by the early 1920s there was some union activity. This union activity was violently repressed during the later 1920s and 1930s when a more conservative political elite and the military became increasingly powerful again as Japan moved toward World War II.

Occupation Reforms and the Rise of Modern Japan

The A-bombs that fell on Hiroshima and Nagasaki not only brought an end to the war, but also brought occupation by the United States, and major social, political, and economic reforms known as the *Occupation reforms.* The Occupation reforms are best described as liberal reforms, and in many cases can be called socialist in nature. Whatever they are called, however, they resulted in major changes that were important in leading to the economic dominance Japan was to achieve by the 1990s.

With respect to political reforms, the most important was the rewriting of Japan's constitution—a constitution, it is interesting to add, that was originally written in English, and which still creates problems of judicial interpretation for the Japanese (Kishimoto 1988). All citizens, including women, were given the right to vote. The upper house, controlled by an invented aristocracy under the Meiji constitution, was eliminated and replaced by a weak upper house that is democratically elected.

Two economic changes are most important for our subject of social stratification. First, the old *zaibatsu* corporate groups were broken up. This was accomplished through laws forcing the sale of much of the upper-class, family-held stock of the *zaibatsu,* restrictions on interlocking directorates, and the elimination of holding companies that had allowed these *zaibatsu* to form (Clark 1979:43). After a few years, some people claim that the *zaibatsu* re-emerged in Japan, with some good evidence to back up the claim (Caves and Uekusa 1976; Fukutake 1981; Steven 1983; Woronoff 1986). But these *zaibatsu* are in a much altered form if they can be said to still exist, as we will consider in some detail below.

Second, there was extensive land reform resulting from the Occupation Force changes. In the rural areas these changes had especially beneficial results for peasants and farmers who received land and support by the government, eliminating the long-standing inequality between rural and urban areas. Since this time farmers have become relatively well-off in Japan. They are a conservative force in politics, hoping to keep the economic gains they have obtained (and also to prevent redistricting of the political boundaries which at present give farmers more proportional representation in the Japanese parliament, the Diet).

THE STRUCTURAL BASES OF SOCIAL STRATIFICATION IN JAPAN

We have seen that the most important bases of social stratification in the United States are the occupational structure, authority structure (economic and political), and property structure. We found that most kinds of rewards (such as income) are distributed through these structures, and that the intersections of these three structures form the bases for the class positions in our industrial society.

What about Japan? If the theories are correct that advanced industrial societies, especially capitalist industrial societies, have these similar bases in their stratification systems, then Japan should also fit. Japan is clearly an advanced industrial society as figures on Japan's GPN and competitive position in the world economy indicate today. And in Chapter 6 we found that Japan was closest to the United States with respect to the percentage of private (in contrast to state) ownership of basic industries.

In summary, Japan does generally fit the pattern, but with some important differences. As pointed out in previous chapters, all advanced industrial societies are expected to have relatively minor differences in their systems of social stratification. Japan has more of these differences than most, but the differences, as we will see, are as much related to the timing of Japan's economic development as to its differing cultural values. It is time to examine Japan's occupational structure, authority structure, and property structure, in turn.

Occupational Structure

Like all industrial societies, Japan has doctors, lawyers, corporate managers, scientists, medical technicians, computer programmers, truck drivers, etc. This much is rather obvious when we consider how well the Japanese make cars, stereos, VCRs, and just about any other product made in the United States. But we need to consider other aspects of the occupational structure in Japan which are not so apparent. For example, we need to know the distribution of these different kinds of occupations, how people are placed in them, and the relationship between important rewards in the society (such as income) and these occupational positions.

Occupational Distribution   The occupational distributions of Japan and the United States are roughly similar. There are some differences, and these differences do matter; but again, they are relatively minor. For example, we find that more people are in farming occupations in Japan (Ishida, Goldthorpe, and Erikson 1987). Another significant difference in the Japanese occupational distribution is the larger number of retail workers and small shopowners (or petite bourgeoisie). As any visitor to Japan can easily see, Japan is still a country of small shopowners.

Another way to compare the occupational structures of the United States and Japan is to compare the occupational status scales of the two countries. You will remember from Chapter 6 that occupational status studies of the United States and other industrial nations indicate a remarkable consistency through time and across cultures. The meaning of occupational status and what these studies measure can be questioned, but it must be stressed that whatever they measure, they do so consistently. In comparing the occupational status ranking in the United States and Japan. Treiman (1977:87) has found a .90 correlation (+ or −1.00 is a perfect correlation) between the occupational status rankings carried out in Japan and the United States. Also significant is the strong .85 correlation between the educational level of occupants of similar jobs in Japan and the United States (Treiman 1977:110). Again, when we find that all advanced capitalist industrial societies have these high correlations, it is clear that Japan's occupational structure fits.

Dual Economy   Japan's dual economy presents another similarity in United States–Japanese occupational structures. To an even greater extent than the United States, in fact, Japan's economy is divided between large firms with higher profits, more market control, higher wages, and more unionization, and smaller firms having all of these characteristics in much smaller degrees (Clark 1979:143; Woronoff 1980:317; Lincoln and Kalleberg 1985; Kalleberg and Lincoln 1988). This aspect of Japan's dual economy must be kept in mind when we hear stories of "lifetime employment" and extensive worker benefits, such as company housing, in Japanese corporations. These things do exist in Japan (though we must qualify the "lifetime employment" in discussing age below), but primarily for the 30 percent of Japanese workers in the core sector of the dual economy.

Age Ranking   We now come to an interesting difference in the Japanese occupational structure. As with all advanced industrial societies, there is a positive correlation between education and occupational level in Japan: That is, a higher-level job (doctor, lawyer, accountant, etc.) usually requires a higher level of education. However, as we see in Table 13-1, at the younger age level (twenty-five years old) workers with less education actually make *more* money than the college-educated. As we move up the age levels in Table 13-1 we find that higher education pays off. But this payoff operates primarily by the relationship between higher education and attaining a job in the core sector of the dual economy. As we will see in more detail later in this chapter, Japan is a

TABLE 13-1
INCOME BY EDUCATION AND AGE, MALE WORKERS IN JAPAN, 1982 (index, college income = 100)

	Education level		
Age	Elementary or lower secondary	Upper secondary	College
25	102.3	100.6	100.0
30	87.8	93.6	100.0
40	74.3	87.3	100.0
50	56.3	76.2	100.0

Source: Foreign Press Center (1985:78).

highly age-ranked society. Thus, there is a stronger correlation between age and income than education and income (Woronoff 1980:164; Kalleberg and Lincoln 1988). This can also be seen in Table 13-2, which shows that income goes up slowly with age in Japan until the fifty-to-sixty age category, then drops off rather fast.

In what is called the *nenko* system in Japan, once a person lands a good job in a major corporation (because of educational attainment), that person will probably be promoted along with the same age group every year. In other words, merit counts in getting that job, but merit is less important for further promotions in that job (though this is changing in some Japanese corporations, but not in public sector bureaucracies, Clark 1979:45; Abegglen and Stalk 1985; McMillan 1985).[4]

There is an element of merit always at work in the background, however, that we need to consider. When employees in the core sector reach about age fifty-five to sixty, the jobs toward the top suddenly become fewer. Everyone cannot be promoted together after this. Thus, those employees most highly evaluated by the company are promoted and the others are forced to retire. This is the major amendment to the concept of "lifetime employment" noted above.[5]

Income Inequality　We have one last aspect of the occupational structure in Japan that must be explored. This is an aspect of the Japanese occupational structure which is much in contrast to that of the United States, though not necessarily in equal contrast to other industrial nations (which suggests that the United States is as much or more the deviant case compared to other nations than is Japan). We have already seen that during the early 1980s Japan had the lowest level of income inequality of any industrial nation. Most of this

TABLE 13-2
MALES' INCOME BY AGE, JAPAN, 1982
(index, 20–24-year-old income = 100)

Age	Income
to 17	71.0
18–19	82.9
20–24	100.0
25–29	126.5
30–34	156.9
35–39	182.1
40–44	197.7
45–49	202.7
50–54	197.7
55–59	171.5
60–64	138.5
65 & over	126.8

Source: Foreign Press Center (1985:78).

low income inequality is produced within the economy, rather than through government action, such as tax and welfare policies (Verba et al. 1987:274; though there is evidence that tax policies are more involved than Verba et al. claim; see Abegglen and Stalk 1985:192).

We have seen that Abegglen and Stalk (1985:192) present 1980 figures showing that the gap between top executive salaries and the new employee salaries in Japan is about 7 to 1. In another survey of wage differences in the auto industry, the *Wall Street Journal* (April 18, 1984) reports a gap in Japan of 7 to 1, while the same wage gap for the auto industry in the United States is 37 to 1. The figures cannot be dismissed by saying that the many fringe benefits Japanese executives receive are ignored. While U.S. executives receive many extras, such as stock options, which increase their total income, stock options for Japanese executives are prohibited by Japanese law (Abegglen and Stalk 1985:187). In 1984, *Fortune* (March 19) reported that the top executive salaries in Japan ranged from $50,000 to $250,000, and the above authors cite an average top executive salary in Japan of about $100,000 a year. *Fortune* also reported eighty-five American executives who made more than $1 million a year, and *Business Week* (May 7, 1984) reported that twenty-five American executives made more than $2.3 million in 1984.[6]

Bureaucratic Authority Structures

When most people think of bureaucracy they think of countless rules and legions of bureaucrats enforcing these rules, so that it takes a longer time to get anything done, at much greater effort. We think of the rules at the U.S. Post Office, where packages must be the correct size and weight, and we must fill out many forms if anything out of the ordinary is requested. Any U.S. citizen who has lived for a time in Japan will tell you that you haven't experienced anything like bureaucracy in a post office until you come to Japan.[7]

The postal service in Japan, however, should not be singled out, as such bureaucracy is a characteristic of all government and corporate agencies in Japan. We will first look at bureaucratic authority structures in the economy and then in the Japanese government agencies.

Corporate Bureaucracies   Not only does Japan now have many of the largest corporations in the world, such as Toyota, Mitsubishi, Nissan, and Sony, but it also has the largest banks. In 1990 the list of the world's largest banks included seven from Japan—in fact, the top seven. These rankings are in terms of corporate assets, which do not exactly represent the size of the work force or bureaucracy, but they are all usually closely related. We will cover this subject of corporate bureaucracies in other ways when considering the power elite of Japan, which includes the corporate elite. However, several things should be noted at this point.

Corporate bureaucracies in Japan are noted for having more ranks and levels than most others (Woronoff 1980:23). This would follow observations made earlier that the Japanese seem concerned with ranking, and that extensive age ranking exists in core corporations in Japan (that is, there must be many ranks to keep promoting people into). But it is also interesting that there tend to be fewer observable rank distinctions in Japanese corporations (Clark 1979:215). In many ways higher management is not treated so differently; managers eat in the same places as workers, they do not have large and separate offices, or executive washrooms. (However, as we will discuss later, the status difference given to top executives by lower-ranking employees in Japan is more extensive than in the United States.)

We have seen that one of the checks on corporate power at the top can be strong labor unions. In most respects it can be said that labor unions in Japan are weaker than in the United States, though this statement is controversial and must be qualified. The first thing to note is that most unions in Japan are company unions, meaning the union is formed primarily in only one company and does not cross a whole industry, in contrast to, say, United Auto Workers in the United States. There are, however, union coalitions in Japan, but this is not the same thing as a large, strong union.

In the U.S. experience, when someone says "a company union," this usu-ally implies that the union is controlled by the company and has no real power. Generally, this may be the case in Japan, but the Japanese idea of worker–management conflict is different. Thus, the Japanese more often see teamwork rather than an adversary relationship existing in worker–management situa-tions. This may in large part be corporate ideology at work, but the unions in Japan do push management rather hard in what is traditionally called the "spring wage offensive" (*shunto*) to get a contract with higher wages each year. Union coalitions coordinate their demands to try to achieve more strength in this annual negotiation process.

Another aspect of a corporate bureaucracy is the extent to which workers have some influence or say in what happens in the work place. It is commonly believed that, with quality control circles and other management techniques used in Japan, there is intensive group decision making and that workers have much say in how their job is done. Most social scientists studying Japan dis-agree with this idea, however (Clark 1979:126–132; Woronoff 1980:45–48). A leading Japanese sociologist has described how decision making in Japan is ac-tually more centralized (Nakane 1970:51). The common *ringi* system of making decisions in a Japanese bureaucracy involves ideas being passed down to lower managers for discussion and consensus. This system is in fact manipu-lated by top managers, because the decision has probably already been made (Woronoff 1980:46). One important result of this, however, is that it can give workers the impression of collective decision making, thereby making them feel more important. This may also make them feel more responsible for the decision if something goes wrong, and more cooperative in trying to correct mistakes.

Finally, we can ask workers how they feel about their input in the company. When we do this, we find that Japanese workers are *more* likely than American workers to say they feel oppressed at work and are afraid to show disagreement with their boss (Naoi and Schooler 1985).

Political Authority Structures   Like the United States, Japan today has a relatively democratic political system where questions of who gets what, and why are influenced by a process of conflict shaping political policies. And, as in the United States, some groups have more resources with which to try to influence the state to protect their interests. But the Japanese political system is not a carbon copy of the U.S. political system. All political systems have their unique aspects, with Japan having probably more than its share. In this section we will briefly review some basic characteristics of the Japanese political system so that we can understand how this political system influences the process of class conflict and the nature of the Japanese stratification system.

Like Western democratic societies, Japan has three branches of government—judicial, congressional, and administrative branches (often referred to as the government bureaucracy or government ministries). But unlike the United States, Japan has a parliamentary system where their congress, the Diet, elects a prime minister, who then appoints a cabinet of ministers to head the various administrative bureaucracies (such as the Ministry of Health and Welfare, Ministry of Education, Ministry of Transportation, and so on to a total of twelve ministry bureaucracies). And also unlike the United States, but like most other industrial democracies, the Japanese central government has more control over local affairs. There are local governments, but they are weaker compared to the more federalized U.S. system of government, especially because most funding must be obtained from the central government in Japan. Thus, the conflict to influence central government is more concentrated.

Finally, another aspect of the Japanese government that differs from the United States must be noted because of its influence on the process of class conflict. In contrast to most other democracies, Japan's parliament, or Diet, is much less involved in governing and even writing legislation (Kishimoto 1988). Diet members are elected to pass laws which govern the nation, but in Japan bureaucracies have more independence and even write legislation which they then give to the Diet for passage. Unlike U.S. senators or representatives, Diet members have few staff or office resources (Woronoff 1980). The minister of each bureaucratic ministry is a member of the prime minister's cabinet and is appointed by the prime minister and party in control of the Diet, much like the U.S. President's cabinet. But the more stable position of vice minister in each government bureaucracy is a career civil servant position with actually more power than the minister.

In one sense it can be said that there is a greater level of democracy in Japan than in the United States. More Japanese people participate in the political process by at least voting (usually around 80 percent vote in national elections compared to 50 percent or less in the United States). In other ways, however, Japan has been described as having less democracy than Western democratic societies. Much of the activity of Diet members is not open to public observation. In other words, many decisions are made in closed, "smoke-filled rooms" (quite literally! Japan has a high percentage of smokers). And the actual activities and intent of Japanese politicians often seem vague as far as the public goes, in part, some argue, because the Japanese language allows a politician to speak in very ambiguous terms (Christopher 1983). And some Japanese claim that because Japanese psychology and culture teach people to be totally straightforward and clear about true intentions or opinions only with close friends or relatives, politicians can seldom be frank and open in public (Doi 1986:48). As a result of these things the Japanese often refer to their government as a "black box"—they see inputs and outputs, but they don't know what happens on the inside. This aspect of the Japanese government presents more opportunity for a power elite to govern.

Another reason for less democracy has already been mentioned. More government power actually falls to the bureaucracies run by unelected civil servants. In Japanese history these Japanese bureaucrats in the central government ministries have had a very high reputation for professionalism and lack of corruption. (This is one reason that the Recruit Cosmos stock scandal of 1988–1989 was so shocking to many Japanese: Politicians were known for corruption, but in this case some top ministry officials were involved in corruption for personal gain; see Kerbo and Inoue 1990.) However, despite this relative lack of personal corruption, there is increasing recognition of ways that powerful interest groups (especially in the corporate class) can legally have extensive influence on what happens in the government through the bureaucracies. These means of influence, however, must await our discussion of the power elite in Japan.

Property Structure

In the United States we found that one of the major sources of inequality was the ownership of the major means of production by a few versus the lack of such ownership by most people. There are certainly degrees of ownership (in terms of overall amounts), but because most privately held corporate stock is concentrated in the hands of less than 1 percent of the U.S. population, it can realistically be divided into those who own major amounts of corporate stock (which gives them much wealth, income, and power) and those who have very little or none.

As for Japan, the most basic point to begin with is that Japan, like the United States, is a capitalist industrial society. This means that there is little government ownership and/or control of the major means of production. But after this simple point it becomes a bit more complex in the case of Japan. Families who could be said to make up an upper class in Japan (either old upper class or new upper class) own much less stock than in the United States. Whereas half of all corporate stock is still controlled by families and individuals in the United States, this number is estimated to be 30 to 25 percent in Japan, and much less than this when we look only at the largest 1,000 or so corporations in Japan (Caves and Uekusa 1976; Clark 1979:85, 102, 237; Dore 1987:112). There are some Marxian analyses of Japan that continue to use the old term upper class in the original Marxian sense of capitalist ruling families (Halliday 1975; Steven 1983), but this terminology has much less application to the Japan of the 1980s and 1990s (or even since World War II). Let's consider some of the data.

As early as 1966, data on the stock ownership patterns of the largest 466 companies (all with assets of more than 5 billion yen) show that only 8.8 percent (or forty-one) of these companies have enough family-held stock to be considered family or individually controlled. Table 13-3 lists ownership by various categories of owners for all the corporations listed on the stock exchanges in Japan for 1983. We find that of all this corporate stock, only 27 percent of shares are held by families or individuals. The next biggest share is the 26 percent held by industrial and other commercial corporations, then 18 percent held by banks, and 17 percent held by insurance companies. Counting the amounts owned by stockbroking companies and investment and other financial companies, we find that 66 percent of all corporate stock is owned by corporations in Japan. Also, in comparison to the United States we must stress a key point: This stock is really *owned* by these other corporations, in contrast to the huge amounts of stock *controlled* by U.S. financial firms that are in reality owned by worker pension funds. All of these data can be confirmed by the 1989 information on the more than 1,000 largest corporations in Japan published each year under the title of *Japan Company Handbook* (Toyo Keizai Shinposha 1989). Along with other corporate data this book lists the top five to ten stockholders in each company. In page after page of this book of over 1,200 pages, very few names of people are found listed as owning any significant stock in these corporations.

You will remember that before World War II most major corporations in Japan were owned and/or controlled by a few wealthy family firms combined

TABLE 13-3
OWNERSHIP OF CORPORATE STOCK, BY CATEGORY OF OWNER, JAPAN, 1983

	Percent of total stock owned
Individuals	27
Stockbroking companies	2
Pension funds	0
Insurance companies	17
Banks	18
Investment trusts	3
Industrial corporations and commercial companies	26
Foreigners	6
	100%

Source: Constructed from data presented by Dore (1987:112).

into groups called *zaibatsu*. As noted above, these firms were forced to sell off their holdings and reduce their control of the economy by the U.S. Occupation reforms. These firms that were once controlled by families are still in operation and have partially reformed their groups of powerful corporations, but family ownership is no longer significant (Clark 1979:75; Abegglen and Stalk 1985:189). As an example, Table 13-4 lists the main corporations in the Mitsubishi group and the stock they control in each other.

The primary reasons for the lack of ownership by families and individuals today must begin with the forced breakup of the old *zaibatsu* after World War II. When this stock was forced to be sold to break up these family groups, other corporations were among the only ones in a position to buy. Secondly, unlike in the United States, top corporate managers are prevented by law from being paid with stock options in their companies (Abegglen and Stalk 1985:187). Thus, while this practice accounts for some of the individually owned stock in the United States, there is almost none of this manager-owned stock in Japan. Finally, in Japan, when corporations have important business deals with another corporation (as a supplier, retailing the product, holding or giving financial loans, etc.) the practice is to buy significant amounts of stock in the corporate business partner (and vice versa) as a show of support and to maintain good relations.

In Chapters 7 and 8, but especially Chapter 8, we found that institutional investors control most stock in major U.S. corporations. This development has cut into the ownership and power of an old upper class of families and created the bases for what is called the *corporate class* of top executives who control not only their own corporations, but who have extensive influence across major corporations, as well as much influence in the government. To what extent do we find this corporate class in Japan? This is our next subject—Japan's power elite.

TABLE 13-4

THE MITSUBISHI GROUP OF INTERLOCKED CORPORATIONS

Company of stock issue	Percent of stock owned by other top 20 firms in the Mitsubishi group
Mitsubishi Bank	26.9
Mitsubishi Trust Bank	32.3
Tokyo Marine	21.7
Mitsubishi Heavy Industries	23.2
Mitsubishi Corporation	42.2
Mitsubishi Electric	16.3
Asahi Glass	29.3
Kirin Beer	12.7
Mitsubishi Chemical	24.5
N.Y.K. Shipping	27.5

Source: Table constructed from data presented in Clark (1979:75).

JAPAN'S POWER ELITE

We are ready to consider who is at the top of Japan's stratification system as we did for the United States in Chapters 7 and 8. There is less research on elites in Japan (Morioka 1989:140), though we have already seen some prime locations for elite dominance in the political system and corporate structure. However, we have difficult questions remaining before concluding that Mills' thesis of a power elite fits Japan.

The Triumvirate of Elites

It turns out that the elite configuration in Japan is on the numerical level suggested in C. Wright Mills' (1956) view of a set of three interlocking elite groups. In Japan, this triumvirate is composed of the corporate class, the government bureaucracy, and the LDP (Liberal Democratic Party) (Tsurutani 1977; Woronoff 1980:190, 1986:32). In many ways this group forms an interlocked group of elites as Mills suggested for the United States, with the corporate rich, government elite, and military elite. And as Mills suggested for the United States, this Japanese power elite is based upon institutional position, with exchanges of personnel and resources, a common background and world view, and common interests. There is some disagreement over which of these is most powerful, but the best estimate seems to place the corporate class first, then the government bureaucratic elites, and, finally, in distant third, the LDP.

Corporate Class The corporate class of this triumvirate is made up of the top executives and board members of the major corporations in Japan, much like in the United States. There are, however, a few differences. A particularly obvious one is the very low level of interlocking directorates in Japan (Clark 1979:100; Vogel 1979:47; Abegglen and Stalk 1985:185). Most of the directors of Japanese corporations are made up of "inside directors" from management and retired executives of the same corporation. Of all corporate board members in Japan, usually two or three (of a total of twelve to fifteen) are "outside directors," mainly from large banks. As in the United States, groups of corporations with various common interests are often tied through bank interlocks, which the Japanese call *keiretsu*. Also, these new groupings of corporations around banks overlap with the older grouping referred to as the *zaibatsu,* which also tends to have a major bank in the group, if not at the center of the corporate ties. In modern Japan, however, there is no evidence that banks are any more than an equal partner in the *keiretsu* groups, rather than a dominating center (Clark 1979:77–78).

Instead of interlocking directorates tying this corporate class together in Japan, it is united through (1) interlocking ownership of corporations (i.e., each corporation holding stock in the other), and (2) powerful business organizations. We have already seen that as much as 60 to 70 percent of the corporate stock is held by other corporations, and it is obvious how these corporate elites are tied together when they hold extensive stock control in each other's corporations in Japan.

The business organizations need further description because of their more extensive power in comparison to their counterparts in the United States. The most important of these business organizations is the *Keidanren,* which is made up of top executives from the largest corporations and informally described as "the main temple," with its president called the "prime minister" of the corporate elite (Vogel 1979:113; Woronoff 1986:152). The *Keidanren* (which in Japanese stands for "Japan Federation of Economic Organizations") so openly organizes and coordinates corporate class political power that it would probably be considered an illegal monopoly if it existed in the United States. It is made up of the top executives of the more than 800 major corporations that account for over 40 percent of all the profits of Japanese corporations and 50 percent of total corporate assets (Woronoff 1986:152). After considering details on the political activities and policy coordination for the corporate class achieved by *Keidanren* and other (though less powerful) business organizations in Japan, the following statement by Woronoff (1986:158) seems justified: "In fact, there is no equally potent business community anywhere else in the world. It would therefore be quite impossible to grasp the operation of the political system without carefully considering what is done here."

The Bureaucratic Elite   We have noted earlier the power of the government bureaucracy in Japan. It is the bureaucratic elite which actually runs the government, and even writes most of the laws which are finally passed in the Diet (Japan's parliament). These government ministries have a huge staff of underlings who do the research and coordination which the Diet members lack. A result is that of all the laws submitted to the Diet by the government bureaucracy, some 80 percent are passed into law, compared to only 30 percent of the bills submitted by Diet members themselves (Kishimoto 1988:66).

But in addition to actually running the government while they are in top bureaucratic positions, these bureaucratic elites tend to retire early to take top corporate positions or to be elected to the Diet (with strong LDP support), where they end up with major committee positions. So common is this practice of bureaucratic elites retiring to top corporate positions that there is a special name for these people—*amakudari,* which means "descended from heaven" (Woronoff 1986:137). It should be noted that the pay of top government bureaucrats is low, while their power and status are very high. By moving into a top corporate position upon retirement in their fifties, these bureaucrats can clearly increase their economic rewards (though certainly not to the level of U.S. corporate executives).

The extent of movement from government bureaucracy to top corporate positions is indicated in Table 13-5. From just one government ministry, the Ministry of International Trade and Industry, we find that these former bureaucratic elites have obtained extremely powerful positions in the corporate world. Nor is this particular ministry unique: "Each year, up to two hundred

TABLE 13-5
FORMER VICE MINISTERS OF MITI AND THEIR LATER TOP CORPORATE POSITIONS, SINCE WORLD WAR II

Name	Corporate Position
Yamanoto Takayuki	Vice-president, Fuji Iron and Steel
Tamaki Keizo	President and chairman, Toshiba Electric
Hirai Tomisaburo	President, New Japan Steel Corp.
Ishihara Takeo	Vice-president, Tokyo Electric Power
Ueno Koshichi	Vice-president, Kansai Electric Power
Tokunaga Hisatsugo	Vice-president, New Japan Steel Corp.
Matsuo Kinzo	Chairman, Nippon Kokan Steel Corp.
Imai Zen'ei	President, Japan Petrochemical Corp.
Shashi Shigeru	Chairman, Japan Leisure Development Center
Yamanoto Shigenobu	Executive director, Toyota Motor Co.
Kumagai Yoshifumi	President, Sumitomo Metals Corp.
Ojimi Yoshihisa	President, Arabian Oil Co.
Morozumi Yoshihiko	President, Electric Power Development Co.
Yamashita Eimei	Managing director, Mitsui Trading Co.
Komatsu Yugoro	Director, Kobe Steel Corp.

Source: Johnson (1982:72).

retired senior bureaucrats, mostly from what the Japanese call 'the economic ministries' and the National Tax Agency, move into key sectors of the corporate world as top executives, board members, and advisers'' (Tsurutani 1977:76).

As for movement into the Diet from the government bureaucracy, over *30 percent* of LDP Diet members are former bureaucrats. And most important in showing the power of this group, between World War II and the mid-1970s about *80 percent* of Japan's prime ministers had been former members of the bureaucratic elite who retired to be elected as Diet members, and then prime minister (Tsurutani 1977:77). Between the mid-1970s and the early 1990s, this percentage has remained high.

The Liberal Democratic Party There is rather wide agreement that the Liberal Democratic Party (LDP) is the most junior member of the triumvirate, behind the corporate elites and the government bureaucracy. As we saw above, a significant number of the LDP Diet members and the majority of prime ministers have actually retired from the bureaucracy. And as we will see below, the LDP is almost totally dependent on corporate elites for funds. But the LDP is a vital arm of the power elite because, as in all advanced capitalist societies, the government has much involvement in the economy.

It is said that the LDP is a member of this power elite in Japan, rather than the Diet (the Japanese parliament), because the LDP has controlled both the upper and lower houses of the Diet since the LDP was formed in 1955 (with the only exception being the LDP's loss of the weaker upper house in the 1989 election), and thus has selected the prime minister after every election since 1955. It is also important to note another fact about Japanese politics in general, and the LDP in particular, when considering the power of the LDP in the Diet. Unlike American political parties, the members of the LPD elected to the Diet are strictly controlled by the party leadership. This means that when the LDP leadership decides how the party should vote or stand on an issue, LDP members will almost always go along. One reason for this contrast to American political parties has to do with Japanese traditions of falling into line with the group and its leader once a decision has been made, but it also has to do with how the LDP's leadership is able to control campaign funds and the importance of the leadership's endorsement for winning elections to the Diet.

Ties between the LDP and government bureaucracy come from personnel exchanges from the bureaucracy, and from the fact that the bureaucracy writes most of the laws and carries them out through its ministry functions. The ties between the LDP and the corporate elites, however, come mainly through money to support election campaigns. Over 90 percent of the LDP's funds come from major corporations (Woronoff 1986:161). One of the reasons that LDP members spend so little time with Diet business and working on new legislation is that they spend so much time in fund-raising activities (Woronoff 1980:194–206).

The Japan Communist Party is officially listed as collecting more campaign funds than any party in Japan (Kishimoto 1988:136), but it is common knowledge that the LDP raises much more money. Since the mid-1970s in Japan there have been new laws regulating the financing of elections, but as in the United States, these laws are rather ineffective. There are restrictions on how much each person and organization can give to a political candidate, but there is one means of raising funds which is not regulated (Kishimoto 1988:137). In what the Japanese call "fund raisers," a candidate or an already-elected politician invites people to a dinner or speech, charges them perhaps 20,000 to 30,000 yen (about $150 to $230 in 1990) each, and does not have to report how much was actually raised and by whom. Since new laws regulating other types of campaign funding came into existence in the mid-1970s, there has been a 300 percent increase in the number of these fund raisers, with a 2,800 percent increase in the amount of funds raised in this manner (Kishimoto 1988:137).

Elite Backgrounds   As we saw in our discussion of elites in the United States, it is important to consider the backgrounds of elites to examine how these elites may have come to think alike, have many similar interests, and have background ties that enhance their unity (and, thus, their power as a group that can act together). In Japan, however, we have already seen that there is no real upper class of family wealth any longer. We must look elsewhere for elite ties and unity.

In the case of corporate elites, as we have seen, many come from the government bureaucratic ministries in the process called *amakudari* ("descending from heaven"). One study of corporate elites in the late 1970s estimated that from 30 to 40 percent of all major corporate executives came to their positions in this manner, while 35 to 45 percent came up from a career within the corporation, with the remaining number of individuals being founders of the company or the son of a founder (Shimizu 1980; McMillan 1985:128). As for the class backgrounds of corporate elites, another study estimated most came from the upper middle class (61 percent), but less came from the upper middle class than in Europe (and the United States, we can add), while slightly more came from the working (9 percent) and middle classes (30 percent) in Japan compared to Europe (Mannari 1974:224; McMillan 1985:129).

We have already seen the high number of LDP members who came from the government ministries. No studies have been located on the class backgrounds of LDP members or the bureaucratic elite, however. But the consensus among Japanologists (Reischauer 1987) is that these people have class origins similar to the corporate elite, if not somewhat lower. A reason for this assumption, in part, comes from their old school ties. When people refer to old school ties in Japan they are usually referring to a very few top universities, headed by Tokyo University, Kyoto University, Hitotsubashi University, and the private universities Keio and Waseda. A high number of elites from the corporate class and government ministry are graduates from these universities. One study estimated that 32 percent of all corporate elites came from Tokyo University alone (Mannari 1974; McMillan 1985:131), while another study estimated that almost half of the top 3,000 corporate executives came from either Tokyo University, Kyoto University, Hitotsubashi University, Keio, or Waseda (Woronoff 1980:133).

Equally interesting is the high number of government ministry officials with elite school ties. As can be seen in Table 13-6, the number of officials holding the rank of section head or above who have these elite university ties ranges from 88 percent to 40 percent, with the ministries listed toward the top of this table more powerful and with a higher percentage of elite university ties.

The extent to which these old school ties bring elites closer together in their thinking, and the extent to which these ties bring these elites together after graduation, need more research. We also need to consider how these universities work as gatekeepers for elite circles, and how one gets channeled into elite status by getting into one of these universities. These questions will be considered below.

Mass Society   You will remember that C. Wright Mills (1956) argued that a mass society is a critical element in the dominance of a power elite in the United States. By a mass society he meant a population below the elites which was rather unorganized and uninformed about its interests and what power elites were doing that might harm its interests. When Mills' thesis was discussed in Chapter 7, it was noted that much of the criticism of Mills was on this point: People in the United States actually are more organized than Mills realized and class conflict from below the elites has led to reforms and improved conditions over the years. Elite groups in the United States are cer-

TABLE 13-6
PERCENT OF TOP MINISTRY OFFICIALS WHO GRADUATED FROM TOKYO UNIVERSITY

Officials, section chief and above, from	Percent graduated from Tokyo University
Ministry of Finance	88.6%
Ministry of Foreign Affairs	76.0
National Land Agency	73.5
Autonomy Agency	70.5
Ministry of Transportation	68.5
Ministry of Construction	67.5
Ministry of Agriculture & Forestry	64.7
Ministry of International Trade & Industry (MITI)	63.7
Ministry of Labor	61.7
Ministry of Justice	60.7
Economic Planning Agency	60.0
Ministry of Education	60.0
Defense Agency	57.9
Environment Agency	55.9
Ministry of Postal Services	50.8
Ministry of Health & Welfare	48.6
Prime Minister's Office	45.9
National Police Agency	44.9
Science & Technology Agency	44.9
Administrative Management Agency	40.5
Average for all National Government	62.3

Source: Rohlen (1983:91).

tainly still powerful, but they do have to worry about challenges to their power. Useem (1984), for example, has found that the corporate elite mobilization just before and during the Reagan years was a response to the threat from other classes felt by corporate elites.

In Japan, however, most people agree that a mass society view fits their country better than it does the United States (Nakane 1970; Vogel 1971:98, 109; Fukutake 1981; Reischauer 1987:196). In Japan we have seen how the group is more important to people than it is in an individualistic society like the United States, and it would therefore seem logical that the Japanese would form groups around any kind of interest or activity. However, the opposite is actually the case. There are fewer voluntary organizations in Japan than in other industrial nations (Woronoff 1980:36–42; van Wolferen 1989).

It is, in fact, *because* the group is so important in Japan that the Japanese have difficulty forming new interest groups. As one social scientist puts it, "It may be that in the name of groupism some sections of Japanese society have perfected the production of Herbert Marcuse's 'one-dimensional' man, or C. Wright Mills' 'cheerful robot'" (Sugimoto 1986:68–69). Their attachment to the family and work groups is so strong that little time is left to worry about conditions or problems outside these groups (Nakane 1970:149; Doi 1981:42).

Thus, it can be said that the group is so strong in Japan, and loyalty to the group and its leader is so important, it is possible to use this group orientation to manipulate people so that they are less critical of authority, or at least less willing to criticize authority.

This is not to say Japanese people never form interest groups or protest. Especially when the interests of an already existing group are threatened, such as the threat to farm villagers from the building of the Narita airport (Apter and Nagayo 1984), protest in Japan can be very persistent and strong. In 1989 women were surprisingly active in protesting against and voting against the LDP (due to a new sales tax, the Recruit stock scandal, and sex scandals involving politicians), resulting in the loss of control by the LDP of the upper house of the Diet. But with a few exceptions, this type of interest group organization is less common in Japan (Smith 1983).

In this context of a mass society we must finally mention the place of the mass media in Japan. Journalists in Japan can be very critical of the government or corruption, but most observers charge that this does not happen often (Fukutake 1981:99; Christopher 1983; van Wolferen 1989:93–100). It was the Japanese press which kept up the coverage of the Lockheed payoff scandal, which led to the resignation and conviction of Prime Minister Tanaka in the 1970s, and it was the Japanese press which kept the Recruit stock scandal before the nation until arrests and resignations led to the downfall of Prime Minister Takeshita in 1989. But in these cases and others, the stories first broke in lesser-known or foreign newspapers. Journalists in Japan, in other words, are not noted for looking hard behind the scenes of power to keep the Japanese people informed.

Taken together, the above information indicates that C. Wright Mills' idea of a power elite does seem to apply more in Japan than in the United States. However, the question remains as to why, if the power elite is so powerful, the level of inequality remains lower in Japan. But, we have more issues to consider before we can answer this question toward the end of this chapter.

ACHIEVEMENT AND ASCRIPTION IN MODERN JAPAN

We have seen that industrial societies require class systems with relatively more achievement criteria in class placement than do the preindustrial stratification systems of feudalism or caste, which have more extensive ascriptive elements. A modern industrial society simply cannot be competitive if most of its members are given highly skilled or top authority positions mostly because of the status of their birth, race, religion, or some other ascriptive criteria. However, we have also seen that all industrial societies contain a *mixture* of ascriptive and achievement rules determining class placement. It is time to consider the mix of these ascriptive and achievement factors behind Japan's class system. As we did in Chapter 11 for the United States, we will consider the extent of social mobility in Japan and the process of class and status attainment, which must also include an examination of Japan's educational system. We will find that Japan in many ways has a greater degree of equality of opportunity, which is to say there are more achievement factors operating in Japan than in the United States or other industrial societies. However, there are some very important exceptions to the statement that Japan has more equality of opportunity. Let's consider the major exceptions first.

Race, Ethnic, and Sex Discrimination in Japan

Given the rather high degree of meritocracy or equality of opportunity found in post–World War II Japan (considered below), the discrimination against women and ethnic minorities in Japan is even more striking. With respect to the treatment of women in Japan, Westerners usually assume that the status of women is low in all Asian societies and always has been. This view, however, is inaccurate. Japan has what Americans would call the most sexist society of any industrial nation, and even more so than most of its Asian neighbors. But this has not always been the case in Japanese history.

With respect to ethnic minorities, it is necessary to first recognize that Japan's population is 97 to 98 percent racially and ethnically Japanese. The remaining 2 percent of the population are mostly Chinese and Korean minorities. Discrimination based upon ethnicity might be assumed to be a minor problem in this situation, but this assumption is also far from accurate. (We do not say race differs in the case of Japanese, Chinese, and Koreans, though many Japanese like to claim this is the case.)

Sex Discrimination   When speaking of sex discrimination it must be recognized that this concept is rather new to many societies. What would perhaps appear as sex discrimination to some would appear as "normal" or "traditional" sex role divisions to others. For most Japanese men, and even many Japanese women, as opinion polls indicate in Japan, to them what exists in Japan is described as sex role divisions, not necessarily discrimination. This also implies that many women have accepted the position given to them as "natural" because the socialization process has been effective in making them think in this manner (McKinstry and McKinstry 1991). But these ideas are changing among Japanese women (Christopher 1983:114), although women who try to have careers outside of the home face extensive resistance in Japanese society.

This discrimination in Japan begins early in life in the home (Hendry 1987:21–37). Girls in Japan are not encouraged as much as boys to achieve in education. While the mother may work hard to keep her sons' grades from falling, the same degree of attention is not given girls. It is assumed that an education is not as important for girls, and in fact too much education may harm their chances of marriage.

Like boys, about 94 percent of girls attend high school and graduate (Keizai Koho 1988), but they are much more likely to go to a high school which does not prepare students for college (Rohlen 1983; White 1987). A result of this is that men are much more likely to go to four-year universities than women. "Only 12 percent of female high school graduates enter four year universities compared with 39 percent of males. In addition, 90 percent of junior [college] students are females and 40 percent of these take majors in home economics" (Buckley and Mackie 1986:182). At the highest-ranked universities we discussed earlier in relation to Japan's power elite, the percentage of women attending is sometimes less than 10 percent (Rohlen 1983:85).

In Japan, most people marry later than in the United States (at around twenty-five to thirty, though sometimes older for men), and this means that most people meet their marriage partner after their education, and often on the job. What this means for women is that employment usually comes after education and before marriage (and it should be noted that Japan has one of the highest rates of people being married in the world). At marriage, and especially with children, women are expected to stop working. In the past, in fact, women were actually fired from their jobs after marriage. Though forcing women to leave their job after marriage is against Japanese law today, it often continues informally (Cook and Hayashi 1980; Buckley and Mackie 1986). Figure 13-1 indicates a more extensive "M" pattern on the graph for Japanese women in contrast to women in the United States: That is, the labor force participation is high for Japanese women in their early twenties, then drops until women are in their forties and the children are out of the home. The kinds of employment open to women in Japan, therefore, are not likely to be career jobs. There is a high concentration of women in lower white-collar and service jobs considered to be temporary. A result is also a high rate of male/female

FIGURE 13-1
Labor force participation for Japanese women by age, 1983.

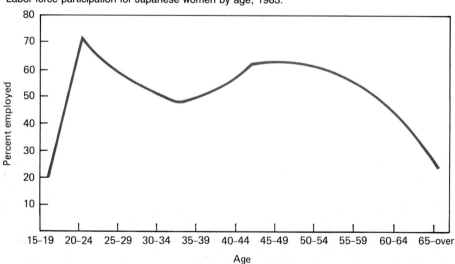

income inequality, as indicated in Table 13-7, when women are in jobs that do not as likely lead to career advancement. Another cause of this pattern of less income for women is a greater concentration of women in the periphery sector rather than the core sector of the economy (Brinton 1989), to an even greater extent than in the United States.

Still another cause of the income inequality between men and women in Japan is related to authority structures. We saw in an earlier chapter that part of the income inequality in the United States is related to the low authority position of women: As seen in Table 13-8, the authority positions of Japanese women in the economy are even lower. A Japanese government study found the actual authority of women in the economy even lower. The survey of 1,000 top corporations in Japan found only 0.3 percent of the real decision-making positions in these corporations to be held by women (Woronoff 1980:91).

We began this section by noting that sex discrimination has not always been so extensive throughout Japanese history. There have been powerful women figures and even some empresses, though the last one ruled in 770 A.D. (Reischauer and Craig 1978:16). And in rural areas women have usually experienced less discrimination (Hane 1982:79). One of the most important factors that increased the practice of sex discrimination and rigid sex role divisions was the institutionalization of the samurai values in the Meiji constitution in the late 1800s. It has only been since World War II with the new constitution that these laws have been changed. Women in Japan can now vote, own property, start their own businesses, and even *keep their children* in the case of divorce (Buckley and Mackie 1986). With this new constitution there has been some slow improvement in opportunities for women in Japan, but traditions are hard to break, especially when women's attitudes still in large degree conform to the values instituted by the old Meiji constitution.

We will close this section with an example of what most people would see as a positive aspect of Japan but which, in fact, has a negative side. Japan has the lowest divorce rate of any industrial nation. But when we ask why, we find that one major reason is the lack of options for women outside of marriage.

TABLE 13-7
MALE/FEMALE INCOME INEQUALITY IN PRIVATE SECTOR, JAPAN, 1985

Size of firm	Male annual income (1,000 yen)	Female annual income (1,000 yen)	Average years employed	
			Male	Female
Under 10 million yen in assets	3,783	1,928	10.7	8.5
10 million yen	3,969	1,997	10.4	7.2
50 million yen	4,190	2,050	10.6	6.6
100 million yen	4,588	2,165	12.4	6.1
1,000 million yen	5,594	2,678	15.9	7.4
Total average	4,510	2,147	12.4	7.4

Source: Keizai Koho (1988:69).

TABLE 13-8
COMPARATIVE PERCENTAGE OF ADMINISTRATIVE AND MANAGERIAL POSITIONS HELD
BY WOMEN, 1982

Country	Percent administrative/managerial positions held by women
Japan	6.0
United States	28.3
Sweden	19.4
West Germany	17.1
South Korea	3.0

Source: Foreign Press Center (1985:82).

The employment women can find is usually not enough to support themselves and their children. And, as noted above, before recent changes in Japan, when parents divorced the children almost always went to the father. The mother even lacked rights over her children. But though there has been change, currently only half of all mothers in divorce cases are given custody of their children (Vogel 1971; Taylor 1983).

Race and Ethnic Discrimination   We can begin this section with one of the most interesting cases of discrimination—the discrimination against *burakumin*. *Burakumin* are racially indistinguishable from all other Japanese and cannot be considered an ethnic group despite their treatment and separation in past centuries. In the late 1960s, however, a national poll found that about 70 percent of the Japanese think that *burakumin* are a different race (Hame 1982:139).

In our short history of stratification in Japan we saw that *burakumin* are former outcaste members of the quasi-caste system that existed in Tokugawa Japan (1600s to 1863). These people existed as low-status people before this time, probably due to their jobs of killing and dealing with the remains of dead animals, a way of life which violated Buddhist principles. During the Tokugawa period their low status was made permanent and hereditary under the new caste laws. With the fall of the Tokugawa shogunate, the modernization efforts of the new Meiji government led to elimination of their legal status as outcastes in 1871. This change in the legal status of *burakumin* led to many protests and riots against these people, such as the one in Fukuoka, in which 100,000 participants burned about 2,200 homes (Hane 1982:144).

Today it is estimated there are about 2 million Japanese with *burakumin* background. They continue to experience extensive discrimination, even though one must look very hard to find out that a person has this background. But they do look hard. As Coser (1956, 1967), among others, has pointed out, when there is a strong in-group sense and stress on conformity in any society there seems to be a need for an out-group of deviants to be looked down upon. The *burakumin* seem to fill this role in Japanese society. For example, before marriage or hiring a new employee it is still common to have a detective agency check the background of a person for *burakumin* ancestors. This is a primary reason that the rate of intramarriage for *burakumin* is still about 90 percent today (Hane 1982:149).

Two other groups receiving extensive discrimination are Koreans and the relatively few Chinese who live in Japan. Both groups came to Japan primarily in the twentieth century, with most Chinese coming from Taiwan, which was held by Japan as a colony from 1895 until the end of World War II. Koreans also came to Japan primarily after Japan took control of Korea in 1910, with many coming as forced laborers in mines during World War II. The prejudice and discrimination directed against Koreans was symbolized in the riots which broke out against Koreans living in Japan after the great Tokyo earthquake of 1923. These riots, which started as "scapegoat attacks" from rumors that Koreans were poisoning the drinking water after the earthquake, killed as many as 5,000 Koreans living in Japan (Mitchell 1967; Taylor 1983:60).

Before World War II Koreans in Japan *and* in Korea were forced to speak Japanese and even change their names to Japanese names. And though it was made easier for Koreans who had lived in Japan for many years to become Japanese citizens in the 1970s, very few have been able or willing to do so, even though 75 percent of Koreans in Japan today were born in Japan (Lee and De Vos 1981). The intermarriage rate between Koreans and Japanese has been rising since the 1970s when the rate of Koreans marrying Japanese was around 40 percent, indicating less prejudice among young Japanese and Koreans.

Studies of *burakumin* and Koreans in particular show that the material and psychological effects of discrimination are similar to those found among minorities in the United States (De Vos and Wagatsuma 1966; Lee and De Vos 1981). For minorities, discrimination leads to poverty and psychological problems of self-identity and self-evaluation, which further lead to lower education, delinquency, and poverty.

Social Mobility and Status Attainment in Japan

Since World War II in Japan there has been an increasing number of sociologists doing research on social mobility. Kunio Odaka, his student Kin'ichi Tominaga, and finally his student Atsushi Naoi, all originally from Tokyo University, have been pursuing a number of studies of social mobility and status attainment.

Because the results of these studies are mostly similar to those in the United States (that we covered in Chapter 11), at this point we need only consider some of the important differences. In short, we find that there is somewhat more social mobility from lower-class positions in Japan, and some increase in the overall circulation mobility rate since the 1950s, all indicating a bit more equality of opportunity in Japan than in the United States or Europe today.

In particular, Naoi and Ojima (1989) have found circulation mobility (mobility up and down due to equality of opportunity and not simply an increase of jobs at the top) increased in Japan from the 1950s through the 1960s, and began to level off in the 1970s to 1985. In this same period they found a similar pattern for income inequality—it was first reduced and than leveled off more recently. Through examination of this Japanese data, Ishida, Goldthorpe, and Erikson (1987) have found a higher rate of mobility out of the working class and into the middle class, and less movement down to working-class positions from people born above compared to other industrial nations. The rate of working-class inheritance in Japan is especially low compared to Europe, where 39 to 78 percent of those born in the working class stay in that class, compared to only 21 percent in Japan. It appears that much of the mobility out of the working class and into middle-class positions in Japan is related to Japan's recent and rapid growth. Japan's industrialization started after that of Europe and the United States, allowing it to copy some advanced technology during its industrial takeoff. Japan therefore skipped over some of the early stages of industrialization that create more working-class jobs.

There is also evidence that class background is somewhat less important to status attainment (both educational attainment and occupational attainment) in Japan compared to the United States (Tominaga and Naoi 1978). This, of course, means more equality of opportunity, which is partly explained by the lower degree of inequality in Japan to begin with, but also by the homogeneous society and culture which has already been discussed. In other words, when there is less separation between classes, class is therefore a less important factor influencing where people end up in life. However, we can also see that part of the reason that there is somewhat more equality of opportunity in Japan relates to their educational system.

Education in Japan   The strengths of the Japanese educational system lie in (1) its ability to cram the heads of Japanese students with an amazing amount of facts and information so that they score above all other nations on comparative math and science tests (Lynn 1988), and (2) the ties between educational institutions and companies or agencies that employ these students (Rosenbaum and Kariya 1989). These ties help assure that Japanese students receive enough math and science to cope with a modern industrial society, and that jobs are waiting for them when they graduate. However, the Japanese educational system is poor in producing creative students and in giving second chances to students who do not do as well in earlier school grades. Whether a student does well or not in school is somewhat less related to class background than in the United States, but once a student's abilities are judged to be high or low, even in the early years of school, this judgment has a very strong effect on what that student's class position will be later in life.

The Japanese school system is much like that in the United States in the grade levels through which a student must pass. For elementary school through the junior high school grades students are required to attend school. These schools are highly regulated by the central government through the Ministry of Education so that all subjects and how they are taught are the same all over Japan. Also important, because these are almost all public schools and because there is little class segregation in housing areas in Japan, students of all class backgrounds are mixed in the same schools (Rohlen 1983:119–129).

With the beginning of high school, however, this changes dramatically. Over 90 percent of Japanese students go on to high school, but now the high schools are ranked by ability level and require tuition payments from parents. Most important are the high school entrance exams which determine which high school a student goes to. The high schools with good records of getting students into the best universities prepare their students well to pass the college entrance exam. Other high schools are not so good at doing so, and then there are schools which do not even try to do so, but rather train students for working-class jobs after high school. Once the student has taken the exam and been placed in a particular high school, it is very difficult to change. Thus, much of the remaining life of a student has been determined by the high school he or she has entered, and therefore which level of university, if any, entered.

As may be expected, there is much pressure on students to do well on these high school entrance exams and then on the college entrance exams. Few Japanese parents are willing to depend upon what their children learn in the public schools. Thus, they spend considerable money on "cram schools" (*juku*) that usually meet several days a week after regular school hours (Rohlen 1983:104). Because of class differences in the ability to pay for *juku* and the motivation and understanding of the importance of doing so, during the high school years we find that a tracking system (through attending separate high schools) by class exists, which tends to reproduce the class system, although less so than in the United States.

A result of this tracking, based on test scores after the junior high school years, leads to class differences in university attendance. There are more students from the working class at top Japanese universities such as Tokyo University (about 14 percent) than there are at elite universities in the United States (Vogel 1979). But like the United States, working-class and even lower-middle-class students are underrepresented at the best Japanese universities. For example, the nine national universities in Japan (Tokyo University, Kyoto University, Hiroshima University, etc.) are among the top in the nation, with only a few private universities included. Even though the government-supported national universities are relatively inexpensive to attend, 34 percent of the students come from the top 20 percent income families and only 14 percent come from the lowest 20 percent income families (Rohlen 1983:138). These data indicate that the percentage of students from upper-income groups in Japan has been slowly increasing since the 1950s when the full force of educational reform of the Occupation began.

In summary, evidence suggests there is more equality of opportunity in Japan than in most other industrial nations, including the United States. However, there are limits to equality of opportunity. Even though the public schools through the junior high grade levels treat students equally (with no tracking, no special programs for bright students or low-achieving students, and no class-segregated schools), there are other factors in the family that give students from higher-class families an advantage.

INEQUALITY AND STATUS RANKING IN JAPAN

In this concluding section on social stratification in Japan we will consider two final questions which are to some degree interrelated. The first pertains to what we can call status ranking in modern Japan, and the second pertains to the relatively low level of income inequality in modern Japan.

In introducing these questions we can reexamine some of the apparent contradictions in the Japanese stratification system noted at the beginning of this chapter. You will remember that we found high stress concerning status ranking and status difference rituals in Japan. We have seen that it is built into the language as well as existing in all kinds of social interactions to a degree not found in other industrial societies. But in the face of this concern for status ranking and ranking things in general, we found much less income inequality in Japan. In the United States this situation is reversed; there is high material inequality but less concern for status rituals in social interaction (Sennett 1974).

We also found evidence that a power elite seems to dominate Japan to a greater extent than in the United States. So why are there fewer extremes of wealth and income in Japan as compared to the United States? Why is the income of top corporate executives in Japan *much less* than the income of corporate executives in the United States? There has not been enough research to fully answer these questions, though we can make some strong inferences. In what follows we must first examine status ranking in Japan in more detail.

Class, Status, and Power in Japan

Max Weber, we have seen, offered a multidimensional view of social stratification in his criticism of Marx's one-dimensional view of stratification. Weber stressed that all three dimensions of stratification (class, status, and power or party) will exist in a society, but that one or two of these dimensions will be more important in a society, depending upon the kind of stratification system that exists in that society. In the early stages of capitalist societies we found that the class dimension (ownership and control of industrial capital) was most important. Then, in advanced industrial societies we found that both class and authority (power) became important. And because of the population size and diversity of advanced industrial societies, we found that the status dimension has become less important.

In Chapter 5 we examined research on religious monasteries (Della Fave and Hillery 1980) and Israeli kibbutzim (Rosenfeld 1951; Spiro 1970) which indicated that the status dimension of social stratification could be dominant only in societies with a very high degree of value consensus. In other words, there must be extensive agreement over values if people are to agree who deserves top status or honor rewards, and such agreement over values usually comes only in a small, homogeneous society. This is one of the reasons we rejected the primary usefulness of functional theories of social stratification in advanced industrial societies.

It must be stressed that social stratification in Japan today must be understood with reference to the class and authority dimensions of social stratification as in the United States. However, to a greater extent than in the United States, it appears that the status dimension of social stratification is important in Japan. Among other ways, this is reflected in the status rituals and the levels of speech in the Japanese language. Top executives of major corporations do not get as much pay as U.S. executives, but when they enter a room the lower-ranking workers will likely bow and speak to them in very respectful language. College professors in Japan receive even less pay than American professors, but when they enter the classroom students will show extreme respect (though they don't often bow in the classroom any more). And even on the street, when a professor is interacting with a stranger, the body language and level of speech will suddenly become very respectful when the professor's status is revealed (as only a small example of the change, "*Tanaka san*" will change to "*Tanaka sensei*" in addressing the professor). In addition, many requests made to store clerks or government agencies may be granted that would not have been before the high status of the person was known.

While it may appear that the importance of status rewards in Japan is in contradiction to our above rejection of the importance of status ranking in advanced industrial societies more generally, we can actually say "it is the exception which fits the rule." To understand this you must remember that status can be important in monasteries or kibbutzim because these groups are small and have a high level of value consensus. Japan, with a population only about half that of the United States, is not small. However, Japan is made up of people who are 97 to 98 percent racially and ethnically Japanese. They are strongly socialized into a common value system by the family and schools, and neither religion nor class differences create significant value conflicts in Japan. Thus, while there are some regional differences in language accents, most Japanologists acknowledge that the nation overall has more value consensus and is unified to a greater degree than any other nation of its size (Reischauer and Craig 1978). These conditions, therefore, would lead us to expect a greater importance for the status dimension of social stratification.

We have also seen that the status dimension of social stratification is primary in a caste system, as in the Indian caste system before British disruption. From about 1600 to 1863 under the Tokugawa shogunate, Japan had a caste system that in many ways was as rigid as that found in early India. It has been only a little more than 100 years since Japan's Tokugawa caste system fell. Traditions and culture change at a slower pace than social organization or technology. Thus, for this reason alone we would expect that status would be a more important dimension of stratification in Japan than in the United States.

A concluding point is that corporate executives, college professors, top ministry officials, and others with high status in Japan can be given extensive deference and respect because people agree that these are the people who have achieved top positions in the status hierarchy. Very few people in these positions of high status are wealthy (including the corporate executives), but you will seldom hear a variation of the phrase "if you are so smart (or well respected), why aren't you rich" in Japan. That phrase would miss the point for most Japanese who see status *in itself* as an important reward.

There is little doubt that Japan is changing in this respect. Some Japanese linguists claim that the formal speech showing respect is used less by Japanese young people today (Ohno 1979; Kerbo and Sha 1987). In Japan the older people complain about this as well as the new materialistic values of the young people. There are opinion polls showing that young people are motivated more by money than loyalty to the company. All of this is in keeping with our view that it is the material or economic substructure of the society which shapes the society more than cultural values in the long run. As Japan has more experience with advanced industrialization, these old deference rituals and the stress on status will be reduced. However, we may have a long time to wait to see if the cultural base of Japan, which has stressed status ranking and extensive deference to those judged to have high status, will continue to keep Japan unusual among advanced industrial societies.

Low Inequality in Japan: Some Causes

It is time to bring some of the things we have learned about Japan to bear on the question of why Japan has lower income inequality than other industrial nations. It must be remembered that inequality in Japan certainly exists, but it sets the lower boundary for the industrial nations and we need to know why. Two things are clear: First, in contrast to a few countries (such as Sweden), Japan's low level of inequality is *not* primarily due to government policies, welfare programs, or other government action (Verba et al. 1987:274; though these authors neglect the small contribution made by Japan's tax policies noted below). Second, we cannot say that Japan's low level of inequality is primarily due to cultural values. These, no doubt, have some effect, but remember that before World War II Japan had probably the highest level of wealth and income inequality of all industrial nations. Cultural effects do not come and go with such speed or ease.

What follows, however, is to some degree speculative. It is clear that some of the factors we will cover below are reasons for Japan's low inequality. But with little research on this question thus far, we do not know which of the following are most important, or how much more important they are than other factors. We will begin with those factors which seem most important.

1. Toward the bottom of society, there is very little poverty in Japan. Though the Japanese government does not measure poverty as often and in a manner similar to the United States, the best estimate is a 1.5 percent poverty rate in Japan compared to 13 to 14 percent rate in the United States (Taylor 1983; Hendry 1987:145; Reischauer 1987). This is not because of adequate welfare programs in Japan. Rather, with a homogeneous culture, a very good educational system treating everybody alike through the junior high school years, a strong family system, and little discrimination against *male* heads of households (except *burakumin,* Ainu, Koreans, and Chinese), there is very little of what we could call an underclass in Japan. Almost everyone is rather competent, with adequate socialization and educational skills and relatively little psychological damage from poverty and/or discrimination. With a strong economy providing jobs (the unemployment rate was around 2 percent in 1989), the vast majority of the population is capable of performing these jobs.

2. Related to this is a labor shortage in Japan's rapidly growing economy. In addition, the country's economy contains many small shops, small farms, and a huge wholesale distribution system which creates many more jobs in these economic functions than in most industrial societies. The Japanese pay for this in higher consumer prices due to the small-scale operations of farms and retail shops, but benefits include less unemployment and less inequality.

3. At the top of the stratification system (in corporations and important government positions) there are restraints on high-income demands. The feeling of being part of the homogeneous group (some say the country seems like an extended kinship system), and norms against being too different from others in the society, have produced norms which restrict pay demands (Vogel 1971:160; Abegglen and Stalk 1985:195; Verba et al. 1987). And it is easier to enforce these norms restricting the pay of elites when both workers and executives are expected to (and do) stay with the company for life, rather than moving around to any job that will offer a higher wage.

It is also argued that the devastation brought on by World War II created a feeling that unity was necessary to rebuild an economy in which a majority of the population was close to starvation. Excessive wages paid to those at the top would have worked against this needed unity. It was also in this context that the *nenko* system of setting wages according to age and need was developed, which did not exist before the war (Kalleberg and Lincoln 1988:126). All of this is combined with a feeling of group commitment, which we have seen is stronger in Japan. Top executives feel this group pressure as well, and it restricts their pay demands. The *zaibatsu* of pre–World War II Japan felt more like the ruling samurai and shogun of old—above the commoners and therefore entitled to more. The arrogance of the old *zaibatsu* and militaristic elite before the war has made anyone who tries to copy it severely criticized in today's Japan (Reischauer 1987).

4. There is less extensive family or individual ownership of the major means of production in post–World War II Japan. This is primarily because of the rather socialistic reforms of the U.S. Occupational Forces in Japan, which re-

duced ownership of the old *zaibatsu* and redistributed the land. We have seen in empirical research on inequality in the United States that the property structure contributes about equally to income inequality compared to the occupational and bureaucratic authority structures. Less private wealth in corporate stock means less income to a rich elite. There is criticism by the Japanese people of a new and growing wealthy group based upon real estate in Japan, which has developed during the late 1980s and 1990s. But so far the few wealthy people in Japan continue to be restricted to the new real estate rich and some private business owners. The vast majority of people in Japan, including corporate executives, receive almost all of their income from a salaried job.

5. It seems likely that the relatively low income of the top position holders is in part possible because of the importance of status inequality in Japan (Kerbo and McKinstry 1987). The extensive consensus over who should be given high status (due to achievement) means that the company's workers, shop clerks, people on the street, in short, almost everyone in society, will treat the top position holders with an abundance of deference. In contrast, American workers and others in positions below the top would be quite likely to say or think, "the SOB only got that job because his family is rich; he isn't any better than I am." We have found that the Davis and Moore (1945) functional theory of stratification can at times be useful, and that people are motivated to attain high positions because of the promise of higher rewards. In Japan this means that abundant status rewards have made abundant material rewards less necessary.

6. Finally, government policies since World War II have had some effect in reducing income inequality. For the average-income person in Japan the tax rate is almost identical to that of the United States, and both countries have low tax rates compared to European nations (Keizai Koho 1988:84). However, for 1987 taxes, the tax rate for low-income people in Japan was *much* lower than in the United States, and the tax rate for upper-income groups was *much* higher in Japan compared to the United States. For example, a $300,000 annual income in Japan (which is rare compared to the United States) was taxed at an effective rate of almost 70 percent, while the same income in the United States had an effective tax rate of around 35 percent. Corporate taxes follow a similar pattern: The effective corporate tax rate in Japan was slightly over 50 percent, but around 30 percent in the United States. We noted earlier that in 1980 the pay gap between corporate executives in Japan and new workers was about 7 to 1 after taxes (about 37 to 1 in the United States): This gap would have been 14 to 1 in Japan without figuring in taxes (Abegglen and Stalk 1985:192).

There is currently a perception of growing income and wealth inequality among the Japanese people that has been producing an angry reaction, according to a 1988 Japanese government study called "White Paper on National Life" (Keizai Kikaku Cho Hen 1988). The anger, at least so far, seems out of proportion to the actual increase in inequality in Japan. But there is no question that the anger existed in Japan in the late 1980s and still exists in the early

1990s. For example, election polls showed that the defeat of the LDP in upper-house elections in 1989 was mostly because the Japanese believed the new 3 percent sales tax (Japan did not have one before), along with tax breaks for upper-income groups which were passed in the Diet at the same time, would further increase inequality. This case, as well as empirical studies (Verba et al. 1987), indicate that normative support for equality is much stronger in Japan than in the United States.

Social Stratification in Japan: A Conclusion

Though modern Japan is an industrial nation with many important cultural differences compared to the United States and Europe, we find more similarities than differences in Japan's system of social stratification. The occupational structure, bureaucratic authority structures, and property structure help determine a person's place in the class system just as in the United States. But there are differences. The property structure generates less inequality since World War II, status ranking is more important, social mobility up from lower positions is somewhat higher, and perhaps most important, income inequality is substantially lower compared to the United States.

Japan has many social problems and conditions that most people in the United States would view in a negative way (Woronoff 1980, 1981, 1986; Taylor 1983). We should, therefore, be cautious not to overidealize Japan as many people have recently because of its economic success, low crime, lack of problems with drugs, and low divorce rate. However, Japan's low level of inequality is important and has many positive functions for the society. We have listed some reasons for less inequality above, but we will close by speculating on some of the possible consequences of less inequality for Japan.

One of the most striking contrasts between Japan and the United States is in the crime rate—the United States has the highest of industrial nations, Japan the lowest. There are clearly many reasons for Japan's low crime rate which we do not have time to consider. Studies of nations and comparisons of U.S. cities, however, indicate that the level of inequality is significantly related to crime (Blau and Blau 1982). The United States has the highest income inequality, Japan has the lowest.

Japan has less welfare spending—in part, because of low inequality. Compared to other major industrial nations, Japan has the lowest rate of welfare spending per capita and as a percentage of GNP. However, a recent study combined the actual rate of welfare spending with a ratio of need (extent of poverty, unemployment, aged in need of care, etc.) and found that Japan moved from last to second (just behind the Netherlands) in welfare support (welfare spending per need) when using this ratio (Gilbert 1987).

Perhaps most important for the United States today, many people now argue that Japan's economic competitiveness is at least partially related to its low inequality (Abegglen and Stalk 1985:196; Dore 1987). Less inequality creates less conflict between management and labor and more unity in the factory. There is more respect for management because of a feeling that management holds its position because of merit rather than a wealthy family or "connections." As well, there is less illiteracy among workers since there is less poverty to create the extensive educational failure which exists in the United States.

Finally, we can conclude this list by reexamining the functional theory of stratification. You will remember that in Chapter 5 we discussed Tumin's (1953) critique of the functional theory of social stratification by listing what he thought were the dysfunctions of social stratification and inequality. Many factors help produce social problems or their lack in a society, but if you reread the list of dysfunctions of inequality listed by Tumin in Chapter 5, you will see they do seem to fit the case of Japan versus the United States rather well.

NOTES

1 We can use the phrase "I will cut it for you" in Japanese to make this point. The following lines all say this same thing, but with changes in the words, verb endings, and honorific status markers to indicate the relative status of the speaker versus the listener—from speaking very formally to someone high in status in the first sentences, to speaking very informally in the last sentences (Goldstein and Tamura 1975:113; Kerbo and Sha 1987):

Watakushi ga o-kiri shite sashiagemasho.
Watakushi ga o-kiri itashimasho.
Watakushi ga o-kiri shimasho.
Watashi ga o-kiri shimasho.
Watashi ga kitte agemasho.
Watashi ga kitte ageru wa yo. (women speakers only)
Watashi ga kitte yaru wa yo. (women speakers only)
Boku ga kitte ageru yo. (men speakers only)
Boku ga kitte yaro. (men speakers only)
Ore ga kitte yaru yo. (men speakers only)

2 There is, however, increasing archeological evidence that very early in Japan's history there was much influence from Korea (Befu 1981:22; Covell and Covell 1984). But because of prejudice against Koreans in Japan, it is charged, this fact has been covered up. A long-standing joke in Japan is that it is difficult to get funding for archeological sites in southwestern Japan, especially on the northern part of Kyushu Island, because they might find that some of the earliest emperors of Japan were Korean in origin.

3 One of the earliest accounts of the Japanese comes from Chinese visitors to Japan around 297 A.D. These Chinese travelers described the Japanese as "law-abiding people, fond of drink, concerned with divination and ritual purity, familiar with agriculture, expert at fishing and weaving, and living in a society of strict social differences indicated by tattooing or other bodily markings" (Reischauer and Craig 1978:5–7). It may well be that all of these things always applied to the Japanese more than some of their Asian neighbors, but the part about a society of strict social differences applied to Japan during the Tokugawa period more than at any other time.

4 This aspect of the Japanese occupational structure sounds unbelievable to most people in the United States. They ask, how can they make workers work hard and where is the incentive for working hard? Two things must be understood about Japan to make the above sound logical: They both involve the age ranking in the society noted earlier and the importance of group relations in Japan discussed in the beginning of this chapter. With age ranking being very important, it would be disruptive to require a worker to take orders from a boss who is younger. This problem is solved by promoting everyone together by age. Then, because group ties are so strong, and the pressure to sacrifice for the group so important in the more collectivist-oriented society of Japan, promotions by some system of objective merit are not so necessary. The group of co-workers applies pressure on each other to perform well for the group. This is one reason that most Japanese workers actually do not take all of their given vacation time (though the young are changing). The Japanese government in the late 1980s was actually involved in a major publicity campaign to make workers stop working so hard and take all of their vacation time! (This is not just being done for humanitarian reasons, I should add. They need more consumption and less saving to help their economy.) Because of the strength and importance of group ties in Japan it is believed that promotion by merit would actually do more harm than good in productivity because it could create hard feelings among the group members when some are promoted and others are not.

5 This practice of forced retirement is especially beneficial to company profits because, as we have seen, younger workers will be hired to replace them at a much lower wage. But this practice is very harmful to older workers because good pensions do *not* go with this retirement in most cases. They must find another job with a smaller company, which explains why there is a steep drop in income for older workers. And this lack of adequate pensions or an extensive Social Security program by the Japanese government is in part why we find that far more people over sixty-five are employed in Japan than in any other major industrial society.

6 It should be noted that two of the most wealthy people in the world in 1989 were Japanese brothers who own the Seibu department store chain. However, this money did not come from executive salaries, and is rather rare in Japan. It came from skyrocketing real estate values in Tokyo, and in many ways this is only paper money. If the owners try to sell this real estate to realize a huge profit, a big percentage of it will be taken away in taxes. There are fewer wealthy people in Japan than in the United States, and the few really wealthy who can be found in Japan are small business owners (who do not work for a salary like the executives in big companies), and people who were lucky enough to have real estate in places such as Tokyo at the right time (Dore 1987:86).

7 To give just one example of many, I have observed at least a 30-minute meeting by five postal workers in Japan over a request that a four-copy form required on thirty-two boxes be filled out in a slightly different way so as to save at least 5 hours of work filling out new forms. The request was finally granted, but not until the indecisive meeting of the five postal workers was resolved by a phone call to a higher authority, presumably to a head office in Tokyo. *That* is bureaucracy.

SOCIAL STRATIFICATION IN COMMUNIST SOCIETIES: THE SOVIET UNION

Early 1990 is not a good time to write about the Soviet Union, or any other communist society, for that matter. What is set down on paper in early 1990 may be old history before the end of the year, or even the month. On March 26, 1989, Gorbachev's *perestroika* (restructuring) and *glasnost* (openness) progressed to the first real national elections in the Soviet Union's seventy-one-year history. With this election of 1,500 representatives to the Congress of People's Deputies, about one-third of the regional Communist Party leaders were voted out of office. Among those elected (through one of the positions reserved for organizational representatives) was the famous scientist and dissident, Andrei Sakharov, who only a short time before had been under house arrest for many years. (And when Sakharov died in December of 1989, there followed one of the biggest funerals, except for those given a head of state, that Moscow has had in many years.) With this first step toward democracy there came a flood of new demands for change and more freedoms from many of the formerly independent republics in the Soviet Union. While some of this change was expected, the degree of change and its speed were *not* expected only a year or so before. But the most dramatic changes of late 1989 came elsewhere.

In communist (and soon to be formerly communist) Eastern Europe, on August 19, 1989, one of Poland's Solidarity leaders (Tadeusz Mazowiecki) became the first noncommunist prime minister of an Eastern European country since World War II. This occurred soon after the communist government of Poland allowed the labor union, Solidarity, to legally exist for the first time, and then called for national elections. Solidarity candidates took a majority of seats in Poland's parliament in this national election during June of 1989. Many of the Solidarity candidates who won office had recently been in jail.

Then, in November and December of 1989, more events began to occur with a rapidity that caused the world to look on in amazement. First, the Berlin Wall fell and the East German communist government resigned; then, the communist government in Czechoslovakia resigned; a popular revolution led to the fall of the communist government in Romania; and other communist governments in Eastern Europe were promising reforms and scheduling multiparty elections. Then, on October 3, 1990, Germany was reunified and East Germany ceased to exist. Just a few months before all of this occurred, however, on the other side of the world a massive reform movement in China was crushed by the old communist leaders. Hundreds, most likely thousands, of young people were killed in and around Tiananmen Square. (And though millions of people throughout the world had watched the massacre on television, the old party leaders tried to make people believe no one was killed.)

All of these countries, and especially those in Eastern Europe and the Soviet Union, will experience more change with the new decade of the 1990s. Nearly all desire to move toward a mixed socialist/capitalist economy and many are attempting to move toward a more predominantly capitalist mixed economy like those existing in Western Europe. As of 1991, there are plans to further open the Soviet economy as well, and all of these changes will affect the system of social stratification in these countries. So what can be written that has any chance of remaining accurate before the ink dries on these pages?

In the previous chapter on Japan, we found that a capitalist industrial society which has developed from an Asian culture will still have a stratification system which is roughly similar to the stratification systems we find in Western capitalist, industrial societies. We will now find that the same is true for a communist industrial society such as the Soviet Union. Even before the 1980s, because of the industrial base of the Soviet Union, there existed a system of stratification that had many similarities to that of the United States. Of course, there were some important differences, and there will continue to be some important differences found in the Soviet stratification system. However, in this chapter we will stress the basic similarities while describing why the differences remain, and then speculate on the directions in which the Soviet Union may move. Let us begin by considering some of the claims made by communist ideology.

Before proceeding, we should also consider the quality and extent of data needed to provide an accurate picture of social stratification in the Soviet Union. The Soviet Union is no doubt less closed and rigid than our popular image would have it (and this is especially so since Gorbachev has been in power), but it is clear that information is more controlled than in the United States. However, although the information we do have is less extensive than we would prefer, since the 1960s we do have much more information of better quality and reliability (Meissner 1972:73; Yanowitch 1977:xiii; Lenski 1978:365).

In a related matter it is interesting to note that sociological research does exist in most communist nations. This point is interesting because the ideal task of social science is an objective analysis of society and social relations. And although this ideal task is difficult and not always met, sociology is sometimes considered something of a threat to elites, especially elites in more authoritarian societies. For example, the study of sociology was actually prohibited in China and the Soviet Union until recently (*Footnotes* 1980; Beliaev and Butorin 1982; Shlapentokh 1987).

In the Soviet Union sociology has been allowed to exist since 1958 for two reasons (Beliaev and Butorin 1982). First, the research usually conducted by Soviet sociologists has been restricted to less sensitive questions, such as demographic changes, occupational distributions, and less political social problems (alcoholism, juvenile delinquency, family instability, and so on). We find no published works by Soviet sociologists on the abuse or outcomes of the concentration of political power. And only recently has research on income equality and unequal access to educational opportunities been published in the Soviet Union, although even here we have only limited data on elites (Yanowitch 1977; Matthews 1978; Vinokur and Ofer 1987).

Second, sociological theory in the Soviet Union (at least up to 1990) has not challenged basic Marxian ideology as interpreted by party elites. Not all sociological theory in the Soviet Union is Marxian theory. In fact, the functional theory of Talcott Parsons has gained wide appeal among Soviet sociologists (Gouldner 1970; Yanowitch 1977:9–11; Collins 1980). And in case this appeal seems puzzling, the general image of society depicted in functional theory should be considered. From the functional perspective (or uncritical order paradigm) society is based upon cooperation, there is little recognition of class conflict, and inequalities of wealth and power are considered functional for the overall society. What better image for a mature communist society that has "eliminated class conflict" could there be?

With Gorbachev in power, however, the second half of the 1980s brought changes that have begun to make the above two points less accurate. Vladimir Shlapentokh (1987), a Soviet sociologist who is now living in the United States, has recorded the history of Soviet sociology since 1958 and described the recent trends of greater freedom for Soviet sociology. And American sociologists who have been hosted by Soviet sociologists and the Soviet government write of the degree to which Gorbachev is promoting sociology, hoping that sociological research will help overcome the many social and economic problems facing Gorbachev's reforms (Molotch 1989; Shelley 1989; Swafford 1989). One of the leading Soviet sociologists and vice-president of the Soviet Sociological Association, Mikk Titma, was even promoted to a high position in the Communist Party in the Soviet Republic of Estonia (though he later resigned from the Communist Party in 1990 during Estonia's independence movement). At present, however, we continue to have only limited research on subjects such as social mobility in the Soviet Union, though enough exists for useful comparisons to be made with the United States.

THE STRUCTURAL BASE OF SOCIAL STRATIFICATION IN THE SOVIET UNION

Throughout this study of social stratification we have stressed that class inequalities are often based upon divisions within occupational, authority, and property structures in the society. In the United States, for example, we have seen how these three structures intersect to form differing class interests. Revolution and historical forces in the Soviet Union have produced only a slight alteration in this pattern; the authority and property structures have been fused. To understand this fusion it is necessary to understand the revolution and the historical forces that brought it about.

While the Russian Revolution of 1917 is a fascinating subject worthy of considerable study, we must give it only brief attention at this point. It was the conscious intent of Lenin, Stalin, Trotsky, and other Bolsheviks to create a communist state without private ownership of the means of production. But history is not made with only the conscious intent of individual leaders. Before the revolution of 1917, Russia was a rather backward country struggling to modernize and industrialize. A push toward industrialization was begun by Alexander II in the 1860s, and although some gains were made, Russia remained behind most of Europe, with much of its industrial capacity foreign-owned (Crankshaw 1976:218; Salisbury 1977:115–119; Skocpol 1979; Kennedy 1987:233–234). It was a weak economic system in the face of foreign competition, and that, combined with World War I, led the czar's government to fall to angry masses in February of 1917 (Skocpol 1979). Lenin and his party had no direct hand in this fall, but they were organized to pick up the pieces in their revolution of October 1917 (Payne 1964; Keep 1976; Solzhenitsyn 1976).

A communist state became possible in part because of the absence of a strong capitalist class (Moore 1966), and forced industrialization became necessary for the state's survival in the face of foreign and internal threats (Skocpol 1976, 1979:215). There has seldom been a revolution resulting in such a thorough break with the past (Skocpol 1979:206), but even in Russia the old traditions had a hand in shaping the future. And these old traditions were an authoritarian state, a strong secret police, and forced labor camps (Crankshaw 1976:63–69). There is abundant evidence (see Fischer 1982) that Lenin, before his death soon after the revolution, attempted to stem the power of a centralized bureaucracy (and Stalin in particular). But of course he failed (Payne 1964; Ulam 1973:217; Howe 1978:86). One reason for differing outcomes of revolution can be found in historical forces rooted in the old regime (Skocpol 1976:284), and these forces, along with military invasion from the West and civil war, resulted in a centralized, authoritarian bureaucracy that controlled the means of production. In our terms, the political authority structure and property structure were merged.

The Occupational Structure

With Stalin's forced industrialization beginning in the late 1920s, the Soviet Union did achieve rapid industrialization to the point where it was second only to the United States in gross national product in the 1980s (though by some measures Japan was second). What this means is that the Soviet Union, like any other industrial nation, has a highly developed division of labor or occupational structure. The centralized state may provide the economic planning and influence the distribution of rewards and resources, but the state cannot provide an output of goods and services without scientists, managers, technicians, and workers of all kinds. In other words, within this occupational structure are divisions based on occupational skill (as described by Weber), much as there are in the United States.

Several kinds of evidence point to basic similarities in the two occupational structures. For example, we find that rapid industrialization in the Soviet Union has produced an equally rapid increase in industrial workers (similar to the United States working class), a rapid increase in nonmanual workers (similar to the United States middle class), and a steady decline in farm laborers (see Jones 1978:523). It will be remembered that this is the precise pattern found with the process of industrialization in the United States. The same general pattern is found in Eastern European nations (see Tellenback 1978:438; Volgyes 1978:501; Chirot 1986).

There are, however, some significant differences with respect to these occupational distributions. Most importantly, Soviet nations continue to have fewer middle-class occupations than industrial working-class occupations (Connor 1988). This difference, compared with the situation in the United States, is the result of forced industrialization focused more on heavy industry and less on services, consumer goods, and marketing. In addition, Soviet nations continue to have a slightly higher proportion of farm workers (Humphrey 1988). This difference is in part the result of the above-mentioned stress on heavy industry, leading to less efficient agricultural technology, which in turn requires more farm workers.

But added to this problem is the much-publicized failure of Stalin's push toward farm collectivization. Farm collectivization, in and of itself, may not be inefficient in every case. But in the Soviet Union it has produced less farm output, requiring more farm workers. All these differences are the products of a state-controlled economy and decisions made by political elites (in the merged authority and property structure). These differences, however, must be recognized as matters of degree within broadly similar occupational structures.

Other evidence of similarities in the occupational structures of the United States and the U.S.S.R. is found with occupational prestige rankings. For example, Inkeles (1968:180–190) compared occupational prestige rankings in the U.S.S.R. with similar studies in Japan, England, New Zealand, the United States, and Germany. Inkeles (1968:180) found that "there exists among the six nations a marked degree of agreement on the relative prestige of matched occupations." A much more extensive comparison of occupational status data from industrial nations around the world by Treiman (1977) presents the same conclusion (also see Swafford 1987).

There is, however, one significant difference with the Soviet rankings when compared with those of the other five nations. In the Soviet Union working-class or skilled manual occupations are consistently ranked above many low-level nonmanual or white-collar occupations by the population (Inkeles 1968:184; Yanowitch 1977:105). As we will see in more detail later, this is no doubt related to the position of the working class in Soviet ideology and its higher income.

Finally, the similarities in occupational structures can be considered in relation to the outcomes of occupational divisions. One important outcome, of course, is income. As in the United States, national and regional data from the Soviet Union show that occupational complexity and prestige ranks are related to income (Inkeles 1968:206; Matthews 1972:81–90; Vinokur and Ofer 1987). And with another important outcome, job satisfaction, there are similarities again (Geiger 1969:287; Yanowitch 1977:151; Lenski 1978:372): "For example, in both the Soviet Union and the United States the proportion enjoying job satisfaction is very high among professional and managerial personnel, and falls steadily as one descends the occupational ladder" (Inkeles 1968:408).

If we knew nothing else about the Soviet Union (for example, if we didn't know about its authoritarian power structure) we might gather from Soviet ideology that work relations would be different from those in the United States. Because of Soviet praise of the working class and because the Soviet Union is supposed to be a nation in which the working class has taken power, we might conclude that workers are more in control of industrial production or at least have a voice in industrial management. With respect to occupational authority relations, however, the Soviet Union and the United States are very similar (Lenski 1978:373). Many Soviet studies show that industrial democracy is as far from reality in the Soviet Union as it is in the United States (Yanowitch 1977:134–161).

The similarities between the occupational structures of the United States and the Soviet Union have led many theorists (for example, Inkeles 1968; Galbraith 1971) to suggest a "convergence theory"—the idea that the United States and the Soviet Union are growing more similar. There are technocrats on top of both industrial systems, with similar occupational divisions below. As Parkin (1971:141) puts it, "Technological advances and the demands of economic progress give rise to a similar reward structure in both types of society; the organization of industry, the system of education and the occupational structure, are all highly responsive to the pressures of modernization." There is much evidence to support a convergence theory, as we will see below, but such a theory can be carried too far. Important differences remain, due to the merging of the authority and property structures in the Soviet Union (see Giddens 1973:21).

The Authority Structure

As was described with respect to social stratification in the United States, people are also divided by divisions within authority structures. Following Dahrendorf's (1959) definition of class divisions in "imperatively coordinated associations," those who give orders to the greatest number of people are on top in authority structures and those who only follow orders are on the bottom. (We can speak of degrees of authority, of course.) Authority structures are found in all aspects of society, but in modern societies those most important are located in the overall political system and the economy. Authority divisions in the political system are most pronounced in the Soviet Union. This is because state elites in the Soviet Union make decisions about what we consider the "traditional" functions of government (military, police, collective needs like education, roads, parks, etc.), as well as decisions about economic matters, because control of the economy is also in the hands of these political elites. It is unlikely that the authority and power of the state in the Soviet Union will be considerably reduced with Gorbachev's planned reforms. In other words, the authority structure of the Soviet state will remain more important compared to that of the United States. What may be changing in the Soviet Union, however, is the process by which one ascends into the political elite, and the extent of its accountability to the Soviet public; that is, a move from totalitarian party control of the state to some degree of democracy. This change to more democracy in and of itself does not mean the authority and power of the state will be reduced, especially as long as the economy remains under state control (though this may also change in the 1990s). This shift toward more democracy merits more of our consideration.

Before the democratic reforms of the late 1980s, the largest government body in the Soviet Union was the Supreme Soviet, composed of 1,500 "elected" members. From this political body were "elected" the thirty-nine representatives on the Presidium. The Supreme Soviet also "elected" the president of the nation. In March of 1979, for example, the members of the Supreme Soviet were reported to be elected with 99.99 percent of the eligible voters casting ballots for these people. The Soviet news agency, *Tass,* reported, "By their unanimous voting for the candidates, the Soviet people expressed complete support for the domestic and foreign policies of the Communist Party and the Soviet state" (quoted in *Time,* June 23, 1980:25).

The most powerful political authority structure in the Soviet Union, however, was the Communist Party, not the constitutional government. The constitutional government is in fact an arm of the party. Top government officials were, and so far still are, almost always top party members. The upper level of the Communist Party consists of 287 members of the Central Committee, who elect the fourteen Politburo members (who are similar to the board of directors of a company) and the general secretary of the Communist Party, who as of 1990 continued to be Gorbachev.

The procedures for selecting Communist Party members do not involve democratic ritual—not even the appearance of democracy is maintained. Much like the process of selection for upper-class social clubs in the United States, candidates for party membership are recommended by current members, and must then pass a screening committee (Harasymiw 1984; Remington 1988). Furthermore, the candidate must have been a member of the communist youth organization (Komsomol), which creates another selective mechanism. This process of selection has kept about 90 percent of the Soviet population out of the Communist Party.

In the past, it was the elite of the Communist Party which determined who would be placed in the state positions that had actual responsibility for running the government and the economy. And this is what has changed to a degree unexpected until the very last years of the 1980s. A new constitution has revised the political bodies in the Soviet Union and allowed real elections by the Soviet people. Candidates for elected office under this new constitution do not have to be Communist Party members (and many elected in 1989 were not party members), though as yet a multiparty system has not been established in the Soviet Union. Under the new constitution the Soviet people elect, by secret ballot, 1,500 members of the Congress of People's Deputies. Added to these 1,500 members are 750 who are selected by official Soviet organizations, such as the Communist Youth League, Soviet Women's Committee, Academy of Sciences, worker organizations, and the Communist Party (which selects 100 deputies). These deputies must run for reelection every five years.

The Congress of People's Deputies meets only twice a year, but is defined by the constitution as having final authority over state policy through approval or disapproval by a majority vote. This political body also elects the president of the nation (the state position to which Gorbachev was elected in 1989) and 450 of its members to make up the Supreme Soviet. The Supreme Soviet is a full-time legislative body, divided into two chambers, somewhat like the U.S. House of Representatives and Senate, though with equal powers. It is in these chambers of the Supreme Soviet that the nation's laws will be debated and passed, while the day-to-day administration of the government will be in the hands of a much smaller body, the Presidium of the Supreme Soviet. The Presidium is much like the U.S. President's cabinet. It is accountable to the Supreme Soviet, and ultimately to the larger Congress of People's Deputies (and, finally, to the Soviet people, as is supposed to be the case for the U.S. population with the U.S. Congress).

As noted in the beginning of this chapter, the Congress of People's Deputies is not made up only of Communist Party officials as in the past. There are multiple candidates running for each seat, and a candidate must receive at least 50 percent of the vote in the district. A runoff election is required if a 50 percent vote is not achieved. In the 1989 election, over 30 percent of the Communist Party candidates lost, and famous antiparty candidates such as Boris Yeltsin (also elected president of the Russian Republic in 1990) and Andrei Sakharov were elected (in Sakharov's case by the Soviet Academy of Sciences). Many of these candidates opposed by the party elites, including Yeltsin and Sakharov, were elected by the Congress of People's Deputies to fill seats on the Supreme Soviet.

It is, of course, too early to tell how well this new political system will work, and the outcomes of political change in the Soviet Union. But in contrast to the Eastern European countries, which have been rejecting their Communist parties since 1989, we must recognize that most of the Soviet population has been more supportive of their political system. And even in 1989 opinion polls in the Soviet Union indicate that many Soviet citizens do not be lieve that Gorbachev's reforms will be beneficial or should be attempted (*Time*, April 10, 1989:62). There has been increasing criticism of elite privilege in the Soviet Union (Yanowitch 1977:26; Matthews 1978), but political legitimacy in a general sense has been relatively high (Lenski 1978:376; Silver 1987). The important difference between the Eastern European communist (and formerly communist) countries, and some formerly independent republics in the Soviet Union (such as Estonia and Lithuania), is that communism was imposed upon the formerly independent republics by a foreign power (the Soviet Union). Thus, in the Eastern European countries and the formerly independent republics of the Soviet Union, the social movements are both anticommunist and nationalist.

To summarize, there does appear to be greater democracy in the Soviet Union with the new Soviet constitution and Gorbachev's reforms. This also means that mobility into the political elite in the Soviet Union has been made possible through the democratic process. Within the Soviet Union, the state remains strong, with a high degree of power and authority. This is in contrast to the Eastern European countries where the withdrawal of Soviet support for the imposed communist governments has led to their fall. But in contrast to capitalist industrial nations, the concentration of power in the Soviet Union is not limited to political power. Because private ownership of the means of production was eliminated after the revolution of 1917, top political authority has been merged with top economic authority. We have found interlocks between political elites and economic elites in the United States, and to some degree political and economic power has been merged in this country, but in the Soviet Union it is more formal and systematic.

At the highest level, political and economic elites are one and the same. In comparison to the United States, top Soviet elites represent an overlap of the upper class, corporate class, and political elites. The imperatives of industrialization have dictated an occupational structure that divides the Soviet population much as it does in the United States. The distribution of valued goods and services—as well as self-esteem, job satisfaction, lifestyles, and education—is shaped by this occupational structure. But unlike the United States, the authority structure is more encompassing.

Class Divisions in the Soviet Union

Class divisions in the United States, as described in Chapter 6, may be drawn by the intersection of occupational, authority, and property structures. In the Soviet Union a similar method of drawing class lines can be employed with consideration for the particular shape of the occupational structure and the merger of the property and authority structures. Divisions or ranks within the occupational and authority structures are not clear-cut and are rather continuous. Thus, as with the United States, class divisions in the Soviet Union are sometimes ambiguous. But also like the United States, meaningful divisions can be located in a general sense, although some disagreement does exist.

Inkeles (1968) suggests ten class divisions for the Soviet Union with attention to divisions in occupational and authority structures. At the top is the ruling elite, or what Djilas (1965) called the *new class,* referring to the replacement by this class of the propertied capitalist upper class. The ruling elite consists of high party members, as well as top government, economic, and military officials (Inkeles 1968:151). Following the ruling elite, in order, are the superior intelligentsia, general intelligentsia, working-class aristocracy, white-collar workers, well-to-do-peasants, average workers, average peasants, disadvantaged workers, and forced laborers (Inkeles 1968:152).

In the Soviet Union the term *intelligentsia* is applied to the educated elite of scientists, technicians, managers, and professionals (similar to the United States upper middle class). Also of note is that many workers or manual laborers (working-class aristocracy) are placed above the lower white-collar nonmanual workers in the Soviet Union. (This higher placement is in terms of both occupational status and rewards.) And finally, the Soviet Union has an extensive population of forced laborers in its system of prison labor or Gulag Archipelago (see Solzhenitsyn 1973).

Meissner (1972) has supplied us with a slightly different set of five class divisions that are perhaps more useful and comparable to the United States. At the top is the upper class, or what Inkeles called the ruling elite, with 3.8 percent of the population. The upper middle class (6.6 percent of the population) contains the educated occupational and professional people who are not top party officials or top bureaucrats (Meissner 1972:130). The lower middle class (15.7 percent) contains the "worker aristocracy" of foremen and highly skilled workers and white-collar employees. The upper lower class (27.5 percent) includes higher peasant and midlevel skilled workers, and the lower lower class (46.4 percent) includes unskilled workers and most peasants. Meissner (1972:129) recognizes the existence of many forced laborers, but decides not to include them in the class divisions because he believes that their numbers have been reduced significantly since Stalin's rule.

Thus, much like the class system in the United States, we can identify class divisions in the Soviet Union based on the intersection of occupational and authority structures. As we will see below, these class divisions have an important impact on the distribution of valued goods and services in the Soviet Union. When answering the questions of who gets what and why we must direct our attention to this class system in the Soviet Union.

THE SOVIET RULING CLASS

We need to add very little about the power of the ruling elite in the Soviet Union; it makes most important decisions and controls the giant bureaucracy and, by doing so, affects the lives of over 280 million Soviet citizens. Elites, of course, never have complete control. The bureaucracy is never totally responsive, there is always some evasion of the rules, and even in the Soviet Union there are popular norms that place restrictions on elite policy. But compared with other industrial nations, it is fair to say that elite power is more extensive in the Soviet Union.

Two subjects do require more attention. In comparison with other industrial nations, and with the United States in particular, what do we know about elite mobility and privilege in the Soviet Union? Throughout the history of advanced societies, movement into and out of elite status has generally been restricted, and elite privilege has usually been extensive. As the first large industrial nation founded on egalitarian principles and claims of a workers' state, what has happened in the Soviet Union as far as elite recruitment and standard of living are concerned?

As noted above, reliable data on the top of the stratification system in the Soviet Union are severely restricted. But recent years have brought surprisingly extensive data. Much information is difficult to hide for many years; it usually comes out in bits and pieces with various documents and emigrants or defectors from the top. The information below comes from many sources, much of it compiled by Matthews (1978) from Soviet documents and interviews during a two-year stay in the Soviet Union.

Elite Recruitment and Mobility

A general conclusion is that recruitment into the Soviet elite from below is quite extensive, more so than in the United States (Nove 1979:196; Harasymiw 1984). Also, the inheritance of top party and bureaucratic positions is low, although inheritance of positions just below the top elite (roughly the upper middle class) is quite high. In one sense this is hardly surprising when we recognize that the stratification system in the Soviet Union is fairly new.

What happens after a revolution is that the old elites are eliminated, with new elites moving in rapidly to take their place—sometimes from positions far down the old stratification system. There is much evidence of this in the Soviet Union, as would be expected, but this recruitment from far below the elite level is slowing down. And as might be expected, such mobility into elite positions in the Soviet Union represents a strict form of sponsored mobility (Harasymiw 1984). That is, those selected for such mobility are hand picked by current elites because of their talent *and* support of current elites and their policies. Still, the Soviet elite appears more open than others (Matthews 1978:163) *in terms of class origins*.

The reasons for this higher level of elite recruitment are no doubt varied, but several seem most important. The Soviet Union is a highly bureaucratized society and, as Weber noted many years ago, bureaucratization means more formal rules pertaining to the attainment of high office. The rules can be bent, but seldom totally ignored. Another source of openness stems from the structural base of Soviet elites. The greatest source of elite closure in the United States is found in the property structure. It is here that great wealth and corporate power can be inherited. This has been eliminated in the Soviet Union.

Finally, rapid elite recruitment in the Soviet Union stems from more room at the top for two reasons. On the one hand, like the United States, with increasing industrialization more room at the top is created by an increased need for specialists and top administrators. And the Soviet Union has been expanding more rapidly in this respect. On the other hand, Stalin hastened this process tremendously with his purges. These purges have been reduced greatly since Stalin's time (he died in 1953), but their effect still lingers with the people currently in power because many gained their positions during these purges.

A bit more information on these purges will be interesting. It is estimated that between 1933 and 1939 about 5 million people were purged from the Communist Party, or from 25 to 30 percent of the membership (Matthews 1978:149). In most cases, of course, the people lost government positions also. In the Politburo in 1939, eight of fifteen members were purged, and in the larger Central Committee, 78 percent of the members were purged. In regional political bodies, the figures are comparable (Matthews 1978:150).

Purges, however, were not limited to the party. In 1940, Matthews reports, 117 of the 151 directors of metallurgy factories were removed. In the Academy of Sciences, all thirteen secretaries between 1921 and 1938 were arrested, as were many university administrators and one-third of the members of the Union of Writers. In the military, a quarter of the officer corps was purged, including 90 percent of the generals and 80 percent of the colonels (Matthews 1978:150–151; Kennedy 1987:325). Many more examples could be given (Matthews 1978:149–154; see also Solzhenitsyn 1973), but the point should be clear. Elite recruitment was drastically opened by Stalin, and although purges of this magnitude are rarer today, they do occur (Matthews 1978:153).

Other indications of elite recruitment and mobility should be examined briefly. Studies by Soviet sociologists in specific industries and regions provide us with some information (Matthews 1978:157–159). For example, one study of a Leningrad factory showed that less than 16 percent of the managers came from families with higher education. In factories in the Urals, only 5 percent of the top "specialists" came from families of that high rank. In a broader study of all ministers and heads of state committees of the U.S.S.R., 70 percent were found to have begun their working life as workers or peasants, while over 50 percent of the directors of the largest industrial enterprises in the Soviet Union began as workers.

In terms of intergenerational inheritance of elite status we have other information. For example, there are data on about half the children of forty Politburo members between 1953 and 1975 (Matthews 1978:159). What these data show is that only seven of fifty-one children attained high elite positions, although most attained upper-middle-class positions.

In summary, the information we do have indicates a relatively open elite in the Soviet Union, although more closure is found just below the elite level. (More detail on mobility below the elite level is included later.) The data, of course, are seldom systematic and their quality is sometimes questionable. To the extent that they are correct, however, they are not very surprising. A high degree of elite recruitment is to be expected with a recent revolution, rapid economic development, political purges, and the elimination of private ownership of the means of production. And as Tellenback (1978:447) points out, the ideology of communist societies and the bureaucratic base of their elites require more mobility into the top to maintain legitimacy. Soviet elites may have extensive control, but they too must worry about legitimacy. Thus, by all indications, recruitment into elite positions in the Soviet Union is more extensive than in the United States, and those moving into these positions are more likely to be from lower-class origins than in the United States.

Soviet Elite Privilege

Following their harsh criticism of elite privilege in the old class system and their egalitarian ideology, Soviet revolutionary leaders saw their task as restricting elite privilege in the new society. For example, Lenin signed laws restricting the income of top administrators and specialists to 150 percent of the income of workers and limiting the inheritance of wealth (with a 90 percent inheritance tax; see Inkeles 1968:160; Matthews 1978:67). Laws were also established creating a high progressive income tax, limiting private property, restricting income from outside sources (from sources other than the primary employment), and placing limits on housing size. Civilian and military ranks were severely restricted or eliminated, and procedures were put into place to create more democracy in the military. But none of this was to last for long.

Soon after Lenin died, and to some extent even before, these restrictions on elite privilege were reversed. During the 1930s, Stalin branded these policies "equality-mongering," and systematically changed these laws or ignored them. It is interesting to note that many of the elite privileges were the result of conditions developing out of the revolution itself. For example, with economic problems and shortages of all kinds, elites got special rations of consumer goods and favored housing. And with the outbreak of civil war at the fall of the old regime, special privilege was given to elites to ensure their loyalty.

We can begin our examination of current elite privilege in the Soviet Union with income. Although elite income was originally not to exceed 150 percent of the average worker income, Matthews (1978:31) estimates that there are currently 227,000 people with incomes 400 percent above the average. (About 60 percent of these people are top party officials.)

Table 14-1 lists the basic monthly income (in rubles) of a few elites compiled by Matthews. These figures are for the early 1970s and can be compared with the monthly income of 130 rubles for the average worker. For example, the general secretary of the party receives a monthly income of about 900 rubles, the secretary of the Central Committee receives from 700 to 800 rubles, top managers in the coal industry receive 400 rubles, and a major general in the Soviet army receives 600 rubles.

The incomes listed in Table 14-1 are much above 150 percent of the average. And these incomes do not take into account extra income or special free benefits as discussed below. For example, we have reports that some military officers receive as much as 2,000 rubles per month in combined income (Matthews 1978:27; *Time*, June 23, 1980:31). However, it is clear that elite income in the Soviet Union is far below that of elites in the United States when

TABLE 14-1
MONTHLY INCOME OF SELECTED SOVIET ELITES

Position	Monthly income in rubles*
Party officials:	
General secretary	900
Secretary of Central Committee	700–800
First secretary of a union republic	600
Assistant to member of Politburo	425
Industry managers:	
In coal	400
In nonferrous	325–375
In ferrous	300–350
In chemical	290–330
In oil and gas	290–300
Military officers:	
Major general	600
Colonel	500
Lieutenant colonel	400
Others:	
Director of research institute	500–700
Professor, chief researcher	325–525
Assistant professor	300–350
First secretary of Union of Composers	800

*The average worker earns 130 rubles per month.
Source: Matthews (1978:23–24).

we consider the top incomes discussed in Chapter 2. A comparison between Gorbachev and President Bush is interesting. Gorbachev's salary is reported to be only $28,000 a year, compared to Bush's official salary of $200,000 a year as President (Remnick 1989). Bush, of course, receives much more money than this from private investments. Gorbachev is reported to have only one other significant source of income, the $600,000 in royalties from Harper & Row for his book *Perestroika*. But it is reported that he gave all of this money to the Communist Party.

The relatively low incomes of the Soviet elite are not necessarily found throughout communist countries, however. There is evidence that most political elites in Eastern European communist countries had modest incomes compared to the incomes of elites in capitalist nations (Parkin 1971; Matthews 1978:165; Tellenback 1978; Volgyes 1978). But at the very top elite positions in these Eastern European communist countries there are stories of vast wealth illegally taken and hidden away in foreign bank accounts. With the fall of some of the Eastern European communist elites in 1989 (for example, in East Germany and Romania), what was rumored was confirmed; they had extensive income and wealth hidden away.

In contrast to this, we have few similar reports of top elite corruption in the Soviet Union, though there have been many cases of corruption and hidden wealth at lower elite levels, especially among some relatives and associates of the Brezhnev ruling elite, discovered after Brezhnev's death (Shlapentokh 1989:203–216; also see Morton 1987:109–110). Estimates of wealth inequality by social scientists also indicate there is less of this type of inequality in the Soviet Union. While we must recognize that the lack of private ownership of the means of production in the Soviet Union will restrict what wealth there is to be unequally divided to begin with, wealth inequality can result from such things as home ownership, cars, and artwork. Vinokur and Ofer (1987:196) calculated that in the late 1970s, the top 1 percent of wealth holders in the Soviet Union held 7 percent of all wealth, compared to 24 percent for the top 1 percent in England, and 26 percent for the top 1 percent of wealth holders in the United States.

Judging elite privilege by income, of course, can be very tricky. This is especially so in the Soviet Union because (1) many services are free to the general population (with elites provided with even more free services), (2) the quality of goods and services purchased can vary greatly, and (3) there are restrictions on what income can buy due to legal restrictions (for example, how many homes or cars can be owned) and a scarcity of goods and services (Schroeder 1987; Teckenberg 1987). Observers of the Soviet Union have often noted that consumer goods are limited, not because people cannot afford them, but because they are scarce. As a result, many Soviet citizens find it difficult to spend the money they have (Geiger 1969:285). So elite privilege in the Soviet Union must be examined further.

Given limits on the quality and quantity of consumer goods, often-cited sources of elite privilege in the Soviet Union include special rations for elites (for example, the Kremlin ration and the academic ration) and restricted consumer outlets (Matthews 1978:38–43). In general, when certain consumer items are in short supply they are rationed—say, by region of the country. The people receiving these goods are those first in line to buy them. However, certain elite groups may be assured a higher ration of these goods. For example, Kremlin party officials may receive more and better quality meat (*Time,* June 23, 1980:40). In a similar fashion, there are special stores in which only party officials can shop, and these stock better-quality items at below-average cost (Matthews 1978:39).

Another form of special elite privilege is found with housing. With a severe housing shortage in many cities like Moscow and Leningrad, there are laws restricting per-capita housing size or laws requiring especially high rents for people living in housing above the authorized size. For example, in the early 1970s the average housing size in the Soviet Union was six square meters per head, and in Leningrad a family must have less than 4 1/2 square meters per head to be placed on a waiting list for alternative housing (Matthews 1978:43). "By 1982, per capita living space in urban areas had increased to 9 square meters (about 9.7 by 9.7 feet) for the Soviet Union as a whole and to 11.3 for Moscow" (Morton 1987:95). The elite, however, receive special privilege with respect to housing. This group is allowed larger housing, and more new housing is now being built for private purchase—at much above the price range affordable by workers (Morton 1987:109). In fact, many elites own country dachas in addition to their primary residences (*Time,* June 23, 1980:40).

Other examples of elite privilege include private transportation, better medical care, and better education. Private autos are very restricted in the Soviet Union, and the highly paid elite are among the few who can afford the standard auto, priced at 3 1/2 times the average worker's yearly income (Matthews 1978:48; see also *Time,* June 23, 1980:48; Schroeder 1987).

Medical attention in the Soviet Union is essentially free to all citizens (Field 1987). The Soviet Union has made tremendous progress in medical care since 1917 (*Time,* June 23, 1980:61–63), but medical facilities are often overcrowded and services may come only after a long waiting period. As might be expected, however, elites can go to special medical facilities of better quality (Matthews 1978:47; Field 1987:70).

Educational institutions in the Soviet Union have also been greatly improved since 1917, with the education level showing a rapid increase among the general population (Yanowitch 1977). But educational quality and access to higher education are quite restricted. Elites are able to send their children to special schools and afford private educational coaching, so their children are in a better position to pass difficult college entrance exams (Yanowitch 1977; Matthews 1978:47–48; *Time,* June 23, 1980:76–77).

Other examples of elite privilege in the Soviet Union could be listed, but the basic point has been made. Despite this group's legacy of a workers' state where elite privilege has been restricted, the extensive power of this elite has resulted in many privileges. In capitalist industrial nations elite privilege is the result of greater wealth and income. In the United States this means scarce goods and services are *distributed by access to wealth and income,* whereas scarce goods and services in the Soviet Union are often *distributed through bureaucratic mechanisms* (such as rationing and special outlets).

Two obvious, but very difficult, questions may be considered in closing this discussion of elite privilege. We may ask if the Soviet elite is better or worse off than its United States counterpart and if the Soviet elite is less above the average Soviet citizen than the United States elite is above the average United States citizen. The two questions are very difficult to answer because there are many separate dimensions to be considered, and cross-national living standards prove difficult to estimate.

After compiling extensive data on Soviet elites, Matthews (1978:176–177) concludes that the material standard of living for most Soviet elites is about equal to that of the *average* United States citizen. What this means is that the material standard of living of Soviet elites is far below that of United States elites in most respects. However, we should qualify further what is meant by material standard of living. The data we have reviewed pertain only to material conditions such as housing, consumer goods, food, transportation, and vacation travel. Pride in accomplishments and the satisfaction of being respected are among nonmaterial rewards perhaps impossible to measure cross-nationally. But it is no doubt with respect to such nonmaterial rewards that Soviet and United States elites are most similar.

And, of course, there is power, which both elites have in abundance. Direct comparisons in this respect are even more difficult. Soviet power is more concentrated in a state bureaucracy, although bureaucracies are known for their obstructions. An order may be given, but that order may not be completely implemented as it moves down the bureaucracy.

As for the second question, although the Soviet elite is about equal to the United States middle class in material existence, the average Soviet citizen is far below the United States middle class in many respects (Schroeder 1987; Teckenberg 1987). But what we want to know is the relative elite–average gap within each country. We have seen that income inequality is less in the Soviet Union, although for the reasons discussed above, income is not always an accurate measure of privilege in the Soviet Union (Belknap 1987). Thus, we may suspect that standards of living are more equal in the Soviet Union (Lenski 1978:369–370), but we have only limited means of making an accurate estimate.

Perhaps most important, however, is that elites broadly similar to those in the United States do exist in the Soviet Union. They do have privilege and extensive power denied the average Soviet citizen; and in the Soviet Union such elite privilege exists within a state that emerged with the pretext of eliminating or severely restricting such privilege.

SOCIAL MOBILITY IN THE SOVIET UNION

Our discussion of the extent and means of social mobility at this point will concern nonelites. We want to know the extent to which intergenerational mobility in the Soviet Union is similar to that found in Chapter 11 for the United States. And, in a related question, we want to know the process by which intergenerational mobility, or the lack of it, occurs. Until very recently we had almost no information on these subjects, but as Soviet sociologists have become freer to pursue such questions and publish their research findings, we do have more information. We do not have massive studies similar to those of Blau and Duncan (1967) or Featherman and Hauser (1978) for the United States, but Yanowitch (1977) and Connor (1988) have compiled evidence from many smaller studies published in Soviet journals.

The Pattern of Social Mobility in the Soviet Union

We can begin by noting the conclusions of several American sociologists who have studied the system of stratification in the Soviet Union and Eastern European communist nations. As we saw with elite recruitment, in the early years after communist rule began, social mobility was extensive. But as the system matured, mobility slowed, although it remains higher than that found in the United States (Inkeles 1968:162–165; Yanowitch 1977; Jones 1978:530–531; Tellenback 1978:438).

The destruction of an old class system often results in a burst of social mobility; but as those who find their new niche in the class system settle in, they become more like the upper middle class, middle class, working class, and lower class in other industrial societies. Those higher in the class system soon find ways to ensure that their offspring are advantaged, while those lower in the class system find it difficult to give their offspring a boost.

Those lower in the class system in communist societies may find that a boost for their children is more possible than in capitalist societies, but it remains difficult. To some extent this more favorable opportunity structure is related to the communist ideology of classlessness, but it is perhaps equally related to the rapid industrialization that the Soviet Union and Eastern European nations have experienced (at least until the 1970s and 1980s). Let us consider some evidence.

Among the many Soviet studies discussed by Yanowitch (1977:109–111) are three conducted in Kazan (in 1967), Ufa (in 1970), and Leningrad (in 1970). In contrast to the standard manual–nonmanual class division employed in most comparative studies of mobility, studies from the Soviet Union generally employ a three-class comparison (workers, lower-level nonmanual, and specialists). The first two occupational categories need no explanation, although we should note that "specialist" is comparable to upper-middle-class occupations in the United States. One reason for such a trichotomy is that (as described above) the occupational status and income of many manual workers in the Soviet Union are higher than those of many lower nonmanual (white-collar) workers. Thus, these differences may affect the pattern of social mobility, and a trichotomy is necessary.

Table 14-2 presents findings on occupational recruitment (an inflow table) from these three Soviet cities. In a pattern similar to that found in the United States, workers are much more likely to have worker or peasant origins. How-

TABLE 14-2

CLASS ORIGINS OF INCUMBENTS OF VARIOUS OCCUPATIONAL POSITIONS IN THREE SOVIET CITIES

Current occupation	Occupation of father (%)					
	Peasant	Worker	Lower nonmanual	Specialist	No answer	Total
Kazan, 1967:						
Workers	31.9	49.0	4.8	6.9	7.4	100
Lower nonmanual	24.3	49.7	7.9	11.2	6.9	100
Specialists	11.7	29.6	14.9	37.5	6.2	99
Ufa, 1970:						
Workers	33.0	44.6	8.0	7.2	7.2	100
Lower nonmanual	21.7	35.1	9.3	18.6	15.3	100
Specialists	17.8	28.1	14.5	32.8	4.8	98
Leningrad, 1970:						
Workers	14.5	54.7	6.7	14.5	9.6	100
Lower nonmanual	8.4	55.4	8.9	16.4	10.9	100
Specialists	6.2	42.4	13.6	31.3	6.4	99

Source: Yanowitch (1977:109).

ever, these studies show considerable recruitment from below into specialist positions. For example, in Leningrad 42.4 percent of the specialists came from worker origins, 13.6 percent from lower nonmanual origins, and 31.3 percent from specialist origins. A similar pattern is found in the other two cities, although the percentage of specialists with worker origins is somewhat lower.

As might be expected considering United States studies, however, when we look higher in the occupational structure (toward the top of the specialist category) we find recruitment from below is much less extensive. In another Soviet study (Yanowitch 1977:114), 70 percent of the scientists and top engineers and 60 percent of the university faculty and physicians had nonmanual or middle-class origins. Several other Soviet studies show this same pattern (Yanowitch 1977:112–114).

Another primary question in the study of social mobility is the degree of occupational inheritance. Inflow tables (such as Table 14-2) and studies discussed above pertain to occupational recruitment, and provide no clear picture of inheritance because of changes in the occupational structure, differing occupational distributions, and differing class fertility. While occupational recruitment from below is apparently high in the Soviet Union (more so than in the United States), occupational inheritance is also quite high (Inkeles 1968:162–169; Jones 1978; Nove 1979:197), as it was in other European communist nations (Tellenback 1978:438). What this indicates is that, much like in the United States, industrialization has produced relatively more occupational positions toward the top. Thus, along with more recruitment to the top from below, there is also much inheritance at the top.

Yanowitch (1977:117) presents other data (in the form of an outflow table) that indicate the degree of occupational inheritance in the city of Ufa for 1970. The data show that 72.5 percent of the children of intelligentsia fathers remained in the intelligentsia. Similarly, 59.1 percent of the children of workers remained workers. Both figures are comparable with, but a bit higher than, figures found for the United States.

Somewhat surprising, however, is the pattern of inheritance for children of lower nonmanual fathers. It will be remembered that, in contrast to the situation in the United States, lower nonmanual positions receive lower prestige and income than worker positions in the Soviet Union. But in a pattern more similar to that in the United States, the children of lower nonmanual fathers are more likely to end up in higher nonmanual (intelligentsia) positions than are children of workers. As the 1970 Ufa data indicate, 55.2 percent of the children with lower nonmanual fathers end up among the intelligentsia (higher nonmanual), compared with only 31.4 percent from worker origins. A similar pattern is shown in other Soviet studies (Yanowitch 1977:116–121).

This means that although lower nonmanual positions pay less and have less status than worker positions, they provide greater chances for upward intergenerational mobility (more so than in the United States). We can speculate that the children of lower nonmanual workers have a family background better suited for educational success than do children of manual workers, even in the face of lower family income and status.

There is newer evidence, however, that the Soviet Union has been experiencing a slowing rate of social mobility in the 1970s and 1980s, somewhat like the United States in the 1980s. And this lower rate of social mobility in the Soviet Union has some similar causes—relative economic decline, in part because of heavy military spending, according to Paul Kennedy (1987). The Brezhnev years are referred to as the years of stagnation, and it is especially for this reason that we saw in the 1980s the beginning of Gorbachev's reform movement for the polity, economy, and sharp military spending cuts (Lewin 1988).

A consequence of this is that studies of social mobility and class inheritance similar to those discussed by Yanowitch (1977) in more recent years show less mobility and more class inheritance. Several of these studies have been compiled by Connor (1988) from Soviet sociology journals. As shown in Table 14-3, several of these studies from the 1960s to the late 1970s generally indicate that an increasing number born into the working class stay in the working class when they are adults. Connor (1988:36) claims this slowdown in social mobility is due to (1) a slower growth in middle-class jobs than in previous years, and (2) less effort made by the Brezhnev government to assure educational opportunities for the working class and peasants in the Soviet Union.

While the studies of social mobility by Soviet sociologists are smaller in scale and focused on particular cities and industries, the findings from these studies indicate that the social mobility patterns may be growing more similar between the Soviet Union and the United States. Because of relative economic decline we find that fewer jobs created in upper-middle-class positions, and

TABLE 14-3
WORKERS OF WORKING-CLASS ORIGIN AS PERCENT OF ALL WORKERS, VARIOUS REGIONS OF THE SOVIET UNION

Location	Year	Percentage
Ufa-Orenburg	1966	38.0
Ufa-Orenburg	1970	44.6
Kazan	1967	49.0
Sverdlovsk (wood industry)	1967	54.0
Leningrad (machine building)	1970	54.7
Bashkir ASSR	1970s	55.8
Moscow Oblast	1975	55.8
Cheliabinsk	1973–74	56.2
Elista (Kalmyk ASSR)	1975–76	69.4
Magnitogorsk	1970s	70.3
Naberezhnye Cheini	1970s	69.1
Sterlitamak	1970s	51.8

Source: Connor (1988), from original Soviet studies.

less effort in providing equality of education, have reduced the chances for up-ward mobility for the lower classes in the Soviet Union and minorities in the United States.

Educational Opportunities in the Soviet Union

As in any industrial society, the educational system in the Soviet Union provides a link to both occupational mobility and inheritance (Jones 1978:522; Kuebart 1987; Connor 1988:38). From our discussion of the attainment process in the United States it will be remembered that class background influences occupational attainment in part through aspirations and educational attainment. Given ideological differences between the United States and the Soviet Union we may be surprised to find that the process of occupational attainment is quite similar in both nations. The evidence we have, however, indicates that this is precisely the case. There is much competition for higher education in the Soviet Union, but people from families higher in the class system have a strong advantage (Yanowitch 1977:59) as has also been found in Hungary (Simkus and Andorka 1982).

In the early school years we find some interesting similarities between the United States and the Soviet Union (see Yanowitch 1977:61–65). Almost all Soviet children receive an education to the eighth-grade level (about 90 percent), but at this point one of four directions is taken: The children can (1) continue high school in a (highest) college track, (2) move to the higher technical track (for four years of technical training), (3) move to a lower technical training track, or (4) leave school for employment. Since the mid-1970s over 95 percent have gone on to complete the tenth grade, and leaving school for employment is discouraged (Kuebart 1987:83).

As in the United States, track placement of Soviet children is influenced by family class background. The influence of family background is shown by several studies in different cities and regions of the Soviet Union (Yanowitch 1977:63). The general findings are that about 70 percent of children with higher-class origin are placed in the college track, while only 40 to 50 percent of the children with working-class origins are placed in the college track, and about 90 percent of the children in the lower-level technical track are from working-class origins (Yanowitch 1977:69). Track placement is influenced to some extent by grades, but the studies have found that higher-class students with low grades are more likely to get into a college track than lower-class children with high grades (Yanowitch 1977:65).

College track placement in high school does not ensure college attendance. College entrance depends upon passing strict exams. As would be expected, those in the college track have the edge in these exams, no matter what their class background. But children from higher-class families have other advantages. They often attend better high schools and their parents can pay for extra tutoring (an extensive practice) so they can pass the college entrance exams (Yanowitch 1977:85; *Time,* June 23, 1980:40).

Behind this educational attainment process is another factor found important in similar United States studies—higher-class children in the Soviet Union have higher educational aspirations (Yanowitch 1977:70). Thus, as in the United States, there is a self-selection process leading higher-class students to strive for more education and to have greater confidence in their abilities to achieve higher education (Yanowitch 1977:81–82). The result of all this is that higher-class children in the Soviet Union are more likely to pass college entrance exams and go to college (Geiger 1969; Matthews 1972:284–297; Liss 1973; Jones 1978:532).

While a higher proportion of working-class children go to college than in capitalist nations, almost all Soviet universities have only a minority of working-class students (Yanowitch 1977:90–91). Considered another way, although families with working-class or farm-labor status account for about 75 percent of the Soviet population, they account for only 30 percent of the college students.

This state of affairs is contrary to Soviet ideology, given its praise of the working class and value of egalitarianism. And it is not a situation that has been ignored. There is debate over the lack of educational opportunity and criticism of such things as tracking in the Soviet Union strikingly similar to the same debates in the United States (see Yanowitch 1977:75, 91).

Under Khrushchev in the 1960s new educational reforms were instituted in an attempt to increase college attendance by working-class children, reforms that are again strikingly similar to many in the United States in the 1960s and 1970s. These reforms included easing the entrance exam requirements for college attendance, requiring students to work for a time before entering college, and holding special programs for working-class children to increase their academic abilities (Anweiler 1972:194–199; Matthews 1978:116). There is some evidence that many of these reforms were working (Yanowitch 1977:95), but the charge that these reforms were producing lower-quality education (Jones 1978:536) resulted in their reduction when the liberal political climate shifted after Khrushchev's fall from power.

INCOME INEQUALITY IN THE SOVIET UNION

Income inequality was considered briefly with elite privilege in the Soviet Union, but now it is time to broaden our examination. We can begin with the general observation that income inequality is extensive in the Soviet Union, although it appears to be less so than in the United States. As in the United States, the distribution of income is for the most part related to divisions in the occupational and authority structures. Data on income inequality by occupation and industry are quite extensive, but we have no systematic data on income by position in the authority structure as we do in the United States (for example, Wright and Perrone 1977; Robinson and Kelly 1979; Kalleberg and Griffin 1980). Unlike the situation in the United States, property divisions do not create significant income inequality because of the elimination of private ownership of the major means of production in the Soviet Union.

Before considering the data a brief review of income inequality since the revolution will be useful. Lenin originally recognized that income inequality could not be totally eliminated, and that income inequality at moderate levels would persist until the Soviet state matured. But Lenin certainly did not imagine that income inequality would reach its current levels (Inkeles 1968:170).

As noted in our discussion of Soviet elites, "in the early 1930s Stalin launched an attack upon the equalization principles which had formed the basis of Soviet income policies for the first decade or so of Bolshevik rule" (Parkin 1971:143). Ideas of income equality were branded "petit bourgeois" and the work of Trotskyites or other enemies of the state (Yanowitch 1977:24). But after Stalin's death this theme was dropped and more income equality was quietly achieved under Khrushchev's more liberal policies. Income equality per se has not become a major goal of Soviet policy, however, for income inequality remains a means of attaining economic goals (for example, by stimulating growth in select industries) and incentives for productivity. And, of course, with Gorbachev in power, economic policies allowing some small private enterprise have raised the incomes of a few shopowners and farmers. But this has yet to produce much more inequality in contrast to the policies followed in China throughout the 1980s.

We have enough evidence showing the impact of different Soviet policies toward income. For example, in 1932 the average wage of engineering-technical personnel was 263 percent of average worker earnings, and that of white-collar employees was 150 percent of average worker earnings. But by 1960 these figures were 150 percent and 88 percent, respectively (Yanowitch 1969:147). We can also examine this change with a ratio comparing the average income of the top 10 percent to the bottom 10 percent of workers. Several Soviet studies have shown sharp reductions in income inequality since 1956 in this respect (Yanowitch 1977:25). For example, in a study of Leningrad this ratio was shown to drop from 4.6 to 3.3 between 1959 and 1972, and in another study (the location of data collection is not specified by Yanowitch) this ratio is said to have dropped from 8.1 to 4.1 between 1956 and 1975.

While the data are usually old, we have various sources of information indicating that income is distributed by occupational skill level or occupational prestige (Inkeles 1968:203–206). From our earlier discussion, however, it must be remembered that the prestige of skilled manual workers is higher than that of lower white-collar workers in the Soviet Union. Using more general occupational categories, we find in Table 14-4 that income to occupation is fairly consistent throughout European communist nations. Using the income of average manual workers as a base (that is, 100 percent), Table 14-4 shows that the income of clerical workers was 84 percent of average manual workers, and the income of engineering and technical staff was 144 percent in the Soviet Union in 1964.

The distribution of income in the Soviet Union is related to position in the occupational structure, but overall income inequality does tend to be lower in communist nations. Table 14-5 presents income inequality data for 10 percent

TABLE 14-4
INCOME RATIO BY OCCUPATIONAL CATEGORIES IN INDUSTRY, EASTERN EUROPE, 1964

Occupation	Income ratio, %				
	Bulgaria	**Hungary**	**Czechoslovakia**	**Poland**	**Soviet Union**
Manual workers	100.0	100.0	100.0	100.0	100.0
Clerical workers	98.5	94.6	84.3	105.4	84.0
Engineering and technical staff	142.8	155.3	130.3	164.9	144.0

Source: United Nations, *Economic Survey of Europe in 1965,* Geneva, 1966, part II, table 8-18.

population segments from some of the Eastern European communist countries and the United States during the mid-1970s. Collecting income inequality data, of course, presents problems, especially in communist countries where freedom of information is restricted and the ideology of equality would make communist elites reluctant to release data, or more likely to present inaccurate data (Morrisson 1984). It may seem surprising that we have income inequality data for communist countries at all, but it is important to note that organizations such as the World Bank require all countries to provide reasonably good economic data if they are to quality for economic assistance. Many of the Eastern European countries have applied for such aid and have provided the economic figures on such things as income inequality.

As can be seen, Table 14-5 indicates that these Eastern European communist countries and the Soviet Union certainly have income inequality, but as is indicated, this inequality is less than in the United States (see also Jain 1975). It is important to remember that since the 1960s income inequality in the United States (in contrast to all other capitalist industrial nations) has increased substantially. Thus, unless the same has happened in the communist countries listed in Table 14-5 (and we have no indication it has), the differences between the United States and the communist countries with respect to income inequality are now greater. Also indicating the level of income in the nations listed in Table 14-5 is the ratio between the bottom 10 percent income group and the top 10 percent income group on the right. Again, less income inequality is indicated in these communist nations.

In another estimate of income inequality, Lenski (1978:370) provides rough estimates of the highest to lowest wage ratios for a number of communist nations. In the early 1970s the ratio was 40 to 1 in Poland, 40 to 1 in China, 7.3 to 1 in Cuba, and 50 to 1 in the Soviet Union, compared with *at least* 300 to 1 in the United States. And these figures represent highest versus lowest incomes from *wages,* not total incomes. If we consider total incomes (wages plus stock dividends, interest payments, and so on), the figures for communist societies would be affected only somewhat, while the United States' ratio would be greatly increased.

We have other data on income inequality in the Soviet Union which makes us believe that the data in Table 14-5 on the Soviet Union are reasonably accu-

TABLE 14-5
INCOME INEQUALITY IN COMMUNIST NATIONS AND THE UNITED STATES[*]

Country	Bottom 10%	10– 20%	20– 30%	30– 40%	40– 50%	50– 60%	60– 70%	70– 80%	80– 90%	Top 10%	Ratio top 10%/ bottom 10%
					10 percent population segments						
East Germany	4.9	5.3	7.2	8.9	8.9	9.6	10.0	11.0	12.2	23.0	4.7
Hungary	2.7	3.7	6.1	7.3	9.1	10.2	11.7	13.2	15.4	20.6	7.6
Poland	3.0	4.1	6.0	7.5	8.8	9.9	11.1	12.3	15.3	22.0	7.3
Romania-Bulgaria	4.5	5.3	6.5	7.6	9.0	10.1	11.0	12.3	15.6	18.1	4.0
USSR	4.0	4.6	6.0	6.7	7.8	8.7	11.1	12.4	13.7	25.0	6.2
Yugoslavia	2.6	3.3	5.0	6.4	7.4	9.1	11.0	13.5	16.5	25.2	9.7
USA	1.9	3.0	5.4	5.9	7.8	9.0	10.2	12.6	16.2	28.0	14.7

[*]Data are for the mid-1970s.
Source: Table constructed with data presented in Morrisson (1984).

rate. We have already seen some of these data in the previous section on the income of elites compared to average workers in the Soviet Union (Matthews 1978). Other studies on many aspects of Soviet life have been conducted by interviews with former Soviet citizens now living outside the Soviet Union (see Millar 1987). Such studies must be considered with caution, of course, because the individuals who have left the Soviet Union no doubt have many differences that separate them from those who stay behind. But with these and other difficulties in mind (Millar 1987:3–30), Vinokur and Ofer (1987) have attempted to estimate income inequality in the Soviet Union in this manner. In a comparison of the Soviet Union (individuals from urban areas only) with capitalist industrial societies in the early 1970s, Vinokur and Ofer (1987:193) have estimated income inequality (using the Gini index) in the Soviet Union to be less than in most capitalist industrial nations. But they also have evidence that income inequality in the Soviet Union may have increased by the end of the 1970s, giving the Soviet Union a higher than average income inequality compared to capitalist industrial nations. We must, however, stress the limits of the type of research conducted by Vinokur and Ofer.

Increasing inequality in the Soviet Union during the economic problems in the 1970s and early 1980s under Brezhnev does seem to make sense, however. We also have reports that a small class of new rich has developed because of new reforms allowing for some small private businesses in the Soviet Union since the 1970s (Shlapentokh 1989:223). And in the face of this small class of new rich, Matthews (1986, 1987) has used definitions of poverty similar to what we have used for the United States to conclude that poverty is rather extensive in the Soviet Union. With Gorbachev's *glasnost* the Soviet Union has now provided data confirming that the rate of poverty in the Soviet Union is about 20 percent of the population (*Los Angeles Times,* July 3, 1989). But, unlike the United States, this poverty comes less from unemployment, for most people are required to be employed in the Soviet Union (Lane 1988), and over 90 percent of middle-aged women also are in the labor force in the Soviet Union (Anderson 1987). Poverty in the Soviet Union is due to inadequate wages in many jobs, but especially because the pensions received by the retired aged are too low.

A pertinent question at this point is why income inequality seems to be less in most communist nations. We will consider at least three reasons.

1 As noted many times above, communist nations have eliminated private ownership of the major means of production. As many studies in the United states have shown (for example, Wright and Perrone 1977), the private property structure accounts for a significant proportion of income inequality in this country. Thus, eliminating private ownership of the major means of production would be expected to reduce income inequality (Lenski 1978:369).

2 It seems clear that Soviet values place greater stress on equality, or at least less elite privilege, than in the United States. And although values do not always meet reality, some effect is to be expected. Soviet leaders hold their legitimacy on the foundation of an anticapitalist revolutionary ideology, and to some extent they must work within the boundaries of this ideology to maintain legitimacy.

3 Coupled with this is the power of the ruling elite in the Soviet Union. Power alone might be expected to produce greater income inequality; but in the context of elite legitimacy based upon an ideology of greater equality, this power can be used to further this end—at least to some degree (Lenski 1978:379). We may add to this that forcing greater income equality does not necessarily harm the material position of elites when their privilege comes primarily from sources other than income (such as special stores, free travel, and other services). The Soviet elite power to produce greater or lesser amounts of income inequality was shown above with changing income inequality resulting from changes in elite policy. This power is also seen in elite policy that provides greater income for workers in certain industries (Yanowitch 1977:31–32). When Soviet elites determine that certain industries should be favored for greater productivity, they have the power to favor them.

Sex Inequality

Although overall income inequality is less in the Soviet Union than in the United States, such greater equality is not necessarily extended to women. About 90 percent of women between the ages of 30 and 49 are in the labor force, making up about 51 percent of the total labor force (Yanowitch 1977:165–166; Anderson 1987:205). And some of these women have attained high occupational positions. For example, about 75 percent of Soviet physicians are women (Yanowitch 1977:168), along with 75 percent of the teachers and 33 percent of the engineers (*Time,* June 23, 1980:65). However, as for the total female labor force, most are in unskilled manual positions or lower white-collar positions (Yanowitch 1977:167; Swafford 1978; Sacks 1988). And even when Soviet women are in higher occupational positions, they usually have low authority compared with that of men (Swafford 1978:667).

A result of all this is that the overall economic position of women in the Soviet Union is quite similar to that of women in the United States. Several studies estimate the female–male wage ratio to be about 65 to 75 percent in the Soviet Union (Yanowitch 1977:171; Swafford 1978:668). This is slightly higher than the 61 percent ratio for 1976 in the United States, but it is comparable to the 61 to 78 percent range among most capitalist nations (Swafford 1978:670).

And as in the United States, the political position of Soviet women is not much better. Before Gorbachev's political restructuring, although 33 percent of the Supreme Soviet were women, only 25 percent of Communist Party members were women, and no women occupied positions of real power in places such as the Politburo (*Time,* June 23, 1980:65). After the first real elections in the Soviet Union in 1989, however, the number of women in political office was cut by about half. Khrushchev has been reported as admitting, "It turns out that it is men who do the administrating and women who do the work."

Class Inequality and Living Standards

Because some goods and services are subsidized in the Soviet economy, class inequality cannot be judged solely upon income inequality (Teckenberg 1987). We have reviewed some of the special goods and services provided for elites that, given their income, render their standard of living higher than it otherwise would be. In this section, we can consider briefly what occupation level and income mean for the living standards of other Soviet citizens.

We can begin with one of the most basic necessities—food. As noted earlier, elites receive better quality food in special stores, and to some extent are not subjected to the periodic shortages of some items. Other class members have no such privilege, and the food they must buy is often relatively expensive (compared with, say, that in the United States). For example, in a 1980 comparison of food items in New York City and Moscow, an average New York City worker must pay 0.2 percent of his or her weekly income for one pound of chicken, while the average Moscow worker must pay 5 percent. For a loaf of bread, the comparative figures are 0.2 percent in New York City and 0.4 percent in Moscow (*Time,* June 23, 1980:48).

As these figures suggest, a much higher percentage of the Soviet worker's income must go for food (also see Schroeder 1987). And because income is distributed unequally in the Soviet Union, those lower in the class system must spend more of their income on food, with less remaining for other necessities. We have figures for Moscow indicating that low-skilled workers must spend about 55.5 percent of their income on food, while the upper middle class (intelligentsia) must spend about 40 percent of its income on food (Matthews 1972:94).

However, the data presented by Matthews also indicate that spending on other necessities is less differentiated by class in the Soviet Union. For example, after calculating the proportion of income going to all necessities (such as food, clothing, shelter, and household goods), Matthews (1972:94) estimates that the low-skilled worker has 17.2 percent of his or her income remaining for other expenses and savings, while the upper-middle-class worker has 26.9 percent remaining. Thus, although food costs are relatively high and create a division between class living standards, after considering all basic necessities there is not a wide separation in discretionary income.

Housing standards and cost deserve special attention. In our comparison of New York City and Moscow, the average New York City worker would have to pay almost 100 percent of his or her monthly income for an average three-room apartment in New York City. The average Moscow worker must pay only 16 percent of his or her monthly income for the average three-room apartment in Moscow (*Time,* June 23, 1980:48).

What this means is that the average New York City worker cannot afford average housing in the city—or even close to average. The average three-room apartment in New York City is, no doubt, much larger and of better quality than in Moscow. But because housing, like medical care, is subsidized in the

Soviet Union, the average Moscow worker can easily afford the average housing—if the family can find it (Morton 1987).

As noted earlier, there is a severe housing shortage in most Soviet cities. What differentiates Soviet class members most is the quality of housing, not so much its cost or size (Geiger 1969:285–287; Yanowitch 1977:40). And we have information from several Soviet cities indicating that the proportion of families sharing apartments with other families is related to class position (that is, lower-class members share more often; Yanowitch 1977:42).

Finally, we may note that the ownership of many consumer items is related to class in the Soviet Union. Studies indicate that most households have sewing machines, radios, and television sets. However, there are substantial inequalities in the ownership of washing machines, vacuum cleaners, refrigerators, and automobiles (Yanowitch 1977:43–45; also see Teckenberg 1987:33).

In short, we can conclude that the standard of living in the Soviet Union is differentiated by class, and especially so when the elite is included. However, the standard of living does not seem considerably more unequal than income, especially when considering only nonelites. The upper middle class and the lower working class have many goods and services subsidized by the state— such things as medical and dental care, housing, transportation, and even vacations. Thus, their incomes go further than they otherwise would, and what they receive is more equal.

INEQUALITY IN THE SOVIET UNION: A CONCLUSION

Our examination of the Soviet Union has provided us with an interesting comparison with the United States. On the one hand we have a capitalist society with extensive class inequality, while on the other we have a communist society that claims to be classless. Both nations, however, have a stratification system that is in many ways similar. Inequality may be less in the Soviet Union, but it clearly exists. And what is most significant, much as in the United States, inequality in the Soviet Union is for the most part based on divisions within authority and occupational structures.

Similarities are also extensive in the pattern and means of social mobility in both countries. While mobility appears to be somewhat greater in the Soviet Union, the amount of class inheritance seems similar, and the place of the educational system in the process of attainment is (the words must be used again) strikingly similar. We find almost the same wording in debates over unequal access to higher education, we find tracking in both countries, and we find that higher-class offspring are more likely to attend college regardless of grades and test scores.

Other similarities must be noted. For example, sex inequality in income and occupational authority is remarkably comparable in both nations. Studies of occupational prestige find roughly similar results, with the main difference being that highly skilled manual workers are rated higher than lower white-collar workers in the Soviet Union. (This seems partially due to ideology, but also to pay differences. As noted in an earlier chapter, we suspect that pay and skill are more important in such rankings than status per se.) And other studies indicate that neither country has much worker democracy, and job satisfaction and alienation are related to class in both nations.

There are important differences in the two stratification systems. The Soviets have done away with private ownership of the major means of production, and thus the effects of the property structure have been eliminated. We have described how this has had an impact on more income equality in the Soviet Union. But the property structure has not been eliminated so much as merged with the state and party authority structure. And with this merger, elites have become even more concentrated in the Soviet Union. This concentration in part helps to explain the most important form of inequality in the Soviet Union—political power. Political power is certainly stratified and highly unequal in the United States. But in many ways C. Wright Mills' description of a power elite applies to the Soviet Union to an even greater extent.

Perhaps the greatest lesson to be learned from stratification in the Soviet Union is that complex industrial societies are based on conflicting class interests. The Soviet Union began with an attempt to eliminate such class conflict, but class conflict has remained, even though in a slightly altered form. Differing traditions and historical forces, combined with Marxist ideology, help account for this altered form. Other historical forces and traditions may produce other societies with different stratification systems. It is clearly possible that future industrial societies will have more material equality *and* less power inequality. But it is extremely doubtful that class conflict can be eliminated entirely.

A SHORT NOTE ON CHANGE IN COMMUNIST SOCIETIES

As mentioned at the beginning of this chapter, 1989 brought dramatic change and turmoil to societies from China to Eastern Europe and the Soviet Union. In a very real sense the direction of the new decade of the 1990s was set with the last amazing year of the 1980s. At the beginning of this new decade we have no way of knowing how these events will play themselves out, and any predictions are clearly speculation. There are, no doubt, many dangers and hard times ahead for those attempting what has never been attempted before— to move from a totalitarian political system and communist economy to a mixed socialist economy or capitalism. But while we cannot predict what will happen with much confidence, we can at least briefly note a few things related to our subject of social stratification that helped set in motion the dramatic events of 1989.

First, it is important to separate what has happened in the Eastern European countries from the situations in the Soviet Union and China. In the Eastern European countries it was not only important that they had totalitarian communist systems since the late 1940s, but also that these communist systems were for the most part imposed upon them by the Soviet Union under Stalin. Thus, the social movements of the late 1980s against communism in

Eastern Europe were also nationalist movements, and in this context the development and strength of these movements are not difficult to understand. Resource mobilization theory in the study of social movements tells us that social movements and revolutions occur when the balance of power and resources between conflicting groups change (see McCarthy and Zald 1977; Tilly 1978). In other words, conflicts of interest which had not stimulated social movements previously are likely to do so when the resources and power of the previously less powerful group increase and/or the resources of the dominant group decrease.

A primary set of resources held by communist elites in Eastern Europe was Soviet tanks. Hungary was one of the first countries to have Soviet tanks crush its movement in 1956 (the first was East Germany in 1953), and Poland was so far the last at the end of the 1970s. (Though Soviet tanks were not directly involved in stopping the Solidarity movement at that time, the Polish military crushed the movement for at least a few years so that Soviet tanks would not be brought in to do so.) But by the end of the 1980s, Gorbachev was not willing to send in Soviet tanks. There were no doubt many reasons why Gorbachev chose not to do so, but important among these reasons were his economic problems at home and the recent experience of "their Vietnam" in Afghanistan.

The Solidarity movement in Poland was the first to again test the waters in the later years of the 1980s, and slowly, going one step at a time, found that Soviet tanks would not be deployed. After Poland had shown that a break with the Soviet Union and communism could be made, communist elites fell one after another in Eastern Europe. For an Eastern European population that had never showed much happiness with Soviet-imposed communism, Gorbachev had helped change the balance of power and resources necessary for social movement activity. The saying at the end of the 1980s was, "In Poland it took ten years, in Hungary ten months, in East Germany ten weeks, and in Czechoslovakia it will take ten days" (Ash 1990). And this was before the bloody Romanian revolt in December of 1989: It is with only some exaggeration that we can say that with Romania it took ten hours.

In the Soviet Union and China, however, we are primarily discussing social movements for political and economic reforms generated by domestic situations, without nationalistic roots. (The exceptions, of course, are the social movements in some regions of the Soviet Union and China that were forcibly incorporated into these nations.) We can note two important relationships between the class system and politics discussed in earlier chapters to help us understand events in China and the Soviet Union. The first involves the relationship between industrialization and democracy, and the second involves what has been called the "new class."

We have described the statistical relationship that tends to exist between industrialization and political democracy. Over time, it is argued, because of changes in the nature of the type of work most people do and the levels of education attained by the general population, the process of industrialization will lead to at least some increases in the level of democracy. The form of democracy, precise degree of democracy, and timing of the relationship between industrialization and democracy, no doubt, are affected by many other factors. But implied in this theory of the relationship between industrialization and democracy is that economic problems will eventually occur when an authoritarian political regime attempts to force labor from workers who are well educated and who must be creative and highly motivated if they are to perform their jobs well. By the 1980s the Soviet economy was in crisis, and many in the Soviet Communist Party, led by Gorbachev, believed that more openness (*glasnost*) was required if the economy was to improve through restructuring (*perestroika*) (see Lewin 1988), thus indicating some agreement with the above theory.

We have already seen that a major shortcoming of Marxian theory was Marx's neglect of major sources of conflict and exploitation outside the economy. This is especially the case with Marx's neglect of the state and the importance of bureaucratic power. With the rise of bureaucratic authority structures in advanced industrial societies, first Max Weber, and then others such as Ralf Dahrendorf, explained that the state can be the new focus of conflict in stratification systems. If the capitalist elite is eliminated, as occurred in the Soviet Union and China, class conflicts centered around control of the state apparatus become more important. Without any form of democratic input, the "new class" of state or bureaucratic elites can come to exploit other classes. At the center of protest in the Soviet Union, and especially in China, has been criticism of this new class and its wealth, as well as the new class's tendency to develop mechanisms for passing its advantages on to the next generations of the new class.

A final comment must be directed to the differences between the Soviet Union and China. *Glasnost* and *perestroika* may continue in the Soviet Union, while the Chinese political elites killed hundreds, and most likely thousands, of their students who called for similar reforms in China. We must be cautious with broad generalities, but one key difference in these countries is the *level of industrialization*. With approximately 80 percent of China's population still made up of rural people with little education, students dedicated to ideas foreign to a peasant society could not maintain a sufficient following. The student movement in 1989 was very strong and was supported by perhaps a majority of the people in the major urban areas in China. But in this society, with limited industrialization and only about 1 percent of its young people ever attending a university (Foreign Press Center 1985:88), the political elite could find enough peasant soldiers (though it took some time) not affected by these new ideas who could be called upon to kill their own people.

POLITICAL EQUALITY VERSUS ECONOMIC EQUALITY

We can conclude this chapter with another observation gained from our examination of stratification in communist societies. It may be suggested that political equality and economic equality represent partially contradictory values. At least initially it takes extensive power in the hands of an elite favoring material equality to induce the privileged to give up their privilege.

As Lenski (1978:380) puts it in an excellent analysis of communist achievements and failures, "This may well be one of those unpleasant situations where two noble ideals are mutually subversive, and some kind of unpleasant tradeoff is required. In other words, gains in *political* equality come at the expense of losses in *economic* equality—and vice versa." Principles of freedom and political equality actually mean that the privileged are free to keep their privilege and grow even more privileged. Principles of economic equality, when put in action, mean that power inequality is necessary if the privileged are forced to give up their privilege.

Marx was aware of the necessity of force and a strong state in making the transition from a political economy with high material inequality. This recognition was made in his call for a "dictatorship of the proletariat." But he also believed that when the transition was complete, or at least well on its way, this dictatorship would no longer be necessary, and the state would wither away.

He neglected two other possible, and interrelated, outcomes. On the one hand, new elites, especially after the original revolutionaries, may emerge with less dedication to principles of equality. They may simply grow accustomed to elite privilege and prefer to guard such privilege. Recent events and new evidence in the Eastern European countries and China support this view. On the other hand, when force is required to remove old elites and deprive large numbers of once powerful people of their property, Lenski (1978:380) notes that "it is never clear what is fair and just—or even good tactics—in this situation." Thus, cleavage often develops within the revolutionary elite over such matters, and because such cleavage can threaten the revolution, repression may be used against dissidents within the party. "And this, in turn, seems to lead to the institutionalization of coercive authoritarian rule." What was at first necessary becomes tradition.

Lenski, however, may be charged with overestimating the degree of political equality in capitalist countries like the United States. Formal political equality and freedom must be distinguished from actual political equality. All may have some freedom—freedom to criticize political and economic elites, freedom to form voluntary associations, freedom to vote, and so on. But the actual result of this freedom and formal democracy is that the interests of the more privileged are favored—the privileged have the freedom to use their greater influence.

Lenski's observation continues to be useful nonetheless. It is useful in understanding the differing nature of communist and capitalist societies, as well as the inability of capitalist nations to achieve greater equality without strong elites on the side of greater equality. The *small* advances to achieve more racial equality in the United States, for example, have come with national elite coercion (stimulated with pressure from black activism) to change hiring and promotion policies of private and local government employers and university admission policies. There has indeed been a trade-off between freedom to discriminate and more racial equality.

Finally, we can consider some of the information from Japan in the previous chapter. We saw that Japan went from having perhaps the highest level of inequality in the world (or at least the highest of industrial societies) before World War II to having one of the lowest levels of income inequality of any industrial nation. While Japan is certainly a capitalist nation with private ownership of the means of production, the Japanese had something in common with communist societies: The wealthy *zaibatsu* families had their wealth drastically reduced after World War II. And while other factors, compared to present Western capitalist societies, also are involved in producing low inequality for Japan (such as a very homogeneous society where norms of relative material equality can be maintained), this forced reduction in wealth inequality has been one of the important reasons that economic recovery was achieved by the 1970s with very low inequality in Japan.

THE WORLD STRATIFICATION SYSTEM

The major capitalist nations account for about 20 percent of the world's population but receive about 66 percent of the world's income. The bottom 30 percent of the world's population receive 3 percent of the world's income, whereas the bottom 50 percent of the people receive only 13 percent of the income (Harrington 1977). In the United States, the per-capita GNP is about $17,000 (U.S. Bureau of the Census, *Statistical Abstracts of the United States, 1989*). In forty-five nations around the world, however, the per-capita GNP is less than $300. In even some of the "most affluent" of these periphery or semiperiphery nations such as Brazil, over 60 percent of the population are undernourished (MacDougal 1984).

Not only is the wealth and income gap between the rich and poor nations increasing, the gap between the rich and poor within these poor countries is increasing. Again using the example of Brazil, we note that between 1960 and 1980 the most affluent 10 percent of the population increased their income share from 40 percent to 48 percent. In Mexico, where the richest one-fifth of the people had an average income ten times that of the poorest one-fifth in 1950, the gap had grown to 20 to 1 by 1977 (MacDougal 1984). In nations where land is so important for economic survival, in Latin America, for example, 10 percent of the farmers own about 90 percent of all farmland.

Thus far our concern has been the traditional subject matter of social stratification—that is, structured inequalities *within* national boundaries. But certainly, as the figures above demonstrate, there is a wider framework within which the nature of inequality can be examined. And most recently, the inequalities that exist within this *international* framework are recognized as de-

riving from a *system of stratification* that in many ways resembles social stratification on the national level. As we will see, not every nation in the world is
equally integrated into this international system of stratification (although most
are). However, the scope of this international system clearly suggests the term
world stratification.

From this perspective we will conclude our examination of social stratification with the international focus of the present chapter. Specifically, we will
examine the world stratification system and its characteristics, development,
and maintenance, with a primary focus on the effects of this world system on
inequality within poor nations in the second half of this chapter.

CHARACTERISTICS OF THE WORLD STRATIFICATION SYSTEM

Soon after the first industrial societies took root in the declining bed of Western feudalism, there was, no doubt, an increasing awareness that separate nations were more and more tied through economic exchange. But the extent of
these economic ties grew more rapidly than the full awareness of their importance. In the early works of economists such as Adam Smith, for example,
such awareness was not yet sufficient. In the mid-1800s Karl Marx did have
something to say about the worldwide growth of capitalism (see Chase-Dunn
1975:721–722), but he left the task of specifying how advanced capitalist nations would dominate others to Lenin (1965) some fifty years later. Still,
Lenin's work on imperialism remained incomplete in many details. It was not
until after the middle of this century that an abundance of literature on what
we know as the world stratification system emerged.

To understand the basic nature of the world stratification system we must
begin by recognizing the worldwide division of labor. As differentiated from
the traditional view of economic systems corresponding with political or national boundaries, an economic division of labor cuts across these boundaries,
bringing national territories within a worldwide economic system (see
Wallerstein 1974:348–349).

Snyder and Kick (1979:1099–1100) summarize three main points in the
world-system perspective:

> First, the world system is the appropriate point of conceptual orientation. The be-
> havior and experiences of its constituent geopolitical units depend fundamentally on
> features of the system as a whole (e.g., a capitalist world economy) which reflect
> transnational linkages. Second, the modern world system is composed of three
> structural positions: core, semiperiphery, and periphery. Third, these labels are not
> merely descriptive. They indicate an international division of labor in which the core
> is linked to the periphery (and semiperiphery) in dynamic and exploitative ways.

We will have much more to say about the structural positions in this modern
world system (that is, core, semiperiphery, and periphery). But for now we
must stress the important implications of this world system for understanding
world stratification.

In earlier chapters we showed how a capitalist property structure and occupational division of labor (along with a bureaucratic power structure) can be located behind the system of social stratification in the United States. Among the results of interaction between property and occupational relations are the following:

1 Rather distinct classes are found in relation to the objective divisions created by ownership of the means of production and position in the occupational structure.

2 There is an upper class that owns and/or controls the means of production, with a working class having no ownership and performing occupational tasks for owners. In between these two classes we find a middle class with little or no ownership of the means of production, but with a higher occupational position.

3 The distribution of valued resources is in large measure based on these class positions.

4 There are dynamics of class conflict and change based on the differing distribution of rewards in the class system.

5 Finally, there are various mechanisms to maintain the favored position of those on top of the stratification system.

The key point is that once we recognize that capitalist property relations and an occupational division of labor exist *beyond national boundaries,* we must also recognize that there is a *world stratification system* with characteristics similar to the five listed above. The primary unit of analysis, however, has shifted from classes within nations to nations that are in many respects like classes (see Wallerstein 1974:351; Rubinson 1976; Chirot 1977:8). Let us proceed by examining the three primary class positions in the world stratification system.

What can be considered as similar to the upper class are the *core* nations (for the characteristics of all three see Wallerstein 1974:349–351; Chirot 1986). Among the core nations we find those most economically diversified, wealthy, and powerful (economically and militarily). These core nations are highly industrialized and specialize in producing manufactured goods rather than raw materials for export. They also have a more complex occupational structure with comparatively less income inequality. In addition, these core nations have relatively more complex and stronger state institutions that help manage economic affairs internally and externally. Finally, these core nations have many means of influence over noncore nations, but are themselves relatively independent of outside control (see Table 15-1 for examples of these nations).

Similar to the lower or working class are the *periphery* nations. Among the periphery nations we find those least economically diversified. They tend to depend on one type of economic activity, such as extracting and exporting raw materials to the core nations. These nations are relatively poor economically, with less division of labor, and a high level of income inequality. There is commonly a wide division between wealthy elites and a poor common mass of peo-

TABLE 15-1
EXAMPLES OF CORE, SEMIPERIPHERY, AND PERIPHERY
NATIONS IN THE WORLD SYSTEM, 1965*

Core	Semiperiphery	Periphery
United States	Venezuela	Chad
United Kingdom	Argentina	Uganda
Canada	South Korea	Morocco
Netherlands	Ireland	Panama
Belgium	Finland	Bolivia
France	Saudi Arabia	Paraguay
Spain	Taiwan	Chile
West Germany	India	Haiti
Austria	Pakistan	Dominican Republic
Italy	Philippines	El Salvador
Japan		Nicaragua
		Thailand

*This table is a representative listing of nations in the structural positions in the world system. For a more complete list of 118 nations see Snyder and Kick (1979:1110). The partial list of nations in this table is from Snyder and Kick's study using trade relations, military interventions, and diplomatic and treaty ties as indicators of world system positions.

ple in the country. These nations have relatively weak state institutions, and are strongly influenced by outside nations (both economically and militarily).

Semiperiphery nations represent those midway between the core and periphery, similar to a middle class. These are nations moving toward industrialization and a diversified economy. They also can be considered as midway between core and periphery nations with respect to state strength, a complex occupational structure, national wealth, and income inequality. In short, "While they are weaker than core societies, they are trying to overcome this weakness and are not as subject to outside manipulation as peripheral societies" (Chirot 1977:13).

It is worth emphasizing that the world stratification system is a type of class system based on the relationship of a nation to world production forces. Class position in the world system is defined with respect to (1) Marx's perspective of class (ownership versus nonownership of the means of production) and (2) Weber's perspective of class, which, in addition to ownership, stressed economic exchange relations and occupational skill level in the production process.

The core nations (through their major corporations) primarily own and control the major means of production in the world *and* perform the higher-level production tasks (for example, the more complex industrial production of cars, computers, aircraft, and electronic equipment). The periphery nations own very little of the world's means of production (even when these are located in periphery nations) *and* provide the less skilled labor of, for example, extracting raw materials (which are usually exported to core nations for production into a finished product). And the semiperiphery nations are in a mixed or middle position in the world's production system.

Like a class system within a nation, class positions in relation to the world economic system result in an unequal distribution of rewards or resources. The upper-class or core nations receive the greatest share of surplus production, while periphery nations receive the least. Furthermore, because of the economic power of core nations they are usually able to purchase raw materials and other goods from the noncore nations at low prices, while demanding higher prices for their exports to noncore nations. Chirot (1986) lists the five most important benefits coming to core societies from their domination of the periphery: (1) access to a large quantity of raw material, (2) cheap labor, (3) enormous profits from direct capital investments, (4) a market for exports, and (5) skilled professional labor through migration from the noncore.

For noncore nations, and especially the periphery, there is an unequal exchange or exploitative relationship with core domination. It might appear (and the ideology pushed by core nations maintains) that periphery nations benefit from their relation with core nations. For example, the periphery nations get a market for their raw materials, military aid, factories built (and owned) by core multinational corporations providing jobs for their people, and technical equipment and expertise—all of which *could* help further economic development in the poor nation.

However, although some benefits for periphery nations *may* be realized, the total impact of core domination actually *harms* the economic and political well-being of the majority of people in periphery nations, especially in the long run. The empirical evidence that has been building in the past few years is quite consistent on this point. Much of this evidence will be examined below. But first we must consider how this system developed.

DEVELOPMENT OF THE WORLD ECONOMIC SYSTEM

It should be noted in beginning this section that Wallerstein (1974, 1980, 1989) argues that there have been only two types of world systems in existence. The first type has existed in several periods of world history, as what he calls a *world empire*. Although never covering such a large area of the world as today's *world economic system* (using Wallerstein's term), these world empires did include major parts of the world—for example the Roman Empire, the Near Eastern empire of Alexander the Great, and the Egyptian and Babylonian empires much earlier.

The major distinction between world empire and a world economy is that in the former a main goal is political, as well as economic, domination (see Wallerstein 1974:60). As Chirot (1977:20) puts it, "In classical empires, a political elite, as opposed to a business elite, dominated policy. This elite was composed of soldiers, glory-seeking emperors, and learned but antibusiness religious officials." Core elites in the world economy, by contrast, are economic elites concerned with economic *profit*. A subjected country in the world economy is not usually controlled in every detail by core elites, occupied by a foreign army, or forced to pay taxes to the dominant country. All of this is rather inefficient in terms of the main goal, which is to extract profits for dominant core elites.

The distinction between world empire and world economy is also important in understanding the *development* of the world economic system. When conditions became ripe for a world economic system about 1450, Spain and Portugal took the lead. They were the first to establish extensive overseas colonies and explore the world for new territories. But Spain and Portugal soon lost their early lead, with England, the Netherlands, and France becoming dominant. Primarily this was because the latter nations learned a lesson that Spain and Portugal did not; it becomes too expensive to dominate many countries politically and militarily around the world (Wallerstein 1974:157–179; Chirot 1977:18–20). In short, Spain and Portugal became overextended with empire building and lost their earlier positions of power in the modern world system.

This is not to say that some core countries within the modern world system today never attempt to gain extensive control over periphery nations, and control them as their colonies. It is a matter of degree when comparing the control a dominant country tried to achieve in a world empire (say, the Roman Empire) compared to the modern world system. Research by Boswell (1989) on historical trends in the world system since the 1600s has shown that there is variance in the amount of control over periphery nations and colonization. Boswell (1989) found that when the world economy is expanding and core nations are experiencing good economic times, there is less colonization, meaning core nations are not trying to achieve as much control over "their periphery nations." But during poor economic times these core nations tend to attempt more extensive colonial control to keep other core nations from having economic relations with "their periphery nations."

A Brief History of Core Conflict and Hegemony

As described above, the modern world system is in many ways similar to an international stratification system, with conflict over competing interests, much like class conflict. This conflict is centered especially around the differing interests of rich and poorer nations, but it is also clearly evident among the core nations themselves. It must be stressed that all core nations are not equal in wealth and power, and the processes of change in this modern world system lead to continual alterations in the fortunes of the core nations. This places these core nations in conflict with each other, especially over their competing claims of hegemony in periphery areas of the world.

We will consider briefly this history of core conflict, some results of this conflict for the rise and fall of core nations, and some of the political and economic principles that Wallerstein and others believe are behind the changes in the modern world system. And, as a related issue, we will consider the current position of the United States in the modern world system, along with this country's relative economic decline and growing inequality.

Since the beginning of this modern world system there has always been a collection of core nations in competition with each other for economic dominance, hegemony over periphery nations, and access to the world's resources. At times the conflict is more overt and deadly, with shifting core alliances as nations try to gain better positions in the process of core conflict. At other times, however brief, there has been one core nation with clear economic dominance over other core nations in the world system.

Wallerstein (1980) considers a core nation as dominant over all others when it has a simultaneous lead in three economic rankings over an extended period of time. First, *productivity* dominance is important. The nation with productivity dominance can produce products of higher quality and at a lower price compared with other nations. Second, productivity dominance can lead to *trade* dominance. In this situation the balance of trade favors the dominant nation because more nations are buying the products of the dominant nation than it is buying from them. Third, trade dominance can lead to *financial* dominance. With a favorable balance of trade, more money is coming into the nation than is going out. The bankers of the dominant nation tend to become the bankers of the world, with greater control of the world's financial resources.

When a nation achieves these three forms of economic dominance, military dominance is also likely. With a stronger economic base, and with interests tied to a world status quo worth protecting, the dominant core nation tends to build a strong military. However, it must be stressed that during this modern world system no country has been able to use military strength as a *means to gain* economic dominance. In fact, each of the previously dominant core nations has achieved economic dominance with relatively small levels of military spending as each rose to the top, and each began to lose economic dominance with later military expansion (Kennedy 1987).

From the time that this modern world system began in the 1400s to 1500s, Wallerstein (1980) argues, there have been only three brief periods in which one core nation has come to dominate, with each period lasting less than 100 years. The first country to have this clear dominance was the Netherlands during the 1600s. As noted above, Spain and Portugal tried to achieve this dominant position but failed when they became overextended with too many military commitments and colonial territories to protect around the world (Kennedy 1987:47–48). By the 1600s, however, the Dutch achieved this dominance after their political revolution led to a modernized state supporting capitalists, a new financial system some historians call "revolutionary" (Kennedy 1987:76), and the development of new technologies, especially with respect to efficient shipbuilding (Chirot 1986:36). The Dutch shipbuilding industry also helped foster an economic lead through more exports to other nations, and their fleet of ships provided them with an advantage in the race for colonies (Wallerstein 1974; Kennedy 1987:67–86).

By becoming the dominant core nation, however, the Dutch set in motion a process that eventually led to their relative economic decline. First, other nations were able to copy the innovative production and banking methods created by the Dutch. With even newer production methods that were developed since the rise of the Dutch, and knowledge of what originally worked and did not work for the Dutch, other industrializing nations began to challenge Dutch economic dominance, particularly England and France. The productivity edge held by the Dutch also declined with the rise in their standard of living, a result of their dominant core status. This relatively high standard of living pushed up production costs, making Dutch products somewhat less competitive (Wallerstein 1980:268–269). With loss of productivity dominance, the Dutch trade dominance was soon lost. And with trade dominance gone, financial dominance was eroded.

But although the Dutch continued to hold financial power, their bankers, seeking profitable investments, went outside the country to a greater degree than in the past. With the development of other industrial nations, Dutch bankers saw more profit potential in these other nations, and the flow of investment capital moved, especially to England (Kennedy 1987:81). This outflow of investment capital further harmed the Dutch economic position even though it helped the profits of Dutch bankers.

With the Dutch in relative decline by the end of the 1600s, conflict among the core nations increased. There had always been wars among core nations, but now (1) the power of the Dutch to enforce world order was reduced, and (2) other nations were fighting for advantage to take the lead once held by the Dutch. The two main nations in this conflict at the time of Dutch decline were England and France. The Dutch had often fought the British, but by the early 1700s they were allies. It was Dutch financial investment that helped the English advance in productivity and trade, and it was Dutch military support that helped the English defeat the French.

It should also be noted, however, that it was an outdated political structure and a rigid stratification system still dominated by the old agrarian aristocracy that hurt the French. The Dutch had what has been called the first "bourgeois revolution" in the 1560s that gave them more independence from the Hapsburgs in Spain, resulting in a new political system which favored the new capitalist class (Wallerstein 1974:181). In England, the capitalist class had achieved dominance over the old landed aristocracy by the 1700s, though this had happened more slowly, over an extended period of time compared to the Netherlands. But in France, the bourgeois revolution of 1789 came too late for French dominance in the new era of the modern world and capitalist competition. Before 1789 the French government was still dominated by the old landed aristocracy, which resisted economic policies and financial reform that could have made their economy more competitive with England.

With British dominance there was again relative stability in the world system during the 1800s. It was especially a time of British expansion all over the world, with many colonies in Asia, Africa, and the New World. But following the earlier pattern of the Dutch, the British also slid into a relative economic decline. The overextended colonial system placed a strain on the British military, the cost of which also contributed to British economic decline. Thus, like the Dutch, the British held clear dominance in the world system for a relatively short time—from about 1815 to the 1870s (Kennedy 1987:226).

As in the 1700s, there was again extensive core conflict after the English lost their clear dominance. This time the British and France were allies, with Germany and later, Japan and Italy, providing the new threat to their hegemony in the world. Germany, and then Japan and Italy, were late developers among the industrial nations. It was German and Italian unification in the late 1800s that helped the rise of these two nations, and the Meiji Restoration noted in the previous chapter which brought industrialization to Japan.

By 1900, however, there was a major difference in the modern world system compared to 100 or 200 years before. Most of the periphery areas of the world had already been claimed by one of the older core nations (Chirot 1986). In 1800 the old European core claimed 35 percent of the world's territory, whereas by 1914 this European core claimed an amazing 85 percent of the world's territory (Kennedy 1987:150). This meant that if a new core nation wanted periphery areas to exploit for economic resources as the French, Dutch, and British had done before, the areas would have to be taken from one of the core nations. And this the Germans, and then the Italians and Japanese, began to do in the first half of the twentieth century, setting the stage for World War I and World War II.

While the Germans, Italians, and Japanese were moving into core status in the world system in the late 1800s, of course, so was the United States. The defeat of the agrarian south in the American Civil War led to more power for industrial elites in the north who could pressure the government for policies favoring industrial expansion. British bankers at this time were also directing more of their financial investment toward the United States as the British economy was in relative decline (as did the Dutch bankers when their relative decline was in process). *And,* like the Dutch and British at the time of their rise to core dominance, the United States had a very small military budget compared to all other industrial nations (Kennedy 1987:248).

It was American entry into World Wars I and II that resulted in Allied victory over Germany, and then Italy and Japan. A key factor in Allied victory during World War II was the early capture of the secret coding machine developed by the Germans, who also gave it to the Japanese. The result of this was that the U.S. and British forces had advance knowledge of most German and some Japanese military moves (Winterbotham 1974). But it was U.S. industrial capacity by the time of World War II that was very important in defeating the Germans, Italians, and Japanese. By 1943 the United States was producing military equipment at a breathtaking pace. For example, a new airplane was produced every 5 minutes and a new ship every day (Kennedy 1987:355).

The United States began taking the place of England as the new dominant core nation after World War I. But with Europe and Japan destroyed after World War II, the United States was able to dominate the world system more than any other nation in the history of this world system. For example, soon after World War II, the United States alone accounted for over half of all the industrial production in the world, supplied one-third of all the world's exports, and owned two-thirds of the world's supply of gold reserves (Kennedy 1987:358). And along with this economic dominance, the United States took over military dominance, becoming "policeman of the world" in protecting periphery areas seen as important to U.S. economic elites and their capitalist allies around the world (Kolko 1988).

The 1970s came as a big shock to the United States. From the highs of world military and economic dominance during the twenty-five years immediately after World War II, the U.S. economy hit a period of relative decline and also lost its first war, in Vietnam. This is not the place to go into all the reasons for this relative economic decline (for discussions of this economic decline, see Vogel 1979, 1985; Blumberg 1980; Bluestone and Harrison 1982; Etzioni 1982; Halberstam 1986; Dore 1987; Harrison and Bluestone 1988). What we have already seen about the relative economic declines of previous core leaders, which were never able to hold core dominance for as long as 100 years (actually only between fifty and seventy-five years), should give us an idea of what has been happening.

Table 15-2 indicates the relative decline of U.S. productivity by the end of the 1970s. Looking at the base year of 1967 for all these countries in Table 15-2, we can see that U.S. productivity was growing, but not at nearly the rate as some of the other industrial nations in the world, especially Japan. United States corporate elites lost the competitive edge due to, among other things, a lack of real competition in a highly concentrated domestic economy, examined in Chapters 7 and 8; a lack of reinvestment as well as research and development; and high costs because of the highest standard of living in the world. By the late 1980s and early 1990s it became evident that Japanese companies could come to the United States and build better cars using *American* workers than could American auto companies (for example, see several research articles in the *Los Angeles Times* from January 14 to January 27, 1990).

TABLE 15-2
COMPARATIVE PRODUCTIVITY GROWTH, 1970–1979 (base productivity in 1967 = 100)*

	1970	1975	1979
United States	104.5	118.2	129.2
Canada	114.7	133.3	156.3
France	121.2	150.7	189.9
West Germany	116.1	151.3	183.8
Japan	146.5	174.6	230.5
United Kingdom	108.8	124.2	133.0

*Note that the base year of productivity in 1967 is set at 100 for every nation. Then each following year's productivity is compared with this base year. Thus, for the United States the 104.5 productivity figure in 1970 showed a slight increase over the 100 level for the 1967 base year.
Source: Statistical Abstracts of the United States, 1980, Table 1591, p.913.

After this relative decline in U.S. productivity became evident in the 1970s, the U.S. trade deficit grew to huge proportions in the 1980s. The U.S. trade imbalance was negative every year in the 1980s, and was well over $100 billion in the red for most years of the decade. And soon, added to this was the U.S. loss of financial dominance. At the beginning of the 1980s, the United States had the largest banks in the world, and more banks listed as among the ten largest in the world than any other nation. By the end of the decade, however, the United States had only one bank among the world's top ten, while the top eight banks in the world were all Japanese banks.

In 1987 and 1988 a scholarly historical work on the subject of the rise and fall of nations in this world system by Paul Kennedy (1987) was among the best-selling books in the United States and Japan. The major theme of the book is how the relative economic decline of the United States, as well as previous leading nations, is due to the huge level of defense spending and overextended military commitments around the world.

The popularity of this book in Japan is evident when we see its prediction that Japan may be the next leading core nation. Japan is rising much like the Netherlands, England, and the United States before, with hard work, innovative technology, support and protection from the previous dominant core nation, and very low defense spending (like the United States in the late 1800s, Japan spends about 1 percent of its GNP on defense). Japan has already taken a leading financial position sooner than any other core nation which rose to the top, and may soon have the world's largest economy with only 3 percent of the world's population and 0.3 percent of the world's usable land (Kennedy 1987:466–467).

We can end this discussion of the history of core dominance in the world system with a brief mention of two final, though important, points. First, much of the increasing inequality within the United States which we have discussed throughout previous chapters is related to the relative economic decline of the United States. Because many U.S. industries are no longer as competitive as the foreign competition, hundreds of thousands, if not millions, of well-paying working-class jobs have been lost (Harrison and Bluestone 1988). But jobs have also been lost due to automation and robots that American companies are introducing into the work place in an attempt to reduce labor costs. Other American workers have had to accept lower pay (1) in attempts to make U.S. companies more competitive, and (2) because of competition from low-wage labor in periphery and semiperiphery nations. United States companies have left and will leave the country if wages for U.S. workers are not brought down. While these things have been happening, the United States has been competitive in some new high-technology industries that pay high wages, widening the pay gap between these highly skilled workers and those workers in industries losing to foreign competition.

Second, we must not leave this discussion of the core in the world system without noting the position of the Soviet Union. With Japan, Germany, and Italy defeated after World War II and brought into the Western capitalist alliance, the new core competition was centered around the United States and its allies and the Soviet bloc countries (Kennedy 1987). But the Soviet Union was attempting to achieve a dominant position through empire building and military power, something we have seen has not been successful in the modern world system since it was attempted by the Spanish in the 1500s and 1600s. Growing economic problems in the Soviet Union and their lost war in Afghanistan made this more evident for enlightened Soviet leaders such as Gorbachev. We can say, therefore, that the dynamics of the modern world system are also behind the changes we have seen in the Soviet Union and other communist bloc countries considered in the previous chapter.

THE IMPACT OF WORLD STRATIFICATION ON NONCORE SOCIETIES

In earlier chapters we examined the impact of domestic social stratification on the distribution of resources, achievement opportunities, and more general life chances of people in differing class positions in the United States. We found those in the upper classes to be better off with respect to opportunities and the distribution of rewards in general, while the lower classes are less advantaged. We are now prepared to indicate the same pattern for world stratification. The very important topic of economic development will be considered first, with the impact of this world system on the internal stratification system in noncore societies our second topic.

The World System and Economic Development in Noncore Nations

For many years economists had assumed that nations in the world would follow a similar pattern of economic development. With some initial capital investment, it was believed, nations would proceed on a path from preindustrial agrarian societies, like the very early history of today's industrial societies, to industrialization (for example, see Rostow 1960).

But we now know that these theories of economic development are highly misleading when applied to less developed nations today (see Portes 1976). The realities faced by today's undeveloped and developing societies in the periphery and semiperiphery are far different from those faced by the already developed (or core) nations when they were in the process of economic development. Among these new realities are fewer natural resources, a much larger population, and poorer climate (see Myrdal 1970:32–37). But perhaps most important, the nations that are now developed economically *did not have other developed nations to contend with in their early process of development.* The result is that the noncore nations today find it much more difficult to achieve economic development.

Many studies have consistently shown that most periphery nations that have extensive aid and investment from the core have *less long-term economic growth* (Chase-Dunn 1975; Bornschier, Chase-Dunn, and Rubinson 1978; Snyder and Kick 1979; Stokes and Jaffee 1982, 1985; Nolan 1983). There is, of course, some economic growth in the short term—fewer than five years—because of the aid and investment coming from the core. But the longer-term prospects for growth may actually be harmed by the kinds of outside aid and investment these nations have received.

Although there are many reasons for these harmful economic effects, three reasons seem the most important. The first involves a problem of *structural distortion* in the economy. For example, in a more normal economic process some natural resource, human or nonhuman, leads to a chain of economic activity. We can use the case of a *core* nation with extensive copper deposits. Mining the copper provides jobs and profits. The copper is then refined into metal, again providing some people with jobs and profits. The metal is then used by another firm to make consumer products, again providing jobs and profits. Finally, the products are sold by retail firms, again providing jobs and profits. From the mining process to the retail sales of the products, there is a chain of jobs and profits providing economic growth.

Now consider what may happen when the copper is mined in a *periphery* nation with extensive ties to the core. The copper may be mined by native workers, but the ore or metal is shipped to core nations where the remainder of the economic chain is completed. The additional jobs and profits from the chain of economic activities are lost to the periphery nation—they go to the core. Thus, economic growth is harmed in the periphery nation (Chase-Dunn 1975).

The second factor harming economic growth in the periphery is related to political and economic power. When periphery nations are heavily tied to multinational corporations from the core, a small, wealthy elite that depends upon multinational corporations develops in the periphery nation. This elite makes sure multinational corporations are happy with the relationship. The multinationals are allowed extensive tax breaks, they are allowed to take most of the profits out of the country, and wages to domestic workers are kept low. All this is likely to keep multinational corporations in the periphery nation and, consequently, the small elite wealthy. But long-term economic growth is harmed. Profits go to the core and the very low wages paid to workers leave them with no buying power to stimulate the domestic periphery economy.

The third negative effect on the economy of periphery nations is related to agricultural disruption. Export agriculture often becomes an important economic activity of a periphery nation brought into the world system. Before this time traditional agriculture was directed toward local consumption and there was no incentive to introduce capital-intensive methods of farming. As a result of traditional agricultural methods and lack of an extensive market for agricultural products, some land was left for poor peasants, food was cheaper, and jobs were more plentiful. But with export agriculture and capital-intensive farming methods, food is now more expensive, poor peasants are being pushed off the land so more land can be used to grow crops for the world market, and more machines are doing the work, resulting in fewer jobs for poor peasants. This also means exaggerated urbanization as peasants lose jobs and land, since they move to the cities in hopes of finding work there (Kentor 1981).

The above is not meant to suggest that all periphery nations are equally hurt by investments from the core, or are hurt in the same way. For example, Lenski and Nolan (1984, 1986) have found that the level of technology within the periphery nation at the time it is brought into the world system is important in influencing whether or not the periphery nation can achieve economic growth. Periphery nations that have more advanced agriculture when brought into the world system through core investments are more likely to have some economic growth.

In other periphery nations, the state may for some reason be stronger and more concerned with domestic economic development, thus making sure that multinationals do not harm the domestic economy. A good example of this is found in Taiwan, an exception to the tendency of less economic growth when there is extensive multinational involvement in the economy (Gold 1986). Since the country of Taiwan became dominated by the Nationalist Party of China fleeing Mao's revolution on mainland China in 1949, Taiwan has had a strong state supported by the United States as a showcase against communism. Among other differences compared to most other periphery nations (Barrett and Whyte 1982, 1984; Hammer 1984), this has helped provide strong economic growth for Taiwan, and a move into semiperiphery status.

World System Effects on Noncore Stratification Systems

The position of noncore societies in the world system has a very important impact on (1) the existence and power of a small group of elites, (2) the degree of working-class powerlessness, (3) the type of political system maintained, and (4) the level of income inequality within noncore nations. These four factors are important aspects of the overall stratification system within a nation. They all tend to be interrelated *and* influence many other conditions, such as inequalities of ownership or wealth, health and health care, social services for those in need, opportunities for social mobility, and so on through a long list of conditions often related to the nature of stratification within a society. In this section we will focus on the four interrelated aspects of social stratification that have received most research attention.

We may begin with a basic condition of *income inequality*. From what we have already examined in Chapters 3 and 6, it can be predicted that noncore societies will have more income inequality than core societies simply because they are *less industrialized*. There is a less developed occupational structure that creates a wider gap between the rich and poor, with fewer occupational positions in between.

The *internal class relations* shaped by the world system must also be recognized as influencing income inequality and other aspects of domestic stratification. On the one hand, we have the *power of elites* in noncore societies.

These elites have a strong interest in keeping multinational corporations in the nation, primarily because their favored economic position is dependent upon multinational investment and trade. One outcome of domestic elite ties to multinationals is that wages are kept low so as to attract multinational investment and trade. Furthermore, these domestic elites work to keep corporate taxes and other duties low. This helps attract multinationals, but also keeps government redistribution to the poor very low.

On the other hand, *the power of the working and lower classes is very low.* This is because industrial workers are a smaller proportion of the labor force and kept unorganized (unions are usually lacking or very weak due to repression), while agricultural workers are often isolated, unorganized, and powerless (see Paige 1975). All of this conspires to produce a lower class with low political and economic influence. And the *state bureaucratic structures,* which *could* help produce less income inequality, are usually dominated by wealthy elites (domestic and/or core elites). A typical result is a very low level of democracy, with the state working to serve the interests of elites rather than other classes in noncore societies. We must now examine what recent research indicates with respect to these internal class dynamics.

Chase-Dunn's (1975) study of economic stagnation in heavily dependent periphery nations was discussed above. In this study Chase-Dunn also examined the relation between core influence in the economy and income inequality. His most important finding is that both heavy foreign investment and foreign debt dependency are related to greater income inequality.

Also of major interest is that in periphery nations with more foreign investment in the economy and greater debt dependence to the core, the *top 5 percent* of the population had a much higher income. This latter finding conforms to the argument that a small elite is formed in periphery nations that depends on core multinationals and that has strong interests in continued core domination.

In a similar but somewhat more detailed study, Rubinson's (1976) findings support those of Chase-Dunn's reported above. With a sample of forty-seven nations, Rubinson measured core influence on other nations by (1) the degree of foreign control over internal economic production, (2) dependence on external markets, and (3) the magnitude of foreign debt dependence in the economy. All three conditions were significantly related to greater income inequality in periphery nations.

In addition, Rubinson (1976) was able to specify further the relation between economic development and income inequality. In Chapter 6 we discussed Jackman's (1975) large study showing that greater economic development is related to less income inequality over time. The effect of economic development on less income inequality has been an important *historical* factor shaping the nature of social stratification in today's industrial societies. However, as we have already discussed, the poorer and less developed nations have at present a reality *not* faced by today's developed nations *when they were in the process of development* many years ago. This new reality for less developed nations is the influence of core or already developed nations.

Rubinson's (1976) data from forty-seven nations *did* find that greater economic development is related to less income inequality (as did Jackman 1975). *But*—and this is the key point—when we divide nations into core and noncore standing in the world system, the effect of economic development on less income inequality *is greatly reduced*. Even when noncore nations are able to achieve some economic growth, the effect of the world system (and core interests) on their economy in large measure *prevents* more economic development from resulting in less income inequality (also see Fiala 1983; Nolan 1983).

Bornschier, Chase-Dunn, and Rubinson (1978) have examined several studies similar to the two above. All these studies are consistent in showing that greater foreign investment and greater aid or debt dependency in a noncore nation produce more income inequality. However, these studies have been criticized in part because they tend to ignore the internal class processes (in large part also related to world system influences) that affect income inequality.

One suggested area of neglect in these studies is class influences on the *political system*. As noted above, when a small but wealthy and powerful elite is able to dominate the state (no doubt because of its role in core dominance), we may expect less democracy and less state aid (or at least no reform measures) to reduce income inequality. With this in mind, Stack (1978b) reanalyzed Rubinson's (1976) data from a smaller sample of thirty-six nations. This reanalysis continued to support Rubinson's findings that core influence in the economy (investment and debt dependency) produce greater income inequality. But Stack found that the democratic performance of the state in these nations also was related independently to the degree of income inequality; that is, less democracy was significantly related to greater income inequality.

Another study is especially interesting in specifying the internal class process that produces greater income inequality in noncore nations. In our examination of the United States stratification system, we pointed out that (1) the property structure (ownership or nonownership of the means of production), (2) bureaucratic authority structures, and (3) the occupational structure are all important in producing class divisions and shaping the nature of social stratification. Most of these world system studies discussed above focus on the first—significant ownership of the means of production by core multinationals—as related to income inequality.

With data from fifty nations, Bornschier and Ballmer-Cao (1979) conducted a more complete examination of factors producing noncore income inequality:

1 In line with previous studies, they found that greater multinational investment in the noncore economy was related to more income inequality.

2 They found that less bureaucratic development in the noncore nations was related to greater income inequality. In other words, with fewer ranks within bureaucratic power structures or a greater separation between bureaucratic elites and the masses, there is greater income inequality. And in relation to the bureaucratic power of the state, when there was more multinational influence in the nation, Bornschier and Ballmer-Cao found that state resources are used to help industry more than the needs of the poor. This strongly suggests the influence of class interests on state behavior.

3 The less developed occupational structure in noncore societies was found to be related to greater income inequality. In this study, the less developed occupational structure was indicated by fewer technical experts and a smaller, powerless, and controlled industrial labor force. Thus, Bornschier and Ballmer-Cao's study specified in more detail the internal class process that helps produce more income inequality in noncore societies. And this study conforms in large degree to our earlier review of the important processes (the three structures) producing class inequality in the United States. *But* all the structures producing income inequality in noncore nations are influenced to a large degree by the nation's position in the *world stratification system* (as indicated in Figure 15-1).

Figure 15-1 roughly indicates what various empirical studies have shown with respect to the world stratification system's impact on internal stratification in noncore societies. However, the health and well-being of the majority of people in noncore societies are not limited to core influence on economic stagnation, class divisions, and income inequality. These effects may be most pervasive and consistent, but there are other negative outcomes of core dominance.

For example, multinational influence may support conditions of racism in noncore nations like South Africa (Riley 1980). These multinational corporations may also promote the dumping of unsafe products on an unaware noncore population when these products have been banned (and are unmarketable) in core nations (Margulies 1980; Dowie 1980). And perhaps most important, the influence of core nations often promotes economic production for the needs of multinationals

FIGURE 15-1
World system influence on internal stratification in noncore societies.

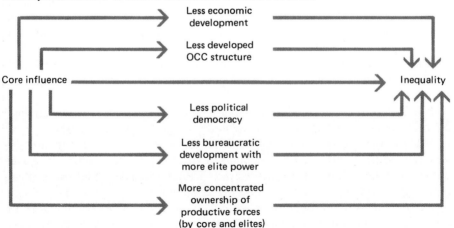

and the core population, *rather than for the needs of the working class and peas-ants in the noncore nations*. Many cases can be found in which people in noncore nations must go hungry because it is more profitable to grow crops that can be exported to core nations than crops that can be used for domestic consumption (see Johnson 1973:7–11).

We may conclude this section by noting briefly some negative and positive effects of core dominance of the world system *for core nations*. As suggested by the unequal exchange and power relation between core and periphery na-tions, core nations are favored. However, the benefits flowing to core nations are not equally distributed within core nations, and in many respects the work-ing class in core nations is harmed by core dominance.

For corporate elites in core nations, there are greater profits, cheap raw ma-terials, and a market for export, all of which strengthen core economic perfor-mance. Some of these benefits work their way down to nonelites in core na-tions in the form of a higher standard of living and some cheaper consumer goods. But there are important negative effects for core nonelites in the form of over a million jobs lost because of multinational moves to periphery nations with cheap labor costs (Barnet and Müller 1974:303–304; Stillman 1980:76; Blumberg 1980:128–129) and the military costs (in tax dollars and lives lost) of maintaining core dominance in the world system.

Figure 15-2 presents a summary of some of the means of core dominance over periphery nations and some of the consequences of this dominance for both core and periphery nations. Given the unequal exchange between core and periphery nations we might expect that nonelites in periphery nations would attempt to re-sist core dominance. This is the general topic of our next section, in which we must also consider core elite attempts to counter this resistance.

THE WORLD STRATIFICATION SYSTEM IN CHANGE

A key point about world stratification is worth restatement. As with domestic stratification, there is class formation based on differing group (that is, na-tional) interests that are in *conflict*. It is in the interests of elites in core nations to retain their favored positions in the world system, while keeping the noncore in their place. Conversely, it is in the interests of noncore nations (ex-cept, perhaps, for small elites tied to the core) to change their position in the world system, either by moving up as an individual nation or by altering the system as a whole.

As already seen, many obstacles work against upward movement by indi-vidual periphery nations, although semiperiphery nations do have a more re-alistic chance of economic growth, given better internal economic conditions (Wallerstein 1974:349–351). Thus, many periphery nations may find it in their interests to opt out of the world system and/or change this system through na-tionalist revolutions.

Given the dynamics of class conflict in the world system (Wallerstein 1974:351); Chase-Dunn and Rubinson 1977:474), there are continuous pres-

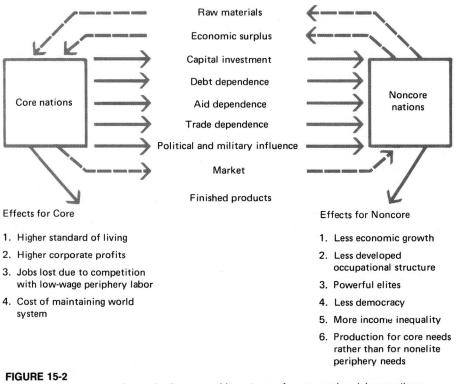

Core nations	→	Raw materials	←	Noncore nations
		Economic surplus		
	→	Capital investment	→	
	→	Debt dependence	→	
	→	Aid dependence	→	
	→	Trade dependence	→	
	→	Political and military influence	→	
	→	Market	→	
		Finished products		

Effects for Core

1. Higher standard of living
2. Higher corporate profits
3. Jobs lost due to competition with low-wage periphery labor
4. Cost of maintaining world system

Effects for Noncore

1. Less economic growth
2. Less developed occupational structure
3. Powerful elites
4. Less democracy
5. More income inequality
6. Production for core needs rather than for nonelite periphery needs

FIGURE 15-2
Summary of the means of core dominance and its outcome for core and periphery nations.

sures for change—in some periods more than others—due to changing conditions that alter the balance of power among nations. In this section the topic will be current pressures toward change in the periphery.

Throughout the 1960s, 1970s, and 1980s, the level of political violence in the periphery was high (Feierabend et al. 1969; Gurr 1969). Most predict it will remain high (see Chirot 1986). We have seen nationalist revolutions or violent class struggle in Vietnam, Angola, Cuba, Chile, Algeria, Ethiopia, Nicaragua, El Salvador, Zimbabwe, and Afghanistan, to name only a few. We have already examined the level of inequality and economic stagnation from core dominance of periphery nations that, when recognized, could produce a desire to change the world system status quo. We may now examine periphery class conflict more specifically.

Several reasons can be listed for the increased willingness and ability of popular resistance to core and domestic elite dominance in periphery nations (see Chirot 1977:122–145).

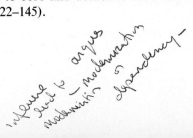

1 Commercialization of agriculture has disrupted traditional peasant life. New technical and labor methods of agricultural production have been employed to produce agricultural goods for export rather than local consumption. A result has been land taken away from peasants and new agricultural working conditions that can make peasant-based revolts more possible (see Moore 1966; Paige 1975). Furthermore, with more of the population pushed off the land into overcrowded cities (Kentor 1981), urban-based resistance movements are more likely.

2 More contact by the noncore lower classes with other societies and segments of the domestic population that live under much better economic conditions can produce a greater awareness of deprivation and increase expectations, in turn producing more anger and frustration. This is a condition called *relative deprivation* (see Gurr 1970) that, with added conditions, such as some described below, can lead to increased political violence (see Korpi 1974; Isaac, Mutran, and Stryker 1980). If this popular anger is channeled through organized nationalist movements it may present, and of course has presented, serious challenges to the status quo.

3 Virtually all revolutionary movements, while made up primarily of nonelite (working-class, lower-class, peasant, and so on) participants, are led and maintained by more educated quasi-elite (or elite) people (Gurr 1970; Hagopian 1974). Such people have been supplied unwittingly by old colonial systems established by core nations. To help manage colonial regimes in periphery nations, the core helped to educate an administrative elite from within these periphery nations. But increasingly this better-educated administrative elite has recognized the exploitative relation between their nation and the core. A result has been the existence of people willing and able to lead periphery resistance to the core and its domestic supporters.

4 A growing number of communist states have emerged, showing that it is possible to escape core dominance, though few of the countries have good prospects for much economic growth as yet (Lenski 1978). But to the extent that these countries *can* opt out of the world system and away from core dominance, they can set an example for other countries where people feel oppressed by multinational corporations and core nations. This is a major reason that the U.S. government has been so concerned with communist governments in Nicaragua and Cuba. Cuba has made great improvements in health care, housing, and education, but not much progress with economic development (Lewis-Beck 1979), in part because of a continuing U.S. economic boycott of Cuba. A similar economic boycott of Nicaragua was in effect throughout the 1980s, and millions were spent on military equipment for the counterrevolutionaries trying to overthrow the communist government in that country. The concern of the U.S. government is that these countries might become positive examples for other people in periphery nations where U.S. multinational corporations have economic interests.

5 In addition to providing examples, new communist governments have become strong enough to provide needed material and military support for core resistance. This kind of aid was not possible for revolutionary movements before World War II. It is clear that such nations as Cuba, Nicaragua, Angola, and Vietnam could not have achieved or maintained revolutionary success without outside support from the Soviet Union or China.

Thus, with the Soviet Union emerging as a core competitor since World War II, if a periphery nation is dominated by the capitalist bloc, the Soviets often have been willing to supply aid to the revolutionaries in these countries so they can break from the capitalist bloc (with the Soviets then bringing them into their bloc). While this is happening, the U.S. bloc will supply more military aid to the government elites in the periphery nation to put down the revolution and keep the periphery nations on the capitalist side. And, conversely, if the periphery nation is in the Soviet bloc, the U.S. government supplies the revolutionaries or counterrevolutionaries with military equipment (as has been done in Cuba, Nicaragua, Angola, Afghanistan, and Ethiopia), while the Soviets supply the government. Thus, it is in this manner that the superpowers have been fighting each other, but more often with people in periphery nations dying.

6 In addition to the above, there is increasing inequality between the rich and poor nations, greater inequality within the periphery nations dominated by the core, and political repression, all of which can stimulate or motivate revolutionary movements in the poor nations. We have already seen several studies indicating that core economic involvement in the periphery increases the inequality within these countries. Muller (1988) has shown that this inequality is related to more political violence in these nations (though London and Robinson, 1989, suggest it is not just because of the inequality, but other things as well that go with being a dependent, poor country that causes the political violence).

Other studies have shown that being in a periphery status in the world system is related to having less democracy (Bollen 1983), or more specifically that multinational corporate involvement in the economy of a periphery nation produces less democracy and more political repression (Timberlake and Williams 1984). There is a very complex process that operates between (1) political repression that is effective in holding back rebellion, and (2) repression that can further provoke rebellion. In addition, it is often difficult to distinguish between the two, so that "successful" repression, when reduced, may help spread revolutionary action. Core nations like the United States have long supported repressive periphery governments. But recognizing that such support may be counterproductive to core interests, during the late 1970s the United States pushed a human rights campaign in periphery nations (although repressive governments typically continued to receive core support). It is interesting to note that President Carter's human rights policy for periphery nations was developed in multinational business organizations such as the Trilateral Commission and the Council on Foreign Relations (see Dye 1979:217). This human rights policy was rejected by President Reagan, with the belief that periphery stability requires repressive periphery governments.

Core Resistance to Change

With these forces and others producing revolution and threatened change in the exploitative relation between the core and the periphery, it is important to consider the response by core nations to this international class conflict. There has been much talk in core nations of reform for periphery populations, new aid programs, and loans to stimulate economic growth. But as studies on economic growth reviewed above have shown, such aid and more debt has seldom helped. (In fact, aid and debt are related to less growth; Chase-Dunn 1975.)

President Carter's human rights campaign, gestures such as returning the Panama Canal to Panama in 1979, and in the same year some weak support for rebels in Nicaragua (in hopes they would not turn to communists) are other examples of core management techniques. However, the main line of action by the core has typically been overt, and increasingly covert, *military and police action* to counter periphery rebellion against the core. President Reagan moved toward more military support for periphery dictators to prevent change in the world system.

With the many cases of United States military action around the world—in places such as Vietnam, Korea, the Dominican Republic, Panama, and so on—the use of military force to counter periphery rebellion does appear to be a common response. More detailed studies of military action by the United States support this appearance. For example, Johnson (1973:6) notes that the United States military has intervened twenty-nine times in Latin American nations between 1806 and 1940. Table 15-3 presents a partial list of military action by the United States in Latin American nations between 1850 and 1965. (With this list in mind we can understand why Latin American nations were unhappy about the United States continuing this behavior with President Bush's invasion of Panama again in 1989, even though the invasion was directed against an unpopular dictator.) And in a study sponsored by the Pentagon it was found that the United States military was involved in a show of force in other nations (for example, sending the navy within striking distance or building up troops in the area) *a total of 215 times* since 1945 (*The Washington Post,* January 3, 1979). The only other nation close to the United States in such activity was the Soviet Union, with 115 cases of military display since 1945.

But this study also showed that overt military threats by the United States are decreasing, while such activity by the Soviet Union is increasing. There was an average of 13.4 per year during John Kennedy's presidency, 9.7 during Johnson's and 5 or less per year during the Nixon and Ford years. For whatever reason (counterpressure by the Soviet Union, lack of success, a counterproductive image, or the Vietnam disaster for United States foreign policy), it seems that the threat and use of overt military action to prevent periphery challenge (while certainly still options, as Bush showed in 1989) are being reduced. However, the covert action approach remains.

Covert actions are secret operations to achieve political and/or economic objectives. Included in such actions are assassination of political actors seen as a threat to core interests, bribes to periphery politicians or other people who

TABLE 15-3
U.S. MILITARY INTERVENTIONS IN LATIN AMERICAN NATIONS, 1850–1965

Year(s)	Nation	Year(s)	Nation
1852–3	Argentina	1912	Cuba
1853–4	Nicaragua	1912–25	Nicaragua
1855	Uruguay	1914	Haiti
1856	Panama	1914	Dominican Republic
1858	Uruguay	1915–34	Haiti
1865	Colombia	1916–24	Dominican Republic
1867	Nicaragua	1919	Honduras
1868	Uruguay	1920	Guatemala
1869–71	Dominican Republic	1924–5	Honduras
1890	Argentina	1926–33	Nicaragua
1891	Chile	1965	Dominican Republic
1894	Nicaragua		
1896	Nicaragua		
1898	Nicaragua		
1899	Nicaragua		
1903	Honduras		
1903	Dominican Republic		
1903	Panama		
1904	Dominican Republic		
1907	Honduras		
1907	Nicaragua		
1910	Nicaragua		
1910	Honduras		

Source: Table constructed from data in L. Gordon Crovitz, "Presidents Have a History of Unilateral Moves," *The Wall Street Journal,* Jan. 15, 1987, p. 24.

may further core interests, helping to stage coups, propaganda, rigged elections, and all kinds of "dirty tricks" that are limited only by the imagination (such as plans by the CIA in the 1960s to "hurt Castro's public image" by giving him LSD before a major speech or secretly "dusting" Castro with a chemical to make his beard fall out. These and more were *really* considered by the CIA; see U.S. Senate Select Committee 1975a:72).

When these types of covert action are successful they can achieve political and economic objectives at much less expense—less expense in the use of military resources, lives lost, and world opinion. Only recently the extensive use of covert actions by the United States against noncore nations such as Nicaragua, Cuba, Chile, Iran, the Congo, the Dominican Republic, and Vietnam became widely known through the release of government documents and congressional investigations (for example, see U.S. Senate Select Committee 1975a, 1975b; Kolko 1988).

The objectives of covert action can be quite varied, but they generally fall into three main categories. First, and no doubt most common, covert action can be directed toward suppressing opposition groups attempting to change governments in the periphery supportive of core interests. Second, covert action can be directed more specifically toward supporting periphery governments favorable to core interests. The distinction between the first and second is often difficult to make, but with the second we mean action such as the spread of propaganda that helps the friendly government. Third, and more complex, are actions directed toward disrupting an unfavorable periphery government so as to place in power a more favorable government—one that is anticommunist, procore, and receptive to more multinational investment and trade.

Because of the importance of complex covert action by the core to disrupt new governments in the periphery unfavorable to core interests it is worth considering in more detail. We can use the case of Chile to show (1) what the extent of dependence of many periphery nations is and (2) how the core is able to make sure these periphery nations *remain* economically dependent on core interests. (For more detail on United States activity in the Chile coup, see Kerbo 1978.)

The Case of Chile

The increasing political violence in Chile during 1970–1973 preceding the military coup in September 1973 has been chosen to emphasize core dominance of the periphery for several reasons. It is first important to note that we now know that the plan of action described below to overthrow the Chilean government was used many times before by the CIA and was first developed to overthrow the prime minister's government in Iran in 1953 (Kolko 1988; and see the book written by the CIA agent in charge of this covert action to overthrow the Iranian government in 1953, Roosevelt 1979). Another reason to focus on the case of Chile is that we have more information pertaining to the CIA-sponsored coup. Because of the political debate in the United States at the time and the subsequent investigations (see U.S. Senate Select Committee 1975a, 1975b), and because of the Allende government's willingness to help with research in that country (see, for example, Zeitlin et al. 1974), much is now known about the political and economic conditions leading up to the political violence in Chile that helped bring about the 1973 military coup.

Also, for two other reasons Chile is probably one of the best cases that can be used to illustrate the above arguments. As many have noted (for example, Zeitlin et al. 1974; Goldberg 1975; Petras and Morley 1975), Chile had one of the strongest traditions of democracy in the Third World. Thus, we can suggest that a foreign power will have a more difficult time in helping to create and exploit conditions leading to a rejection of that constitutional government.

In addition, Chile provides us with an example of a country highly dependent on economic actors from the outside. For example, before Allende (the socialist president) took office, Chile had the second highest foreign debt in the world (Goldberg 1975:101; U.S. Senate Select Committee 1975b:35). In terms of foreign aid, "Between 1961 and 1970, Chile was the largest recipient of any country in Latin America, on a per capita basis, of U.S. Alliance for Progress loans, approximately $1.3 to $1.4 billion'' (U.S. Senate Select Committee 1975b:32; Petras and Morley 1975:22; for a summary of United States aid to Chile before and after Allende took office, see Table 15-4).

As Petras and Morley's (1975:8–9) research shows: "U.S. direct private investment in Chile in 1970 stood at $1.1 billion, out of a total estimated foreign investment of $1.672 billion." Most United States corporate investment in Chile was in the mining and smelting sector (over 50 percent). "However, U.S. and foreign corporations controlled almost all of the most dynamic and critical areas of the economy by the end of 1970." The foreign-controlled industry included machinery and equipment (50 percent); iron, steel, and metal products (60 percent); petroleum products and distribution (over 50 percent); industrial and other chemicals (60 percent); rubber products (45 percent); automotive assembly (100 percent); radio and television (nearly 100 percent); and advertising (90 percent). "Furthermore, U.S. corporations controlled 80 percent of the production of Chile's only important foreign exchange earner—copper."

Chile's internal class structure fits closely that of a highly dependent country on the periphery described by Wallerstein (1974), Chirot (1977), and Rubinson (1976) above, with a small but powerful and united upper class with strong ties to private interests in core societies. (For detailed figures on this class structure, see Zeitlin et al. 1974, 1976).

Before discussing how the preconditions for political violence in Chile developed with the help of foreign influence, we must look at the relative absence of these preconditions before 1970. The consensus has generally been that Chile had one of the most stable political systems in Latin America up to 1970. As Needler (1968:891) shows, Chile had the longest history of constitutional democracy of any Latin American country. His predictions in 1968 were that the future for democracy and political stability in Chile looked good (Needler 1968:896).

Even more support for this conclusion in 1968 comes from the empirical work of Duff and McCamant (1968) and Ayres (1973). In their comparative study of Latin American countries, Duff and McCamant attempted to build a model that could explain the stability or lack of stability among these countries. Using variables that can be placed under the general headings of "social welfare, social mobilization, economic growth, distribution of income, government extractive capability, government distributive capability, and political party organization," they ranked Chile third among nineteen Latin American countries in terms of overall "system stability" (Duff and McCamant 1968:1138).

In summary, therefore, we find the preconditions for, and actual level of, political violence low in Chile before 1970 (Feierabend et al. 1969; Gurr 1969). We can concur with Ayres' (1973:502) statement that before 1970, "Among Latin American countries, Chile [continued] to be distinguished by the relative absence of sizable social aggregates capable of taking the law into their own hands as well as by the relative absence of official repression. The general impression in Chile was one of relative absence of overt civil strife and civil disorder."

TABLE 15-4
FOREIGN AID TO CHILE FROM SELECTED UNITED STATES AGENCIES AND INTERNATIONAL ORGANIZATIONS

Agency	Millions of dollars							
	1966	**1967**	**1968**	**1969**	**1970**	**1971**	**1972**	**1973**
U.S. AID	93.2	15.5	57.9	35.4	18.0	1.5	1.0	0.8
U.S. Food for Peace	14.4	7.9	23.0	15.0	7.2	6.3	5.9	2.5
U.S. military assistance	10.2	4.2	7.8	11.7	0.8	5.7	12.3	15.0
U.S. Export–Import Bank	0.1	212.3	13.4	28.7	—	—	1.6	3.1
World Bank	2.7	60.0	—	11.6	19.3	—	—	—
Inter-American Development Bank	62.2	31.0	16.5	31.9	45.6	12.0	2.1	5.2

Source: U.S. Senate Select Committee (1975b:34); see also Petras and Morley (1975:166–167).

Chile, by 1970, although industrialized by Third World standards, was dominated economically by core nations (Petras 1969; U.S. Senate Select Committee 1975b:32). It was a country in which outside interests, mainly from the United States, could apply pressures that had the potential of seriously disrupting that country's economy and basic social structure. Rather than simply sending support for one side in the conflict after it had broken out, these foreign interests had the potential to exacerbate chronic economic imbalances already existing due to its periphery status, as well as help create new ones that could lead to serious political violence. The only thing lacking in Chile before 1970 was the motivation for outside interests to apply these pressures. With a newly elected Marxist president, one who moved toward policies viewed as highly unfavorable by these foreign interests (see U.S. Senate Select Committee 1975b:44–45), that motivation soon materialized.

Not long after Allende was elected president a concerted effort was mounted from outside to disrupt the highly dependent economy and government. We are not suggesting that these foreign interests alone created the conditions leading to political violence in Chile, but as a Senate investigation (U.S. Senate Select Committee 1975b:32) maintains, these outside pressures were very important (see also Goldberg 1975:116; Petras and Morley 1975:6; Sanford 1976:150). After a coup supported by the United States failed to prevent Allende from assuming office in 1970 (U.S. Senate Select Committee 1975b:2), the efforts, mainly from the United States government and private industry, were directed toward two goals: to disrupt the economy and then aid segments within the country mobilized and mobilizing to oppose Allende's government.

Several actions were taken by multinationals and the United States government that helped disrupt the Chilean economy.

1 The various types of foreign aid coming from the United States before Allende took office were cut back severely (see Table 15-4; see also U.S. Senate Select Committee 1975b:33–35; Sanford 1976:147–148).

2 Short-term credits to Chile from American commercial banks were virtually cut off (see U.S. Senate Select Committee 1975b:33–35; Goldberg 1975:109).

3 Funds from the World Bank and Inter-American Development Bank were cut (see U.S. Senate Select Committee 1975b:33–35; Petras and Morley 1975:94).

4 Multinationals such as ITT worked with other multinationals and the United States government to organize these pressures (see Sampson 1973:283; U.S. Senate Select Committee 1975b:13–14).

5 Supplies necessary to Chile's industry were withheld, such as parts for their primarily United States–made machinery (see U.S. Senate Select Committee 1975b:33; Petras and Morley 1975:98; Goldberg 1975:109).

6 Pressure was applied to other countries to prevent them from trading with Chile (see Petras and Morley 1975:111; Farnsworth et al. 1976:362; Sanford 1976:149).

The above measures contributed to limiting industrial output in Chile severely by 1972 (see Petras and Morley 1975:12; Farnsworth et al. 1976). And in Goldberg's (1975:109–110) words: "The United States' credit blockage aroused intense consumer dissatisfaction which the opposition parties succeeded in mobilizing against the government. ... Producers whose imports were also curtailed joined newly deprived consumers in protest strikes and demonstrations against the government."

The next step for foreign powers working within Chile was fairly simple—to provide support for old and newly emerging protest groups (U.S. Senate Select Committee 1975b:29–30). In this regard, the CIA was authorized to spend $8 million between 1970 and 1973, $3 million of this spent in 1973 alone (U.S. Senate Select Committee 1975b:1). It is interesting to note that while all other aid to Chile from the United States was cut, the aid going specifically to the military in Chile was maintained at a high level (U.S. Senate Select Committee 1975b:37–39; Petras and Morley 1975:126; Sanford 1976:149; see also Table 15-4). In line with this the United States military also attempted to cultivate stronger personal ties with the Chilean military (U.S. Senate Select Committee 1975b:28; Petras and Morley 1975:119; Sanford 1976:52, 78, 192) in an attempt to make it known that the United States would not look unfavorably on a coup (U.S. Senate Select Committee 1975b:26).

In conclusion, what we find in the case of Chile is a concerted effort by actors in a core society that contributed to the disruption of Chile's social structure. This disruption helped create the preconditions for collective violence. Rather than sitting back and taking advantage of the internal political violence that may or may not have arisen, foreign interests were working to help create the preconditions that could lead to political violence.

Three main factors were important in the development of political violence in Chile during Allende's term in office. Due to the vested interests of those favored by the previous status quo of Chile's dependent relationship, opposition groups developed (aided by the CIA) as soon as Allende was elected. Newly deprived groups later arose to oppose Allende because of the economic disruption promoted by the United States government and multinational economic actions against Chile. Then both of these opposition groups were aided by CIA covert actions, which further contributed to an increasingly vicious cycle of political and economic breakdown.

The result was the coup of September 1973 that killed President Allende and thousands more (Sanford 1976). A military dictatorship took power that reopened Chile to economic investment and trade from the core, and reestablished the place of wealthy Chilean elites tied to the core interests. The United States government more than restored the aid and loans that were cut or eliminated when Allende took office in 1970 (Petras and Morley 1975:141), and top United States banks sent huge loans to revitalize the economy (Letelier and Moffitt 1980). Chile was welcomed back to its place in the world economic system.

THE WORLD STRATIFICATION SYSTEM: A CONCLUSION

We can conclude by first emphasizing what has *not* been suggested by world system theorists. Most important, the world system and multinational corporations *cannot* be held accountable for all of the world's inequality. To state the obvious, there was world inequality before the modern world system developed, and there are pockets of poverty around the world untouched by the world economic system. Culture, climate, and lack of resources, among many other factors not directly related to world stratification, can help produce and maintain poverty.

However, to a very large degree, all regions of the world are increasingly interrelated in a worldwide economic system. And because of differing economic interests in this system, and because of differing amounts of power to ensure that these interests are met, there is a world stratification system that produces inequality among nations and inequality among classes within the nations.

It must also be recognized that no easy solutions to underdevelopment can be identified. Many problems are faced by Third World nations that will not be solved by simply removing core dominance (as Myrdal 1970, among others, has shown). And even if a Third World nation is successful in opting out of the capitalist world system, thus reducing multinational corporate exploitation within the Third World nation, the nation may face economic isolation sponsored by core nations and/or a new form of imperialism when forced to turn to other powerful nations, like the Soviet Union.

The reader should also be cautioned not to overly reify the world stratification system. Core elites are not all-powerful, and there is no grand plan with people working out designs in something like a war room to make sure periphery nations do not develop economically, trade with noncore nations, or pay their workers living wages. Rather, the dominance of core nations and their elites comes from many decisions and actions, not always seen as related by dominant actors, that over time add up to a system of exploitation as described in this chapter.

At times, of course, there may be planned coordinated policies to maintain some aspect of the world stratification system. For example, as noted earlier, the complex covert action used against Chile was first used against Iran in 1953 (Mosley 1978:325; Roosevelt 1979). The director of the CIA at the time, Allen Dulles, and his brother in the State Department, John Foster Dulles, liked the plan so well it was used again and again. But it is doubtful that these core actors viewed their plan as maintaining a world stratification exactly as described here. They saw their activity as furthering specific United States interests around the world, which to them meant above all "fighting communism."

Finally, we must not take the simplistic view that these core elites, along with their supporters among noncore elites, are evil people seeking to profit from starving children in poor nations. As C. Wright Mills (1956:284) wrote in reference to the United States power elite, "We are sure that they are honorable men. But what is honor? Honor can only mean living up to a code that one believes to be honorable. There is no one code upon which we are all agreed.''

These core elites no doubt view their duty as seeking profits for their respective corporations or seeing to it that their country remains strong in the world. And there is just enough validity (although, as we have seen, it is slight) in the view that multinational corporations are creating jobs and better living conditions in poor countries to justify their profit-seeking activities around the world as good for poor nations, while ignoring the negative consequences.

What we find in the ever more interrelated activities of people around the world is a stratification system that is in many ways similar to domestic systems of stratification. There are, of course, some differences between the two types of systems. For one, the phenomenon of nationalism can produce less international class unity and more overt class conflict between the core, semiperiphery, and periphery. Also, it is more difficult to maintain the world stratification system through ideological justification because of nationalism, cultural differences, and communication limitations. And although there are a property structure and occupational division of labor stretching around most of the world, we do not find extensive bureaucratic authority structures that create divisions related to international class interests.

There are other differences between domestic and world stratification, most of which were described earlier in this chapter. What is most striking, however, are the similarities. We find that the world is divided into something quite similar to classes, and the differing interests of these classes result in class conflict—conflict that is sometimes hidden and sometimes open, but always threatening to undermine the advantaged position of those at the top.

REFERENCES

Abegglen, James C., and George Stalk, Jr. 1985. *Kaisha: The Japanese Corporation.* New York: Basic Books.

Abrahamson, Mark. 1973. "Functionalism and the Functional Theory of Stratification: An Empirical Assessment." *American Journal of Sociology,* 78:1236–1246.

Abrahamson, Mark. 1979. "A Functional Theory of Organizational Stratification." *Social Forces,* 58:128–145.

Acker, Joan. 1973. "Women and Social Stratification: A Case of Intellectual Sexism." *American Journal of Sociology,* 78:936–945.

Adorno, T. W., E. Frenkel-Brunswik, D. J. Levinson, and R. N. Sanford. 1950. *The Authoritarian Personality.* New York: Harper & Row.

Ajami, Fouad. 1972. "Corporate Giants: Some Global Social Costs." Pp. 109–125 in G. Modelski (ed.), *Multinational Corporations and World Order.* Beverly Hills, Calif.: Stage Publications.

Alba, Richard, and Gwen Moore. 1982. "Ethnicity in the American Elite." *American Sociological Review,* 47:373–383.

Aldrich, Howard, and Jane Weiss. 1981. "Differentiation Within the U.S. Capitalist Class: Workforce Size and Income Differences." *American Sociological Review,* 46:279–289.

Alexander, Karl, Bruce Eckland, and Larry Griffin. 1975. "The Wisconsin Model of Socioeconomic Achievement." *American Journal of Sociology,* 81:324–342.

Alexander, Karl, and Martha Cook. 1982. "Curricula and Coursework: A Surprise Ending to a Familiar Story." *American Sociological Review,* 47:626–640.

Alexander, Karl, Martha Cook, and Edward McDill. 1978. "Curriculum Tracking and Educational Stratification: Some Further Evidence." *American Sociological Review,* 43:47–66.

Allen, Michael. 1974. "The Structure of Interorganizational Elite Cooptation: Interlocking Corporate Directorates." *American Sociological Review,* 39:393–406.

Allen, Michael. 1977. "Economic Interest Groups and the Corporate Elite Structure." *Social Science Quarterly,* 58:597–615.

Allen, Michael. 1978. "Continuity and Change Within the Core Corporate Elite." *Sociological Quarterly,* 19:510–521.

Allen, Michael Patrick, and Philip Broyles. 1989. "Class Hegemony and Political Finance: Presidential Campaign Contributions of Wealthy Capitalist Families." *American Sociological Review,* 54:275–287.

Althusser, Louis. 1969. *For Marx.* Harmondsworth, England: Penguin.

Althusser, Louis. 1977. *Politics and History.* London: NLB.

Alves, Wayne, and Peter Rossi, 1978. "Who Should Get What? Fairness Judgments of Distribution of Earnings." *American Journal of Sociology,* 84:541–564.

American Almanac. 1970. New York: Grosset and Dunlap.

Armory, Cleveland, 1960. *Who Killed Society?* New York: Harper & Row.

Anderson, Barbara A. 1987. "The Life Course of Soviet Women Born 1905–1960." Pp. 203–240, in James R. Millar (ed.), *Politics, Work, and Daily Life in the USSR: A Survey of Former Soviet Citizens.* Cambridge: Cambridge University Press.

Anderson, Charles. 1974. *The Political Economy of Social Class.* Englewood Cliffs, N.J.: Prentice-Hall.

Anderson, Martin. 1978. *Welfare: The Political Economy of Welfare Reform in the United States.* Stanford: Hoover Institution Press.

Andrews, Frank, and Stephen Withey. 1976. *Social Indicators of Well-Being*. New York: Plenum.

Antonio, Robert. 1979. "The Contradiction of Domination and Production in Bureaucracy: The Contribution of Organizational Efficiency to the Decline of the Roman Empire." *American Sociological Review*, 44:895–912.

Anweiler, Oskar. 1972. "Educational Policy and Social Structure in the Soviet Union." Pp. 173–210 in Boris Meissner (ed.), *Social Change in the Soviet Union*. Notre Dame, Ind.: University of Notre Dame Press.

Appelbaum, Richard. 1978a. "Marxist Method: Structural Constraints and Social Praxis." *The American Sociologist*, 13:73–81.

Appelbaum, Richard. 1978b. "Marx's Theory of the Falling Rate of Profit: Towards a Dialectical Analysis of Structural Social Change." *American Sociological Review*, 43:67–80.

Apter, David E., and Nagayo Sawa. 1984. *Against the State: Politics and Social Protest in Japan*. Cambridge, Mass.: Harvard University Press.

Aptheker, Herbert. 1963. *American Negro Slave Revolts*. New York: International Publishers.

Archer, Jules. 1973. *The Plot to Seize the White House*. New York: Hawthorn Books.

Aronowitz, Stanley. 1974. *False Promises: The Shaping of American Working Class Consciousness*. New York: McGraw-Hill.

Ash, Timothy Garton. 1990. "The Revolution of the Magic Lantern." *New York Review of Books*, 35 (January 18):42–51.

Atkinson, Dick. 1972. *Orthodox Consensus and Radical Alternative*. New York: Basic Books.

Auletta, Ken. 1983. *The Under Class*. New York: Vintage.

Ayres, Robert. 1973. "Political History, Institutional Structure, and Prospects for Socialism in Chile." *Comparative Politics*, 5:497–522.

Bachrach, Peter. 1967. *The Theory of Democratic Elitism*. Boston: Little, Brown.

Baker, P. M. 1977. "On the Use of Psychophysical Methods in the Study of Social Status: A Replication, and Some Theoretical Problems." *Social Forces*, 55:898–920.

Balkwell, James, Frederick Bates, and Albeno Garbin. 1980. "On the Intersubjectivity of Occupational Status Evaluations: A Test of a Key Assumption Underlying the 'Wisconsin Model' of Status Attainment." *Social Forces*, 58:865–881.

Baltzell, E. Digby. 1958. *Philadelphia Gentlemen: The Making of a National Upper Class*. New York: Free Press.

Baltzell, E. Digby. 1964. *The Protestant Establishment: Aristocracy and Caste in America*. New York: Random House.

Barash, David. 1977. "Reflections on a Premature Burial." *The American Sociologist*, 12:62–68.

Barger, Ben, and Everett Hall. 1965. "The Interaction of Ability Levels and Socioeconomic Variables in Prediction of College Dropouts and Grade Achievement." *Educational and Psychological Measurement*, 25:501–508.

Barnet, Richard, and Ronald Müller. 1974. *Global Reach*. New York: Simon & Schuster.

Barnet, Richard, and Ronald Müller. 1980. "The Global Shopping Center." Pp. 381–398 in Mark Green and Robert Massie (eds.), *The Big Business Reader: Essays in Corporate America*. New York: The Pilgrim Press.

Baron, James, and William Bielby. 1980. "Bringing the Firms Back In: Stratification,

Segmentation, and the Organization of Work." *American Sociological Review,* 45:737–766.

Baron, James, and William Bielby. 1984. "The Organization of Work in a Segmented Economy." *American Sociological Review,* 49:454–473.

Barrett, Richard, and Martin King Whyte. 1982. "Dependency Theory and Taiwan: Analysis of a Deviant Case." *American Journal of Sociology,* 87:1064–1089.

Barrett, Richard, and Martin King Whyte. 1984. "What is Dependency? Reply to Hammer." *American Journal of Sociology,* 89:937–940.

Barton, Allen. 1985. "Determinants of Economic Attitudes in the American Business Elite." *American Journal of Sociology,* 91:54–87.

Baughman, F. Earl. 1971. *Black Americans.* New York: Academic Press.

Bayer, Alan. 1968. "The College Dropout: Factors Affecting Senior College Completion." *Sociology of Education,* 41:305–316.

Beck, E. M., Patrick Horan, and Charles Tolbert, 1978. "Stratification in a Dual Economy: A Structural Model of Earnings Determination." *American Sociological Review,* 43:704–720.

Beck, E. M., Patrick Horan, and Charles Tolbert. 1980. "Social Stratification in Industrial Society: Further Evidence for a Structural Alternative." *American Sociological Review,* 45:712–719.

Befu, Harumi. 1981. *Japan: An Anthropological Introduction.* New York: Chandler Publishing Co.

Beliaev, Edward, and Pavel Butorin. 1982. "The Institutionalization of Soviet Sociology: Its Social and Political Context." *Social Forces,* 61:418–435.

Belknap, Robert. 1987. "On Quantifying Quality." Pp. 7–12 in Horst Herlemann (ed.), *Quality of Life in the Soviet Union.* Boulder, Colo.: Westview Press.

Bell, Daniel. 1976. *The Coming of Post-Industrial Society.* New York: Basic Books.

Bell, Wendell, and Robert Robinson. 1980. "Cognitive Maps of Class and Racial Inequalities in England and the United States." *American Journal of Sociology,* 86:320–349.

Bellah, Robert. 1970. *Beyond Belief.* New York: Harper & Row.

Bellah, Robert N., Richard Madsen, William M. Sullivan, Ann Swidler, and Steven M. Tipton. 1985. *Habits of the Heart: Individualism and Commitment in American Life.* New York: Harper & Row.

Bendix, Reinhard. 1960. *Max Weber: An Intellectual Portrait.* New York: Doubleday.

Bendix, Reinhard. 1978. *Kings or People: Power and the Mandate to Rule.* Berkeley: University of California Press.

Bendix, Reinhard, and Frank Howton. 1959. "Social Mobility and the American Business Elite." Pp. 114–143 in Reinhard Bendix and Seymour Lipset (eds.), *Social Mobility in Industrial Society.* Berkeley: University of California Press.

Benedict, Ruth. 1947. *The Chrysanthemum and the Sword: Patterns of Japanese Culture.* New York: Houghton Mifflin.

Berger, J., M. Zelditch, B. Anderson, and B. P. Cohen. 1972. "Structural Aspects of Distributive Justice: A Status Value Formulation." Pp. 111–129 in J. Berger, M. Zelditch, and B. Anderson (eds.), *Sociological Theories in Progress,* vol. 2. Boston: Houghton Mifflin.

Berger, Peter, and Thomas Luchman. 1966. *The Social Construction of Reality.* Garden City, N.Y.: Doubleday.

Berle, Adolf. 1959. *Power Without Property*. New York: Harcourt Brace & Jovanovich.

Berle, Adolf, and Gardiner Means. 1932. *The Modern Corporation and Private Property*. New York: Macmillan.

Berlin, Isaiah. 1963. *Karl Marx: His Life and Environment*. New York: Oxford University Press.

Bernstein, Carl. 1977. "The CIA and the Media." *Rolling Stone*, October 20, pp. 55–67.

Berry, John. 1986. "U.S. Wealth Becomes More Concentrated." *Washington Post* (July 26, D1b).

Betz, Michael. 1974. "Riots and Welfare: Are They Related?" *Social Problems*, 21:345–355.

Bielby, William T., and James N. Baron. 1986. "Men and Women at Work: Sex Segregation and Statistical Discrimination." *American Journal of Sociology*, 91:759–799.

Blair, John. 1976. *The Control of Oil*. New York: Vintage Books.

Blau, Judith, and Peter Blau. 1982. "The Cost of Inequality: Metropolitan Structure and Violent Crime." *American Sociological Review*, 47:114–129.

Blau, Peter, and Otis Dudley Duncan. 1967. *The American Occupational Structure*. New York: John Wiley & Sons.

Bloch, Marc. 1961. *Feudal Society*. London: Routledge & Kegan Paul.

Bloomquist, Leonard, and Gene Summer. 1982. "Organization of Production and Community Income Distributions." *American Sociological Review*, 47:325–338.

Bluestone, Barry. 1988. "The Great U-Turn: An Inquiry into Recent U.S. Economic Trends in Employment, Earnings and Family Income." Paper presented to the Sapporo Seminar in American Studies, Sapporo, Japan, Hokkaido University, August, 1988.

Bluestone, Barry, and Bennett Harrison. 1982. *The Deindustrialization of America*. New York: Basic Books.

Blumberg, Paul. 1980. *Inequality in an Age of Decline*. New York: Oxford University Press.

Blumberg, Paul, and P. W. Paul. 1975. "Continuities and Discontinuities in Upper-Class Marriages." *Journal of Marriage and Family*, 37:63–77.

Boies, John L. 1989. "Money, Business, and the State: Material Interests. *Fortune 500* Corporations, and the Size of Political Action Committees." *American Sociological Review*, 54:821–833.

Bolin, Robert, and Susan Bolton Bolin. 1980. "Sociobiology and Paradigms in Evolutionary Theory." *American Sociological Review*, 45:154–159.

Bollen, Kenneth. 1983. "World System Position, Dependency, and Democracy: The Cross-National Evidence." *American Sociological Review*, 48:468–479.

Bornschier, Volker, and Thank-Huyen Ballmer-Cao. 1979. "Income Inequality: A Cross-National Study of the Relationships Between MNC-Penetration, Dimensions of the Power Structure and Income Distribution." *American Sociological Review*, 44:487–506.

Bornschier, Volker, Christopher Chase-Dunn, and Richard Rubinson. 1978. "Cross-National Evidence of the Effects of Foreign Investment and Aid on Economic Growth and Inequality: A Survey of Findings and a Reanalysis." *American Journal of Sociology*, 84:651–683.

Boswell, Terry. 1989. "Colonial Empires and the Capitalist World-Economy: A Time Series Analysis of Colonization, 1640–1960." *American Sociological Review,* 54:169–180.

Bottomore, Thomas B. 1964. *Elites and Society.* Baltimore: Penguin Books.

Bottomore, Thomas B. 1966. *Classes in Modern Society.* New York: Vintage Books.

Bottomore, Thomas B. (ed.). 1973. *Karl Marx.* Englewood Cliffs, N.J.: Prentice-Hall.

Bowker, Lee. 1972. "Red and Black in Contemporary American History Texts: A Content Analysis." Pp. 101–109 in Howard Bahr, Bruce Chadwick, and Robert Day (eds.), *Native Americans Today: Sociological Perspectives.* New York: Harper & Row.

Bowles, Samuel. 1983. *Beyond the Wasteland: A Democratic Alternative to Economic Decline.* New York: Anchor.

Bowles, S., and H. Gintis. 1976. *Schooling in Capitalist America: Educational Reform and the Contradictions of Economic Life.* New York: Basic Books.

Bradburn, N. M., and David Caplovitz. 1965. *Reports on Happiness.* Chicago: Aldine.

Bradshaw, York W. 1988. "Reassessing Economic Dependency and Uneven Development: The Kenyan Experience." *American Sociological Review,* 53:693–708.

Breedlove, William L., and Patrick D. Nolan. 1988. "International Stratification and Inequality 1960–1980." *International Journal of Contemporary Sociology,* 25:105–123.

Briar, Scott. 1966. "Welfare From Below: Recipients' Views of the Public Welfare System." Pp. 73–95 in Jacobus Ten Broek (ed.), *The Law of the Poor.* San Francisco: Chandler.

Brint, Steven. 1984. "'New-Class' and Cumulative Trend Explanations of the Liberal Political Attitudes of Professionals." *American Journal of Sociology,* 60:30–71.

Brinton, Mary C. 1989. "Gender Stratification in Contemporary Urban Japan." *American Sociological Review,* 54:549–564.

Broadbent, Jeffery. 1986. "Environmental Politics in Japan: An Integrated Structural Analysis." *Sociological Forum,* 4:179–202.

Broadbent, Jeffery. 1989. "Strategies and Structural Contradictions: Growth Coalition Politics in Japan." *American Sociological Review,* 54:707–721.

Broom, Leonard, and Robert Cushing, 1977. "A Modest Test of an Immodest Theory: The Functional Theory of Stratification." *American Sociological Review,* 42:157–169.

Broom, Leonard, F. L. Jones, Patrick McDonnell, and Trevor Williams. 1980. *The Inheritance of Inequality.* London: Routledge & Kegan Paul.

Broom, Leonard, and F. Lancaster Jones. 1976. *Opportunity and Attainment in Australia.* Canberra: Australian National University/Stanford University Press.

Brown, Dee. 1970. *Bury My Heart at Wounded Knee: An Indian History of the American West.* New York: Holt, Rinehart and Winston.

Brown, J. Larry. 1987. "Hunger in the U.S." *Scientific American,* (February) 256:37–41.

Brown, Lester. 1976. "World Population Trends: Signs of Hope, Signs of Distress." *Worldwatch Papers,* 8:1–10.

Brownstein, Ronald, and Nina Easton. 1983. *Reagan's Ruling Class: Portraits of the President's Top One Hundred Officials.* New York: Pantheon.

Bruce-Briggs, B. (ed.). 1979. *The New Class?* New Brunswick, N.J.: Transaction.

Brunt, P. A. 1971. *Social Conflicts in the Roman Republic.* London: Chatto & Windus.

Buckley, Sandra, and Vera Mackie. 1986. "Women in the New Japanese State." Pp.

173–185 in Gavan McCormack and Yoshio Sugimoto (eds.), *Democracy in Contemporary Japan*. New York: M. E. Sharpe.

Bunting, David. 1976. "Corporate Interlocking, Part III. Interlocks and Return on Investment." *Directors and Boards*, 1:4–11.

Burbank, Garin. 1976. *When Farmers Voted Red: The Gospel of Socialism in the Oklahoma Countryside, 1910–1924*. Westport, Conn.: Greenwood Press.

Burch, Philip. 1973. "The N.A.M. as an Interest Group." *Politics and Society*, 4:97–130.

Burch, Philip H. 1981. *Elites in American History*, vols. 1–3. New York: Holmes and Meier.

Burger, Thomas. 1977. "Talcott Parsons, the Problem of Order in Society, and the Program of an Analytical Sociology," *American Journal of Sociology*, 83:320–334.

Burnham, James. 1941. *The Managerial Revolution*. New York: Day.

Burnham, Walter. 1974. "Equality in Voting." Pp. 288–298 in Lee Rainwater (ed.), *Social Problems and Public Policy: Inequality and Justice*. Chicago: Aldine.

Burris, Val. 1987. "The Political Partisanship of American Business: A Study of Corporate Political Action Committees." *American Sociological Review*, 52:732–744.

Burt, Ronald S. 1983. "Corporate Philanthropy as a Cooptive Relation." *Social Forces*, 62:419–449.

Burt, Ronald S., Kenneth P. Christman, and Harold C. Kilburn, Jr. 1980. "Testing a Structural Theory of Corporate Cooptation: Inter-Organizational Directorate Ties as a Strategy for Avoiding Market Constraints on Profits." *American Sociological Review*, 45:821–841.

Burtless, Gary. 1986. "Public Spending for the Poor: Trends, Prospects, and Economic Limits." Pp. 18–49, in Sheldon H. Danziger and Daniel H. Weinberg (eds.), *Fighting Poverty: What Works and What Doesn't*. Cambridge, Mass.: Harvard University Press.

Campbell, A. 1971. *White Attitudes Toward Black People*. Ann Arbor: Institute for Social Research.

Carcopino, Jerome. 1973. *Daily Life in Ancient Rome*. New Haven: Yale University Press.

Caudill, Harry. 1962. *Night Comes to the Cumberlands: A Biography of a Depressed Area*. New York: Little, Brown.

Caudill, Harry. 1980. "Unsafe in Any Mine—The Story of Big Black Mountain." Pp. 140–153 in Mark Green and Robert Massie (eds.), *The Big Business Reader: Essays on Corporate America*. New York: The Pilgrim Press.

Caves, Richard E., and Masu Uekusa. 1976. "Industrial Organization." Pp. 459–524 in Hugh Patrick and Henry Rosovsky (eds.), *Asia's New Giant: How the Japanese Economy Works*. Washington, D.C.: The Brookings Institution.

Centers, Richard. 1949. *The Psychology of Social Classes*. Princeton, N.J.: Princeton University Press.

Cerulo, Karen. 1984. "Television, Magazine Covers, and the Shared Symbolic Environment: 1948–1970." *American Sociological Review*, 49:566–570.

Chartier, Roger (ed.). 1989. *A History of Private Life: Passions of the Renaissance*. Cambridge, Mass.: Belknap/Harvard University Press.

Chase, Ivan. 1975. "A Comparison of Men's and Women's Intergenerational Mobility in the United States." *American Sociological Review*, 40:483–505.

Chase-Dunn, Christopher. 1975. "The Effects of International Economic Dependence on Development and Inequality: A Cross-National Study." *American Sociological Review*, 40:720–738.

Chase-Dunn, Christopher, and Richard Rubinson. 1977. "Toward a Structural Perspective on the World-System." *Politics and Society,* 7:453–476.

Childe, V. Gordon. 1952. *New Light on the Most Ancient East.* London: Routledge & Kegan Paul.

Chirot, Daniel. 1977. *Social Change in the Twentieth Century.* New York: Harcourt Brace Jovanovich.

Chirot, Daniel. 1978. "Social Change in Communist Romania." *Social Forces,* 57:457–499.

Chirot, Daniel. 1986. *Social Change in the Modern Era.* New York: Harcourt Brace Jovanovich.

Chirot, Daniel. 1984. "The Rise of the West." *American Sociological Review,* 50:181–195.

Christopher, Robert. 1983. *The Japanese Mind: The Goliath Explained.* New York: Simon & Schuster.

Claiborn, W. L. 1969. "Expectancy Effects in the Classroom: A Failure to Replicate." *Journal of Educational Psychology,* 60:377–383.

Clark, Rodney. 1979. *The Japanese Company.* Tokyo: Tuttle.

Clark, Ronald. 1971. *Einstein: The Life and Times.* New York: Times Mirror World Publishing.

Coe, Richard. 1978. "Dependency and Poverty in the Short and Long Run." In G. J. Duncan and J. N. Morgan (eds.), *Five Thousand American Families—Patterns of Economic Progress,* vol. 6. Ann Arbor: Institute for Social Research, University of Michigan Press.

Cohen, Albert K., and Harold Hodges. 1963. "Characteristics of the Lower-Blue-Collar Classes." *Social Problems,* 10:303–334.

Cohen, Jere. 1980. "Rational Capitalism in Renaissance Italy." *American Journal of Sociology,* 85:1340–1355.

Cohen, Jere, Lawrence Hazelrigg, and Whitney Pope. 1975. "De-Parsonizing Weber." *American Sociological Review,* 40:229–241.

Cohen, Mark. 1977. *The Food Crisis in Prehistory: Overpopulation and the Origins of Agriculture.* New Haven: Yale University Press.

Cohen, Percy. 1968. *Modern Sociological Theory.* New York: Basic Books.

Cole, Stephen, and Robert Lejeune. 1972. "Illness and the Legitimization of Failure." *American Sociological Review,* 37:347–356.

Collier, Peter, and David Horowitz. 1976. *The Rockefellers: An American Dynasty.* New York: Holt, Rinehart and Winston.

Collins, Norman, and Lee Preston. 1961. "The Size Structure of the Largest Industrial Firms, 1909–1958." *American Economic Review,* 51:986–1011.

Collins, Randall. 1971. "Functional and Conflict Theories of Educational Stratification." *American Sociological Review,* 36:1002–1019.

Collins, Randall. 1975. *Conflict Sociology.* New York: Academic Press.

Collins, Randall. 1980. "Comment on Ifskhokin's 'The Dual System.'" *American Journal of Sociology,* 85:1337–1339.

Collins, Robert. 1977. "Positive Business Responses to the New Deal: The Roots of the Committee for Economic Development, 1933–1942." *Business History Review,* 22:103–119.

Connor, Walter D. 1988. "The Soviet Working Class: Change and Its Political Impact." Pp. 31–52, in Michael Paul Sacks and Jerry G. Pankhurst (eds.), *Understanding Soviet Society.* Boston: Unwin Hyman.

Cook, Alice H., and Hiroko Hayashi. 1980. *Working Women in Japan: Discrimination, Resistance, and Reform*. Ithaca, N.Y.: Cornell University Press.

Cookson, Peter W., Jr., and Caroline Hodges Persell. 1985. *Preparing for Power: America's Elite Boarding Schools*. New York: Basic Books.

Coser, Lewis. 1956. *The Functions of Social Conflict*. New York: Free Press.

Coser, Lewis. 1967. *Continuities in the Study of Social Conflict*. New York: Free Press.

Covell, Jon Carter, and Alan Covell. 1984. *Korean Impact on Japanese Culture: Japan's Hidden History*. Elizabeth, N.J., and Seoul, Korea: Hollym International.

Cox, Oliver. 1948. *Caste, Class and Race*. Garden City, N.Y.: Doubleday.

Coxon, A. P. M., P. M. Davies, and C. L. Jones. 1986. *Images of Social Stratification: Occupational Structures and Class*. London: Sage.

Crankshaw, Edward. 1976. *The Shadow of the Winter Palace: Russia's Drift to Revolution, 1825–1917*. New York: Viking Press.

Crovitz, Gordon. 1987. "Presidents Have a History of Unilateral Moves." *Wall Street Journal*, (Jan. 15):24.

Cuber, John, and William Kenkel. 1954. *Social Stratification in the United States*. New York: Appleton-Century-Crofts.

Cummings, Scott, and Del Taebel. 1978. "The Economic Socialization of Children: A Neo-Marxist Analysis." *Social Problems*, 26:198–210.

Curtis, Richard F. 1986. "Household and Family in Theory on Inequality." *American Sociological Review*, 51:168–183.

Cutright, Phillips. 1968. "Occupational Inheritance: A Cross-Nation Analysis." *American Journal of Sociology*, 73:400–416.

Dahl, Robert. 1958. "A Critique of the Ruling Elite Model." *American Political Science Review*, 52:463–469.

Dahl, Robert. 1961. *Who Governs?* New Haven: Yale University Press.

Dahl, Robert. 1967. *Pluralist Democracy in the United States*. Chicago: Rand McNally.

Dahrendorf, Ralf. 1959. *Class and Class Conflict in Industrial Society*. Stanford, Calif.: Stanford University Press.

Dahrendorf, Ralf. 1968. *Essays in the Theory of Society*. Stanford, Calif.: Stanford University Press.

Dahrendorf, Ralf. 1969. "Review of Lenski's 'Power and Privilege.'" *American Sociological Review*, 34:248–249.

Danziger, Sheldon, and Robert Haveman. 1982. "Poverty in the United States: Where Do We Stand." *Focus*, 5:1–16. Institute for Research on Poverty, Madison: University of Wisconsin.

Danziger, Sheldon, Robert H. Haveman, and Robert D. Plotnick. 1986. "Antipoverty Policy: Effects on the Poor and the Nonpoor." Pp. 50–77 in Sheldon H. Danziger and Daniel H. Weinberg (eds.), *Fighting Poverty: What Works and What Doesn't*. Cambridge, Mass.: Harvard University Press.

Davies, James. 1962. "Toward a Theory of Revolution." *American Sociological Review*, 27:5–19.

Davis, Kingsley, 1948. *Human Societies*. New York: Macmillan.

Davis, Kingsley, and Wilbert Moore. 1945. "Some Principles of Stratification." *American Sociological Review*, 10:242–249.

Davis, Nancy, and Robert Robinson. 1988. "Class Identification of Men and Women in the 1970s and 1980s." *American Sociological Review*, 53:103–112.

De Jong, Peter, Milton Brawer, and Stanley Robin. 1971. "Patterns of Female Intergenerational Occupational Mobility: A Comparison with Male Patterns of Intergenerational Occupational Mobility." *American Sociological Review,* 36:1035–1042.

Della Fave, L. Richard. 1974a. "Success Values: Are They Universal or Class-Differentiated?" *American Journal of Sociology,* 80:153–169.

Della Fave, L. Richard. 1974b. "The Culture of Poverty Revisited: A Strategy for Research." *Social Problems,* 21:609–621.

Della Fave, L. Richard. 1974c. "On the Structure of Egalitarianism." *Social Problems,* 22:199–213.

Della Fave, L. Richard. 1980. "The Meek Shall Not Inherit the Earth: Self-Evaluation and the Legitimacy of Stratification." *American Sociological Review,* 45:955–971.

Della Fave, L. Richard. 1986. "Toward an Explication of the Legitimation Process." *Social Forces,* 65:476–500.

Della Fave, L. Richard, and George Hillery. 1980. "Status Inequality in a Religious Community: The Case of a Trappist Monastery." *Social Forces,* 59:62–84.

Demo, David, and Ritch Savin-Williams. 1983. "Early Adolescent Self-Esteem as a Function of Social Class: Rosenberg and Pearlin Revisited." *American Journal of Sociology,* 88:763–774.

de Tocqueville, Alexis. 1969. *Democracy in America.* New York: Doubleday.

Devine, Joel A. 1983. "Fiscal Policy and Class Income Inequality: The Distributional Consequences of Governmental Revenues and Expenditures in the United States. 1949–1976." *American Sociological Review,* 48:606–622.

De Vos, George, and Hiroshi Wagatsuma. 1966. *Japan's Invisible Race: Caste in Culture and Personality.* Berkeley: University of California Press.

Diamond, D. E., and H. Bedrosian. 1970. *Hiring Standards and Job Performance.* Washington, D.C.: U.S. Government Printing Office.

DiMaggio, Paul J., and Walter W. Powell. 1983. "The Iron Cage Revisited: Institutional Isomorphism and Collective Rationality in Organizational Fields." *American Sociological Review,* 48:147–160.

Djilas, Milovan. 1965. *The New Class.* New York: Praeger.

Doi, Takeo. 1981. *The Anatomy of Dependence.* Tokyo: Kodansha.

Doi, Takeo. 1986. *The Anatomy of Self: The Individual Versus Society.* Tokyo: Kodansha.

Domhoff, G. William. 1967. *Who Rules America?* Englewood Cliffs, N.J.: Prentice-Hall.

Domhoff, G. William. 1970. *The Higher Circles.* New York: Random House.

Domhoff, G. William. 1974. *The Bohemian Grove and Other Retreats.* New York: Harper & Row.

Domhoff, G. William. 1975. "Social Clubs, Policy-Planning Groups, and Corporations: A Network Study of Ruling-Class Cohesiveness." *The Insurgent Sociologist,* 5:173–184.

Domhoff, G. William. 1979. *The Powers That Be.* New York: Vintage Press.

Domhoff, G. William. 1981. "Politics Among the Redwoods: Ronald Reagan's Bohemian Grove Connection." *The Progressive,* (January): 32–36.

Domhoff, G. William. 1983. *Who Rules America Now?: A View for the '80s.* Englewood Cliffs, N.J.: Prentice-Hall.

Domhoff, G. William, and Hoyt Ballard (eds.). 1968. *C. Wright Mills and 'The Power Elite.'* Boston: Beacon Press.

Domhoff, G. William. 1990. *The Power Elite and the State*. New York: Aldine de Gruyter.

Dooley, Peter. 1969. "The Interlocking Directorate." *American Economic Review*, 59:314–323.

Dore, Ronald. 1987. *Taking Japan Seriously*. Stanford: Stanford University Press.

Dowie, Mark. 1980. "The Dumping of Hazardous Products on Foreign Markets." Pp. 430–444 in Mark Green and Robert Massie (eds.), *The Big Business Reader: Essays on Corporate America*. New York: The Pilgrim Press.

Downes, Bryan T. 1970. "A Critical Reexamination of the Social and Political Characteristics of Riot Cities." *Social Science Quarterly*, 51:349–360.

Duby, Georges (ed.). 1988. *A History of Private Life: Revelations of the Medieval World*. Cambridge, Mass.: Belknap/Harvard University Press.

Duff, E. A., and M. McCamant. 1968. "Measuring Social and Political Requirements for System Stability in Latin America." *American Political Science Review*, 62:1125–1143.

Dukas, Helen, and Banesh Hoffman. 1979. *Albert Einstein: The Human Side, New Glimpses From His Archives*. Princeton: Princeton University Press.

Dumont, Louis. 1970. *Homo Hierarchieus: The Caste System and Its Implications*. Chicago: University of Chicago Press.

Duncan, Greg. 1976. "Food Expenditure Changes Between 1972 and 1974." Pp. 196–212 in Greg Duncan and James Morgan (eds.), *Five Thousand American Families—Patterns of Economic Progress*, vol. IX. Ann Arbor: Institute for Social Research, University of Michigan.

Duncan, Otis Dudley. 1965. "The Trend of Occupational Mobility in the United States." *American Sociological Review*, 30:491–498.

Duncan, Otis Dudley. 1966. "Methodological Issues in the Analysis of Social Mobility." Pp. 51–97 in Niel Smelser and Seymour Lipset (eds.), *Social Structure and Mobility in Economic Development*. Chicago: Aldine.

Duncan-Jones, Richard. 1974. *The Economy of the Roman Empire*. Cambridge, Mass.: Cambridge University Press.

Dunn, Patricia. 1984. "Reagan's Solution for Aiding Families With Dependent Children." Pp. 88–110, in Anthony Champagne and Edward Harpham (eds.), *The Attack on the Welfare State*. Prospect Heights, Ill.: Waveland Press.

Durkheim, Émile. 1951. *Suicide*. New York: Free Press.

Durkheim, Émile. 1962. *Socialism*. Edited with an Introduction by Alvin Gouldner. New York: Collier Books.

Durkheim, Émile. 1964. *The Division of Labor in Society*. New York: Free Press.

Dutton, Diana. 1978. "Explaining the Low Use of Health Services by the Poor: Costs, Attitudes, or Delivery Systems?" *American Sociological Review*, 43:348–367.

Dye, Thomas R. 1978. "Oligarchic Tendencies in National Policy-Making: The Role of the Private Policy-Planning Organizations." *Journal of Politics*, 40:309–331.

Dye, Thomas R. 1979. *Who's Running America?* Englewood Cliffs, N.J.: Prentice-Hall.

Dye, Thomas R. 1983. *Who's Running America?: The Reagan Years*. Englewood Cliffs, N.J.: Prentice-Hall.

Effrat, Andrew. 1972. "Power to the Paradigms." Pp. 3–34 in Andrew Effrat (ed.), *Perspectives in Political Sociology*. New York: Bobbs-Merrill.

Ehrlich, Paul, and Anne Ehrlich. 1979. "What Happened to the Population Bomb?" *Human Nature*, 2:88–92.

Ellis, Dean. 1967. "Speech and Social Status in America." *Social Forces,* 45:431–437.

Ellis, Godfrey, Gary Lee, and Larry Peterson. 1978. "Supervision and Conformity: A Cross-Cultural Analysis of Parental Socialization Values." *American Journal of Sociology,* 84:386–403.

Ellis, Lee. 1977. "The Decline and Fall of Sociology, 1975–2000." *The American Sociologist,* 12:56–66.

England, Paula, George Farkas, Barbara Stanek Kilbourne, and Thomas Dou. 1988. "Explaining Occupational Sex Segregation and Wages: Findings from a Model with Fixed Effects." *American Sociological Review,* 53:544–558.

Epstein, Samuel. 1980. "The Asbestos 'Pentagon Papers.'" Pp. 154–166 in Mark Green and Robert Massie (eds.), *The Big Business Reader: Essays on Corporate America.* New York: The Pilgrim Press.

Erlanger, Howard. 1974. "Social Class and Corporal Punishment in Childrearing: A Reassessment." *American Sociological Review,* 39:68–85.

Etzioni, Amitai. 1984. *An Immodest Agenda: Rebuilding America Before the 21st Century.* New York: McGraw-Hill.

Evanson, Elizabeth. 1981. "The Dynamics of Poverty." *Focus,* 5:9–11, 19–20.

Farnsworth, Elizabeth, Richard Feinberg, and Eric Leenson. 1976. "The Invisible Blockage: The United States Reacts." Pp. 338–373 in Arturo Valenzuela and J. Samuel Valenzuela (eds.), *Chile: Politics and Society.* New Brunswick, N.J.: Transaction Books.

Feagin, Joe R. 1972. "When It Comes to Poverty, It's Still 'God Helps Those Who Help Themselves.'" *Psychology Today,* (November) 6:101–129.

Feagin, Joe R. 1975. *Subordinating the Poor.* Englewood Cliffs, N.J.: Prentice-Hall.

Featherman, David L., F. Lancaster Jones, and Robert M. Hauser. 1975. "Assumptions of Social Mobility Research in the U.S.: A Case of Occupational Status." *Social Science Research,* 4:329–360.

Featherman, David, and Robert Hauser. 1978. *Opportunity and Change.* New York: Academic Press.

Feierabend, I. K., R. L. Feierabend, and Betty Nesvold. 1969. "Social Change and Political Violence: Cross National Patterns." Pp. 157–183 in H. Graham and Ted Gurr (eds.), *Violence in America.* New York: Signet Books.

Festinger, Leon. 1957. *A Theory of Cognitive Dissonance.* Stanford, Calif.: Stanford University Press.

Fiala, Robert. 1983. "Inequality and the Service Sector in Less Developed Countries: A Reanalysis and Respecification." *American Sociological Review,* 48:421–428.

Field, Mark G. 1987. "Medical Care in the Soviet Union: Promises and Realities." Pp. 65–82, in Horst Herlemann (eds.), *Quality of Life in the Soviet Union.* Boulder, Colo.: Westview Press.

Finley, M. I. 1973. *The Ancient Economy.* London: Chatto & Windus.

Fischer, Ruth. 1982. *Stalin and German Communism.* New Brunswick, N.J.: Transaction Press.

Flannery, Kent. 1972. "The Origins of the Village as a Settlement Type in Mesoamerica and the Near East: A Comparative Study." Pp. 117–132 in Peter Ucko, Ruth Tringham, and G. W. Dimbleday (eds.), *Man, Settlement, and Urbanism.* London: Duckworth.

Focus. 1982. "Valuing In-Kind Transfers." 6:13–14. Madison: University of Wisconsin: Institute for Research on Poverty.

Focus. 1984. "Poverty in the United States: Where Do We Stand Now?" 7:1–13. Madison: University of Wisconsin: Institute for Research on Poverty.

Focus. 1986. "The Changing Economic Circumstances of Children: Families Losing Ground." 9:6–11. Madison: University of Wisconsin: Institute for Research on Poverty.

Footnotes. 1980. "Sociology in China: Its Restoration and Future Role." (October) 8:4.

Forbis, William H. 1976. *Japan Today: People, Places, Power,* Tokyo: Tuttle.

Foreign Press Center. 1985. *Facts and Figures of Japan.* Tokyo: Foreign Press Center.

Form, William. 1985. *Divided We Stand: Working-Class Stratification in America.* Urbana: University of Illinois Press.

Fortune. 1940. "The People of the U.S.A.—A Self Portrait." 21:14.

Fortune. 1981. "The Fortune Directory of the 500 Largest Industrial Corporations." (May 14):324–339.

Fortune. 1981. "The Fortune Directory of the 50 Largest Commercial-Banking Companies." (July 13):318.

Fox, Thomas, and S. M. Miller. 1965a. "Intra-Country Variations: Occupational Stratification and Mobility." *Society/Transactions,* 1:23–38.

Fox, Thomas, and S. M. Miller. 1965b. "Economic, Political, and Social Determinants of Mobility: An International Cross-Sectional Analysis." *Acta Sociologica,* 9:73–91.

Frazier, E. Franklin. 1932. *The Negro Family in Chicago.* Chicago: University of Chicago Press.

Freitag, Peter. 1975. "The Cabinet and Big Business: A Study of Interlocks." *Social Problems,* 23:137–152.

Fried, Morton. 1973. "On the Evolution of Social Stratification and the State." Pp. 15–25 in John C. Leggett (ed.), *Taking State Power: The Sources and Consequences of Political Challenge.* New York: Harper & Row.

Friedlander, Walter. 1968. *Introduction to Social Welfare.* Englewood Cliffs, N.J.: Prentice-Hall.

Friedrichs, Robert. 1970. *A Sociology of Sociology.* New York: Free Press.

Fukutake, Tadashi. 1981. *Japanese Society Today.* Tokyo: Tokyo University Press.

Galaskiewicz, Joseph, Stanley Wasserman, Barbara Rauschenbach, Wolfgang Bielefeld, and Patti Mullaney. 1985. "The Influence of Corporate Power, Social Status, and Market Position on Corporate Interlocks in a Regional Network." *Social Forces,* 64:403–432.

Galaskiewicz, Joseph, and Stanley Wasserman. 1981. "A Dynamic Study of Change in a Regional Corporate Network." *American Sociological Review,* 46:475–484.

Galbraith, John Kenneth. 1971. *The New Industrial State.* Boston: Houghton Mifflin.

Galbraith, John Kenneth. 1973. *Economics and the Public Purpose.* Boston: Houghton Mifflin.

Galliher, John, and James McCartney. 1973. "The Influence of Funding Agencies on Juvenile Delinquency Research." *Social Problems,* 21:77–90.

Gallman, R. E. 1969. "Trends in the Size Distribution of Wealth in the Nineteenth Century." Pp. 1–31 in L. Soltow (ed.), *Six Papers on the Distribution of Wealth.* New York: National Bureau of Economic Research.

Gallup Opinion Index. 1979. Princeton: Gallup International.

Gamoran, Adam, and Robert D. Mare. 1989. "Secondary School Tracking and Educational Inequality: Compensation, Reinforcement, or Neutrality?" *American Journal of Sociology,* 94:1146–1183.

Gamson, William. 1975. *The Strategy of Social Protest.* Homewood, Ill.: Dorsey Press.

Gans, Herbert. 1969. "Culture and Class in the Study of Poverty: An Approach to Anti-Poverty Research." Pp. 201–228 in Daniel P. Moynihan (ed.), *On Understanding Poverty.* New York: Basic Books.

Gans, Herbert. 1972. "Positive Functions of Poverty." *American Journal of Sociology,* 78:275–289.

Gans, Herbert. 1979. *Deciding What's News.* New York: Pantheon.

Garfinkel, Harold. 1967. *Studies in Ethnomethodology.* Englewood Cliffs, N.J.: Prentice-Hall.

Garner, Roberta Ash. 1977. *Social Movements in America.* Chicago: Rand McNally.

Geiger, H. Kent. 1969. "Social Class Differences in Family Life in the USSR." Pp. 284–295 in Celia S. Heller (ed.), *Structured Social Inequality.* New York: Macmillan.

George, Vic, and Roger Lawson (eds.). 1980. *Poverty and Inequality in Common Market Countries.* London: Routledge & Kegan Paul.

Gerth, Hans, and C. Wright Mills. 1946. *From Max Weber: Essays in Sociology.* New York: Oxford University Press.

Giddens, Anthony. 1973. *The Class Structure of the Advanced Societies.* New York: Harper & Row.

Giddens, Anthony. 1976. "Classical Social Theory and Modern Sociology." *American Journal of Sociology,* 81:703–729.

Giddens, Anthony. 1978. *Émile Durkheim.* New York: Penguin Books.

Gilbert, Neil. 1987. "How to Rate a Social Welfare System." January 13, *The Wall Street Journal.*

Gilder, George. 1981. *Wealth and Poverty.* New York: Basic Books.

Gitlin, Todd. 1979. "Prime Time Ideology: The Hegemonic Process in Television Entertainment." *Social Problems,* 26:251–268.

Glenn, Norval, Andreain Ross, and Judy Corder Tully. 1974. "Patterns of Intergenerational Mobility of Females Through Marriage." *American Sociological Review,* 39:683–699.

Goffman, Erving. 1959. *The Presentation of Self in Everyday Life.* Garden City, N.Y.: Doubleday.

Gold, Thomas B. 1986. *State and Society in the Taiwan Miracle.* Armonk, N.Y.: M. E. Sharpe.

Goldberg, P. 1975. "The Politics of the Allende Overthrow in Chile." *Political Science Quarterly,* 90:93–116.

Goldman, Robert, and Ann Tickamyer. 1984. "Status Attainment and the Commodity Form: Stratification in Historical Perspective." *American Sociological Review,* 49:196–209.

Goldstein, Bernice, and Kyoka Tamura. 1975. *Japan and America: A Comparative Study in Language and Culture.* Tokyo: Tuttle.

Goldthorpe, John H., with Catriona Llewellyn and Clive Payne. 1987. *Social Mobility and Class Structure in Modern Britain.* 2d ed. Oxford: Oxford University Press.

Good, T., and J. Brophy. 1973. *Looking in Class-Rooms.* New York: Harper & Row.

Goodwin, Leonard. 1972. *Do the Poor Want to Work? A Social-Psychological Study of Work Orientations.* Washington, D.C.: Brookings Institution.

Gordon, Milton. 1963. *Social Class in American Sociology.* New York: McGraw-Hill.

Gortmaker, Steven. 1979. "Poverty and Infant Mortality in the United States." *American Sociological Review,* 44:280–297.

Gouldner, Alvin. 1970. *The Coming Crisis in Western Sociology.* New York: Basic Books.

Gouldner, Alvin. 1973. *For Sociology: Renewal and Critique in Sociology Today.* New York: Basic Books.

Gouldner, Alvin. 1979. *The Future of Intellectuals and the Rise of the New Class.* New York: Seabury.

Gouldner, Alvin, and Richard A. Peterson. 1962. *Notes on Technology and the Moral Order*. Indianapolis: Bobbs-Merrill.

Grandjean, Burke, and Frank Bean. 1975. "The Davis-Moore Theory and Perceptions of Stratification." *Social Forces,* 54:166–180.

Granovetter, Mark. 1984. "Small is Bountiful: Labor Markets and Establishment Size." *American Sociological Review,* 49:323–334.

Grier, William, and Price Cobbs. 1968. *Black Rage*. New York: Basic Books.

Griffin, Larry, and Karl Alexander. 1978. "Schooling and Socioeconomic Attainments: High School and College Influences." *American Journal of Sociology,* 84:319–347.

Griffin, Larry, Michael Wallace, and Beth Rubin. 1986. "Capitalist Resistance to the Organization of Labor Before the New Deal: Why? How? Success?" *American Sociological Review,* 51:147–167.

Gross, Neal. 1953. "Social Class of Identification in the Urban Community." *American Sociological Review,* 18:398–404.

Grusky, David. 1983. "Industrialization and the Status Attainment Process: The Thesis of Industrialism Reconsidered." *American Sociological Review,* 48:494–506.

Grusky, David, and Robert Hauser. 1984. "Comparative Social Mobility Revisited: Models of Convergence and Divergence in 16 Countries." *American Sociological Review,* 49:19–38.

Guest, Avery M., Nancy S. Landale, and James C. McCann. 1989. "Intergenerational Occupational Mobility in the Late 19th Century United States." *Social Forces,* 68:351–378.

Guppy, L. Neil. 1982. "On Intersubjectivity and Collective Conscience in Occupational Prestige Research: A Comment on Balkwell-Bates-Garbin and Kraus-Schild-Hodge." *Social Forces,* 60:1178–1182.

Guppy, L. Neil, and John C. Goyder. 1984. "Consensus on Occupational Prestige: A Reassessment of the Evidence." *Social Forces,* 62:709–726.

Gurr, Ted. 1969. "A Comparative Study of Civil Strife." Pp. 203–235 in H. Graham and Ted Gurr (eds.), *Violence in America*. New York: Signet Books.

Gurr, Ted. 1970. *Why Men Rebel*. Princeton: Princeton University Press.

Gusfield, J. R., and M. Schwartz. 1963. "The Meanings of Occupational Prestige: Reconsideration of the NORC Scale." *American Sociological Review,* 28:265–271.

Habermas, Jurgen. 1984. *Reason and the Rationalization of Society*. Boston: Beacon Press.

Habermas, Jurgen. 1975. *Legitimation Crisis*. Boston: Beacon Press.

Hacker, Andrew. 1975. "What Rules America?" *The New York Review of Books* 22(May 1):9–13. Reprinted pp. 363–371 in Maurice Zeitlin (ed.), *American Society, Inc*. 2d ed. Chicago: Rand McNally. 1977.

Hagopian, Mark. 1974. *The Phenomenon of Revolution*. New York: Dodd-Mead.

Halberstam, David. 1979. *The Powers That Be*. New York: Alfred Knopf.

Halberstam, David. 1986. *The Reckoning*. New York: Morrow.

Hall, P. M., and J. P. Hewitt. 1970. "The Quasi Theory of Communication and Management of Dissent." *Social Problems,* 18:17–26.

Halliday, Jon. 1975. *A Political History of Japanese Capitalism*. New York: Monthly Review Press.

Hamilton, Richard. 1972. *Class and Politics in the United States*. New York: John Wiley & Sons.

Hammer, Heather-Jo. 1984. "Comment of 'Dependency Theory and Taiwan: Analysis of a Deviant Case.'" *American Journal of Sociology,* 89:932–936.

Handler, Joel, and Ellen Jane Hollingsworth. 1971. *The 'Deserving Poor': A Study of Welfare Administration*. Chicago: Markham.

Hane, Mikiso. 1982. *Peasants, Rebels, And Outcastes: The Underside of Modern Japan*. New York: Pantheon.

Harasymiw, Bohdan. 1984. *Political Elite Recruitment in the Soviet Union*. New York: St. Martin's Press.

Harms, L. S. 1961. "Listener Judgments of Status Cues in Speech." *Quarterly Journal of Speech*, 47:164–168.

Harrington, Michael. 1976. *The Twilight of Capitalism*. New York: Simon & Schuster.

Harrington, Michael. 1977. *The Vast Majority: A Journey to the World's Poor*. New York: Touchstone Books.

Harrington, Michael. 1984. *The New American Poverty*. New York: Holt, Rinehart and Winston.

Harris, David. 1977. "Alternative Pathways Toward Agriculture." Pp. 231–248 in Charles Reed (ed.), *Origins of Agriculture*. The Hague, Netherlands: Mouton.

Harrison, Bennett, and Barry Bluestone. 1988. *The Great U-Turn: Corporate Restructuring and the Polarizing of America*. New York: Basic Books.

Hauser, Robert. 1980. "On Stratification in a Dual Economy." *American Sociological Review*, 45:702–711.

Hauser, Robert, and David Featherman. 1977. *The Process of Stratification*. New York: Academic Press.

Hauser, Robert, and David Grusky. 1988. "Cross-National Variation in Occupational Distributions, Relative Mobility Chances, and Intergenerational Shifts in Occupational Distributions." *American Sociological Review*, 53:723–741.

Havinghurst, Robert. 1978. "Indian Education Since 1960." *The Annals*, 436:13–26.

Hazelrigg, Lawrence, and Maurice Garnier. 1976. "Occupational Mobility in Industrial Societies: A Comparative Analysis of Different Access to Occupational Ranks in Seventeen Countries." *American Sociological Review*, 41:498–510.

Hechter, Michael, and William Brustein. 1980. "Regional Modes of Production and Patterns of State Formation in Western Europe." *American Journal of Sociology*, 85:1061–1094.

Heise, David, Gerhard Lenski, and John Wardwell. 1976. "Further Notes on Technology and the Moral Order." *Social Forces*, 55:316–337.

Heller, Celia (ed.). 1969. *Structured Social Inequality*. New York: Macmillan.

Heller, Celia S. (ed.). 1987. *Structured Social Inequality: A Reader in Comparative Social Stratification*. 2d ed. New York: Macmillan.

Hendry, Joy. 1987. *Understanding Japanese Society*. London: Croom Helm.

Herberg, Will. 1960. *Protestant, Catholic, Jew*. New York: Doubleday.

Herman, Edward. 1973. "Do Banks Control Corporations?" *Monthly Review*, 24:17–29.

Herman, Edward. 1975. *Conflicts of Interest: Commercial Bank Trust Departments*. New York: Twentieth Century Fund.

Herman, Edward S., and Noam Chomsky. 1988. *Manufacturing Consent: The Political Economy of the Mass Media*. New York: Pantheon.

Hewitt, Christopher. 1977. "The Effect of Political Democracy and Social Democracy on Equality in Industrial Societies: A Cross-National Comparison." *American Sociological Review*, 42:450–463.

Heyns, B. 1974. "Social Selection and Stratification Within Schools." *American Journal of Sociology*, 79:1434–1451.

Hicks, Alexander. 1984. "Elections, Keynes, Bureaucracy and Class: Explaining U.S. Budget Deficits. 1961–1978." *American Sociological Review,* 49:165–181.

Hicks, Alexander, Roger Friedland, and Edwin Johnson. 1978. "Class Power and State Policy: The Case of Large Business Corporations, Labor Unions and Governmental Redistribution in the American States." *American Sociological Review,* 43:302–315.

Hill, Martha. 1981. "Some Dynamic Aspects of Poverty." In M. Hill, D. Hill, and J. N. Morgan (eds.), *Five Thousand American Families—Patterns of Economic Progress,* vol. 9. Ann Arbor: Institute for Social Research, University of Michigan Press.

Himelstein, Philip. 1965. "Validities and Intercorrelations of MMPI Subscales Predictive of College Achievement." *Educational and Psychological Measurement,* 25:1125–1128.

Hirsch, Glenn. 1975. "Only You Can Prevent Ideological Hegemony: The Advertising Council and Its Place in the American Power Structure." *Insurgent Sociologist,* 5:64–82.

Hodge, Robert, Paul Siegel, and Peter Rossi. 1964. "Occupational Prestige in the United States." *American Journal of Sociology,* 70:286–302.

Hodge, Robert, Paul Siegel, and Peter Rossi. 1966. "Occupational Prestige in the United States, 1925–1963." Pp. 322–334 in R. Bendix and S. M. Lipset (eds.), *Class, Status, and Power.* New York: Free Press.

Hodge, Robert, and Donald Treiman. 1968a. "Social Participation and Social Status." *American Sociological Review,* 33:578–593.

Hodge, Robert, and Donald Treiman, 1968b. "Class Identification in the United States." *American Journal of Sociology,* 73:535–542.

Hodge, Robert, Donald Treiman, and Peter Rossi. 1966. "A Comparative Study of Occupational Prestige." Pp. 309–321 in R. Bendix and S. M. Lipset (eds.), *Class, Status, and Power.* New York: Free Press.

Hollingshead, August. 1949. *Elmtown's Youth.* New York: John Wiley & Sons.

Hollingshead, August, and Frederick Redlich. 1958. *Social Class and Mental Illness.* New York: John Wiley & Sons.

Homans, George. 1961. *Social Behavior: Its Elementary Forms.* New York: Harcourt, Brace, & World.

Homans, George. 1974. *Social Behavior: Its Elementary Forms.* (Revised ed.). New York: Harcourt, Brace, & World.

Hope, Keith. 1982. "A Liberal Theory of Prestige." *American Journal of Sociology,* 87:1011–1031.

Hopkins, Mark. 1970. *Mass Media in the Soviet Union.* New York: Pegasus.

Horan, Patrick. 1978. "Is Status Attainment Research Atheoretical?" *American Sociological Review,* 43:534–541.

Horton, John. 1966. "Order and Conflict Theories of Social Problems as Competing Ideologies." *American Journal of Sociology,* 71:701–713.

Hout, Michael. 1984. "Occupational Mobility of Black Men: 1962 to 1973." *American Sociological Review,* 49:308–322.

Hout, Michael. 1988. "More Universalism, Less Structural Mobility: The American Occupational Structure in the 1980s." *American Journal of Sociology,* 93:1358–1400.

Howe, Irving. 1978. *Leon Trotsky.* New York: Viking.

Huber, Joan, and William H. Form. 1973. *Income and Ideology: An Analysis of the American Political Formula.* New York: Free Press.

Humphrey, Caroline. 1988. "Rural Society in the Soviet Union." Pp. 53–70, in Michael

Paul Sacks and Jerry G. Pankhurst (eds.), *Understanding Soviet Society*. Boston: Allen & Unwin.

Hunter, Alfred A. 1988. "Formal Education and Initial Employment: Unravelling the Relationships Between Schooling and Skills Over Time." *American Sociological Review*, 53:753–765.

Hunter, Floyd. 1953. *Community Power Structure: A Study of Decision Makers*. Chapel Hill: University of North Carolina Press.

Hyman, Herbert, and Charles R. Wright. 1971. "Trends in Voluntary Association Memberships of American Adults: Replication Based on Secondary Analysis of National Sample Surveys." *American Sociological Review*, 36:191–206.

Ingham, John. 1978. *The Iron Barons*. Chicago: University of Chicago Press.

Inkeles, Alex. 1950. "Social Stratification and Mobility in the Soviet Union: 1940–1950." *American Sociological Review*, 15:465–479.

Inkeles, Alex. 1968. *Social Change in Soviet Russia*. Cambridge, Mass.: Harvard University Press.

Institute for Social Research. 1986/1987. "Wealth in America." *IRS Newsletter* (Winter) 14:3–5.

Isaac, Larry, and William Kelly. 1981. "Racial Insurgency, the State, and Welfare Expansion: Local and National Level Evidence from the Postwar United States." *American Journal of Sociology*, 86:1348–1386.

Isaac, Larry, Elizabeth Mutran, and Sheldon Stryker. 1980. "Political Protest Orientations Among Black and White Adults." *American Sociological Review*, 45:191–213.

Ishida, Hiroshi, John H. Goldthorpe, and Robert Erikson. 1987. "Intergenerational Class Mobility in Post War Japan: Conformity or Peculiarity in Cross-National Perspective." Paper presented to the Research Committee on Social Stratification of the International Sociological Association, Berkeley: August.

Jackman, Robert. 1974. "Political Democracy and Social Equality: A Comparative Analysis." *American Sociological Review*, 39:29–45.

Jackman, Robert. 1975. *Politics and Social Equality: A Comparative Analysis*. New York: John Wiley & Sons.

Jacobs, David. 1988. "Corporate Economic Power and the State: A Longitudinal Assessment of Two Explanations." *American Journal of Sociology*, 93:852–881.

Jacobs, David. 1985. "Unequal Organizations or Unequal Attainment? An Empirical Comparison of Sectoral and Individualistic Explanations for Aggregate Inequality." *American Sociological Review*, 50:166–180.

Jacobs, David. 1982. "Competition, Scale, and Political Explanations for Inequality: An Integrated Study of Sectoral Explanations at the Aggregate Level." *American Sociological Review*, 47:600–614.

Jacobs, David. 1979. "Inequality and Police Strength: Conflict Theory and Coercive Control in Metropolitan Areas." *American Sociological Review*, 44:913–924.

Jacobs, Jerry. 1983. "Industrial Sector and Career Mobility Reconsidered." *American Sociological Review*, 48:415–421.

Jacques, Jeffrey, and Karen Chason. 1977. "Self-Esteem and Low Status Groups: A Changing Scene?" *Sociological Quarterly*, 18:399–412.

Jaffee, David. 1985. "Export Dependence and Economic Growth: A Reformulation and Respecification." *Social Forces*, 64:102–118.

Jain, Shail. 1975. *Size Distribution of Income: A Compilation of Data*. Washington, D.C.: The World Bank.

James, David, and Michael Soref. 1981. "Profit Constraints on Managerial Autonomy:

Managerial Theory and the Unmaking of the Corporation President.'' *American Sociological Review*, 46:1–18.

Jasso, Guillermina, and Peter Rossi. 1977. ''Distributive Justice and Earned Income.'' *American Sociological Review*, 42:639–651.

Jencks, Christopher, et al. 1972. *Inequality: A Reassessment of the Effect of Family and Schooling in America*. New York: Harper & Row.

Jencks, Christopher, et al. 1979. *Who Gets Ahead? The Determinants of Economic Success in America*. New York: Basic Books.

Jenkins, J. Craig, and Barbara G. Brents. 1989. ''Social Protest. Hegemonic Competition, and Social Reform: A Political Struggle Interpretation of the Origins of the American Welfare State.'' *American Sociological Review*, 54:891–909.

Jenkins, J. Craig, and Charles Perrow. 1977. ''Insurgency of the Powerless: Farm Worker Movements.'' *American Sociological Review*, 42:249–268.

Jennings, Edward T. 1983. ''Racial Insurgency, the State, and Welfare Expansion: A Critical Comment and Reanalysis.'' *American Journal of Sociology*, 88:1220–1236.

Johnson, Chalmers. 1982. *MITI and the Japanese Miracle*. Stanford: Stanford University Press.

Johnson, Dale. 1973. *The Sociology of Change and Reaction in Latin America*. New York: Bobbs-Merrill.

Jones, A. H. M. 1974. *The Roman Economy*. Oxford: Basil Blackwell.

Jones, T. Anthony. 1978. ''Modernization and Education in the USSR.'' *Social Forces*, 57:522–548.

Kahl, Joseph, and James A. Davis. 1955. ''A Comparison of Indexes of Socio-Economic Status.'' *American Sociological Review*, 20:317–325.

Khan, Alfred, and Shelia Kamerman. 1977. *Not for the Poor Alone: European Social Services*. New York: Harper Colophon Books.

Kalleberg, Arne, and Larry Griffin. 1980. ''Class, Occupation, and Inequality in Job Rewards.'' *American Journal of Sociology*, 85:731–768.

Kalleberg, Arne L., and James R. Lincoln. 1988. ''The Structure of Earnings Inequality in the United States and Japan.'' *American Journal of Sociology*, 94:5121–5153.

Kamata, Satoshi. 1982. *Japan in the Passing Lane: An Insider's Account of Life in a Japanese Auto Factory*. New York: Pantheon Books.

Kane, Michael. 1970. *Minorities in Textbooks*. Chicago: Quadrangle.

Kaplan, H. Roy, and Curt Travsky. 1972. ''Work and the Welfare Cadillac: The Function and Commitment to Work Among the Hard-Core Unemployed.'' *Social Problems*, 19:469–483.

Kaplan, H. Roy, and Curt Travsky. 1974. ''The Meaning of Work Among the Hard-Core Unemployed.'' *Pacific Sociological Review*, 17:185–198.

Kaufman, Robert L. 1983. ''A Structural Decomposition of Black–White Earnings Differentials.'' *American Journal of Sociology*, 89:585–611.

Kaufman, Robert, Harry Chernotsky, and Daniel Geller. 1975. ''A Preliminary Test of the Theory of Dependency.'' *Comparative Politics*, 7:303–330.

Keep, John. 1976. *The Russian Revolution: A Study in Mass Mobilization*. New York: Norton.

Keizai Kikaku Cho Hen. 1988. *Kokumein Seikatsu Hakusho* (White Paper on National Life). Tokyo: Okura Sho Insatsu Kyoku Hakko.

Keizai Koho. 1988. *Japan 1988: An International Comparison*. Tokyo: Keizai Koho Center (Japan Institute for Social and Economic Affairs).

Keller, Suzanne. 1953. "The Social Origins and Career Lines of Three Generations of American Business Leaders." Unpublished Ph.D. dissertation, Columbia University.

Keller, Suzanne. 1963. *Beyond the Ruling Class: Strategic Elites in Modern Society.* New York: Random House.

Keller, Suzanne, and M. Zavalloni. 1964. "Ambition and Social Class: A Respecification." *Social Forces,* 43:58–70.

Kelly, William, and David Snyder, 1980. "Racial Violence and Socioeconomic Changes among Blacks in the United States." *Social Forces,* 58:739–760.

Kennedy, Paul. 1987. *The Rise and Fall of the Great Powers: Economic Change and Military Conflict From 1500 to 2000.* New York: Random House.

Kentor, Jeffrey. 1981. "Structural Determinants of Peripheral Urbanization: The Effects of International Dependence." *American Sociological Review,* 46:201–211.

Kerbo, Harold. 1976a. "Marxist and Functionalist Theories in the Study of Social Stratification: A Comment." *Social Forces,* 55:191–192.

Kerbo, Harold. 1976b. "The Stigma of Welfare and a Passive Poor." *Sociology and Social Research,* 60:173–187.

Kerbo, Harold. 1978. "Foreign Involvement in the Preconditions for Political Violence: The World System and the Case of Chile." *Journal of Conflict Resolution,* 22:363–392.

Kerbo, Harold. 1981a. "Characteristics of the Poor: A Continuing Focus in Social Research." *Sociology and Social Research,* 65:323–331.

Kerbo, Harold. 1981b. "College Achievement Among Native Americans: A Research Note." *Social Forces,* 59:1275–1280.

Kerbo, Harold, and L. Richard Della Fave. 1979. "The Empirical Side of the Power Elite Debate: An Assessment and Critique of Recent Research." *Sociological Quarterly,* 20:5–22.

Kerbo, Harold R., and L. Richard Della Fave. 1983. "Corporate Linkage and Control of the Corporate Economy: New Evidence and a Reinterpretation." *Sociological Quarterly,* 24:201–218.

Kerbo, Harold R., and L. Richard Della Fave. 1984. "Further Notes on the Evolution of Corporate Control and Institutional Investors: A Response to Niemonen." *Sociological Quarterly,* 25:279–283.

Kerbo, Harold R., and Mariko Inoue. 1990. "Japanese Social Structure and White Collar Crime: Recruit Cosmos and Beyond." *Deviant Behavior,*11:139–154.

Kerbo, Harold R., and John McKinstry. 1987. "Social Stratification in Modern Japan: A Comparative Analysis." Paper presented to meetings of the Western Society of Asian Studies, October 1987. Tucson, Arizona.

Kerbo, Harold R., and Meika Sha. 1987. "Language and Social Stratification in Japan." Paper presented to meetings of the Eastern Sociological Association, May, 1987. Boston.

Kerbo, Harold R., and Richard A. Shaffer. 1986. "Unemployment and Protest in the United States: 1890–1940: A Methodological Critique and Research Note." *Social Forces,* 64:1046–1056.

Kerbo, Harold R., and Richard A. Shaffer. 1986. "Elite Recognition of Unemployment as a Working Class Issue in the United States. 1890–1940." *Sociology and Social Research,* 70:294–298.

Kerckhoff, Alan. 1976. "The Status Attainment Process: Socialization or Allocation?" *Social Forces,* 55:368–381.

Kerckhoff, Alan C. 1989. "On the Social Psychology of Social Mobility Processes." *Social Forces*, 68:17–25.

Kerckhoff, Alan, Richard Campbell, and Jerry Trott. 1982. "Dimensions of Educational and Occupational Attainment in Great Britain." *American Sociological Review*, 47:347–364.

Kirkpatrick, Jeanne J. 1976. *The Presidential Elite*. New York: Russell Sage.

Kishimoto, Koichi. 1988. *Politics In Modern Japan: Development and Organization*. 3d ed. Tokyo: Japan Echo Inc.

Kluegel, James. 1978. "The Causes and Cost of Racial Exclusion from Job Authority." *American Sociological Review*, 43:285–301.

Kluegel, James, Royce Singleton, and Charles Starnes. 1977. "Subjective Class Identification: A Multiple Indicator Approach." *American Sociological Review*, 42:599–611.

Kluegel, James, and Eliot Smith. 1982. "White's Beliefs About Blacks' Opportunity." *American Sociological Review*, 47:518–532.

Komarovsky, Mirra. 1962. *Blue-Collar Marriage*. New York: Random House.

Korpi, Walter. 1974. "Conflict, Power, and Relative Deprivation." *American Political Science Review*, 68:1569–1578.

Knoke, David, and Michael Hout. 1974. "Social and Demographic Factors in American Political Party Affiliations." *American Sociological Review*, 39:700–713.

Knottnerus, J. David. 1987. "Status Attainment Research and Its Image of Society." *American Sociological Review*, 52:113–121.

Kohn, Melvin. 1969. *Class and Conformity*. Homewood, Ill.: Dorsey Press.

Kohn, Melvin. 1976. "Occupational Structure and Alientation." *American Journal of Sociology*, 82:111–130.

Kohn, Melvin, and Carmi Schooler. 1982. "Job Conditions and Personality: A Longitudinal Assessment of their Reciprocal Effects." *American Journal of Sociology*, 87:1257–1286.

Kolko, Gabriel. 1988. *Confronting the Third World: United States Foreign Policy, 1945–1980*. New York: Pantheon.

Krader, Lawrence. 1975. *The Asiatic Mode of Production: Sources, Development and Critique in the Writings of Karl Marx*. Assen, The Netherlands: Van Gorcum.

Kristol, Irving. 1972. "About Equality." *Commentary*, 54:41–74.

Kropi, Walter. 1989. "Power, Politics, and State Autonomy in the Development of Social Citizenship: Social Rights During Sickness in Eighteen OECD Countries Since 1953." *American Sociological Review*, 54:309–328.

Kuczynski, Jürgen. 1967. *The Rise of the Working Class*. New York: McGraw-Hill.

Kuebart, Friedrich. 1987. "Aspects of Soviet Secondary Education: School Performance and Teacher Accountability." Pp. 83–94, in Horst Herlemann (ed.), *Quality of Life in the Soviet Union*. Boulder, Colo.: Westview Press.

Kuhn, Thomas. 1962. *The Structure of Scientific Revolutions*. Chicago: University of Chicago Press.

Kuhn, Thomas. 1970. *The Structure of Scientific Revolutions*. 2d ed. Chicago: University of Chicago Press.

Kutz, Myer. 1974. *Rockefeller Power: America's Chosen Family*. New York: Simon & Schuster.

Labovitz, Eugene. 1974. "Fulfillment of College Aspirations: A Simple Causal Analysis." *Pacific Sociological Review*, 17:379–397.

Labovitz, Eugene. 1975. "Race, SES Contexts and Fulfillment of College Aspirations." *Sociological Quarterly*, 16:241–249.

Lane, David. 1988. "Full Employment and Labor Utilization in the USSR." Pp. 221–238, in Michael Paul Sacks and Jerry G. Pankhurst (eds.), *Understanding Soviet Society*. Boston: Allen & Unwin.

Lane, Robert. 1962. *Political Ideology*. New York: Free Press.

Larner, Robert. 1970. *Management Control and the Large Corporation*. Cambridge, Mass.: Dunellen.

Lasson, Kenneth. 1971. *The Workers: Portraits of Nine American Job Holders*. New York: Grossman.

Laumann, Edward, David Knoke, and Yon-Hak Kim. 1985. "An Organizational Approach to State Policy Formation: A Comparative Study of Energy and Health Domains." *American Sociological Review,* 50:1–19.

Leakey, Richard, and Roger Lewin. 1977. *Origins*. New York: Dutton.

Leakey, Richard, and Roger Lewin. 1978. *The People of the Lake*. New York: Doubleday.

Leavy, Marvin. 1974. "Commentary" *American Journal of Sociology,* 80:723–727.

Lee, Changsoo, and George De Vos. 1981. *Koreans in Japan: Ethnic Conflict and Accommodation*. Berkeley: University of California Press.

Lefebvre, Georges. 1973. *The Great Fear of 1789*. New York: Vintage.

Leggett, John C. 1972. *Race, Class, and Political Consciousness*. Cambridge, Mass.: Schenkman.

Leggett, John C., Deborah Vidi DeJames, Joe Somma, and Tom Menendez. 1978. *Allende, His Exit, and Our 'Times.'* New Brunswick, N.J.: New Brunswick Cooperative Press.

Le Masters, E. E. 1975. *Blue-Collar Aristocrats: Life-Styles at a Working-Class Tavern*. Madison: University of Wisconsin Press.

Lenin, V. I. 1965. *Imperialism: The Highest Stage of Capitalism*. New York: International Publishers.

Lenski, Gerhard. 1966. *Power and Privilege*. New York: McGraw-Hill.

Lenski, Gerhard. 1977. "Sociology and Sociobiology: An Alternative View." *The American Sociologist,* 12:72–75.

Lenski, Gerhard. 1978. "Marxist Experiments in Destratification: An Appraisal." *Social Forces,* 57:364–383.

Lenski, Gerhard, and Jean Lenski. 1982. *Human Socities,* 4th ed. New York: McGraw-Hill.

Lenski, Gerhard, and Patrick Nolan. 1984. "Trajectories of Development: A Test of Ecological–Evolutionary Theory." *Social Forces,* 63:1–23.

Lenski, Gerhard, and Patrick Nolan. 1986. "Trajectories of Development: A Further Test." *Social Forces,* 64:794–795.

Le Roy Ladurie, Emmanuel. 1978. *Montaillou: The Promised Land of Error*. New York: George Braziller.

Le Roy Ladurie, Emmanuel. 1979. *Carnival in Romans*. New York: George Braziller.

Lester, Marilyn. 1980. "Generating Newsworthiness: The Interpretive Construction of Public Events." *American Sociological Review,* 45:984–994.

Letelier, Isabel, and Michael Moffitt. 1980. "How American Banks Keep the Chilean Junta Going." Pp. 399–412 in Mark Green and Robert Massie (eds.), *The Big Business Reader: Essays on Corporate America*. New York: The Pilgrim Press.

Leventhal, G. 1975. "The Distribution of Rewards and Resources in Groups and Organizations." Pp. 132–143 in L. Berkowitz and E. Walster (eds.), *Advances in Experimental Social Psychology*. New York: Academic Press.

Leventhal, G., J. W. Michaels, and C. Sanford. 1972. "Inequality and Interpersonal Conflict: Reward Allocation and Secrecy About Rewards as Methods of Preventing Conflict." *Journal of Personality and Social Psychology,* 23:88–102.

Levinson, Andrew. 1975. *The Working-Class Majority.* New York: Penguin Books.

Levy, Fred. 1977. "How Big is the American Underclass?" Working Paper 0090–1. Urban Institute, Washington, D.C.

Lewin, Moshe. 1988. *The Gorbachev Phenomenon: A Historical Interpretation.* Berkeley: University of California Press.

Lewis, Oscar. 1959. *Five Families: Mexican Case Studies in the Culture of Poverty.* New York: Basic Books.

Lewis, Oscar. 1961. *The Children of Sanchez.* New York: Random House.

Lewis, Oscar. 1966. *La Vida: A Puerto Rican Family in the Culture of Poverty.* New York: Random House.

Lewontin, R. C., Steven Rose, and Leon J. Kamin. 1984. *Not in Our Genes.* New York: Pantheon.

Lichter, Daniel T. 1988. "Racial Differences in Underemployment in American Cities." *American Journal of Sociology,* 93:771–792.

Liebow, Elliot. 1967. *Tally's Corner.* Boston: Little, Brown.

Lin, Nan, and Wen Xie. 1988. "Occupational Prestige in Urban China." *American Journal of Sociology,* 93:793–833.

Lincoln, James. 1978. "Community Structure and Industrial Conflict: An Analysis of Strike Activity in SMSAs." *American Sociological Review,* 43:199–220.

Lincoln, James R., and Arne L. Kalleberg. 1985. "Work Organization and Work Force Commitment: A Study of Plants and Employees in the U.S. and Japan." *American Sociological Review,* 50:738–760.

Lipset, Seymour. 1960. *Political Man.* New York: Doubleday.

Lipset, Seymour. 1963. "The Value Patterns of Democracy: A Case Study in Comparative Analysis." *American Sociological Review,* 28:515–531.

Lipset, Seymour, and Reinhard Bendix. 1964. *Social Mobility in Industrial Society.* Berkeley: University of California Press.

Lipset, Seymour, and Earl Raab. 1970. *The Politics of Unreason.* New York: Harper & Row.

Lipsitz, L. 1965. "Working-Class Authoritarianism: A Re-evaluation." *American Sociological Review,* 30:103–109.

Liska, Allen. 1977. "The Dissipation of Sociological Social Psychology." *The American Sociologist,* 12:2–8.

Liss, L. F. 1973. "The Social Conditioning of Occupational Choice." *International Journal of Sociology,* 3:275–288. Reprinted pp. 339–347 in Mark Abrahamson, Ephraim Mizruchi, and Carlton Horning, *Stratification and Mobility.* New York: Macmillan. 1976.

London, Bruce, and Thomas Robinson. 1989. "The Effect of International Dependence on Income Inequality and Political Violence." *American Sociological Review,* 54:305–308.

London, Bruce, and Bruce Williams. 1988. "Multinational Corporate Penetration, Protest, and Basic Needs Provision in Non-Core Nations: A Cross-National Analysis." *Social Forces,* 66:747–773.

Lopreato, Joseph, and Lionel Lewis. 1963. "An Analysis of Variables in the Functional Theory of Stratification." *Sociological Quarterly,* 4:301–310.

Lord, George, and William Falk. 1980. "An Exploratory Analysis of Individualist Versus Structuralist Explanations of Income." *Social Forces,* 59:376–391.

Loscocco, Karyn, and Arne L. Kalleberg. 1988. "Age and the Meaning of Work in the United States and Japan." *Social Forces,* 67:337–356.

Lowi, Theodore. 1973. "Foreword." Pp. vii–xii in Kenneth Prewitt and Alan Stone. *The Ruling Elites.* New York: Harper & Row.

Lukes, Steven. 1973a. *Émile Durkheim: His Life and Work: A Historical and Critical Study.* New York: Penguin Books.

Lukes, Steven. 1973b. *Individualism.* New York: Harper & Row.

Lundberg, Ferdinand. 1968. *The Rich and the Super-Rich.* New York: Bantam Books.

Lynd, Robert, and Helen Lynd. 1929. *Middletown.* New York: Harcourt Brace Jovanovich.

Lynd, Robert, and Helen Lynd. 1937. *Middletown in Transition.* New York: Harcourt Brace Jovanovich.

Lynn, Richard. 1988. *Educational Achievement in Japan.* Armonk, N.Y.: M. E. Sharpe.

McAteer, J. Davitt. 1971. *Safety in Mines: A Look at the World's Most Hazardous Occupation.* Washington, D.C.: Center for Study of Responsive Law.

McCartney, James. 1970. "On Being Scientific: Changing Styles of Presentation of Sociological Research." *The American Sociologist,* 5:30–35.

McCarthy, John D., and Mayer N. Zald. 1977. "Resource Mobilization and Social Movements: A Partial Theory." *American Journal of Sociology,* 82:1212–1241.

MacDougal, A. Kent. 1984. "Progress Is Harbinger of Inequality." *Los Angeles Times.* (November 15):1.

MacDougal, A. Kent. 1984. "Rich–Poor Gap in U.S. Widens During Decade." *Los Angeles Times.* (October 25):1.

McKinstry, John, and Asako McKinstry. 1991. *Jinsei Annai: "Life's Guide," Glimpses of Japan Through a Popular Advice Column.* Armonk, N.Y.: M. E. Sharpe.

McLaughlin, Steven. 1978. "Occupational Sex Identification and the Assessment of Male and Female Earnings Inequality." *American Sociological Review,* 43:909–921.

McLellan, David. 1973. *Karl Marx: His Life and Thought.* New York: Harper & Row.

MacMillan, Charles J. 1985. *The Japanese Industrial System.* New York: Walter de Gruyter.

MacMullen, Ramsay. 1974. *Roman Social Relations.* New Haven: Yale University Press.

McNall, Scott. 1977. "Does Anybody Rule America?: A Critique of Elite Theory and Method." Paper presented at the annual meeting of the America Sociological Association, Chicago.

McPortland, J. 1968. *The Segregated Students in Desegregated Schools: Sources of Influence on Negro Secondary Students.* Baltimore, Md.: John Hopkins University Press.

Magaziner, Ira C., and Robert B. Reich. 1982. *Minding America's Business.* New York: Harcourt Brace Jovanovich.

Mandel, Ernest. 1971. *The Formation of the Economic Thought of Karl Marx: 1843 to 'Capital.'* New York: Monthly Review Press.

Mankoff, Milton. 1970. "Power in Advanced Capitalist Society: A Review Essay on Recent Elitist and Marxist Criticism of Pluralist Society." *Social Problems,* 17:418–429.

Mann, Michael. 1970. "The Social Cohesion of Liberal Democracy." *American Sociological Review,* 35:423–439.

Mannari, Hiroshi. 1974. *The Japanese Business Leaders*. Tokyo: Tokyo University Press.

Marchetti, Victor, and John Marks. 1974. *The CIA and the Cult of Intelligence*. New York: Knopf.

Marcuse, Herbert. 1964. *One-Dimensional Man*. Boston: Beacon Press.

Marcuse, Herbert. 1971. "Industrialization and Capitalism." Pp. 133–150 in Otto Stammer (ed.), *Max Weber and Sociology Today*. New York: Free Press.

Marger, Martin. 1987. *Elites and Masses: An Introduction to Political Sociology*. 2d ed. Belmont, Calif.: Wadsworth.

Margulies, Leah. 1980. "Babies, Bottles, and Breast Milk: The Nestles Syndrome." Pp. 418–429 in Mark Green and Robert Massie (eds.) *The Big Business Reader: Essays on Corporate America*. New York: The Pilgrim Press.

Mariolis, Peter. 1975. "Interlocking Directorates and the Control of Corporations: The Theory of Bank Control." *Social Science Quarterly*, 56:425–439.

Martindale, Don. 1972. "The Theory of Stratification." Pp. 209–228 in Gerald Thielbar and Saul Feldman (eds.), *Issues in Social Inequality*. Boston: Little, Brown.

Marx, Gary T. 1974. "Thoughts on a Neglected Category of Social Movement Participant: The Agent Provocateur and the Informant." *American Journal of Sociology*, 80:402–442.

Marx, Karl. 1906. *Capital: A Critique of Political Economy*. New York: Random House.

Marx, Karl. 1964. *Karl Marx: Early Writings*. Edited by T. B. Bottomore. New York: McGraw-Hill.

Marx, Karl. 1971. *The Grundrisse*. Edited by David McLellan. New York: Harper Torchbooks.

Marx, Karl. 1973. *The Grundrisse*. Translated by Martin Nicolaus. New York: Vintage.

Marx, Karl, and Friedrich Engels. 1965. *The German Ideology*. New York: International Publishers.

Matras, Judah. 1980. "Comparative Social Mobility." *Annual Review of Sociology*, 6:401–431.

Matthews, Mervyn. 1972. *Class and Society in Soviet Russia*. New York: Walker.

Matthews, Mervyn. 1978. *Privilege in the Soviet Union: A Study of Elite Life-Styles Under Communism*. London: Allen & Unwin.

Matthews, Mervyn. 1987. "Aspects of Poverty in the Soviet Union." Pp. 43–64, in Horst Herlemann (ed.), *Quality of Life in the Soviet Union*. Boulder, Colo.: Westview Press.

Matthews, Mervyn. 1986. *Poverty in The Soviet Union*. Cambridge: Cambridge University Press.

Mayer, A. J., and T. F. Hoult. 1950. "Social Stratification and Combat Survival." *Social Forces*, 34:155–159.

Mayer, Kurt, and Walter Buckley. 1955. *Class and Society*. New York: Random House.

Mayhew, Bruce. 1980. "Structuralism Versus Individualism: Part I, Shadowboxing in the Dark." *Social Forces*, 59:335–375.

Mayhew, Bruce. 1981. "Structuralism Versus Individualism: Part II, Ideological and Other Obfuscations." *Social Forces*, 59:627–648.

Mead, George Herbert. 1935. *Mind, Self and Society*. Chicago: University of Chicago Press.

Meissner, Boris. 1972. "Social Change in Bolshevik Russia." Pp. 23–172 in Boris

Meissner (ed.), *Social Change in the Soviet Union*. Notre Dame, Ind.: University of Notre Dame Press.

Menard, Scott. 1986. "A Research Note on International Comparisons of Inequality of Income." *Social Forces*, 64:778–793.

Mercy, James, and Lala Carr Steelman. 1982. "Familial Influence on the Intellectual Attainment of Children." *American Sociological Review*, 47:532–542.

Mermelstein, David. 1969. "Large Industrial Corporations and Asset Shares." *American Economic Review*, 59:531–541.

Messner, Steven F. 1982. "Societal Development, Social Equality, and Homicide: A Cross-National Test of A Durhkeimian Model." *Social Forces*, 61:225–240.

Milgram, Stanley. 1974. *Obedience in Authority*. New York: Harper Colophon Books.

Miliband, Ralph. 1969. *The State in Capitalist Society*. New York: Basic Books.

Miliband, Ralph. 1977. *Marxism and Politics*. New York: Oxford University Press.

Millar, James R. (ed.). 1987. *Politics, Work, and Daily Life in the USSR: A Survey of Former Soviet Citizens*. Cambridge: Cambridge University Press.

Miller, Delbert. 1977. *Handbook of Research Design and Social Measurement*. New York: David McKay.

Miller, Roy Andrew. 1967. *The Japanese Language*. Chicago: University of Chicago Press.

Miller, S. M. 1960. "Comparative Social Mobility." *Current Sociology*, 9:81–89.

Miller, S. M. 1975. "Notes on Neo-Capitalism. *Theory and Society*, 2:1–36.

Miller, S. M. 1976. "The Political Economy of Social Problems: From the Sixties to the Seventies." *Social Problems*, 24:131–141.

Miller, S. M., and David Riessman. 1961. "The Working Class Subculture: A New View." *Social Problems*, 9:86–97.

Miller, S. M., David Riessman, and A. Seagull. 1971. "Poverty and Self-Indulgence: A Critique of the Non-Deferred Gratification Pattern." Pp. 285–302 in Louis Ferman, Joyce Kornbluh, and Alan Harber (eds.), *Poverty in America*. Ann Arbor: University of Michigan Press.

Miller, Walter. 1969. "The Elimination of the American Lower Class as National Policy: A Critique of the Ideology of the Poverty Movement of the 1960s." Pp. 260–315 in Daniel P. Moynihan (ed.), *On Understanding Poverty*. New York: Basic Books.

Miller, Walter. 1971. "Is the Income Gap Closed—No!" Pp. 61–66 in Louis Ferman, Joyce Kornbluh, and Alan Harber (eds.), *Poverty in America*. Ann Arbor: University of Michigan Press.

Mills, C. Wright. 1953. *White Collar*. New York: Oxford University Press.

Mills, C. Wright. 1956. *The Power Elite*. New York: Oxford University Press.

Mills, C. Wright. 1962. *The Marxists*. New York: Dell.

Mills, C. Wright. 1963. *Power, Politics, and People*. Edited by I. L. Horowitz. New York: Oxford University Press.

Mintz, Beth. 1975. "The President's Cabinet, 1897–1972: A Contribution to the Power Structure Debate." *Insurgent Sociologist*, 5:131–148.

Mintz, Beth. 1989. "United States." Pp. 207–226 in Tom Bottomore and Robert J. Brym (eds.), *The Capitalist Class: An International Study*. New York: New York University Press.

Mintz, Beth, Peter Freitag, Carol Hendricks, and Michael Schwartz. 1976. "Problems of Proof in Elite Research." *Social Problems*, 23:314–324.

Mintz, Beth, and Michael Schwartz. 1985. *The Power Structure of American Business*. Chicago: University of Chicago Press.

Mintz, Morton, and Jerry Cohen. 1971. *America, Inc.: Who Owns and Operates the United States*. New York: Dell.

Mintz, Morton, and Jerry Cohen. 1976. *Power, Inc.: Public and Private Rulers and How to Make Them Accountable*. New York: Viking.

Mitchell, Richard. 1967. *The Korean Minority in Japan*. Berkeley: University of California Press.

Mitzman, Arthur. 1969. *The Iron Cage*. New York: Grosset and Dunlap.

Mizurchi, Mark S. 1989. "Similarity of Political Behavior among Large American Corporations." *American Journal of Sociology*, 95:401–424.

Mizruchi, Mark, and Thomas Koening. 1986. "Economic Sources of Corporate Political Consensus: An Examination of Interindustry Relations." *American Sociological Review*, 51:482–489.

Molotch, Harvey. 1989. "Lecturing in the USSR." *Footnotes*. 17(November):3–6.

Moore, Barrington. 1966. *Social Origins of Dictatorship and Democracy: Lord and Peasant in the Making of the Modern World*. Boston: Beacon.

Moore, Barrington. 1978. *Injustice: The Social Bases of Obedience and Revolt*. White Plains, N.Y.: M. E. Sharpe.

Morgan, Edmund. 1956. *The Birth of the Republic, 1763–89*. Chicago: University of Chicago Press.

Morioka, Koji. 1989. "Japan." Pp. 140–176 in Tom Bottomore and Robert J. Brym (eds.), *The Capitalist Class: An International Study*. New York: New York University Press.

Morris, Robert. 1979. *Social Policy of the American Welfare State*. New York: Harper & Row.

Morrisson, Christian. 1984. "Income Distribution in East European and Western Countries." *Journal of Comparative Economics*, 8:121–138.

Morton, Henry W. 1987. "Housing Quality and Housing Classes in the Soviet Union." Pp. 95–116, in Horst Herlemann (ed.), *Quality of Life in the Soviet Union*. Boulder, Colo.: Westview Press.

Mosley, Leonard. 1978. *Dulles*. New York: The Dial Press.

Moynihan, Daniel Patrick. 1973. *The Politics of a Guaranteed Income*. New York: Vintage.

Mudrick, Nancy. 1978. "The Use of AFDC by Previously High and Low Income Households." *Social Service Review*, 52:107–115.

Muller, Edward. 1985. "Income Inequality, Regime Repressiveness, and Political Violence." *American Sociological Review*, 50:47–61.

Muller, Edward. 1988. "Democracy, Economic Development, and Income Inequality." *American Sociological Review*, 53:50–68.

Muller, Georg P., and Volker Bornschier. 1988. *Comparative World Data: A Statistical Handbook for Social Science*. Baltimore, Md.: Johns Hopkins University Press.

Mullins, Nicholas. 1973. *Theories and Theory Groups in Contemporary American Sociology*. New York: Harper & Row.

Murdock, George. 1949. *Social Structure*. New York: Macmillan.

Murdock, George. 1957. "World Ethnographic Sample." *American Anthropologist*, 59:664–687.

Myrdal, Gunnar. 1970. *The Challenge of World Poverty*. New York: Pantheon.

Nakao, Keiko, and Judith Treas. 1990. "Occupational Prestige in the United States Revisited: Twenty-Five Years of Stability and Change." Paper presented at the annual meetings of the American Sociological Association. August, Washington, D.C.

Nakane, Chie. 1970. *Japanese Society*. Berkeley: University of California Press.

Naoi, Atsushi, and Fumiaki Ojima. 1989. "Industrialization and Social Stratification: Reexamination of Treiman's Industrialization Thesis." Paper presented to the meetings of Research Stratification Committee of the International Sociological Association, Stanford, Calif., Aug. 1989.

Naoi, Atsushi, and Carmi Schooler. 1985. "Occupational Conditions and Psychological Functions in Japan." *American Journal of Sociology*, 90:729–752.

Needler, M. C. 1968. "Political Development and Socioeconomic Development: The Case of Latin America." *American Political Science Review*, 62:889–897.

Nisbet, Robert. 1959. "The Decline and Fall of Social Class." *Pacific Sociological Review*, 2:11–17.

Nolan, Patrick D. 1983. "Status in the World System, Income Inequality, and Economic Growth." *American Journal of Sociology*, 89:410–419.

Nolan, Patrick D. 1983. "Status in the World Economy and National Structure and Development." *International Journal of Contemporary Sociology*, 24:109–120.

Nolan, Patrick D. 1983. "Status in the World System, Income Inequality, and Economic Growth." *American Journal of Sociology*, 89:410–419.

North, C. C., and P. K. Hatt. 1947. "Jobs and Occupations: A Popular Evaluation." *Opinion News*, 9:3–13.

Nove, Alec. 1979. *Political Economy and Soviet Socialism*. London: Allen & Unwin.

Nulty, Leslie Ellen. 1977. *Understanding the New Inflation: The Importance of the Basic Necessities*. Washington, D.C.: Exploratory Project for Economic Alternatives.

Nutter, G. Warren. 1978. *Growth of Government in the West*. Washington, D.C.: American Enterprise Institute for Public Policy Research.

Ofshe, L., and R. Ofshe. 1970. *Utility and Choice in Social Interaction*. Englewood Cliffs, N.J.: Prentice-Hall.

Ohno, Susumo. 1979. *Nihongo ni Tsuite* (About the Japanese Language). Tokyo: Kadokawa Shuten.

Olsen, Nancy. 1973. "Family Structure and Independence Training in a Taiwanese Village." *Journal of Marriage and Family*, 35:512–519.

Oppenheimer, Martin. 1969. *The Urban Guerrilla*. Chicago: Quadrangle Books.

Orloff, Ann Shola, and Theda Skocpol. 1984. "Why Not Equal Protection? Explaining the Politics of Public Social Spending in Britain, 1900–1911, and the United States, 1800s–1920." *American Sociological Review*, 49:726–750.

Ostrander, Susan A. 1984. *Women of the Upper Class*. Philadelphia: Temple University Press.

Ozawa, Martha. 1978. "Issues in Welfare Reform." *Social Service Review*, 52:37–55.

Page, Charles H. 1969. *Class and American Sociology*. New York: Schocken Books.

Paige, Jeffrey. 1975. *Agrarian Revolution*. New York: Free Press.

Pampel, Fred, Kenneth Land, and Marcus Felson. 1977. "A Social Indicator Model of Changes in the Occupational Structure of the United States: 1947–1974." *American Sociological Review*, 42:951–964.

Pampel, Fred, and John Williamson. 1985. "Age Structure, Politics and Cross-National Patterns of Public Pension Expenditures." *American Sociological Review*, 50:782–799.

Pampel, Fred C., and John B. Williamson. 1988. "Welfare Spending in Advanced Industrial Democracies, 1950–1980." *American Journal of Sociology*, 93:1424–1456.

Parcel, Toby. 1979. "Race, Regional Labor Markets and Earnings." *American Sociological Review*, 44:262–279.

Parcel, Toby L., and Charles W. Mueller. 1989. "Temporal Change in Occupational Earnings Attainment, 1970–1980." *American Sociological Review,* 54:622–634.

Parkin, Frank. 1971. *Class Inequality and Political Order: Social Stratification in Capitalist and Communist Societies.* New York: Praeger.

Parsons, Talcott. 1937. *The Structure of Social Action.* New York: Free Press.

Parsons, Talcott. 1951. *The Social System.* New York: Free Press.

Parsons, Talcott. 1960. "Authority, Legitimization, and Political Action." Pp. 170–198 in *Structure and Process in Modern Societies.* New York: Free Press.

Parsons, Talcott. 1964. *Essays in Sociological Theory.* New York: Free Press.

Parsons, Talcott. 1964a. "A Revised Analytical Approach to the Theory of Social Stratification." Pp. 386–440 in *Essays in Sociological Theory.* New York: Free Press.

Parsons, Talcott. 1964b. "Social Classes and Class Conflict in Light of Recent Sociological Theory." Pp. 323–335 in *Essays in Sociological Theory.* New York: Free Press.

Parsons, Talcott. 1968. "The Distribution of Power in American Society." Pp. 60–87 in G. William Domhoff and Hoyt B. Ballard (eds.), *C. Wright Mills and the Power Elite.* Boston: Beacon.

Parsons, Talcott. 1970. "Equality and Inequality in Modern Society, or Social Stratification Revisited." Pp. 13–72 in Edward O. Laumann (ed.), *Social Stratification.* New York: Bobbs-Merrill.

Parsons, Talcott. 1977. "Comment on Burger's Critique." *American Journal of Sociology,* 83:335–339.

Patchen, M. 1970. "Social Class and Dimensions of Foreign Policy Attitudes." *Social Science Quarterly,* 51:649–667.

Patterson, James T. 1986. *America's Struggle Against Poverty, 1900–1985.* Cambridge, Mass.: Harvard University Press.

Payne, Robert. 1964. *The Life and Death of Lenin.* New York: Simon & Schuster.

Pearlin, Leonard. 1971. *Class Context and Family Relations: A Cross-National Study.* Boston: Little, Brown.

Pearson, Jessica. 1978. "Organizational Response to Occupational Injury and Disease: The Case of the Uranium Industry." *Social Forces,* 57:23–41.

Pease, John, William Form, and Joan Huber. 1970. "Ideological Currents in American Stratification Literature." *American Sociologist,* 5:127–137.

Persell, C. H. 1977. *Education and Inequality: A Theoretical and Empirical Synthesis.* New York: Free Press.

Petras, James. 1969. *Politics and Social Forces in Chilean Development.* Berkeley: University of California Press.

Petras, James, and Morris Morley. 1975. *The United States and Chile.* New York: Monthly Review Press.

Pettigrew, Thomas. 1964. *A Profile of the Negro American.* Princeton, N.J.: Van Nostrand.

Pfautz, Harold. 1953. "The Current Literature on Social Stratification: Critique and Bibliography." *American Journal of Sociology,* 58:391–418.

Pfeffer, Richard. 1979. *Working for Capitalism.* New York: Columbia University Press.

Pfeiffer, John. 1977. *The Emergence of Society: A Prehistory of the Establishment.* New York: McGraw-Hill.

Piven, Frances Fox, and Richard Cloward. 1971. *Regulating the Poor: The Functions of Public Welfare.* New York: Pantheon Books.

Piven, Frances Fox, and Richard Cloward. 1977. *Poor People's Movements: Why They Succeed, Why They Fail*. New York: Pantheon Books.

Piven, Frances Fox, and Richard Cloward. 1982. *The New Class War: Reagan's Attack on the Welfare State and Its Consequences*. New York: Pantheon.

Piven, Frances Fox, and Richard Cloward. 1988. *Why Americans Don't Vote*. New York: Pantheon.

Portes, Alejandro. 1976. "On the Sociology of National Development: Theories and Issues." *American Journal of Sociology*, 85:55–85.

Poulantzas, Nicos. 1975. *Classes and Contemporary Capitalism*. London: NLB.

Poulantzas, Nicos. 1973. *Political Power and Social Classes*. London: Verso.

Putnam, Robert. 1976. *The Comparative Study of Elites*. Englewood Cliffs, N.J.: Prentice-Hall.

Quadagno, Jill. 1979. "Paradigms in Evolutionary Theory: The Sociobiological Model of Natural Selection." *American Sociological Review*, 44:100–109.

Quadagno, Jill S. 1984. "Welfare Capitalism and the Social Security Act of 1935." *American Sociological Review*, 49:632–647.

Raabe, Phyllis Hutton. 1973. *Status and Its Impact: New Orlean's Carnival. The Social Upper Class and Upper-Class Power*. Ph.D. dissertation, Department of Sociology, Pennsylvania State University.

Radcliffe-Brown, A. R. 1948. *The Andaman Islanders*. New York: Free Press.

Rainwater, Lee. 1969. "The Problem of Lower-Class Culture and Poverty-War Strategy." Pp. 229–259 in Daniel P. Moynihan (ed.), *On Understanding Poverty*. New York: Basic Books.

Ransford, Edward H. 1972. "Blue-Collar Anger: Reactions to Student and Black Protest." *American Sociological Review*, 37:333–346.

Rawlins, V. L., and L. Ulman. 1974. "The Utilization of College Trained Manpower in the United States." In M. S. Gordon (ed.), *Higher Education and the Labor Market*. New York: McGraw-Hill.

Redman, Charles. 1978. *The Rise of Civilization: From Early Farmers to Urban Society in the Ancient Near East*. San Francisco: Freeman.

Rein, Martin. 1971. "Problems in the Definition and Measurement of Poverty." Pp. 116–131 in Louis Ferman, Joyce Kornbluh, and Alan Harber (eds.), *Poverty in America*. Ann Arbor: University of Michigan Press.

Reischauer, Edwin O., and Albert M. Craig. 1978. *Japan: Tradition and Transformation*. New York: Houghton Mifflin.

Reischauer, Edwin O. 1987. *The Japanese*. Cambridge, Mass.: Harvard University Press.

Reiss, Albert, O. D. Duncan, Paul Hatt, and C. C. North. 1961. *Occupations and Social Status*. New York: Free Press.

Remington, Thomas F. 1988. "Words and Deeds: CPSU Ideological Work." Pp. 147–166 in Michael Paul Sacks and Jerry G. Pankhurst (ed.), *Understanding Societ Society*. Boston: Allen & Unwin.

Remnick, David. 1989. "Gorbachev's Pay: He's Not Rich." *International Herald Tribune*, February 1, p. 1.

Riley, George. 1980. "U.S. Investment in South Africa: An Overview." Pp. 413–418 in Mark Green and Robert Massie (eds.), *The Big Business Reader: Essays on Corporate America*. New York: The Pilgrim Press.

Rist, R. C. 1970. "Student Social Class and Teachers; Expectations: The Self-fulfilling Prophecy in Ghetto Education." *Harvard Educational Review*, 40:411–450.

Ritzer, George. 1975. *Sociology: A Multiple Paradigm Science*. Boston: Allyn and Bacon.

Ritzer, George. 1980. *Sociology: A Multiple Paradigm Science*. (Revised Edition) Boston: Allyn and Bacon.

Robinson, Robert V. 1984. "Reproducing Class Relations in Industrial Capitalism." *American Sociological Review*, 49:182–196.

Robinson, Robert, and Wendell Bell. 1978. "Equality, Success, and Social Injustice in England and the United States." *American Sociological Review*, 43:125–143.

Robinson, Robert V. and Maurice A. Garnier. 1985. "Class Reproduction among Men and Women in France: Reproduction Theory on Its Home Ground." *American Journal of Sociology*, 91:250–281.

Robinson, Robert, and Jonathan Kelley. 1979. "Class as Conceived by Marx and Dahrendorf: Effects on Income Inequality, Class Consciousness, and Class Conflict in the United States and Great Britain." *American Sociological Review*, 44:38–58.

Rodman, Hyman. 1963. "The Lower Class Value Stretch." *Social Forces*, 42:205–215.

Rogoff, Natalie. 1953a. "Recent Trends in Occupational Mobility." Pp. 442–454 in Reinhard Bendix and Seymour Lipset (eds.), *Class, Status, and Power*. New York: Free Press.

Rogoff, Natalie. 1953b. *Recent Trends in Occupational Mobility*. New York: Free Press.

Rohlen, Thomas P. 1982. *Japan's High Schools*. Berkeley: University of California Press.

Roosevelt, Kermit. 1979. *Counter Coup: The Struggle for the Control of Iran*. New York: McGraw-Hill.

Rose, Arnold. 1967. *The Power Structure*. New York: Oxford University Press.

Rosen, Lawrence, and Robert Bell. 1966. "Mate Selection in the Upper Class." *Sociological Quarterly*, 7:157–166.

Rosenau, James. 1961. *Public Opinion and Foreign Policy*. New York: Random House.

Rosenbaum, J. E. 1975. "The Stratification of the Socialization Processes." *American Sociological Review*, 40:48–54.

Rosenbaum, James, and Takehiko Kariya. 1989. "From High School to Work: Market and Institutional Mechanisms in Japan." *American Journal of Sociology*, 94:1334–1365.

Rosenberg, Morris, and Leonard I. Pearlin. 1978. "Social Class and Self-Esteem Among Children and Adults." *American Journal of Sociology*, 84:53–77.

Rosenberg, Morris, and Roberta Simmons. 1972. *Black and White Self-Esteem: The Urban School Child*. Washington, D.C.: American Sociological Association, Rose Monograph Series.

Rosenfeld, Eva. 1951. "Social Stratification in a 'Classless' Society." *American Sociological Review*, 16:766–774.

Rosenthal, R., and L. Jacobson. 1968. *Pygmalion in the Classroom*. New York: Holt, Rinehart, and Winston.

Rossi, Peter, and Zahava Blum. 1969. "Class, Status, and Poverty." Pp. 36–63 in Daniel P. Moynihan (ed.), *On Understanding Poverty*. New York: Basic Books.

Rossi, Peter, and Katharine Lyall. 1976. *Reforming Public Welfare*. New York: Russell Sage.

Rostow, Walter. 1960. *The Stages of Economic Growth*. New York: Cambridge University Press.

Roy, William G. 1981. "The Vesting of Interests and the Determinants of Political

Power: Size, Network Structure, and Mobilization of American Industries, 1886–1905.'' *American Journal of Sociology,* 86:1287–1310.

Roy, William G. 1983. ''The Unfolding of the Interlocking Directorate Structure in the United States.'' *American Sociological Review,* 48:248–257.

Rubin, Beth. 1986. ''Class Struggle American Style: Unions, Strikes, and Wages.'' *American Sociological Review,* 51:618–631.

Rubinson, Richard. 1976. ''The World Economy and the Distribution of Income Within States: A Cross-National Study.'' *American Sociological Review,* 41:638–659.

Rubinson, Richard. 1986. ''Class Formation, Politics, and Institutions: Schooling in the United States.'' *American Journal of Sociology,* 92:519–538.

Rubinson, Richard, and Dan Quinlan. 1977. ''Democracy and Social Inequality: A Reanalysis.'' *American Sociological Review,* 42:611–623.

Rudé, George. 1964. *The Crowd in History, 1730–1848.* New York: John Wiley & Sons.

Ryan, William. 1971. *Blaming the Victim.* New York: Vintage.

Sacks, Michael Paul. 1988. ''Women, Work, and Family in the Soviet Union.'' Pp. 71–96, in Michael Paul Sacks and Jerry G. Pankhurst (eds.), *Understanding Soviet Society.* Boston: Allen & Unwin.

Sahlins, Marshall, and Elman Service. 1960. *Evolution and Culture.* Ann Arbor: University of Michigan Press.

Salamon, Lester, and John Siegfried. 1977. ''Economic Power and Political Influence: The Impact of Industry Structure on Public Policy.'' *American Political Science Review,* 71:1026–1043.

Salert, Barbara, and John Sprague. 1980. *The Dynamics of Riots.* Ann Arbor, Mich.: Inter-University Consortium for Political and Social Research.

Salisbury, Harrison. 1977. *Black Night, White Snow: Russia's Revolutions, 1905–1917.* New York: Doubleday.

Sallach, David. 1974. ''Class Domination and Ideological Hegemony.'' *Sociological Quarterly,* 15:38–50.

Sampson, Anthony. 1973. *The Sovereign State of I.T.&T.* New York: Stein and Day.

Sampson, Anthony. 1975. *The Seven Sisters.* New York: Viking.

Sanford, Rojas. 1976. *The Murder of Allende: The End of the Chilean Way to Socialism.* New York: Harper & Row.

Schafer, W. E., and C. Olexa. 1971. *Tracking and Opportunity: The Locking-Out Process and Beyond.* Scranton, Pa.: Chandler.

Schama, Simon. 1989. *Citizens: A Chronicle of the French Revolution.* New York: Knopf.

Schattschneider, E. E. 1960. *The Semi-Sovereign People: A Realist's View of Democracy in America.* New York: Holt, Rinehart, and Winston.

Schermerhorn, R. A. 1970. *Comparative Ethnic Relations.* New York: Random House.

Scheuerman, William. 1975. ''Economic Power in the United States: The Case of Steel.'' *Politics and Society,* 5:337–366.

Schooler, Carmi, and Atsushi Naoi. 1988. ''The Psychological Effects of Traditional and of Economically Peripheral Job Settings in Japan.'' *American Journal of Sociology,* 94:335–355.

Schram, Sanford F., and J. Patrick Turbett. 1983. ''Civil Disorder and the Welfare Explosion: A Two Step Process.'' *American Sociological Review,* 48:408–414.

Schriftgiesser, Karl. 1967. *Business and Public Policy.* Englewood Cliffs, N.J.: Prentice-Hall.

Schroeder, Gertrude E. 1987. ''Soviet Living Standards in Comparative Perspective.''

Pp. 13–30, in Horst Herlemann (ed.), *Quality of Life in the Soviet Union*. Boulder, Colo.: Westview Press.

Schwartz, B. 1974. "Waiting, Exchange, and Power: The Distribution of Time in Social System." *American Journal of Sociology*, 79:841–870.

Scott, John. 1979. *Corporations, Classes and Capitalism*. London: Hutchinson.

Semyonov, Moshe, and Noah Lewin-Epstein. 1986. "Economic Development, Investment Dependence, and the Rise of Services in Less Developed Nations." *Social Forces*, 64:582–598.

Sennett, Richard, and Jonathan Cobb. 1973. *The Hidden Injuries of Class*. New York: Vintage.

Sennett, Richard. 1974. *The Fall of Public Man: On the Social Psychology of Capitalism*. New York: Vintage.

Sewell, William. 1971. "Inequality of Opportunity for Higher Education." *American Sociological Review*, 36:793–809.

Sewell, William, A. O. Haller, and G. W. Ohlendorf. 1970. "The Educational and Early Occupational Status Attainment Process: A Replication and Revision." *American Sociological Review*, 35:1014–1027.

Sewell, William, and Robert Hauser. 1975. *Education, Occupation, and Earnings: Achievement in the Early Career*. New York: Academic Press.

Sewell, William, and Vimal Shah. 1968. "Parents' Education and Children's Education Aspirations and Achievements." *American Sociological Review*, 33:191–209.

Shaffer, Richard A., and Harold R. Kerbo. 1987. "Welfare Development in the Untied States, 1890–1940: An Empirical Test of Competing Theories." Paper presented at the meetings of the Research Committee on Social Stratification of the International Sociological Association. Berkeley: August.

Shelley, Louise. 1989. "Soviet Sociology Today: Possibilities for Cooperation." *Footnotes*, 17(November):3.

Shimizu, Ryuei. 1980. *The Growth of Firms in Japan*. Tokyo: Keio Tsushin Ltd.

Shlapentokh, Vladimir. 1989. *Public and Private Life of the Soviet People: Changing Values in Post-Stalin Russia*. New York: Oxford University Press.

Shlapentokh. Vladimir. 1987. *The Politics of Sociology in the Soviet Union*. Boulder, Colo.: Westview Press.

Shoup, Laurence. 1975. "Shaping the Postwar World: The Council of Foreign Relations and U.S. War Aims During WW II." *Insurgent Sociologist*, 5:9–52.

Shoup, Laurence, and William Minter. 1977. *Imperial Brain Trust*. New York: Monthly Review Press.

Siegel, Paul. 1971. "Prestige in the American Occupational Structure." Ph.D. dissertation, The University of Chicago.

Silver, Brian D. 1987. "Political Beliefs of the Soviet Citizen: Sources of Support for Regime Norms." Pp. 100–141, in Hames R. Millar (ed.), *Politics, Work, and Daily Life in the USSR: A Survey of Former Soviet Citizens*. Cambridge: Cambridge University Press.

Simkus, Albert, and Rudolf Andorka. 1982. "Inequality in Educational Attainment in Hungary, 1923–1973." *American Sociological Review*, 47:740–751.

Simkus, Albert, and Peter Robert. 1989. "Attitudes Toward Inequality Under a Kind of Socialism: Hungary, 1987." Paper presented at the meeting of the Research Committee on Social Stratification of the International Sociological Association, Stanford University, August.

Singelmann, Joachim. 1978. "The Sectoral Transformation of the Labor Force in

Seven Industrialized Countries, 1920–1970.'' *American Journal of Sociology,* 83:1224–1234.

Sio, Arnold. 1969. "Interpretations of Slavery: The Slave Status in the Americas." Pp. 63–73 in Celia Heller (ed.), *Structured Social Inequality.* New York: Macmillan.

Skinner, Elliot (ed.). 1973. *Peoples and Cultures of Africa.* New York: Doubleday.

Skocpol, Theda. 1976. "Old Regime Legacies and Communist Revolutions in Russia and China." *Social Forces,* 55:284–315.

Skocpol, Theda. 1979. *States and Social Revolutions: A Comparative Analysis of France, Russia, and China.* New York: Cambridge University Press.

Skocpol, Theda, and Edwin Amenta. 1985. "Did Capitalists Shape Social Security?" *American Sociological Review,* 50:572–575.

Slomczynski, Kazimierz, and Tadeusz K. Krauze. 1987. "Cross-National Similarity in Social Mobility Patterns: A Direct Test of the Fatherman–Jones–Hauser Hypothesis." *American Sociological Review,* 52:598–611.

Slomczynski, Kazimierz, Joanne Miller, and Melvin Kohn. 1981. "Stratification, Work, and Values: A Polish–United States Comparison." *American Sociological Review,* 46:720–744.

Smith, David. 1974. *Who Rules the Universities?* New York: Monthly Review Press.

Smith, Robert J. 1983. *Japanese Society: Tradition, Self and the Social Order.* Cambridge: Cambridge University Press.

Smith, James D. 1986. *The Distribution of Wealth.* Ann Arbor: Survey Research Center.

Snyder, David. 1975. "Institutional Setting and Industrial Conflict: Comparative Analysis of France, Italy, and the United States." *American Sociological Review,* 40:259–278.

Snyder, David, and Edward Kick. 1979. "Structural Position in the World System and Economic Growth, 1955–1970: A Multiple Analysis of Transnational Interactions." *American Journal of Sociology,* 84:1096–1128.

Soboul, Albert. 1974. *The French Revolution, 1787–1799: From the Storming of the Bastille to Napoleon.* New York: Random House.

Solzhenitsyn, Aleksandr. 1973. *The Gulag Archipelago.* New York: Harper & Row.

Solzhenitsyn, Aleksandr. 1976. *Lenin in Zurich.* New York: Farrar, Straus, & Giroux.

Solzhenitsyn, Aleksandr. 1980. *The Oak and the Calf.* New York: Harper & Row.

Sonquist, John, and Thomas Koening. 1975. "Interlocking Directorates in the Top U.S. Corporations: A Graph Theory Approach." *Insurgent Sociologist,* 5:196–229.

Soref, Michael. 1976. "Social Class and a Division of Labor Within the Corporate Elite: A Note on Class, Interlocking, and Executive Committee Membership of Directors of U.S. Firms." *Sociological Quarterly,* 17:360–368.

Sorkin, Alan. 1978. "The Economic Base of Indian Life." *The Annals,* 436:1–12.

Sorokin, Pitirim. 1959. *Social and Cultural Mobility.* New York: Free Press.

Spaeth, Joe. 1976. "Cognitive Complexity: A Dimension Underlying the Socioeconomic Achievement Process." Pp. 153–189 in William Sewell, Robert Hauser, and David Featherman (eds.), *Schooling and Achievement in American Society.* New York: Academic Press.

Spaeth, Joe. 1979. "Vertical Differentiation Among Occupations." *American Sociological Review,* 44:746–762.

Spiro, Melford. 1970. *Kibbutz: Venture in Utopia.* New York: Schocken Books.

Stack, Steven. 1978a. "The Effect of Direct Government Involvement in the Economy on the Degree of Income Inequality: A Cross-National Study." *American Sociological Review,* 43:880–888.

Stack, Steven. 1978b. "Internal Political Organization and the World Economy of Income Inequality." *American Sociological Review,* 42:271–272.

Stanfiel, James. 1973. "Socioeconomic Status as Related to Aptitude, Attrition, and Achievement of College Students." *Sociology of Education,* 46:480–488.

Stein, A. 1971. "Strategies for Failure." *Harvard Educational Review,* 41:158–204.

Steiner, Gilbert. 1971 *The State of Welfare.* Washington, D.C.: The Brookings Institution.

Steinmetz, George, and Erik Olin Wright. 1989. "The Fall and Rise of the Petty Bourgeoisie: Changing Patterns of Self-Employment in the Postwar United States." *American Journal of Sociology,* 94:973–1018.

Stern, Philip. 1973. *The Rape of the Taxpayer.* New York: Random House.

Steven, Rob. 1983, *Classes in Contemporary Japan.* Cambridge: Cambridge University Press.

Stillman, Don. 1980. "The Devastating Impact of Plant Relocations." Pp. 72–88 in Mark Green and Robert Massie (eds.), *The Big Business Reader: Essays on Corporate America.* New York: The Pilgrim Press.

Stohl, Michael. 1976. *War and Domestic Political Violence.* Beverly Hills, Calif.: Sage Publications.

Stokes, Randall, and David Jaffee. 1982. "Another Look at the Export of Raw Materials and Economic Growth." *American Sociological Review,* 47:402–407.

Stolte, John F. 1983. "The Legitimation of Structural Inequality: Reformulation and Test of the Self-Evaluation Argument." *American Sociological Review,* 48:331–342.

Stolzenberg, Ross. 1978. "Bringing the Boss Back In: Employer Size, Employee Schooling, and Socioeconomic Achievement." *American Sociological Review,* 43:813–828.

Strasser, Hermann. 1976. *The Normative Structure of Sociology: Conservative and Emancipatory Themes in Social Thought.* London: Routledge & Kegan Paul.

Sugimoto, Yoshio. 1986. "The Manipulative Bases of 'Consensus' in Japan." Pp. 65–75 in Gavan McCormack and Yoshio Sugimoto (eds.), *Democracy in Contemporary Japan.* New York: M. E. Sharpe.

Survey, Stanley. 1973. *Pathways to Tax Reform.* Cambridge, Mass.: Harvard University Press.

Swafford, Michael. 1978. "Sex Differences in Soviet Earnings." *American Sociological Review,* 43:657–673.

Swafford, Michael. 1987. "Perceptions of Social Status in the USSR." Pp. 279–300, in James R. Millar (ed.), *Politics, Work, and Daily life in the USSR: A Survey of Former Soviet Citizens.* Cambridge: Cambridge University Press.

Swafford, Michael. 1989. "The Face, and Pace, of Change in the Soviet Union." *Footnotes,* 17(November):6–8.

Swatos, William. 1980. "Five More Years: Introductory Text Citations Revisited." *The Southern Sociologist,* 11:15–18.

Sztompka, Piotr. 1974. *System and Function: Toward a Theory of Society.* New York: Academic Press.

Szymanski, Albert. 1978. *The Capitalist State and the Politics of Class.* Cambridge, Mass.: Winthrop Publishers.

Taeuber, Cynthia, and Victor Valdisera. 1987. "Women in the American Economy." Current Population Reports: Special Studies, Washington, D.C.: U.S. Government Printing Office.

Tax, Sol. 1978. "The Impact of Urbanization on American Indians." *The Annals,* 436:121–136.

Taylor, Jared. 1983. *Shadows of the Rising Sun: A Critical View of the "Japanese Miracle."* Tokyo: Tuttle.

Teckenberg, Wolfgang. 1987. "Consumer Goods and Services: Contemporary Problems and Their Impact on the Quality of Life in the Soviet Union." Pp. 31–42, in Horst Herlemann (ed.), *Quality of Life in the Soviet Union.* Boulder, Colo.: Westview Press.

Telenback, Sten. 1978. "The Logic of Development in Socialist Poland." *Social Forces,* 57:436–456.

Terkel, Studs. 1972. *Working.* New York: Pantheon.

Therborn, Göran. 1978. *What Does the Ruling Class Do When It Rules?* London NLB.

Thernstrom, Stephen. 1964. *Poverty and Progress: Social Mobility in a Nineteenth Century City.* Cambridge, Mass.: Harvard University Press.

Thernstrom, Stephen. 1970. "Immigrants and Wasps: Ethnics Differences in Occupational Mobility in Boston, 1890–1940." Pp. 125–164 in Stephen Thernstrom and Richard Sennett (eds.), *Nineteenth Century Cities.* New Haven: Yale University Press.

Thurow, Lester. 1980. *The Zero-Sum Society.* New York: Basic Books.

Thurow, Lester. 1987. "A Surge in Inequality." *Scientific American,* 256:31–37.

Tigges, Leann M. 1988. "Age Earnings, and Change Within the Dual Economy." *Social Forces,* 66:676–698.

Tilly, Charles. 1978. *From Mobilization to Revolution.* Reading, Mass.: Addison-Wesley.

Timberlake, Michael, and Kirk R. Williams. 1984. "Dependence, Political Exclusion, and Government Repression: Some Cross-National Evidence." *American Sociological Review,* 49:141–146.

Tiryakian, Edward. 1975. "Neither Marx Nor Durkheim . . . Perhaps Weber." *American Journal of Sociology,* 81:1–33.

Tolbert, Charles. 1983. "Industrial Segmentation and Men's Intergenerational Mobility." *Social Forces,* 61:1119–1138.

Tolbert, Charles. 1982. "Industrial Segmentation and Men's Career Mobility." *American Sociological Review,* 47:457–477.

Tolbert, Charles, Patrick Horan, and E. M. Beck. 1980. "The Structure of Economic Segmentation: A Dual Economy Approach." *American Journal of Sociology,* 85:1095–1116.

Tominaga, Ken'ichi, and Atsushi Naoi. 1978. "A Comparative Analysis of Social Mobility: Tokyo and Chicago." Pp. 201–231 in Wlodzimierz Wesolowski, Kazimierz Slomczynski, and Bogdan Mach (eds.), *Social Mobility in Comparative Perspective.* Wroclaw: Polish Academy of Science.

Tominaga, Ken'ichi. 1979. *Nihon no Kaiao Kozo* (The Structure of Japanese Social Stratification). Tokyo: Tokyo University Press.

Tompkins, Gary. 1975. "A Causal Model of State Welfare Expenditures." *Journal of Politics,* 37:392–416.

Toyo Keizai Shinposha. 1989. *Japan Company Handbook* (2 volumes). Tokyo: Toyo Keizai Shinposha.

Trattner, Walter I. (eds.). 1983. *Social Welfare or Social Control? Some Historical Reflections on "Regulating the Poor."* Knoxville, Tenn.: University of Tennessee Press.

Treas, Judith. 1983. "Trickle Down or Transfers?: Post War Determinants of Family Income Inequality." *American Sociological Review,* 48:546–559.

Treiman, Donald J. 1977. *Occupational Prestige in Comparative Perspective*. New York: Academic Press.

Treiman, Donald J., and Patricia Roos. 1983. "Sex and Earning in Industrial Society: A Nine-Nation Comparison." *American Journal of Sociology*, 89:612–650.

Treiman, Donald, and Kermitt Terrell. 1975. "Sex and the Process of Status Attainment: A Comparison of Working Women and Men." *American Sociological Review*, 40:174–200.

Tsurutani, Taketsugu. 1977. *Political Change in Japan*. New York: David McKay.

Tufte, Edward. 1978. *Political Control of the Economy*. Princeton: Princeton University Press.

Tully, J. C., E. F. Jackson, and R. F. Curtis. 1970. "Trends in Occupational Mobility in Indianapolis." *Social Forces*, 49:186–200.

Tumin, Melvin M. 1953. "Some Principles of Stratification: A Critical Analysis." *American Sociological Review*, 18:387–394.

Tumin, Melvin M. 1963. "On Inequality." *American Sociological Review*, 28:19–26.

Turnbull, Colin. 1961. *The Forest People*. New York: Simon & Schuster.

Turner, Jonathan. 1970. "Entrepreneurial Environments and the Emergence of Achievement Motivation in Adolescent Males." *Sociometry*, 33:147–166.

Turner, Jonathan, and Charles Starnes. 1976. *Inequality: Privilege and Poverty in America*. Santa Monica, Calif.: Goodyear.

Turner, Ralph. 1960. "Sponsored and Contest Mobility and the School System." *American Sociological Review*, 25:855–867.

Tyree, Andrea, and Robert Hodge. 1978. "Editorial Foreword: Five Empirical Landmarks." *Social Forces*, 56:761–769.

Tyree, Andrea, Moshe Semyonov, and Robert Hodge. 1979. "Gaps and Glissandes: Inequality, Economic Development, and Social Mobility in 24 Countries." *American Sociological Review*, 44:410–424.

Tyree, Andrea, and Judith Treas. 1974. "The Occupational and Marital Mobility of Women." *American Sociological Review*, 39:293–302.

Ulam, Adam. 1973. *Stalin: The Man and His Era*. New York: Viking Press.

U.S. Bureau of the Census. 1980. *Statistical Abstracts of the United States*. Washington, D.C.: U.S. Government Printing Office.

U.S. Bureau of the Census. 1986. *Household Wealth and Asset Ownership: 1984*. Current Population Reports, Household Economic Studies, series P–70, no. 7. Washington, D.C.: U.S. Government Printing Office.

U.S. Bureau of the Census. 1987. *Male-Female Differences in Work Experience, Occupation and Earnings: 1984*. Current Population Reports, Household Economic Studies, series P–70, no. 10, Washington, D.C.: U.S. Government Printing Office.

U.S. Bureau of the Census. 1987. *Statistical Abstracts of the United States*. Washington, D.C.: U.S. Government Printing Office.

U.S. Bureau of the Census. 1988. *Statistical Abstracts of the United States*. Washington, D.C.: U.S. Government Printing Office.

U.S. Bureau of the Census. 1988. *Measuring the Effect of Benefits and Taxes on Income and Poverty: 1986*. Current Population Report. Consumer Income, series P–60, no. 164–RD–1, Washington, D.C.: U.S. Government Printing Office.

U.S. Bureau of the Census. 1989. *Poverty in the United States, 1987*. Current Population Reports, Consumer Income, series P–60, no. 163, Washington, D.C.: U.S. Government Printing Office.

U.S. Bureau of the Census. 1989. *Money Income of Households, Families, and Per-*

sons in the United States: 1987. Current Population Reports, Consumer Income, series P–60, no. 162, Washington, D.C.: U.S. Government Printing Office.

U.S. Bureau of the Census. 1989. *Money Income and Poverty Status in the United States: 1988.* Current Population Reports, Consumer Income, series P–60, Washington, D.C.: U.S. Government Printing Office.

U.S. Bureau of the Census. 1989. *Characteristics of Persons Receiving Benefits From Major Assistance Programs.* Current Population Reports. Household Economic Studies, series P–70, no. 14, Washington, D.C.: U.S. Government Printing Office.

U.S. Bureau of the Census. 1989. *Spells of Job Search and Layoff . . . and Their Outcomes.* Current Population Reports, Household Economic Studies, series P–70, no. 16–RD–2, Washington, D.C.: U.S. Government Printing Office.

U.S. Bureau of the Census. 1989. *Statistical Abstracts of the United States.* Washington, D.C.: U.S. Government Printing Office.

U.S. Bureau of the Census. 1989. *Voting and Registration in the Election of November 1988.* Current Population Reports, series P–20, No. 440. Washington, D.C.: U.S. Government Printing Office.

U.S. Commission on Civil Rights. 1978. *Social Indicators of Equality for Minorities and Women.* Washington, D.C.: U.S. Government Printing Office.

U.S. Department of Commerce. 1960. *Historical Statistics of the United States.* Washington, D.C.: U.S. Government Printing Office.

U.S. Department of Commerce. 1974. *Statistical Abstracts of the United States.* Washington, D.C.: U.S. Government Printing Office.

U.S. Internal Revenue Service. 1980. *Individual Income Tax Return.* Washington, D.C.: U.S. Government Printing Office.

U.S. Office of Management and Budget. 1973. *Social Indicators.* Washington, D.C.: U.S. Government Printing Office.

U.S. Senate Committee on Governmental Affairs. 1978a. *Voting Rights in Major Corporations.* Washington, D.C.: U.S. Government Printing Office.

U.S. Senate Committee on Governmental Affairs. 1978b. *Interlocking Directorates among the Major U.S. Corporations.* Washington, D.C.: U.S. Government Printing Office.

U.S. Senate Committee on Governmental Affairs. 1980. *Structure of Corporate Concentration.* 2 vols. Washington, D.C.: U.S. Government Printing Office.

U.S. Senate Select Committee to Study Governmental Operations with Respect to Intelligence Activities. 1975a. *Alleged Assassination Plots Involving Foreign Leaders.* Washington, D.C.: U.S. Government Printing Office.

U.S. Senate Select Committee to Study Governmental Operations with Respect to Intelligence Activities. 1975b. *Covert Action in Chile, 1963–1973.* Washington, D.C.: U.S. Government Printing Office.

Useem, Michael. 1976a. "State Production of Social Knowledge: Patterns in Government Financing of Academic Social Research." *American Sociological Review,* 41:613–629.

Useem, Michael. 1976b. "Government Influence on the Social Science Paradigm." *Sociological Quarterly,* 17:146–161.

Useem, Michael. 1978. "The Inner Group of the American Capitalist Class." *Social Problems,* 25:225–240.

Useem, Michael. 1979a. "Studying the Corporation and the Corporate Elite." *American Sociologist,* 14:97–107.

Useem, Michael. 1979b. "The Social Organization of the American Business Elite." *American Sociological Review,* 44:553–571.

Useem, Michael. 1984. *The Inner Circle: Large Corporations and the Rise of Business Political Activity in the U.S. and U.K.* New York: Oxford University Press.

Useem, Michale, John Hoops, and Thomas Moore. 1976. "Class and Corporate Relations with the Private College System." *Insurgent Sociologist,* 5:27–35.

Valentine, Charles. 1968. *Culture and Poverty.* Chicago: University of Chicago Press.

Valentine, Charles. 1971. "The 'Culture of Poverty': Its Scientific Significance and Its Implications for Action." Pp. 193–225 in E. B. Leacock (ed.), *The Culture of Poverty: A Critique.* New York: Simon & Schuster.

van den Berghe, Pierre. 1963. "Dialectic and Functionalism: Toward a Theoretical Synthesis." *American Sociological Review,* 28:695–705.

van den Berghe, Pierre. 1974. "Bringing Beasts Back In: Toward a Biosocial Theory of Aggression." *American Sociological Review,* 39:777–788.

van den Berghe, Pierre. 1977. "Response to Ellis' 'The Decline and Fall of Sociology.'" *American Sociologist,* 12:76–79.

van den Berghe, Pierre. 1978. *Man in Society: A Biosocial View.* New York: Elsevier.

Vanfossen, Beth, and R. I. Rhodes. 1974. "Commentary." *American Journal of Sociology,* 80:727–732.

Vanneman, Reeve. 1977. "The Occupational Composition of American Classes: Results from Cluster Analysis." *American Journal of Sociology,* 82:783–807.

Vanneman, Reeve. 1980. "US and British Perceptions of Class." *American Journal of Sociology,* 85:769–790.

Vanneman, Reeve, and Lynn Weber Cannon. 1987. *The American Perception of Class.* Philadelphia, Pa.: Temple University Press.

Vanneman, Reeve, and Fred Pampel. 1977. "The American Perception of Class and Status." *American Sociological Review,* 42:422–437.

van Wolferen, Karel. 1989. *The Enigma of Japanese Power.* New York: Knopf.

Veblen, Thorstein. 1899. *The Theory of the Leisure Class.* New York: Macmillan.

Verba, Sidney, et al. 1987. *Elites and the Idea of Equality.* Cambridge, Mass.: Harvard University Press.

Verba, Sidney, and Gary R. Orren. 1985. *Equality in America: The View from the Top.* Cambridge, Mass.: Harvard University Press.

Veyne, Paul (ed.). 1987. *A History of Private Life: From Pagan Rome to Byzantium.* Cambridge, Mass.: Belknap/Harvard University Press.

Vidmar, Neil, and Milton Rokeach. 1974. "Archie Bunker's Bigotry: A Study in Selective Perception and Exposure." *Journal of Communication,* 38:36–47.

Vinokur, Aaron, and Gur Ofer. 1987. "Inequality of Earnings, Household Income, and Wealth in the Soviet Union in the 1970s." Pp. 171–202, in James R. Millar (ed.), *Politics, Work, and Daily Life in the USSR: A Survey of Former Soviet Citizens.* Cambridge: Cambridge University Press.

Vise, David A. 1986. "Report Overstated Gains of Super Rich." *Washington Post* (August 22, C9c).

Vogel, Ezra. 1971. *Japan's New Middle Class.* Berkeley: University of California Press.

Vogel, Ezra. 1979. *Japan As Number One: Lessons for America.* Cambridge, Mass.: Harvard University Press.

Vogel, Ezra. 1985. *Come Back: Building the Resurgence of American Business.* New York: Simon & Schuster.

Volgyes, Ivan. 1978. "Modernization, Stratification, and Elite Development in Hungary." *Social Forces,* 57:500–522.

Wallace, Walter. 1969. *Sociological Theory.* Chicago: Aldine.

Wallerstein, Immanual. 1974. *The Modern World-System*. New York: Academic Press.

Wallerstein, Immanual. 1977. "How Do We Know Class Struggle When We See It?" *Insurgent Sociologist*, 7:104–106.

Wallerstein, Immanual. 1980. *The Modern World-System II: Mercantilism and the Consolidation of the European World Economy, 1600–1750*. New York: Academic Press.

Wallerstein, Immanual. 1989. *The Modern World-System III: The Second Era of Great Expansion of the Capitalist World-Economy, 1730–1840s*. New York: Academic Press.

Warner, W. Lloyd. 1953. *American Life*. Chicago: University of Chicago Press.

Warner, W. Lloyd, et al. 1949. *Democracy in Jonesville*. New York: Harper & Brothers.

Warner, W. Lloyd, and J. O. Low. 1947. *The Social System of a Modern Factory*. Yankee City Series, vol. IV. New Haven: Yale University Press.

Warner, W. Lloyd, and Paul S. Lunt. 1941. *The Social Life of a Modern Community*. Yankee City Series, vol. I. New Haven: Yale University Press.

Warner, W. Lloyd, and Paul S. Lunt. 1942. *The Status System of a Modern Community*. Yankee City Series, vol. II. New Haven: Yale University Press.

Warner, W. Lloyd, Marchia Meeker, and Kenneth Eells. 1949. *Social Class in America*. Chicago: Science Research Associates, Inc.

Warner, W. Lloyd, and Leo Srole. 1949. *The Social Systems of American Ethnic Groups*. Yankee City Series, vol. III. New Haven: Yale University Press.

Warner, W. Lloyd, and Darab Unwalla. 1967. "The System of Interlocking Directorates." Pp. 121–157 in W. Lloyd Warner, Darab Unwalla, and John Trimm (eds.), *The Emergent American Society*. New Haven: Yale University Press.

Wax, Murray. 1971. *Indian Americans*. Englewood Cliffs, N.J.: Prentice-Hall.

Weber, Marianne. 1975. *Max Weber: A Biography*. Translated by Harry Zohn. New York: John Wiley & Sons.

Weber, Max. 1946. *From Max Weber: Essays in Sociology*. Edited and Translated by Hans Gerth and C. Wright Mills. New York: Oxford University Press.

Weber, Max. 1947. *The Theory of Social and Economic Organization*. Edited by Talcott Parsons. New York: Free Press.

Weber, Max. 1958. *The Protestant Ethic and the Spirit of Capitalism*. Translated by Talcott Parsons. New York: Charles Scribner's Sons.

Webster, M. J., and J. E. Driskell. 1978. "Status Generalization: A Review of Some New Data." *American Sociological Review*, 43:22–236.

Weede, Erich. 1980. "Beyond Misspecification in Sociological Analysis of Income Inequality." *American Sociological Review*, 45:497–501.

Weinberg, Martin, and Colin Williams. 1980. "Sexual Embourgeoisement? Social Class and Sexual Activity: 1938–1970." *American Sociological Review*, 45:33–48.

Wells, H. G. 1971. *The Outline of History*. New York: Doubleday.

Wenke, Robert. 1980. *Patterns in Prehistory: Mankind's First Three Million Years*. New York: Oxford University Press.

West, J. C. 1945. *Plainville, USA*. New York: Columbia University Press.

White, Merry. 1987. *The Japanese Educational Challenge*. New York: Free Press.

Whitt, J. Allen. 1979. "Toward a Class-Dialectical Model of Power: An Empirical Assessment of Three Competing Models of Political Power." *American Sociological Review*, 44:81–99.

Whyte, William H. 1956. *The Organization Man*. New York: Simon & Schuster.

Wilensky, Harold. 1975. *The Welfare State and Equality*. Berkeley: The University of California Press.

Willhelm, Sidney. 1979. "Opportunities are Diminishing." *Society (Trans-action)*, 16:5, 12–17.

Williams, Kirk. 1984. "Economic Sources of Homicide: Reestimating the Effects of Poverty and Inequality." *American Sociological Review*, 49:283–289.

Wilson, Edmond O. 1975. *Sociobiology: The New Synthesis*. Cambridge, Mass.: Harvard University Press.

Wilson, Kenneth. 1978. "Toward an Improved Explanation of Income Attainment: Recalibrating Education and Occupation." *American Journal of Sociology*, 84:83–4:684–697.

Wilson, Kenneth, and Alejandro Portes. 1975. "The Educational Attainment Process: Results from a National Sample." *American Journal of Sociology*, 81:343–363.

Wilson, William Julius. 1980. *The Declining Significance of Race: Blacks and Changing American Institutions*. 2d ed. Chicago: University of Chicago Press.

Wilson, William Julius. 1987. *The Truly Disadvantaged: The Inner City, the Underclass, and Public Polity*. Chicago: University of Chicago Press.

Winterbotham, F. W. 1974. *The Ultra Secret*. New York: Harper & Row.

Wittfogel, Karl A. 1957. *Oriental Despotism: A Comparative Study of Total Power*. New Haven: Yale University Press.

Wolf, Wendy, and Neil Fligstein. 1979. "Sex and Authority in the Work Place: The Causes of Sexual Inequality." *American Sociological Review*, 44:235–252.

Wolff, Kurt (ed.). 1971. *From Karl Mannheim*. New York: Oxford University Press.

World Bank. 1986. *World Development Report 1986*. New York: Oxford University Press.

Woronoff, Jon. 1980. *Japan: The Coming Social Crisis*. Tokyo: Yohan Lotus Press.

Woronoff, Jon. 1981. *Japan's Wasted Workers*. Tokyo: Lotus Press.

Woronoff, Jon. 1986. *Politics The Japanese Way*. Tokyo: Lotus Press.

Wright, Erik Olin. 1978a. *Class, Crisis and the State*. New York: Schocken Books.

Wright, Erik Olin. 1978b. "Race, Class, and Income Inequality." *American Journal of Sociology*, 83:1368–1388.

Wright, Erik Olin. 1979. *Class Structure and Income Determination*. New York: Academic Press.

Wright, Erik Olin, Cynthia Costello, David Hachen, and Joey Sprague. 1982. "The American Class Structure." *American Sociological Review*, 47:709–726.

Wright, Erik Olin, and Bill Martin. 1987. "The Transformation of the American Class Structure, 1960–1980." *American Sociological Review*, 93:1–29.

Wright, Erik Olin, and Luca Peronne. 1977. "Marxist Class Categories and Income Inequality." *American Sociological Review*, 42:32–55.

Wright, James D. 1972. "Working Class, Authoritarianism, and the War in Vietnam." *Social Problems*, 20:133–150.

Wright, James D., and Sonia Wright. 1976. "Social Class and Parental Values for Children: A Partial Replication and Extension of the Kohn Thesis." *American Sociological Review*, 41:527–537.

Wright, Sonia. 1975. "Work Response to Income Maintenance." *Social Forces*, 53:553–562.

Wrong, Dennis. 1959. "The Functional Theory of Stratification: Some Neglected Considerations." *American Sociological Review*, 24:772–782.

Wrong, Dennis. 1964. "Social Inequality Without Social Stratification." *Canadian Review of Sociology and Anthropology*, 1:5–16.

Yanaga, Chitoshi. 1949. *Japan Since Perry*. New York: McGraw-Hill.

Yanowitch, Murray. 1969. "The Soviet Income Revolution." Pp. 143–153 in Celia Heller (ed.), *Structured Social Inequality*. New York: Macmillan.

Yanowitch, Murray. 1977. *Social and Economic Inequality in the Soviet Union*. White Plains, N.Y.: Sharpe.

Zeitlin, Irving M. 1968. *Ideology and the Development of Sociological Theory*. Englewood Cliffs, N.J.: Prentice-Hall.

Zeitlin, Maurice. 1974. "Corporate Ownership and Control: The Large Corporation and the Capitalist Class." *American Journal of Sociology*, 79:1073–1119.

Zeitlin, Maurice, L. Ewen, and Richard Ratcliff. 1974. "New Princes for Old? The Large Corporations and the Capitalist Class in Chile." *American Journal of Sociology*, 80:87–123.

Zeitlin, Maurice, Kenneth Lutterman, and James Russel. 1973. "Death in Vietnam: Class, Poverty, and the Risks of War." *Politics and Society*, 3:313–328.

Zeitlin, Maurice, W. L. Neuman, and Richard Ratcliff. 1976. "Class Segments: Agrarian Property and Political Leadership in the Capitalist Class in Chile." *American Sociological Review*, 41:1006–1029.

Zipp, John, Richard Landerman, and Paul Luebke. 1982. "Political Parties and Political Participation: A Reexamination of the Standard Socioeconomic Model." *Social Forces*, 60:1140–1153.

Zorbaugh, H. W. 1929. *The Gold Coast and the Slum*. Chicago: University of Chicago Press.

NAME INDEX

SUBJECT INDEX